BOLLINGEN SERIES XX

THE COLLECTED WORKS

OF

C. G. JUNG

VOLUME 10

EDITORS

SIR HERBERT READ

MICHAEL FORDHAM, M.D., M.R.C.P.

GERHARD ADLER, PH.D.

WILLIAM MC GUIRE, *executive editor*

CIVILIZATION

IN

TRANSITION

C. G. JUNG

SECOND EDITION

TRANSLATED BY R. F. C. HULL

BOLLINGEN SERIES XX

PRINCETON UNIVERSITY PRESS

Third printing, 1978

THIS EDITION IS BEING PUBLISHED IN THE
UNITED STATES OF AMERICA BY PRINCETON
UNIVERSITY PRESS AND IN ENGLAND BY
ROUTLEDGE AND KEGAN PAUL, LTD. IN THE
AMERICAN EDITION, ALL THE VOLUMES COM-
PRISING THE COLLECTED WORKS CONSTITUTE
NUMBER XX IN BOLLINGEN SERIES, SPON-
SORED BY BOLLINGEN FOUNDATION. THE
PRESENT VOLUME IS NUMBER 10 OF THE
COLLECTED WORKS, AND WAS THE THIR-
TEENTH TO APPEAR.

LIBRARY OF CONGRESS CATALOG CARD NUMBER: 75–156
ISBN 0–691–09762–3
MANUFACTURED IN THE UNITED STATES OF AMERICA

EDITORIAL NOTE

In 1918 Jung published a paper, "The Role of the Unconscious," which sounds the keynote of the present volume. There he put forward the arresting theory that the conflict in Europe, then almost exclusively interpreted in materialistic terms, was basically a psychological crisis originating in the collective unconscious of the individuals that form groups and nations. Subsequently he wrote a considerable number of essays bearing on the contemporary scene and, in particular, on the relation of the individual to society.

The first two sections of this volume, written during the years between the World Wars, develop the themes broached in the opening essay, and are largely concerned with modern man's discovery of his unconscious premises and the importance of self-knowledge in enabling the individual to maintain himself against social pressures. Specific questions, such as the influence of social changes on the relations between the sexes and of ethnic factors on the development of psychological theories, are also discussed. The third section presents four papers previously published in *Essays on Contemporary Events* (1947). In these Jung shows that the dreams and fantasies of individual patients, no less than social and political upheavals, which he explains as psychic epidemics, can reflect tendencies in the unconscious life of nations. In an essay first published in 1936 Wotan is presented as an archetypal figure symbolizing the unconscious agencies active in Germany which found expression in the Nazi movement.

The psychodynamics which Jung inferred from the behaviour of individuals and groups, though easier to perceive in Germany, had, however, a much wider application, as he made clear in two major essays written in his last years. In "The Undiscovered Self" (1957) he reverts to the relation between the individual and a mass society, and in "Flying Saucers" (1958) he examines the birth of a myth which he regards as compensating the scientistic trends of our technological era. Since the crisis in civilization is maintained by Jung to be moral, his late views on good and evil and on the psychological function of conscience, in section six, are necessary and relevant amplifications of his theme.

The reviews and short articles in section seven present Jung's lively and emotional responses to the pronouncements of his contemporary, Count Hermann Keyserling, on national problems, and to his own visits to the United States and India. Finally, the appendix brings together the documents relating to the years when Jung was president of the International General Medical Society for Psychotherapy and editor of its organ, the *Zentralblatt für Psychotherapie*. His energetic nature and feelings of obligation both to society and to his colleagues compelled him to accept this position as a vantage point from which to combat, to the best of his ability, the threat to psychotherapy in Germany under the Nazis. Unjustly, he was subjected to a barrage of tendentious and largely uninformed criticism because of his action. The aims he consistently sought to achieve are now set forth fully for the first time, with the necessary documentation.

*

Grateful acknowledgment is made to the American-Scandinavian Foundation, New York, for permission to quote from the Bellows translation of *The Poetic Edda;* to the Viking Press, New York, for permission to quote from *The Portable Nietzsche,* translated by Walter Kaufmann and copyright 1954 by the Viking Press, Inc.; and to Otto Müller Verlag, Salzburg, for permission to reproduce an illustration from Maria Böckeler, *Hildegard von Bingen: Wissen die Wege.* For advice and assistance, the Editors are grateful to C. A. Meier, M.D., of Zurich; Walter Cimbal, M.D., of Hamburg; W. Morgenthaler, M.D., of Bern; Miss Liselotte Bendix, librarian of the New York Psychoanalytic Society and Institute; and the staff of the Warburg Institute, London.

EDITORIAL NOTE TO THE SECOND EDITION

For this edition essential corrections have been made in the text, and the bibliographical references have been brought up to date.

TABLE OF CONTENTS

EDITORIAL NOTE   v

LIST OF PLATES   xii

I

The Role of the Unconscious   3
Translated from "Über das Unbewusste," *Schweizerland* (Zurich), IV (1918).

Mind and Earth   29
Translated from "Seele und Erde," *Seelenprobleme der Gegenwart* (Zurich: Rascher, 1931).

Archaic Man   50
Translated from "Der archaische Mensch," *Seelenprobleme der Gegenwart* (Zurich: Rascher, 1931).

The Spiritual Problem of Modern Man   74
Translated from "Das Seelenproblem des modernen Menschen," *Seelenprobleme der Gegenwart* (Zurich: Rascher, 1931).

II

The Love Problem of a Student   97
Translated from an unpublished ms. (1922?).

Woman in Europe   113
Translated from "Die Frau in Europa," *Europäische Revue* (Berlin), III (1927).

The Meaning of Psychology for Modern Man   134
Translated from "Die Bedeutung der Psychologie für die Gegenwart," *Wirklichkeit der Seele* (Zurich: Rascher, 1934).

The State of Psychotherapy Today   157
Translated from "Zur gegenwärtigen Lage der Psychotherapie," *Zentralblatt für Psychotherapie und ihre Grenzgebiete* (Leipzig), VII (1934).

III

Preface to *Essays on Contemporary Events*   177
Translated from Vorwort to *Aufsätze zur Zeitgeschichte* (Zurich: Rascher, 1946).

Wotan   179
Translated from "Wotan," *Neue Schweizer Rundschau* (Zurich), n.s., III (1936).

After the Catastrophe   194
Translated from "Nach der Katastrophe," *Neue Schweizer Rundschau* (Zurich), n.s., XIII (1945).

The Fight with the Shadow   218
Originally published in English in *The Listener* (London), XXXVI (1946).

Epilogue to *Essays on Contemporary Events*   227
Translated from Nachwort to *Aufsätze zur Zeitgeschichte* (Zurich: Rascher, 1946).

IV

The Undiscovered Self (Present and Future)   245
Translated from *Gegenwart und Zukunft* (Zurich: Rascher, 1957).
     1. The Plight of the Individual in Modern Society, 247

2. Religion as the Counterbalance to Mass-Mindedness, 256
3. The Position of the West on the Question of Religion, 263
4. The Individual's Understanding of Himself, 269
5. The Philosophical and the Psychological Approach to Life, 284
6. Self-Knowledge, 293
7. The Meaning of Self-Knowledge, 302

V

Flying Saucers: A Modern Myth of Things Seen in the Skies   307

Translated from *Ein moderner Mythus: Von Dingen, die am Himmel gesehen werden* (Zurich and Stuttgart: Rascher, 1958).

Preface to the First English Edition, 309

Introductory, 311

1. Ufos as Rumours, 314
2. Ufos in Dreams, 330
3. Ufos in Modern Painting, 383
4. Previous History of the Ufo Phenomenon, 401
5. Ufos Considered in a Non-Psychological Light, 413

Epilogue, 418

VI

A Psychological View of Conscience   437

Translated from "Das Gewissen in psychologischer Sicht," in *Das Gewissen* (Studien aus dem C. G. Jung-Institut, VII; Zurich: Rascher, 1958).

Good and Evil in Analytical Psychology   456

Translated from "Gut und Böse in der analytischen Psychologie," in *Gut und Böse in der Psychotherapie,* ed. by Wilhelm Bitter (Stuttgart: "Arzt und Seelsorger," 1959).

Introduction to Toni Wolff's *Studies in Jungian Psychology*   469
Translated from the Vorrede to Wolff, *Studien zu C. G. Jung's Psychologie* (Zurich: Rhein, 1959).

VII

The Swiss Line in the European Spectrum   479
Translated from "Die Bedeutung der schweizerischen Linie im Spektrum Europas," *Neue Schweizer Rundschau* (Zurich), XXIV (1928).

The Rise of a New World   489
Translated from "Der Aufgang einer neuen Welt," *Neue Zürcher Zeitung* (Zurich), 1930.

La Révolution Mondiale   496
Translated from "Ein neues Buch von Keyserling," *Basler Nachrichten*, XXVIII (1934).

The Complications of American Psychology   502
Originally published in English as "Your Negroid and Indian Behavior," *Forum* (New York), LXXXIII (1930).

The Dreamlike World of India   515
Originally published in English in *Asia* (New York), XXXIX (1939).

What India Can Teach Us   525
Originally published in English in *Asia* (New York), XXXIX (1939).

APPENDIX

Editorial   533
Translated from the *Zentralblatt*, VI (1933).

A Rejoinder to Dr. Bally   535
Translated from the *Neue Zürcher Zeitung*, CLV (1934).

Circular Letter   545
Translated from the *Zentralblatt,* VII (1934).

Editorial   547
Translated from the *Zentralblatt,* VIII (1935).

Editorial Note   552
Translated from the *Zentralblatt,* VIII (1935).

Presidential Address to the 8th General Medical
Congress for Psychotherapy, Bad Nauheim, 1935   554
Translated from an unpublished ms.

Contribution to a Discussion on Psychotherapy   557
Translated from "Votum C. G. Jung," *Schweizerische Aerzte-
zeitung für Standesfragen* (Bern), XVI (1935).

Presidential Address to the 9th International Medical Congress for Psychotherapy, Copenhagen, 1937   561
Translated from an unpublished ms.

Presidential Address to the 10th International Medical Congress for Psychotherapy, Oxford, 1938   564
Written in English; not previously published.

BIBLIOGRAPHY   569
INDEX   581

LIST OF PLATES

The plates follow p. 404

I. A Ufo Vision
Painting by a patient

II. E. Jakoby: *The Fire Sower*
Author's collection

III. P. Birkhäuser: *The Fourth Dimension*
Private collection

IV. Yves Tanguy: Painting, 1927
Title unknown. Private collection

V. Basel Broadsheet, 1566
Wickiana Collection, Zentralbibliothek, Zurich

VI. Nuremberg Broadsheet, 1561
Wickiana Collection, Zentralbibliothek, Zurich

VII. "The Spiritual Pilgrim Discovering Another World"
Woodcut, 19th(?) cent. Van Houten Collection, Bergen,
Netherlands

VIII. "The Quickening of the Child in the Womb"
From the *Scivias,* by Hildegard von Bingen, Rupertsberg
Codex, 12th cent., as reproduced in M. Böckeler, *Hildegard
von Bingen: Wissen die Wege: Scivias* (Salzburg, 1954)

xii

I

THE ROLE OF THE UNCONSCIOUS

MIND AND EARTH

ARCHAIC MAN

THE SPIRITUAL PROBLEM OF MODERN MAN

THE ROLE OF THE UNCONSCIOUS [1]

1   To the layman's ears, the word "unconscious" has an undertone of something metaphysical and rather mysterious. This peculiarity, attaching to the whole concept of the unconscious, is primarily due to the fact that the term found its way into ordinary speech as a designation for a metaphysical entity. Eduard von Hartmann, for instance, called the unconscious the "Universal Ground." Again, the word was taken up by occultism, because people with these leanings are extremely fond of borrowing scientific terms in order to dress their speculations in a "scientific" guise. In contradiction to this, the experimental psychologists, who for a long time regarded themselves—not unjustly—as the representatives of the only truly scientific psychology, adopted a negative attitude towards the concept of the unconscious, on the ground that everything psychic is conscious and that consciousness alone deserves the name "psyche." They admitted that conscious psychic contents showed varying degrees of clarity, some being "brighter" or "darker" than others, but the existence of unconscious contents was denied as being a contradiction in terms.

2   This view stemmed very largely from the circumstance that work in the laboratory was confined exclusively to "normal" subjects, and also from the nature of the experiments themselves. These were concerned so far as possible with the most elementary psychic processes, while the investigation of the more complex psychic functions, which by their very nature do not lend themselves to experimental procedures based on exact measurement, was almost entirely absent. But a factor far transcending both these reasons in importance was the segregation

1 [Originally published as "Ueber das Unbewusste," *Schweizerland: Monatshefte für Schweizer Art und Arbeit* (Zurich), IV (1918), no. 9, 464–72, and no. 11–12, 548–58.—EDITORS.]

of experimental psychology from psychopathology. In France, ever since the time of Ribot, psychologists had kept an alert eye on abnormal psychic phenomena, and one of their most eminent representatives, Binet, even made the pronouncement that the pathological psyche exaggerated certain deviations from the normal which were difficult to understand, and, by throwing them into relief, made them more comprehensible. Another French psychologist, Pierre Janet, working at the Salpêtrière, devoted himself almost exclusively and with great success to the study of psychopathological processes. But it is just the abnormal psychic processes which demonstrate most clearly the existence of an unconscious. For this reason it was the medical men, and above all the specialists in the field of psychic illnesses, who supported the hypothesis of the unconscious and defended it most vigorously. But whereas in France psychology was considerably enriched by the findings of psychopathology and was led to accept the notion of "unconscious" processes, in Germany it was psychology that enriched psychopathology, supplying it with a number of valuable experimental methods—without, however, taking over from psychopathology its interest in pathological phenomena. This explains in large part why psychopathological research underwent a different development in German science from that followed in France. It became—except for the interest it aroused in academic circles—a task for the medical practitioner, who by his professional work was compelled to understand the complex psychic phenomena exhibited by his patients. In this way there came into being that complex of theoretical views and practical techniques which is known as "psychoanalysis." The concept of the unconscious underwent a broad development in the psychoanalytic movement, far more so than in the French school, which was more concerned with the various forms in which unconscious processes manifested themselves than with their causation and their specific content. Fifteen years ago, independently of the Freudian school and on the basis of my own experimental researches, I satisfied myself as to the existence and significance of unconscious processes, indicating at the same time the methods by which these processes might be demonstrated. Later, in collaboration with a number of my pupils, I also demonstrated the significance of unconscious processes in the mentally insane.

4

3   As a result of this—at first—purely medical development the concept of the unconscious took on a coloration derived from the natural sciences. It has remained a purely medical concept in the Freudian school. According to the views of this school, man, as a civilized being, is unable to act out a large number of instinctive impulses and wishes, for the simple reason that they are incompatible with law and morality. In so far, therefore, as he wants to adapt himself to society, he is obliged to suppress these wishes. The assumption that man has such wishes is altogether plausible, and the truth of it can be seen at any time by every individual with a little application of honesty. But this insight amounts as a rule only to the general statement that socially incompatible and inadmissible wishes exist. Experience shows, however, that the facts are quite different when we come down to individual cases. It then proves, remarkably enough, that very often, as a result of the suppression of an inadmissible wish, the thin wall between wishing and being conscious of the wish is broken, so that the wish becomes unconscious. It is forgotten, and its place is taken by a more or less rational justification—if, indeed, any motivation is sought at all. This process, whereby an inadmissible wish becomes unconscious, is called *repression,* as distinct from *suppression,* which presupposes that the wish remained conscious. Although repressed and forgotten, the incompatible content—whether it consist of wishes or of painful memories—nevertheless exists, and its unperceived presence influences the conscious processes. This influence expresses itself in the form of peculiar disturbances of the conscious, normal functions; we call these disturbances nervous or *psychogenic* disturbances. The remarkable thing is that they do not confine themselves to purely psychological processes but extend also to physiological ones. In the latter case, as Janet emphasizes, it is never the elementary components of the function that are disturbed, but only the voluntary application of the function under various complex conditions. For instance, an elementary component of the nutritive function consists in the act of swallowing. If choking were regularly to occur whenever food in solid or liquid form was taken, then it would be an anatomical or organic disturbance. But if the choking occurred only in the case of certain foods or at certain meals, or only in the presence of certain persons, or only in certain moods, then it would be a

nervous or psychogenic disturbance. The psychogenic disturbance therefore affects merely the act of eating under certain psychological and not physical conditions.

4   Such disturbances of physiological functions are particularly frequent in hysteria. In another, equally large group of illnesses which French doctors call psychasthenia, their place is taken by purely psychological disturbances. These can assume a great variety of forms, such as obsessional ideas, anxiety states, depressions, moods, fantasies, pathological affects and impulses, and so on. At the root of all these disturbances we find repressed psychic contents, i.e., contents that have become unconscious. On the basis of these purely empirical findings, the concept of the unconscious as the sum-total of all incompatible and repressed wishes, including all painful and repressed memories, gradually took form.

5   Now it is an easily demonstrated fact that the overwhelming majority of these incompatible contents have to do with the phenomenon of sexuality. Sexuality is a fundamental instinct which, as everyone knows, is the most hedged about with secrecy and with feelings of delicacy. In the form of love, it is the cause of the stormiest emotions, the wildest longings, the profoundest despairs, the most secret sorrows, and, altogether, of the most painful experiences. Sexuality is an important physical and widely ramified psychic function on which the whole future of humanity depends. It is thus at least as important as the function of nutrition, even though it is an instinct of another kind. But whereas we can allow the nutritive function, from the devouring of a simple piece of bread to a guild banquet, to be seen by all eyes in all its variations, and at most must hold it in check because of an attack of intestinal catarrh or a general food shortage, sexuality comes under a moral taboo and has to submit to a large number of legal regulations and restrictions. It is not, like the nutritive function, at the free disposal of the individual. It is therefore understandable that a great many pressing interests and powerful emotions congregate round this question, for as a rule affects are found at places where adaptation is least complete. Furthermore, sexuality, as I have said, is a fundamental instinct in every human being, and this is reason enough for the well-known Freudian theory which reduces everything to sexuality, and sketches a picture of the unconscious which makes it

6

appear as a kind of lumber-room where all the repressed and inadmissible infantile wishes and all the later, inadmissible sexual wishes are stored. Distasteful as such a view is, we must give it its due if we want to discover all the things that Freud has smuggled into the concept of sexuality. We shall then see that he has widened its boundaries far beyond the permitted limits, so that a better word for what he actually means would be "Eros" in the old, philosophical sense of a Pan-Eros who permeates all nature as a creative and procreative force. "Sexuality" is a most unhappy expression for this. But, such as it is, the concept of sexuality has now been coined and appears to have such definite limits that one even hesitates to use the word "love" as a synonym. And yet Freud, as can easily be shown from numerous passages in his writings, very often means "love" when he speaks merely of sexuality.

6   The whole Freudian movement has settled firmly for the sexual theory. There is certainly no unprejudiced thinker or investigator who would not instantly acknowledge the extraordinary importance of sexual or erotic experiences and conflicts. But it will never be proved that sexuality is *the* fundamental instinct and *the* activating principle of the human psyche. Any unprejudiced scientist will, on the contrary, admit that the psyche is an extremely complex structure. Though we can approach it from the biological standpoint and seek to explain it in terms of biological factors, it presents us with a great many other puzzles whose solution makes demands which no isolated science, such as biology, is in a position to satisfy. No matter what instincts, drives or dynamisms biologists may postulate or assume both now and in the future, it will assuredly be quite impossible to set up a sharply defined instinct like sexuality as a fundamental principle of explanation. Biology, indeed science in general, has got beyond this stage: we no longer reduce everything to a single manifest force, as the earlier scientists did with phlogiston and electricity. We have learned to employ a modest abstraction, named energy, as an explanatory principle for all quantitative changes.

7   I am convinced that a truly scientific attitude in psychology must likewise lead to the conclusion that the dynamic processes of the psyche cannot be reduced to this or that concrete instinct —we should merely find ourselves back at the stage of the phlo-

giston theory. We shall be obliged to take the instincts as constituent parts of the psyche, and then abstract our principle of explanation from their mutual relationship. I have therefore pointed out that we would do well to posit a hypothetical quantity, an "energy," as a psychological explanatory principle, and to call it "libido" in the classical sense of the word, without harbouring any prejudice with regard to its substantiality. With the help of such a quantity, the psychodynamic processes could be explained in an unobjectionable manner, without that unavoidable distortion which a concrete ground of explanation necessarily entails. Thus, when the Freudian school explains that religious feelings or any other sentiments that pertain to the spiritual sphere are "nothing but" inadmissible sexual wishes which have been repressed and subsequently "sublimated," this procedure would be equivalent to a physicist's explanation that electricity is "nothing but" a waterfall which someone had bought up and piped into a turbine. In other words, electricity is nothing but a "culturally deformed" waterfall—an argument which might conceivably be raised by the Society for the Preservation of Wild Nature but is hardly a piece of scientific ratiocination. In psychology such an explanation would be appropriate only if it could be proved that the dynamic ground of our being is nothing but sexuality, which amounts to saying, in physics, that falling water alone can produce electricity. In that case it could rightly be maintained that electricity is nothing but a waterfall conducted along wires.

8   So if we reject the exclusively sexual theory of the unconscious and put in its place an energic view of the psyche, we must say that the unconscious contains everything psychic that has not reached the threshold of consciousness, or whose energy-charge is not sufficient to maintain it in consciousness, or that will reach consciousness only in the future. We can then picture to ourselves how the unconscious must be constituted. We have already taken cognizance of repressions as contents of the unconscious, and to these we must add *everything that we have forgotten*. When a thing is forgotten, it does not mean that it is extinguished; it simply means that the memory has become subliminal. Its energy-charge has sunk so low that it can no longer appear in consciousness; but, though lost to consciousness, it is not lost to the unconscious. It will naturally be objected that

this is no more than a *façon de parler*. I would like to make what I mean clear by a hypothetical example. Suppose there are two people, one of whom has never read a book and the other has read a thousand. From the minds of both of them we expunge all memory of the ten years in which the first was merely living and the second was reading his thousand books. Each now knows as little as the other, and yet anyone will be able to find out which of them has read the books and, be it noted, understood them. The experience of reading, though long forgotten, leaves traces behind it, and from these traces the previous experience can be recognized. This long-lasting, indirect influence is due to a fixing of impressions, which are still preserved even when they are no longer capable of reaching consciousness.

9   Besides things that have been forgotten, subliminal perceptions form part of the contents of the unconscious. These may be sense perceptions occurring below the stimulus-threshold of conscious hearing, or in the peripheral field of vision; or they may be apperceptions, by which are meant perceptions of endopsychic or external processes.

10   All this material constitutes the *personal unconscious*. We call it personal because it consists entirely of acquisitions deriving from personal life. Therefore, when anything falls into the unconscious it is taken up in the network of associations formed by this unconscious material. Associative connections of high intensity may then be produced, which cross over or rise up into consciousness in the form of inspirations, intuitions, "lucky ideas," and so on.

11   The concept of a personal unconscious does not, however, enable us fully to grasp the nature of the unconscious. If the unconscious were only personal, it would in theory be possible to trace all the fantasies of an insane person back to individual experiences and impressions. No doubt a large proportion of the fantasy-material could be reduced to his personal history, but there are certain fantasies whose roots in the individual's previous history one would seek for in vain. What sort of fantasies are these? They are, in a word, *mythological fantasies*. They are elements which do not correspond to any events or experiences of personal life, but only to myths.

12   Where do these mythological fantasies come from, if they do not spring from the personal unconscious and hence from the

experiences of personal life? Indubitably they come from the brain—indeed, precisely from the brain and not from personal memory-traces, but from the inherited brain-structure itself. Such fantasies always have a highly original and "creative" character. They are like new creations; obviously they derive from the creative activity of the brain and not simply from its mnemonic activity. We receive along with our body a highly differentiated brain which brings with it its entire history, and when it becomes creative it creates out of this history—out of the history of mankind. By "history" we usually mean the history which we "make," and we call this "objective history." The truly creative fantasy activity of the brain has nothing to do with this kind of history, but solely with that age-old natural history which has been transmitted in living form since the remotest times, namely, the history of the brain-structure. And this structure tells its own story, which is the story of mankind: the unending myth of death and rebirth, and of the multitudinous figures who weave in and out of this mystery.

13   This unconscious, buried in the structure of the brain and disclosing its living presence only through the medium of creative fantasy, is the *suprapersonal unconscious*. It comes alive in the creative man, it reveals itself in the vision of the artist, in the inspiration of the thinker, in the inner experience of the mystic. The suprapersonal unconscious, being distributed throughout the brain-structure, is like an all-pervading, omnipresent, omniscient spirit. It knows man as he always was, and not as he is at this moment; it knows him as myth. For this reason, also, the connection with the suprapersonal or *collective* unconscious means an extension of man beyond himself; it means death for his personal being and a rebirth in a new dimension, as was literally enacted in certain of the ancient mysteries. It is certainly true that without the sacrifice of man as he is, man as he was—and always will be—cannot be attained. And it is the artist who can tell us most about this sacrifice of the personal man, if we are not satisfied with the message of the Gospels.

14   It should on no account be imagined that there are such things as *inherited ideas*. Of that there can be no question. There are, however, innate possibilities of ideas, *a priori* conditions for fantasy-production, which are somewhat similar to the Kantian categories. Though these innate conditions do not

produce any contents of themselves, they give definite form to contents that have already been acquired. Being a part of the inherited structure of the brain, they are the reason for the identity of symbols and myth-motifs in all parts of the earth. The collective unconscious forms the dark background against which the adaptive function of consciousness stands out in sharp relief. One is almost tempted to say that everything of value in the psyche is taken up into the adaptive function, and that everything useless goes to form that inchoate background from which, to the terror of primitive man, menacing shadows and nocturnal spectres detach themselves, demanding sacrifices and ceremonies which to our biologically oriented minds seem futile and meaningless. We laugh at primitive superstitions, thinking ourselves superior, but we completely forget that we are influenced in just as uncanny a fashion as the primitive by this background, which we are wont to scoff at as a museum of stupidities. Primitive man simply has a different theory—the theory of witchcraft and spirits. I find this theory very interesting and very sensible— actually more sensible than the academic views of modern science. Whereas the highly educated modern man tries to figure out what diet best suits his nervous intestinal catarrh and to what dietetic mistakes the new attack may be due, the primitive, quite correctly, looks for psychological reasons and seeks a psychically effective method of cure. The processes in the unconscious influence us just as much as they do primitives; we are possessed by the demons of sickness no less than they, our psyche is just as much in danger of being struck by some hostile influence, we are just as much the prey of malevolent spirits of the dead, or the victims of a magic spell cast by a strange personality. Only, we call all these things by different names, and that is the only advantage we have over primitive man. It is, as we know, a little thing, yet it makes all the difference. For mankind it was always like a deliverance from a nightmare when the new name was found.

15   This mysterious background, which from time immemorial peopled the nocturnal shadows of the primeval forest with the same yet ever-changing figures, seems like a distorted reflection of life during the day, repeating itself in the dreams and terrors of the night. Shadowily they crowd round, the revenants, the spirits of the dead, fleeting memory-images risen from the prison

11

of the past whence no living thing returns, or feelings left behind by some impressive experience and now personified in spectral form. All this seems but the bitter aftertaste from the emptied beaker of the day, the unwelcome lees, the useless sediment of experience. But if we look closer, we discover that this apparently hostile background sends out powerful emissaries which influence the behaviour of primitives in the highest degree. Sometimes these agencies take on a magical, sometimes a religious form, and sometimes the two forms appear inextricably mixed. Both of them are the most important factors in the primitive mentality after the struggle for existence. In them the spiritual element manifests itself autonomously to the primitive psyche—whose reflexes are purely animal—in projected, sensuous form, and we Europeans must sometimes be struck with wonder at the tremendous influence the experience of the spirit can have on primitive man. For him, the sensuous immediacy of the object attaches to spiritual phenomena as well. A thought *appears to him,* he does not think it; it appears to him in the form of a projected sensuous perception, almost like an hallucination, or at least like an extremely vivid dream. For this reason a thought, for the primitive, can superimpose itself on sensuous reality to such an extent that if a European were to behave in the same way we should say he was mad.

16 These peculiarities of primitive psychology, which I can only touch lightly on here, are of great importance for an understanding of the collective unconscious. A simple reflection will bear this out. As civilized human beings, we in Western Europe have a history reaching back perhaps 2,500 years. Before that there is a prehistoric period of considerably greater duration, during which man reached the cultural level of, say, the Sioux Indians. Then come the hundreds of thousands of years of neolithic culture, and before that an unimaginably vast stretch of time during which man evolved from the animal. A mere fifty generations ago many of us in Europe were no better than primitives. The layer of culture, this pleasing patina, must therefore be quite extraordinarily thin in comparison with the powerfully developed layers of the primitive psyche. But it is these layers that form the collective unconscious, together with the vestiges of animality that lose themselves in the nebulous abyss of time.

17 Christianity split the Germanic barbarian into an upper and

12

a lower half, and enabled him, by repressing the dark side, to domesticate the brighter half and fit it for civilization. But the lower, darker half still awaits redemption and a second spell of domestication. Until then, it will remain associated with the vestiges of the prehistoric age, with the collective unconscious, which is subject to a peculiar and ever-increasing activation. As the Christian view of the world loses its authority, the more menacingly will the "blond beast" be heard prowling about in its underground prison, ready at any moment to burst out with devastating consequences. When this happens in the individual it brings about a psychological revolution, but it can also take a social form.

18   In my opinion this problem does not exist for the Jews. The Jew already had the culture of the ancient world and on top of that has taken over the culture of the nations amongst whom he dwells. He has two cultures, paradoxical as that may sound. He is domesticated to a higher degree than we are, but he is badly at a loss for that quality in man which roots him to the earth and draws new strength from below. This chthonic quality is found in dangerous concentration in the Germanic peoples. Naturally the Aryan European has not noticed any signs of this for a very long time, but perhaps he is beginning to notice it in the present war; and again, perhaps not. The Jew has too little of this quality—where has he his own earth underfoot? The mystery of earth is no joke and no paradox. One only needs to see how, in America, the skull and pelvis measurements of all the European races begin to indianize themselves in the second generation of immigrants. That is the mystery of the American earth.

19   The soil of every country holds some such mystery. We have an unconscious reflection of this in the psyche: just as there is a relationship of mind to body, so there is a relationship of body to earth. I hope the reader will pardon my figurative way of speaking, and will try to grasp what I mean. It is not easy to describe, definite though it is. There are people—quite a number of them—who live outside and above their bodies, who float like bodiless shadows above their earth, their earthy component, which is their body. Others live wholly in their bodies. As a rule, the Jew lives in amicable relationship with the earth, but without feeling the power of the chthonic. His receptivity to this

seems to have weakened with time. This may explain the specific need of the Jew to reduce everything to its material beginnings; he needs these beginnings in order to counterbalance the dangerous ascendency of his two cultures. A little bit of primitivity does not hurt him; on the contrary, I can understand very well that Freud's and Adler's reduction of everything psychic to primitive sexual wishes and power-drives has something about it that is beneficial and satisfying to the Jew, because it is a form of simplification. For this reason, Freud is perhaps right to close his eyes to my objections. But these specifically Jewish doctrines are thoroughly unsatisfying to the Germanic mentality; we still have a genuine barbarian in us who is not to be trifled with, and whose manifestation is no comfort for us and not a pleasant way of passing the time. Would that people could learn the lesson of this war! The fact is, our unconscious is not to be got at with over-ingenious and grotesque interpretations. The psychotherapist with a Jewish background awakens in the Germanic psyche not those wistful and whimsical residues from the time of David, but the barbarian of yesterday, a being for whom matters suddenly become *serious* in the most unpleasant way. This annoying peculiarity of the barbarian was apparent also to Nietzsche —no doubt from personal experience—which is why he thought highly of the Jewish mentality and preached about dancing and flying and not taking things seriously. But he overlooked the fact that it is not the barbarian in us who takes things seriously —they become serious for him. He is gripped by the daemon. And who took things more seriously than Nietzsche himself?

20   It seems to me that we should take the problem of the unconscious very seriously indeed. The tremendous compulsion towards goodness and the immense moral force of Christianity are not merely an argument in the latter's favour, they are also a proof of the strength of its suppressed and repressed counterpart —the antichristian, barbarian element. The existence within us of something that can turn against us, that can become a serious matter for us, I regard not merely as a dangerous peculiarity, but as a valuable and congenial asset as well. It is a still untouched fortune, an uncorrupted treasure, a sign of youthfulness, an earnest of rebirth. Nevertheless, to value the unconscious exclusively for the sake of its positive qualities and to regard it as a source of revelation would be fundamentally wrong.

14

The unconscious is, first and foremost, the world of the past, which is activated by the one-sidedness of the conscious attitude. Whenever life proceeds one-sidedly in any given direction, the self-regulation of the organism produces in the unconscious an accumulation of all those factors which play too small a part in the individual's conscious existence. For this reason I have put forward the compensation theory of the unconscious as a complement to the repression theory.

21   The role of the unconscious is to act compensatorily to the conscious contents of the moment. By this I do not mean that it sets up an opposition, for there are times when the tendency of the unconscious coincides with that of consciousness, namely, when the conscious attitude is approaching the optimum. The nearer it approaches the optimum, the more the autonomous activity of the unconscious is diminished, and the more its value sinks until, at the moment when the optimum is reached, it falls to zero. We can say, then, that so long as all goes well, so long as a person travels the road that is, for him, the individual as well as the social optimum, there is no talk of the unconscious. The very fact that we in our age come to speak of the unconscious at all is proof that everything is not in order. This talk of the unconscious cannot be laid entirely at the door of analytical psychology; its beginnings can be traced back to the time of the French Revolution, and the first signs of it can be found in Mesmer. It is true that in those days they did not speak of the unconscious but of "animal magnetism." This is nothing but a rediscovery of the primitive concept of soul-force or soul-stuff, awakened out of the unconscious by a reactivation of archaic forms of thought. At the time when animal magnetism was spreading throughout the Western world as a regular epidemic of table-turning, amounting in the end to a recrudescence of the belief in fetishes (animation of an inanimate object), Robert Mayer elevated the primitive dynamic idea of energy, which rose up from the unconscious and forced itself on him like an inspiration—as he himself describes—to the level of a scientific concept. Meanwhile, the table-turning epidemic burst its bounds altogether and proliferated into spiritualism, which is a modern belief in spirits and a rebirth of the shamanistic form of religion practised by our remote forefathers. This development of reactivated contents from the unconscious is still going on today,

and during the last few decades has led to a popularizing of the next higher stage of differentiation—the eclectic or Gnostic systems of Theosophy and Anthroposophy. At the same time, it laid the foundations of French psychopathology, and in particular of the French school of hypnotism. These, in turn, became the main sources of analytical psychology, which now seeks to investigate scientifically the phenomena of the unconscious—the same phenomena which the theosophical and Gnostic sects made accessible to the simple-minded in the form of portentous mysteries.

22   It is evident from this development that analytical psychology does not stand in isolation but finds itself in a definite historical setting. The fact that this whole disturbance or reactivation of the unconscious took place around the year 1800 is, in my view, connected with the French Revolution. This was less a political revolution than a revolution of minds. It was a colossal explosion of all the inflammable matter that had been piling up ever since the Age of Enlightenment. The official deposition of Christianity by the Revolution must have made a tremendous impression on the unconscious pagan in us, for from then on he found no rest. In the greatest German of the age, Goethe, he could really live and breathe, and in Hölderlin he could at least cry loudly for the glory that was Greece. After that, the dechristianization of man's view of the world made rapid progress despite occasional reactionaries. Hand in hand with this went the importation of strange gods. Besides the fetishism and shamanism already mentioned, the prime import was Buddhism, retailed by Schopenhauer. Mystery religions spread apace, including that higher form of shamanism, Christian Science. This picture reminds us vividly of the first centuries of our era, when Rome began to find the old gods ridiculous and felt the need to import new ones on a large scale. As today, they imported pretty well everything that existed, from the lowest, most squalid superstition to the noblest flowerings of the human spirit. Our time is fatally reminiscent of that epoch, when again everything was not in order, and again the unconscious burst forth and brought back things immemorially buried. If anything, the chaos of minds was perhaps less pronounced then than it is today.

23   As the reader will have remarked, I have omitted to speak

here of the medical aspect of the unconscious, for instance the question of how the unconscious produces nervous symptoms. But I have touched on this question in the earlier pages and can now leave it alone. At all events, I am not getting away from my subject, because psychotherapy is concerned not only with family quarrels, unhappy love-affairs, and the like, but with the question of psychological adaptation in general, and the attitude we are to take towards people and things, and also towards ourselves. A doctor who treats the body must know the body, and a doctor who treats the psyche must know the psyche. If he knows the psyche only under the aspect of sexuality or of the personal lust for power, he knows it only in part. This part has to be known, of course, but the other parts are equally important, and particularly the question I have touched on here concerning the relation between conscious and unconscious. A biologically trained eye is not sufficient to grasp this problem, for in practice it is more than a matter of eugenics, and the observation of human life in the light of self-preservation and propagation is too one-sided. Certainly the unconscious presents us with very different aspects; but so far we have fixed our attention too much on certain outward peculiarities, for instance the archaic language of the unconscious, and have taken it all quite literally. The language of the unconscious is particularly rich in images, as our dreams prove. But it is a primitive language, a faithful reflection of the colourful, ever-changing world. The unconscious is of like nature: it is a compensatory image of the world. In my view it cannot be maintained either that the unconscious has a merely sexual nature or that it is a metaphysical reality, nor can it be exalted into a "universal ground." It is to be understood as a psychic phenomenon, like consciousness. We no more know what the psyche is than we know what life is. They are interpenetrating mysteries, giving us every reason for uncertainty as to how much "I" am the world, and how much "world" is "I". The unconscious at any rate is real, because it *works*. I like to visualize the unconscious as a world seen in a mirror: our consciousness presents to us a picture of the outer world, but also of the world within, this being a compensatory mirror-image of the outer world. We could also say that the outer world is a compensatory mirror-image of the inner world. At all events we stand between two worlds, or between two totally different psychological systems of perception; between perception of external sensory stimuli and perception of the unconscious. The picture we have of the outer world makes us understand everything as the effect of physical and physiological forces; the picture of the inner world shows everything as the effect of spiritual agencies. Then, it is no longer the force of gravity that welds the stars together, but the creative hand of a demiurge; love is no longer the effect of a sexual stimulus, but of psychic predestination, and so forth.

24 The right way may perhaps be found in the approximation of the two worlds. Schiller thought he had found this way in art, in what he called the "symbol" of art. The artist, therefore, should know the secret of the middle path. My own experiences led me to doubt this. I am of the opinion that the union of rational and irrational truth is to be found not so much in art as in the symbol *per se;* for it is the essence of the symbol to contain both the rational and the irrational. It always expresses the one through the other; it comprises both without being either.

25 How does a symbol originate? This question brings us to the most important function of the unconscious: the *symbol-creating function.* There is something very remarkable about this function, because it has only a relative existence. The compensatory function, on the other hand, is the natural, automatic function of the unconscious and is constantly present. It owes its existence to the simple fact that all the impulses, thoughts, wishes, and tendencies which run counter to the rational orientation of daily life are denied expression, thrust into the background, and finally fall into the unconscious. There all the things which we have repressed and suppressed, which we have deliberately ignored and devalued, gradually accumulate and, in time, acquire such force that they begin to influence consciousness. This influence would be in direct opposition to our conscious orientation if the unconscious consisted only of repressed and suppressed material. But this, as we have seen, is not the case. The unconscious also contains the dark springs of instinct and intuition, it contains all those forces which mere reasonableness, propriety, and the orderly course of bourgeois existence could never call awake, all those creative forces which lead man onwards to new developments, new forms, and new goals. I therefore call the influence of the unconscious not merely complementary but

compensatory, because it adds to consciousness everything that has been excluded by the drying up of the springs of intuition and by the fixed pursuit of a single goal.

26   This function, as I say, works automatically, but, owing to the notorious atrophy of instinct in civilized man, it is often too weak to swing his one-sided orientation of consciousness in a new direction against the pressures of society. Therefore, artificial aids have always been needed to bring the healing forces of the unconscious into play. It was chiefly the religions that performed this task. By taking the manifestations of the unconscious as divine or daemonic signs, revelations, or warnings, they offered it some idea or view that served as a favourable gradient. In this way they directed particular attention to all phenomena of unconscious origin, whether they were dreams, visions, feelings, fantasies, or projections of the same in strange or unusual personalities, or in any striking processes of organic and inorganic nature. This concentration of attention enabled the unconscious contents and forces to overflow into conscious life, thereby influencing it and altering it. From this standpoint, religious ideas are an artificial aid that benefits the unconscious by endowing its compensatory function—which, if disregarded, would remain ineffective—with a higher value for consciousness. Faith, superstition, or any strongly feeling-toned idea gives the unconscious content a value which ordinarily it does not possess, but which it might in time attain, though in a very unpleasant form. When, therefore, unconscious contents accumulate as a result of being consistently ignored, they are bound to exert an influence that is pathological. There are just as many neurotics among primitives as among civilized Europeans. Hysterical Africans are by no means rare in Africa. These disagreeable manifestations of the unconscious account in large measure for the primitive fear of demons and the resultant rites of propitiation.

27   The compensatory function of the unconscious naturally does not contain in itself the conscious valuation, although it is wholly dependent on the conscious way of thinking. The unconscious can supply, at most, the germs of conscious convictions or of symbol-formation. We can say, therefore, that the symbol-creating function of the unconscious exists and does not exist, depending on the conditions. It shares this paradoxical quality

19

with symbols in general. One is reminded of the story of the young rabbi who was a pupil of Kant's. One day an old rabbi came to guide him back to the faith of his fathers, but all arguments were in vain. At last the old rabbi drew forth the ominous *shofar*, the horn that is blown at the cursing of heretics (as happened to Spinoza), and asked the young man if he knew what it was. "Of course I know," answered the young man coolly, "it is the horn of a ram." At that the old rabbi reeled back and fell to the ground in horror.

28   What is the *shofar*? It is *also* only the horn of a ram. Sometimes a symbol can be no more than that, but only when it is dead. The symbol is killed when we succeed in reducing the *shofar* to a ram's horn. But again, through symbolization a ram's horn can become the *shofar*.

29   The compensatory function expresses itself in quite definite arrangements of psychic material, for instance in dreams, in which nothing "symbolic" is to be found any more than in a ram's horn. In order to discover their symbolic quality a quite definite conscious attitude is needed, namely, the willingness to understand the dream-content symbolically, first of all as a mere hypothesis, and then leave experience to decide whether it is necessary or desirable to understand the dream in this way. I will give a brief example which may help to elucidate this difficult question. An elderly woman-patient, who, like many others, was upset by the problem of the war, once told me the following dream which she had shortly before she visited me:

30   *She was singing hymns that put particular emphasis on her belief in Christ, among others the hymn that goes:*

> Christ's blood and righteousness shall be
> My festal dress and jewellery;
> So shall I stand before the Lord
> When heaven shall grant me my reward.
> They shall be saved at Judgment Day
> Who put their trust in Christ alway.

While she was singing it, she saw a bull tearing around madly in front of the window. Suddenly it gave a jump and broke one of its legs. She saw that the bull was in agony, and thought, turning her eyes away, that somebody ought to kill it. Then she awoke.

31   The bull's agony reminded her of the torturings of animals

whose unwilling witness she had been. She abominated such things and was extraordinarily upset by them because of her unconscious identification with the tortured animal. There was something in her that could be expressed by the image of an animal being tortured. This image was evidently evoked by the special emphasis on the belief in Christ in the hymns she was singing, for it was while she was singing that the bull got excited and broke its leg. This odd combination of ideas immediately led to an association concerning the profound religious disquiet she had felt during the war, which shook her belief in the goodness of God and in the adequacy of the Christian view of the world. This shock should have been assuaged by the emphasis on Christian faith in the hymn, but instead it aroused that animal element in the unconscious which was personified by the bull. This is just the element that is represented by the Christian symbol as having been conquered and offered up in sacrifice. In the Christian mystery it is the sacrificed Lamb, or more correctly, the "little ram." In its sister-religion, Mithraism, which was also Christianity's most successful rival, the central symbol of the cult was the sacrifice not of a ram but of a bull. The usual altarpiece showed the overcoming of the bull by the divine saviour Mithras. We have, therefore, a very close historical connection between Christianity and the bull sacrifice. Christianity suppressed this animal element, but the moment the absolute validity of the Christian faith is shaken, that element is thrust into the foreground again. The animal instinct seeks to break out, but in so doing breaks a leg—in other words, instinct cripples itself. From the purely animal drives there also come all those factors which limit the sway of instinct. From the same root that produces wild, untamed, blind instinct there grow up the natural laws and cultural forms that tame and break its pristine power. But when the animal in us is split off from consciousness by being repressed, it may easily burst out in full force, quite unregulated and uncontrolled. An outburst of this sort always ends in catastrophe—the animal destroys itself. What was originally something dangerous now becomes something to be pitied, something that really needs our compassion. The tremendous forces unleashed by the war bring about their own destruction because there is no human hand to preserve and guide them. Our view of the world has proved too narrow to channel these forces into a cultural form.

32   Had I tried to explain to my elderly woman-patient that the bull was a sexual symbol, she would have got nothing out of it; on the contrary, she would merely have lost her religious point of view and been none the better off. In such cases it is not a question of an either/or explanation. If we are willing to adopt a symbolical standpoint, even if only as an hypothesis, we shall see that the dream is an attempt on the part of the unconscious to bring the Christian principle into harmony with its apparently irreconcilable opposite—animal instinct—by means of understanding and compassion. It is no accident that official Christianity has no relation to the animal. This omission, particularly striking in comparison with Buddhism, is often felt by sensitive people and has moved one modern poet to sing of a Christ who sacrifices his life for the sufferings of dumb animals. The Christian love of your neighbour can extend to the animal too, the *animal in us,* and can surround with love all that a rigidly anthropomorphic view of the world has cruelly repressed. By being repressed into the unconscious, the source from which it originated, the animal in us only becomes more beastlike, and that is no doubt the reason why no religion is so defiled with the spilling of innocent blood as Christianity, and why the world has never seen a bloodier war than the war of the Christian nations. The repressed animal bursts forth in its most savage form when it comes to the surface, and in the process of destroying itself leads to international suicide. If every individual had a better relation to the animal within him, he would also set a higher value on life. Life would be the absolute, the supreme moral principle, and he would react instinctively against any institution or organization that had the power to destroy life on a large scale.

33   This dream, then, simply shows the dreamer the value of Christianity and contrasts it with an untamed force of nature, which, left to its raging, hurts itself and demands pity. A purely analytical reduction that traced the religious emotion back to the repression of animal instinct would, in this particular case, be sterile and uselessly destructive. If, on the other hand, we assert that the dream is to be understood symbolically and is trying to give the dreamer an opportunity to become reconciled with herself, we have taken the first step in an interpretation which will bring the contradictory values into harmony and open up a new path of inner development. Subsequent dreams would then, in

22

keeping with this hypothesis, provide the means for understanding the wider implications of the union of the animal component with the highest moral and intellectual achievements of the human spirit. In my experience this is what actually happens, for the unconscious is continuously compensatory in its action upon the conscious situation of the moment. It is therefore not a matter of indifference *what* our conscious attitude is towards the unconscious. The more negative, critical, hostile, or disparaging we are, the more it will assume these aspects, and the more the true value of the unconscious will escape us.

34   Thus the unconscious has a symbol-creating function only when we are willing to recognize in it a symbolic element. The products of the unconscious are pure nature. *Naturam si sequemur ducem, nunquam aberrabimus,*[2] said the ancients. But nature is not, in herself, a guide, for she is not there for man's sake. Ships are not guided by the phenomenon of magnetism. We have to make the compass a guide and, in addition, allow for a specific correction, for the needle does not even point exactly to the north. So it is with the guiding function of the unconscious. It can be used as a source of symbols, but with the necessary conscious correction that has to be applied to every natural phenomenon in order to make it serve our purpose.

35   Many people will find this view extremely unscientific, for nowhere do they see any reduction to fundamental causes, so that they could declare with certainty that such-and-such a thing is "nothing but" this or that. For all those who seek to explain things in this way, sexuality as a causative factor is very convenient. Indeed, in the case I have described a sexual explanation could be offered without much difficulty. But—what would the patient get out of it? What use is it to a woman on the threshold of old age if her problem is answered in this way? Or should psychotherapy be reserved for patients under forty?

36   Naturally we can ask in return: What does the patient get out of an answer that takes religious problems seriously? What is a religious problem anyway? And what has a scientific method to do with religion?

37   It seems to me that the patient is the proper authority to deal with questions of this sort. What does he get out of them

2 "If we take Nature for our guide, we shall never go astray."

however they are answered? Why should he bother his head about science? If he is a religious person, his relationship to God will mean infinitely more to him than any scientifically satisfactory explanation, just as it is a matter of indifference to a sick man *how* he gets well so long as he does get well. Our patient, indeed any patient, is treated correctly only when he is treated as an individual. This means entering into his particular problem and not giving him an explanation based on "scientific" principles that goes clean over his head although it may be quite correct biologically.

38   In my view the first duty of a scientific psychologist is to keep close to the living facts of the psyche, to observe these facts carefully, and thus open himself to those deeper experiences of which at present he has absolutely no knowledge. When, therefore, this or that individual psyche has a sexual conflict, and another one has a religious problem, the true scientist will first of all acknowledge the patent difference between them. He will devote himself as much to the religious problem as to the sexual problem, regardless of whether the biologist's credo allows room for the gods or not. The really unprejudiced investigator will not let his subjective credo influence or in any way distort the material lying before him, and pathological material is no exception to this. Nowadays it is a piece of unwarranted naïveté to regard a neurotic conflict as exclusively a sexual or as exclusively a power problem. This procedure is just as arbitrary as the assertion that there is no such thing as the unconscious and no neurotic conflicts. When we see all round us how powerful ideas can be, we must admit that they must be equally powerful in the psyche of the individual, whether or not he is aware of it. No one doubts that sexuality is a psychologically effective factor, and it cannot be doubted that ideas are psychologically effective factors too. Between the world of ideas and the world of instinct there is, however, a polar difference, so that as a rule only one pole is conscious. The other pole then dominates the unconscious. Thus, when anyone in his conscious life is wholly under the sway of instinct, his unconscious will place just as one-sided an emphasis on the value of ideas. And since the influence of the unconscious does in the end reach consciousness indirectly, and secretly determines its attitude, it gives rise to a compromise formation: instinct surreptitiously becomes a fixed idea, it loses

its reality and is blown up by the unconscious into a one-sided, universal principle. We see the contrary often happening too, when a person consciously takes his stand on the world of ideas and is gradually forced to experience how his instinct secretly makes his ideas the instrument of unconscious wishes.

39   As the contemporary world and its newspapers present the spectacle of a gigantic psychiatric clinic, every attentive observer has ample opportunity to see these formulations being enacted before his eyes. A principle of cardinal importance in studying these phenomena is the one already stressed by analytical psychology: that the unconscious of one person is projected upon another person, so that the first accuses the second of what he overlooks in himself. This principle is of such alarming general validity that everyone would do well, before railing at others, to sit down and consider very carefully whether the brick should not be thrown at his own head.

40   This seemingly irrelevant aside brings us to one of the most remarkable features of the unconscious: it is, as it were, present before our eyes in all its parts, and is accessible to observation at any time.

41   The reason for this paradoxical quality is that the unconscious, in so far as it is activated in any way by small amounts of energy, is projected upon certain more or less suitable objects. The reader will ask how anyone can know this. The existence of projections was gradually recognized when it was found that the process of psychological adaptation was marked by disturbances and defects whose cause appeared to lie in the object. Closer investigation revealed that the "cause" was an unconscious content of the subject, which, because not recognized by him, apparently transferred itself to the object, and there magnified one of its peculiarities to such proportions that it seemed a sufficient cause of the disturbance.

42   The fact of projection was first recognized from disturbances of psychological adaptation. Later, it was recognized also from what *promoted* adaptation, that is to say from the apparently positive qualities of the object. Here it was the valuable qualities of the subject's own personality which he had overlooked that appeared in the object and made it especially desirable.

43   But the full extent of these projections from the unconscious became known through analysis of those obscure and inexplic-

able feelings and emotions which give some intangible, magical quality to certain places, certain moods of nature, certain works of art, and also to certain ideas and certain people. This magic likewise comes from projection, but a projection of the collective unconscious. If it is inanimate objects that have the "magical" quality, often their mere statistical incidence is sufficient to prove that their significance is due to the projection of a mythological content from the collective unconscious. Mostly these contents are motifs already known to us from myths and fairytales. I would mention as an example the mysterious house where a witch or magician dwells, where some monstrous crime is being committed or has been committed, where there is a ghost, where a hidden treasure lies buried, and so on. The projection of this primordial image can be recognized when, one day, a person somehow comes upon this mysterious house—when, in other words, a real but quite ordinary house makes a magical impression upon him. Generally, too, the whole atmosphere of the place seems symbolic and is, therefore, the projection of a coherent unconscious system.

44   We find this phenomenon beautifully developed in primitive man. The country he inhabits is at the same time the topography of his unconscious. In that stately tree dwells the thundergod; this spring is haunted by the Old Woman; in that wood the legendary king is buried; near that rock no one may light a fire because it is the abode of a demon; in yonder pile of stones dwell the ancestral spirits, and when any woman passes it she must quickly utter an apotropaic formula lest she become pregnant, for one of the spirits could easily enter her body. All kinds of objects and signs mark these places, and pious awe surrounds the marked spot. Thus does primitive man dwell in his land and at the same time in the land of his unconscious. Everywhere his unconscious jumps out at him, alive and real. How different is our relationship to the land we dwell in! Feelings totally strange to us accompany the primitive at every step. Who knows what the cry of a bird means to him, or the sight of that old tree! A whole world of feeling is closed to us and is replaced by a pale aestheticism. Nevertheless, the world of primitive feeling is not entirely lost to us; it lives on in the unconscious. The further we remove ourselves from it with our enlightenment and our rational superiority, the more it fades into the distance, but is

made all the more potent by everything that falls into it, thrust out by our one-sided rationalism. This lost bit of nature seeks revenge and returns in faked, distorted form, for instance as a tango epidemic, as Futurism, Dadaism, and all the other crazes and crudities in which our age abounds.

45   Even the primitive's distrust of the neighbouring tribe, which we thought we had long ago outgrown thanks to our global organizations, has come back again in this war, swollen to gigantic proportions. It is no longer a matter of burning down the neighbouring village, or of making a few heads roll: whole countries are devastated, millions are slaughtered. The enemy nation is stripped of every shred of decency, and our own faults appear in others, fantastically magnified. Where are the superior minds, capable of reflection, today? If they exist at all, nobody heeds them: instead there is a general running amok, a universal fatality against whose compelling sway the individual is powerless to defend himself. And yet this collective phenomenon is the fault of the individual as well, for nations are made up of individuals. Therefore the individual must consider by what means he can counteract the evil. Our rationalistic attitude leads us to believe that we can work wonders with international organizations, legislation, and other well-meant devices. But in reality only a change in the attitude of the individual can bring about a renewal in the spirit of the nations. Everything begins with the individual.

46   There are well-meaning theologians and humanitarians who want to break the power principle—in others. We must begin by breaking it in ourselves. Then the thing becomes credible. We should listen to the voice of nature that speaks to us from the unconscious. Then everyone will be so preoccupied with himself that he will give up trying to put the world to rights.

47   The layman may feel somewhat astonished that I have included these general problems in my discussion of a psychological concept. They are not a digression from my theme, as might appear, but are an essential part of it. The question of the relations between conscious and unconscious is not a special question, but one which is bound up in the most intimate way with our history, with the present time, and with our view of the world. Very many things are unconscious for us only because our view of the world allows them no room; because by education

and training we have never come to grips with them, and, whenever they came to consciousness as occasional fantasies, have instantly suppressed them. The borderline between conscious and unconscious is in large measure determined by our view of the world. That is why we must talk about general problems if we wish to deal adequately with the concept of the unconscious. And if we are to grasp its nature, we must concern ourselves not only with contemporary problems, but also with the history of the human mind.

48   This preoccupation with the unconscious is a problem of practical as well as theoretical importance. For just as our view of the world up till now has been a decisive factor in the shaping of the unconscious and its contents, so the remoulding of our views in accordance with the active forces of the unconscious is laid upon us as a practical necessity. It is impossible to cure a neurosis permanently with individual nostrums, for man cannot exist merely as an isolated individual outside the human community. The principle on which he builds his life must be one that is generally acceptable, otherwise it will lack that natural morality which is indispensable to man as a member of the herd. But such a principle, if it is not left in the darkness of the unconscious, becomes a formulated view of the world which is felt as a necessity by all who are in the habit of consciously scrutinizing their thoughts and actions. This may explain why I have touched on questions each one of which would need for its full presentation more than one head and more than one lifetime.

MIND AND EARTH [1]

49   The phrase "mind and earth" has a slightly poetic ring. Involuntarily we think, by contrast, of the mind [2] as subject to the influences of heaven, in much the same way as the Chinese distinguish between a *shen*-soul and a *kwei*-soul, the one relating to heaven, the other to earth. But since we Westerners know nothing about the substance of the mind, and therefore cannot venture to say whether it has in it something of a heavenly nature and something of an earthly nature, we must be content to speak of two different ways of viewing, or two different aspects of, the complicated phenomenon we call mind. Instead of postulating a heavenly *shen*-soul, we could regard mind as a causeless and creative principle; and instead of a *kwei*-soul, mind could be conceived as a product of cause and effect. The latter point of view would be the more appropriate in regard to our theme, for mind would then be understood as a *system of adaptation determined by the conditions of an earthly environment.* I need hardly emphasize that this causal view must necessarily be one-sided, because only one aspect of the mind is properly grasped by it. The other side of the problem must be left out of account as not belonging to my theme.

1 [Originally published as part of an essay, "Die Erdbedingtheit der Psyche," in *Mensch und Erde,* edited by Count Hermann Keyserling (Darmstadt, 1927), pp. 83–137. That essay was later divided and largely rewritten as two: "Die Struktur der Seele," for the bibliographical history of which see its translation, "The Structure of the Psyche," *Coll. Works,* Vol. 8, p. 139, n. 1; and the present paper, "Seele und Erde," in *Seelenprobleme der Gegenwart* (Zurich, 1931). The original (1927) paper was translated by C. F. and H. G. Baynes as "Mind and the Earth," *Contributions to Analytical Psychology* (London and New York, 1928), and that version has been consulted.—EDITORS.]
2 [The word used throughout this essay is "Seele," which in this context can be translated either as "mind" or as "psyche." Cf. *The Structure and Dynamics of the Psyche,* p. 300, note.—TRANS.]

50   In approaching the subject of our discussion, it would be as well to define accurately what is to be understood by "mind." Certain views would limit "mental" or "psychic" strictly to consciousness. But such a limitation would no longer satisfy us today. Modern psychopathology has in its possession a wealth of observations regarding psychic activities that are entirely analogous to conscious functions and yet are unconscious. One can perceive, think, feel, remember, decide, and act, unconsciously. Everything that happens in consciousness can under certain conditions also occur unconsciously. How this is possible can best be seen if one pictures the psychic functions and contents as a night landscape over which the beam of a searchlight is playing. Whatever appears in this light of perception is conscious; what lies in the darkness beyond is unconscious, though none the less real and effective. If the beam of light shifts, the contents that till now were conscious sink into the unconscious, and new contents come into the lighted area of consciousness. The contents that have vanished in the darkness continue to be active and make themselves felt indirectly, most commonly as symptoms. Freud has described these symptomatic disturbances in *The Psychopathology of Everyday Life*. The unconscious aptitudes and inhibitions can also be demonstrated experimentally, by means of association tests.

51   If, then, we take the investigations of psychopathology into account, the mind appears as an extended area of psychic phenomena which are partly conscious and partly unconscious. The unconscious portion of the mind is not directly accessible—otherwise it would not be unconscious—but can only be inferred from the effects which unconscious processes have on consciousness. Our inferences can never go beyond an "as if."

52   Here I must go rather more closely into the nature and structure of the unconscious if I am to deal adequately with the conditioning of the mind by the earth. It is a question that concerns the very beginnings and foundations of the mind—things that from time immemorial have lain buried in the darkness, and not merely the banal facts of sense-perception and conscious adaptation to the environment. These belong to the psychology of consciousness, and, as I have said, I do not equate consciousness with the psyche. The latter is a much more comprehensive and darker

field of experience than the narrow, brightly lit area of consciousness, for the psyche also includes the unconscious.

53   In another essay[3] I tried to give a general view of the structure of the unconscious. Its contents, the archetypes, are as it were the hidden foundations of the conscious mind, or, to use another comparison, the roots which the psyche has sunk not only in the earth in the narrower sense but in the world in general. Archetypes are systems of readiness for action, and at the same time images and emotions. They are inherited with the brain-structure—indeed, they are its psychic aspect. They represent, on the one hand, a very strong instinctive conservatism, while on the other hand they are the most effective means conceivable of instinctive adaptation. They are thus, essentially, the chthonic portion of the psyche, if we may use such an expression—that portion through which the psyche is attached to nature, or in which its link with the earth and the world appears at its most tangible. The psychic influence of the earth and its laws is seen most clearly in these primordial images.

54   This problem is not only very complicated but also a very subtle one. We shall have to reckon with quite unusual difficulties in dealing with it, and the first of these is that the archetype and its function must be understood far more as a part of man's prehistoric, irrational psychology than as a rationally conceivable system. Perhaps I may be allowed a comparison: it is as though we had to describe and explain a building whose upper storey was erected in the nineteenth century, the ground floor dates back to the sixteenth century, and careful examination of the masonry reveals that it was reconstructed from a tower built in the eleventh century. In the cellar we come upon Roman foundations, and under the cellar a choked-up cave with neolithic tools in the upper layer and remnants of fauna from the same period in the lower layers. That would be the picture of our psychic structure. We live on the upper storey and are only aware that the lower storey is slightly old-fashioned. As to what lies beneath the earth's surface, of that we remain totally unconscious.

55   This is a lame analogy, like all analogies, for in the psyche there is nothing that is just a dead relic. Everything is alive, and

3 ["The Structure of the Psyche" (cf. supra, n. 1), which immediately preceded the present essay in *Seelenprobleme der Gegenwart.*—EDITORS.]

our upper storey, consciousness, is continually influenced by its living and active foundations. Like the building, it is sustained and supported by them. And just as the building rises freely above the earth, so our consciousness stands as if above the earth in space, with a wide prospect before it. But the deeper we descend into the house the narrower the horizon becomes, and the more we find ourselves in the darkness, till finally we reach the naked bed-rock, and with it that prehistoric time when reindeer hunters fought for a bare and wretched existence against the elemental forces of wild nature. The men of that age were still in full possession of their animal instincts, without which life would have been impossible. The free sway of instinct is not compatible with a strongly developed consciousness. The consciousness of primitive man, like that of the child, is sporadic, and his world, like the child's, is very limited. Indeed, in accordance with phylogenetic law, we still recapitulate in childhood reminiscences of the prehistory of the race and of mankind in general. Phylogenetically as well as ontogenetically we have grown up out of the dark confines of the earth; hence the factors that affected us most closely became archetypes, and it is these primordial images which influence us most directly, and therefore seem to be the most powerful. I say "seem" because what seems to us the most important thing psychically is not necessarily the most important, or at least need not remain so.

56   What, then, are the most immediate archetypes? This question leads us straight to the problem of archetypal functioning, and so to the heart of the difficulty. From what standpoint should we answer the question? From that of the child, or of the primitive, or of our adult modern consciousness? How can we recognize an archetype? And when is it necessary to have recourse to this hypothesis at all?

57   *I would like to suggest that every psychic reaction which is out of proportion to its precipitating cause should be investigated as to whether it may be conditioned at the same time by an archetype.*[4]

58   What I mean by this can best be illustrated by an example. Suppose a child is afraid of its mother. We have first to assure ourselves that there is no rational cause for this, a bad con-

4 [Cf. "Instinct and the Unconscious," in *The Structure and Dynamics of the Psyche.*—EDITORS.]

science, for instance, on the child's part, or violence on the mother's, or something else that may have happened to the child. If there is nothing of this kind to explain the fear, then I would suggest that the situation be regarded as an archetypal one. Usually such fears occur at night, and are wont to show themselves in dreams. The child now dreams of the mother as a witch who pursues children. The conscious material behind these dreams is in some cases the story of Hänsel and Gretel. It is then said that the child should not have been told such a fairytale, because the tale is thought to be the cause of the fear. That is an erroneous rationalization, but it nevertheless contains a core of truth in so far as the witch-motif is the most suitable expression for childish fears, and always has been. That is why such fairytales exist. Children's night-terrors are a typical event that is constantly repeating itself and has always been expressed in typical fairytale motifs.

59   But fairytales are only infantile forms of legends, myths, and superstitions taken from the "night religion" of primitives. What I call "night religion" is the magical form of religion, the meaning and purpose of which is intercourse with the dark powers, devils, witches, magicians, and spirits. Just as the childish fairytale is a phylogenetic repetition of the ancient night religion, so the childish fear is a re-enactment of primitive psychology, a phylogenetic relic.

60   The fact that this relic displays a certain vitality is in no sense abnormal, for nocturnal fears, even in adults living under civilized conditions, are not necessarily an abnormal phenomenon. Only an intensified degree of night-fear can be regarded as abnormal. The question then is, under what circumstances is this night-fear increased? Can the increase be explained solely by the archetype of the witch expressed in the fairytale, or must some other explanatory cause be adduced?

61   We should make the archetype responsible only for a definite, minimal, normal degree of fear; any pronounced increase, felt to be abnormal, must have special causes. Freud, as we know, explains this fear as due to the collision of the child's incestuous tendency with the incest prohibition. He thus explains it from the standpoint of the child. I have no doubt that children can have "incestuous" tendencies in the extended sense used by Freud, but I doubt very much whether these tendencies

can be attributed without more ado to the child's psychology *sui generis*. There are very good reasons for the view that the child-psyche is still under the spell of the parents' psyche, especially the mother's, and to such a degree that the psyche of the child must be regarded as a functional appendage of that of the parents. The psychic individuality of the child develops only later, after a reliable continuity of consciousness has been established. The fact that the child begins by speaking of himself in the third person is in my view a clear proof of the impersonality of his psychology.

62   I am therefore inclined to explain the possible incestuous tendencies of the child rather from the standpoint of the psychology of the parents, just as every childish neurosis should be considered first and foremost in the light of the parental psychology. Thus, a frequent cause of increased infantile terrors is an especial "complex-proneness" on the part of the parents, that is, their repression and disregard of certain vital problems. Anything that falls into the unconscious takes on a more or less archaic form. If, for example, the mother represses a painful and terrifying complex, she will feel it as an evil spirit pursuing her —a "skeleton in the cupboard," as the English say. This formulation shows that the complex has already acquired archetypal force. It sits on her like an incubus, she is tormented by nightmares. Whether she tells "nightmare-stories" to the child or not, she none the less infects the child and awakens in its mind archetypal terror images from her own psychology. Perhaps she has erotic fantasies about a man other than her husband. The child is the visible sign of their marriage tie, and her resistance to the tie is unconsciously directed against the child, who has to be repudiated. On the archaic level this corresponds to child-murder. In this way the mother becomes a wicked witch who devours children.

63   As in the mother, so in the child the possibilities of archaic representation lie dormant, and the same cause which first produced and laid down the archetype during the course of human history reactivates it again and again today.

64   This example of the manifestation of an archetype in a child has not been chosen at random. We began with the question of what are the most immediate archetypes. The most immediate is the primordial image of the mother; she is in every way the

nearest and most powerful experience, and the one which occurs during the most impressionable period of man's life. Since consciousness is as yet only poorly developed in childhood, one cannot speak of an "individual" experience at all. On the contrary, the mother is an archetypal experience; she is experienced by the more or less unconscious child not as a definite, individual feminine personality but as *the* mother, an archetype charged with an immensity of possible meanings. As life proceeds the primordial image fades and is replaced by a conscious, relatively individual image, which is assumed to be the only mother-image we have. But in the unconscious the mother always remains a powerful primordial image, colouring and even determining throughout life our relations to woman, to society, to the world of feeling and fact, yet in so subtle a way that, as a rule, there is no conscious perception of the process. We think all this is only a metaphor. But it becomes a very concrete fact when a man marries a wife only because in some way she resembles his mother, or else because she very definitely does not. Mother Germania is for the Germans, like *la douce France* for the French, a figure of the utmost importance behind the political scene, who could be overlooked only by blinkered intellectuals. The all-embracing womb of Mother Church is anything but a metaphor, and the same is true of Mother Earth, Mother Nature, and "matter" in general.

65   The archetype of the mother is the most immediate one for the child. But with the development of consciousness the father also enters his field of vision, and activates an archetype whose nature is in many respects opposed to that of the mother. Just as the mother archetype corresponds to the Chinese *yin,* so the father archetype corresponds to the *yang.* It determines our relations to man, to the law and the state, to reason and the spirit and the dynamism of nature. "Fatherland" implies boundaries, a definite localization in space, whereas the land itself is Mother Earth, quiescent and fruitful. The Rhine is a father, as is the Nile, the wind and storm, thunder and lightning. The father is the "auctor" and represents authority, hence also law and the state. He is that which moves in the world, like the wind; the guide and creator of invisible thoughts and airy images. He is the creative wind-breath—the spirit, pneuma, *atman.*

66   Thus the father, too, is a powerful archetype dwelling in the

psyche of the child. At first he is *the* father, an all-encompassing God-image, a dynamic principle. In the course of life this authoritarian imago recedes into the background: the father turns into a limited and often all-too-human personality. The father-imago, on the other hand, develops to the full its potential significance. Just as man was late in discovering nature, so he only gradually discovered law, duty, responsibility, the state, the spirit. As the nascent consciousness becomes more capable of understanding, the importance of the parental personality dwindles. The place of the father is taken by the society of men, and the place of the mother by the family.

67   It would be wrong, in my view, to say that all those things which take the place of the parents are nothing but a substitute for the unavoidable loss of the primordial parental imagos. What appears in their stead is not just a substitute, but a reality that is interwoven with the parents and has impressed itself on the mind of the child through the parental imago. The mother who gives warmth, protection, and nourishment is also the hearth, the sheltering cave or hut, and the surrounding vegetation. She is the provident field, and her son is the godlike grain, the brother and friend of man. She is the milk-giving cow and the herd. The father goes about, talks with other men, hunts, travels, makes war, lets his bad moods loose like thunderstorms, and at the behest of invisible thoughts he suddenly changes the whole situation like a tempest. He is the war and the weapon, the cause of all changes; he is the bull provoked to violence or prone to apathetic laziness. He is the image of all the helpful or harmful elemental powers.

68   All these things are the early immediacies of the child's life, impinging on him, directly or indirectly, through the parents. And as the parental imago shrinks and becomes humanized, all those things, which at first seemed only like a background or like marginal effects, begin to stand out more clearly. The earth he plays with, the fire he warms himself at, the rain and wind that chill him, were always realities, but because of his twilight consciousness they were seen and understood only as qualities of the parents. Then, as out of a mist, there emerge the material and dynamic aspects of the earth, revealing themselves as powers in their own right, and no longer wearing the masks of the

parents. They are thus not a substitute but a reality that corresponds to a higher level of consciousness.

69   Nevertheless something is lost in this development, and that is the irreplaceable feeling of immediate oneness with the parents. This feeling is not just a sentiment, but an important psychological fact which Lévy-Bruhl, in an altogether different context, has called *participation mystique*. The fact denoted by this not immediately understandable expression plays a great role in the psychology of primitives as well as in analytical psychology. To put it briefly, it means *a state of identity in mutual unconsciousness*. Perhaps I should explain this further. If the same unconscious complex is constellated in two people at the same time, it produces a remarkable emotional effect, a projection, which causes either a mutual attraction or a mutual repulsion. When I and another person have an unconscious relation to the same important fact, I become in part identical with him, and because of this I orient myself to him as I would to the complex in question were I conscious of it.

70   This state of *participation mystique* obtains between parents and children. A well-known example is the stepmother who identifies herself with the daughter and, through her, marries the son-in-law; or the father who thinks he is considering his son's welfare when he naïvely forces him to fulfil his—the father's—wishes, for instance in marriage or in the choice of a profession. The son who identifies himself with the father is an equally well-known figure. But there is an especially close bond between mother and daughter, which in certain cases can actually be demonstrated by the association method.[5] Although the *participation mystique* is an unconscious fact to the person concerned, he nevertheless feels the change when it no longer exists. There is always a certain difference between the psychology of a man whose father is still living and one whose father is dead. So long as a *participation mystique* with the parents persists, a relatively infantile style of life can be maintained. Through the *participation mystique* life is pumped into us from outside in the form of unconscious motivations, for which, since they are unconscious, no responsibility is felt. Because of this infantile unconsciousness

5 ["Statistical Investigations on Word-Associations and on Familial Agreement in Reaction Type among Uneducated Persons," by Emma Fürst, in *Studies in Word Association* (trans. by Eder).—EDITORS.]

the burden of life is lightened, or at least seems so. One is not alone, but exists unconsciously in twos or threes. In imagination the son is in his mother's lap, protected by the father. The father is reborn in the son—at least as a link in the chain of eternal life. The mother has rejuvenated her father in her youthful husband and so has not lost her youth. I need not cite examples from primitive psychology. A reference to them must suffice.

71   All this drops away with the broadening and intensification of consciousness. The resultant extension of the parental imagos over the face of the world, or rather, the world's breaking through the mists of childhood, severs the unconscious union with the parents. This process is even performed consciously in the primitive rites of initiation into manhood. The archetype of the parents is thereby driven into the background; it is, as we say, no longer "constellated." Instead, a new kind of *participation mystique* begins with the tribe, society, Church, or nation. This participation is general and impersonal, and above all it gives unconsciousness very little scope. If anyone should incline to be too unconscious and too guilelessly trusting, law and society will quickly shake him into consciousness. But sexual maturity also brings with it the possibility of a new personal *participation mystique,* and hence of replacing that part of the personality which was lost in identification with the parents. A new archetype is constellated: in a man it is the archetype of woman, and in a woman the archetype of man. These two figures were likewise hidden behind the mask of the parental imagos, but now they step forth undisguised, even though strongly influenced by the parental imagos, often overwhelmingly so. I have given the feminine archetype in man the name "anima," and the masculine archetype in woman the name "animus," for specific reasons which I shall discuss later.[6]

72   The more a man or woman is unconsciously influenced by the parental imago, the more surely will the figure of the loved one be chosen as either a positive or a negative substitute for the parents. The far-reaching influence of the parental imago should not be considered abnormal; on the contrary, it is a very normal and therefore very common phenomenon. It is, indeed, very important that this should be so, for otherwise the parents are not

[6] Cf. *Two Essays on Analytical Psychology*, pars. 296ff.

reborn in the children, and the parental imago becomes so completely lost that all continuity in the life of the individual ceases. He cannot connect his childhood with his adult life, and therefore remains unconsciously a child—a situation that is the best possible foundation for a neurosis. He will then suffer from all those ills that beset parvenus without a history, be they individuals or social groups.

73   It is normal that children should in a certain sense marry their parents. This is just as important, psychologically, as the biological necessity to infuse new blood if the ancestral tree is to produce a good breed. It guarantees continuity, a reasonable prolongation of the past into the present. Only too much or too little in this direction is harmful.

74   So long as a positive or negative resemblance to the parents is the deciding factor in a love choice, the release from the parental imago, and hence from childhood, is not complete. Although childhood has to be brought along for the sake of historical continuity, this should not be at the expense of further development. When, towards middle life, the last gleam of childhood illusion fades—this it must be owned is true only of an almost ideal life, for many go as children to their graves—then the archetype of the mature man or woman emerges from the parental imago: an image of man as woman has known him from the beginning of time, and an image of woman that man carries within him eternally.

75   There are indeed many men who can describe exactly, even to individual details, the image of woman that they carry in their minds. (I have met few women who could give as exact a picture of the masculine archetype.) Just as the primordial image of the mother is a composite image of all previous mothers, so the image of the anima is a supra-individual image. So true is this that the image reveals closely corresponding features in men who are individually very different, and one can almost reconstruct from it a definite type of woman. The most striking feature about the anima-type is that the maternal element is entirely lacking. She is the companion and friend in her favourable aspect, in her unfavourable aspect she is the courtesan. Often these types are described very accurately, with all their human and daemonic qualities, in fantastic romances, such as Rider Haggard's *She* and *Wisdom's Daughter*, Benoît's *L'Atlan-*

tide, and, fragmentarily, in the second part of *Faust,* in the figure of Helen. But the anima-type is presented in the most succinct and pregnant form in the Gnostic legend of Simon Magus, a caricature of whom appears in the Acts of the Apostles.[7] Simon Magus was always accompanied on his travels by a girl, whose name was Helen. He had found her in a brothel in Tyre; she was a reincarnation of Helen of Troy. I do not know whether Goethe's Faust-Helen motif was consciously derived from the Simon legend. A similar relationship occurs in Rider Haggard's *Wisdom's Daughter,* where we can be certain that there was no conscious continuity.

76   The absence of the maternal element demonstrates, on the one hand, the complete release from the mother-imago, and, on the other, the idea of a purely human relationship lacking the natural incentive of procreation. The overwhelming majority of men on the present cultural level never advance beyond the maternal significance of woman, and this is the reason why the anima seldom develops beyond the infantile, primitive level of the prostitute. Consequently, prostitution is one of the main by-products of civilized marriage. In the legend of Simon, however, and in the second part of *Faust* anima symbols of complete maturity are found. This growth of adulthood is synonymous with growth away from nature. Christian and Buddhist monastic ideals grappled with the same problem, but always the flesh was sacrificed. Goddesses and demigoddesses took the place of the personal, human woman who should carry the projection of the anima.

77   Here we touch on highly controversial territory into which I do not wish to venture further at this point. We shall do better to return to the simpler problem of how we can recognize the existence of such a feminine archetype.

78   As long as an archetype is not projected and not loved or hated in an object, it is still wholly identical with the individual, who is thus compelled to act it out himself. A man will then act out his own anima. We have a word that aptly characterizes this attitude: it is "animosity." This expression can best be interpreted as "anima possession," denoting a condition of uncontrolled emotion. The word "animosity" is used only for un-

7 8:9-24. For the Helen legend see Irenaeus, *Adv. haer.* 9, xxiii.

pleasant emotions, but actually the anima can induce pleasant ones as well.[8]

79 Self-control is a typically masculine ideal, to be achieved by the repression of feeling. Feeling is a specifically feminine virtue, and because a man in trying to attain his ideal of manhood represses all feminine traits—which are really part of him, just as masculine traits are part of a woman's psychology—he also represses certain emotions as womanish weakness. In so doing he piles up effeminacy or sentimentality in the unconscious, and this, when it breaks out, betrays in him the existence of a feminine being. As we know, it is just the "he-men" who are most at the mercy of their feminine feelings. This might explain the very much greater number of suicides among men, and, conversely, the extraordinary strength and toughness often developed by very feminine women. If we carefully examine the uncontrolled emotions of a man and try to reconstruct the probable personality underlying them, we soon arrive at a feminine figure which I call, as I said, the anima. On the same ground the ancients conceived of a feminine soul, a "psyche" or "anima," and not without good psychological reasons did the ecclesiastics of the Middle Ages propound the question, *Habet mulier animam?*

80 With women the case is reversed. When the animus breaks out in a woman, it is not feelings that appear, as in a man, but she begins to argue and to rationalize. And just as his anima-feelings are arbitrary and capricious, so these feminine arguments are illogical and irrational. One can speak of an animus-thinking that is always right and must have the last word, and always end up with "That's just the reason!" If the anima is irrational feeling, the animus is irrational thinking.

81 So far as my experience goes, a man always understands fairly easily what is meant by the anima; indeed, as I said, he frequently has a quite definite picture of her, so that from a varied collection of women of all periods he can single out the one who comes closest to the anima-type. But I have, as a rule, found it very difficult to make a woman understand what the animus is, and I have never met any woman who could tell me anything definite about his personality. From this I conclude

[8] *Two Essays*, pars. 335ff. [Cf. also *Aion*, ch. III, esp. pars. 23–33.—EDS.]

41

that the animus does not have a definite personality at all; in other words, he is not so much a unity as a plurality. This fact must somehow be connected with the specific psychology of men and women. On the biological level a woman's chief interest is to hold a man, while a man's chief interest is to conquer a woman, and because of his nature he seldom stops at one conquest. Thus one masculine personality plays a decisive role for a woman, but a man's relation to a woman is much less definite, as he can look on his wife as one among many women. This makes him lay stress on the legal and social character of marriage, whereas a woman sees it as an exclusively personal relationship. Hence, as a rule, a woman's consciousness is restricted to one man, whereas a man's consciousness has a tendency to go beyond the one personal relationship—a tendency that is sometimes opposed to any personal limitations. In the unconscious, therefore, we may expect a compensation by contraries. The man's sharply defined anima figure fulfils this expectation perfectly, as also does the indefinite polymorphism of the woman's animus.

82   The description of anima and animus that I have given here is necessarily a brief one. But I should be carrying brevity too far if I described the anima merely as a primordial image of woman consisting of irrational feelings, and the animus merely as a primordial image of man consisting of irrational views. Both figures present far-reaching problems, since they are elementary forms of that psychic phenomenon which from primitive times has been called the "soul." They are also the cause of that deep human need to speak of souls or daemons at all.

83   Nothing that is autonomous in the psyche is impersonal or neutral. Impersonality is a category pertaining to consciousness. All autonomous psychic factors have the character of personality, from the "voices" of the insane to the control-spirits of mediums and the visions of the mystics. Anima and animus, likewise, have a personality character, and this cannot be better expressed than by the word "soul."

84   Here I would like to guard against a misunderstanding. The concept of "soul" which I am now using can be compared more with the primitive idea of the soul, for instance the *ba*-soul and *ka*-soul of the Egyptians, than with the Christian idea of it, which is an attempt to make a philosophical construct out of a

metaphysical individual substance. My conception of the soul has absolutely nothing to do with this, since it is purely phenomenological. I am not indulging in any psychological mysticism, but am simply trying to grasp scientifically the elementary psychic phenomena which underlie the belief in souls.

85   Since the complex of facts represented by anima and animus best corresponds to what has been described as soul at all times and by all peoples, it is hardly surprising that they bring an uncommonly mystical atmosphere along with them as soon as one tries to examine their contents more closely. Whenever the anima is projected, she immediately surrounds herself with a peculiar historical feeling which Goethe expressed in the words: "In times gone by you were my wife or sister." [9] Rider Haggard and Benoît had to go back to Greece and Egypt in order to give expression to this insistent historical feeling.

86   Curiously enough, the animus seems to be lacking in this mystical sense of history. I would almost say that he is more concerned with the present and the future. He has nomothetical proclivities, preferring to speak grandiosely of things as they should be, or to give an apodictic judgment on the most obscure and controversial matters, and in such positive terms that the woman is relieved of all further (and possibly all too painful) reflection.

87   Once again, I can only explain this difference as a compensation by contraries. A man, in his conscious activity, plans ahead and seeks to create the future, while it is a specifically feminine trait to rack one's brains over such questions as who was somebody's great-great-aunt. But it is just this feminine passion for genealogies that comes out very clearly in Rider Haggard, garnished with Anglo-Saxon sentiment, and in Benoît the same thing is served up with the spicy admixture of a *chronique scandaleuse*. Intimations of reincarnation in the form of irrational feelings hang very strongly about a man's anima, while a woman will sometimes consciously admit such feelings if she is not too much under the domination of the man's rationalism.

88   This historical feeling always has the quality of momentousness and fatefulness, and therefore leads directly to the problems

9 Untitled poem ("Warum gabst du uns die tiefen Blicke?") in *Werke*, II, p. 43.

of immortality and divinity. Even the rationalistic, sceptical Benoît describes those who have died of love as being preserved for all eternity by a peculiarly effective method of mummification, not to mention the full-blown mysticism of Rider Haggard in *Ayesha: The Return of She*—altogether a psychological document of the first rank.

89   The animus, not having these emotional qualities, seems to lack entirely the aspect I have been describing, yet in his deepest essence he is just as historically-minded as the anima. Unfortunately there are no good literary examples of the animus. Women writers seem to be deficient in a certain naïve introspection, or at least they prefer to keep the results of their introspection in another compartment, possibly because no feeling is connected with it. I know of only one unprejudiced document of this sort, a novel by Marie Hay, *The Evil Vineyard*. In this very unpretentious story the historical element in the animus comes out in a clever disguise that was surely not intended by the author.

90   The animus consists of *a priori* assumptions based on unconsidered judgments. The existence of such judgments can only be inferred from the woman's conscious attitude to certain things. I must give you an example. A woman I knew surrounded her son with the most solemn care and lent him an importance he in no way deserved, with the result that soon after puberty he became neurotic. The reason for her senseless attitude was not at first discernible. Closer investigation, however, revealed the existence of an unconscious dogma that said: My son is the coming Messiah. This is a very ordinary instance of the widespread hero-archetype in women, which is projected on the father or the husband or the son, in the form of an opinion which then unconsciously regulates the woman's behaviour. A well-known example is Annie Besant, who also discovered a saviour.

91   In Marie Hay's novel the heroine drives her husband insane by her attitude which is based on the unconscious and unspoken assumption that he is a horrible tyrant who holds her captive in much the same way as . . . The uncompleted simile she left to the interpretation of her husband, who finally discovered the appropriate figure for it in a *cinquecento* tyrant with whom he identified himself, and lost his reason in consequence. The his-

44

torical factor, therefore, is by no means lacking to the animus. But it expresses itself in a way fundamentally different from that of the anima. Similarly, in the religious problems connected with the animus the judging faculties predominate, just as the feeling faculties do in the case of a man.

92   Finally, I would like to remark that the anima and animus are not the only autonomous figures or "souls" in the unconscious, though in practice they are the most immediate and most important. But, since I would like to touch on still another aspect of the problem of mind and earth, perhaps I may leave this difficult field of extremely subtle inward experience and turn to that other side where we shall no longer grope laboriously in the dark background of the mind, but pass into the wide world of everyday things.

93   Just as, in the process of evolution, the mind has been moulded by earthly conditions, so the same process repeats itself under our eyes today. Imagine a large section of some European nation transplanted to a strange soil and another climate. We can confidently expect this human group to undergo certain psychic and perhaps also physical changes in the course of a few generations, even without the admixture of foreign blood. We can observe in the Jews of the various European countries marked differences which can only be explained by the peculiarities of the people they live amongst. It is not difficult to tell a Spanish Jew from a North African Jew, a German Jew from a Russian Jew. One can even distinguish the various types of Russian Jew, the Polish from the North Russian and Cossack type. In spite of the similarity of race, there are pronounced differences whose cause is obscure. It is extremely hard to define these differences exactly, though a student of human nature feels them at once.

94   The greatest experiment in the transplantation of a race in modern times was the colonization of the North American continent by a predominantly Germanic population. As the climatic conditions vary very widely, we would expect all sorts of variations of the original racial type. The admixture of Indian blood is increasingly small, so it plays no role. Boas has shown that anatomical changes begin already in the second generation of immigrants, chiefly in the measurements of the skull. At all events the "Yankee" type is formed, and this is so similar to the

45

Indian type that on my first visit to the Middle West,[10] while watching a stream of workers coming out of a factory, I remarked to my companion that I should never have thought there was such a high percentage of Indian blood. He answered, laughing, that he was willing to bet that in all these hundreds of men there would not be found a drop of Indian blood. That was many years ago when I had no notion of the mysterious Indianization of the American people. I got to know of this mystery only when I had to treat many American patients analytically. Remarkable differences were revealed in comparison with Europeans.

95   Another thing that struck me was the great influence of the Negro, a psychological influence naturally, not due to the mixing of blood. The emotional way an American expresses himself, especially the way he laughs, can best be studied in the illustrated supplements of the American papers; the inimitable Teddy Roosevelt laugh is found in its primordial form in the American Negro. The peculiar walk with loose joints, or the swinging of the hips so frequently observed in Americans, also comes from the Negro. American music draws its main inspiration from the Negro, and so does the dance. The expression of religious feeling, the revival meetings, the Holy Rollers and other abnormalities are strongly influenced by the Negro, and the famous American naïveté, in its charming as well as its more unpleasant form, invites comparison with the childlikeness of the Negro. The vivacity of the average American, which shows itself not only at baseball games but quite particularly in his extraordinary love of talking—the ceaseless gabble of American papers is an eloquent example of this—is scarcely to be derived from his Germanic forefathers, but is far more like the chattering of a Negro village. The almost total lack of privacy and the all-devouring mass sociability remind one of primitive life in open huts, where there is complete identity with all members of the tribe. It seemed to me that American houses had their doors open all the time, just as there are no hedges round the gardens in American towns and villages. Everything seems to be street.

96   It is naturally very difficult to decide how much of all this is due to symbiosis with the Negro, and how much to the fact

10 [*Sic,* but Buffalo, New York, is meant. Cf. infra, par. 948.—EDITORS.]

that America is still a pioneering nation on virgin soil. But taken all in all, the wide influence of the Negro on the general character of the people is unmistakable.

97   This infection by the primitive can, of course, be observed just as well in other countries, though not to the same degree and in this form. In Africa, for example, the white man is a diminishing minority and must therefore protect himself from the Negro by observing the most rigorous social forms, otherwise he risks "going black." If he succumbs to the primitive influence he is lost. But in America the Negro, just because he is in a minority, is not a degenerative influence, but rather one which, peculiar though it is, cannot be termed unfavourable—unless one happens to have a jazz phobia.

98   The remarkable thing is that one notices little or nothing of the Indian influence. The above-mentioned physiognomical similarities do not point to Africa but are specifically American. Does the body react to America, and the psyche to Africa? I must answer this question by saying that only the outward behaviour is influenced by the Negro, but what goes on in the psyche must be the subject of further investigation.

99   It is natural that in the dreams of my American patients the Negro should play no small role as an expression of the inferior side of their personality. A European might similarly dream of tramps or other representatives of the lower classes. But as the great majority of dreams, especially those in the early stages of analysis, are superficial, it was only in the course of very thorough and deep analyses that I came upon symbols relating to the Indian. The progressive tendency of the unconscious, as expressed for instance in the hero-motif, chooses the Indian as its symbol, just as certain coins of the Union bear an Indian head. This is a tribute to the once-hated Indian, but it also testifies to the fact that the American hero-motif chooses the Indian as an ideal figure. It would certainly never occur to any American administration to place the head of Cetewayo or any other Negro hero on their coins. Monarchies prefer the head of the sovereign, democratic states honour other symbols of their ideals. I have given a detailed example of a similar American hero-fantasy in my book *Symbols of Transformation,* and I could add dozens of others.

100   The hero is always the embodiment of man's highest and

most powerful aspiration, or of what this aspiration ought ideally to be and what he would most gladly realize. It is therefore of importance what kind of fantasy constitutes the hero-motif. In the American hero-fantasy the Indian's character plays a leading role. The American conception of sport goes far beyond the notions of the easy-going European; only the Indian rites of initiation can compare with the ruthlessness and savagery of a rigorous American training. The performance of American athletes is therefore admirable. In everything on which the American has really set his heart we catch a glimpse of the Indian. His extraordinary concentration on a particular goal, his tenacity of purpose, his unflinching endurance of the greatest hardships—in all this the legendary virtues of the Indian find full expression.[11]

101   The hero-motif affects not only the general attitude to life but also the problems of religion. Any absolutist attitude is always a religious attitude, and in whatever respect a man becomes absolute, there you see his religion. I have found in my American patients that their hero-figure possesses traits derived from the religion of the Indians. The most important figure in their religion is the shaman, the medicine-man or conjurer of spirits. The first American discovery in this field—since taken up in Europe—was spiritualism, and the second was Christian Science and other forms of mental healing. Christian Science is an exorcistic ritual. The demons of sickness are denied, suitable incantations are sung over the refractory body, and Christianity, the product of a high level of culture, is used as healing-magic. Though the poverty of its spiritual content is appalling, Christian Science is a living force; it possesses a strength derived from the soil, and can therefore work those miracles that are sought for in vain in the official churches.

102   There is no country on earth where the "power-word," the magic formula, the slogan or advertisement is more effective than in America. We Europeans laugh about this, but we forget that faith in the magical power of the word can move more than mountains. Christ himself was a word, the Word. We have become estranged from this psychology, but in the American it is still alive. It has yet to be seen what America will do with it.

11 See "The Complications of American Psychology," infra, pp. 502ff.

103   Thus the American presents a strange picture: a European
with Negro behaviour and an Indian soul. He shares the fate of
all usurpers of foreign soil. Certain Australian primitives assert
that one cannot conquer foreign soil, because in it there dwell
strange ancestor-spirits who reincarnate themselves in the new-
born. There is a great psychological truth in this. The foreign
land assimilates its conqueror. But unlike the Latin conquerors
of Central and South America, the North Americans preserved
their European standards with the most rigid puritanism, though
they could not prevent the souls of their Indian foes from becoming theirs. Everywhere the virgin earth causes at least the unconscious of the conqueror to sink to the level of its indigenous
inhabitants. Thus, in the American, there is a discrepancy between conscious and unconscious that is not found in the European, a tension between an extremely high conscious level of
culture and an unconscious primitivity. This tension forms a
psychic potential which endows the American with an indomi-
table spirit of enterprise and an enviable enthusiasm which we
in Europe do not know. The very fact that we still have our ancestral spirits, and that for us everything is steeped in history,
keeps us in contact with our unconscious, but we are so caught
in this contact and held so fast in the historical vice that the
greatest catastrophes are needed in order to wrench us loose and
to change our political behaviour from what it was five hundred
years ago. Our contact with the unconscious chains us to the
earth and makes it hard for us to move, and this is certainly no
advantage when it comes to progressiveness and all the other desirable motions of the mind. Nevertheless I would not speak ill
of our relation to good Mother Earth. *Plurimi pertransibunt—*
but he who is rooted in the soil endures. Alienation from the
unconscious and from its historical conditions spells rootlessness.
That is the danger that lies in wait for the conqueror of foreign
lands, and for every individual who, through one-sided allegiance to any kind of -ism, loses touch with the dark, maternal,
earthy ground of his being.

49

ARCHAIC MAN [1]

104   The word "archaic" means primal, original. While it is one of the most difficult and thankless of tasks to say anything of importance about the civilized man of today, we are apparently in a more favourable position when it comes to archaic man. In the first case, the speaker finds himself caught in the same presuppositions and is blinded by the same prejudices as those whom he wishes to view from a superior standpoint. In the case of archaic man, however, we are far removed from his world in time, our mental equipment, being more differentiated, is superior to his, so that from this more elevated coign of vantage it is possible for us to survey his world and the meaning it held for him.

105   With this sentence I have set limits to the subject to be covered in my lecture. Unless I restricted myself to the psychic life of archaic man, I could hardly paint a sufficiently comprehensive picture of him in so small a space. I should like to confine myself to this picture, and shall say nothing about the findings of anthropology. When we speak of man in general, we do not have his anatomy, the shape of his skull, or the colour of his skin in mind, but mean rather his psychic world, his state of consciousness, and his mode of life. Since all this belongs to the subject-matter of psychology, we shall be dealing here chiefly with the psychology of archaic man and with the primitive mentality. Despite this limitation we shall find we have actually widened our theme, because it is not only primitive man

1 [First published as "Der archaische Mensch," *Europäische Revue* (Berlin), VII (1931), 182–203. Revised and republished in *Seelenprobleme der Gegenwart* (Zurich, 1931), pp. 211–47; trans. by W. S. Dell and Cary F. Baynes in *Modern Man in Search of a Soul* (London and New York, 1933), pp. 143–74. The latter trans. has been consulted.—EDITORS.]

whose psychology is archaic. It is the psychology also of modern, civilized man, and not merely of individual "throw-backs" in modern society. On the contrary, every civilized human being, however high his conscious development, is still an archaic man at the deeper levels of his psyche. Just as the human body connects us with the mammals and displays numerous vestiges of earlier evolutionary stages going back even to the reptilian age, so the human psyche is a product of evolution which, when followed back to its origins, shows countless archaic traits.

106   When we first come into contact with primitive peoples or read about primitive psychology in scientific works, we cannot fail to be deeply impressed with the strangeness of archaic man. Lévy-Bruhl himself, an authority in the field of primitive psychology, never wearies of emphasizing the striking difference between the "prelogical" state of mind and our own conscious outlook. It seems to him, as a civilized man, inexplicable that the primitive should disregard the obvious lessons of experience, should flatly deny the most evident causal connections, and instead of accounting for things as simply due to chance or on reasonable grounds of causality, should take his "collective representations" as being intrinsically valid. By "collective representations" Lévy-Bruhl means widely current ideas whose truth is held to be self-evident from the start, such as the primitive ideas concerning spirits, witchcraft, the power of medicines, and so forth. While it is perfectly understandable to us that people die of advanced age or as the result of diseases that are recognized to be fatal, this is not the case with primitive man. When old persons die, he does not believe it to be the result of age. He argues that there are persons who have lived to be much older. Likewise, no one dies as the result of disease, for there have been other people who recovered from the same disease, or never contracted it. To him, the real explanation is always magic. Either a spirit has killed the man, or it was sorcery. Many primitive tribes recognize death in battle as the only natural death. Still others regard even death in battle as unnatural, holding that the enemy who caused it must either have been a sorcerer or have used a charmed weapon. This grotesque idea can on occasion take an even more impressive form. For instance, two anklets were found in the stomach of a crocodile shot by a European. The natives recognized the anklets as the property of two women

51

who, some time before, had been devoured by a crocodile. At once the charge of witchcraft was raised; for this quite natural occurrence, which would never have aroused the suspicions of a European, was given an unexpected interpretation in the light of one of those presuppositions which Lévy-Bruhl calls "collective representations." The natives said that an unknown sorcerer had summoned the crocodile, and had bidden it catch the two women and bring them to him. The crocodile had carried out this command. But what about the anklets in the beast's stomach? Crocodiles, they explained, never ate people unless bidden to do so. The crocodile had merely received the anklets from the sorcerer as a reward.

107   This story is a perfect example of that capricious way of explaining things which is characteristic of the "prelogical" state of mind. We call it prelogical, because to us such an explanation seems absurdly illogical. But it seems so to us only because we start from assumptions wholly different from those of primitive man. If we were as convinced as he is of the existence of sorcerers and other mysterious powers, instead of believing in so-called natural causes, his inferences would seem to us perfectly logical. As a matter of fact, primitive man is no more logical or illogical than we are. Only his presuppositions are different, and that is what distinguishes him from us. His thinking and his conduct are based on assumptions quite unlike our own. To all that is in any way out of the ordinary and that therefore disturbs, frightens or astonishes him, he ascribes what we would call a supernatural origin. For him, of course, these things are not supernatural, but belong to his world of experience. We feel we are stating a natural sequence of events when we say: This house was burned down because it was struck by lightning. Primitive man senses an equally natural sequence of events when he says: A sorcerer used the lightning to set fire to this house. There is absolutely nothing in the world of the primitive —provided that it is at all unusual or impressive—that will not be accounted for on essentially similar grounds. But in explaining things in this way he is acting just like ourselves: he does not examine his assumptions. To him it is an unquestionable truth that disease and other ills are caused by spirits or witchcraft, just as for us it is a foregone conclusion that an illness has a natural cause. We would no more put it down to sorcery than

he to natural causes. His mental functioning does not differ in any fundamental way from ours. It is, as I have said, his assumptions alone that distinguish him from ourselves.

108   It is also supposed that primitive man has other feelings than we, and another kind of morality—that he has, so to speak, a "prelogical" temperament. Undoubtedly he has a different code of morals. When asked about the difference between good and evil, a Negro chieftain declared: "When I steal my enemy's wives, it is good, when he steals mine, it is bad." In many regions it is a terrible insult to tread on a person's shadow, and in others it is an unpardonable sin to scrape a sealskin with an iron knife instead of a flint one. But let us be honest. Do we not think it a sin to eat fish with a steel knife, for a man to keep his hat on in a room, or to greet a lady with a cigar in his mouth? With us, as well as with primitives, such things have nothing to do with ethics. There are good and loyal head-hunters, and there are others who piously and conscientiously perform cruel rites, or commit murder from sacred conviction. The primitive is no less prompt than we are to value an ethical attitude. His good is just as good as ours, and his evil is just as bad as ours. Only the forms under which they appear are different; the process of ethical judgment is the same.

109   It is likewise thought that primitive man has keener senses than we, or that they are somehow different. But his highly re-fined sense of direction or of hearing and sight is entirely a matter of professional differentiation. If he is confronted with things that are outside his experience, he is amazingly slow and clumsy. I once showed some native hunters, who were as keen-sighted as hawks, magazine pictures in which any child of ours would instantly have recognized human figures. But my hunt-ers turned the pictures round and round until one of them, tracing the outline with his finger, finally exclaimed: "These are white men!" It was hailed by all as a great discovery.

110   The incredibly accurate sense of direction shown by many primitives is essentially occupational. It is absolutely necessary that they should be able to find their way in forests and in the bush. Even the European, after a short while in Africa, begins to notice things he would never have dreamed of noticing before —and from fear of going hopelessly astray in spite of his compass.

111   There is nothing to show that primitive man thinks, feels, or

perceives in a way fundamentally different from ours. It is relatively unimportant that he has, or seems to have, a smaller area of consciousness than we, and that he has little or no aptitude for concentrated mental activity. This last, it is true, strikes the European as strange. For instance, I could never hold a palaver for longer than two hours, since by that time the natives declared themselves tired. They said it was too difficult, and yet I had asked only quite simple questions in the most desultory way. But these same people were capable of astonishing concentration and endurance when out hunting or on a journey. My letter-carrier, for instance, could run seventy-five miles at a stretch. I saw a woman in her sixth month of pregnancy, carrying a baby on her back and smoking a long pipe of tobacco, dance almost the whole night through round a blazing fire when the temperature was 95°, without collapsing. It cannot be denied that primitives are quite capable of concentrating on things that interest them. If we have to give our attention to uninteresting matters, we soon notice how feeble our powers of concentration are. We are just as dependent as they are on emotional impulses.

112   It is true that primitives are simpler and more childlike than we, in good and evil alike. This in itself does not impress us as strange. And yet, when we approach the world of archaic man, we have the feeling of something prodigiously strange. As far as I have been able to analyse it, this feeling comes predominantly from the fact that the primary assumptions of archaic man are essentially different from ours, so that he lives in a different world. Until we come to know his presuppositions, he is a hard riddle to read; but when we know them, all is relatively simple. We might equally well say that primitive man ceases to be a riddle for us as soon as we get to know our *own* presuppositions.

113   It is a rational presupposition of ours that everything has a natural and perceptible cause. We are convinced of this right from the start. Causality is one of our most sacred dogmas. There is no legitimate place in our world for invisible, arbitrary, and so-called supernatural powers—unless, indeed, we descend with the modern physicist into the obscure, microcosmic world inside the atom, where, it appears, some very curious things happen. But that lies far from the beaten track. We distinctly resent the idea of invisible and arbitrary forces, for it is not so long ago

that we made our escape from that frightening world of dreams and superstitions, and constructed for ourselves a picture of the cosmos worthy of our rational consciousness—that latest and greatest achievement of man. We are now surrounded by a world that is obedient to rational laws. It is true that we do not know the causes of everything, but in time they will be discovered, and these discoveries will accord with our reasoned expectations. There are, to be sure, also chance occurrences, but they are merely accidental, and we do not doubt that they have a causality of their own. Chance happenings are repellent to the mind that loves order. They disturb the regular, predictable course of events in the most absurd and irritating way. We resent them as much as we resent invisible, arbitrary forces, for they remind us too much of Satanic imps or of the caprice of a *deus ex machina*. They are the worst enemies of our careful calculations and a continual threat to all our undertakings. Being admittedly contrary to reason, they deserve all our abuse, and yet we should not fail to give them their due. The Arab shows them greater respect than we. He writes on every letter *Insha' allah*, "If God wills," for only then will the letter arrive. In spite of our resentment and in spite of the fact that events run true to general laws, it is undeniable that we are always and everywhere exposed to incalculable accidents. And what is more invisible and capricious than chance? What is more unavoidable and more annoying?

114   If we consider the matter, we could as well say that the causal connection of events according to general laws is a theory which is borne out about half the time, while for the rest the demon of chance holds sway. Chance events certainly have their natural causes, and all too often we must discover to our sorrow how commonplace they are. It is not this causality that annoys us; the irritating thing about chance events is that they have to befall us here and now in an apparently arbitrary way. At least that is how it strikes us, and even the most obdurate rationalist may occasionally be moved to curse them. However we interpret chance makes no difference to its power. The more regulated the conditions of life become, the more chance is excluded and the less we need to protect ourselves against it. But despite this everyone in practice takes precautions against chance occur-

rences or hopes for them, even though there is nothing about chance in the official credo.

115   It is our assumption, amounting to a positive conviction, that everything has a "natural" cause which, at least in theory, is perceptible. Primitive man, on the other hand, assumes that everything is brought about by invisible, arbitrary powers—in other words, that everything is chance. Only he does not call it chance, but intention. Natural causation is to him a mere pretence and not worthy of mention. If three women go to the river to draw water, and a crocodile seizes the one in the middle and pulls her under, our view of things leads us to the verdict that it was pure chance that that particular woman was seized. The fact that the crocodile seized her at all seems to us quite natural, for these beasts do occasionally eat human beings.

116   For primitive man such an explanation completely obliterates the facts and accounts for no aspect of the whole exciting story. He rightly finds our explanation superficial or even absurd, for according to this view the accident could just as well not have happened and the same explanation would fit that case too—that it was "pure chance" it did not. The prejudice of the European does not allow him to see how little he is saying when he explains things in that way.

117   Primitive man expects far more of an explanation. What we call pure chance is for him wilful intention. It was therefore the intention of the crocodile—as everyone could observe—to seize the middle one of the three women. If it had not had this intention it would have taken one of the others. But why did the crocodile have this intention? Ordinarily these creatures do not eat human beings. That is quite correct—as correct as the statement that it does not ordinarily rain in the Sahara. Crocodiles are rather timid animals, easily frightened. Considering their numbers, they kill astonishingly few people, and it is an unexpected and unnatural event when they devour a man. Such an event calls for an explanation. Of his own accord the crocodile would not take a human life. By whom, then, was he ordered to do so?

118   It is on the facts of the world around him that primitive man bases his verdicts. When the unexpected occurs he is justifiably astonished and wishes to know the specific causes. To this extent he behaves exactly as we do. But he goes further than we. He has

one or more theories about the arbitrary power of chance. We say: Pure chance. He says: Calculating intention. He lays the chief stress on the confusing and confused breaks in the chain of causation, which we call chance—on those occurrences that fail to show the neat causal connections which science expects, and that constitute the other half of happenings in general. He has long ago adapted himself to nature in so far as it conforms to general laws; what he fears is unpredictable chance whose power makes him see in it an arbitrary and incalculable agent. Here again he is right. It is quite understandable that everything out of the ordinary should frighten him. Anteaters are fairly numerous in the regions south of Mount Elgon where I stayed for some time. The anteater is a shy, nocturnal animal that is rarely seen. If one happens to be seen by day, it is an extraordinary and unnatural event which astonishes the natives as much as the discovery of a brook that occasionally flows uphill would astonish us. If we knew of actual cases in which water suddenly overcame the force of gravity, such a discovery would be exceedingly disquieting. We know that tremendous masses of water surround us, and can easily imagine what would happen if water no longer conformed to gravitational law. This is the situation in which primitive man finds himself with respect to the happenings in his world. He is thoroughly familiar with the habits of anteaters, but when one of them suddenly transgresses the natural order of things it acquires for him an unknown sphere of action. Primitive man is so strongly impressed by things as they are that a transgression of the laws of his world exposes him to incalculable possibilities. It is a portent, an omen, comparable to a comet or an eclipse. Since such an unnatural event as the appearance of an anteater by day can have no natural causes, some invisible power must be behind it. And the alarming manifestation of a power which can transgress the natural order obviously calls for extraordinary measures of placation or defence. The neighbouring villages must be aroused, and the anteater must be dug up with their concerted efforts and killed. The oldest maternal uncle of the man who saw the anteater must then sacrifice a bull. The man descends into the sacrificial pit and receives the first piece of the animal's flesh, whereupon the uncle and the other participants in the ceremony also eat. In this way the dangerous caprice of nature is expiated.

119   As for us, we should certainly be alarmed if water suddenly began to run uphill for unknown reasons, but are not when an anteater is seen by day, or an albino is born, or an eclipse takes place. We know the meaning and sphere of action of such happenings, while primitive man does not. Ordinary events constitute for him a coherent whole in which he and all other creatures are embraced. He is therefore extremely conservative, and does what others have always done. If something happens, at any point, to break the coherence of this whole, he feels there is a rift in his well-ordered world. Then anything may happen—heaven knows what. All occurrences that are in any way striking are at once brought into connection with the unusual event. For instance, a missionary set up a flagstaff in front of his house so that he could fly the Union Jack on Sundays. But this innocent pleasure cost him dear, for when shortly after his revolutionary action a devastating storm broke out, the flagstaff was of course made responsible. This sufficed to start a general uprising against the missionary.

120   It is the regularity of ordinary occurrences that gives primitive man a sense of security in his world. Every exception seems to him a threatening act of an arbitrary power that must somehow be propitiated. It is not only a momentary interruption of the ordinary course of things, but a portent of other untoward events. This seems absurd to us, inasmuch as we forget how our grandparents and great-grandparents still felt about the world. A calf is born with two heads and five legs. In the next village a cock has laid an egg. An old woman has had a dream, a comet appears in the sky, there is a great fire in the nearest town, and the following year a war breaks out. In this way history was always written from remote antiquity down to the eighteenth century. This concatenation of events, so meaningless to us, is significant and convincing to primitive man. And, contrary to all expectation, he is right to find it so. His powers of observation can be trusted. From age-old experience he knows that such concatenations actually exist. What seems to us a wholly senseless heaping-up of single, haphazard occurrences—because we pay attention only to single events and their particular causes—is for the primitive a completely logical sequence of omens and of happenings indicated by them. It is a fatal outbreak of demonic power showing itself in a thoroughly consistent way.

121   The calf with two heads and the war are one and the same, for the calf was only an anticipation of the war. Primitive man finds this connection so unquestionable and convincing because the whims of chance seem to him a far more important factor in the happenings of the world than regularity and conformity to law. Thanks to his close attention to the unusual, he discovered long before us that chance events arrange themselves in groups or series. The law of the duplication of cases is known to all doctors engaged in clinical work. An old professor of psychiatry at Würzburg always used to say of a particularly rare clinical case: "Gentlemen, this case is absolutely unique—tomorrow we shall have another just like it." I myself often observed the same thing during my eight years' practice in an insane asylum. On one occasion a person was committed for a very rare twilight state of consciousness—the first case of this kind I had ever seen. Within two days we had a similar case, and that was the last. "Duplication of cases" is a joke with us in the clinics, but it was also the first object of primitive science. A recent investigator has ventured the statement: "Magic is the science of the jungle." Astrology and other methods of divination may certainly be called the science of antiquity.

122   What happens regularly is easily observed because we are prepared for it. Knowledge and skill are needed only in situations where the course of events is interrupted in a way hard to fathom. Generally it is one of the shrewdest and wiliest men of the tribe who is entrusted with the observation of meteorological events. His knowledge must suffice to explain all unusual occurrences, and his art to combat them. He is the scholar, the specialist, the expert on chance, and at the same time the keeper of the archives of the tribe's traditional lore. Surrounded by respect and fear, he enjoys great authority, yet not so great but that his tribe is secretly convinced that the neighbouring tribe has a sorcerer who is stronger than theirs. The best medicine is never to be found close at hand, but as far away as possible. I stayed for some time with a tribe who held their old medicine-man in the greatest awe. Nevertheless he was consulted only for the minor ailments of cattle and men. In all serious cases a foreign authority was called in—a *M'ganga* who was brought at a high fee from Uganda—just as with us.

123   Chance events occur most often in larger or smaller series or

groups. An old and well-tried rule for foretelling the weather is this, that when it has rained for several days it will also rain tomorrow. A proverb says, "Misfortunes never come singly." Another has it that "It never rains but it pours." This proverbial wisdom is primitive science. The common people still believe it and fear it, but the educated man smiles at it—until something unusual happens to him. I will tell you a disagreeable story. A woman I know was awakened one morning by a peculiar tinkling on her night-table. After looking about her for a while she discovered the cause: the rim of her tumbler had snapped off in a ring about a quarter of an inch wide. This struck her as peculiar, and she rang for another glass. About five minutes later she heard the same tinkling, and again the rim of the glass had broken off. This time she was greatly disquieted, and had a third glass brought. Within twenty minutes the rim broke off again with the same tinkling noise. Three such accidents in immediate succession were too much for her. She gave up her belief in natural causes on the spot and brought out in its place a primitive "collective representation"—the conviction that an arbitrary power was at work. Something of this sort happens to many modern people—provided they are not too thick-skulled—when they are confronted with events which natural causation fails to explain. We naturally prefer to deny such occurrences. They are unpleasant because they disrupt the orderly course of our world and make anything seem possible, thus proving that the primitive mind in us is not yet dead.

124   Primitive man's belief in an arbitrary power does not arise out of thin air, as was always supposed, but is grounded in experience. The grouping of chance occurrences justifies what we call his superstition, for there is a real measure of probability that unusual events will coincide in time and place. We must not forget that our experience is apt to leave us in the lurch here. Our observation is inadequate because our point of view leads us to overlook these matters. For instance, it would never seriously occur to us to take the following events as a sequence: in the morning a bird flies into your room, an hour later you witness an accident in the street, in the afternoon a relative dies, in the evening the cook drops the soup tureen, and, on coming home at night, you find that you have lost your key. Primitive man would not have overlooked a single item in this chain of

events. Every new link would have confirmed his expectations, and he would be right—much more nearly right than we are willing to admit. His anxious expectations are fully justified and serve a purpose. Such a day is ill-omened, and on it nothing should be undertaken. In our world this would be reprehensible superstition, but in the world of the primitive it is highly appropriate shrewdness. In that world man is far more exposed to accidents than we are in our sheltered and well-regulated existence. When you are in the bush you dare not take too many chances. The European soon comes to appreciate this.

125   When a Pueblo Indian does not feel in the right mood, he stays away from the men's council. When an ancient Roman stumbled on the threshold as he left his house, he gave up his plans for the day. This seems to us senseless, but under primitive conditions such an omen inclines one at least to be cautious. When I am not in full control of myself, I am hampered in my movements, my attention wanders, I get absent-minded. As a result I knock against something, stumble, drop something, forget something. Under civilized conditions all these are mere trifles, but in the primeval forest they mean mortal danger. I make a false step on a slippery tree-trunk that serves as a bridge over a river teeming with crocodiles. I lose my compass in the high grass. I forget to load my rifle and blunder into a rhinoceros trail in the jungle. I am preoccupied with my thoughts and step on a puff-adder. At nightfall I forget to put on my mosquito-boots in time and eleven days later I die from an onset of tropical malaria. To forget to keep one's mouth shut while bathing is enough to bring on a fatal attack of dysentery. For us accidents of this kind have their recognizable natural cause in a somewhat distracted psychological state, but for the primitive they are objectively conditioned omens, or sorcery.

126   It may be rather more than a question of inattention, however. In the Kitoshi region south of Mount Elgon, in East Africa, I went on an expedition into the Kabras forest. There, in the thick grass, I nearly stepped on a puff-adder, and only managed to jump away just in time. That afternoon my companion returned from a hunt, deathly pale and trembling in every limb. He had narrowly escaped being bitten by a seven-foot mamba which darted at him from behind a termite hill. He would undoubtedly have been killed had he not been able to wound the

61

brute with a shot at the last moment. At nine o'clock that night our camp was attacked by a pack of ravenous hyenas which had surprised a man in his sleep the day before and torn him to pieces. In spite of the fire they swarmed into the hut of our cook, who fled screaming over the stockade. Thenceforth there were no accidents throughout the whole of our journey. Such a day gave our Negroes food for thought. For us it was a simple multiplication of chance events, but for them the inevitable fulfilment of an omen that had occurred on the first day of our journey into the wilds. It so happened that we had fallen, Ford car, bridge, and all, into a stream we were trying to cross. Our boys had exchanged glances as if to say: "Well, that's a fine start." To cap this calamity, a tropical thunderstorm blew up and soaked us so thoroughly that I was prostrated with fever for several days. On the evening of the day when my friend had had such a narrow escape out hunting, I could not help saying to him as we white men sat looking at one another: "You know, it seems to me as if the trouble had begun still further back. Do you remember the dream you told me in Zurich just before we left?" At that time he had had a very impressive nightmare. He dreamed he was hunting in Africa, and was suddenly attacked by a huge mamba, so that he woke up with a cry of terror. The dream had disturbed him greatly, and he now confessed to me that he had thought it portended the death of one of us. He had of course assumed that it was my death, because we always hope it is the other fellow. But it was he who later fell ill of a severe malarial fever that brought him to the brink of the grave.

127   To read of such a conversation in a corner of the world where there are no mambas and no anopheles mosquitoes means very little. One must imagine the velvety blue of a tropical night, the overhanging black masses of gigantic trees standing in the primeval forest, the mysterious voices of the nocturnal spaces, a lonely fire with loaded rifles stacked beside it, mosquito-nets, boiled swamp-water to drink, and above all the conviction expressed by an old Afrikander who knew what he was talking about: "This isn't man's country—it's God's country." There man is not king; it is rather nature, the animals, plants, and the microbes. Given the mood that goes with the place, one understands how it is that we found a dawning significance in things that anywhere else would provoke a smile. That is the world of

unrestrained capricious powers which primitive man has to deal with every day. The unusual event is no joke to him. He draws his own conclusions. "This is not a good place," "The day is unfavourable"—and who knows what dangers he avoids by following such warnings?

128 "Magic is the science of the jungle." The portent brings about an immediate alteration of a course of action, the abandonment of a planned undertaking, a change of psychic attitude. These are all highly expedient reactions in view of the fact that chance occurrences tend to fall into sequences and that primitive man is wholly unconscious of psychic causality. Thanks to our one-sided emphasis on so-called natural causes, we have learned to differentiate what is subjective and psychic from what is objective and "natural." For primitive man, on the contrary, the psychic and the objective coalesce in the external world. In the face of something extraordinary it is not he who is astonished, but rather the thing which is astonishing. It is *mana*—endowed with magic power. What we would call the powers of imagination and suggestion seem to him invisible forces which act on him from without. His country is neither a geographical nor a political entity. It is that territory which contains his mythology, his religion, all his thinking and feeling in so far as he is unconscious of these functions. His fear is localized in certain places that are "not good." The spirits of the departed inhabit such and such a wood. That cave harbours devils who strangle any man who enters. In yonder mountain lives the great serpent; that hill is the grave of the legendary king; near this spring or rock or tree every woman becomes pregnant; that ford is guarded by snake-demons; this towering tree has a voice that can call certain people. Primitive man is unpsychological. Psychic happenings take place outside him in an objective way. Even the things he dreams about are real to him; that is his only reason for paying attention to dreams. Our Elgonyi porters maintained in all seriousness that they never had dreams —only the medicine-man had them. When I questioned the medicine-man, he declared that he had stopped having dreams when the British entered the land. His father had still had "big" dreams, he told me, and had known where the herds strayed, where the cows took their calves, and when there was going to be a war or a pestilence. It was now the District Com-

missioner who knew everything, and they knew nothing. He was as resigned as certain Papuans who believe that the crocodiles have for the most part gone over to the British Government. It happened that a native convict who had escaped from the authorities had been badly mangled by a crocodile while trying to cross a river. They therefore concluded that it must have been a police crocodile. God now speaks in dreams to the British, and not to the medicine-man of the Elgonyi, he told me, because it is the British who have the power. Dream activity has emigrated. Occasionally the souls of the natives wander off too, and the medicine-man catches them in cages as if they were birds, or strange souls come in as immigrants and cause peculiar diseases.

129   This projection of psychic happenings naturally gives rise to relations between men and men, or between men and animals or things, that to us are inconceivable. A white man shoots a crocodile. At once a crowd of people come running from the nearest village and excitedly demand compensation. They explain that the crocodile was a certain old woman in their village who had died at the moment when the shot was fired. The crocodile was obviously her bush-soul. Another man shot a leopard that was lying in wait for his cattle. Just then a woman died in a neighbouring village. She and the leopard were identical.

130   Lévy-Bruhl has coined the expression *participation mystique* for these remarkable relationships. It seems to me that the word "mystical" is not happily chosen. Primitive man does not see anything mystical in these matters, but considers them perfectly natural. It is only we who find them so strange, because we appear to know nothing about the phenomena of psychic dissociation. In reality, however, they occur in us too, not in this naïve but in a rather more civilized form. In daily life it happens all the time that we presume that the psychology of other people is the same as ours. We suppose that what is pleasing or desirable to us is the same to others, and that what seems bad to us must also seem bad to them. It is only recently that our courts of law have nerved themselves to admit the psychological relativity of guilt in pronouncing sentence. The tenet *quod licet Jovi non licet bovi* still rankles in the minds of all unsophisticated people; equality before the law is still a precious

achievement. And we still attribute to the other fellow all the evil and inferior qualities that we do not like to recognize in ourselves, and therefore have to criticize and attack him, when all that has happened is that an inferior "soul" has emigrated from one person to another. The world is still full of *bêtes noires* and scapegoats, just as it formerly teemed with witches and werewolves.

131   Projection is one of the commonest psychic phenomena. It is the same as *participation mystique,* which Lévy-Bruhl, to his great credit, emphasized as being an especially characteristic feature of primitive man. We merely give it another name, and as a rule deny that we are guilty of it. Everything that is unconscious in ourselves we discover in our neighbour, and we treat him accordingly. We no longer subject him to the test of drinking poison; we do not burn him or put the screws on him; but we injure him by means of moral verdicts pronounced with the deepest conviction. What we combat in him is usually our own inferior side.

132   The simple truth is that primitive man is somewhat more given to projection than we because of the undifferentiated state of his mind and his consequent inability to criticize himself. Everything to him is absolutely objective, and his speech reflects this in a drastic way. With a touch of humour we can picture to ourselves what a leopard-woman is like, just as we do when we call a person a goose, a cow, a hen, a snake, an ox, or an ass. These uncomplimentary epithets are familiar to us all. But when primitive man attributes a bush-soul to a person, the poison of moral judgment is absent. He is too naturalistic for that; he is too much impressed by things as they are and much less prone to pass judgment than we. The Pueblo Indians declared in a matter-of-fact way that I belonged to the Bear Totem —in other words, that I was a bear—because I did not come down a ladder standing up like a man, but bunched up on all fours like a bear. If anyone in Europe said I had a bearish nature this would amount to the same thing, but with a rather different shade of meaning. The theme of the bush-soul, which seems so strange to us when we meet with it among primitives, has become with us a mere figure of speech, like so much else. If we take our metaphors concretely we return to the primitive point of view. For instance, we have the expression "to handle

a patient." In concrete terms this means "to lay hands on" a person, "to work at with the hands," "to manipulate." And this is precisely what the medicine-man does with his patients.

133   We find the bush-soul hard to understand because we are baffled by such a concrete way of looking at things. We cannot conceive of a "soul" that splits off completely and takes up its abode in a wild animal. When we describe someone as an ass, we do not mean that he is in every aspect the quadruped called an ass. We mean that he resembles an ass in some particular respect. We split off a bit of his personality or psyche and personify it as an ass. So, too, for primitive man the leopard-woman is a human being, only her bush-soul is a leopard. Since all unconscious psychic life is concrete and objective for him, he supposes that a person describable as a leopard has the soul of a leopard. If the splitting and concretizing go still further, he assumes that the leopard-soul lives in the bush in the form of a real leopard.

134   These identifications, brought about by projection, create a world in which man is completely contained psychically as well as physically. To a certain extent he coalesces with it. In no way is he master of this world, but only a fragment of it. Primitive man is still far from the glorification of human powers. He does not dream of regarding himself as the lord of creation. In Africa, for instance, his zoological classification does not culminate in *Homo sapiens,* but in the elephant. Next comes the lion, then the python or the crocodile, then man and the lesser creatures. Man is still dovetailed into nature. It never occurs to him that he might be able to rule her; all his efforts are devoted to protecting himself against her dangerous caprices. It is civilized man who strives to dominate nature and therefore devotes his greatest energies to the discovery of natural causes which will give him the key to her secret laboratory. That is why he strongly resents the idea of arbitrary powers and denies them. Their existence would amount to proof that his attempt to dominate nature is futile after all.

135   Summing up, we may say that the outstanding trait of archaic man is his attitude towards the arbitrary power of chance, which he considers a far more important factor in the world-process than natural causes. It consists on the one hand in the observed tendency of chance occurrences to take place in a

66

series, and on the other in the projection of unconscious psychic contents through *participation mystique*. For archaic man this distinction does not exist, because psychic happenings are projected so completely that they cannot be distinguished from objective, physical events. For him the vagaries of chance are arbitrary and intentional acts, interventions by animate beings. He does not realize that unusual events stir him so deeply only because he invests them with the power of his own astonishment or fear. Here, it is true, we move on treacherous ground. Is a thing beautiful because I attribute beauty to it? Or is it the objective beauty of the thing that compels me to acknowledge it? As we know, great minds have wrestled with the problem whether it is the glorious sun that illuminates the world, or the sunlike human eye. Archaic man believes it to be the sun, and civilized man believes it to be the eye—so far, at any rate, as he reflects at all and does not suffer from the disease of the poets. He must de-psychize nature in order to dominate her; and in order to see his world objectively he must take back all his archaic projections.

136   In the archaic world everything has soul—the soul of man, or let us say of mankind, the collective unconscious, for the individual has as yet no soul of his own. We must not forget that what the Christian sacrament of baptism purports to do is a landmark of the utmost significance in the psychic development of mankind. Baptism endows the individual with a living soul. I do not mean that the baptismal rite in itself does this, by a unique and magical act. I mean that the idea of baptism lifts man out of his archaic identification with the world and transforms him into a being who stands above it. The fact that mankind has risen to the level of this idea is baptism in the deepest sense, for it means the birth of the spiritual man who transcends nature.

137   In the psychology of the unconscious it is an axiom that every relatively independent portion of the psyche has the character of personality, that it is personified as soon as it is given an opportunity for independent expression. We find the clearest instances of this in the hallucinations of the insane and in mediumistic communications. Whenever an autonomous component of the psyche is projected, an invisible person comes into being. In this way the spirits arise at an ordinary spiritual-

67

istic séance. So too among primitives. If an important psychic component is projected on a human being, he becomes *mana*, extraordinarily effective—a sorcerer, witch, werewolf, or the like. The primitive idea that the medicine-man catches the souls that have wandered away by night and puts them in cages like birds is a striking illustration of this. These projections give the medicine-man his mana, they cause animals, trees, and stones to speak, and because they are his own psychic components they compel the projicient to obey them absolutely. For this reason an insane person is helplessly at the mercy of his voices; they are projections of his own psychic activity whose unconscious subject he is. He is the one who speaks through his voices, just as he is the one who hears, sees, and obeys.

138   From a psychological point of view, therefore, the primitive theory that the arbitrary power of chance is the outcome of the intentions of spirits and sorcerers is perfectly natural, because it is an unavoidable inference from the facts as primitive man sees them. Let us not delude ourselves in this connection. If we explain our scientific views to an intelligent native he will accuse us of ludicrous superstitiousness and a disgraceful want of logic, for he believes that the world is lighted by the sun and not by the human eye. My friend Mountain Lake, a Pueblo chief, once called me sharply to account because I had made insinuating use of the Augustinian argument: "Not this sun is our Lord, but he who made this sun." Pointing to the sun he cried indignantly: "He who goes there is our father. You can see him. From him comes all light, all life—there is nothing that he has not made." He became greatly excited, struggled for words, and finally cried out: "Even a man in the mountains, who goes alone, cannot make his fire without him." The archaic standpoint could hardly be more beautifully expressed than by these words. The power that rules us is outside, in the external world, and through it alone are we permitted to live. Religious thought keeps alive the archaic state of mind even today, in a time bereft of gods. Untold millions of people still think like this.

139   Speaking earlier of primitive man's attitude to the arbitrary power of chance, I expressed the view that this attitude serves a purpose and therefore has a meaning. Shall we, for the moment at least, venture the hypothesis that the primitive belief

in arbitrary powers is justified by the facts and not merely from a psychological point of view? This sounds alarming, but I have no intention of jumping from the frying-pan into the fire and trying to prove that witchcraft actually works. I merely wish to consider the conclusions to which we shall be led if we follow primitive man in assuming that all light comes from the sun, that things are beautiful in themselves, and that a bit of the human soul is a leopard—in other words, that the mana theory is correct. According to this theory, beauty moves *us,* it is not we who create beauty. A certain person *is* a devil, we have not projected our own evil on him and in this way made a devil out of him. There are people—mana personalities—who are impressive in their own right and in no way thanks to our imagination. The mana theory maintains that there is something like a widely distributed power in the external world that produces all those extraordinary effects. Everything that exists acts, otherwise it would not *be.* It can *be* only by virtue of its inherent energy. Being is a field of force. The primitive idea of mana, as you can see, has in it the beginnings of a crude theory of energy.

140 So far we can easily follow this primitive idea. The difficulty arises when we try to carry its implications further, for they reverse the process of psychic projection of which I have spoken. It is then not my imagination or my awe that makes the medicine-man a sorcerer; on the contrary, he *is* a sorcerer and projects his magical powers on me. Spirits are not hallucinations of my mind, but appear to me of their own volition. Although such statements are logical derivatives of the mana idea, we hesitate to accept them and begin to look around for a comfortable theory of psychic projection. The question is nothing less than this: Does the psychic in general—the soul or spirit or the unconscious—originate in *us,* or is the psyche, in the early stages of conscious evolution, actually outside us in the form of arbitrary powers with intentions of their own, and does it gradually take its place within us in the course of psychic development? Were the split-off "souls"—or dissociated psychic contents, as we would call them—ever parts of the psyches of individuals, or were they from the beginning psychic entities existing in themselves according to the primitive view as ghosts, ancestral spirits, and the like? Were they only by degrees embodied in man in the course of development, so that they gradu-

ally constituted in him that world which we now call the psyche?

141   This whole idea strikes us as dangerously paradoxical, but, at bottom, it is not altogether inconceivable. Not only the religious instructor but the educator as well assumes that it is possible to implant something psychic in man that was not there before. The power of suggestion and influence is a fact; indeed, the modern behaviourists have extravagant expectations in this respect. The idea of a complex building-up of the psyche is expressed on a primitive level in a variety of forms, for instance in the widespread belief in possession, the incarnation of ancestral spirits, the immigration of souls, and so forth. When someone sneezes, we still say: "God bless you," by which is meant: "I hope your new soul will do you no harm." When in the course of our own development we feel ourselves achieving a unified personality out of a multitude of contradictory tendencies, we experience something like a complex growing-together of the psyche. Since the human body is built up by heredity out of a multitude of Mendelian units, it does not seem altogether out of the question that the human psyche is similarly put together.

142   The materialistic views of our day have one tendency which they share with archaic thought: both lead to the conclusion that the individual is a mere resultant. In the first case he is the resultant of natural causes, and in the second of chance occurrences. According to both accounts, human individuality is nothing in its own right, but rather the accidental product of forces contained in the objective environment. This is thoroughly consistent with the archaic view of the world, in which the ordinary individual is never important, but always interchangeable with any other and easily dispensable. By the roundabout way of strict causalism, modern materialism has returned to the standpoint of archaic man. But the materialist is more radical, because he is more systematic. Archaic man has the advantage of being inconsistent: he makes an exception of the mana personality. In the course of history these mana personalities were exalted to the position of divine figures; they became heroes and kings who shared the immortality of the gods by eating the food of eternal youth. This idea of the immortality of the individual and of his imperishable worth can be found

on the earliest archaic levels, first of all in the belief in spirits, and then in myths of the age when death had not yet gained entry into the world through human carelessness or folly.

143   Primitive man is not aware of this contradiction in his views. My Elgonyi porters assured me that they had no idea what would happen to them after death. According to them a man is simply dead, he does not breathe any more, and the corpse is carried into the bush where the hyenas eat it. That is what they think by day, but the night teems with spirits of the dead who bring diseases to cattle and men, who attack and strangle the nocturnal traveller and indulge in other forms of violence. The primitive mind is full of such contradictions. They could worry a European out of his skin, and it would never occur to him that something quite similar is to be found in our civilized midst. We have universities where the very thought of divine intervention is considered beneath dispute, but where theology is a part of the curriculum. A research worker in natural science who thinks it positively obscene to attribute the smallest variation of an animal species to an act of divine arbitrariness may have in another compartment of his mind a full-blown Christian faith which he likes to parade on Sundays. Why should we excite ourselves about primitive inconsistency?

144   It is impossible to derive any philosophical system from the fundamental thoughts of primitive man. They provide only antinomies, but it is just these that are the inexhaustible source of all spiritual problems in all times and in all civilizations. We may ask whether the "collective representations" of archaic man are really profound, or do they only seem so? I cannot answer this most difficult of questions, but I would like, in conclusion, to tell you of an observation I made among the mountain tribe of the Elgonyi. I searched and inquired far and wide for traces of religious ideas and ceremonies, and for weeks on end I discovered nothing. The natives let me see everything and were willing to give me any information. I could talk with them without the hindrance of a native interpreter, for many of the old men spoke Swahili. At first they were rather reserved, but once the ice was broken I had the friendliest reception. They knew nothing of religious customs. But I did not give up, and finally, at the end of one of many fruitless palavers, an old man suddenly exclaimed: "In the morning, when the sun comes up,

we go out of the huts, spit in our hands, and hold them up to the sun." I got them to perform the ceremony for me and describe it exactly. They hold their hands before their faces and spit or blow into them vigorously. Then they turn their hands round and hold the palms towards the sun. I asked them the meaning of what they did—why they blew or spat in their hands. My question was futile. "That is how it has always been done," they said. It was impossible to get an explanation, and it became clear to me that they knew only what they did and not why they did it. They see no meaning in their action. They greet the new moon with the same gesture.

145   Now let us suppose that I am a total stranger in Zurich and have come to this city to explore the customs of the place. First I settle down on the outskirts near some suburban homes, and come into neighbourly contact with their owners. I then say to Messrs. Müller and Meyer: "Please tell me something about your religious customs." Both gentlemen are taken aback. They never go to church, know nothing about it, and emphatically deny that they practise any such customs. It is spring, and Easter is approaching. One morning I surprise Mr. Müller at a curious occupation. He is busily running about the garden, hiding coloured eggs and setting up peculiar rabbit idols. I have caught him *in flagrante.* "Why did you conceal this highly interesting ceremony from me?" I ask him. "What ceremony?" he retorts. "This is nothing. Everybody does it at Eastertime." "But what is the meaning of these idols and eggs, and why do you hide them?" Mr. Müller is stunned. He does not know, any more than he knows the meaning of the Christmas-tree. And yet he does these things, just like a primitive. Did the distant ancestors of the Elgonyi know any better what they were doing? It is highly improbable. Archaic man everywhere does what he does, and only civilized man knows what he does.

146   What is the meaning of the Elgonyi ceremony just cited? Clearly it is an offering to the sun, which for these natives is *mungu*—that is, *mana,* or divine—only at the moment of rising. If they have spittle on their hands, this is the substance which, according to primitive belief, contains the personal *mana,* the life-force, the power to heal and to make magic. If they breathe into their hands, breath is wind and spirit—it is *roho,* in Arabic *ruch,* in Hebrew *ruach,* and in Greek *pneuma.* The action

means: I offer my living soul to God. It is a wordless, acted prayer, which could equally well be spoken: "Lord, into thy hands I commend my spirit."

147   Does this merely happen so, or was this thought brooded and willed even before man existed? I must leave this question unanswered.

THE SPIRITUAL PROBLEM OF MODERN MAN [1]

148   The spiritual problem of modern man is one of those questions which are so much a part of the age we live in that we cannot see them in the proper perspective. Modern man is an entirely new phenomenon; a modern problem is one which has just arisen and whose answer still lies in the future. In speaking of the spiritual problem of modern man we can at most frame a question, and we should perhaps frame it quite differently if we had but the faintest inkling of the answer the future will give. The question, moreover, seems rather vague; but the truth is that it has to do with something so universal that it exceeds the grasp of any single individual. We have reason enough, therefore, to approach such a problem in all modesty and with the greatest caution. This open avowal of our limitations seems to me essential, because it is these problems more than any others which tempt us to the use of high-sounding and empty words, and because I shall myself be forced to say certain things which may sound immoderate and incautious, and could easily lead us astray. Too many of us already have fallen victim to our own grandiloquence.

149   To begin at once with an example of such apparent lack of caution, I must say that the man we call modern, the man who is aware of the immediate present, is by no means the average man. He is rather the man who stands upon a peak, or at the very edge of the world, the abyss of the future before him, above him the heavens, and below him the whole of mankind with a

1 [First pub. as "Das Seelenproblem des modernen Menschen," *Europäische Revue* (Berlin), IV (1928), 700–715. Revised and expanded in *Seelenprobleme der Gegenwart* (Zurich, 1931), pp. 401–35. Trans. by W. S. Dell and Cary F. Baynes in *Modern Man in Search of a Soul* (London and New York, 1933), pp. 226–54. The latter version has been consulted.—EDITORS.]

history that disappears in primeval mists. The modern man—or, let us say again, the man of the immediate present—is rarely met with, for he must be conscious to a superlative degree. Since to be wholly of the present means to be fully conscious of one's existence as a man, it requires the most intensive and extensive consciousness, with a minimum of unconsciousness. It must be clearly understood that the mere fact of living in the present does not make a man modern, for in that case everyone at present alive would be so. He alone is modern who is fully conscious of the present.

150   The man who has attained consciousness of the present is solitary. The "modern" man has at all times been so, for every step towards fuller consciousness removes him further from his original, purely animal *participation mystique* with the herd, from submersion in a common unconsciousness. Every step forward means tearing oneself loose from the maternal womb of unconsciousness in which the mass of men dwells. Even in a civilized community the people who form, psychologically speaking, the lowest stratum live in a state of unconsciousness little different from that of primitives. Those of the succeeding strata live on a level of consciousness which corresponds to the beginnings of human culture, while those of the highest stratum have a consciousness that reflects the life of the last few centuries. Only the man who is modern in our meaning of the term really lives in the present; he alone has a present-day consciousness, and he alone finds that the ways of life on those earlier levels have begun to pall upon him. The values and strivings of those past worlds no longer interest him save from the historical standpoint. Thus he has become "unhistorical" in the deepest sense and has estranged himself from the mass of men who live entirely within the bounds of tradition. Indeed, he is completely modern only when he has come to the very edge of the world, leaving behind him all that has been discarded and outgrown, and acknowledging that he stands before the Nothing out of which All may grow.[2]

151   This sounds so grand that it borders suspiciously on bathos, for nothing is easier than to affect a consciousness of the present. A great horde of worthless people do in fact give themselves

2 ["In this, your Nothing, I may find my All!" *Faust, Part Two.*—TRANS.]

75

a deceptive air of modernity by skipping the various stages of development and the tasks of life they represent. Suddenly they appear by the side of the truly modern man—uprooted wraiths, bloodsucking ghosts whose emptiness casts discredit upon him in his unenviable loneliness. Thus it is that the few present-day men are seen by the undiscerning eyes of the masses only through the dismal veil of those spectres, the pseudo-moderns, and are confused with them. It cannot be helped; the "modern" man is questionable and suspect, and has been so at all times, beginning with Socrates and Jesus.

152   An honest admission of modernity means voluntarily declaring oneself bankrupt, taking the vows of poverty and chastity in a new sense, and—what is still more painful—renouncing the halo of sanctity which history bestows. To be "unhistorical" is the Promethean sin, and in this sense the modern man is sinful. A higher level of consciousness is like a burden of guilt. But, as I have said, only the man who has outgrown the stages of consciousness belonging to the past, and has amply fulfilled the duties appointed for him by his world, can achieve full consciousness of the present. To do this he must be sound and proficient in the best sense—a man who has achieved as much as other people, and even a little more. It is these qualities which enable him to gain the next highest level of consciousness.

153   I know that the idea of proficiency is especially repugnant to the pseudo-moderns, for it reminds them unpleasantly of their trickery. This, however, should not prevent us from taking it as our criterion of the modern man. We are even forced to do so, for unless he is proficient, the man who claims to be modern is nothing but a trickster. He must be proficient in the highest degree, for unless he can atone by creative ability for his break with tradition, he is merely disloyal to the past. To deny the past for the sake of being conscious only of the present would be sheer futility. Today has meaning only if it stands between yesterday and tomorrow. It is a process of transition that forms the link between past and future. Only the man who is conscious of the present in this sense may call himself modern.

154   Many people call themselves modern—especially the pseudo-moderns. Therefore the really modern man is often to be found among those who call themselves old-fashioned. They do this

firstly in order to make amends for their guilty break with tradition by laying all the more emphasis on the past, and secondly in order to avoid the misfortune of being taken for pseudo-moderns. Every good quality has its bad side, and nothing good can come into the world without at once producing a corresponding evil. This painful fact renders illusory the feeling of elation that so often goes with consciousness of the present—the feeling that we are the culmination of the whole history of mankind, the fulfilment and end-product of countless generations. At best it should be a proud admission of our poverty: we are also the disappointment of the hopes and expectations of the ages. Think of nearly two thousand years of Christian Idealism followed, not by the return of the Messiah and the heavenly millennium, but by the World War among Christian nations with its barbed wire and poison gas. What a catastrophe in heaven and on earth!

155   In the face of such a picture we may well grow humble again. It is true that modern man is a culmination, but tomorrow he will be surpassed. He is indeed the product of an age-old development, but he is at the same time the worst conceivable disappointment of the hopes of mankind. The modern man is conscious of this. He has seen how beneficent are science, technology, and organization, but also how catastrophic they can be. He has likewise seen how all well-meaning governments have so thoroughly paved the way for peace on the principle "in time of peace prepare for war" that Europe has nearly gone to rack and ruin. And as for ideals, neither the Christian Church, nor the brotherhood of man, nor international social democracy, nor the solidarity of economic interests has stood up to the acid test of reality. Today, ten years after the war,[3] we observe once more the same optimism, the same organizations, the same political aspirations, the same phrases and catchwords at work. How can we but fear that they will inevitably lead to further catastrophes? Agreements to outlaw war leave us sceptical, even while we wish them every possible success. At bottom, behind every such palliative measure there is a gnawing doubt. I believe I am not exaggerating when I say that modern

3 [This essay was originally written in 1928.—EDITORS.]

man has suffered an almost fatal shock, psychologically speaking, and as a result has fallen into profound uncertainty.

156 These statements make it clear enough that my views are coloured by a professional bias. A doctor always spies out diseases, and I cannot cease to be a doctor. But it is essential to the physician's art that he should not discover diseases where none exists. I will therefore not make the assertion that Western man, and the white man in particular, is sick, or that the Western world is on the verge of collapse. I am in no way competent to pass such a judgment.

157 Whenever you hear anyone talking about a cultural or even about a human problem, you should never forget to inquire who the speaker really is. The more general the problem, the more he will smuggle his own, most personal psychology into the account he gives of it. This can, without a doubt, lead to intolerable distortions and false conclusions which may have very serious consequences. On the other hand, the very fact that a general problem has gripped and assimilated the whole of a person is a guarantee that the speaker has really experienced it, and perhaps gained something from his sufferings. He will then reflect the problem for us in his personal life and thereby show us a truth. But if he projects his own psychology into the problem, he falsifies it by his personal bias, and on the pretence of presenting it objectively so distorts it that no truth emerges but merely a deceptive fiction.

158 It is of course only from my own experience with other persons and with myself that I draw my knowledge of the spiritual problem of modern man. I know something of the intimate psychic life of many hundreds of educated persons, both sick and healthy, coming from every quarter of the civilized, white world; and upon this experience I base my statements. No doubt I can draw only a one-sided picture, for everything I have observed lies in the psyche—it is all *inside*. I must add at once that this is a remarkable fact in itself, for the psyche is not always and everywhere to be found on the inside. There are peoples and epochs where it is found *outside,* because they were wholly unpsychological. As examples we may choose any of the ancient civilizations, but especially that of Egypt with its monumental objectivity and its naïve confession of sins that have not been committed. We can no more feel psychic problems lurking

78

behind the Apis tombs of Saqqara and the Pyramıds than we can behind the music of Bach.

159   Whenever there exists some external form, be ıt an ideal or a ritual, by which all the yearnings and hopes of the soul are adequately expressed—as for instance in a living religion—then we may say that the psyche is outside and that there is no psychic problem, just as there is then no unconscious in our sense of the word. In consonance with this truth, the discovery of psychology falls entirely within the last decades, although long before that man was introspective and intelligent enough to recognize the facts that are the subject-matter of psychology. It was the same with technical knowledge. The Romans were familiar with all the mechanical principles and physical facts which would have enabled them to construct a steam engine, but all that came of it was the toy made by Hero of Alexandria. The reason for this is that there was no compelling necessity to go further. This need arose only with the enormous division of labour and the growth of specialization in the nineteenth century. So also a spiritual need has produced in our time the "discovery" of psychology. The psychic facts still existed earlier, of course, but they did not attract attention—no one noticed them. People got along without them. But today we can no longer get along unless we pay attention to the psyche.

160   It was men of the medical profession who were the first to learn this truth. For the priest, the psyche can only be something that needs fitting into a recognized form or system of belief in order to ensure its undisturbed functioning. So long as this system gives true expression to life, psychology can be nothing but a technical adjuvant to healthy living, and the psyche cannot be regarded as a factor *sui generis*. While man still lives as a herd-animal he has no psyche of his own, nor does he need any, except the usual belief in the immortality of the soul. But as soon as he has outgrown whatever local form of religion he was born to—as soon as this religion can no longer embrace his life in all its fullness—then the psyche becomes a factor in its own right which cannot be dealt with by the customary measures. It is for this reason that we today have a psychology founded on experience, and not upon articles of faith or the postulates of any philosophical system. The very fact that we have such a psychology is to me symptomatic of a profound

79

convulsion of the collective psyche. For the collective psyche shows the same pattern of change as the psyche of the individual. So long as all goes well and all our psychic energies find an outlet in adequate and well-regulated ways, we are disturbed by nothing from within. No uncertainty or doubt besets us, and we *cannot* be divided against ourselves. But no sooner are one or two channels of psychic activity blocked up than phenomena of obstruction appear. The stream tries to flow back against the current, the inner man wants something different from the outer man, and we are at war with ourselves. Only then, in this situation of distress, do we discover the psyche as something which thwarts our will, which is strange and even hostile to us, and which is incompatible with our conscious standpoint. Freud's psychoanalytic endeavours show this process in the clearest way. The very first thing he discovered was the existence of sexually perverse and criminal fantasies which at their face value are wholly incompatible with the conscious outlook of civilized man. A person who adopted the standpoint of these fantasies would be nothing less than a rebel, a criminal, or a madman.

161   We cannot suppose that the unconscious or hinterland of man's mind has developed this aspect only in recent times. Probably it was always there, in every culture. And although every culture had its destructive opponent, a Herostratus who burned down its temples, no culture before ours was ever forced to take these psychic undercurrents in deadly earnest. The psyche was merely part of a metaphysical system of some sort. But the conscious, modern man can no longer refrain from acknowledging the might of the psyche, despite the most strenuous and dogged efforts at self-defence. This distinguishes our time from all others. We can no longer deny that the dark stirrings of the unconscious are active powers, that psychic forces exist which, for the present at least, cannot be fitted into our rational world order. We have even elevated them into a science—one more proof of how seriously we take them. Previous centuries could throw them aside unnoticed; for us they are a shirt of Nessus which we cannot strip off.

162   The revolution in our conscious outlook, brought about by the catastrophic results of the World War, shows itself in our inner life by the shattering of our faith in ourselves and our

own worth. We used to regard foreigners as political and moral reprobates, but the modern man is forced to recognize that he is politically and morally just like anyone else. Whereas formerly I believed it was my bounden duty to call others to order, I must now admit that I need calling to order myself, and that I would do better to set my own house to rights first. I admit this the more readily because I realize only too well that my faith in the rational organization of the world—that old dream of the millennium when peace and harmony reign—has grown pale. Modern man's scepticism in this respect has chilled his enthusiasm for politics and world-reform; more than that, it is the worst possible basis for a smooth flow of psychic energies into the outer world, just as doubt concerning the morality of a friend is bound to prejudice the relationship and hamper its development. Through his scepticism modern man is thrown back on himself; his energies flow towards their source, and the collision washes to the surface those psychic contents which are at all times there, but lie hidden in the silt so long as the stream flows smoothly in its course. How totally different did the world appear to medieval man! For him the earth was eternally fixed and at rest in the centre of the universe, circled by a sun that solicitously bestowed its warmth. Men were all children of God under the loving care of the Most High, who prepared them for eternal blessedness; and all knew exactly what they should do and how they should conduct themselves in order to rise from a corruptible world to an incorruptible and joyous existence. Such a life no longer seems real to us, even in our dreams. Science has long ago torn this lovely veil to shreds. That age lies as far behind as childhood, when one's own father was unquestionably the handsomest and strongest man on earth.

163   Modern man has lost all the metaphysical certainties of his medieval brother, and set up in their place the ideals of material security, general welfare and humanitarianism. But anyone who has still managed to preserve these ideals unshaken must have been injected with a more than ordinary dose of optimism. Even security has gone by the board, for modern man has begun to see that every step forward in material "progress" steadily increases the threat of a still more stupendous catastrophe. The imagination shrinks in terror from such a picture. What are we to think when the great cities today are

perfecting defence measures against gas attacks, and even practise them in dress rehearsals? It can only mean that these attacks
have already been planned and provided for, again on the principle "in time of peace prepare for war." Let man but accumulate sufficient engines of destruction and the devil within him
will soon be unable to resist putting them to their fated use. It
is well known that fire-arms go off of themselves if only enough
of them are together.

164   An intimation of the terrible law that governs blind contingency, which Heraclitus called the rule of *enantiodromia* (a
running towards the opposite), now steals upon modern man
through the by-ways of his mind, chilling him with fear and
paralysing his faith in the lasting effectiveness of social and
political measures in the face of these monstrous forces. If he
turns away from the terrifying prospect of a blind world in
which building and destroying successively tip the scales, and
then gazes into the recesses of his own mind, he will discover a
chaos and a darkness there which everyone would gladly ignore.
Science has destroyed even this last refuge; what was once a
sheltering haven has become a cesspool.

165   And yet it is almost a relief to come upon so much evil in
the depths of our own psyche. Here at least, we think, is the
root of all the evil in mankind. Even though we are shocked
and disillusioned at first, we still feel, just because these things
are part of our psyche, that we have them more or less in hand
and can correct them or at any rate effectively suppress them.
We like to assume that, if we succeeded in this, we should at
least have rooted out some fraction of the evil in the world.
Given a widespread knowledge of the unconscious, everyone
could see when a statesman was being led astray by his own bad
motives. The very newspapers would pull him up: "Please have
yourself analysed; you are suffering from a repressed father-
complex."

166   I have purposely chosen this grotesque example to show to
what absurdities we are led by the illusion that because something is psychic it is under our control. It is, however, true that
much of the evil in the world comes from the fact that man in
general is hopelessly unconscious, as it is also true that with increasing insight we can combat this evil at its source in our-

selves, in the same way that science enables us to deal effectively with injuries inflicted from without.

167   The rapid and worldwide growth of a psychological interest over the last two decades shows unmistakably that modern man is turning his attention from outward material things to his own inner processes. Expressionism in art prophetically anticipated this subjective development, for all art intuitively apprehends coming changes in the collective unconsciousness.

168   The psychological interest of the present time is an indication that modern man expects something from the psyche which the outer world has not given him: doubtless something which our religion ought to contain, but no longer does contain, at least for modern man. For him the various forms of religion no longer appear to come from within, from the psyche; they seem more like items from the inventory of the outside world. No spirit not of this world vouchsafes him inner revelation; instead, he tries on a variety of religions and beliefs as if they were Sunday attire, only to lay them aside again like worn-out clothes.

169   Yet he is somehow fascinated by the almost pathological manifestations from the hinterland of the psyche, difficult though it is to explain how something which all previous ages have rejected should suddenly become interesting. That there is a general interest in these matters cannot be denied, however much it offends against good taste. I am not thinking merely of the interest taken in psychology as a science, or of the still narrower interest in the psychoanalysis of Freud, but of the widespread and ever-growing interest in all sorts of psychic phenomena, including spiritualism, astrology, Theosophy, parapsychology, and so forth. The world has seen nothing like it since the end of the seventeenth century. We can compare it only to the flowering of Gnostic thought in the first and second centuries after Christ. The spiritual currents of our time have, in fact, a deep affinity with Gnosticism. There is even an "Église gnostique de la France," and I know of two schools in Germany which openly declare themselves Gnostic. The most impressive movement numerically is undoubtedly Theosophy, together with its continental sister, Anthroposophy; these are pure Gnosticism in Hindu dress. Compared with them the interest in scientific psychology is negligible. What is striking about these

Gnostic systems is that they are based exclusively on the manifestations of the unconscious, and that their moral teachings penetrate into the dark side of life, as is clearly shown by the refurbished European version of *Kundalini-yoga*. The same is true of parapsychology, as everyone acquainted with this subject will agree.

170   The passionate interest in these movements undoubtedly arises from psychic energy which can no longer be invested in obsolete religious forms. For this reason such movements have a genuinely religious character, even when they pretend to be scientific. It changes nothing when Rudolf Steiner calls his Anthroposophy "spiritual science," or when Mrs. Eddy invents a "Christian Science." These attempts at concealment merely show that religion has grown suspect—almost as suspect as politics and world-reform.

171   I do not believe that I am going too far when I say that modern man, in contrast to his nineteenth-century brother, turns to the psyche with very great expectations, and does so without reference to any traditional creed but rather with a view to Gnostic experience. The fact that all the movements I have mentioned give themselves a scientific veneer is not just a grotesque caricature or a masquerade, but a positive sign that they are actually pursuing "science," i.e., *knowledge,* instead of *faith,* which is the essence of the Western forms of religion. Modern man abhors faith and the religions based upon it. He holds them valid only so far as their knowledge-content seems to accord with his own experience of the psychic background. He wants to *know*—to experience for himself.

172   The age of discovery has only just come to an end in our day, when no part of the earth remains unexplored; it began when men would no longer *believe* that the Hyperboreans were one-footed monsters, or something of that kind, but wanted to find out and see with their own eyes what existed beyond the boundaries of the known world. Our age is apparently setting out to discover what exists in the psyche beyond consciousness. The question asked in every spiritualistic circle is: What happens after the medium has lost consciousness? Every Theosophist asks: What shall I experience at the higher levels of consciousness? The question which every astrologer asks is: What are the operative forces that determine my fate despite

my conscious intention? And every psychoanalyst wants to know: What are the unconscious drives behind the neurosis?

173   Our age wants to experience the psyche for itself. It wants original experience and not assumptions, though it is willing to make use of all the existing assumptions as a means to this end, including those of the recognized religions and the authentic sciences. The European of yesterday will feel a slight shudder run down his spine when he gazes more deeply into these delvings. Not only does he consider the subject of this so-called research obscure and shuddersome, but even the methods employed seem to him a shocking misuse of man's finest intellectual attainments. What is the professional astronomer to say when he is told that at least a thousand times more horoscopes are cast today than were cast three hundred years ago? What will the educator and advocate of philosophical enlightenment say about the fact that the world has not grown poorer by a single superstition since the days of antiquity? Freud himself, the founder of psychoanalysis, has taken the greatest pains to throw as glaring a light as possible on the dirt and darkness and evil of the psychic background, and to interpret it in such a way as to make us lose all desire to look for anything behind it except refuse and smut. He did not succeed, and his attempt at deterrence has even brought about the exact opposite—an admiration for all this filth. Such a perverse phenomenon would normally be inexplicable were it not that even the scatologists are drawn by the secret fascination of the psyche.

174   There can be no doubt that from the beginning of the nineteenth century—ever since the time of the French Revolution—the psyche has moved more and more into the foreground of man's interest, and with a steadily increasing power of attraction. The enthronement of the Goddess of Reason in Notre Dame seems to have been a symbolic gesture of great significance for the Western world—rather like the hewing down of Wotan's oak by Christian missionaries. On both occasions no avenging bolt from heaven struck the blasphemer down.

175   It is certainly more than an amusing freak of history that just at the time of the Revolution a Frenchman, Anquetil du Perron, should be living in India and, at the beginning of the nineteenth century, brought back with him a translation of the *Oupnek'hat,* a collection of fifty Upanishads, which gave the

West its first deep insight into the baffling mind of the East. To the historian this is a mere coincidence independent of the historical nexus of cause and effect. My medical bias prevents me from seeing it simply as an accident. Everything happened in accordance with a psychological law which is unfailingly valid in personal affairs. If anything of importance is devalued in our conscious life, and perishes—so runs the law—there arises a compensation in the unconscious. We may see in this an analogy to the conservation of energy in the physical world, for our psychic processes also have a quantitative, energic aspect. No psychic value can disappear without being replaced by another of equivalent intensity. This is a fundamental rule which is repeatedly verified in the daily practice of the psychotherapist and never fails. The doctor in me refuses point blank to consider the life of a people as something that does not conform to psychological law. For him the psyche of a people is only a somewhat more complex structure than the psyche of an individual. Moreover, has not a poet spoken of the "nations of his soul"? And quite correctly, it seems to me, for in one of its aspects the psyche is not individual, but is derived from the nation, from the collectivity, from humanity even. In some way or other we are part of a single, all-embracing psyche, a single "greatest man," the *homo maximus,* to quote Swedenborg.

176   And so we can draw a parallel: just as in me, a single individual, the darkness calls forth a helpful light, so it does in the psychic life of a people. In the crowds that poured into Notre Dame, bent on destruction, dark and nameless forces were at work that swept the individual off his feet; these forces worked also upon Anquetil du Perron and provoked an answer which has come down in history and speaks to us through the mouths of Schopenhauer and Nietzsche. For he brought the Eastern mind to the West, and its influence upon us we cannot as yet measure. Let us beware of underestimating it! So far, indeed, there is little of it to be seen on the intellectual surface: a handful of orientalists, one or two Buddhist enthusiasts, a few sombre celebrities like Madame Blavatsky and Annie Besant with her Krishnamurti. These manifestations are like tiny scattered islands in the ocean of mankind; in reality they are the peaks of submarine mountain-ranges. The cultural Philis-

tines believed until recently that astrology had been disposed of long since and was something that could safely be laughed at. But today, rising out of the social deeps, it knocks at the doors of the universities from which it was banished some three hundred years ago. The same is true of Eastern ideas; they take root in the lower levels and slowly grow to the surface. Where did the five or six million Swiss francs for the Anthroposophist temple at Dornach come from? Certainly not from one individual. Unfortunately there are no statistics to tell us the exact number of avowed Theosophists today, not to mention the unavowed. But we can be sure there are several millions of them. To this number we must add a few million Spiritualists of Christian or Theosophist leanings.

177   Great innovations never come from above; they come invariably from below, just as trees never grow from the sky downward, but upward from the earth. The upheaval of our world and the upheaval of our consciousness are one and the same. Everything has become relative and therefore doubtful. And while man, hesitant and questioning, contemplates a world that is distracted with treaties of peace and pacts of friendship, with democracy and dictatorship, capitalism and Bolshevism, his spirit yearns for an answer that will allay the turmoil of doubt and uncertainty. And it is just the people from the obscurer levels who follow the unconscious drive of the psyche; it is the much-derided, silent folk of the land, who are less infected with academic prejudices than the shining celebrities are wont to be. Looked at from above, they often present a dreary or laughable spectacle; yet they are as impressively simple as those Galileans who were once called blessed. Is it not touching to see the offscourings of man's psyche gathered together in compendia a foot thick? We find the merest babblings, the most absurd actions, the wildest fantasies recorded with scrupulous care in the volumes of *Anthropophyteia*,[4] while men like Havelock Ellis and Freud have dealt with like matters in serious treatises which have been accorded all scientific honours. Their reading public is scattered over the breadth of the civilized, white world. How are we to explain this zeal, this almost fanatical worship of everything unsavoury? It is because these

4 [See bibliography.]

things are psychological—they are of the substance of the psyche and therefore as precious as fragments of manuscript salvaged from ancient middens. Even the secret and noisome things of the psyche are valuable to modern man because they serve his purpose. But what purpose?

178   Freud prefixed to his *Interpretation of Dreams* the motto: *Flectere si nequeo superos Acheronta movebo*—"If I cannot bend the gods on high, I will at least set Acheron in uproar." But to what purpose?

179   The gods whom we are called upon to dethrone are the idolized values of our conscious world. Nothing, as we know, discredited the ancient gods so much as their love-scandals, and now history is repeating itself. People are laying bare the dubious foundations of our belauded virtues and incomparable ideals, and are calling out to us in triumph: "There are your man-made gods, mere snares and delusions tainted with human baseness—whited sepulchres full of dead men's bones and of all uncleanness." We recognize a familiar strain, and the Gospel words which we failed to digest at Confirmation come to life again.

180   I am deeply convinced that these are not just vague analogies. There are too many persons to whom Freudian psychology is dearer than the Gospels, and to whom Bolshevism means more than civic virtue. And yet they are all our brothers, and in each of us there is at least one voice which seconds them, for in the end there is one psyche which embraces us all.

181   The unexpected result of this development is that an uglier face is put upon the world. It becomes so ugly that no one can love it any longer; we cannot even love ourselves, and in the end there is nothing in the outer world to draw us away from the reality of the life within. Here, no doubt, we have the true significance of this whole development. After all, what does Theosophy, with its doctrines of *karma* and reincarnation, seek to teach except that this world of appearance is but a temporary health-resort for the morally unperfected? It depreciates the intrinsic value of the present-day world no less radically than does the modern outlook, but with the help of a different technique; it does not vilify our world, but grants it only a relative meaning in that it promises other and higher worlds. The result in either case is the same.

182   I admit that all these ideas are extremely unacademic, the truth being that they touch modern man on the side where he is least conscious. Is it again a mere coincidence that modern thought has had to come to terms with Einstein's relativity theory and with nuclear theories which lead us away from determinism and border on the inconceivable? Even physics is volatilizing our material world. It is no wonder, then, in my opinion, if modern man falls back on the reality of psychic life and expects from it that certainty which the world denies him.

183   Spiritually the Western world is in a precarious situation, and the danger is greater the more we blind ourselves to the merciless truth with illusions about our beauty of soul. Western man lives in a thick cloud of incense which he burns to himself so that his own countenance may be veiled from him in the smoke. But how do we strike men of another colour? What do China and India think of us? What feelings do we arouse in the black man? And what about all those whom we rob of their lands and exterminate with rum and venereal disease?

184   I have an American Indian friend who is a Pueblo chieftain. Once when we were talking confidentially about the white man, he said to me: "We don't understand the whites. They are always wanting something, always restless, always looking for something. What is it? We don't know. We can't understand them. They have such sharp noses, such thin, cruel lips, such lines in their faces. We think they are all crazy."

185   My friend had recognized, without being able to name it, the Aryan bird of prey with his insatiable lust to lord it in every land, even those that concern him not at all. And he had also noted that megalomania of ours which leads us to suppose, among other things, that Christianity is the only truth and the white Christ the only redeemer. After setting the whole East in turmoil with our science and technology, and exacting tribute from it, we send our missionaries even to China. The comedy of Christianity in Africa is really pitiful. There the stamping out of polygamy, no doubt highly pleasing to God, has given rise to prostitution on such a scale that in Uganda alone twenty thousand pounds are spent annually on preventives of venereal infection. And the good European pays his missionaries for these edifying achievements! Need we also mention the story of suffering in Polynesia and the blessings of the opium trade?

186   That is how the European looks when he is extricated from the cloud of his own moral incense. No wonder that unearthing the psyche is like undertaking a full-scale drainage operation. Only a great idealist like Freud could devote a lifetime to such unclean work. It was not he who caused the bad smell, but all of us—we who think ourselves so clean and decent from sheer ignorance and the grossest self-deception. Thus our psychology, the acquaintance with our own souls, begins in every respect from the most repulsive end, that is to say with all those things which we do not wish to see.

187   But if the psyche consisted only of evil and worthless things, no power on earth could induce the normal man to find it attractive. That is why people who see in Theosophy nothing but lamentable intellectual superficiality, and in Freudian psychology nothing but sensationalism, prophesy an early and inglorious end to these movements. They overlook the fact that such movements derive their force from the fascination of the psyche, and that it will express itself in these forms until they are replaced by something better. They are transitional or embryonic stages from which new and riper forms will emerge.

188   We have not yet realized that Western Theosophy is an amateurish, indeed barbarous imitation of the East. We are just beginning to take up astrology again, which to the Oriental is his daily bread. Our studies of sexual life, originating in Vienna and England, are matched or surpassed by Hindu teachings on this subject. Oriental texts ten centuries old introduce us to philosophical relativism, while the idea of indeterminacy, newly broached in the West, is the very basis of Chinese science. As to our discoveries in psychology, Richard Wilhelm has shown me that certain complicated psychic processes are recognizably described in ancient Chinese texts. Psychoanalysis itself and the lines of thought to which it gives rise—a development which we consider specifically Western—are only a beginner's attempt compared with what is an immemorial art in the East. It may not perhaps be known that parallels between psychoanalysis and yoga have already been drawn by Oscar Schmitz.[5]

189   Another thing we have not realized is that while we are turn-

5 [*Psychoanalyse und Yoga.* See bibliography.]

ing the material world of the East upside down with our technical proficiency, the East with its superior psychic proficiency is throwing our spiritual world into confusion. We have never yet hit upon the thought that while we are overpowering the Orient from without, it may be fastening its hold on us from within. Such an idea strikes us as almost insane, because we have eyes only for obvious causal connections and fail to see that we must lay the blame for the confusion of our intellectual middle class at the doors of Max Müller, Oldenberg, Deussen, Wilhelm, and others like them. What does the example of the Roman Empire teach us? After the conquest of Asia Minor, Rome became Asiatic; Europe was infected by Asia and remains so today. Out of Cilicia came the Mithraic cult, the religion of the Roman legions, and it spread from Egypt to fog-bound Britain. Need I point out the Asiatic origin of Christianity?

190   The Theosophists have an amusing idea that certain Mahatmas, seated somewhere in the Himalayas or Tibet, inspire and direct every mind in the world. So strong, in fact, can be the influence of the Eastern belief in magic that Europeans of sound mind have assured me that every good thing I say is unwittingly inspired in me by the Mahatmas, my own inspirations being of no account whatever. This myth of the Mahatmas, widely circulated in the West and firmly believed, far from being nonsense, is—like every myth—an important psychological truth. It seems to be quite true that the East is at the bottom of the spiritual change we are passing through today. Only, this East is not a Tibetan monastery full of Mahatmas, but lies essentially within us. It is our own psyche, constantly at work creating new spiritual forms and spiritual forces which may help us to subdue the boundless lust for prey of Aryan man. We shall perhaps come to know something of that narrowing of horizons which has grown in the East into a dubious quietism, and also something of that stability which human existence acquires when the claims of the spirit become as imperative as the necessities of social life. Yet in this age of Americanization we are still far from anything of the sort; it seems to me that we are only at the threshold of a new spiritual epoch. I do not wish to pass myself off as a prophet, but one can hardly attempt to sketch the spiritual problem of modern man without mentioning the longing for rest in a period of unrest, the longing

for security in an age of insecurity. It is from need and distress that new forms of existence arise, and not from idealistic requirements or mere wishes.

191   To me the crux of the spiritual problem today is to be found in the fascination which the psyche holds for modern man. If we are pessimists, we shall call it a sign of decadence; if we are optimistically inclined, we shall see in it the promise of a far-reaching spiritual change in the Western world. At all events, it is a significant phenomenon. It is the more noteworthy because it is rooted in the deeper social strata, and the more important because it touches those irrational and—as history shows —incalculable psychic forces which transform the life of peoples and civilizations in ways that are unforeseen and unforeseeable. These are the forces, still invisible to many persons today, which are at the bottom of the present "psychological" interest. The fascination of the psyche is not by any means a morbid perversity; it is an attraction so strong that it does not shrink even from what it finds repellent.

192   Along the great highways of the world everything seems desolate and outworn. Instinctively modern man leaves the trodden paths to explore the by-ways and lanes, just as the man of the Greco-Roman world cast off his defunct Olympian gods and turned to the mystery cults of Asia. Our instinct turns outward, and appropriates Eastern theosophy and magic; but it also turns inward, and leads us to contemplate the dark background of the psyche. It does this with the same scepticism and the same ruthlessness which impelled the Buddha to sweep aside his two million gods that he might attain the original experience which alone is convincing.

193   And now we must ask a final question. Is what I have said of modern man really true, or is it perhaps an illusion? There can be no doubt whatever that to many millions of Westerners the facts I have adduced are wholly irrelevant and fortuitous, and regrettable aberrations to a large number of educated persons. But—did a cultivated Roman think any differently when he saw Christianity spreading among the lower classes? Today the God of the West is still a living person for vast numbers of people, just as Allah is beyond the Mediterranean, and the one believer holds the other an inferior heretic, to be pitied and tolerated failing all else. To make matters worse, the en-

lightened European is of the opinion that religion and such things are good enough for the masses and for women, but of little consequence compared with immediate economic and political questions.

194   So I am refuted all along the line, like a man who predicts a thunderstorm when there is not a cloud in the sky. Perhaps it is a storm below the horizon, and perhaps it will never reach us. But what is significant in psychic life always lies below the horizon of consciousness, and when we speak of the spiritual problem of modern man we are speaking of things that are barely visible—of the most intimate and fragile things, of flowers that open only in the night. In daylight everything is clear and tangible, but the night lasts as long as the day, and we live in the night-time also. There are people who have bad dreams which even spoil their days for them. And for many people the day's life is such a bad dream that they long for the night when the spirit awakes. I believe that there are nowadays a great many such people, and this is why I also maintain that the spiritual problem of modern man is much as I have presented it.

195   I must plead guilty, however, to the charge of one-sidedness, for I have passed over in silence the spirit of the times, about which everyone has so much to say because it is so clearly apparent to us all. It shows itself in the ideal of internationalism and supernationalism, embodied in the League of Nations and the like; we see it also in sport and, significantly, in cinema and jazz. These are characteristic symptoms of our time, which has extended the humanistic ideal even to the body. Sport puts an exceptional valuation on the body, and this tendency is emphasized still further in modern dancing. The cinema, like the detective story, enables us to experience without danger to ourselves all the excitements, passions, and fantasies which have to be repressed in a humanistic age. It is not difficult to see how these symptoms link up with our psychological situation. The fascination of the psyche brings about a new self-appraisal, a reassessment of our fundamental human nature. We can hardly be surprised if this leads to a rediscovery of the body after its long subjection to the spirit—we are even tempted to say that the flesh is getting its own back. When Keyserling sarcastically singles out the chauffeur as the culture-hero of our time, he has struck, as he often does, close to the mark. The body lays claim

to equal recognition; it exerts the same fascination as the psyche. If we are still caught in the old idea of an antithesis between mind and matter, this state of affairs must seem like an unbearable contradiction. But if we can reconcile ourselves to the mysterious truth that the spirit is the life of the body seen from within, and the body the outward manifestation of the life of the spirit—the two being really one—then we can understand why the striving to transcend the present level of consciousness through acceptance of the unconscious must give the body its due, and why recognition of the body cannot tolerate a philosophy that denies it in the name of the spirit. These claims of physical and psychic life, incomparably stronger than they were in the past, may seem a sign of decadence, but they may also signify a rejuvenation, for as Hölderlin says:

Where danger is,
Arises salvation also.

196   And indeed we see, as the Western world strikes up a more rapid tempo—the American tempo—the exact opposite of quietism and world-negating resignation. An unprecedented tension arises between outside and inside, between objective and subjective reality. Perhaps it is a final race between aging Europe and young America; perhaps it is a healthier or a last desperate effort to escape the dark sway of natural law, and to wrest a yet greater and more heroic victory of waking consciousness over the sleep of the nations. This is a question only history can answer.

II

THE LOVE PROBLEM OF A STUDENT

———

WOMAN IN EUROPE

———

THE MEANING OF PSYCHOLOGY
FOR MODERN MAN

———

THE STATE OF
PSYCHOTHERAPY TODAY

THE LOVE PROBLEM OF A STUDENT [1]

197   It is, I assure you, with no light heart that I undertake the task of opening your discussion of the love problem of a student by reading a general paper on this subject. Such a discussion is an unusual one, and presents difficulties if taken in a spirit of seriousness and with a fitting sense of responsibility.

198   Love is always a problem, whatever our age may be. In childhood, the love of one's parents is a problem, and for the old man the problem is what he has made of his love. Love is a force of destiny whose power reaches from heaven to hell. We must, I think, understand love in this way if we are to do any sort of justice to the problems it involves. They are of immense scope and complexity, not confined to any particular province but covering every aspect of human life. Love may be an ethical, a social, a psychological, a philosophical, an aesthetic, a religious, a medical, a legal, or a physiological problem, to name only a few aspects of this many-sided phenomenon. This invasion of love into all the collective spheres of life is, however, only a minor difficulty in comparison with the fact that love is also an intensely individual problem. For it means that every general criterion and rule loses its validity, in exactly the same way that religious beliefs, although constantly codified in the course of history, are always, in essence, an individual experience which bows to no traditional rule.

199   The very word "love" is itself an obstacle to our discussion. What, indeed, has not been called "love"! Beginning with the highest mystery of the Christian religion, we encounter, on the

1 [A lecture to Zurich University students, probably in Dec., 1922. Originally published in English as "The Love Problem of the Student," trans. by C. F. and H. G. Baynes from the unpublished German ms., in *Contributions to Analytical Psychology* (London and New York, 1928). For the present trans. the Baynes version has been consulted.—EDITORS.]

97

next-lower stages, the *amor Dei* of Origen, the *amor intellectualis Dei* of Spinoza, Plato's love of the Idea, and the *Gottesminne* of the mystics. Goethe's words introduce us to the human sphere of love:

> Let now the savage instincts sleep
> And all the violence they do;
> When human love stirs in the deep
> The love of God is stirring too.

200   Here we find the love of one's neighbour, in the Christian sense as well as in the Buddhist sense of compassion, and the love of mankind as expressed in social service. Next there is love of one's country, and the love for ideal institutions such as the Church. Then comes parental love, above all mother-love, then filial love. When we come to conjugal love we leave the sphere of the spiritual and enter that intermediate realm between spirit and instinct. Here the pure flame of Eros sets fire to sexuality, and the ideal forms of love—love of parents, of country, of one's neighbour, etc.—are mingled with the lust for personal power and the desire to possess and to rule. This does not mean that all contact with instinct debases love. On the contrary, its beauty and truth and strength become the more perfect the more instinct it can absorb into itself. Only if instinct predominates does the animal come to the surface. Conjugal love can be of the kind of which Goethe says at the end of *Faust:*

> Spirit by attraction draws
> Elemental matter,
> Forges bonds no man can force
> And no angel shatter.
> Double natures single grown,
> Inwardly united,
> By Eternal Love alone
> Can it be divided.

201   But it need not necessarily be such a love. It may recall Nietzsche's words: "Two animals have lighted on each other." The love of the lover is again different. Even though the sacrament of marriage be lacking, and the pledge of a life together, this love may be transfigured by the power of fate or by its own

tragic nature. But as a rule instinct predominates, with its dark glow or its flickering fires.

202   Even this has not brought us to the limits of love. By "love" we also mean the sexual act on all levels, from officially sanctioned, wedded cohabitation to the physiological need which drives a man to prostitutes and to the mere business they make or are forced to make of love.

203   We also speak of "the love of boys," meaning homosexuality, which since classical times has lost its glamour as a social and educative institution, and now ekes out a miserable, terror-stricken existence as a so-called perversion and punishable offence, at least where men are concerned. In Anglo-Saxon countries it seems on the other hand that female homosexuality means rather more than Sapphic lyricism, since it somehow acts as a stimulus to the social and political organization of women, just as male homosexuality was an important factor in the rise of the Greek *polis*.

204   Finally, the word "love" must be stretched still further to cover all sexual perversions. There is incestuous love, and a masturbatory self-love that goes by the name of narcissism. The word "love" includes every kind of morbid sexual abomination as well as every kind of greed that has ever degraded man to the level of a beast or a machine.

205   Thus we find ourselves in the awkward position of beginning a discussion about a matter or concept whose outlines are of the vaguest and whose extent is well-nigh illimitable. At least for the purposes of the present discussion, one would like to restrict the concept of love to the problem of how a young student should come to terms with sex. But this just cannot be done, because all the meanings of the word "love" which I have already mentioned enter actively into the love problem of a student.

206   We can, however, agree to discuss the question of the way in which the average so-called normal person behaves under the conditions I have described. Disregarding the fact the "normal" person does not exist, we find, nevertheless, sufficient similarities even among individuals of the most varied types to warrant a discussion of the "average" problem. As always, the practical solution of the problem depends on two factors: the

demands and capacities of the individual, and the environmental conditions.

207   It is the duty of a speaker to present a general survey of the question under discussion. Naturally this can be done only if, as a doctor, I can give an objective account of things as they are, and abstain from that stale, moralizing talk which veils the subject with a mixture of bashfulness and hypocrisy. Moreover, I am not here to tell you what ought to be done. That must be left to those who always know what is better for other people.

208   Our theme is "The Love Problem of a Student," and I assume that "love problem" means the relation of the two sexes and is not to be construed as the "sexual problem" of a student. This provides a useful limitation of our theme, for the question of sex would need considering only so far as it is a love problem, or a problem of relationship. Hence we can exclude all those sexual phenomena that have nothing to do with relationship, such as sexual perversions (with the exception of homosexuality), masturbation, and intercourse with prostitutes. We cannot exclude homosexuality because very often it is a problem of relationship; but we can exclude prostitution because usually it does not involve a relationship, though there are exceptions which prove the rule.

209   The average solution of the love problem is, as you know, marriage. But experience shows that this statistical truth does not apply to the student. The immediate reason for this is that a student is generally not in a position to set up house. A further reason is the youthful age of most students, which, partly because of their unfinished studies, and partly because of their need for freedom to move from place to place, does not yet permit the social fixation entailed by marriage. Other factors to be considered are psychological immaturity, childish clinging to home and family, relatively undeveloped capacity for love and responsibility, lack of experience of life and the world, the typical illusions of youth, and so on. A reason that should not be underestimated is the sagacious reserve of the girl students. Their first aim is to complete their studies and take up a profession. They therefore abstain from marriage, especially from marriage with a student, who so long as he remains a student is not a desirable marriage partner for the reasons already mentioned. Another, very important, reason for the infrequency of

student marriages is the question of children. As a rule when a girl marries she wants a child, whereas a man can manage well enough for a time without children. A marriage without children has no special attraction for a woman; she prefers to wait.

210   In recent years, it is true, student marriages have become more frequent. This is due partly to the psychological changes in our modern outlook, and partly to the spread of contraceptive measures. The psychological changes that have produced, among other things, the phenomenon of the student marriage are probably the result of the spiritual upheavals of the last few decades, the total significance of which we are as yet unable to grasp. All we can say is that, as a consequence of the general dissemination of scientific knowledge and a more scientific way of thinking, a change in the very conception of the love problem has come about. Scientific objectivity has effected a rapprochement between the sacrosanct idea of man as a superior being and man as a natural being, and made it possible for *Homo sapiens* to take his place as part of the natural order. The change has an emotional as well as an intellectual aspect. Such a view works directly on the feelings of the individual. He feels released from the confines of a metaphysical system and from those moral categories which characterized the medieval outlook on the world. The taboos erected on man's exclusion from nature no longer prevail, and the moral judgments which in the last analysis always have their roots in the religious metaphysic of the age have lost their force. Within the traditional moral system everyone knows perfectly why marriage is "right" and why any other form of love is to be abhorred. But outside the system, on the playground and battlefield of nature, where man feels himself to be the most gifted member of the great family of animals, he must orient himself anew. The loss of the old standards and values amounts, at first, to moral chaos. All the hitherto accepted forms are doubted, people begin to discuss things that have long sheltered behind a moral prejudice. They boldly investigate the actual facts and feel an irresistible need to take stock of experience, to know and to understand. The eyes of science are fearless and clear; they do not flinch from gazing into moral darknesses and dirty corners. The man of today can no longer rest content with a traditional judg-

ment; he must know why. This search leads to the creation of new standards of value.

211   One of these is an evaluation of love in terms of hygiene. Through a franker and more objective discussion of sex a knowledge of the immense dangers of venereal disease has become much more widespread. The obligation to keep oneself healthy has superseded the guilty fears of the old morality. But this process of moral sanitation has not yet progressed to the point where public conscience would allow the same civic measures to be taken for dealing with venereal diseases as with other infectious diseases. Venereal diseases are still considered "indecent," unlike smallpox and cholera, which are morally acceptable in the drawing room. No doubt these fine distinctions will raise a smile in a more enlightened age.

212   The widespread discussion of the sexual question has brought the extraordinary importance of sexuality in all its psychic ramifications to the forefront of our social consciousness. A major contribution was made during the last twenty-five years by the much-decried psychoanalytic movement. Today it is no longer possible to brush aside the tremendous psychological importance of sex with a bad joke or a display of moral indignation. People are beginning to see the sexual question in the context of the great human problems and to discuss it with the seriousness it deserves. The natural result of this is that much that was formerly held to be beyond dispute is now open to doubt. There is, for instance, a doubt as to whether the officially sanctioned form of sexuality is the only one that is morally possible, and whether all other forms are to be condemned out of hand. The arguments for and against are gradually losing their moral acerbity, practical considerations force themselves into the discussion, and finally we are beginning to discover that legitimized sex is not *eo ipso* the equivalent of moral superiority.

213   In addition to this, the marriage problem with its usually sombre background has become a theme for romantic literature. Whereas the romance of the old style concluded with a happy betrothal or a wedding, the modern novel often begins after the marriage. In these novels, which get into everybody's hands, the most intimate problems are often treated with a lack of reticence that is positively painful. Of the veritable flood of

more or less undisguised pornographic writings we need hardly speak. A popular scientific book, Forel's *The Sexual Question,* not only had an enormous sale but found a good many imitators. In scientific literature, compilations have been produced which both in scope and in the dubious nature of their contents exceed anything found in Krafft-Ebing's *Psychopathia Sexualis,* in a way that would have been inconceivable thirty or forty years ago.

214   These widespread and widely known phenomena are a sign of the times. They make it possible for young people today to grasp the full importance of the problem of sex much earlier than they could have at any time during the last two decades. There are some who maintain that this early preoccupation with sex is unhealthy, a sign of urban degeneration. I remember reading an article fifteen years ago in Ostwald's *Annalen der Naturphilosophie,* which said, quite literally: "Primitive people like the Eskimos, Swiss, etc., have no sexual problem." It scarcely needs much reflection to see why primitives have no sexual problem; beyond the concerns of the stomach they have no other problems to worry about. Problems are the prerogative of civilized man. Here in Switzerland we have no great cities and yet such problems exist. I do not think that discussion of the sexual question is unhealthy or in the least degenerate; I see it rather as a symptom of the great psychological revolution of our time and the changes it has brought about. It seems to me that the more seriously and thoroughly we discuss this question, which is of such vital importance for man's health and happiness, the better it will be for all of us.

215   It is no doubt the serious interest shown in this question that has led to the hitherto unknown phenomenon of student marriages. Such a very recent phenomenon is difficult to judge for lack of sufficient data. In former times there were early marriages in abundance, also marriages that must have seemed socially very unstable. In itself, therefore, the student marriage is perfectly permissible. The question of children, however, is another matter. If both partners are studying, children must obviously be ruled out. But a marriage that remains artificially childless is always rather problematical. Children are the cement that holds it together as nothing else could. And it is the parents' concentration on the children which in innumera-

ble instances keeps alive the feeling of companionship so essential for the stability of a marriage. When there are no children the interest of each partner is directed to the other, which in itself might be a good thing. In practice, unfortunately, this mutual preoccupation is not always of an amiable kind. Each blames the other for the dissatisfaction felt by both. In these circumstances it is probably better for the wife to be studying, otherwise she is left without an object; for there are many women who cannot endure marriage without children and become unendurable themselves. If she is studying, she at least has a life outside her marriage that is sufficiently satisfying. A woman who is very set on children, and for whom children are more important than a husband, should certainly think twice before embarking on a student marriage. She should also realize that the urge to maternity often appears in imperative form only later, that is, after she is married.

216   As to whether student marriages are premature, we must take note of a fact that applies to all early marriages, namely, that a girl of twenty is usually older than a man of twenty-five, as far as maturity of judgment is concerned. With many men of twenty-five the period of psychological puberty is not yet over. Puberty is a period of illusion and only partial responsibility. The psychological difference is due to the fact that a boy, up to the time of sexual maturity, is as a rule quite childish, whereas a girl develops much earlier than he does the psychological subtleties that go hand in hand with adolescence. Into this childishness sexuality often breaks with brutal force, while, despite the onset of puberty, it often goes on slumbering in a girl until the passion of love awakens it. There are a surprising number of women whose real sexuality, even though they are married, remains virginal for years; they become conscious of it only when they fall in love with another man. That is the reason why very many women have no understanding at all of masculine sexuality—they are completely unconscious of their own. With men it is different. Sexuality bursts on them like a tempest, filling them with brute desires and needs, and there is scarcely one of them who escapes the painful problem of masturbation. But a girl can masturbate for years without knowing what she is doing.

217   The onrush of sexuality in a boy brings about a powerful

change in his psychology. He now has the sexuality of a grown man with the soul of a child. Often the flood of obscene fantasies and smutty talk with schoolfellows pours like a torrent of dirty water over all his delicate and childish feelings, sometimes smothering them for ever. Unexpected moral conflicts arise, temptations of every description lie in wait for him and weave themselves into his fantasies. The psychic assimilation of the sexual complex causes him the greatest difficulties even though he may not be conscious of its existence. The onset of puberty also brings about considerable changes in his metabolism, as can be seen from the pimples and acne that so often afflict adolescents. The psyche is disturbed in a similar manner and thrown off its balance. At this age the young man is full of illusions, which are always a sign of psychic disequilibrium. They make stability and maturity of judgment impossible. His tastes, his interests, his plans alter fitfully. He can suddenly fall head over heels in love with a girl, and a fortnight later he cannot conceive how anything of the sort could have happened to him. He is so riddled with illusions that he actually needs these mistakes to make him conscious of his own taste and individual judgment. He is still experimenting with life, and *must* experiment with it in order to learn how to judge things correctly. Hence there are very few men who have not had sexual experience of some kind before they are married. During puberty it is mostly homosexual experiences, and these are much more common than is generally admitted. Heterosexual experiences come later, not always of a very beautiful kind. For the less the sexual complex is assimilated to the whole of the personality, the more autonomous and instinctive it will be. Sexuality is then purely animal and recognizes no psychological distinctions. The most inferior woman will do; it is enough if she has the typical secondary sexual characteristics. A false step of this kind does not entitle us to draw conclusions about a man's character, as the act can easily occur at a time when the sexual complex is still split off from the psyche's influence. Nevertheless, too many experiences of this nature have a bad effect on the formation of the personality, as by force of habit they fix sexuality on too low a level and make it unacceptable to moral judgment. The result is that though the man in question is outwardly a respectable citizen, inwardly he is prey to sexual fantasies of the lowest kind, or else he represses them and on some festive occasion they come leaping to the surface in their primitive form, much to the astonishment of his unsuspecting wife—assuming, of course, that she notices what is going on. A frequent accompaniment is premature coldness towards the wife. Women are often frigid from the first day of marriage because their sensation function does not respond to this kind of sexuality in their husbands. The weakness of a man's judgment at the time of psychological puberty should prompt him to reflect very deeply on the premature choice of a wife.

218   Let us now turn to other forms of relationship between the sexes that are customary during the student period. There are, as you know, characteristic liaisons between students, chiefly in the great universities of other countries. These relationships are sometimes fairly stable and may even have a psychological value, as they do not consist entirely of sexuality but also, in part, of love. Occasionally the liaison is continued into marriage. The relationship stands, therefore, considerably higher than prostitution. But as a rule it is limited to those students who were careful in the choice of their parents. It is usually a question of money, for most of the girls are dependent on their lovers for financial help, though they could not be said to sell their love for money. Very often the relationship is a beautiful episode in the girl's life, otherwise poor and empty, while for the man it may be his first intimate acquaintance with a woman, and in later life a memory on which he looks back with emotion. Often, again, there is nothing valuable in these affairs, partly owing to the man's crude sensuality, thoughtlessness, and lack of feeling, and partly owing to the frivolity and fickleness of the girl.

219   Over all these relationships hangs the Damoclean sword of their transitoriness, which prevents the formation of real values. They are passing episodes, experiments of very limited validity. Their injurious effect on the personality is due to the fact that the man gets the girl too easily, so that the value of the love-object is depreciated. It is convenient for him to dispose of his sexual problem in such a simple and irresponsible way. He becomes spoilt. But even more, the fact that he is sexually satisfied robs him of a driving-force which no young man can do without. He becomes blasé and can afford to wait. Meanwhile he

can calmly review the massed femininity passing before him until the right party turns up. Then the wedding comes along and the latest date is thrown over. This procedure adds little of advantage to his character. The low level of relationship tends to keep sexuality on a correspondingly low level of development, and this can easily lead to difficulties in marriage. Or if his sexual fantasies are repressed, the result is only too likely to be a neurotic or, worse still, a moral zealot.

220   Homosexual relations between students of either sex are by no means uncommon. So far as I can judge of this phenomenon, I would say that these relationships are less common with us, and on the continent generally, than in certain other countries where boy and girl college students live in strict segregation. I am speaking here not of pathological homosexuals who are incapable of real friendship and meet with little sympathy among normal individuals, but of more or less normal youngsters who enjoy such a rapturous friendship that they also express their feelings in sexual form. With them it is not just a matter of mutual masturbation, which in all school and college life is the order of the day among the younger age groups, but of a higher and more spiritual form which deserves the name "friendship" in the classical sense of the word. When such a friendship exists between an older man and a younger its educative significance is undeniable. A slightly homosexual teacher, for example, often owes his brilliant educational gifts to his homosexual disposition. The homosexual relation between an older and a younger man can thus be of advantage to both sides and have a lasting value. An indispensable condition for the value of such a relation is the steadfastness of the friendship and their loyalty to it. But only too often this condition is lacking. The more homosexual a man is, the more prone he is to disloyalty and to the seduction of boys. Even when loyalty and true friendship prevail the results may be undesirable for the development of personality. A friendship of this kind naturally involves a special cult of feeling, of the feminine element in a man. He becomes gushing, soulful, aesthetic, over-sensitive, etc. —in a word, effeminate, and this womanish behaviour is detrimental to his character.

221   Similar advantages and disadvantages can be pointed out in friendships between women, only here the difference in age

and the educative factor are not so important. The main value lies in the exchange of tender feelings on the one hand and of intimate thoughts on the other. Generally they are high-spirited, intellectual, and rather masculine women who are seeking to maintain their superiority and to defend themselves against men. Their attitude to men is therefore one of disconcerting self-assurance, with a trace of defiance. Its effect on their character is to reinforce their masculine traits and to destroy their feminine charm. Often a man discovers their homosexuality only when he notices that these women leave him stone-cold.

222   Normally, the practice of homosexuality is not prejudicial to later heterosexual activity. Indeed, the two can even exist side by side. I know a very intelligent woman who spent her whole life as a homosexual and then at fifty entered into a normal relationship with a man.

223   Among the sexual relations of the student period we must mention yet another, which is quite normal even if rather peculiar. This is the attachment of a young man to an older woman, possibly married or at any rate widowed. You will perhaps remember Jean Jacques Rousseau and his connection with Mme de Warens; this is the kind of relationship I have in mind. The man is usually rather shy, unsure of himself, inwardly afraid, sometimes infantile. He naturally seeks a mother, perhaps because he has had too much or too little love in his own family. Many women like nothing better than a man who is rather helpless, especially when they are considerably older than he is; they do not love a man's strength, his virtues and his merits, but his weaknesses. They find his infantilisms charming. If he stammers a little, he is enchanting; or perhaps he has a limp, and this excites maternal compassion and a little more besides. As a rule the woman seduces him, and he willingly submits to her mothering.

224   Not always, however, does a timid youth remain half a child. It may be that this surfeit of maternal solicitude was just what was needed to bring his undeveloped masculinity to the surface. In this way the woman educates his feeling and brings it to full consciousness. He learns to understand a woman who has experience of life and the world, is sure of herself, and thus he has a rare opportunity for a glimpse behind the scenes. But he

can take advantage of it only if he quickly outgrows this relationship, for should he get stuck in it her mothering would ruin him. Maternal tenderness is the most pernicious poison for anyone who has to equip himself for the hard and pitiless struggle of life. If he cannot let go of her apron-strings he will become a spineless parasite—for most of these women have money—and sink to the level of a lap-dog or a pet cat.

225   We must now discuss those forms of relationship which offer no solution of the sexual question for the reason that they are asexual or "platonic." If there were any reliable statistics on this subject, I believe they would show that in Switzerland the majority of students prefer a platonic relationship. Naturally, this raises the question of sexual abstinence. One often hears that abstaining from sexual intercouse is injurious to health. This view is incorrect, at least for people of the student age. Abstinence is injurious to health only when a man has reached the age when he could win a woman for himself, and should do so according to his individual inclinations. The extraordinary intensification of the sexual need that is so often felt at this time has the biological aim of forcibly eliminating the man's scruples, misgivings, doubts, and hesitations. This is very necessary, because the very idea of marriage, with all its doubtful possibilities, often makes a man panicky. It is only to be expected, therefore, that nature will push him over the obstacle. Abstention from sexual intercourse may certainly have injurious effects under these conditions, but not when there is no urgent physical or psychological need for it.

226   This brings us to the very similar question concerning the injurious effects of masturbation. When for physical or psychological reasons normal intercouse is impossible, masturbation as a safety-valve has no ill effects. Young people who come to the doctor suffering from the harmful effects of masturbation are not by any means excessive masturbationists—these usually have no need of a doctor because they are not in any sense ill —rather, their masturbation has harmful effects because it shows psychic complications and is attended by pangs of conscience or by a riot of sexual fantasies. The latter are particularly common among women. Masturbation with psychic complications is harmful, but not the ordinary, uncomplicated kind. If, however, it is continued up to the age when normal intercourse

109

becomes physically, psychologically, and socially possible, and is indulged in merely in order to avoid the necessary tasks of life, then it is harmful.

227   Platonic relationships are very important during the student period. The form they most commonly take is flirting. Flirting is the expression of an experimental attitude which is altogether appropriate at this age. It is a voluntary activity which, by tacit agreement, puts neither side under an obligation. This is an advantage and at the same time a disadvantage. The experimental attitude enables both parties to get to know each other without any immediately undesirable results. Both exercise their judgment and their skill in self-expression, adaptation, and defence. An enormous variety of experiences which are uncommonly valuable in later life can be picked up from flirting. On the other hand, the absence of any obligation can easily lead to one's becoming an habitual flirt, shallow, frivolous, and heartless. The man turns into a drawing-room hero and professional heart-breaker, never dreaming what a boring figure he cuts; the girl a coquette, and a serious man instinctively feels that she is not to be taken seriously.

228   A phenomenon that is as rare as flirting is common is the conscious cultivation of a serious love. We might call this simply the ideal, without, however, identifying it with traditional romanticism. For the development of personality, there can be no doubt that the timely awakening and conscious cultivation of deeply serious and responsible feelings are of the utmost value. A relationship of this kind can be the most effective shield against the temptations that beset a young man, as well as being a powerful incentive to hard work, loyalty, and reliability. However, there is no value so great that it does not have its unfavourable side. A relationship that is too ideal easily becomes exclusive. Through his love the young man is too much cut off from the acquaintance of other women, and the girl does not learn the art of erotic conquest because she has got her man already. Woman's instinct for possession is a dangerous thing, and it may easily happen that the man will regret all the experiences he never had with women before marriage and will make up for them afterwards.

229   Hence it must not be concluded that every relationship of this kind is ideal. There are cases where the exact opposite is

THE LOVE PROBLEM OF A STUDENT

true—when, for instance, a man or girl trails round with a school sweetheart for no intelligible reason, from mere force of habit. Whether from inertia, or lack of spirit, or helplessness they simply cannot get rid of each other. Perhaps the parents on both sides find the match suitable, and the affair, begun in a moment of thoughtlessness and prolonged by habit, is passively accepted as a *fait accompli*. Here the disadvantages pile up without a single advantage. For the development of personality, acquiescence and passivity are harmful because they are an obstacle to valuable experience and to the exercise of one's specific gifts and virtues. Moral qualities are won only in freedom and prove their worth only in morally dangerous situations. The thief who refrains from stealing merely because he is in prison is not a moral personality. Though the parents may gaze benignly on this touching marriage and add their children's respectability to the tale of their own virtues, it is all a sham and a delusion, lacking real strength, and sapped by moral inertia.

230   After this brief survey of the problems as we meet them in actual life, I will, in conclusion, turn to the land of heart's desire and utopian possibilities.

231   Nowadays we can hardly discuss the love problem without speaking of the utopia of free love, including trial marriage. I regard this idea as a wishful fantasy and an attempt to make light of a problem which in actual life is invariably very difficult. It is no more possible to make life easy than it is to grow a herb of immortality. The force of gravity can be overcome only by the requisite application of energy. Similarly, the solution of the love problem challenges all our resources. Anything else would be useless patchwork. Free love would be conceivable only if everyone were capable of the highest moral achievement. The idea of free love was not invented with this aim in view, but merely to make something difficult appear easy. Love requires depth and loyalty of feeling; without them it is not love but mere caprice. True love will always commit itself and engage in lasting ties; it needs freedom only to effect its choice, not for its accomplishment. Every true and deep love is a sacrifice. The lover sacrifices all other possibilities, or rather, the illusion that such possibilities exist. If this sacrifice is not made, his illusions prevent the growth of any deep and responsible

feeling, so that the very possibility of experiencing real love is denied him.

232 Love has more than one thing in common with religious faith. It demands unconditional trust and expects absolute surrender. Just as nobody but the believer who surrenders himself wholly to God can partake of divine grace, so love reveals its highest mysteries and its wonder only to those who are capable of unqualified devotion and loyalty of feeling. And because this is so difficult, few mortals can boast of such an achievement. But, precisely because the truest and most devoted love is also the most beautiful, let no man seek to make it easy. He is a sorry knight who shrinks from the difficulty of loving his lady. Love is like God: both give themselves only to their bravest knights.

233 I would offer the same criticism of trial marriages. The very fact that a man enters into a marriage on trial means that he is making a reservation; he wants to be sure of not burning his fingers, to risk nothing. But that is the most effective way of forestalling any real experience. You do not experience the terrors of the Polar ice by perusing a travel-book, or climb the Himalayas in a cinema.

234 Love is not cheap—let us therefore beware of cheapening it! All our bad qualities, our egotism, our cowardice, our worldly wisdom, our cupidity—all these would persuade us not to take love seriously. But love will reward us only when we do. I must even regard it as a misfortune that nowadays the sexual question is spoken of as something distinct from love. The two questions should not be separated, for when there is a sexual problem it can be solved only by love. Any other solution would be a harmful substitute. Sexuality dished out as sexuality is brutish; but sexuality as an expression of love is hallowed. Therefore, never ask what a man does, but how he does it. If he does it from love or in the spirit of love, then he serves a god; and whatever he may do is not ours to judge, for it is ennobled.

235 I trust that these remarks will have made it clear to you that I pass no sort of moral judgment on sexuality as a natural phenomenon, but prefer to make its moral evaluation dependent on the way it is expressed.

WOMAN IN EUROPE [1]

> You call yourself free? Your domi-
> nant thought I would hear, and
> not that you have escaped from a
> yoke. Are you one of those who
> had the right to escape from a
> yoke? There are some who threw
> away their last value when they
> threw away their servitude.
>
> *Thus Spake Zarathustra*

236   To write about woman in Europe today is such a hazardous undertaking that I would scarcely have ventured to do so without a pressing invitation. Have we anything of fundamental importance to say about Europe? Is anyone sufficiently detached? Are we not all involved in some programme or experiment, or caught in some critical retrospect that clouds our judgment? And in regard to woman, cannot the same questions be asked? Moreover, what can a man say about woman, his own opposite? I mean of course something sensible, that is outside the sexual programme, free of resentment, illusion, and theory. Where is the man to be found capable of such superiority? Woman always stands just where the man's shadow falls, so that he is only too liable to confuse the two. Then, when he tries to repair this misunderstanding, he overvalues her and

1 [Originally published as "Die Frau in Europa," *Europäische Revue* (Berlin), III: 7 (Oct., 1927); republished by the *Neue Schweizer Rundschau* as a pamphlet (Zurich, 1929), which was reprinted by Rascher Verlag in 1932, 1948, and 1959 (cf. n. 2, infra). Trans. by C. F. and H. G. Baynes in *Contributions to Analytical Psychology* (London and New York, 1928), pp. 164–88, which version has been consulted here. The motto is from the trans. of Nietzsche by Common.—EDITORS.]

believes her the most desirable thing in the world. Thus it is with the greatest misgivings that I set out to treat of this theme.

237   One thing, however, is beyond doubt: that woman today is in the same process of transition as man. Whether this transition is a historical turning-point or not remains to be seen. Sometimes, when we look back at history, it seems as though the present time had analogies with certain periods in the past, when great empires and civilizations had passed their zenith and were hastening irresistibly towards decay. But these analogies are deceptive, for there are always renaissances. What *does* move more clearly into the foreground is Europe's position midway between the Asiatic East and the Anglo-Saxon—or shall we say American?—West. Europe now stands between two colossi, both uncouth in their form but implacably opposed to one another in their nature. They are profoundly different not only racially but in their ideals. In the West there is the maximum political freedom with the minimum personal freedom; in the East it is just the opposite. We see in the West a tremendous development of Europe's technological and scientific tendencies, and in the Far East an awakening of all those spiritual forces which, in Europe, these tendencies hold in check. The power of the West is material, that of the East ideal.[2] The struggle between these opposites, which in the world of the European man takes place in the realm of the scientifically applied intellect and finds expression on the battlefield and in the state of his bank balance, is, in woman, a psychic conflict.

238   What makes it so uncommonly difficult to discuss the problem of the modern European woman is that we are necessarily writing about a minority. There is no "modern European woman" properly speaking. Or is the peasant's wife of today different from her forbears of a hundred years ago? There is, in fact, a large body of the population that only to a very limited extent lives in the present and participates in present-day problems. We speak of a "woman's problem," but how many women have problems? In proportion to the sum-total of European women only a dwindling minority really live in the Europe of

[2] In the thirty years since this essay was written the significance of the "East" has changed and has largely assumed the form of the "Russian Empire." This already reaches as far as central Germany, but it has lost nothing of its Asiatic character. [Author's footnote in 1959 pamphlet edition.—EDITORS.]

today; and these are city dwellers and belong—to put it cautiously—to the more complicated of their kind. This must always be so, for it is only the few who clearly express the spirit of the present in any age. In the fourth and fifth centuries of our era there were only a very few Christians who in any way understood the spirit of Christianity, the rest were still practically pagan. The cultural process that is characteristic of an epoch operates most intensely in cities, for it needs large agglomerations of men to make civilization possible, and from these agglomerations culture gradually spreads to the smaller, backward groups. Thus we find the present only in the large centres, and there alone do we encounter the "European woman," the woman who expresses the social and spiritual aspect of contemporary Europe. The further we go from the influence of the great centres, the more we find ourselves receding into history. In the remote Alpine valleys we can meet people who have never seen a railway, and in Spain, which is also a part of Europe, we plunge to a dark medieval age lacking even an alphabet. The people of those regions, or of the corresponding social strata, do not live in our Europe but in the Europe of 1400, and their problems are those of the bygone age in which they dwell. I have analysed such people, and have found myself carried back into an ambience that was not wanting in historical romance.

239   The "present" is a thin surface stratum that is laid down in the great centres of civilization. If it is very thin, as in Tsarist Russia, it has no meaning, as events have shown. But once it has attained a certain strength, we can speak of civilization and progress, and then problems arise that are characteristic of an epoch. In this sense Europe has a present, and there are women who live in it and suffer its problems. About these, and these only, are we entitled to speak. Those who are satisfied with a medieval life have no need of the present and its experiments. But the man of the present cannot—no matter what the reason—turn back again to the past without suffering an essential loss. Often this turning back is altogether impossible, even if he were prepared to make the sacrifice. The man of the present must work for the future and leave others to conserve the past. He is therefore not only a builder but also a destroyer. He and his world have both become questionable and ambiguous. The

ways that the past shows him and the answers it gives to his questions are insufficient for the needs of the present. All the old, comfortable ways are blocked, new paths have been opened up, and new dangers have arisen of which the past knew nothing. It is proverbial that one never learns anything from history, and in regard to present-day problems it usually teaches us nothing. The new path has to be made through untrodden regions, without presuppositions and often, unfortunately, without piety. The only thing that cannot be improved upon is morality, for every alteration of traditional morality is by definition an immorality. This *bon mot* has an edge to it, against which many an innovator has barked his shins.

240   All the problems of the present form a tangled knot, and it is hardly possible to single out one particular problem and treat it independently of the others. Thus there is no problem of "woman in Europe" without man and his world. If she is married, she usually has to depend economically on her husband; if she is unmarried and earning a living, she is working in some profession designed by a man. Unless she is prepared to sacrifice her whole erotic life, she again stands in some essential relationship to man. In numerous ways woman is indissolubly bound up with man's world and is therefore just as exposed as he is to all the shocks of his world. The war, for instance, has affected woman just as profoundly as it has man, and she has to adapt to its consequences as he must. What the upheavals of the last twenty or thirty years mean for man's world is apparent to everyone; we can read about it every day in the newspapers. But what it means for woman is not so evident. Neither politically, nor economically, nor spiritually is she a factor of visible importance. If she were, she would loom more largely in man's field of vision and would have to be considered a rival. Sometimes she is seen in this role, but only as a man, so to speak, who is accidentally a woman. But since as a rule her place is on man's intimate side, the side of him that merely feels and has no eyes and does not want to see, woman appears as an impenetrable mask behind which everything possible and impossible can be conjectured—and actually seen!—without his getting anywhere near the mark. The elementary fact that a person always thinks another's psychology is identical with his own effectively prevents a correct understanding of feminine psychology. This is

abetted by woman's own unconsciousness and passivity, useful
though these may be from the biological point of view: she
allows herself to be convinced by the man's projected feelings.
Of course this is a general human characteristic, but in woman
it is given a particularly dangerous twist, because in this respect
she is not naïve and it is only too often her *intention* to let herself be convinced by them. It fits in with her nature to keep her
ego and her will in the background, so as not to hinder the man
in any way, and to invite him to realize his intentions with
regard to her person. This is a sexual pattern, but it has far-
reaching ramifications in the feminine psyche. By maintaining
a passive attitude with an ulterior purpose, she helps the man
to realize his ends and in that way holds him. At the same time
she is caught in her own toils, for whoever digs a pit for others
falls into it himself.

241 I admit that this is a rather unkind description of a process
which might well be sung in more lyrical strains. But all natural
things have two sides, and when something has to be made conscious we must see the shadow side as well as the light.

242 When we observe the way in which women, since the second
half of the nineteenth century, have begun to take up masculine
professions, to become active in politics, to sit on committees,
etc., we can see that woman is in the process of breaking with
the purely feminine sexual pattern of unconsciousness and passivity, and has made a concession to masculine psychology by
establishing herself as a visible member of society. She no longer
hides behind the mask of Mrs. So-and-so, with the obliging intention of having all her wishes fulfilled by the man, or to
make him pay for it if things do not go as she wishes.

243 This step towards social independence is a necessary response
to economic and other factors, but in itself it is only a symptom
and not the thing about which we are most concerned. Certainly the courage and capacity for self-sacrifice of such women
is admirable, and only the blind could fail to see the good that
has come out of all these efforts. But no one can get round the
fact that by taking up a masculine profession, studying and
working like a man, woman is doing something not wholly in
accord with, if not directly injurious to, her feminine nature.
She is doing something that would scarcely be possible for a
man to do, unless he were a Chinese. Could he, for instance, be

a nursemaid or run a kindergarten? When I speak of injury, I do not mean merely physiological injury but above all psychic injury. It is a woman's outstanding characteristic that she can do anything for the love of a man. But those women who can achieve something important for the love of a *thing* are most exceptional, because this does not really agree with their nature. Love for a thing is a man's prerogative. But since masculine and feminine elements are united in our human nature, a man can live in the feminine part of himself, and a woman in her masculine part. None the less the feminine element in man is only something in the background, as is the masculine element in woman. If one lives out the opposite sex in oneself one is living in one's own background, and one's real individuality suffers. A man should live as a man and a woman as a woman. The contrasexual element in either sex is always dangerously close to the unconscious. It is even typical that the effects of the unconscious upon the conscious mind have a contrasexual character. For instance the soul (anima, psyche) has a feminine character which compensates the masculine consciousness. (Mystical instruction among primitives is exclusively a masculine concern, corresponding to the function of the Catholic priest.)

244 The immediate presence of the unconscious exerts a magnetic influence on the conscious processes. This explains the fear or even horror we have of the unconscious. It is a purposeful defence-reaction of the conscious mind. The contrasexual element has a mysterious charm tinged with fear, perhaps even with disgust. For this reason its charm is particularly attractive and fascinating, even when it comes to us not directly from outside, in the guise of a woman, but from within, as a psychic influence—for instance in the form of a temptation to abandon oneself to a mood or an affect. This example is not characteristic of women, for a woman's moods and emotions do not come to her directly from the unconscious but are peculiar to her feminine nature. They are therefore never naïve, but are mixed with an unacknowledged purpose. What comes to a woman from the unconscious is a sort of *opinion,* which spoils her mood only secondarily. These opinions lay claim to being absolute truths, and they prove to be the more fixed and incorrigible the less they are subjected to conscious criticism. Like the moods and feelings of a man, they are somewhat hazy and often

totally unconscious, and are seldom recognized for what they are. They are in fact collective, having the character of the opposite sex, as though a man—the father, for example—had thought of them.

245   Thus it can happen—indeed it is almost the rule—that the mind of a woman who takes up a masculine profession is influenced by her unconscious masculinity in a way not noticeable to herself but quite obvious to everybody in her environment. She develops a kind of rigid intellectuality based on so-called principles, and backs them up with a whole host of arguments which always just miss the mark in the most irritating way, and always inject a little something into the problem that is not really there. Unconscious assumptions or opinions are the worst enemy of woman; they can even grow into a positively demonic passion that exasperates and disgusts men, and does the woman herself the greatest injury by gradually smothering the charm and meaning of her femininity and driving it into the background. Such a development naturally ends in profound psychological disunion, in short, in a neurosis.

246   Naturally, things need not go to this length, but long before this point is reached the mental masculinization of the woman has unwelcome results. She may perhaps be a good comrade to a man without having any access to his feelings. The reason is that her animus (that is, her masculine rationalism, assuredly not true reasonableness!) has stopped up the approaches to her own feeling. She may even become frigid, as a defence against the masculine type of sexuality that corresponds to her masculine type of mind. Or, if the defence-reaction is not successful, she develops, instead of the receptive sexuality of woman, an aggressive, urgent form of sexuality that is more characteristic of a man. This reaction is likewise a purposeful phenomenon, intended to throw a bridge across by main force to the slowly vanishing man. A third possibility, especially favoured in Anglo-Saxon countries, is optional homosexuality in the masculine role.

247   It may therefore be said that, whenever the attraction of the animus becomes noticeable, there is a quite special need for the woman to have an intimate relationship with the other sex. Many women in this situation are fully aware of this necessity and proceed—*faute de mieux*—to stir up another of those

present-day problems that is no less painful, namely, the marriage problem.

248   Traditionally, man is regarded as the marriage breaker. This legend comes from times long past, when men still had leisure to pursue all sorts of pastimes. But today life makes so many demands on men that the noble hidalgo, Don Juan, is to be seen nowhere save in the theatre. More than ever man loves his comfort, for ours is an age of neurasthenia, impotence, and easy chairs. There is no energy left for window-climbing and duels. If anything is to happen in the way of adultery it must not be too difficult. In no respect must it cost too much, hence the adventure can only be of a transitory kind. The man of today is thoroughly scared of jeopardizing marriage as an institution. He is a firm believer in doing things on the quiet, and therefore supports prostitution. I would wager that in the Middle Ages, with its notorious bagnios and unrestricted prostitution, adultery was relatively more frequent than it is today. In this respect marriage should be safer now than it ever was. But in reality it is beginning to be discussed. It is a bad sign when doctors begin writing books of advice on how to achieve the "perfect marriage." Healthy people need no doctors. Marriage today has indeed become rather precarious. In America about a quarter of the marriages end in divorce. And the remarkable thing is that this time the scapegoat is not the man but the woman. She is the one who doubts and feels uncertain. It is not surprising that this is so, for in post-war Europe there is such an alarming surplus of unmarried women that it would be inconceivable if there were no reaction from that quarter. Such a piling up of misery has inescapable consequences. It is no longer a question of a few dozen voluntary or involuntary old maids here and there, but of millions. Our legislation and our social morality give no answer to this question. Or can the Church provide a satisfactory answer? Should we build gigantic nunneries to accommodate all these women? Or should tolerated prostitution be increased? Obviously this is impossible, since we are dealing neither with saints nor sinners but with ordinary women who cannot register their spiritual requirements with the police. They are decent women who want to marry, and if this is not possible, well—the next best thing. When it comes to the question of love, laws and institutions and ideals mean less to

woman than ever before. If things cannot go straight they will have to go crooked.

249   At the beginning of our era, three-fifths of the population of Italy consisted of slaves—human chattels without rights. Every Roman was surrounded by slaves. The slave and his psychology flooded ancient Italy, and every Roman became inwardly a slave. Living constantly in the atmosphere of slaves, he became infected with their psychology. No one can shield himself from this unconscious influence. Even today the European, however highly developed, cannot live with impunity among the Negroes in Africa; their psychology gets into him unnoticed and unconsciously he becomes a Negro. There is no fighting against it. In Africa there is a well-known technical expression for this: "going black." It is no mere snobbery that the English should consider anyone born in the colonies, even though the best blood may run in his veins, "slightly inferior." There are facts to support this view.

250   A direct result of slave influence was the strange melancholy and longing for deliverance that pervaded imperial Rome and found striking expression in Virgil's Fourth Eclogue. The explosive spread of Christianity, a religion which might be said to have risen from the sewers of Rome—Nietzsche called it a "slave insurrection in morals"—was a sudden reaction that set the soul of the lowest slave on a par with that of the divine Caesar. Similar though perhaps less momentous processes of psychological compensation have repeatedly occurred in the history of the world. Whenever some social or psychological monstrosity is created, a compensation comes along in defiance of all legislation and all expectation.

251   Something similar is happening to women in present-day Europe. Too much that is inadmissible, that has not been lived, is accumulating in the unconscious, and this is bound to have an effect. Secretaries, typists, shop-girls, all are agents of this process, and through a million subterranean channels creeps the influence that is undermining marriage. For the desire of all these women is not to have sexual adventures—only the stupid could believe that—but to get married. The possessors of that bliss must be ousted, not as a rule by naked force, but by that silent, obstinate desire which, as we know, has magical effects, like the fixed stare of a snake. This was ever the way of women.

252   What is the attitude of the married woman to all this? She clings to the old idea that man is the scapegoat, that he switches from one love-affair to another as he pleases, and so on. On the strength of these outworn conceptions she can wrap herself still more deeply in her jealousies. But all this is only on the surface. Neither the pride of the Roman patrician nor the thick walls of the imperial palace availed to keep out the slave infection. In the same way, no woman can escape the secret, compelling atmosphere with which her own sister, perhaps, is enveloping her, the stifling atmosphere of a life that has never been lived. Unlived life is a destructive, irresistible force that works softly but inexorably. The result is that the married woman begins to have doubts about marriage. The unmarried believe in it because they want it. Equally, the man believes in marriage because of his love of comfort and a sentimental belief in institutions, which for him always tend to become objects of feeling.

253   Since women have to be down to earth in matters of feeling, a certain fact should not escape our notice. This is the possibility of contraceptive measures. Children are one of the main reasons for maintaining a responsible attitude towards marriage. If this reason disappears, then the things that are "not done" happen easily enough. This applies primarily to unmarried women, who thus have an opportunity to contract an "approximate" marriage. But it is a consideration that counts also with all those married women who, as I have shown in my essay "Marriage as a Psychological Relationship," [3] are the "containers." By this I mean women whose demands as individuals are not satisfied, or not wholly satisfied, by their husbands. Finally, contraception is a fact of enormous importance to women in general, because it does away with the constant fear of pregnancy and the care of an ever-increasing number of children. This deliverance from bondage to nature brings a release of psychic energies that inevitably seek an outlet. Whenever a sum of energy finds no congenial goal it causes a disturbance of the psychic equilibrium. Lacking a conscious goal, it reinforces the unconscious and gives rise to uncertainty and doubt.

254   Another factor of great importance is the more or less open

[3] In *The Development of Personality, Coll. Works*, Vol. 17.

discussion of the sexual problem. This territory, once so obscure, has now become a focus of scientific and other interests. Things can be heard and said in society that formerly would have been quite impossible. Large numbers of people have learned to think more freely and honestly, and have come to realize how important these matters are. The discussion of the sexual problem is, however, only a somewhat crude prelude to a far deeper question, and that is the question of the psychological relationship between the sexes. In comparison with this the other pales into insignificance, and with it we enter the real domain of woman.

255   Woman's psychology is founded on the principle of Eros, the great binder and loosener, whereas from ancient times the ruling principle ascribed to man is Logos. The concept of Eros could be expressed in modern terms as psychic relatedness, and that of Logos as objective interest. In the eyes of the ordinary man, love in its true sense coincides with the institution of marriage, and outside marriage there is only adultery or "platonic" friendship. For woman, marriage is not an institution at all but a human love-relationship—at least that is what she would like to believe. (Since her Eros is not naïve but is mixed with other, unavowed motives—marriage as a ladder to social position, etc.—the principle cannot be applied in any absolute sense.) Marriage means to her an exclusive relationship. She can endure its exclusiveness all the more easily, without dying of ennui, inasmuch as she has children or near relatives with whom she has a no less intimate relationship than with her husband. The fact that she has no sexual relationship with these others means nothing, for the sexual relationship is of far less importance to her than the psychic relationship. It is enough that she and her husband both believe their relationship to be unique and exclusive. If he happens to be the "container" he feels suffocated by this exclusiveness, especially if he fails to notice that the exclusiveness of his wife is nothing but a pious fraud. In reality she is distributed among the children and among as many members of the family as possible, thus maintaining any number of intimate relationships. If her husband had anything like as many relationships with other people she would be mad with jealousy. Most men, though, are erotically blinded—they commit the unpardonable mistake of confusing

Eros with sex. A man thinks he possesses a woman if he has her sexually. He never possesses her less, for to a woman the Eros-relationship is the real and decisive one. For her, marriage is a relationship with sex thrown in as an accompaniment. Since sex is a formidable thing on account of its consequences, it is useful to have it in a safe place. But when it is less of a danger it also becomes less relevant, and then the question of relationship moves into the foreground.

256   It is just here that the woman runs into great difficulties with her husband, for the question of relationship borders on a region that for him is dark and painful. He can face this question only when the woman carries the burden of suffering, that is, when he is the "contained"—in other words, when she can imagine herself having a relationship with another man, and as a consequence suffering disunion within herself. Then it is she who has the painful problem, and he is not obliged to see his own, which is a great relief to him. In this situation he is not unlike a thief who, quite undeservedly, finds himself in the enviable position of having been forestalled by another thief who has been caught by the police. Suddenly he becomes an honourable, impartial onlooker. In any other situation a man always finds the discussion of personal relations painful and boring, just as his wife would find it boring if he examined her on the *Critique of Pure Reason*. For him, Eros is a shadow-land which entangles him in his feminine unconscious, in something "psychic," while for woman Logos is a deadly boring kind of sophistry if she is not actually repelled and frightened by it.

257   Just as woman began, towards the end of the nineteenth century, to make a concession to masculinity by taking her place as an independent factor in the social world, so man has made, somewhat hesitantly, a concession to femininity by creating a new psychology of complex phenomena, inaugurated by the sexual psychology of Freud. What this psychology owes to the direct influence of women—psychiatrists' consulting-rooms are packed with women—is a theme that would fill a large volume. I am speaking here not only of analytical psychology but of the beginnings of psychopathology in general. By far the greatest number of "classic" cases, beginning with the "Seeress of Prevorst," were women, who, perhaps unconsciously, took enor-

mous trouble to put their own psychology on view in the most dramatic fashion, and thus demonstrated to the world the whole question of psychic relationship. Women like Frau Hauffe and Hélène Smith [4] and Miss Beauchamp have assured for themselves a kind of immortality, rather like those worthy folk whose miraculous cures brought fame and prosperity to the wonder-working spot.

258   An astonishingly high percentage of this material comes from women. This is not as remarkable as it might seem, for women are far more "psychological" than men. A man is usually satisfied with "logic" alone. Everything "psychic," "unconscious" etc., is repugnant to him; he considers it vague, nebulous, and morbid. He is interested in things, in facts, and not in the feelings and fantasies that cluster round them or have nothing to do with them. To a woman it is generally more important to know how a man feels about a thing than to know the thing itself. All those things which are merely futile impedimenta to a man are important to her. So it is naturally woman who is the most direct exponent of psychology and gives it its richest content. Very many things can be perceived in her with the utmost distinctness which in a man are mere shadowy processes in the background, whose very existence he is unwilling to admit. But, unlike the objective discussion and verification of facts, a human relationship leads into the world of the psyche, into that intermediate realm between sense and spirit, which contains something of both and yet forfeits nothing of its own unique character.

259   Into this territory a man must venture if he wishes to meet woman half way. Circumstances have forced her to acquire a number of masculine traits, so that she shall not remain caught in an antiquated, purely instinctual femininity, lost and alone in the world of men. So, too, man will be forced to develop his feminine side, to open his eyes to the psyche and to Eros. It is a task he cannot avoid, unless he prefers to go trailing after woman in a hopelessly boyish fashion, worshipping from afar but always in danger of being stowed away in her pocket.

260   For those in love with masculinity or femininity *per se* the traditional medieval marriage is enough—and a thoroughly

4 [See *Psychiatric Studies, Coll. Works*, Vol. 1, index, s. vv.—EDITORS.]

praiseworthy, well-tried, useful institution it is. But the man of today finds it extremely difficult to return to it, and for many the way back is simply impossible, because this sort of marriage can exist only by shutting out all contemporary problems. Doubtless there were many Romans who could shut their eyes to the slave problem and to Christianity, and spend their days in a more or less pleasant unconsciousness. They could do this because they had no relation to the present, only to the past. All those for whom marriage contains no problem are not living in the present, and who shall say they are not blessed! Modern man finds marriage only too problematical. I recently heard a German scholar exclaim before an audience of several hundred people: "Our marriages are sham marriages!" I admired his courage and sincerity. Usually we express ourselves less directly, cautiously offering good advice as to what might be done—in order not to tarnish the ideal. But for the modern woman—let men take note of this—the medieval marriage is an ideal no longer. True, she keeps her doubts to herself, and hides her rebelliousness; one woman because she is married and finds it highly inconvenient if the door of the safe is not hermetically sealed, another because she is unmarried and too virtuous to look her own tendencies squarely in the face. Nevertheless, their newly-won masculinity makes it impossible for either of them to believe in marriage in its traditional form ("He shall be thy master"). Masculinity means knowing what one wants and doing what is necessary to achieve it. Once this lesson has been learned it is so obvious that it can never again be forgotten without tremendous psychic loss. The independence and critical judgment she acquires through this knowledge are positive values and are felt as such by the woman. She can never part with them again. The same is true of the man who, with great efforts, wins that needful feminine insight into his own psyche, often at the cost of much suffering. He will never let it go again, because he is thoroughly aware of the importance of what he has won.

261   At first glance it might be thought that such a man and woman would be especially likely to make the "perfect marriage." In reality this is not so; on the contrary, a conflict begins immediately. What the woman, in her new-found self-assurance, wants to do is not at all pleasing to the man, while the feelings

he has discovered in himself are far from agreeable to the woman. What both have discovered in themselves is not a virtue or anything of intrinsic value; it is something comparatively inferior, and it might justly be condemned if it were understood as the outcome of a personal choice or mood. And that, indeed, is what usually happens. The masculinity of the woman and the femininity of the man *are* inferior, and it is regrettable that the full value of their personalities should be contaminated by something that is less valuable. On the other hand, the shadow belongs to the wholeness of the personality: the strong man must somewhere be weak, somewhere the clever man must be stupid, otherwise he is too good to be true and falls back on pose and bluff. Is it not an old truth that woman loves the weaknesses of the strong man more than his strength, and the stupidity of the clever man more than his cleverness? Her love wants the whole man—not mere masculinity as such but also its negation. The love of woman is not sentiment, as is a man's, but a will that is at times terrifyingly unsentimental and can even force her to self-sacrifice. A man who is loved in this way cannot escape his inferior side, for he can only respond to the reality of her love with his own reality. And this reality is no fair semblance, but a faithful reflection of that eternal human nature which links together all humanity, a reflection of the heights and depths of human life which are common to us all. In this reality we are no longer differentiated persons (*persona* means a mask), but are conscious of our common human bonds. Here I strip off the distinctiveness of my own personality, social or otherwise, and reach down to the problems of the present day, problems which do not arise out of myself—or so at least I like to imagine. Here I can no longer deny them; I feel and know myself to be one of many, and what moves the many moves me. In our strength we are independent and isolated, and are masters of our own fate; in our weakness we are dependent and bound, and become unwilling instruments of fate, for here it is not the individual will that counts but the will of the species.

262   What the two sexes have won through mutual assimilation is an inferiority when viewed from the two-dimensional, personal world of appearances, and an immoral pretension if regarded as a personal claim. But in its truest meaning for life

and society it is an overcoming of personal isolation and selfish reserve in order to take an active part in the solution of present-day problems. If, therefore, the woman of today consciously or unconsciously loosens the cohesion of the marriage bond by her spiritual or economic independence, this is not the expression of her personal will, but of the will of the species, which makes her, the individual woman, its tool.

263   The institution of marriage is such a valuable thing, both socially and morally—religious people even regard it as a sacrament—that it is quite understandable that any weakening of it should be felt as undesirable, indeed scandalous. Human imperfection is always a discord in the harmony of our ideals. Unfortunately, no one lives in the world as we desire it, but in the world of actuality where good and evil clash and destroy one another, where no creating or building can be done without dirtying one's hands. Whenever things get really bad, there is always some one to assure us amid great applause that nothing has happened and everything is in order. I repeat, anyone who lives and thinks like this is not living in the present. If we examine any marriage with a really critical eye, we shall find—unless acute pressure of circumstances has completely extinguished all signs of "psychological" trouble—symptoms of its weakening and clandestine disruption, "marriage problems" ranging from unbearable moods to neurosis and adultery. Unfortunately, those who can still bear to remain unconscious cannot be imitated; their example is not infectious enough to induce more conscious people to descend again to the level of mere unconsciousness.

264   As to all those—and they are many—who are not obliged to live in the present, it is extremely important that they should believe in the ideal of marriage and hold fast to it. Nothing is gained if a valuable ideal is merely destroyed and not replaced by something better. Therefore even the women hesitate, whether they are married or not, to go over openly to the side of rebellion. But at least they do not follow the lead of that well-known authoress who, after trying out all sorts of experiments, ended up in the secure haven of matrimony, whereupon marriage became the best solution, and all those who did not achieve it could brood on their mistakes and end their days in pious renunciation. For the modern woman marriage is not as

easy as that. Her husband would have something to say on this score.

265 So long as there are legalistic clauses that lay down exactly what adultery is, women will have to remain with their doubts. But do our legislators really know what "adultery" is? Is their definition of it the final embodiment of the truth? From the psychological standpoint, the only one that counts for a woman, it is a wretched piece of bungling, like everything else contrived by men for the purpose of codifying love. For a woman, love has nothing to do with "marital misconduct," "extramarital intercourse," "deception of the husband," or any of the less savoury formulas invented by the erotically blind masculine intellect and echoed by the self-opinionated demon in woman. Nobody but the absolute believer in the inviolability of traditional marriage could perpetrate such breaches of good taste, just as only the believer in God can really blaspheme. Whoever doubts marriage in the first place cannot infringe against it; for him the legal definition is invalid because, like St. Paul, he feels himself beyond the law, on the higher plane of love. But because the believers in the law so frequently trespass against their own laws, whether from stupidity, temptation, or mere viciousness, the modern woman begins to wonder whether she too may not belong to the same category. From the traditional standpoint she does, and she has to realize this in order to smash the idol of her own respectability. To be "respectable" means, as the word tells us, to allow oneself to be seen; a respectable person is one who comes up to public expectations, who wears an ideal mask—in short, is a fraud. "Good form" is not a fraud, but when respectability represses the psyche, the God-given essence of man, then one becomes what Christ called a whited sepulchre.

266 The modern woman has become conscious of the undeniable fact that only in the state of love can she attain the highest and best of which she is capable, and this knowledge drives her to the other realization that love is beyond the law. Her respectability revolts against this, and one is inclined to identify this reaction with public opinion. That would be the lesser evil; what is worse is that public opinion is in her blood. It comes to her like a voice from within, a sort of conscience, and this is the power that holds her in check. She is unaware that love, her most personal, most prized possession, could bring her into

conflict with history. Such a thing would seem to her most unexpected and absurd. But who, if it comes to that, has fully realized
that history is not contained in thick books but lives in our very
blood?

267   So long as a woman lives the life of the past she can never
come into conflict with history. But no sooner does she begin to
deviate, however slightly, from a cultural trend that has dominated the past than she encounters the full weight of historical
inertia, and this unexpected shock may injure her, perhaps
fatally. Her hesitation and her doubt are understandable
enough, for, if she submits to the law of love, she finds that she
is not only in a highly disagreeable and dubious situation,
where every kind of lewdness and depravity abounds, but actually caught between two universal forces—historical inertia and
the divine urge to create.

268   Who, then, will blame her for hesitating? Do not most men
prefer to rest on their laurels rather than get into a hopeless
conflict as to whether they shall or shall not make history? In
the end it boils down to this: is one prepared to break with
tradition, to be "unhistorical" in order to make history, or not?
No one can make history who is not willing to risk everything
for it, to carry the experiment with his own life through to the
bitter end, and to declare that his life is not a continuation of
the past, but a new beginning. Mere continuation can be left to
the animals, but inauguration is the prerogative of man, the one
thing he can boast of that lifts him above the beasts.

269   There is no doubt that the woman of today is deeply concerned with this problem. She gives expression to one of the
cultural tendencies of our time: the urge to live a completer
life, a longing for meaning and fulfilment, a growing disgust
with senseless one-sidedness, with unconscious instinctuality
and blind contingency. The psyche of the modern European
has not forgotten the lesson of the last war, however much it has
been banished from his consciousness. Women are increasingly
aware that love alone can give them full stature, just as men are
beginning to divine that only the spirit can give life its highest
meaning. Both seek a psychic relationship, because love needs
the spirit, and the spirit love, for its completion.

270   Woman nowadays feels that there is no real security in marriage, for what does her husband's faithfulness mean when she

knows that his feelings and thoughts are running after others and that he is merely too calculating or too cowardly to follow them? What does her own faithfulness mean when she knows that she is simply using it to exploit her legal right of possession, and warping her own soul? She has intimations of a higher fidelity to the spirit and to a love beyond human weakness and imperfection. Perhaps she will yet discover that what seems like weakness and imperfection, a painful disturbance, or an alarming deviation, must be interpreted in accordance with its dual nature. These are steps that lead down to the lowest human level and finally end in the morass of unconsciousness if the individual lets go of his personal distinctiveness. But if he can hold on to it, he will experience for the first time the meaning of selfhood, provided that he can simultaneously descend below himself into the undifferentiated mass of humanity. What else can free him from the inner isolation of his personal differentiation? And how else can he establish a psychic bridge to the rest of mankind? The man who stands on high and distributes his goods to the poor is separated from mankind by the height of his own virtue, and the more he forgets himself and sacrifices himself for others the more he is inwardly estranged from them.

271   The word "human" sounds very beautiful, but properly understood it does not mean anything particularly beautiful, or virtuous, or intelligent, but just a low average. This is the step which Zarathustra could not take, the step to the "Ugliest Man," who is real man. Our resistance to taking this step, and our fear of it, show how great is the attraction and seductive power of our own depths. To cut oneself off from them is no solution; it is a mere sham, an essential misunderstanding of their meaning and value. For where is a height without depth, and how can there be light that throws no shadow? There is no good that is not opposed by evil. "No man can be redeemed from a sin he has not committed," says Carpocrates; a deep saying for all who wish to understand, and a golden opportunity for all those who prefer to draw false conclusions. What is down below is not just an excuse for more pleasure, but something we fear because it demands to play its part in the life of the more conscious and more complete man.

272   What I am saying here is not for the young—it is precisely
what they ought not to know—but for the more mature man
whose consciousness has been widened by experience of life. No
man can begin with the present; he must slowly grow into it,
for there would be no present but for the past. A young person
has not yet acquired a past, therefore he has no present either.
He does not create culture, he merely exists. It is the privilege
and the task of maturer people, who have passed the meridian
of life, to create culture.

273   The European psyche has been torn to shreds by the hellish
barbarism of the war. While man turns his hand to repairing
the outer damage, woman—unconsciously as ever—sets about
healing the inner wounds, and for this she needs, as her most
important instrument, a psychic relationship. But nothing
hampers this more than the exclusiveness of the medieval marriage, for it makes relationship altogether superfluous. Relationship is possible only if there is a psychic distance between
people, in the same way that morality presupposes freedom.
For this reason the unconscious tendency of woman aims at
loosening the marriage structure, but not at the destruction of
marriage and the family. That would be not only immoral but
a thoroughly pathological misuse of her powers.

274   It would take volumes of case-material to describe the innumerable ways in which this goal is achieved. It is the way of
woman, as of nature, to work indirectly, without naming her
goal. To anything unsatisfactory she reacts purposively, with
moods, outbursts of affects, opinions, and actions that all have
the same end in view, and their apparent senselessness, viru-
lence, and cold-blooded ruthlessness are infinitely distressing to
the man who is blind to Eros.

275   The indirect method of woman is dangerous, for it can hopelessly compromise her aim. That is why she longs for greater
consciousness, which would enable her to name her goal and
give it meaning, and thus escape the blind dynamism of nature.
In any other age it would have been the prevailing religion that
showed her where her ultimate goal lay; but today religion
leads back to the Middle Ages, back to that soul-destroying un-
relatedness from which came all the fearful barbarities of war.
Too much soul is reserved for God, too little for man. But God

himself cannot flourish if man's soul is starved. The feminine psyche responds to this hunger, for it is the function of Eros to unite what Logos has sundered. The woman of today is faced with a tremendous cultural task—perhaps it will be the dawn of a new era.

THE MEANING OF PSYCHOLOGY FOR
MODERN MAN [1]

276   I have always found it uncommonly difficult to make the meaning of psychology intelligible to a wider public. This difficulty dates back to the time when I was a doctor in a mental hospital. Like every psychiatrist, I made the astonishing discovery that it is not we who hold competent opinions on mental health and sickness, but the public, who always know much better than we do. They tell us that the patient does not really climb up the walls, that he knows where he is, that he recognizes his relatives, that he hasn't forgotten his name, that, consequently, he is not really ill but only a little depressed or a little excited, and that the psychiatrist's notion that the man is suffering from such and such an illness is entirely incorrect.

277   This very common experience introduces us to the field of psychology proper, where things are even worse. Everyone thinks that psychology is what he himself knows best—psychology is always *his* psychology, which he alone knows, and at the time his psychology is everybody else's psychology. Instinctively he supposes that his own psychic constitution is the general one, and that everyone is essentially like everyone else, that is to say like himself. Husbands suppose this of their wives, wives suppose it of their husbands, parents of their children, and children of their parents. It is as though everyone had the most direct access to what is going on inside him, was intimately acquainted with it and competent to pass an opinion on it; as though his own psyche were a kind of master-psyche which suited all and sundry, and entitled him to suppose that his own situation was the general rule. People are profoundly aston-

[1] [Originally a lecture delivered in Cologne and Essen, February 1933. Published as "Ueber Psychologie," *Neue Schweizer Rundschau* (Zurich), I (1933), no. 1, 21–28, and no. 2, 98–106. Revised and expanded as "Die Bedeutung der Psychologie für die Gegenwart," *Wirklichkeit der Seele* (Zurich, 1934), pp. 32–67.—EDITORS.]

ished, or even horrified, when this rule quite obviously does not fit—when they discover that another person really is different from themselves. Generally speaking, they do not feel these psychic differences as in any way curious, let alone attractive, but as disagreeable failings that are hard to bear, or as unendurable faults that have to be condemned. The painfully obvious difference seems like a contravention of the natural order, like a shocking mistake that must be remedied as speedily as possible, or a misdemeanour that calls for condign punishment.

278   As you know, there actually are widely accepted psychological theories which start from the assumption that the human psyche is the same everywhere and can therefore be explained in the same way regardless of circumstances. The appalling monotony presupposed by these theories, however, is contradicted by the fact that individual psychic differences do exist and are capable of almost infinite variation. In addition to this, one of the theories explains the world of psychic phenomena mainly in terms of the sexual instinct, and the other in terms of the power drive. The result of this inconsistency is that both theories cling all the more rigidly to their principles and show clear tendencies to set themselves up as the one and only source of salvation. Each denies the other, and one asks oneself in vain which of them is right. But although the adherents of both views try their utmost to ignore each other's existence, these tactics do nothing to resolve the contradiction. And yet the answer to the riddle is absurdly simple. It amounts to this: both of them are right, in so far as each theory describes a psychology which resembles that of its adherents. We can well say with Goethe that it "matches the spirit that it comprehends." [2]

279   Turning back to our theme, let us consider more closely the well-nigh ineradicable prejudice of simple-minded persons that everybody is exactly the same as them. Although it is true in general that psychic differences are admitted as a theoretical possibility, in practice one always forgets that the other person is different from oneself, that he thinks differently, feels differently, sees differently, and wants quite different things. Even scientific theories, as we have seen, start from the assumption that the shoe pinches everyone in the same place. Quite apart

[2] *Faust, Part One,* trans. by Wayne, p. 48.

from this entertaining domestic quarrel among psychologists, there are other egalitarian assumptions of a social and political nature which are much more serious, because they forget the existence of the individual psyche altogether.

280   Instead of vexing myself to no purpose over such narrow-minded and short-sighted views, I began to wonder why they should exist at all, and I tried to discover what the reasons might be. This inquiry led me to study the psychology of primitive peoples. I had long been struck by the fact that there is a certain naïveté and childlikeness about those who are most prejudiced in favour of psychic uniformity. In primitive society one does in fact find that this assumption extends not only to human beings, but to all the objects of nature, the animals, plants, rivers, mountains, and so on. They all have something of man's psychology in them, even trees and stones can speak. And just as there are certain human beings who obviously do not conform to the general rule and are honoured as magicians, witches, chiefs, and medicine-men, so among the animals there are doctor-coyotes, doctor-birds, werewolves, and the like, whose honorific title is conferred whenever an animal behaves in any way out of the ordinary and upsets the tacit assumption of uniformity. This prejudice is evidently a vestige—but a very potent one—of a primitive frame of mind which is based essentially on an insufficiently differentiated consciousness. Individual consciousness or ego-consciousness is a late product of man's development. Its primitive form is a mere group-consciousness, and among the primitive societies that still exist today this is often so poorly developed that many tribes do not even give themselves a name that would distinguish them from other tribes. For instance, in East Africa I came across a tribe who simply called themselves "the people who are there." This primitive group-consciousness goes on living in our own family-consciousness, and we often find that members of a family can give no account of themselves other than that they are called by such and such a name—which seems entirely satisfactory to the person concerned.

281   But a group-consciousness in which individuals are interchangeable is still not the lowest level of consciousness, for it already shows traces of differentiation. At the lowest and most primitive level we would find a sort of generalized or cosmic

consciousness, with complete unconsciousness of the subject. On this level there are only events, but no acting persons.

282   Our assumption that what pleases me must necessarily please everybody else is therefore an obvious relic from that primordial night of consciousness where there was no perceptible difference between I and You, and where everyone thought, felt, and acted in the same way. But if anything happened which showed that somebody was not of like mind, there was an immediate disturbance. Nothing arouses so much panic among primitives as something out of the ordinary; it is at once suspected of being dangerous and hostile. This primitive reaction survives in us too: how prompt we are to take offence when somebody does not share our convictions! We are insulted when somebody finds our idea of beauty detestable. We still persecute anyone who thinks differently from ourselves, we still try to force our opinions on others, to convert poor heathens in order to save them from the hell that indubitably lies in wait for them, and we are all abysmally afraid of standing alone with our beliefs.

283   The psychic equality of all men is an unspoken assumption deriving from the individual's original unconsciousness of himself. In that far-off world there was no individual consciousness, but only a collective psyche from which gradually an individual consciousness emerged on the higher levels of development. The indispensable condition for the existence of an individual consciousness is its difference from other consciousnesses. One could liken the process of conscious development to a rocket that rises up from the darkness and dissolves in a shower of multicoloured stars.

284   Psychology as an empirical science is of very recent origin. It is not yet fifty years old, and is therefore still in its swaddling-clothes. The premise of equality prevented it from being born earlier. From this we can see how young any kind of differentiated consciousness is. It has just crept out of its long sleep, slowly and clumsily taking cognizance of its own existence. It would be a delusion to imagine that we have attained anything like a high level of consciousness. Our present-day consciousness is a mere child that is just beginning to say "I."

285   It was one of the greatest experiences of my life to discover how enormously different people's psyches are. If the collective

equality of the psyche were not a primordial fact, the origin and matrix of all individual psyches, it would be a gigantic illusion. But despite our individual consciousness it unquestionably continues to exist as the *collective unconscious*—the sea upon which the ego rides like a ship. For this reason also, nothing of the primordial world of the psyche has ever been lost. Just as the sea stretches its broad tongues between the continents and laps them round like islands, so our original unconsciousness presses round our individual consciousness. In the catastrophe of mental disease the storm-tide of the sea surges over the island and swallows it back into the depths. In neurotic disturbances there is at least a bursting of dikes, and the fruitful lowlands are laid waste by flood. Neurotics are all shore-dwellers—they are the most exposed to the dangers of the sea. So-called normal people live inland, on higher, drier ground, near placid lakes and streams. No flood however high reaches them, and the circumambient sea is so far away that they even deny its existence. Indeed, a person can be so identified with his ego that he loses the common bond of humanity and cuts himself off from all others. As nobody wants to be entirely like everybody else, this is quite a common occurrence. For primitive egoism, however, the standing rule is that it is never "I" who must change, but always the other fellow.

286   Individual consciousness is surrounded by the treacherous sea of the unconscious. This consciousness of ours has the appearance of being stable and reliable, but in reality it is a fragile thing and rests on very insecure foundations. Often no more than a strong emotion is needed to upset the sensitive balance of consciousness. Our turns of speech are an indication of this. We say that a person was "beside himself" with rage, he "forgot himself completely," one "couldn't recognize him," "the devil had got into him," etc. Something makes you "jump out of your skin," "drives you mad," so that you "no longer know what you are doing." All these familiar phrases show how easily our ego-consciousness is disrupted by affects. These disturbances do not show themselves only in acute form; often they are chronic and can bring about a lasting change of consciousness. As a result of some psychic upheaval whole tracts of our being can plunge back into the unconscious and vanish from the surface for years and decades. Permanent changes of

character are not uncommon. We therefore say, quite correctly, that after some such experience a person was a "changed man." These things happen not only to people with a bad heredity or to neurotics, but to normal people as well. Disturbances caused by affects are known technically as *phenomena of dissociation,* and are indicative of a psychic split. In every psychic conflict we can discern a split of this kind, which may go so far as to threaten the shattered structure of consciousness with complete disintegration.

287   But even the inland dwellers, the inhabitants of the normal world who forgot the sea, do not live on firm ground. The soil is so friable that at any moment the sea can rush in through continental fissures and maroon them. Primitive man knows this danger not only from the life of his tribe but from his own psychology. The most important of these "perils of the soul," as they are technically called, are loss of soul and possession. Both are phenomena of dissociation. In the first case, he will say that a soul has wandered away from him, and in the second, that a strange soul has taken up its abode in him, generally in some unpleasant form. This way of putting it may sound odd, but it describes exactly the symptoms which today we call phenomena of dissociation or schizoid states. They are not by any means purely pathological symptoms, for they are found just as much in normal people. They may take the form of fluctuations in the general feeling of well-being, irrational changes of mood, unpredictable affects, a sudden distaste for everything, psychic inertia, and so on. Even the schizoid phenomena that correspond to primitive possession can be observed in normal people. They, too, are not immune to the demon of passion; they, too, are liable to possession by an infatuation, a vice, or a one-sided conviction; and these are all things that dig a deep grave between them and those they hold most dear, and create an aching split in their own psyche.

288   Primitive man feels the splitting of the psyche as something unseemly and morbid, just as we do. Only, we call it a conflict, nervousness, or a mental breakdown. Not for nothing did the Bible story place the unbroken harmony of plant, animal, man, and God, symbolized as Paradise, at the very beginning of all psychic development, and declare that the first dawning of consciousness—"Ye shall be as gods, knowing good and evil"—

was a fatal sin. To the naïve mind it must indeed seem a sin to shatter the divine unity of consciousness that ruled the primal night. It was the Luciferian revolt of the individual against the One. It was a hostile act of disharmony against harmony, a separation from the fusion of all with all. Therefore God cursed the serpent and said: "I will put enmity between thee and the woman, and between thy seed and her seed; it shall bruise thy head, and thou shalt bruise his heel."

289   And yet the attainment of consciousness was the most precious fruit of the tree of knowledge, the magical weapon which gave man victory over the earth, and which we hope will give him a still greater victory over himself.

290   The fact that individual consciousness means separation and opposition is something that man has experienced countless times in his long history. And just as for the individual a time of dissociation is a time for sickness, so it is in the life of nations. We can hardly deny that ours is a time of dissociation and sickness. The political and social conditions, the fragmentation of religion and philosophy, the contending schools of modern art and modern psychology all have one meaning in this respect. And does anyone who is endowed with the slightest sense of responsibility feel any satisfaction at this turn of events? If we are honest, we must admit that no one feels quite comfortable in the present-day world; indeed, it becomes increasingly uncomfortable. The word "crisis," so often heard, is a medical expression which always tells us that the sickness has reached a dangerous climax.

291   When man became conscious, the germ of the sickness of dissociation was planted in his soul, for consciousness is at once the highest good and the greatest evil. It is difficult to estimate the sickness of the age in which we live. But if we glance back at the clinical history of mankind, we shall find earlier bouts of sickness which are easier to survey. One of the worst attacks was the malaise that spread through the Roman world in the first centuries after Christ. The dissociation showed itself in an unexampled breakdown of the political and social conditions, in religious and philosophical dissension, and in a deplorable decline of the arts and sciences. If we reduced humanity as it then was to a single individual, we would see before us a highly differentiated personality who, after mastering his environment

with sublime self-assurance, split himself up in the pursuit of his separate occupations and interests, forgetting his own origins and traditions, and even losing all memory of his former self, so that he seemed to be now one thing and now another, and thus fell into a hopeless conflict with himself. In the end the conflict led to such a state of enfeeblement that the world he had conquered broke in like a devastating flood and completed the process of destruction.

292　　After long years spent in the investigation of the psyche, there gradually took shape in me, as it had in the minds of other investigators, the fundamental axiom that a psychic phenomenon should never be looked at from one side only, but from the other side as well. Experience has shown that everything has at least two sides, and sometimes several more. Disraeli's maxim that not too much importance should be attached to important things, and that unimportant things are not so unimportant as they seem, is another formulation of the same truth. A third version would be the hypothesis that every psychic phenomenon is compensated by its opposite, in agreement with the proverb, "Les extrêmes se touchent," or, "There is no misfortune so great that no good may come of it."

293　　Thus, the sickness of dissociation in our world is at the same time a process of recovery, or rather, the climax of a period of pregnancy which heralds the throes of birth. A time of dissociation such as prevailed during the Roman Empire is simultaneously an age of rebirth. Not without reason do we date our era from the age of Augustus, for that epoch saw the birth of the symbolical figure of Christ, who was invoked by the early Christians as the Fish, the Ruler of the aeon of Pisces which had just begun.[3] He became the ruling spirit of the next two thousand years. Like the teacher of wisdom in Babylonian legend, Oannes, he rose up from the sea, from the primeval darkness, and brought a world-period to an end. It is true that he said, "I am come not to bring peace but a sword." But that which brings division ultimately creates union. Therefore his teaching was one of all-uniting love.

294　　Our distance in time puts us in the favourable position of being able to see these historical events quite clearly. Had we

3 [Cf. *Aion,* passim.—EDITORS.]

lived in those days we would probably have been among the many who overlooked them. The Gospel, the joyful tidings, were known only to the humble few; on the surface everything was politics, economic questions, and sport. Religion and philosophy tried to assimilate the spiritual riches that poured into the Roman world from the newly conquered East. Few noticed the grain of mustard-seed that was destined to grow into a great tree.

295   In classical Chinese philosophy there are two contrary principles, the bright *yang* and the dark *yin*. Of these it is said that always when one principle reaches the height of its power, the counter-principle is stirring within it like a germ. This is another, particularly graphic formulation of the psychological law of compensation by an inner opposite. Whenever a civilization reaches its highest point, sooner or later a period of decay sets in. But the apparently meaningless and hopeless collapse into a disorder without aim or purpose, which fills the onlooker with disgust and despair, nevertheless contains within its darkness the germ of a new light.

296   But let us go back for a moment to our earlier attempt to construct a single individual from the period of classical decay. I tried to show you how he disintegrated psychologically, how in a disastrous fit of weakness he lost control of his environment, and finally succumbed to the forces of destruction. Let us suppose that this man came to me for a consultation. I would make the following diagnosis: "You are suffering from overstrain as a result of your numerous activities and boundless extraversion. In the profusion and complexity of your business, personal, and human obligations you have lost your head. You are a kind of Ivar Kreuger,[4] who is a typical representative of the modern European spirit. You must realize, my dear Sir, that you are rapidly going to the dogs."

297   This latter realization would be particularly important for him, because patients have in any case a pernicious tendency to go on muddling through in the same old way, even though it has long since proved ineffective, and to make their situation only worse. Waiting is useless. Therefore the question immediately arises: "What is to be done?"

4 [Swedish financier (1880–1932), known as "The Match King," whose complicated peculations led to his financial collapse and suicide.—EDITORS.]

298   Our patient is an intelligent man. He has tried all the patent medicines, both good and bad, every kind of diet, and all the bits of advice given him by all the clever people. We must therefore proceed with him as with Till Eulenspiegel, who always laughed when the way went uphill, and wept when it went down, in shocking defiance of sound commonsense. But hidden beneath his fool's garment was a wise man, who when going uphill was rejoicing in the coming descent.

299   We must direct our patient's attention to the place where the germ of unity is growing within him, the place of creative birth, which is the deepest cause of all the rifts and schisms on the surface. A civilization does not decay, it regenerates. In the early centuries of our era a man of discernment could have cried out with unshakable certainty amid the political intrigue and wild speculation of the Caesar-worshipping, circus-besotted Roman world: "The germ of the coming era has even now been born in the darkness, behind all this aimless confusion; the seed of the Tree that will overshadow the nations from Thule in the far West to Poland, from the mountains of the North to Sicily, and unite them in one belief, one culture, and one language."

300   That is the psychological law. My patient, in all probability, will not believe a word of it. At the very least he will want to have experienced these things for himself. And here our difficulties begin, for the compensation always makes its appearance just where one would least expect it, and where, objectively considered, it seems least plausible. Let us now suppose that our patient is not the pale abstraction of a long-dead civilization, but a flesh-and-blood man of our own day, who has the misfortune to be a typical representative of our modern European culture. We shall then find that our compensation theory means nothing to him. He suffers most of all from the disease of knowing everything better; there is nothing that he cannot classify and put in the correct pigeonhole. As to his psyche, it is essentially his *own* invention, his *own* will, and it obeys *his* reason exclusively; and if it should happen that it does not do so, if he should nevertheless have psychic symptoms, such as anxiety-states, obsessional ideas, and so on, then it is a clinically identifiable disease with a thoroughly plausible, scientific name. Of the psyche as an original experience which cannot be reduced to anything else he has no knowledge at all and does not know what I am talking about,

but he thinks he has understood it perfectly and even writes articles and books in which he bemoans the evils of "psychologism."

301   This kind of mentality, barricading itself behind a thick wall of books, newspapers, opinions, social institutions, and professional prejudices, cannot be argued with. Nothing can break through its defences, least of all that little germ of the new which would make him at one with the world and himself. It is so small and ridiculous that for modesty's sake it would rather give up the ghost at once. Where, then, must we lead our patient in order to give him at least a glimmer of an inkling of something different, something that would counterbalance the everyday world he knows only too well? We must guide him, by devious ways at first, to a dark, ridiculously insignificant, quite unimportant corner of his psyche, following a long-disused path to the longest-known illusion, which as all the world knows is nothing but . . . That corner of the psyche is *the dream,* which is nothing but a fleeting, grotesque phantom of the night, and the path is the understanding of dreams.

302   With Faustian indignation my patient will cry out:

> This witch's quackery disgusts my soul!
> Is this your promise then, that I be healed
> By crooked counsel in this crazy hole,
> In truth by some decrepit dame revealed?
> . . . .
> Cannot you brew an ichor of your own? [5]

303   To which I shall reply: "Haven't you tried one remedy after another? Haven't you seen for yourself that all your efforts have only led you round in a circle, back to the confusion of your present life? So where will you get that other point of view from, if it cannot be found anywhere in your world?"

304   Here Mephistopheles murmurs approvingly, "That's where the witch comes in," thus giving his own devilish twist to Nature's secret and perverting the truth that the dream is an inner vision, "mysterious still in open light of day." The dream is a little hidden door in the innermost and most secret recesses of the soul, opening into that cosmic night which was psyche long

---

[5] *Faust, Part One,* trans. by Wayne, pp. 110f.

144

before there was any ego-consciousness, and which will remain psyche no matter how far our ego-consciousness extends. For all ego-consciousness is isolated; because it separates and discriminates, it knows only particulars, and it sees only those that can be related to the ego. Its essence is limitation, even though it reach to the farthest nebulae among the stars. All consciousness separates; but in dreams we put on the likeness of that more universal, truer, more eternal man dwelling in the darkness of primordial night. There he is still the whole, and the whole is in him, indistinguishable from nature and bare of all egohood.

305   It is from these all-uniting depths that the dream arises, be it never so childish, grotesque, and immoral. So flowerlike is it in its candour and veracity that it makes us blush for the deceitfulness of our lives. No wonder that in all the ancient civilizations an impressive dream was accounted a message from the gods! It remained for the rationalism of our age to explain the dream as the remnants left over from the day, as the crumbs that fell into the twilit world from the richly laden table of our consciousness. These dark depths are then nothing but an empty sack, containing no more than what falls into it from above. Why do we always forget that there is nothing majestic or beautiful in the wide domain of human culture that did not grow originally from a lucky idea? What would become of mankind if nobody had lucky ideas any more? It would be far truer to say that our consciousness is that sack, which has nothing in it except what chances to fall into it. We never appreciate how dependent we are on lucky ideas—until we find to our distress that they will not come. A dream is nothing but a lucky idea that comes to us from the dark, all-unifying world of the psyche. What would be more natural, when we have lost ourselves amid the endless particulars and isolated details of the world's surface, than to knock at the door of dreams and inquire of them the bearings which would bring us closer to the basic facts of human existence?

306   Here we encounter the obstinate prejudice that dreams are so much froth, they are not real, they lie, they are mere wish-fulfilments. All this is but an excuse not to take dreams seriously, for that would be uncomfortable. Our intellectual hybris of consciousness loves isolation despite all its inconveniences, and for this reason people will do anything rather than admit

145

that dreams are real and speak the truth. There are some saints who had very rude dreams. Where would their saintliness be, the very thing that exalts them above the vulgar rabble, if the obscenity of a dream were a real truth? But it is just the most squalid dreams that emphasize our blood-kinship with the rest of mankind, and most effectively damp down the arrogance born of an atrophy of the instincts. Even if the whole world were to fall to pieces, the unity of the psyche would never be shattered. And the wider and more numerous the fissures on the surface, the more this unity is strengthened in the depths.

307   No one, of course, who has not experienced it himself will be convinced that there could be any independent psychic activity outside consciousness, and certainly not an activity that takes place not only in me but simultaneously in all men. But when we compare the psychology of modern art with the findings of psychological research, and this again with the products of mythology and philosophy, we shall discover irrefutable proofs of the existence of this collective, unconscious factor.

308   Our patient, however, is so accustomed to treat his psyche as something he has under his control that he will retort that he has never yet observed anything objective about his psychic processes. They are, on the contrary, the most subjective things one can possibly imagine. To this I rejoin: "Then you can make your anxiety-states and your obsessional ideas disappear at once. The bad moods you are riddled with will be no more. You have only to speak the magic word."

309   Naturally, in his modern naïveté, he has entirely failed to notice that he is as much possessed by his pathological states as any witch or witch-hunter in the darkest Middle Ages. It is merely a difference of name. In those days they spoke of the devil, today we call it a neurosis. But it comes to the same thing, to the same age-old experience: something objectively psychic and strange to us, not under our control, is fixedly opposed to the sovereignty of our will. We are in no better case than the Proktophantasmist in *Faust*, when he exclaimed:

> Preposterous! You still intend to stay?
> Vanish at once, you've been explained away!
> By rules this devil's crew is nothing daunted:
> For all our wisdom, Tegel still is haunted.[6]

6 Cf. Wayne trans., p. 178.

10   If our patient can submit to the logic of this argument, much will have been gained. The way to experience of the psyche is open. But soon one comes to another prejudice that blocks further progress. "Granted," he will say, "that I am experiencing a psychic force that thwarts my will, an objective-psychic factor, if you like to call it that. But it still remains something purely psychological, vague, unreliable, and of no importance in the practical affairs of life."

11   It is amazing how people get caught in words. They always imagine that the name postulates the thing—just as if we were doing the devil a serious wrong when we call him a neurosis! This touchingly childlike trait is another remnant left over from the year 1, when mankind still operated with magical words. But what is behind the devil or the neurosis does not bother about the name we give it. Naturally we do not know what the psyche is. We speak of the "unconscious" merely because we are not conscious of what it is in reality. We know this as little as the physicist knows what matter is. He simply has theories about it, certain views, picturing it now in one way and now in another. For a time the picture fits, then a new discovery brings quite a different view. But that has no effect on matter. Or is the reality of matter in some way diminished?

12   We simply do not know what we are dealing with when we encounter this strange and disturbing factor which we call the unconscious or the objective psyche. With some semblance of justification, it has been defined as the sexual instinct or the power drive. But this does nothing like justice to its real significance. What is behind these instincts, which are certainly not the be-all and end-all of existence, but merely represent the limits of our understanding? In this field every interpretation has free play. You can also take the unconscious as a manifestation of the life-instinct, and equate the force which creates and sustains life with Bergson's *élan vital*, or even with his *durée créatrice*. Another parallel would be Schopenhauer's Will. I know people who feel that the strange power in their own psyche is something divine, for the very simple reason that it has given them an understanding of what is meant by religious experience.

13   I admit that I fully understand the disappointment of my patient and of my public when I point to dreams as a source of information in the spiritual confusion of our

modern world. Nothing is more natural than that such a paradoxical gesture should strike one as completely absurd. What
can a dream do, this utterly subjective and nugatory thing, in
a world brimful of overpowering realities? Realities must be
countered with other, equally palpable realities, and not with
dreams, which merely disturb our sleep or put us in a bad mood
the next day. You cannot build a house with dreams, or pay
taxes, or win battles, or overcome the world crisis. Therefore
my patient, like all other sensible people, will want me to tell
him what can be done in this insufferable situation, and with
appropriate, common-sense methods. The only snag is that all
the methods that seem appropriate have already been tried out
with no success whatever, or consist of wishful fantasies that are
impossible in practice. These methods were all chosen with a
view to meeting the existing situation. For instance, when someone gets his business into a mess, he naturally considers how he
can set it on its feet again, and he employs all the remedies that
are designed to restore his languishing business to health. But
what happens when all these remedies have been tried, when,
contrary to all reasonable expectations, the situation only slith-
ers from bad to worse? In that case he will be compelled to give
up the use of these so-called reasonable methods as speedily as
possible.

314   My patient, and perhaps our whole age, is in this situation.
Anxiously he asks me, "What can I do?" And I must answer, "I
don't know either." "Then there's nothing to be done?" I reply
that mankind has got into these blind alleys countless times during the course of evolution, and no one knew what to do because
everybody was busy hatching out clever plans to meet the situation. No one had the courage to admit that they had all taken
the wrong turning. And then, suddenly, things somehow began
to move again, so that the same old humanity still exists, though
somewhat different from before.

315   When we look at human history, we see only what happens
on the surface, and even this is distorted in the faded mirror of
tradition. But what has really been happening eludes the in-
quiring eye of the historian, for the true historical event lies
deeply buried, experienced by all and observed by none. It is the
most private and most subjective of psychic experiences. Wars,
dynasties, social upheavals, conquests, and religions are but the

superficial symptoms of a secret psychic attitude unknown even to the individual himself, and transmitted by no historian; perhaps the founders of religions give us the most information in this regard. The great events of world history are, at bottom, profoundly unimportant. In the last analysis, the essential thing is the life of the individual. This alone makes history, here alone do the great transformations first take place, and the whole future, the whole history of the world, ultimately spring as a gigantic summation from these hidden sources in individuals. In our most private and most subjective lives we are not only the passive witnesses of our age, and its sufferers, but also its makers. We make our own epoch.

316   So when I counsel my patient to pay attention to his dreams, I mean: "Turn back to the most subjective part of yourself, to the source of your being, to that point where you are making world history without being aware of it. Your apparently insoluble difficulty must, it is obvious, remain insoluble, for otherwise you would wear yourself out seeking for remedies of whose ineptitude you are convinced from the start. Your dreams are an expression of your inner life, and they can show you through what false attitude you have landed yourself in this blind alley."

317   Dreams are impartial, spontaneous products of the unconscious psyche, outside the control of the will. They are pure nature; they show us the unvarnished, natural truth, and are therefore fitted, as nothing else is, to give us back an attitude that accords with our basic human nature when our consciousness has strayed too far from its foundations and run into an impasse.

318   To concern ourselves with dreams is a way of reflecting on ourselves—a way of self-reflection. It is not our ego-consciousness reflecting on itself; rather, it turns its attention to the objective actuality of the dream as a communication or message from the unconscious, unitary soul of humanity. It reflects not on the ego but on the self; it recollects that strange self, alien to the ego, which was ours from the beginning, the trunk from which the ego grew. It is alien to us because we have estranged ourselves from it through the aberrations of the conscious mind.

319   But even if we accept the proposition that dreams are not arbitrary inventions but are natural products of unconscious psychic activity, we shall still, when confronted with a real dream, lack the courage to see in it a message of any importance.

Dream-interpretation was one of the accomplishments of witch-craft, and was therefore among the black arts persecuted by the Church. Even though we of the twentieth century are rather more broad-minded in this respect, so much historical prejudice still attaches to the whole idea of dream-interpretation that we do not take kindly to it. Is there, one may ask, any reliable method of dream-interpretation? Can we put faith in any of the various speculations? I admit that I share these misgivings to the full, and I am convinced that there is in fact no absolutely reliable method of interpretation. Absolute reliability in the interpretation of natural events is found only within the narrowest limits —that is to say, when no more comes out of the interpretation than we have put in. Every attempt to explain nature is a hazard. A reliable method does not come into being until long after the pioneer work has been accomplished. We know that Freud has written a book on dream-interpretation, but his interpretation is an example of what we have just said: no more comes out of it than what his theory allows to be put into the dream. This view naturally does not do anything like justice to the boundless freedom of dream-life, with the consequence that the meaning of the dream is concealed rather than revealed. Also, when we consider the infinite variety of dreams, it is difficult to conceive that there could ever be a method or a technical procedure which would lead to an infallible result. It is, indeed, a good thing that no valid method exists, for otherwise the meaning of the dream would be limited in advance and would lose precisely that virtue which makes dreams so valuable for therapeutic pur-poses—their ability to offer new points of view.

320   One would do well, therefore, to treat every dream as though it were a totally unknown object. Look at it from all sides, take it in your hand, carry it about with you, let your imagination play round it, and talk about it with other people. Primitives tell each other impressive dreams, in a public palaver if possible, and this custom is also attested in late antiquity, for all the ancient peoples attributed great significance to dreams. Treated in this way, the dream suggests all manner of ideas and associations which lead us closer to its meaning. The ascertainment of the meaning is, I need hardly point out, an entirely arbitrary affair, and this is where the hazards begin. Narrower or wider limits will be set to the meaning, according to one's experience, tem-

perament, and taste. Some people will be satisfied with little, for others much is still not enough. Also the meaning of the dream, or our interpretation of it, is largely dependent on the intentions of the interpreter, on what he expects the meaning to be or requires it to do. In eliciting the meaning he will involuntarily be guided by certain presuppositions, and it depends very much on the scrupulousness and honesty of the investigator whether he gains something by his interpretation or perhaps only becomes still more deeply entangled in his mistakes. So far as presuppositions are concerned, we may take it as certain that the dream is not an idle invention of the conscious mind but an involuntary, natural phenomenon, even though it should prove true that dreams are in some way distorted by becoming conscious. Anyway this distortion occurs so quickly and automatically that it is barely perceptible. It is therefore safe to assume that it is an integral part of the dream-function. And it is equally safe to assume that dreams arise from the unconscious part of our being and are, consequently, its symptoms, allowing us to make inferences as to the nature of this being. If we wish to investigate our own nature, dreams are the most suitable media for this purpose.

321   During the work of interpretation one must abstain from all presuppositions that smack of superstition, such as, first and foremost, the notion that the protagonists in dreams are nothing other than these same persons in real life. One should never forget that one dreams in the first place, and almost to the exclusion of all else, of oneself. (Any exceptions are governed by quite definite rules, but I cannot go into this here.) If we acknowledge this truth we shall sometimes find ourselves faced with very interesting problems. I remember two instructive cases: one of my patients dreamed of a drunken tramp who lay in a ditch, and another of a drunken prostitute who rolled about in the gutter. The first patient was a theologian, the second a distinguished lady in high society. Both of them were outraged and horrified, and absolutely refused to admit that they had dreamed of themselves. I gave them both the well-meant advice that they should spend an hour in self-reflection, diligently and devoutly considering in what ways they were not much better than their drunken brother in the ditch and their drunken sister in the gutter. The subtle process of self-knowledge often begins with

a bomb-shell like this. The "other" person we dream of is not our friend and neighbour, but the other in us, of whom we prefer to say: "I thank thee, Lord, that I am not as this publican and sinner." Certainly the dream, being a child of nature, has no moralizing intention; it merely exemplifies the well-known law that no trees reach up to heaven.

322   If, in addition to this, we bear in mind that the unconscious contains everything that is lacking to consciousness, that the unconscious therefore has a compensatory tendency, then we can begin to draw conclusions—provided, of course, that the dream does not come from too deep a psychic level. If it is a dream of this kind, it will as a rule contain mythological motifs, combinations of ideas or images which can be found in the myths of one's own folk or in those of other races. The dream will then have a collective meaning, a meaning which is the common property of mankind.

323   This does not contradict my earlier remark that we always dream of ourselves. As individuals we are not completely unique, but are like all other men. Hence a dream with a collective meaning is valid in the first place for the dreamer, but it expresses at the same time the fact that his momentary problem is also the problem of other people. This is often of great practical importance, for there are countless people who are inwardly cut off from humanity and oppressed by the thought that nobody else has their problems. Or else they are those all-too-modest souls who, feeling themselves nonentities, have kept their claim to social recognition on too low a level. Moreover, every individual problem is somehow connected with the problem of the age, so that practically every subjective difficulty has to be viewed from the standpoint of the human situation as a whole. But this is permissible only when the dream really is a mythological one and makes use of collective symbols.

324   Such dreams are called by primitives "big" dreams. The primitives I observed in East Africa took it for granted that "big" dreams are dreamed only by "big" men—medicine-men, magicians, chiefs, etc. This may be true on a primitive level. But with us these dreams are dreamed also by simple people, more particularly when they have got themselves, mentally or spiritually, in a fix. It is obvious that in handling "big" dreams intuitive guesswork will lead nowhere. Wide knowledge is required,

such as a specialist ought to possess. But no dream can be interpreted with knowledge alone. This knowledge, furthermore, should not be dead material that has been memorized; it must possess a living quality, and be infused with the experience of the person who uses it. Of what use is philosophical knowledge in the head, if one is not also a philosopher at heart? Anyone who wishes to interpret a dream must himself be on approximately the same level as the dream, for nowhere can he see anything more than what he is himself.

325   The art of interpreting dreams cannot be learnt from books. Methods and rules are good only when we can get along without them. Only the man who can do it anyway has real skill, only the man of understanding really understands. No one who does not know himself can know others. And in each of us there is another whom we do not know. He speaks to us in dreams and tells us how differently he sees us from the way we see ourselves. When, therefore, we find ourselves in a difficult situation to which there is no solution, he can sometimes kindle a light that radically alters our attitude—the very attitude that led us into the difficult situation.

326   The more I engrossed myself in these problems over the years, the stronger became my impression that our modern education is morbidly one-sided. No doubt we are right to open the eyes and ears of our young people to the wide world, but it is the maddest of delusions to think that this really equips them for the task of living. It is the kind of training that enables a young person to adapt himself outwardly to the world and reality, but no one gives a thought to the necessity of adapting to the self, to the powers of the psyche, which are far mightier than all the Great Powers of the earth. A system of education does indeed exist, but it has its origins partly in antiquity and partly in the early Middle Ages. It styles itself the Christian Church. But it cannot be denied that in the course of the last two centuries Christianity, no less than Confucianism in China and Buddhism in India, has largely forfeited its educative activity. Human iniquity is not to blame for this, but rather a gradual and widespread spiritual change, the first symptom of which was the Reformation. It shattered the authority of the Church as a teacher, and thereafter the authoritarian principle itself began to crumble away. The inevitable consequence was an increase in

the importance of the individual, which found expression in the modern ideals of humanity, social welfare, democracy, and equality. The decidedly individualistic trend of these latest developments is counterbalanced by a compensatory reversion to the collective man, whose authority at present is the sheer weight of the masses. No wonder that nowadays there is a feeling of catastrophe in the air, as though an avalanche had broken loose which nothing can stop. The collective man threatens to stifle the individual man, on whose sense of responsibility everything valuable in mankind ultimately depends. The mass as such is always anonymous and always irresponsible. So-called leaders are the inevitable symptoms of a mass movement. The true leaders of mankind are always those who are capable of self-reflection, and who relieve the dead weight of the masses at least of their own weight, consciously holding aloof from the blind momentum of the mass in movement.

327   But who can resist this all-engulfing force of attraction, when each man clings to the next and each drags the other with him? Only one who is firmly rooted not only in the outside world but also in the world within.

328   Small and hidden is the door that leads inward, and the entrance is barred by countless prejudices, mistaken assumptions, and fears. Always one wishes to hear of grand political and economic schemes, the very things that have landed every nation in a morass. Therefore it sounds grotesque when anyone speaks of hidden doors, dreams, and a world within. What has this vapid idealism got to do with gigantic economic programmes, with the so-called problems of reality?

329   But I speak not to nations, only to the individual few, for whom it goes without saying that cultural values do not drop down like manna from heaven, but are created by the hands of individuals. If things go wrong in the world, this is because something is wrong with the individual, because something is wrong with me. Therefore, if I am sensible, I shall put myself right first. For this I need—because outside authority no longer means anything to me—a knowledge of the innermost foundations of my being, in order that I may base myself firmly on the eternal facts of the human psyche.

330   If I spoke before chiefly of dreams, I did so because I wished to draw attention to one of the most immediate approaches to

the world of inner experience. But there are many things besides dreams which I cannot discuss here. The investigation of the deeper levels of the psyche brings to light much that we, on the surface, can at most dream about. No wonder, then, that sometimes the strongest and most original of all man's spiritual activities—the religious activity—is also discovered from our dreams. This is the activity which, more even than sexuality or social adaptation, is thwarted in modern man. I know people for whom the encounter with the strange power within themselves was such an overwhelming experience that they called it "God." So experienced, "God" too is a "theory" in the most literal sense, a way of looking at the world, an image which the limited human mind creates in order to express an unfathomable and ineffable experience. The experience alone is real, not to be disputed; but the image can be soiled or broken to pieces.

331   Names and words are sorry husks, yet they indicate the quality of what we have experienced. When we call the devil a neurosis, we are signifying that we feel this demonic experience as a sickness which is characteristic of our age. When we call it repressed sexuality or the will to power, this shows that it seriously disturbs even these fundamental instincts. When we call it God, we are trying to describe its profound and universal significance, because this is what we have glimpsed in the experience. Looking at it soberly, and bearing in mind the vast, unknowable background, we must admit that this latter designation is the most cautious and also the most modest, because it sets no limits to the experience and does not squeeze it into any conceptual schema. Unless, of course, someone should hit upon the singular idea that he knew exactly what God is.

332   Whatever name we may put to the psychic background, the fact remains that our consciousness is influenced by it in the highest degree, and all the more so the less we are conscious of it. The layman can hardly conceive how much his inclinations, moods, and decisions are influenced by the dark forces of his psyche, and how dangerous or helpful they may be in shaping his destiny. Our cerebral consciousness is like an actor who has forgotten that he is playing a role. But when the play comes to an end, he must remember his own subjective reality, for he can no longer continue to live as Julius Caesar or as Othello, but only as himself, from whom he has become estranged by a

momentary sleight of consciousness. He must know once again that he was merely a figure on the stage who was playing a piece by Shakespeare, and that there was a producer as well as a director in the background who, as always, will have something very important to say about his acting.

THE STATE OF PSYCHOTHERAPY TODAY [1]

333   In earlier days, when people were less sophisticated in their
ideas, psychotherapy was regarded as a technique which could be
applied to practically anybody who had learnt it by heart. In
medical treatises and text-books you would come across the
wonderful remark: ". . . in addition, the following may be of
use: massage, cold baths, mountain air, and psychotherapy." The
nature of this "psychotherapy" was prudently never specified in
detail. Certainly, so long as it consisted of hypnotism, suggestion,
persuasion, "rééducation de la volonté," Couéism, and so forth,
anybody could learn the art by rote and say his piece in season
and out of season. The medical profession generally—and this
includes psychiatrists and neurologists—is notoriously slow to
learn and needs a long period of incubation. And so it happened
that, long after psychotherapy had grown to a psychology, and
therapeutics had ceased to be a mere technique, the illusion still
continued to flourish that psychological treatment was some
kind of technical procedure. It would be decidedly too optimistic to say that this illusion has ceased to exist even among
the ranks of psychotherapists, nor would it accord with the facts.
All that has happened is that now and again voices are heard
which demur at the mechanization of psychotherapy and aspire
to rescue it from the soullessness of a mere technical procedure.
Their aim is to raise it to the higher plane of psychological and
philosophical dialectic, where it becomes a discussion between
two psychic systems, that is, two human beings confronting one
another in their totality.

334   These doubts and aims were not, as one might think, dragged
down from the airless realm of eternal ideas by pernickety minds
overloaded with philosophy. On the contrary, they sprang from

1 [Translated from "Zur gegenwärtigen Lage der Psychotherapie," *Zentralblatt
für Psychotherapie und ihre Grenzgebiete* (Leipzig), VII (1934):1, 1–16.—EDITORS.]

the deep impression which the unedifying confusion of psychological and therapeutic views cannot fail to make today even on the distant observer. A glance at the chaotic profusion of psychotherapeutic literature is sufficient confirmation of this. Not only are there different schools which until very recently have anxiously avoided any serious communication with one another, there are also groups—self-styled "Societies"—who barricade themselves like cenobites against unbelievers, not to mention the numerous solitaries who are not a little proud of being the only members of their church, to use the well-known *mot* of Coleridge. No doubt this state of affairs is a sure sign of vitality and of the many pressing problems still to be solved in the field of psychotherapy. But it is far from gratifying; and it ill accords with the dignity of science when bigoted dogmatism and personal touchiness hamper the free discussion so necessary to its growth.

335   What, indeed, could shed a more glaring light on the fact that psychotherapy is anything but a technique than the very multiplicity of techniques, points of view, "psychologies," and philosophical premises (or lack of them)? Does not this welter of contradictions show in the most striking way that what we are concerned with is far more than a technique? A technique can be modified and improved by all sorts of recipes and dodges, and everybody would welcome a change for the better. But, far from that being the case, we find all too many people entrenching themselves behind precepts which they envelop with the sacrosanct halo of dogma. Ostensibly they are guarding the ultimate scientific truth; but has it ever—except in the most benighted periods of history—been observed that a scientific truth needed to be elevated to the rank of a dogma? Truth can stand on its own feet, only shaky opinions require the support of dogmatization. Fanaticism is ever the brother of doubt.

336   What is the lesson of these characteristic and, for the history of any science, very noteworthy signs? Beyond a doubt they point to the incontrovertible fact that psychotherapy has outgrown the stage of technique and has already broken into the realm of *opinion*. We can easily agree about a technique, but hardly ever about opinions. Hence the heatedness of discussion —indeed if there be any—or the equally eloquent silence.

337   It has long been imagined that psychotherapy can be prac-

tised "technically," as though it were a formula, a method of operation, or a colour-test. The general practitioner can use a wide assortment of medical techniques without hesitation, whatever his personal opinions may be about his patients and irrespective of his psychological theories or even of his philosophical and religious assumptions. Psychotherapy cannot be used like that. Whether he likes it or not, the doctor and his assumptions are involved just as much as the patient. It is in fact largely immaterial what sort of technique he uses, for the point is not the technique but the person who uses the technique. The object to which the technique is applied is neither an anatomical specimen nor an abscess nor a chemical substance; it is the totality of the suffering individual. The object of therapy is not the neurosis but the man who has the neurosis. We have long known, for instance, that a cardiac neurosis comes not from the heart, as the old medical mythology would have it, but from the mind of the sufferer. Nor does it come from some obscure corner of the unconscious, as many psychotherapists still struggle to believe; it comes from the totality of a man's life and from all the experiences that have accumulated over the years and decades, and finally, not merely from his life as an individual but from his psychic experience within the family or even the social group.

338   In dealing with a neurosis, the doctor is not confronted with a delimited field of illness; he is faced with a sick person who is sick not in one particular mechanism or focus of disease but in his whole personality. "Technique" cannot cope with that. The personality of the patient demands all the resources of the doctor's personality and not technical tricks.

339   Very early on, therefore, I required that the doctor himself should be analysed. Freud seconded this requirement, obviously because he could not escape the conviction that the patient should be confronted by a doctor and not by a technique. It is certainly very laudable in a doctor to try to be as objective and impersonal as possible and to refrain from meddling with the psychology of his patient like an overzealous saviour. But if this attitude is carried to artificial lengths it has unfortunate consequences. The doctor will find that he cannot overstep the bounds of naturalness with impunity. Otherwise he would be setting a bad example to his patient, who certainly did not get

ill from an excess of naturalness. Besides, it would be dangerously to underestimate the patients if one imagined that they were all too stupid to notice the artifices of the doctor, his security measures and his little game of prestige. Nor can it conceivably be the doctor's intention to strengthen the patient everywhere in his natural functioning, and yet to keep him as much as possible in the dark when it comes to the one crucial spot—which concerns the doctor himself—and so in a state of helpless dependence or "transference." Such a mistake could only be made by an extremely unanalysed doctor whose personal prestige counted for more than the welfare of his patient.

340   Because the personality and attitude of the doctor are of supreme importance in therapy—whether he appreciates this fact or not—his personal opinions stand out in a disproportionately strong light in the history of psychotherapy and are the cause of apparently irreconcilable schisms. Freud took his stand with fanatical one-sidedness on sexuality, concupiscence—in a word, on the "pleasure principle." Everything turns on the question of whether one can do what one wants. Repression, sublimation, regression, narcissism, wish-fulfilment and the rest are all concepts that relate to the grand drama of the pleasure principle. It almost looks as if man's desire and greed have been made the cardinal principle of psychology.

341   Adler also drew on the wide field of human concupiscence and discovered the need for self-assertion. This tendency of human nature was likewise made a cardinal principle of psychology, and with the same one-sidedness so regrettable in Freud.

342   Now, there is no doubt that the principle of concupiscence can explain a very large number of cases of neurosis. Indeed, the same case can be explained both in the manner of Freud and in the manner of Adler, nor is either explanation lacking in conviction. As a matter of fact, the one explanation complements the other, which in itself would be a very satisfactory state of affairs did it not also prove that neither explanation can lay claim to absolute validity. Both are relative, heuristic points of view, and as such unfitted to be universal concepts. But at least they have a bearing on essential partial aspects. The theory of repression is based on certain psychic facts which are met with everywhere, and the same is true of the need for self-assertion

or the will to power. Clearly everyone would like to enjoy all he can and at the same time be "on top," and it is equally obvious that so long as he has this primitive, naïve, infantile attitude he will not be able to avoid a neurosis if ever he makes an attempt to adapt himself to his surroundings. This last condition is very much to the point, for without it there is no neurosis but simply moral insanity or the higher idiocy.

343   If, then, at least two conditions are necessary to produce a neurosis, both must be of aetiological significance. It is out of the question for only the infantile attitude to be causal, but not the will to adapt. Not only *can* the latter be an aetiological factor, it always is so. Freud and Adler explain a neurosis exclusively from the infantile angle. A more comprehensive explanation would be forced to take account of the will to adapt as well. There need not always be simply an excess of infantilism; there can also be an excess of adaptation. Nor must this latter possibility necessarily be understood as a mere repression of infantilism or as a "substitute formation"; we could equally well explain infantilism as repression of adaptation and call it a "substitute formation." Neither Freud nor Adler would welcome this reversal, although it is logically unavoidable once we take the aetiological significance of the will to adapt into account. And this we must do—even Freud needs a factor that represses, that does not fulfil wishes, that arouses anxiety, etc. Adler needs something that keeps a man down. If there is no aetiological opposite of equal strength, then all that infantile concupiscence is without object.

344   Having discovered that every neurotic suffers from infantile concupiscence, we must still ask how it is with his will to adapt, for perhaps he has developed infantile concupiscence merely as a "substitute formation." In this case it would be purely symptomatic and not genuine at all; and, if explained from the infantile angle, the explanation would be quite beside the point. More, an unforgiveable blunder would have been committed. Unfortunately such blunders are very frequent, because the doctor's attention is turned too exclusively to the infantile traits. The patient is then automatically charged with inferiority.

345   Infantilism, however, is something extremely ambiguous. First, it can be either genuine or purely symptomatic; and second, it can be either residuary or embryonic. There is an

enormous difference between something that has *remained* infantile and something that is in the process of growth. Both can take an infantile or embryonic form, and more often than not it is impossible to tell at first glance whether we are dealing with a regrettably persistent fragment of infantile life or with a vitally important creative beginning. To deride these possibilities is to act like a dullard who does not know that the future is more important than the past. For this reason it would be more advisable to examine these "infantile-perverse" fantasies for their creative content than to trace them back to the cradle, and to understand all neurosis more as an attempt at adaptation than as an unsuccessful or otherwise distorted wish-fulfilment.

346   Naturally, the theory of infantilism has the inestimable advantage of always putting the doctor "on top" as the representative of sound, healthy, superior insight, while the poor patient lies there helpless, the victim of unconscious infantile-perverse wish-fulfilments. This also gives the doctor the opportunity to know better, to avoid meeting the patient's personality face to face, and to hide behind a technique.

347   It is not hard to see how much this attitude is aided and abetted by all manner of conscious and unconscious tendencies, and why a theory of infantilism is welcomed by the doctor from the start, even if, as a human being, he were quite ready to acknowledge the personality of his patient. The tremendous influence Freud's ideas have exerted rests not merely on their agreement with the real or supposed facts, but very largely on the easy opportunity they afford of touching the other fellow on his sore spot, of deflating him and hoisting oneself into a superior position. What a blessed relief it is when one can say in a tight corner, "That's nothing but resistance!" or when one need no longer take one's opponent's argument seriously because it can so easily be explained away as "symbolical"—without, be it noted, ever asking him whether this explanation is acceptable to his psychology.

348   Besides which, there are numberless patients who, with a great show of coyness, are at bottom only too ready to subscribe to the infantilism theory, because it gives them a broad hint of how to pass off the disturbing "infantilism" as a "nothing but." And in many cases the theory offers a heaven-sent way out of the unpleasantly acute problems of real life into the blissful mead-

ows of childhood, where, having invoked the aetiological bogy, the patient pretends to discover why he is no good in the present and how it is all the fault of his parents and his upbringing.

349   Admittedly there is nothing that cannot be used to illegitimate advantage. But one ought to note where the misuse creeps in and how it is being exploited. These things depend very largely on the doctor, who must take his patient with great seriousness in order to detect abuses of this kind. A technique notices nothing, but a human being does—and he alone can develop the sensitiveness necessary to decide whether a neurosis should be treated from the infantile angle or from the adaptation angle.

350   I need hardly say that technique is necessary up to a point—we are all sufficiently convinced of that. But behind every method there stands the man, who is so much more important because, irrespective of his technique, he has to arrive at decisions which are at least as vital to the patient as any technique however adroitly applied. It is therefore the duty of the psychotherapist to exercise self-knowledge and to criticize his personal assumptions, whether religious or philosophical, just as asepsis is obligatory for a surgeon. The doctor must know his "personal equation" in order not to do violence to his patient. To this end I have worked out a critical psychology which would enable the psychiatrist to recognize the various typical attitudes, even though the Freudian school asserts that this has nothing to do with psychoanalysis. Psychoanalysis is evidently a technique behind which the human being vanishes, and which always remains the same no matter who practises it. Consequently, the psychoanalyst needs no self-knowledge and no criticism of his assumptions. Apparently the purpose of his training analysis is to make him not a human being but a correct applier of technique.

351   But even regarded as a technique psychoanalysis is far from simple. In actual fact it is a very complicated and fiendishly tricky affair compared even with the most elaborate chemical procedure, subject to endless variation and well-nigh unpredictable in its results. Anyone who finds that hard to believe should peruse the "technique" of a Freudian dream-analysis in *The Interpretation of Dreams*—for instance, the dream of "Irma's injection." To call such a procedure a "technique" requires a

strong dose of optimism. And yet dreams are supposed to be the *"via regia* to the unconscious" and to play a not uncertain role in psychoanalysis! Truly one must be smitten with blindness not to see that this kind of "technique" is first and foremost an expression of the man who applies it and of all his subjective assumptions.

352   These reflections lead us back to the problem of the doctor's attitude and to the need for criticism of subjective premises. A subjective view of the world should not be imported uncritically into his conception of neurosis, as was the case, for instance, with Freud's view of the unconscious and with his materialistic bias in regard to the religious function of the psyche. The psychotherapist should no longer labour under the delusion that the treatment of neurosis demands nothing more than the knowledge of a technique; he should be absolutely clear in his own mind that psychological treatment of the sick is a *relationship* in which the doctor is involved quite as much as the patient. True psychological treatment can only be individual, and this is why even the best technique has only a relative value. All the more significance, therefore, falls to the general attitude of the doctor, who must know himself well enough not to destroy the peculiar values of the patient entrusted to his care, whatever these may be. If Alfred Adler were to request analytical treatment of his old teacher Freud, Freud would have to adjust himself to seeing Adler's peculiar psychology, even to the point of admitting its general right to exist; for there are innumerable people whose psychology is that of the son in need of prestige. If, on the other hand, I were to analyse Freud, I would be doing him a great and irreparable wrong if I failed to take elaborate account of the very real historical significance of the nursery, the importance of the entanglements of the family romance, the bitterness and gravity of early-acquired resentments, and their compensatory accompaniment by wish-fantasies which—unhappily—cannot be fulfilled, and to accept all this as a *fait accompli*. Freud would certainly take it amiss if I told him that resentments are all nothing but a "substitute" for failure to love one's neighbour, or something of that sort. True as such an assertion might be in other cases, it would be incorrect here, even if I should succeed in persuading Freud of the truth of my idea. Doubtless Freud means what he says, consequently we must take

him as the type of person who says such things. Only then is his particular case accepted, and with it all those whose psychology is similarly constituted. But since we can hardly suppose that either Freud or Adler is a universally valid representative of European man, there is some hope that I too may possess my own peculiar psychology, and, with me, all those who cannot subscribe to the primacy of infantile-perverse wish-fantasies or to that of the urge to power.

353   It goes without saying that this should not be a matter for naïve self-deception; on the contrary, no psychotherapist should let slip the opportunity to study himself critically in the light of these negative psychologies. Freud and Adler have beheld very clearly the shadow that accompanies us all. The Jews have this peculiarity in common with women; being physically weaker, they have to aim at the chinks in the armour of their adversary, and thanks to this technique which has been forced on them through the centuries, the Jews themselves are best protected where others are most vulnerable. Because, again, of their civilization, more than twice as ancient as ours, they are vastly more conscious than we of human weaknesses, of the shadow-side of things, and hence in this respect much less vulnerable than we are. Thanks to their experience of an old culture, they are able, while fully conscious of their frailties, to live on friendly and even tolerant terms with them, whereas we are still too young not to have "illusions" about ourselves. Moreover, we have been entrusted by fate with the task of creating a civilization—and indeed we have need of it—and for this "illusions" in the form of one-sided ideals, convictions, plans, etc. are indispensable. As a member of a race with a three-thousand-year-old civilization, the Jew, like the cultured Chinese, has a wider area of psychological consciousness than we. Consequently it is *in general* less dangerous for the Jew to put a negative value on his unconscious. The "Aryan" unconscious, on the other hand, contains explosive forces and seeds of a future yet to be born, and these may not be devalued as nursery romanticism without psychic danger. The still youthful Germanic peoples are fully capable of creating new cultural forms that still lie dormant in the darkness of the unconscious of every individual—seeds bursting with energy and capable of mighty expansion. The Jew, who is something of a nomad, has never yet

created a cultural form of his own and as far as we can see never will, since all his instincts and talents require a more or less civilized nation to act as host for their development.

354   The Jewish race as a whole—at least this is my experience—possesses an unconscious which can be compared with the "Aryan" only with reserve. Creative individuals apart, the average Jew is far too conscious and differentiated to go about pregnant with the tensions of unborn futures. The "Aryan" unconscious has a higher potential than the Jewish; that is both the advantage and the disadvantage of a youthfulness not yet fully weaned from barbarism. In my opinion it has been a grave error in medical psychology up till now to apply Jewish categories—which are not even binding on all Jews—indiscriminately to Germanic and Slavic Christendom. Because of this the most precious secret of the Germanic peoples—their creative and intuitive depth of soul—has been explained as a morass of banal infantilism, while my own warning voice has for decades been suspected of anti-Semitism. This suspicion emanated from Freud. He did not understand the Germanic psyche any more than did his Germanic followers. Has the formidable phenomenon of National Socialism, on which the whole world gazes with astonished eyes, taught them better? Where was that unparalleled tension and energy while as yet no National Socialism existed? Deep in the Germanic psyche, in a pit that is anything but a garbage-bin of unrealizable infantile wishes and unresolved family resentments. A movement that grips a whole nation must have matured in every individual as well. That is why I say that the Germanic unconscious contains tensions and potentialities which medical psychology must consider in its evaluation of the unconscious. Its business is not with neuroses but with human beings—that, in fact, is the grand privilege of medical psychology: to treat the whole man and not an artificially segregated function.[2] And that is why its scope must be widened to reveal to the physician's gaze not just the pathological aberrations of a disturbed psychic development, but the creative powers of the psyche labouring at the future; not just a dreary fragment but the meaningful whole.

[2] Similar views are expressed by von Weizsäcker in regard to internal medicine. [Viktor von Weizsäcker (1886–1957), professor of medicine at Heidelberg University. He pioneered in psychosomatic medicine.—EDITORS.]

355   A neurosis is by no means merely a negative thing, it is also something positive. Only a soulless rationalism reinforced by a narrow materialistic outlook could possibly have overlooked this fact. In reality the neurosis contains the patient's psyche, or at least an essential part of it; and if, as the rationalist pretends, the neurosis could be plucked from him like a bad tooth, he would have gained nothing but would have lost something very essential to him. That is to say, he would have lost as much as the thinker deprived of his doubt, or the moralist deprived of his temptation, or the brave man deprived of his fear. To lose a neurosis is to find oneself without an object; life loses its point and hence its meaning. This would not be a cure, it would be a regular amputation; and it would be cold comfort indeed if the psychoanalyst then assured the patient that he had lost nothing but his infantile paradise with its wishful chimeras, most of them perverse. Very much more would have been lost, for hidden in the neurosis is a bit of still undeveloped personality, a precious fragment of the psyche lacking which a man is condemned to resignation, bitterness, and everything else that is hostile to life. A psychology of neurosis that sees only the negative elements empties out the baby with the bath-water, since it neglects the positive meaning and value of these "infantile"— i.e., creative—fantasies. So often its main endeavour seems to lie in trying to explain everything backwards and downwards, and there is of course nothing that is not capable of some obscene caricature. But this will never prove that the symbol or symptom so explained really has that meaning; it merely demonstrates the adolescent smutty-mindedness of the explainer.

356   And here I cannot refrain from remarking how often it happens that otherwise serious-minded physicians, in complete disregard of all the fundamental tenets of scientific caution, will interpret psychological material in the light of subjective conjectures, of which one can make absolutely nothing except that they are all attempts to discover by what obscene joke the material can be related to some oral, anal, urethral, or other sexual abnormality. The poison of the "low-down" interpretation has bitten so deeply into the marrow of these people's bones that they can no longer think at all except in the infantile-perverse jargon of certain neurotics who display all the peculiarities of a Freudian psychology. It is positively grotesque that the doc-

tor should himself fall into a way of thinking which in others he rightly censures as infantile and wants to cure for that reason. Certainly it is much easier to make conjectures over the head of the patient than to see what the empirical material really means. Nevertheless, one must assume that the patient came to the analyst in order to rid himself of his morbid way of thinking and looking at things, and we may therefore infer—as everywhere else in modern medicine—that the symptom is really the effort of the diseased system to cure itself. But if the analyst's thoughts, spoken or unspoken, are as negative and disparaging as the patient's, and if he degrades everything to the level of a "dirty joke" psychology, then we must not be surprised if the patient becomes spiritually blighted and compensates for this blight by incurable intellectualism.

357   Unfortunately it is true that there are far too many people who justify our mistrust. Too many of them use ideals and meretricious values to pull wool over their own eyes. Often the analyst has to reduce them to a very unpleasant formula indeed in order to bring home to them the truth about themselves. But not all people are like that. At least as many patients need anything rather than distrust and disparagement. They are fundamentally decent folk who play fair and do not prostitute ideals for the adornment of their inferiorities. To treat such people reductively, to impute ulterior motives to them, and to suspect their natural wholesomeness of unnatural obscenities is not only sinfully stupid but positively criminal. A technique is always a soulless mechanism, and whoever takes psychotherapy for a technique and vaunts it as such runs the risk, at the very least, of committing an unpardonable blunder. A conscientious doctor must be able to doubt all his skills and all his theories, otherwise he is befooled by a system. But all systems mean bigotry and inhumanity. Neurosis—let there be no doubt about this—may be any number of things, but never a "nothing but." It is the agony of a human soul in all its vast complexity—so vast, indeed, that any and every theory of neurosis is little better than a worthless sketch, unless it be a gigantic picture of the psyche which not even a hundred Fausts could conceive.

358   The fundamental rule for the psychotherapist should be to consider each case new and unique. That, probably, is the nearest we can get to the truth.

359   The proper handling of psychic material requires supreme
tact and an almost artistic sensitiveness. Without these, it is
hardly possible to distinguish what is valuable from what is not.
A neurosis, as I have said, consists of two things: infantile un-
willingness and the will to adapt. Hence one has first to feel
one's way until one is sure on which side the accent lies, for
the road goes on from there. If the accent is on the will to adapt,
there is no sense in decrying the attempt at adaptation as an
infantile wish-fantasy. The analyst is very liable to make this
mistake with his patient, and the patient—to his own great
injury—is ever so delighted because he is then protected on
medical authority against the feared or hated demands of his
neurosis, that is, against the demands of that part of his personality which is concealed in it. But this "other" personality
is the very thing he ought never to lose sight of, for it is his own
inner antithesis, the conflict that must be fought out again and
again if life is to go on. Without this initial opposition there is
no flow of energy, no vitality. Lack of opposition brings life to
a standstill wherever that lack reaches. But beyond that reach
life flows on unconsciously in ever-renewed and ever-changing
forms of neurosis. Only if we understand and accept the neurosis as our truest and most precious possession can we be sure
of avoiding stagnation and of not succumbing to rigidity and
neurotic subterfuge. In the neurosis is hidden one's worst enemy
and best friend. One cannot rate him too highly, unless of course
fate has made one hostile to life. There are always deserters, but
they have nothing to say to us, nor we to them.

360   Neurotic symbolism is ambiguous, pointing at once forward
and back, downward and up. In general the forward movement
is the more important, because the future is coming and the past
retreating. Only those who are preparing a retreat will do better
to look back. The neurotic has no need to feel himself beaten;
he has merely misjudged his necessary adversary, thinking that
he could give him the slip. The whole task of his personality
lies in the very thing he sought to avoid. Any doctor who deludes
him on that score is doing him a disservice. *The patient has not
to learn how to get rid of his neurosis, but how to bear it.* His
illness is not a gratuitous and therefore meaningless burden; it
is *his own self,* the "other" whom, from childish laziness or fear,
or for some other reason, he was always seeking to exclude from

his life. In this way, as Freud rightly says, we turn the ego into a "seat of anxiety," which it would never be if we did not defend ourselves against ourselves so neurotically. When the ego has been made a "seat of anxiety," someone is running away from himself and will not admit it. That dreaded "other self" is the main target of psychoanalysis with its depreciating, undermining technique which is always seeking to wear down the enemy and cripple him for good.

361   We should not try to "get rid" of a neurosis, but rather to experience what it means, what it has to teach, what its purpose is . We should even learn to be thankful for it, otherwise we pass it by and miss the opportunity of getting to know ourselves as we really are. A neurosis is truly removed only when it has removed the false attitude of the ego. We do not cure it—it cures us. A man is ill, but the illness is nature's attempt to heal him. From the illness itself we can learn so much for our recovery, and what the neurotic flings away as absolutely worthless contains the true gold we should never have found elsewhere. The psychoanalyst's every second word is "nothing but"—just what a dealer would say of an article he wanted to buy on the cheap. In this case it is man's soul, his hope, his boldest flight, his finest adventure.

362   No, it will not do, this attempt to buy off the sick man's neurosis and with it his soul. Moreover it is, at bottom, an impossible undertaking, a fraud: in the long run nobody can dodge his shadow unless he lives in eternal darkness. What the patient encounters in a neurotic dissociation is a strange, unrecognized part of his personality, which seeks to compel his recognition in exactly the same way that any other part of the body, if obstinately denied, would insist on its presence. If anyone set out to deny the existence of his left hand, he would inevitably get entangled in a fantastic web of "nothing but" explanations, just as happens to the neurotic—except that the psychoanalyst dignifies them with the name of a "theory." The infantile-perverse "nothing but" fantasies are the patient's efforts to deny his left hand. These efforts are themselves his morbid deviation, and they are interesting only inasmuch as all fantasies contain a secret allusion to the left hand. Everything else about them is unreal, because it is merely contrived for the purpose of concealment. Freud, of course, thinks that the thing concealed is the

thing these fantasies more or less openly allude to, i.e., sexuality and all the rest of it. But this is just what that kind of patient is aiming at all the time. He rides the same hobby-horse as his analyst, who may even have handed him a helpful idea or two— the famous infantile sexual trauma, for instance, which we can spend so much time chasing, only to find that we are as far from the truth as ever.

363   The true reason for a neurosis always lies in the present, since the neurosis exists in the present. It is definitely not a hangover from the past, a *caput mortuum;* it is fed and as it were new-made every day. And it is only in the today, not in our yesterdays, that the neurosis can be "cured." Because the neurotic conflict has to be fought today, any historical deviation is a detour, if not actually a wrong turning. And because the neurosis contains a part of one's own personality, an excursus into the thousand and one possibilities of obscene fantasy and unfulfillable infantile wishes is just a pretext for avoiding the essential question.

364   The essential question is: what will pierce through this fog of verbiage to the conscious personality of the patient, and what must be the nature of his attitude if he is to integrate that split-off fragment, supposing it were ever part of him? But how could it trouble him so much unless it were like his left hand, like the other half of himself? Something, therefore, that belongs to him in the deepest sense, completes him, creates organic balance, and yet for some reason is feared, perhaps because it makes life complicated and sets apparently impossible tasks?

365   Obviously, the best way to evade these tasks is to replace them by something that can rightly be called impossible—for instance, that world of obscenities whose speediest sublimation is recommended by Freud himself. Freud, it seems, took these neurotic conjectures quite seriously and thus fell into the same trap as the neurotic: on the one hand he seeks a wrong turning at any price, and on the other hand he cannot find the right way out of the maze. He was obviously taken in by the neurotic trick of *euphemistic disparagement.* He undervalued the neurosis and thereby won the applause of patients and doctors alike, who want nothing better than to hear that neurosis is "nothing but . . ."

366   The very word "psychogenic," however, tells us that certain

disturbances come from the psyche. Unfortunately the psyche is not a hormone but a world of almost cosmic proportions. Scientific rationalism completely overlooked this fact. Have psychotherapists ever seriously reflected that they have quite other forbears than Mesmer, Faria, Liébeault, Charcot, Bernheim, Janet, Forel, and the rest?

367　　For thousands of years the mind of man has worried about the sick soul, perhaps even earlier than it did about the sick body. The propitiation of gods, the perils of the soul and its salvation, these are not yesterday's problems. Religions are psychotherapeutic systems in the truest sense of the word, and on the grandest scale. They express the whole range of the psychic problem in mighty images; they are the avowal and recognition of the soul, and at the same time the revelation of the soul's nature. From this universal foundation no human soul is cut off; only the individual consciousness that has lost its connection with the psychic totality remains caught in the illusion that the soul is a small circumscribed area, a fit subject for "scientific" theorizing. The loss of this great relationship is the prime evil of neurosis, and that is why the neurotic loses his way among ever more tortuous back-streets of dubious repute, because he who denies the great must blame the petty. In his book *The Future of an Illusion* Freud has unwittingly shown his hand. He wants to put an end once and for all to the larger aspect of the psychic phenomenon, and in the attempt he continues the baleful work that is going on in every neurotic: destruction of the bond between men and the gods, severance from the universally felt and known bases of the psyche, and hence "denial of the left hand," of the counterpart man needs for his psychic existence.

368　　Let us not ask who has *not* preached to deaf ears! But did Goethe really write his *Faust* in vain? Hasn't Faust a neurosis as big as your fist? For surely the devil has been proved nonexistent. Consequently his psychic counterpart doesn't exist either—a mystery still to be unriddled, born of Faust's dubious internal secretions! That at least is the opinion of Mephistopheles, who is himself not altogether above reproach sexually—inclined to be bisexual, if anything. This devil who, according to *The Future of an Illusion*, does not exist is yet the scientific object of psychoanalysis, which gleefully busies itself with his non-existent ways of thought. Faust's fate in heaven and on earth may well be "left to the poets," but meanwhile the topsy-turvy view[3] of the human soul is turned into a theory of psychic suffering.

369   Psychotherapy today, it seems to me, still has a vast amount to unlearn and relearn if it is to do even rough justice to its subject, the full range of the human psyche. But first it must cease thinking neurotically and see the psychic processes in true perspective. Not only the whole conception of neurosis, but our ideas about the psychic functions themselves—for instance the function of dreams—stand in need of radical revision. Very notable blunders have occurred here, as when the perfectly normal function of dreams was viewed from the same angle as disease. It will then become clear that psychotherapy made approximately the same mistake as did the old school of medicine when it attacked the fever in the belief that this was the noxious agent.

370   It is the fate and misfortune of psychotherapy to have been born in an age of enlightenment, when self-distrust had made the old cultural values inaccessible and there was no psychology anywhere that went much beyond the level of Herbart or Condillac—none at any rate that would have done anything like justice to the complexities and perplexities with which the innocent and wholly unprepared physician was suddenly faced. In this respect we must be grateful to Freud, for at least he created a certain sense of direction in this chaos, and gave the physician sufficient courage to take a case of hysteria seriously, as a scientific proposition. Criticism after the event is easy enough, but all the same there is no sense in an entire generation of doctors going to sleep on Freud's laurels. Much has still to be learnt about the psyche, and our especial need today is liberation from outworn ideas which have seriously restricted our view of the psyche as a whole.

3 ["Afterbild."—TRANS.]

III

PREFACE TO
"ESSAYS ON CONTEMPORARY EVENTS"

―――

WOTAN

―――

AFTER THE CATASTROPHE

―――

THE FIGHT WITH THE SHADOW

―――

EPILOGUE TO
"ESSAYS ON CONTEMPORARY EVENTS"

PREFACE TO
"ESSAYS ON CONTEMPORARY EVENTS" [1]

Medical psychotherapy, for practical reasons, has to deal with the whole of the psyche. Therefore it is bound to come to terms with all those factors, biological as well as social and mental, which have a vital influence on psychic life.

We are living in times of great disruption: political passions are aflame, internal upheavals have brought nations to the brink of chaos, and the very foundations of our *Weltanschauung* are shattered. This critical state of things has such a tremendous influence on the psychic life of the individual that the doctor must follow its effects with more than usual attention. The storm of events does not sweep down upon him only from the great world outside; he feels the violence of its impact even in the quiet of his consulting-room and in the privacy of the medical consultation. As he has a responsibility towards his patients, he cannot afford to withdraw to the peaceful island of undisturbed scientific work, but must constantly descend into the arena of world events, in order to join in the battle of conflicting passions and opinions. Were he to remain aloof from the tumult, the calamity of his time would reach him only from afar, and his patient's suffering would find neither ear nor understanding. He would be at a loss to know how to talk to him, and to help him out of his isolation. For this reason the psychologist cannot avoid coming to grips with contemporary history, even if his very soul shrinks from the political uproar, the lying propaganda, and the jarring speeches of the demagogues. We need not mention his duties as

1 [Originally published as the Vorwort to *Aufsätze zur Zeitgeschichte* (Zurich, 1946). Trans. by Elizabeth Welsh in *Essays on Contemporary Events* (London, 1947); this version has been consulted. The latter volume contained the four papers that follow this preface and two more that were published in Vol. 16 of the *Coll. Works*: "Psychotherapy Today" (pars. 212ff.) and "Psychotherapy and a Philosophy of Life" (pars. 175ff.). Also see "Marginalia on Contemporary Events" (1945), CW 18, pars. 1349ff.—EDITORS.]

a citizen, which confront him with a similar task. As a physician, he has a higher obligation to humanity in this respect.

From time to time, therefore, I have felt obliged to step beyond the usual bounds of my profession. The experience of the psychologist is of a rather special kind, and it seemed to me that the general public might find it useful to hear his point of view. This was hardly a far-fetched conclusion, for surely the most naïve of laymen could not fail to see that many contemporary figures and events were positively asking for psychological elucidation. Were psychopathic symptoms ever more conspicuous than in the contemporary political scene?

It has never been my wish to meddle in the political questions of the day. But in the course of the years I have written a few papers which give my reactions to current events. The present book contains a collection of these occasional essays, all written between 1936 and 1946. It is natural enough that my thoughts should have been especially concerned with Germany, which has been a problem to me ever since the first World War. My statements have evidently led to all manner of misunderstandings, which are chiefly due, no doubt, to the fact that my psychological point of view strikes many people as new and therefore strange. Instead of embarking upon lengthy arguments in an attempt to clear up these misunderstandings, I have found it simpler to collect all the passages in my other writings which deal with the same theme and to put them in an epilogue.[2] The reader will thus be in a position to get a clear picture of the facts for himself.

[2] [Infra, pars. 458ff.]

WOTAN [1]

En Germanie naistront diverses sectes,
S'approchans fort de l'heureux paganisme:
Le cœur captif et petites receptes
Feront retour à payer la vraye disme.
—*Prophéties de Maistre Michel Nostradamus,* 1555

371   When we look back to the time before 1914, we find ourselves living in a world of events which would have been inconceivable before the war. We were even beginning to regard war
between civilized nations as a fable, thinking that such an absurdity would become less and less possible in our rational, inter-
nationally organized world. And what came after the war was a
veritable witches' sabbath. Everywhere fantastic revolutions, violent alterations of the map, reversions in politics to medieval or
even antique prototypes, totalitarian states that engulf their
neighbours and outdo all previous theocracies in their absolutist
claims, persecutions of Christians and Jews, wholesale political
murder, and finally we have witnessed a light-hearted piratical
raid on a peaceful, half-civilized people.[2]

372   With such goings on in the wide world it is not in the least

---

1 [First published as "Wotan," *Neue Schweizer Rundschau* (Zurich), n.s., III
(March, 1936), 657–69. Republished in *Aufsätze zur Zeitgeschichte* (Zurich, 1946),
1–23. Trans. by Barbara Hannah in *Essays on Contemporary Events* (London,
1947), 1–16; this version has been consulted. The author added footnotes 3, 4, 15,
and 16 (first par.) to the London edn. Motto, trans. by H. C. Roberts:

    "In Germany shall divers sects arise,
    Coming very near to happy paganism.
    The heart captivated and small receivings
    Shall open the gate to pay the true tithe."
                         —EDITORS.]

2 Abyssinia.

surprising that there should be equally curious manifestations on a smaller scale in other spheres. In the realm of philosophy we shall have to wait some time before anyone is able to assess the kind of age we are living in. But in the sphere of religion we can see at once that some very significant things have been happening. We need feel no surprise that in Russia the colourful splendours of the Eastern Orthodox Church have been superseded by the Movement of the Godless—indeed, one breathed a sigh of relief oneself when one emerged from the haze of an Orthodox church with its multitude of lamps and entered an honest mosque, where the sublime and invisible omnipresence of God was not crowded out by a superfluity of sacred paraphernalia. Tasteless and pitiably unintelligent as it is, and however deplorable the low spiritual level of the "scientific" reaction, it was inevitable that nineteenth-century "scientific" enlightenment should one day dawn in Russia.

373   But what is more than curious—indeed, piquant to a degree—is that an ancient god of storm and frenzy, the long quiescent Wotan, should awake, like an extinct volcano, to new activity, in a civilized country that had long been supposed to have outgrown the Middle Ages. We have seen him come to life in the German Youth Movement, and right at the beginning the blood of several sheep was shed in honour of his resurrection. Armed with rucksack and lute, blond youths, and sometimes girls as well, were to be seen as restless wanderers on every road from the North Cape to Sicily, faithful votaries of the roving god. Later, towards the end of the Weimar Republic, the wandering role was taken over by the thousands of unemployed, who were to be met with everywhere on their aimless journeys. By 1933 they wandered no longer, but marched in their hundreds of thousands. The Hitler movement literally brought the whole of Germany to its feet, from five-year-olds to veterans, and produced the spectacle of a nation migrating from one place to another. Wotan the wanderer was on the move. He could be seen, looking rather shamefaced, in the meeting-house of a sect of simple folk in North Germany, disguised as Christ sitting on a white horse. I do not know if these people were aware of Wotan's ancient connection with the figures of Christ and Dionysus, but it is not very probable.

374   Wotan is a restless wanderer who creates unrest and stirs up

strife, now here, now there, and works magic. He was soon changed by Christianity into the devil, and only lived on in fading local traditions as a ghostly hunter who was seen with his retinue, flickering like a will o' the wisp through the stormy night. In the Middle Ages the role of the restless wanderer was taken over by Ahasuerus, the Wandering Jew, which is not a Jewish but a Christian legend. The motif of the wanderer who has not accepted Christ was projected on the Jews, in the same way as we always rediscover our unconscious psychic contents in other people. At any rate the coincidence of anti-Semitism with the reawakening of Wotan is a psychological subtlety that may perhaps be worth mentioning.

375   The German youths who celebrated the solstice with sheep-sacrifices were not the first to hear a rustling in the primeval forest of the unconscious. They were anticipated by Nietzsche, Schuler, Stefan George, and Ludwig Klages.[3] The literary tradition of the Rhineland and the country south of the Main has a classical stamp that cannot easily be got rid of; every interpretation of intoxication and exuberance is apt to be taken back to classical models, to Dionysus, to the *puer aeternus* and the cosmogonic Eros.[4] No doubt it sounds better to academic ears to interpret these things as Dionysus, but Wotan might be a more

---

[3] Ever since Nietzsche (1844–1900) there has been consistent emphasis on the "Dionysian" aspect of life in contrast to its "Apollonian" opposite. Since "The Birth of Tragedy" (1872), the dark, earthy, feminine side, with its mantic and orgiastic characteristics, has possessed the imagination of philosophers and poets. Irrationality gradually came to be regarded as the ideal; this is found, for example, all through the research of Alfred Schuler (d. 1923) into the mystery religions, and particularly in the writings of Klages (b. 1872 [d. 1956]), who expounded the philosophy of "irrationalism." To Klages, logos and consciousness are the destroyers of creative preconscious life. In these writers we witness the origin of a gradual rejection of reality and a negation of life as it is. This leads in the end to a cult of ecstasy, culminating in the self-dissolution of consciousness in death, which meant, to them, the conquest of material limitations.

The poetry of Stefan George (1868–1933) combines elements of classical civilization, medieval Christianity, and oriental mysticism. George deliberately attacked nineteenth- and twentieth-century rationalism. His aristocratic message of mystical beauty and of an esoteric conception of history had a deep influence on German youth. His work has been exploited by unscrupulous politicians for propaganda purposes.

[4] *Vom kosmogonischen Eros* is the title of one of Klages' main works (first pub. 1922).

correct interpretation. He is the god of storm and frenzy, the unleasher of passions and the lust of battle; moreover he is a superlative magician and artist in illusion who is versed in all secrets of an occult nature.

376 Nietzsche's case is certainly a peculiar one. He had no knowledge of Germanic literature; he discovered the "cultural Philistine"; and the announcement that "God is dead" led to Zarathustra's meeting with an unknown god in unexpected form, who approached him sometimes as an enemy and sometimes disguised as Zarathustra himself. Zarathustra, too, was a soothsayer, a magician, and the storm-wind:

And like a wind shall I come to blow among them, and with my spirit shall take away the breath of their spirit; thus my future wills it.
Truly, a strong wind is Zarathustra to all that are low; and this counsel gives he to his enemies and to all that spit and spew:
"Beware of spitting against the wind." [5]

377 And when Zarathustra dreamed that he was guardian of the graves in the "lone mountain fortress of death," and was making a mighty effort to open the gates, suddenly

A roaring wind tore the gates asunder; whistling, shrieking, and keening, it cast a black coffin before me.
And amid the roaring and whistling and shrieking the coffin burst open and spouted a thousand peals of laughter.

378 The disciple who interpreted the dream said to Zarathustra:

Are you not yourself the wind with shrill whistling, which bursts open the gates of the fortress of death?
Are you not yourself the coffin filled with life's gay malice and angel-grimaces? [6]

379 In 1863 or 1864, in his poem "To the Unknown God," Nietzsche had written:

I shall and will know thee, Unknown One,
Who searchest out the depths of my soul,
And blowest through my life like a storm,
Ungraspable, and yet my kinsman!
I shall and will know thee, and serve thee.

[5] *Thus Spake Zarathustra*, trans. by Kaufmann, p. 211 (mod.).
[6] Ibid., p. 247 (mod.).

380 Twenty years later, in his "Mistral Song," he wrote:

> Mistral wind, chaser of clouds,
> Killer of gloom, sweeper of the skies,
> Raging storm-wind, how I love thee!
> Are we not both the first-fruits
> Of the same womb, forever predestined
> To the same fate? [7]

381 In the dithyramb known as "Ariadne's Lament," Nietzsche is completely the victim of the hunter-god:

> Stretched out, shuddering,
> Like a half-dead thing whose feet are warmed,
> Shaken by unknown fevers,
> Shivering with piercing icy frost arrows,
> Hunted by thee, O thought,
> Unutterable! Veiled! horrible one!
> Thou huntsman behind the clouds.
> Struck down by thy lightning bolt,
> Thou mocking eye that stares at me from the dark!
> Thus I lie,
> Writhing, twisting, tormented
> With all eternal tortures,
> Smitten
> By thee, cruel huntsman,
> Thou unknown—God! [8]

382 This remarkable image of the hunter-god is not a mere dithyrambic figure of speech but is based on an experience which Nietzsche had when he was fifteen years old, at Pforta. It is described in a book by Nietzsche's sister, Elizabeth Foerster-Nietzsche.[9] As he was wandering about in a gloomy wood at night, he was terrified by a "blood-curdling shriek from a neighbouring lunatic asylum," and soon afterwards he came face to face with a huntsman whose "features were wild and uncanny." Setting his whistle to his lips "in a valley surrounded by wild scrub," the huntsman "blew such a shrill blast" that Nietzsche lost consciousness—but woke up again in Pforta. It was a nightmare. It is significant that in his dream Nietzsche, who in reality

---

[7] *Werke*, V, pp. 457f. and 495; trans. by R.F.C.H.
[8] *Thus Spake Zarathustra*, Kaufmann trans., p. 365.
[9] *Der werdende Nietzsche*, pp. 84ff.

intended to go to Eisleben, Luther's town, discussed with the huntsman the question of going instead to "Teutschenthal" (Valley of the Germans). No one with ears to hear can misunderstand the shrill whistling of the storm-god in the nocturnal wood.

383   Was it really only the classical philologist in Nietzsche that led to the god being called Dionysus instead of Wotan—or was it perhaps due to his fateful meeting with Wagner?

384   In his *Reich ohne Raum,* which was first published in 1919, Bruno Goetz saw the secret of coming events in Germany in the form of a very strange vision. I have never forgotten this little book, for it struck me at the time as a forecast of the German weather. It anticipates the conflict between the realm of ideas and life, between Wotan's dual nature as a god of storm and a god of secret musings. Wotan disappeared when his oaks fell and appeared again when the Christian God proved too weak to save Christendom from fratricidal slaughter. When the Holy Father at Rome could only impotently lament before God the fate of the *grex segregatus,* the one-eyed old hunter, on the edge of the German forest, laughed and saddled Sleipnir.

385   We are always convinced that the modern world is a reasonable world, basing our opinion on economic, political, and psychological factors. But if we may forget for a moment that we are living in the year of Our Lord 1936, and, laying aside our well-meaning, all-too-human reasonableness, may burden God or the gods with the responsibility for contemporary events instead of man, we would find Wotan quite suitable as a causal hypothesis. In fact I venture the heretical suggestion that the unfathomable depths of Wotan's character explain more of National Socialism than all three reasonable factors put together. There is no doubt that each of these factors explains an important aspect of what is going on in Germany, but Wotan explains yet more. He is particularly enlightening in regard to a general phenomenon which is so strange to anybody not a German that it remains incomprehensible even after the deepest reflection.

386   Perhaps we may sum up this general phenomenon as *Ergriffenheit*—a state of being seized or possessed. The term postulates not only an *Ergriffener* (one who is seized) but also an *Ergreifer* (one who seizes). Wotan is an *Ergreifer* of men, and, unless one

wishes to deify Hitler—which has indeed actually happened—he is really the only explanation. It is true that Wotan shares this quality with his cousin Dionysus, but Dionysus seems to have exercised his influence mainly on women. The maenads were a species of female storm-troopers, and, according to mythical reports, were dangerous enough. Wotan confined himself to the berserkers, who found their vocation as the Blackshirts of mythical kings.

387 A mind that is still childish thinks of the gods as metaphysical entities existing in their own right, or else regards them as playful or superstitious inventions. From either point of view the parallel between Wotan *redivivus* and the social, political, and psychic storm that is shaking Germany might have at least the value of a parable. But since the gods are without doubt personifications of psychic forces, to assert their metaphysical existence is as much an intellectual presumption as the opinion that they could ever be invented. Not that "psychic forces" have anything to do with the conscious mind, fond as we are of playing with the idea that consciousness and psyche are identical. This is only another piece of intellectual presumption. "Psychic forces" have far more to do with the realm of the unconscious. Our mania for rational explanations obviously has its roots in our fear of metaphysics, for the two were always hostile brothers. Hence anything unexpected that approaches us from that dark realm is regarded either as coming from outside and therefore as real, or else as an hallucination and therefore not true. The idea that anything could be real or true which does *not* come from outside has hardly begun to dawn on contemporary man.

388 For the sake of better understanding and to avoid prejudice, we could of course dispense with the name "Wotan" and speak instead of the *furor teutonicus*. But we should only be saying the same thing and not as well, for the *furor* in this case is a mere psychologizing of Wotan and tells us no more than that the Germans are in a state of "fury." We thus lose sight of the most peculiar feature of this whole phenomenon, namely, the dramatic aspect of the *Ergreifer* and the *Ergriffener*. The impressive thing about the German phenomenon is that one man, who is obviously "possessed," has infected a whole nation to such an extent that everything is set in motion and has started rolling on its course towards perdition.

389   It seems to me that Wotan hits the mark as an hypothesis. Apparently he really was only asleep in the Kyffhäuser mountain until the ravens called him and announced the break of day. He is a fundamental attribute of the German psyche, an irrational psychic factor which acts on the high pressure of civilization like a cyclone and blows it away. Despite their crankiness, the Wotan-worshippers seem to have judged things more correctly than the worshippers of reason. Apparently everyone had forgotten that Wotan is a Germanic datum of first importance, the truest expression and unsurpassed personification of a fundamental quality that is particularly characteristic of the Germans. Houston Stewart Chamberlain is a symptom which arouses suspicion that other veiled gods may be sleeping elsewhere. The emphasis on the Germanic race (vulgarly called "Aryan"), the Germanic heritage, blood and soil, the Wagalaweia songs,[10] the ride of the Valkyries, Jesus as a blond and blue-eyed hero, the Greek mother of St. Paul, the devil as an international Alberich in Jewish or Masonic guise, the Nordic aurora borealis as the light of civilization, the inferior Mediterranean races—all this is the indispensable scenery for the drama that is taking place and at bottom they all mean the same thing: a god has taken possession of the Germans and their house is filled with a "mighty rushing wind." It was soon after Hitler seized power, if I am not mistaken, that a cartoon appeared in *Punch* of a raving berserker tearing himself free from his bonds. A hurricane has broken loose in Germany while we still believe it is fine weather.

390   Things are comparatively quiet in Switzerland, though occasionally there is a puff of wind from the north or south. Sometimes it has a slightly ominous sound, sometimes it whispers so harmlessly or even idealistically that no one is alarmed. "Let sleeping dogs lie"—we manage to get along pretty well with this proverbial wisdom. It is sometimes said that the Swiss are singularly averse to making a problem of themselves. I must rebut this accusation: the Swiss do have their problems but they would not admit it for anything in the world, even though they see which way the wind is blowing. We thus pay our tribute to the time

10 [After the meaningless refrains sung by the Rhine maidens in Wagner's *Ring* cycle: "*Weia! Waga! Wagala weia!*," etc.—EDITORS.]

of storm and stress in Germany, but we never mention it, and this enables us to feel vastly superior.

391   It is above all the Germans who have an opportunity, perhaps unique in history, to look into their own hearts and to learn what those perils of the soul were from which Christianity tried to rescue mankind. Germany is a land of spiritual catastrophes, where nature never makes more than a pretence of peace with world-ruling reason. The disturber of the peace is a wind that blows into Europe from Asia's vastness, sweeping in on a wide front from Thrace to the Baltic, scattering the nations before it like dry leaves, or inspiring thoughts that shake the world to its foundations. It is an elemental Dionysus breaking into the Apollonian order. The rouser of this tempest is named Wotan, and we can learn a good deal about him from the political confusion and spiritual upheaval he has caused throughout history. For a more exact investigation of his character, however, we must go back to the age of myths, which did not explain everything in terms of man and his limited capacities but sought the deeper cause in the psyche and its autonomous powers. Man's earliest intuitions personified these powers as gods, and described them in the myths with great care and circumstantiality according to their various characters. This could be done the more readily on account of the firmly established primordial types or images which are innate in the unconscious of many races and exercise a direct influence upon them. Because the behaviour of a race takes on its specific character from its underlying images we can speak of an archetype "Wotan." [11] As an autonomous psychic factor, Wotan produces effects in the collective life of a people and thereby reveals his own nature. For Wotan has a peculiar biology of his own, quite apart from the nature of man. It is only from time to time that individuals fall under the irresistible influence of this unconscious factor. When it is quiescent, one is no more aware of the archetype Wotan than of a latent epilepsy. Could the Germans who were adults in 1914 have foreseen what they would be today? Such amazing transformations are the effect of the god of wind, that "bloweth where it listeth, and thou hearest the sound thereof, but canst

11 One should read what Bruno Goetz (*Deutsche Dichtung*, pp. 36ff. and 72ff.) has to say about Odin as the German wanderer-god. Unfortunately I only read this book after I had finished my article.

not tell whence it cometh, nor whither it goeth." It seizes everything in its path and overthrows everything that is not firmly rooted. When the wind blows it shakes everything that is insecure, whether without or within.

392   Martin Ninck has recently published a monograph [12] which is a most welcome addition to our knowledge of Wotan's nature. The reader need not fear that this book is nothing but a scientific study written with academic aloofness from the subject. Certainly the right to scientific objectivity is fully preserved, and the material has been collected with extraordinary thoroughness and presented in unusually clear form. But over and above all this one feels that the author is vitally interested in it, that the chord of Wotan is vibrating in him too. This is no criticism—on the contrary it is one of the chief merits of the book, which without this enthusiasm might easily have degenerated into a tedious catalogue.

393   Ninck sketches a really magnificent portrait of the German archetype Wotan. He describes him in ten chapters, using all the available sources, as the berserker, the god of storm, the wanderer, the warrior, the *Wunsch-* and *Minne*-god, the lord of the dead and of the *Einherier*,[13] the master of secret knowledge, the magician, and the god of the poets. Neither the Valkyries nor the *Fylgja* [14] are forgotten, for they form part of the mythological background and fateful significance of Wotan. Ninck's inquiry into the name and its origin is particularly instructive. He shows that Wotan is not only a god of rage and frenzy who embodies the instinctual and emotional aspect of the unconscious. Its intuitive and inspiring side also manifests itself in him, for he understands the runes and can interpret fate.

394   The Romans identified Wotan with Mercury, but his character does not really correspond to any Roman or Greek god, although there are certain resemblances. He is a wanderer like Mercury, for instance, rules over the dead like Pluto and Kronos, and is connected with Dionysus by his emotional frenzy, particularly in its mantic aspect. It is surprising that Ninck does not mention Hermes, the god of revelation, who as *pneuma* and

12 *Wodan und germanischer Schicksalsglaube.*
13 [*Wunsch,* magical wish; *Minne,* remembrance, love; *Einherier,* the dead heroes in Valhalla (*Meyers Konversations-Lexikon*).—EDITORS.]
14 [*Fylgja,* attendant spirit in the form of an animal (Hastings, *Encyclopedia*).]

nous is associated with the wind. He would be the connecting-link with the Christian pneuma and the miracle of Pentecost. As Poimandres (the shepherd of men) Hermes is an *Ergreifer* like Wotan. Ninck rightly points out that Dionysus and the other Greek gods always remained under the supreme authority of Zeus, which indicates a fundamental difference between the Greek and the Germanic temperament. Ninck assumes an inner affinity between Wotan and Kronos, and the latter's defeat may perhaps be a sign that the Wotan-archetype was once overcome and split up in prehistoric times. At all events, the Germanic god represents a totality on a very primitive level, a psychological condition in which man's will was almost identical with the god's and entirely at his mercy. But the Greeks had gods who helped man against other gods; indeed, All-Father Zeus himself is not far from the ideal of a benevolent, enlightened despot.

395   It was not in Wotan's nature to linger on and show signs of old age. He simply disappeared when the times turned against him, and remained invisible for more than a thousand years, working anonymously and indirectly. Archetypes are like river-beds which dry up when the water deserts them, but which it can find again at any time. An archetype is like an old water-course along which the water of life has flowed for centuries, digging a deep channel for itself. The longer it has flowed in this channel the more likely it is that sooner or later the water will return to its old bed. The life of the individual as a member of society and particularly as part of the State may be regulated like a canal, but the life of nations is a great rushing river which is utterly beyond human control, in the hands of One who has always been stronger than men. The League of Nations, which was supposed to possess supranational authority, is regarded by some as a child in need of care and protection, by others as an abortion. Thus the life of nations rolls on unchecked, without guidance, unconscious of where it is going, like a rock crashing down the side of a hill, until it is stopped by an obstacle stronger than itself. Political events move from one impasse to the next, like a torrent caught in gullies, creeks, and marshes. All human control comes to an end when the individual is caught in a mass movement. Then the archetypes begin to function, as happens also in the lives of individuals when they are confronted with situations that cannot be dealt with in any of the familiar ways.

But what a so-called Führer does with a mass movement can plainly be seen if we turn our eyes to the north or south of our country.

396   The ruling archetype does not remain the same for ever, as is evident from the temporal limitations that have been set to the hoped-for reign of peace, the "thousand-year Reich." The Mediterranean father-archetype of the just, order-loving, benevolent ruler has been shattered over the whole of northern Europe, as the present fate of the Christian Churches bears witness. Fascism in Italy and the civil war in Spain show that in the south as well the cataclysm has been far greater than one expected. Even the Catholic Church can no longer afford trials of strength.

397   The nationalist God has attacked Christianity on a broad front. In Russia he is called technology and science, in Italy, Duce, and in Germany, "German Faith," "German Christianity," or the State. The "German Christians" [15] are a contradiction in terms and would do better to join Hauer's "German Faith Movement." [16] These are decent and well-meaning people

[15] A National Socialist movement inside the Protestant Church, which tried to eliminate all vestiges of the Old Testament from Christianity.

[16] Wilhelm Hauer (b. 1881), first a missionary and later professor of Sanskrit at the University of Tübingen, was the founder and leader of the "German Faith Movement." It tried to establish a "German Faith" founded on German and Nordic writings and traditions, e.g., those of Eckhart and Goethe. This movement sought to combine a number of different and often incompatible trends: some of its members accepted an expurgated form of Christianity, others were opposed not only to Christianity in any form but to every kind of religion or god. One of the common articles of faith, which the movement adopted in 1934, was: "The German Faith Movement aims at the religious renaissance of the nation out of the hereditary foundations of the German race."

The spirit of this movement may be contrasted with a sermon preached by Dr. Langmann, an evangelical clergyman and high dignitary of the Church, at the funeral of the late Gustloff. Dr. Langmann gave the address "in S.A. uniform and jackboots." He sped the deceased on his journey to Hades, and directed him to Valhalla, to the home of Siegfried and Baldur, the heroes who "nourish the life of the German people by the sacrifice of their blood"—like Christ among others. "May this god send the nations of the earth *clanking on their way* through history." "Lord bless our struggle. Amen." Thus the reverend gentleman ended his address, according to the *Neue Zürcher Zeitung* (1936, no. 249). As a service held to Wotan it is no doubt very edifying—and remarkably tolerant towards believers in Christ! Are our Churches inclined to be equally tolerant and to preach that Christ shed his blood for the salvation of mankind, like Siegfried, Baldur, and Odin among others?! One can ask unexpectedly grotesque questions these days.

who honestly admit their *Ergriffenheit* and try to come to terms with this new and undeniable fact. They go to an enormous amount of trouble to make it look less alarming by dressing it up in a conciliatory historical garb and giving us consoling glimpses of great figures such as Meister Eckhart, who was also a German and also *ergriffen*. In this way the awkward question of who the *Ergreifer* is is circumvented. He was always "God." But the more Hauer restricts the world-wide sphere of Indo-European culture to the "Nordic" in general and to the *Edda* in particular, and the more "German" this faith becomes as a manifestation of *Ergriffenheit*, the more painfully evident it is that the "German" god is the god of the Germans.

398   One cannot read Hauer's book [17] without emotion, if one regards it as the tragic and really heroic effort of a conscientious scholar who, without knowing how it happened to him, was violently summoned by the inaudible voice of the *Ergreifer* and is now trying with all his might, and with all his knowledge and ability, to build a bridge between the dark forces of life and the shining world of historical ideas. But what do all the beauties of the past from totally different levels of culture mean to the man of today, when confronted with a living and unfathomable tribal god such as he has never experienced before? They are sucked like dry leaves into the roaring whirlwind, and the rhythmic alliterations of the *Edda* become inextricably mixed up with Christian mystical texts, German poetry, and the wisdom of the *Upanishads*. Hauer himself is *ergriffen* by the depths of meaning in the primal words lying at the root of the Germanic languages, to an extent that he certainly never knew before. Hauer the Indologist is not to blame for this, nor yet the *Edda;* it is rather the fault of *kairos*—the present moment in time—whose name on closer investigation turns out to be Wotan. I would therefore advise the German Faith Movement to throw aside their scruples. Intelligent people will not confuse them with the crude Wotan-worshippers whose faith is a mere pretence. There are people in the German Faith Movement who are intelligent enough not only to *believe* but to *know* that the god of the *Germans* is Wotan and not the Christian God. This is a tragic experience and no disgrace. It has always been terrible to fall

[17] *Deutsche Gottschau: Grundzüge eines deutschen Glaubens* [German Vision of God: Basic Elements of a German Faith].

into the hands of a living god. Yahweh was no exception to this rule, and the Philistines, Edomites, Amorites, and the rest, who were outside the Yahweh experience, must certainly have found it exceedingly disagreeable. The Semitic [18] experience of Allah was for a long time an extremely painful affair for the whole of Christendom. We who stand outside judge the Germans far too much as if they were responsible agents, but perhaps it would be nearer the truth to regard them also as *victims*.

399   If we apply our admittedly peculiar point of view consistently, we are driven to conclude that Wotan must, in time, reveal not only the restless, violent, stormy side of his character, but also his ecstatic and mantic qualities—a very different aspect of his nature. If this conclusion is correct, National Socialism would not be the last word. Things must be concealed in the background which we cannot imagine at present, but we may expect them to appear in the course of the next few years or decades. Wotan's reawakening is a stepping back into the past; the stream was dammed up and has broken into its old channel. But the obstruction will not last for ever; it is rather a *reculer pour mieux sauter,* and the water will overleap the obstacle. Then at last we shall know what Wotan is saying when he "murmurs with Mimir's head."

> Fast move the sons   of Mim, and fate
> Is heard in the note   of the Gjallarhorn;
> Loud blows Heimdall,   the horn is aloft,
> In fear quake all   who on Hel-roads are.
>
> Yggdrasil shakes   and shivers on high
> The ancient limbs,   and the giant is loose;
> Wotan murmurs   with Mimir's head
> But the kinsman of Surt   shall slay him soon.
>
> How fare the gods?   how fare the elves?
> All Jotunheim groans,   the gods are at council;
> Loud roar the dwarfs   by the doors of stone,
> The masters of the rocks: would you know yet more?

18 [Using the word to connote those peoples within the Semitic language-group. —Trans.]

Now Garm howls loud   before Gnipahellir;
The fetters will burst,   and the wolf run free;
Much do I know,   and more can see
Of the fate of the gods,   the mighty in fight.

From the east comes Hrym   with shield held high;
In giant-wrath   does the serpent writhe;
O'er the waves he twists,   and the tawny eagle
Gnaws corpses screaming;   Naglfar is loose.

O'er the sea from the north   there sails a ship
With the people of Hel,   at the helm stands Loki;
After the wolf   do wild men follow,
And with them the brother   of Byleist goes.[19]

[19] *Voluspo* (*The Poetic Edda,* trans. by Bellows, pp. 20f.; line 7 mod.).

AFTER THE CATASTROPHE [1]

400   This is the first time since 1936 that the fate of Germany again drives me to take up my pen. The quotation from the *Voluspo* with which I ended the article [2] I wrote at that time, about Wotan "murmuring with Mimir's head," pointed prophetically to the nature of the coming apocalyptic events. The myth has been fulfilled, and the greater part of Europe lies in ruins.

401   Before the work of reconstruction can begin, there is a good deal of clearing up to be done, and this calls above all for *reflection*. Questions are being asked on all sides about the meaning of the whole tragedy. People have even turned to me for an explanation, and I have had to answer them there and then to the best of my ability. But as the spoken word very quickly gives rise to legends, I have decided—not without considerable hesitations and misgivings—to set down my views once again in the form of an article. I am only too well aware that "Germany" presents an immense problem, and that the subjective views of a medical psychologist can touch on only a few aspects of this gigantic tangle of questions. I must be content with a modest contribution to the work of clearing up, without even attempting to look as far ahead as reconstruction.

402   While I was working on this article I noticed how churned up one still is in one's own psyche, and how difficult it is to reach anything approaching a moderate and relatively calm point of view in the midst of one's emotions. No doubt we should be cold-blooded and superior; but we are, on the whole,

---

1 [First published as "Nach der Katastrophe," *Neue Schweizer Rundschau* (Zurich), n.s., XIII (1945), 67–88; reprinted in *Aufsätze zur Zeitgeschichte* (Zurich, 1946), pp. 73–116. Previously trans. by Elizabeth Welsh in *Essays on Contemporary Events* (London, 1947), pp. 45–72.—EDITORS.]

2 [See previous paper.]

much more deeply involved in the recent events in Germany than we like to admit. Nor can we feel compassion, for the heart harbours feelings of a very different nature, and these would like to have the first say. Neither the doctor nor the psychologist can afford to be *only* cold-blooded—quite apart from the fact that they would find it impossible. Their relationship to the world involves them and all their affects, otherwise their relationship would be incomplete. That being so, I found myself faced with the task of steering my ship between Scylla and Charybdis, and —as is usual on such a voyage—stopping my ears to one side of my being and lashing the other to the mast. I must confess that no article has ever given me so much trouble, from a moral as well as a human point of view. I had not realized how much I myself was affected. There are others, I am sure, who will share this feeling with me. This inner identity or *participation mystique* with events in Germany has caused me to experience afresh how painfully wide is the scope of the psychological concept of *collective guilt*. So when I approach this problem it is certainly not with any feelings of cold-blooded superiority, but rather with an avowed sense of inferiority.

403   The psychological use of the word "guilt" should not be confused with guilt in the legal or moral sense. Psychologically, it connotes the irrational presence of a subjective feeling (or conviction) of guilt, or an objective imputation of, or imputed share in, guilt. As an example of the latter, suppose a man belongs to a family which has the misfortune to be disgraced because one of its members has committed a crime. It is clear that he cannot be held responsible, either legally or morally. Yet the atmosphere of guilt makes itself felt in many ways. His family name appears to have been sullied, and it gives him a painful shock to hear it bandied about in the mouths of strangers. Guilt can be restricted to the lawbreaker only from the legal, moral, and intellectual point of view, but as a psychic phenomenon it spreads itself over the whole neighbourhood. A house, a family, even a village where a murder has been committed feels the psychological guilt and is made to feel it by the outside world. Would one take a room where one knows a man was murdered a few days before? Is it particularly pleasant to marry the sister or daughter of a criminal? What father is not deeply wounded if his son is sent to prison, and does he not feel injured in his

family pride if a cousin of the same name brings dishonour on his house? Would not every decent Swiss feel ashamed—to put it mildly—if our Government had erected a human slaughter-house like Maidenek in our country? Would we then be surprised if, travelling abroad with our Swiss passports, we heard such remarks at the frontier as "Ces cochons de Suisses!"? Indeed, are we not all a little ashamed—precisely because we are patriots—that Switzerland should have bred so many traitors?

404   Living as we do in the middle of Europe, we Swiss feel comfortably far removed from the foul vapours that arise from the morass of German guilt. But all this changes the moment we set foot, as Europeans, on another continent or come into contact with an Oriental people. What are we to say to an Indian who asks us: "You are anxious to bring us your Christian culture, are you not? May I ask if Auschwitz and Buchenwald are examples of European civilization?" Would it help matters if we hastened to assure him that these things did not take place where we live, but several hundred miles further east—not in our country at all but in a neighbouring one? How would we react if an Indian pointed out indignantly that India's black spot lay not in Travancore but in Hyderabad? Undoubtedly we'd say, "Oh well, India is India!" Similarly, the view all over the East is, "Oh well, Europe is Europe!" The moment we so-called innocent Europeans cross the frontiers of our own continent we are made to feel something of the collective guilt that weighs upon it, despite our good conscience. (One might also ask: Is Russia so primitive that she can still feel our "guilt-by-contagion"—as collective guilt might also be called—and for that reason accuses us of Fascism?) The world sees Europe as the continent on whose soil the shameful concentration camps grew, just as Europe singles out Germany as the land and the people that are enveloped in a cloud of guilt; for the horror happened in Germany and its perpetrators were Germans. No German can deny this, any more than a European or a Christian can deny that the most monstrous crime of all ages was committed in his house. The Christian Church should put ashes on her head and rend her garments on account of the guilt of her children. The shadow of their guilt has fallen on her as much as upon Europe, the mother of monsters. Europe must account for herself before the world, just as Germany must before Europe. The European

can no more convince the Indian that Germany is no concern of his, or that he knows nothing at all about that country, than the German can rid himself of his collective guilt by protesting that he did not know. In that way he merely compounds his collective guilt by the sin of unconsciousness.

405   Psychological collective guilt is a *tragic fate*. It hits everybody, just and unjust alike, everybody who was anywhere near the place where the terrible thing happened. Naturally no reasonable and conscientious person will lightly turn collective into individual guilt by holding the individual responsible without giving him a hearing. He will know enough to distinguish between the individually guilty and the merely collectively guilty. But how many people are either reasonable or conscientious, and how many take the trouble to become so? I am not very optimistic in this respect. Therefore, although collective guilt, viewed on the archaic and primitive level, is a state of *magical uncleanness*, yet precisely because of the general unreasonableness it is a very real fact, which no European outside Europe and no German outside Germany can leave out of account. If the German intends to live on good terms with Europe, he must be conscious that in the eyes of Europeans he is a guilty man. As a German, he has betrayed European civilization and all its values; he has brought shame and disgrace on his European family, so that one must blush to hear oneself called a European; he has fallen on his European brethren like a beast of prey, and tortured and murdered them. The German can hardly expect other Europeans to resort to such niceties as to inquire at every step whether the criminal's name was Müller or Meier. Neither will he be deemed worthy of being treated as a gentleman until the contrary has been proved. Unfortunately, for twelve long years it has been demonstrated with the utmost clarity that the official German was no gentleman.

406   If a German is prepared to acknowledge his moral inferiority as collective guilt before the whole world, without attempting to minimize it or explain it away with flimsy arguments, then he will stand a reasonable chance, after a time, of being taken for a more or less decent man, and will thus be absolved of his collective guilt at any rate in the eyes of individuals.

407   It may be objected that the whole concept of psychological collective guilt is a prejudice and a sweepingly unfair condemna-

tion. Of course it is, but that is precisely what constitutes the irrational nature of collective guilt: it cares nothing for the just and the unjust, it is the dark cloud that rises up from the scene of an unexpiated crime. It is a psychic phenomenon, and it is therefore no condemnation of the German people to say that they are collectively guilty, but simply a statement of fact. Yet if we penetrate more deeply into the psychology of this phenomenon, we shall soon discover that the problem of collective guilt has another and more questionable aspect than that merely of a collective judgment.

408   Since no man lives within his own psychic sphere like a snail in its shell, separated from everybody else, but is connected with his fellow-men by his unconscious humanity, no crime can ever be what it appears to our consciousness to be: an isolated psychic happening. In reality, it always happens over a wide radius. The sensation aroused by a crime, the passionate interest in tracking down the criminal, the eagerness with which the court proceedings are followed, and so on, all go to prove the exciting effect which the crime has on everybody who is not abnormally dull or apathetic. Everybody joins in, feels the crime in his own being, tries to understand and explain it. Something is set aflame by that great fire of evil that flared up in the crime. Was not Plato aware that the sight of ugliness produces something ugly in the soul? Indignation leaps up, angry cries of "Justice!" pursue the murderer, and they are louder, more impassioned, and more charged with hate the more fiercely burns the fire of evil that has been lit in our souls. It is a fact that cannot be denied: the wickedness of others becomes our own wickedness because it kindles something evil in our own hearts. The murder has been suffered by everyone, and everyone has committed it; lured by the irresistible fascination of evil, we have all made this collective psychic murder possible; and the closer we were to it and the better we could see, the greater our guilt. In this way we are unavoidably drawn into the uncleanness of evil, no matter what our conscious attitude may be. No one can escape this, for we are all so much a part of the human community that every crime calls forth a secret satisfaction in some corner of the fickle human heart. It is true that, in persons with a strong moral disposition, this reaction may arouse contrary feelings in a neighbouring compartment of the

mind. But a strong moral disposition is a comparative rarity, so that when the crimes mount up, indignation may easily get pitched too high, and evil then becomes the order of the day. Everyone harbours his "statistical criminal" in himself, just as he has his own private madman or saint. Owing to this basic peculiarity in our human make-up, a corresponding suggestibility, or susceptibility to infection, exists everywhere. It is our age in particular—the last half century—that has prepared the way for crime. Has it never occurred to anybody, for instance, that the vogue for the thriller has a rather questionable side?

409 Long before 1933 there was a smell of burning in the air, and people were passionately interested in discovering the locus of the fire and in tracking down the incendiary. And when denser clouds of smoke were seen to gather over Germany, and the burning of the Reichstag gave the signal, then at last there was no mistake where the incendiary, evil in person, dwelt. Terrifying as this discovery was, in time it brought a sense of relief: now we knew for certain where all unrighteousness was to be found, whereas we ourselves were securely entrenched in the opposite camp, among respectable people whose moral indignation could be trusted to rise higher and higher with every fresh sign of guilt on the other side. Even the call for mass executions no longer offended the ears of the righteous, and the saturation bombing of German cities was looked upon as the judgment of God. Hate had found respectable motives and had ceased to be a personal idiosyncrasy, indulged in secret. And all the time the esteemed public had not the faintest idea how closely they themselves were living to evil.

410 One should not imagine for a moment that anybody could escape this play of opposites. Even a saint would have to pray unceasingly for the souls of Hitler and Himmler, the Gestapo and the S.S., in order to repair without delay the damage done to his own soul. The sight of evil kindles evil in the soul—there is no getting away from this fact. The victim is not the only sufferer; everybody in the vicinity of the crime, including the murderer, suffers with him. Something of the abysmal darkness of the world has broken in on us, poisoning the very air we breathe and befouling the pure water with the stale, nauseating taste of blood. True, we are innocent, we are the victims, robbed, betrayed, outraged; and yet for all that, or precisely because of

it, the flame of evil glowers in our moral indignation. It must be so, for it is necessary that someone should feel indignant, that someone should let himself be the sword of judgment wielded by fate. Evil calls for expiation, otherwise the wicked will destroy the world utterly, or the good suffocate in their rage which they cannot vent, and in either case no good will come of it.

411　　When evil breaks at any point into the order of things, our whole circle of psychic protection is disrupted. Action inevitably calls up reaction, and, in the matter of destructiveness, this turns out to be just as bad as the crime, and possibly even worse, because the evil must be exterminated root and branch. In order to escape the contaminating touch of evil we need a proper *rite de sortie*, a solemn admission of guilt by judge, hangman, and public, followed by an act of expiation.

412　　The terrible things that have happened in Germany, and the moral downfall of a "nation of eighty millions," are a blow aimed at all Europeans. (We used to be able to relegate such things to "Asia!") The fact that one member of the European family could sink to the level of the concentration camp throws a dubious light on all the others. Who are we to imagine that "it couldn't happen here"? We have only to multiply the population of Switzerland by twenty to become a nation of eighty millions, and our public intelligence and morality would then automatically be divided by twenty in consequence of the devastating moral and psychic effects of living together in huge masses. Such a state of things provides the basis for collective crime, and it is then really a miracle if the crime is not committed. Do we seriously believe that *we* would have been immune? We, who have so many traitors and political psychopaths in our midst? It has filled us with horror to realize all that man is capable of, and of which, therefore, we too are capable. Since then a terrible doubt about humanity, and about ourselves, gnaws at our hearts.

413　　Nevertheless, it should be clear to everyone that such a state of degradation can come about only under certain conditions. The most important of these is the accumulation of urban, industrialized masses—of people torn from the soil, engaged in one-sided employment, and lacking every healthy instinct, even that of self-preservation. Loss of the instinct of self-preservation can be measured in terms of dependence on the State, which is a bad symptom. Dependence on the State means that everybody relies on everybody else (= State) instead of on himself. Every man hangs on to the next and enjoys a false feeling of security, for one is still hanging in the air even when hanging in the company of ten thousand other people. The only difference is that one is no longer aware of one's own insecurity. The increasing dependence on the State is anything but a healthy symptom; it means that the whole nation is in a fair way to becoming a herd of sheep, constantly relying on a shepherd to drive them into good pastures. The shepherd's staff soon becomes a rod of iron, and the shepherds turn into wolves. What a distressing sight it was to see the whole of Germany heave a sigh of relief when a megalomaniac psychopath proclaimed, "I take over the responsibility!" Any man who still possesses the instinct of self-preservation knows perfectly well that only a swindler would offer to relieve him of responsibility, for surely no one in his senses would dream of taking responsibility for the existence of another. The man who promises everything is sure to fulfil nothing, and everyone who promises too much is in danger of using evil means in order to carry out his promises, and is already on the road to perdition. The steady growth of the Welfare State is no doubt a very fine thing from one point of view, but from another it is a doubtful blessing, as it robs people of their individual responsibility and turns them into infants and sheep. Besides this, there is the danger that the capable will simply be exploited by the irresponsible, as happened on a huge scale in Germany. The citizen's instinct of self-preservation should be safeguarded at all costs, for, once a man is cut off from the nourishing roots of instinct, he becomes the shuttlecock of every wind that blows. He is then no better than a sick animal, demoralized and degenerate, and nothing short of a catastrophe can bring him back to health.

414   I own that in saying all this I feel rather like the prophet who, according to Josephus, lifted up his voice in lamentation over the city as the Romans laid siege to Jerusalem. It proved not the slightest use to the city, and a stone missile from a Roman ballista put an end to the prophet.

415   With the best will in the world we cannot build a paradise on earth, and even if we could, in a very short time we would

have degenerated in every way. We would take delight in destroying our paradise, and then, just as foolishly, marvel at what we had done. Moreover, if we happened to be a "nation of eighty millions" we would be convinced that the "others" were to blame, and our self-confidence would be at such a low ebb that we would not even think of shouldering the responsibility or taking the blame for anything.

416   This is a pathological, demoralized, and mentally abnormal condition: one side of us does things which the other (so-called decent) side prefers to ignore. This side is in a perpetual state of defence against real and supposed accusations. In reality the chief accuser is not outside, but the judge who dwells in our own hearts. Since this is nature's attempt to bring about a cure, it would be wiser not to persist too long in rubbing the noses of the Germans in their own abominations, lest we drown the voice of the accuser in their hearts—and also in our own hearts and those of our Allies. If only people could realize what an enrichment it is to find one's own guilt, what a sense of honour and spiritual dignity! But nowhere does there seem to be a glimmering of this insight. Instead, we hear only of attempts to shift the blame on to others—"no one will admit to having been a Nazi." The Germans were never wholly indifferent to the impression they made on the outside world. They resented disapproval and hated even to be criticized. Inferiority feelings make people touchy and lead to compensatory efforts to impress. As a result, the German thrusts himself forward and seeks to curry favour, or "German efficiency" is demonstrated with such aplomb that it leads to a reign of terror and the shooting of hostages. The German no longer thinks of these things as murder, for he is lost in considerations of his own prestige. Inferiority feelings are usually a sign of inferior feeling—which is not just a play on words. All the intellectual and technological achievements in the world cannot make up for inferiority in the matter of feeling. The pseudo-scientific race-theories with which it was dolled up did not make the extermination of the Jews any more acceptable, and neither do falsifications of history make a wrong policy appear any more trustworthy.

417   This spectacle recalls the figure of what Nietzsche so aptly calls the "pale criminal," who in reality shows all the signs of hysteria. He simply will not and cannot admit that he is what

he is; he cannot endure his own guilt, just as he could not help incurring it. He will stoop to every kind of self-deception if only he can escape the sight of himself. It is true that this happens everywhere, but nowhere does it appear to be such a national characteristic as in Germany. I am by no means the first to have been struck by the inferiority feelings of the Germans. What did Goethe, Heine, and Nietzsche have to say about their countrymen? A feeling of inferiority does not in the least mean that it is unjustified. Only, the inferiority does not refer to that side of the personality, or to the function, in which it visibly appears, but to an inferiority which none the less really exists even though only dimly suspected. This condition can easily lead to an hysterical dissociation of the personality, which consists essentially in one hand not knowing what the other is doing, in wanting to jump over one's own shadow, and in looking for everything dark, inferior, and culpable *in others*. Hence the hysteric always complains of being surrounded by people who are incapable of appreciating him and who are activated only by bad motives; by inferior mischief-makers, a crowd of submen who should be exterminated neck and crop so that the Superman can live on his high level of perfection. The very fact that his thinking and feeling proceed along these lines is clear proof of inferiority in action. Therefore all hysterical people are compelled to torment others, because they are unwilling to hurt themselves by admitting their own inferiority. But since nobody can jump out of his skin and be rid of himself, they stand in their own way everywhere as their own evil spirit—and that is what we call an hysterical neurosis.

418   All these pathological features—complete lack of insight into one's own character, auto-erotic self-admiration and self-extenuation, denigration and terrorization of one's fellow men (how contemptuously Hitler spoke of his own people!), projection of the shadow, lying, falsification of reality, determination to impress by fair means or foul, bluffing and double-crossing—all these were united in the man who was diagnosed clinically as an hysteric, and whom a strange fate chose to be the political, moral, and religious spokesman of Germany for twelve years. Is this pure chance?

419   A more accurate diagnosis of Hitler's condition would be *pseudologia phantastica*, that form of hysteria which is character-

ized by a peculiar talent for believing one's own lies. For a short spell, such people usually meet with astounding success, and for that reason are socially dangerous. Nothing has such a convincing effect as a lie one invents and believes oneself, or an evil deed or intention whose righteousness one regards as self-evident. At any rate they carry far more conviction than the good man and the good deed, or even than the wicked man and his purely wicked deed. Hitler's theatrical, obviously hysterical gestures struck all foreigners (with a few amazing exceptions) as purely ridiculous. When I saw him with my own eyes, he suggested a psychic scarecrow (with a broomstick for an outstretched arm) rather than a human being. It is also difficult to understand how his ranting speeches, delivered in shrill, grating, womanish tones, could have made such an impression. But the German people would never have been taken in and carried away so completely if this figure had not been a reflected image of the collective German hysteria. It is not without serious misgivings that one ventures to pin the label of "psychopathic inferiority" on to a whole nation, and yet, heaven knows, it is the only explanation which could in any way account for the effect this scarecrow had on the masses. A sorry lack of education, conceit that bordered on madness, a very mediocre intelligence combined with the hysteric's cunning and the power fantasies of an adolescent, were written all over this demagogue's face. His gesticulations were all put on, devised by an hysterical mind intent only on making an impression. He behaved in public like a man living in his own biography, in this case as the sombre, daemonic "man of iron" of popular fiction, the ideal of an infantile public whose knowledge of the world is derived from the deified heroes of trashy films. These personal observations led me to conclude at the time (1937) that, when the final catastrophe came, it would be far greater and bloodier than I had previously supposed. For this theatrical hysteric and transparent impostor was not strutting about on a small stage, but was riding the armoured divisions of the Wehrmacht, with all the weight of German heavy industry behind him. Encountering only slight and in any case ineffective opposition from within, the nation of eighty millions crowded into the circus to witness its own destruction.

420   Among Hitler's closest associates, Goebbels and Göring stand

out as equally striking figures. Göring is the good fellow and *bon vivant* type of cheat, who takes in the simple-minded with his jovial air of respectability; Goebbels, a no-less-sinister and dangerous character, is the typical *Kaffeehausliterat* and card-sharper, handicapped and at the same time branded by nature. Any one partner in this unholy trinity should have been enough to make any man whose instincts were not warped cross himself three times. But what in fact happened? Hitler was exalted to the skies; there were even theologians who looked upon him as the Saviour. Göring was popular on account of his weaknesses; few people would believe his crimes. Goebbels was tolerated because many people think that lying is inseparable from success, and that success justifies everything. Three of these types at one time were really the limit, and one is at a loss to imagine how anything quite so monstrous ever came to power. But we must not forget that we are judging from today, from a knowledge of the events which led to the catastrophe. Our judgment would certainly be very different had our information stopped short at 1933 or 1934. At that time, in Germany as well as in Italy, there were not a few things that appeared plausible and seemed to speak in favour of the regime. An undeniable piece of evidence in this respect was the disappearance of the unemployed, who used to tramp the German highroads in their hundreds of thousands. And after the stagnation and decay of the post-war years, the refreshing wind that blew through the two countries was a tempting sign of hope. Meanwhile, the whole of Europe looked on at this spectacle like Mr. Chamberlain, who was prepared at most for a heavy shower. But it is just this extreme speciousness that is the peculiar genius of *pseudologia phantastica,* and Mussolini also had a touch of it (kept within bounds, however, while his brother Arnaldo was alive). It introduces its plans in the most innocent way in the world, finding the most appropriate words and the most plausible arguments, and there is nothing to show that its intentions are bad from the start. They may even be good, genuinely good. In the case of Mussolini, for instance, it might be difficult to draw a definite line between black and white. Where *pseudologia* is at work one can never be sure that the intention to deceive is the principal motive. Quite often the "great plan" plays the leading role, and it is only when it comes to the ticklish question of bringing this plan into reality that every opportunity is exploited and any means is good enough, on the principle that "the end justifies the means." In other words, things only become dangerous when the pathological liar is taken seriously by a wider public. Like Faust, he is bound to make a pact with the devil and thus slips off the straight path. It is even possible that this is more or less what happened to Hitler—let us give him the benefit of the doubt! But the infamies of his book, once it is shorn of its *Schwabinger* [3] brand of bombast, make one suspicious, and one cannot help wondering if the evil spirit had not already taken possession of this man long before he seized power. Round about 1936, many people in Germany were asking themselves the same question; they expressed fears that the Führer might fall a victim to "evil influences," he dabbled too much in "black magic," etc. Clearly these misgivings came much too late; but even so, it is just conceivable that Hitler himself may have had good intentions at first, and only succumbed to the use of the wrong means, or the misuse of his means, in the course of his development.

421   But I should like to emphasize above all that it is part and parcel of the pathological liar's make-up to be plausible. Therefore it is no easy matter, even for experienced people, to form an opinion, particularly while the plan is still apparently in the idealistic stage. It is then quite impossible to foresee how things are likely to develop, and Mr. Chamberlain's "give-it-a-chance" attitude seems to be the only policy. The overwhelming majority of the Germans were just as much in the dark as people abroad, and quite naturally fell an easy prey to Hitler's speeches, so artfully attuned to German (and not only German) taste.

422   Although we may be able to understand why the Germans were misled in the first place, the almost total absence of any reaction is quite incomprehensible. Were there not army commanders who could have ordered their troops to do anything they pleased? Why then was the reaction totally lacking? I can only explain this as the outcome of a peculiar state of mind, a passing or chronic disposition which, in an individual, we call hysteria.

423   As I cannot take it for granted that the layman knows exactly what is meant by "hysteria," I had better explain that the "hys-

3 [Schwabing is the bohemian quarter of Munich.—EDITORS.]

terical" disposition forms a sub-division of what are known as "psychopathic inferiorities." This term by no means implies that the individual or the nation is "inferior" in every respect, but only that there is a place of least resistance, a peculiar instability, which exists independently of all the other qualities. An hysterical disposition means that the opposites inherent in every psyche, and especially those affecting character, are further apart than in normal people. This greater distance produces a higher energic tension, which accounts for the undeniable energy and drive of the Germans. On the other hand, the greater distance between the opposites produces inner contradictions, conflicts of conscience, disharmonies of character—in short, everything we see in Goethe's Faust. Nobody but a German could ever have devised such a figure, it is so intrinsically, so infinitely German. In Faust we see the same "hungering for the infinite" born of inner contradiction and dichotomy, the same eschatological expectation of the Great Fulfilment. In him we experience the loftiest flight of the mind and the descent into the depths of guilt and darkness, and still worse, a fall so low that Faust sinks to the level of a mountebank and wholesale murderer as the outcome of his pact with the devil. Faust, too, is split and sets up "evil" outside himself in the shape of Mephistopheles, to serve as an alibi in case of need. He likewise "knows nothing of what has happened," i.e., what the devil did to Philemon and Baucis. We never get the impression that he has real insight or suffers genuine remorse. His avowed and unavowed worship of success stands in the way of any moral reflection throughout, obscuring the ethical conflict, so that Faust's moral personality remains misty. He never attains the character of reality: he is not a real human being and cannot become one (at least not in this world). He remains the German idea of a human being, and therefore an image—somewhat overdone and distorted—of the average German.

424   The essence of hysteria is a systematic dissociation, a loosening of the opposites which normally are held firmly together. It may even go to the length of a splitting of the personality, a condition in which quite literally one hand no longer knows what the other is doing. As a rule there is amazing ignorance of the shadow; the hysteric is only aware of his good motives, and when the bad ones can no longer be denied he becomes the unscrupu-

lous Superman and *Herrenmensch* who fancies he is ennobled by the magnitude of his aim.

425   Ignorance of one's other side creates great inner insecurity. One does not really know who one is; one feels inferior somewhere and yet does not wish to know where the inferiority lies, with the result that a new inferiority is added to the original one. This sense of insecurity is the source of the hysteric's prestige psychology, of his need to make an impression, to flaunt his merits and insist on them, of his insatiable thirst for recognition, admiration, adulation, and longing to be loved. It is the cause of that loud-mouthed arrogance, uppishness, insolence, and tactlessness by which so many Germans, who at home grovel like dogs, win a bad reputation for their countrymen abroad. Insecurity is also responsible for their tragic lack of civic courage, criticized by Bismarck (one need only recall the pitiable role of the German generals).

426   The lack of reality, so striking in Faust, produces a corresponding lack of realism in the German. He merely talks of it, boasting of his "ice-cold" realism, which in itself is enough to expose his hysteria. His realism is nothing but a pose, a stage-realism. He merely acts the part of one who has a sense of reality, but what does he actually want to do? He wants to conquer the world in spite of the whole world. Of course, he has no idea how it can be done. But at least he might know that the enterprise had failed once before. Unfortunately a plausible reason, that explains away the failure by means of lies, is immediately invented and believed. How many Germans were taken in by the legend of the "stab in the back" in 1918? And how many "stab in the back" legends are floating around today? Believing one's own lies when the wish is father to the lie is a well-known hysterical symptom and a distinct sign of inferiority. One would have thought that the bloodbath of the first World War would have been enough, but not a bit of it; glory, conquest, and bloodthirstiness acted like a smoke-screen on the German mind, so that reality, only dimly perceived at best, was completely blotted out. In an individual we call this sort of thing an hysterical twilight-state. When a whole nation finds itself in this condition it will follow a mediumistic Führer over the housetops with a sleep-walker's assurance, only to land in the street with a broken back.

427   Supposing we Swiss had started such a war and had thrown all our experience, all warnings and all our knowledge of the world to the winds as blindly as the Germans, and had finally gone to the length of establishing an original edition of Buchenwald in our country. We should no doubt feel very disagreeably surprised if a foreigner declared that the Swiss were one and all completely mad. No reasonable person would be surprised at such a verdict, but can we say it about Germany? I wonder what the Germans themselves think. All I know is that at the time of the censorship in Switzerland we were not permitted to say these things aloud, and now it seems we cannot say them out of consideration for Germany which is laid so low. When on earth, I should like to ask, may one venture to form an opinion of one's own? To my mind, the history of the last twelve years is the casechart of an hysterical patient. The truth should not be withheld from him, for when the doctor makes a diagnosis he does so as part of his effort to find the remedy, and not in order to hurt, degrade, or insult the sufferer. A neurosis or a neurotic disposition is not a disgrace, it is a handicap, and sometimes merely a *façon de parler*. It is not a fatal disease, but it does grow worse to the degree that one is determined to ignore it. When I say that the Germans are psychically ill it is surely kinder than saying that they are criminals. I have no wish to irritate the notorious sensitiveness of the hysteric, but there comes a time when we can no longer afford to gloss over all the painful symptoms and to help the patient forget what has happened, merely in order that his pathological condition should remain undisturbed. I would not like to insult the healthy-minded and decent German by suspecting him of being a coward who runs away from his own image. We should do him the honour of treating him like a man and telling him the truth, and not conceal from him that our soul is cut to the quick by the terrible things that happened in his country and were perpetrated by the Germans in Europe. We are hurt and indignant and have no particular feelings of loving-kindness—nor can any amount of determination and will-power twist these sentiments into a Christian "love of your neighbour." For the sake of the healthy-minded and decent Germans one should not attempt to do so; they would surely prefer the truth to insulting forbearance.

428   Hysteria is never cured by hushing up the truth, whether in

an individual or in a nation. But can we say that a whole nation is hysterical? We can say it as much or as little of a nation as of an individual. Even the craziest person is not completely crazy; quite a number of his functions are still normal, and there may even be times when he himself is fairly normal too. This is even truer of hysteria, where there is really nothing wrong except exaggerations and excesses on the one hand, and weakness or temporary paralysis of normal functions on the other. In spite of his psychopathic condition the hysteric is very nearly normal. We may therefore expect many parts of the psychic body-politic to be entirely normal even though the over-all picture can only be described as hysterical.

429   The Germans undoubtedly have their own peculiar psychology which distinguishes them from their neighbours, in spite of the many human qualities which they share with all mankind. Have they not demonstrated to the world that they consider themselves the *Herrenvolk*, with the right to disregard every human scruple? They have labelled other nations inferior and done their best to exterminate them.

430   In view of these terrible facts, it is a mere bagatelle to turn the tables on the *Herrenvolk* and apply the diagnosis of inferiority to the murderer instead of the murdered, while remaining fully conscious that one is injuring all those Germans who suffered their nation's tribulation with open eyes. It does indeed hurt one to hurt others. But, as Europeans—a brotherhood which includes the Germans—we are wounded, and if we wound in return it is not with the intention of torturing but, as I said earlier, of discovering the truth. As in the case of collective guilt, the diagnosis of its mental condition extends to the whole nation, and indeed to the whole of Europe, whose mental condition for some time past has hardly been normal. Whether we like it or not we are bound to ask: What is wrong with our art, that most delicate of all instruments for reflecting the national psyche? How are we to explain the blatantly pathological element in modern painting? Atonal music? The far-reaching influence of Joyce's fathomless *Ulysses*? Here we already have the germ of what was to become a political reality in Germany.

431   The European, or rather the white man in general, is scarcely in a position to judge of his own state of mind. He is too deeply involved. I had always wanted to see Europeans through other

eyes, and eventually I was able, on my many journeys, to establish sufficiently close relationships with non-Europeans to see the European through their eyes. The white man is nervous, restless, hurried, unstable, and (in the eyes of non-Europeans) possessed by the craziest ideas, in spite of his energy and gifts which give him the feeling of being infinitely superior. The crimes he has committed against the coloured races are legion, though obviously this is no justification for any fresh crime, just as the individual is no better for being in a vast company of bad people. Primitives dread the sharply focussed stare in the eye of the European, which seems to them like the evil eye. A Pueblo chieftain once confided to me that he thought all Americans (the only white men he knew) were crazy, and the reasons he gave for this view sounded exactly like a description of people who were possessed. Well, perhaps we are. For the first time since the dawn of history we have succeeded in swallowing the whole of primitive animism into ourselves, and with it the spirit that animated nature. Not only were the gods dragged down from their planetary spheres and transformed into chthonic demons, but, under the influence of scientific enlightenment, even this band of demons, which at the time of Paracelsus still frolicked happily in mountains and woods, in rivers and human dwelling-places, was reduced to a miserable remnant and finally vanished altogether. From time immemorial, nature was always filled with spirit. Now, for the first time, we are living in a lifeless nature bereft of gods. No one will deny the important role which the powers of the human psyche, personified as "gods," played in the past. The mere act of enlightenment may have destroyed the spirits of nature, but not the psychic factors that correspond to them, such as suggestibility, lack of criticism, fearfulness, propensity to superstition and prejudice—in short, all those qualities which make possession possible. Even though nature is depsychized, the psychic conditions which breed demons are as actively at work as ever. The demons have not really disappeared but have merely taken on another form: they have become unconscious psychic forces. This process of reabsorption went hand in hand with an increasing inflation of the ego, which became more and more evident after the sixteenth century. Finally we even began to be aware of the psyche, and, as history shows, the discovery of the unconscious was a particularly painful episode. Just when people were congratulating themselves on having abolished all spooks, it turned out that instead of haunting the attic or old ruins the spooks were flitting about in the heads of apparently normal Europeans. Tyrannical, obsessive, intoxicating ideas and delusions were abroad everywhere, and people began to believe the most absurd things, just as the possessed do.

432   The phenomenon we have witnessed in Germany was nothing less than the first outbreak of epidemic insanity, an irruption of the unconscious into what seemed to be a tolerably well-ordered world. A whole nation, as well as countless millions belonging to other nations, were swept into the blood-drenched madness of a war of extermination. No one knew what was happening to him, least of all the Germans, who allowed themselves to be driven to the slaughterhouse by their leading psychopaths like hypnotized sheep. Maybe the Germans were predestined to this fate, for they showed the least resistance to the mental contagion that threatened every European. But their peculiar gifts might also have enabled them to be the very people to draw helpful conclusions from the prophetic example of Nietzsche. Nietzsche was German to the marrow of his bones, even to the abstruse symbolism of his madness. It was the psychopath's weakness that prompted him to play with the "blond beast" and the "Superman." It was certainly not the healthy elements in the German nation that led to the triumph of these pathological fantasies on a scale never known before. The weakness of the German character, like Nietzsche's, proved to be fertile soil for hysterical fantasies, though it must be remembered that Nietzsche himself not only criticized the German Philistine very freely but laid himself open to attack on a broad front. Here again the Germans had a priceless opportunity for self-knowledge—and let it slip. And what could they not have learned from the suet-and-syrup of Wagner!

433   Nevertheless, with the calamitous founding of the Reich in 1871, the devil stole a march on the Germans, dangling before them the tempting bait of power, aggrandizement, national arrogance. Thus they were led to imitate their prophets and to take their words literally, but not to understand them. And so it was that the Germans allowed themselves to be deluded by these disastrous fantasies and succumbed to the age-old temptations

of Satan, instead of turning to their abundant spiritual potentialities, which, because of the greater tension between the inner
opposites, would have stood them in good stead. But, their Christianity forgotten, they sold their souls to technology, exchanged
morality for cynicism, and dedicated their highest aspirations to
the forces of destruction. Certainly everybody else is doing much
the same thing, but even so there really are chosen people who
have no right to do such things because they should be striving
for higher treasures. At any rate the Germans are not among
those who may enjoy power and possessions with impunity. Just
think for a moment what anti-Semitism means for the German:
he is trying to use others as a scapegoat for his own greatest
fault! This symptom alone should have told him that he had
got on to a hopelessly wrong track.

434   After the last World War the world should have begun to
reflect, and above all Germany, which is the nerve-centre of
Europe. But the spirit turned negative, neglected the decisive
questions, and sought solutions in its own negation. How different it was at the time of the Reformation! Then the spirit of
Germany rose manfully to the needs of Christendom, though
the answer—as we might expect from the German tension of
opposites—was somewhat too extreme. But at least this spirit did
not shrink from its own problems. Goethe, too, was a prophet
when he held up before his people the example of Faust's pact
with the devil and the murder of Philemon and Baucis. If, as
Burckhardt says, Faust strikes a chord in every German soul,
this chord has certainly gone on ringing. We hear it echoing
in Nietzsche's Superman, the amoral worshipper of instinct,
whose God is dead, and who presumes to be God himself, or
rather a demon "six thousand feet beyond good and evil." And
where has the feminine side, the soul, disappeared to in Nietzsche? Helen has vanished in Hades, and Eurydice will never
return. Already we behold the fateful travesty of the denied
Christ: the sick prophet is himself the Crucified, and, going back
still further, the dismembered Dionysus-Zagreus. The raving
prophet carries us back to the long-forgotten past: he had heard
the call of destiny in the shrill whistling of the hunter, the god
of the rustling forests, of drunken ecstasy, and of the berserkers
who were possessed by the spirits of wild animals.

435   While Nietzsche was prophetically responding to the schism

of the Christian world with the art of thinking, his brother in spirit, Richard Wagner, was doing the same thing with the art of music. Germanic prehistory comes surging up, thunderous and stupefying, to fill the gaping breach in the Church. Wagner salved his conscience with *Parsifal,* for which Nietzsche could never forgive him, but the Castle of the Grail vanished into an unknown land. The message was not heard and the omen went unheeded. Only the orgiastic frenzy caught on and spread like an epidemic. Wotan the storm-god had conquered. Ernst Jünger sensed that very clearly: in his book *On the Marble Cliffs* a wild huntsman comes into the land, bringing with him a wave of possession greater than anything known even in the Middle Ages. Nowhere did the European spirit speak more plainly than it did in Germany, and nowhere was it more tragically misunderstood.

436   Now Germany has suffered the consequences of the pact with the devil, she has experienced madness and is torn in pieces like Zagreus, she has been ravished by the berserkers of her god Wotan, been cheated of her soul for the sake of gold and world-mastery, and defiled by the scum rising from the lowest depths.

437   The Germans must understand why the whole world is outraged, for our expectations had been so different. Everybody was unanimous in recognizing their gifts and their efficiency, and nobody doubted that they were capable of great things. The disappointment was all the more bitter. But the fate of Germany should not mislead Europeans into nursing the illusion that the whole world's wickedness is localized in Germany. They should realize that the German catastrophe was only one crisis in the general European sickness. Long before the Hitler era, in fact before the first World War, there were symptoms of the mental change taking place in Europe. The medieval picture of the world was breaking up and the metaphysical authority that ruled it was fast disappearing, only to reappear in man. Did not Nietzsche announce that God was dead and that his heir was the Superman, that doomed rope-dancer and fool? It is an immutable psychological law that when a projection has come to an end it always returns to its origin. So when somebody hits on the singular idea that God is dead, or does not exist at all, the psychic God-image, which is a dynamic part of the psyche's structure, finds its way back into the subject and produces a condi-

tion of "God-Almightiness," that is to say all those qualities which are peculiar to fools and madmen and therefore lead to catastrophe.

438   This, then, is the great problem that faces the whole of Christianity: where now is the sanction for goodness and justice, which was once anchored in metaphysics? Is it really only brute force that decides everything? Is the ultimate authority only the will of whatever man happens to be in power? Had Germany been victorious, one might almost have believed that this was the last word. But as the "thousand-year Reich" of violence and infamy lasted only a few years before it collapsed in ruins, we might be disposed to learn the lesson that there are other, equally powerful forces at work which in the end destroy all that is violent and unjust, and that consequently it does not pay to build on false principles. But unfortunately, as history shows, things do not always turn out so reasonably in this world of ours.

439   "God-Almightiness" does not make man divine, it merely fills him with arrogance and arouses everything evil in him. It produces a diabolical caricature of man, and this inhuman mask is so unendurable, such a torture to wear, that he tortures others. He is split in himself, a prey to inexplicable contradictions. Here we have the picture of the hysterical state of mind, of Nietzsche's "pale criminal." Fate has confronted every German with his inner counterpart: Faust is face to face with Mephistopheles and can no longer say, "So that was the essence of the brute!" He must confess instead: "That was my other side, my *alter ego,* my all too palpable shadow which can no longer be denied."

440   This is not the fate of Germany alone, but of all Europe. We must all open our eyes to the shadow who looms behind contemporary man. We have no need to hold up the devil's mask before the Germans. The facts speak a plainer language, and anyone who does not understand it is simply beyond help. As to what should be done about this terrifying apparition, everyone must work this out for himself. It is indeed no small matter to know of one's own guilt and one's own evil, and there is certainly nothing to be gained by losing sight of one's shadow. When we are conscious of our guilt we are in a more favourable position—we can at least hope to change and improve ourselves. As we know, anything that remains in the unconscious

is incorrigible; psychological corrections can be made only in consciousness. Consciousness of guilt can therefore act as a powerful moral stimulus. In every treatment of neurosis the discovery of the shadow is indispensable, otherwise nothing changes. In this respect, I rely on those parts of the German body-politic which have remained sound to draw conclusions from the facts. Without guilt, unfortunately, there can be no psychic maturation and no widening of the spiritual horizon. Was it not Meister Eckhart who said: "For this reason God is willing to bear the brunt of sins and often winks at them, mostly sending them to people for whom he has prepared some high destiny. See! Who was dearer to our Lord or more intimate with him than his apostles? Not one of them but fell into mortal sin, and all were mortal sinners." [4]

441   Where sin is great, "grace doth much more abound." Such an experience brings about an inner transformation, and this is infinitely more important than political and social reforms which are all valueless in the hands of people who are not at one with themselves. This is a truth which we are forever forgetting, because our eyes are fascinated by the conditions around us and riveted on them instead of examining our own heart and conscience. Every demagogue exploits this human weakness when he points with the greatest possible outcry to all the things that are wrong in the outside world. But the principal and indeed the only thing that is wrong with the world is man.

442   If the Germans today are having a hard time of it outwardly, fate has at least given them a unique opportunity of turning their eyes inward to the inner man. In this way they might make amends for a sin of omission of which our whole civilization is guilty. Everything possible has been done for the outside world: science has been refined to an unimaginable extent, technical achievement has reached an almost uncanny degree of perfection. But what of man, who is expected to administer all these blessings in a reasonable way? He has simply been taken for granted. No one has stopped to consider that neither morally nor psychologically is he in any way adapted to such changes. As blithely as any child of nature he sets about enjoying these dangerous playthings, completely oblivious of the shadow lurk-

4 *Works,* trans. by Evans, II, pp. 18–19.

ing behind him, ready to seize them in its greedy grasp and turn them against a still infantile and unconscious humanity. And who has had a more immediate experience of this feeling of helplessness and abandonment to the powers of darkness than the German who fell into the clutches of the Germans?

443   If collective guilt could only be understood and accepted, a great step forward would have been taken. But this alone is no cure, just as no neurotic is cured by mere understanding. The question remains: How am I to live with this shadow? What attitude is required if I am to be able to live in spite of evil? In order to find valid answers to these questions a complete spiritual renewal is needed. And this cannot be given gratis, each man must strive to achieve it for himself. Neither can old formulas which once had a value be brought into force again. The eternal truths cannot be transmitted mechanically; in every epoch they must be born anew from the human psyche.

THE FIGHT WITH THE SHADOW [1]

444   The indescribable events of the last decade lead one to suspect that a peculiar psychological disturbance was a possible
cause. If you ask a psychiatrist what he thinks about these things,
you must naturally expect to get an answer from his particular
point of view. Even so, as a scientist, the psychiatrist makes no
claim to omniscience, for he regards his opinion merely as one
contribution to the enormously complicated task of finding a
comprehensive explanation.

445   When one adopts the standpoint of psychopathology, it is not
easy to address an audience which may include people who know
nothing of this specialized and difficult field. But there is one
simple rule that you should bear in mind: the psychopathology
of the masses is rooted in the psychology of the individual.
Psychic phenomena of this class can be investigated in the individual. Only if one succeeds in establishing that certain phenomena or symptoms are common to a number of different
individuals can one begin to examine the analogous mass phenomena.

446   As you perhaps already know, I take account of the psychology both of the conscious and of the unconscious, and this
includes the investigation of dreams. Dreams are the natural
products of unconscious psychic activity. We have known for a
long time that there is a biological relationship between the unconscious processes and the activity of the conscious mind. This
relationship can best be described as a compensation, which

1 [A broadcast talk in the Third Programme of the British Broadcasting Corporation, on November 3, 1946. First published in *The Listener* (London), XXXVI
(1946), no. 930, 615–16; reprinted as an introduction to *Essays on Contemporary
Events* (1947); also published, under the title "Individual and Mass Psychology,"
in *Chimera* (New York and Princeton, N.J.), V (1947):3, 3–11. Here slightly revised.
—EDITORS.]

means that any deficiency in consciousness—such as exaggeration, one-sidedness, or lack of a function—is suitably supplemented by an unconscious process.

447 As early as 1918, I noticed peculiar disturbances in the unconscious of my German patients which could not be ascribed to their personal psychology. Such non-personal phenomena always manifest themselves in dreams as mythological motifs that are also to be found in legends and fairytales throughout the world. I have called these mythological motifs *archetypes*: that is, typical modes or forms in which these collective phenomena are experienced. There was a disturbance of the collective unconscious in every single one of my German patients. One can explain these disorders causally, but such an explanation is apt to be unsatisfactory, as it is easier to understand archetypes by their aim rather than by their causality. The archetypes I had observed expressed primitivity, violence, and cruelty. When I had seen enough of such cases, I turned my attention to the peculiar state of mind then prevailing in Germany. I could only see signs of depression and a great restlessness, but this did not allay my suspicions. In a paper which I published at that time, I suggested that the "blond beast" was stirring in an uneasy slumber and that an outburst was not impossible.[2]

448 This condition was not by any means a purely Teutonic phenomenon, as became evident in the following years. The onslaught of primitive forces was more or less universal. The only difference lay in the German mentality itself, which proved to be more susceptible because of the marked proneness of the Germans to mass psychology. Moreover, defeat and social disaster had increased the herd instinct in Germany, so that it became more and more probable that Germany would be the first victim among the Western nations—victim of a mass movement brought about by an upheaval of forces lying dormant in the unconscious, ready to break through all moral barriers. These forces, in accordance with the rule I have mentioned, were meant to be a compensation. If such a compensatory move of the unconscious is not integrated into consciousness in an individual, it leads to a neurosis or even to a psychosis, and the same would apply to a collectivity. Clearly there must be something

[2] Cf. "The Role of the Unconscious," above, par. 17.

wrong with the conscious attitude for a compensatory move of this kind to be possible; something must be amiss or exaggerated, because only a faulty consciousness can call forth a counter-move on the part of the unconscious. Well, innumerable things were wrong, as you know, and opinions are thoroughly divided about them. Which is the correct opinion will be learned only *ex effectu;* that is, we can only discover what the defects in the consciousness of our epoch are by observing the kind of reaction they call forth from the unconscious.

449   As I have already told you, the tide that rose in the unconscious after the first World War was reflected in individual dreams, in the form of collective, mythological symbols which expressed primitivity, violence, cruelty: in short, all the powers of darkness. When such symbols occur in a large number of individuals and are not understood, they begin to draw these individuals together as if by magnetic force, and thus a mob is formed. Its leader will soon be found in the individual who has the least resistance, the least sense of responsibility and, because of his inferiority, the greatest will to power. He will let loose everything that is ready to burst forth, and the mob will follow with the irresistible force of an avalanche.

450   I had observed the German revolution in the test-tube of the individual, so to speak, and I was fully aware of the immense dangers involved when such people crowd together. But I did not know at the time whether there were enough of them in Germany to make a general explosion inevitable. However, I was able to follow up quite a number of cases and to observe how the uprush of the dark forces deployed itself in the individual test-tube. I could watch these forces as they broke through the individual's moral and intellectual self-control, and as they flooded his conscious world. There was often terrific suffering and destruction; but when the individual was able to cling to a shred of reason, or to preserve the bonds of a human relationship, a new compensation was brought about in the unconscious by the very chaos of the conscious mind, and this compensation could be integrated into consciousness. New symbols then appeared, of a collective nature, but this time reflecting the forces of *order*. There was measure, proportion, and symmetrical arrangement in these symbols, expressed in their peculiar mathematical and geometrical structure. They represent a kind of

axial system and are known as *mandalas*. I am afraid I cannot go into an explanation of these highly technical matters here, but, however incomprehensible they may sound, I must mention them in passing because they represent a gleam of hope, and we need hope very badly in this time of dissolution and chaotic disorder.

451 The world-wide confusion and disorder reflect a similar condition in the mind of the individual, but this lack of orientation is compensated in the unconscious by the archetypes of order. Here again I must point out that if these symbols of order are not integrated into consciousness, the forces they express will accumulate to a dangerous degree, just as the forces of destruction and disorder did twenty-five years ago. The integration of unconscious contents is an individual act of realization, of understanding, and moral evaluation. It is a most difficult task, demanding a high degree of ethical responsibility. Only relatively few individuals can be expected to be capable of such an achievement, and they are not the political but the moral leaders of mankind. The maintenance and further development of civilization depend on such individuals, for it is obvious enough that the consciousness of the masses has not advanced since the first World War. Only certain reflective minds have been enriched, and their moral and intellectual horizon has been considerably enlarged by the realization of the immense and overwhelming power of evil, and of the fact that mankind is capable of becoming merely its instrument. But the average man is still where he was at the end of the first World War. Therefore it is only too obvious that the vast majority are incapable of integrating the forces of order. On the contrary, it is even probable that these forces will encroach upon consciousness and take it by surprise and violence, against our will. We see the first symptoms everywhere: totalitarianism and State slavery. The value and importance of the individual are rapidly decreasing and the chances of his being heard will vanish more and more.

452 This process of deterioration will be long and painful, but I fear it is inevitable. Yet in the long run it will prove to be the only way by which man's lamentable unconsciousness, his childishness and individual weakness, can be replaced by a future man, who knows that he himself is the maker of his fate and that the State is his servant and not his master. But man will reach

this level only when he realizes that, through his unconsciousness, he has gambled away the fundamental *droits de l'homme*. Germany has given us a most instructive example of the psychological development in question. There the first World War released the hidden power of evil, just as the war itself was released by the accumulation of unconscious masses and their blind desires. The so-called "Friedenskaiser" was one of the first victims and, not unlike Hitler, he voiced these lawless, chaotic desires and was thus led into war, and into the inevitable catastrophe. The second World War was a repetition of the same psychic process but on an infinitely greater scale.

453   As I have said, the uprush of mass instincts was symptomatic of a compensatory move of the unconscious. Such a move was possible because the conscious state of the people had become estranged from the natural laws of human existence. Thanks to industrialization, large portions of the population were uprooted and were herded together in large centres. This new form of existence—with its mass psychology and social dependence on the fluctuation of markets and wages—produced an individual who was unstable, insecure, and suggestible. He was aware that his life depended on boards of directors and captains of industry, and he supposed, rightly or wrongly, that they were chiefly motivated by financial interests. He knew that, no matter how conscientiously he worked, he could still fall a victim at any moment to economic changes which were utterly beyond his control. And there was nothing else for him to rely on. Moreover, the system of moral and political education prevailing in Germany had already done its utmost to permeate everybody with a spirit of dull obedience, with the belief that every desirable thing must come from above, from those who by divine decree sat on top of the law-abiding citizen, whose feelings of personal responsibility were overruled by a rigid sense of duty. No wonder, therefore, that it was precisely Germany that fell a prey to mass psychology, though she is by no means the only nation threatened by this dangerous germ. The influence of mass psychology has spread far and wide.

454   The individual's feeling of weakness, indeed of non-existence, was thus compensated by the eruption of hitherto unknown desires for power. It was the revolt of the powerless, the insatiable greed of the "have-nots." By such devious means the

unconscious compels man to become conscious of himself. Unfortunately, there were no values in the conscious mind of the individual which would have enabled him to understand and integrate the reaction when it reached consciousness. Nothing but materialism was preached by the highest intellectual authorities. The Churches were evidently unable to cope with this new situation; they could do nothing but protest and that did not help very much. Thus the avalanche rolled on in Germany and produced its leader, who was elected as a tool to complete the ruin of the nation. But what was his original intention? He dreamed of a "new order." We should be badly mistaken if we assumed that he did not really intend to create an international order of some kind. On the contrary, deep down in his being he was motivated by the forces of order, which became operative in him the moment desirousness and greed had taken complete possession of his conscious mind. Hitler was the exponent of a "new order," and that is the real reason why practically every German fell for him. The Germans wanted order, but they made the fatal mistake of choosing the principal victim of disorder and unchecked greed for their leader. Their individual attitude remained unchanged: just as they were greedy for power, so they were greedy for order. Like the rest of the world, they did not understand wherein Hitler's significance lay, that he symbolized something in every individual. He was the most prodigious personification of all human inferiorities. He was an utterly incapable, unadapted, irresponsible, psychopathic personality, full of empty, infantile fantasies, but cursed with the keen intuition of a rat or a guttersnipe. He represented the shadow, the inferior part of everybody's personality, in an overwhelming degree, and this was another reason why they fell for him.

455   But what could they have done? In Hitler, every German should have seen his own shadow, his own worst danger. It is everybody's allotted fate to become conscious of and learn to deal with this shadow. But how could the Germans be expected to understand this, when nobody in the world can understand such a simple truth? The world will never reach a state of order until this truth is generally recognized. In the meantime, we amuse ourselves by advancing all sorts of external and secondary reasons why it cannot be reached, though we know

well enough that conditions depend very largely on the way we take them. If, for instance, the French Swiss should assume that the German Swiss were all devils, we in Switzerland could have the grandest civil war in no time, and we could also discover the most convincing economic reasons why such a war was inevitable. Well—we just don't, for we learned our lesson more than four hundred years ago. We came to the conclusion that it is better to avoid external wars, so we went home and took the strife with us. In Switzerland we have built up the "perfect democracy," where our warlike instincts expend themselves in the form of domestic quarrels called "political life." We fight each other within the limits of the law and the constitution, and we are inclined to think of democracy as a chronic state of mitigated civil war. We are far from being at peace with ourselves: on the contrary, we hate and fight each other because we have succeeded in introverting war. Our peaceful outward demeanour merely serves to safeguard our domestic quarrels from foreign intruders who might disturb us. Thus far we have succeeded, but we are still a long way from the ultimate goal. We still have enemies in the flesh, and we have not yet managed to introvert our political disharmonies. We still labour under the unwholesome delusion that we should be at peace within ourselves. Yet even our national, mitigated state of war would soon come to an end if everybody could see his own shadow and begin the only struggle that is really worth while: the fight against the overwhelming power-drive of the shadow. We have a tolerable social order in Switzerland because we fight among ourselves. Our order would be perfect if only everybody could direct his aggressiveness inwards, into his own psyche. Unfortunately, our religious education prevents us from doing this, with its false promises of an immediate peace within. Peace may come in the end, but only when victory and defeat have lost their meaning. What did our Lord mean when he said: "I came not to send peace, but a sword"?

456   To the extent that we are able to found a true democracy— a conditional fight among ourselves, either collective or individual—we realize, we make real, the factors of order, because then it becomes absolutely necessary to live in orderly circumstances. In a democracy you simply cannot afford the disturbing complications of outside interference. How can you run a

civil war properly when you are attacked from without? When, on the other hand, you are seriously at variance with yourself, you welcome your fellow human beings as possible sympathizers with your cause, and on this account you are disposed to be friendly and hospitable. But you politely avoid people who want to be helpful and relieve you of your troubles. We psychologists have learned, through long and painful experience, that you deprive a man of his best resource when you help him to get rid of his complexes. You can only help him to become sufficiently aware of them and to start a conscious conflict within himself. In this way the complex becomes a focus of life. Anything that disappears from your psychological inventory is apt to turn up in the guise of a hostile neighbour, who will inevitably arouse your anger and make you aggressive. It is surely better to know that your worst enemy is right there in your own heart. Man's warlike instincts are ineradicable—therefore a state of perfect peace is unthinkable. Moreover, peace is uncanny because it breeds war. True democracy is a highly psychological institution which takes account of human nature as it is and makes allowances for the necessity of conflict within its own national boundaries.

457   If you now compare the present state of mind of the Germans with my argument you will appreciate the enormous task with which the world is confronted. We can hardly expect the demoralized German masses to realize the import of such psychological truths, no matter how simple. But the great Western democracies have a better chance, so long as they can keep out of those wars that always tempt them to believe in external enemies and in the desirability of internal peace. The marked tendency of the Western democracies to internal dissension is the very thing that could lead them into a more hopeful path. But I am afraid that this hope will be deferred by powers which still believe in the contrary process, in the destruction of the individual and the increase of the fiction we call the State. The psychologist believes firmly in the individual as the sole carrier of mind and life. Society and the State derive their quality from the individual's mental condition, for they are made up of individuals and the way they are organized. Obvious as this fact is, it has still not permeated collective opinion sufficiently for people to refrain from using the word "State" as if it referred to a sort of super-individual endowed with inexhaustible power

and resourcefulness. The State is expected nowadays to accomplish what nobody would expect from an individual. The dangerous slope leading down to mass psychology begins with this plausible thinking in large numbers, in terms of powerful organizations where the individual dwindles to a mere cipher. Everything that exceeds a certain human size evokes equally inhuman powers in man's unconscious. Totalitarian demons are called forth, instead of the realization that all that can really be accomplished is an infinitesimal step forward in the moral nature of the individual. The destructive power of our weapons has increased beyond all measure, and this forces a psychological question on mankind: Is the mental and moral condition of the men who decide on the use of these weapons equal to the enormity of the possible consequences?

EPILOGUE TO
"ESSAYS ON CONTEMPORARY EVENTS" [1]

458   Germany has set the world a tremendous problem, a problem that has to be considered from many angles. The psychological aspect is only one of its many facets. As a psychologist, I
am naturally inclined to think it an important facet, but I must
leave it to my reader to form his own opinion on this point.
My professional concern with the psychology of the unconscious
often brings to light things which are still hidden from consciousness but exist in embryonic form; and these contents are
ready to break through into consciousness long before the individual has any idea of what his psyche holds in store for him.
I had an inkling of what was brewing in the unconscious nearly
thirty years ago, for I had Germans among my patients. As early
as 1918 I wrote:

As the Christian view of the world loses its authority, the more
menacingly will the "blond beast" be heard prowling about in its
underground prison, ready at any moment to burst out with
devastating consequences.[2]

459   It hardly requires an Oedipus to guess what is meant by the
"blond beast." I had an idea, however, that this "blond beast"
was not restricted to Germany, but stood for the primitive European in general, who was gradually coming to the surface as a
result of ever-increasing mass organization. In the same article
I went on to say:

1 [Originally published as Nachwort to *Aufsätze zur Zeitgeschichte* (Zurich, 1946),
pp. 117–47. Translated by Elizabeth Welsh in *Essays on Contemporary Events*
(London, 1947), pp. 73–90, which version has been consulted. Unless otherwise indicated, the quotations of and references to Jung's writings are in accordance with
the *Coll. Works*, although the author gives dates of original publication.—EDITORS.]
2 "The Role of the Unconscious," supra, par. 17.

227

Even the primitive's distrust of the neighbouring tribe, which we thought we had long ago outgrown thanks to our global organizations, has come back again in this war, swollen to gigantic proportions. It is no longer a matter of burning down the neighbouring village, or of making a few heads roll: whole countries are devastated, millions are slaughtered. The enemy nation is stripped of every shred of decency, and our own faults appear in others, fantastically magnified. Where are the superior minds, capable of reflection, today? If they exist at all, nobody heeds them: instead there is a general running amok, a universal fatality against whose compelling sway the individual is powerless to defend himself. And yet this collective phenomenon is the fault of the individual as well, for nations are made up of individuals. Therefore the individual must consider by what means he can counter the evil. Our rationalistic attitude leads us to believe that we can work wonders with international organizations, legislation, and other well-meant devices. But in reality only a change in the attitude of the individual can bring about a renewal in the spirit of the nations. Everything begins with the individual. There are well-meaning theologians and humanitarians who want to break the power principle—in others. We must begin by breaking it in ourselves. Then the thing becomes credible.[3]

460   While the first World War was still in progress, I wrote an essay that first appeared in French, which I enlarged and published as a book in Germany in 1928.[4] Dealing among other things with the subject of mass psychology, I said:

It is a notorious fact that the morality of society as a whole is in inverse ratio to its size; the greater the aggregation of individuals, the more the individual factors are blotted out, and with them morality, which depends entirely on the moral sense of the individual and on the freedom necessary for this. Hence every man is, in a certain sense, unconsciously a worse man when he is in society than when acting alone; for he is carried by society and to that extent relieved of his individual responsibility. Any large company composed of wholly admirable persons has the morality and intelligence of an unwieldy, stupid, and violent animal. The bigger the organization, the more unavoidable is its immorality and blind stupidity. (*Senatus bestia, senatores boni viri.*) Society, by automatically stressing all the collective qualities in its individual representatives, puts a premium on

3 Ibid., pars. 45f.
4 "The Structure of the Unconscious," expanded into "The Relations between the Ego and the Unconscious." Both in *Two Essays on Analytical Psychology.*

mediocrity, on everything that settles down to vegetate in an easy, irresponsible way. Individuality will inevitably be driven to the wall. . . . Without freedom there can be no morality. Our admiration for great organizations dwindles when once we become aware of the other side of the wonder: the tremendous piling up and accentuation of all that is primitive in man, and the unavoidable destruction of his individuality in the interests of the monstrosity that every great organization in fact is. The man of today, who resembles more or less the collective ideal, has made his heart into a den of murderers, as can easily be proved by the analysis of his unconscious, even though he himself is not in the least disturbed by this fact. And in so far as he is normally adapted to his environment, it is true that the greatest infamy on the part of his group will not disturb him, so long as the majority of his fellows steadfastly believe in the exalted morality of their social organization.[5]

461   In the same essay I uttered the almost banal truth: "The best, just because it is the best, holds the seed of evil, and there is nothing so bad but good can come of it."[6] I lay particular stress on this sentence, because it always put me in a mood of caution when I had to judge of any particular manifestation of the unconscious. The contents of the collective unconscious, the archetypes, with which we are concerned in any occurrence of psychic mass-phenomena, are always bipolar: they have both a positive and a negative side. Whenever an archetype appears things become critical, and it is impossible to foresee what turn they will take. As a rule this depends on the way consciousness reacts to the situation. During a collective manifestation of archetypes there is always a great danger of a mass movement, and a catastrophe can be avoided only if the effect of the archetype can be intercepted and assimilated by a sufficiently large majority of individuals. At the very least there must be a certain number of individuals who are still capable of making their influence felt.

462   In February 1933, lecturing in Cologne and Essen, I said:

The decidedly individualistic trend of these latest developments is counterbalanced by a compensatory reversion to the collective man, whose authority at present is the sheer weight of the masses. No wonder that nowadays there is a feeling of catastrophe in the air, as

5 *Two Essays*, par. 240.
6 Ibid., par. 289.

though an avalanche had broken loose which nothing can stop. The collective man threatens to stifle the individual man, on whose sense of responsibility everything valuable in mankind ultimately depends. The mass as such is always anonymous and always irresponsible. So-called leaders are the inevitable symptoms of a mass movement. The true leaders of mankind are always those who are capable of self-reflection, and who relieve the dead weight of the masses at least of their own weight, consciously holding aloof from the blind momentum of the mass in movement.

But who can resist this all-engulfing force of attraction, when each man clings to the next and each drags the other with him? Only one who is firmly rooted not only in the outside world but also in the world within.

Small and hidden is the door that leads inward, and the entrance is barred by countless prejudices, mistaken assumptions, and fears. Always one wishes to hear of grand political and economic schemes, the very things that have landed every nation in a morass. Therefore it sounds grotesque when anyone speaks of hidden doors, dreams, and a world within. What has this vapid idealism got to do with gigantic economic programmes, with the so-called problems of reality?

But I speak not to nations, only to the individual few, for whom it goes without saying that cultural values do not drop down like manna from heaven, but are created by the hands of individuals. If things go wrong in the world, this is because something is wrong with the individual, because something is wrong with me. Therefore, if I am sensible, I shall put myself right first. For this I need—because outside authority no longer means anything to me—a knowledge of the innermost foundations of my being, in order that I may base myself firmly on the eternal facts of the human psyche.[7]

463   In the Terry Lectures, which I gave at Yale University in 1937, I said:

We can never be sure that a new idea will not seize either upon ourselves or upon our neighbours. We know from modern as well as from ancient history that such ideas are often so strange, indeed so bizarre, that they fly in the face of reason. The fascination which is almost invariably connected with ideas of this sort produces a fanatical obsession, with the result that all dissenters, no matter how well-meaning or reasonable they are, get burnt alive or have their heads cut off or are disposed of in masses by the more modern machine-gun. We cannot even console ourselves with the thought that such things belong

[7] "The Meaning of Psychology for Modern Man," supra, pars. 326ff.

to the remote past. Unfortunately they seem to belong not only to the present, but, quite particularly, to the future. *Homo homini lupus* is a sad yet eternal truism. There is indeed reason enough for man to be afraid of the impersonal forces lurking in his unconscious. We are blissfully unconscious of these forces because they never, or almost never, appear in our personal relations or under ordinary circumstances. But if people crowd together and form a mob, then the dynamisms of the collective man are let loose—beasts or demons that lie dormant in every person until he is part of a mob. Man in the mass sinks unconsciously to an inferior moral and intellectual level, to that level which is always there, below the threshold of consciousness, ready to break forth as soon as it is activated by the formation of a mass. . . .

The change of character brought about by the uprush of collective forces is amazing. A gentle and reasonable being can be transformed into a maniac or a savage beast. One is always inclined to lay the blame on external circumstances, but nothing could explode in us if it had not been already there. As a matter of fact, we are constantly living on the edge of a volcano, and there is, so far as we know, no way of protecting ourselves from a possible outburst that will destroy everybody within reach. It is certainly a good thing to preach reason and common sense, but what if you have a lunatic asylum for an audience or a crowd in a collective frenzy? There is not much difference between them because the madman and the mob are both moved by impersonal, overwhelming forces. . . .[8]

Now we behold the amazing spectacle of states taking over the age-old totalitarian claims of theocracy, which are inevitably accompanied by the suppression of free opinion. Once more we see people cutting each other's throats in support of childish theories of how to create paradise on earth. It is not very difficult to see that the powers of the underworld—not to say of hell—which in former times were more or less successfully chained up in a gigantic spiritual edifice where they could be of some use, are now creating, or trying to create, a State slavery and a State prison devoid of any mental or spiritual charm. There are not a few people nowadays who are convinced that mere human reason is not entirely up to the enormous task of putting a lid on the volcano. . . .

Look at all the incredible savagery going on in our so-called civilized world: it all comes from human beings and their mental condition! Look at the devilish engines of destruction! They are invented by completely innocuous gentlemen, reasonable, respectable citizens who are everything we could wish. And when the whole thing blows

8 "Psychology and Religion," pars. 23ff.

231

up and an indescribable hell of devastation is let loose, nobody seems to be responsible. It simply happens, and yet it is all man-made. But since everybody is blindly convinced that he is nothing more than his own extremely unassuming and insignificant conscious self, which performs its duties decently and earns a moderate living, nobody is aware that this whole rationalistically organized conglomeration we call a state or a nation is driven on by a seemingly impersonal but terrifying power which nobody and nothing can check. This ghastly power is mostly explained as fear of the neighbouring nation, which is supposed to be possessed by a malevolent fiend. Since nobody is capable of recognizing just where and how much he himself is possessed and unconscious, he simply projects his own condition upon his neighbour, and thus it becomes a sacred duty to have the biggest guns and the most poisonous gas. The worst of it is that he is quite right. All one's neighbours are in the grip of some uncontrollable fear, just like oneself. In lunatic asylums it is a well-known fact that patients are far more dangerous when suffering from fear than when moved by rage or hatred.[9]

464   During the "phoney war," early in 1940, I published a German translation of these lectures. The book was published just in time to reach Germany, but was soon suppressed on account of the passages just quoted, and I myself figured on the Nazi black list. I was a "marked man." After the invasion of France the Gestapo destroyed all the French editions of my books they were able to lay their hands on.

465   I have been blamed in many quarters for allowing myself to speak of German "psychopathy." I am—and always was—of the opinion that the political mass movements of our time are psychic epidemics, in other words, *mass psychoses*. They are, as their inhuman concomitants show, abnormal mental phenomena, and I refuse to regard such things as normal, to say nothing of whitewashing them as excusable blunders. Murder is murder, and the fact that the whole German nation threw itself with all its might into the most infamous war of aggression in history is a crime that nothing can ever wipe out. It is true that very many individuals stood out against it, but they were a small minority. The behaviour of the Germans in general is abnormal; were it not so, we should long since have been ac-

[9] Ibid., pars. 83ff.

customed to look upon this form of war as the normal state of things.

466   Naturally there were plenty of reasons—political, social, economic, and historical—to drive the Germans to war, just as there are in the case of common murder. Every murderer has motives enough to spur him on, or the crime would never be committed. But, in addition to all this, a special psychic disposition is needed to bring matters to such a point. That is why there is such a thing as criminal psychology. Germany was suffering from a mass psychosis which was bound to lead to crime. But no psychosis ever appears out of the blue, it is always the result of a long-standing predisposition which we call a psychopathic inferiority. Nations have their own peculiar psychology, and in the same way they also have their own particular kind of psychopathology. It consists in the accumulation of a large number of abnormal features, the most striking of which is a suggestibility affecting the entire nation. No doubt there are special reasons for this too, otherwise it would not exist. But the existence of reasons does not do away either with the deed or its character. There are plenty of reasons for both crime and madness, but we do not on that account send our criminals and lunatics to recuperate at the seaside.

467   I should like to point out that the idea of speaking of mass psychoses did not suddenly occur to me after May 1945; I had done that long before and had given warnings of this tremendous danger, not once but many times. As early as 1916, before the United States entered the first World War, I wrote:

Is the present war supposed to be a war of economics? That is a neutral American "business-like" standpoint, that does not take the blood, tears, unprecedented deeds of infamy and great distress into account, and which completely ignores the fact that this war is really an *epidemic of madness*.[10]

Once this function [of the irrational] finds itself in the unconscious, it works unceasing havoc, like an incurable disease whose focus cannot be eradicated because it is invisible. Individual and nation alike are then compelled to live the irrational in their own

[10] In *Collected Papers on Analytical Psychology* (1917), p. 416.

lives, even devoting their loftiest ideals and their best wits to expressing its madness in the most perfect form.[11]

468   In a lecture given at the British Society for Psychical Research in 1919, I said:

If this animation [of the collective unconscious] is due to a complete breakdown of all conscious hopes and expectations, the danger arises that the unconscious may take the place of conscious reality. Such a state is morbid. We actually see something of this kind in the present Russian and German mentality. An outbreak of violent desires and impossible fantasies among the lower strata of the population is analogous to an outburst from the lower strata of the unconscious in an individual.[12]

469   In 1927 I expressed myself as follows:

The old religions with their sublime and ridiculous, their friendly and fiendish symbols did not drop from the blue, but were born of this human soul that dwells within us at this moment. All those things, in their primal forms, live on in us and may at any time burst in upon us with annihilating force, in the guise of mass-suggestions against which the individual is defenceless. Our fearsome gods have only changed their names: they now rhyme with -ism. Or has anyone the nerve to claim that the World War or Bolshevism was an ingenious invention? Just as outwardly we live in a world where a whole continent may be submerged at any moment, or a pole be shifted, or a new pestilence break out, so inwardly we live in a world where at any moment something similar may occur, albeit in the form of an idea, but no less dangerous and untrustworthy for that. Failure to adapt to this inner world is a negligence entailing just as serious consequences as ignorance and ineptitude in the outer world. It is after all only a tiny fraction of humanity, living mainly on that thickly populated peninsula of Asia which juts out into the Atlantic Ocean, and calling themselves "cultured," who, because they lack all contact with nature, have hit upon the idea that religion is a peculiar kind of mental disturbance of undiscoverable purport. Viewed from a safe distance, say from central Africa or Tibet, it would certainly look as if this fraction had projected its own unconscious mental derangements upon nations still possessed of healthy instincts.[13]

[11] Two Essays, par. 150; cf. Collected Papers, p. 432.
[12] "The Psychological Foundations of Belief in Spirits," reprinted in Contributions to Analytical Psychology (1928), pp. 265f. In Über die Energetik der Seele (1928) the end of this passage was revised as follows: ". . . the mental state of the people as a whole might well be compared to a psychosis." [Cf. The Structure and Dynamics of the Psyche, par. 595.—EDITORS.]   [13] Two Essays, par. 326.

470　　In 1928 I wrote that "the normal person . . . acts out his psychic disturbances socially and politically, in the form of mass psychoses like wars and revolutions."[14] A year later, in *The Secret of the Golden Flower*, which I published in collaboration with Richard Wilhelm, I remarked:

> If we deny the existence of the autonomous systems, . . . they become an inexplicable source of disturbance which we finally assume must exist somewhere outside ourselves. The resultant projection creates a dangerous situation in that the disturbing effects are now attributed to a wicked will outside ourselves, which is naturally not to be found anywhere but with our neighbor *de l'autre côté de la rivière*. This leads to collective delusions, "incidents," revolutions, war—in a word, to destructive mass psychoses.[15]

471　　In November 1932, the year in which Germany's fate was decided, I gave a lecture at the Austrian *Kulturbund* in Vienna, from which I should like to quote the following passage:

> The gigantic catastrophes that threaten us today are not elemental happenings of a physical or biological order, but psychic events. To a quite terrifying degree we are threatened by wars and revolutions which are nothing other than psychic epidemics. At any moment several millions of human beings may be smitten with a new madness, and then we shall have another world war or devastating revolution. Instead of being at the mercy of wild beasts, earthquakes, landslides, and inundations, modern man is battered by the elemental forces of his own psyche. This is the World Power that vastly exceeds all other powers on earth. The Age of Enlightenment, which stripped nature and human institutions of gods, overlooked the God of Terror who dwells in the human soul. If anywhere, fear of God is justified in face of the overwhelming supremacy of the psychic.
>
> But all this is so much abstraction. Everyone knows that the intellect, that clever jackanapes, can put it this way or any other way he pleases. It is a very different thing when the psyche, as an objective fact, hard as granite and heavy as lead, confronts a man as an inner experience and addresses him in an audible voice, saying, "This is what will and must be." Then he feels himself called, just as the group does when there's a war on, or a revolution, or any other madness. It is not for nothing that our age cries out for the redeemer personality, for the one who can emancipate himself from the grip of the collec-

14 "General Aspects of Dream Psychology," in *The Structure and Dynamics of the Psyche*, par. 518.
15 *Alchemical Studies*, par. 52.

tive and save at least his own soul, who lights a beacon of hope for others, proclaiming that here is at least *one* man who has succeeded in extricating himself from that fatal identity with the group psyche. For the group, because of its unconsciousness, has no freedom of choice, and so psychic activity runs on in it like an uncontrolled force of nature. There is thus set going a chain reaction that comes to a stop only in catastrophe. The people always long for a hero, a slayer of dragons, when they feel the danger of psychic forces; hence the cry for personality.[16]

472   There is no need to burden the reader with further quotations. Of course I never imagined that such observations would have an effect on any large scale, but it certainly never occurred to me that a time would come when I should be reproached for having said absolutely nothing about these things before 1945, that is, before my article "After the Catastrophe." When Hitler seized power it became quite evident to me that a mass psychosis was boiling up in Germany. But I could not help telling myself that this was after all Germany, a civilized European nation with a sense of morality and discipline. Hence the ultimate outcome of this unmistakable mass movement still seemed to me uncertain, just as the figure of the Führer at first struck me as being merely ambivalent. It is true that in July 1933, when I gave a series of lectures in Berlin, I received an extremely unfavourable impression both of the behaviour of the Party and of the person of Goebbels. But I did not wish to assume from the start that these symptoms were decisive, for I knew other people of unquestionable idealism who sought to prove to me that these things were unavoidable abuses such as are customary in any great revolution. It was indeed not at all easy for a foreigner to form a clear judgment at that time. Like many of my contemporaries, I had my doubts.

473   As a psychiatrist, accustomed to dealing with patients who are in danger of being overwhelmed by unconscious contents, I knew that it is of the utmost importance, from the therapeutic point of view, to strengthen as far as possible their conscious position and powers of understanding, so that something is there to intercept and integrate the contents that are breaking through into consciousness. These contents are not necessarily

[16] *The Development of the Personality, Coll. Works*, Vol. 17, pars. 302f.

destructive in themselves, but are ambivalent, and it depends entirely on the constitution of the intercepting consciousness whether they will turn out to be a curse or a blessing.

474   National Socialism was one of those psychological mass phenomena, one of those outbreaks of the collective unconscious, about which I had been speaking for nearly twenty years. The driving forces of a psychological mass movement are essentially archetypal. Every archetype contains the lowest and the highest, evil and good, and is therefore capable of producing diametrically opposite results. Hence it is impossible to make out at the start whether it will prove to be positive or negative. My medical attitude towards such things counselled me to wait, for it is an attitude that allows no hasty judgments, does not always know from the start what is better, and is willing to give things "a fair trial." Far from wishing to give the beleaguered consciousness its death-blow, it tries to strengthen its powers of resistance through insight, so that the evil that is hidden in every archetype shall not seize hold of the individual and drag him to destruction. The therapist's aim is to bring the positive, valuable, and living quality of the archetype—which will sooner or later be integrated into consciousness in any case—into reality, and at the same time to obstruct as far as possible its damaging and pernicious tendencies. It is part of the doctor's professional equipment to be able to summon up a certain amount of optimism even in the most unlikely circumstances, with a view to saving everything that it is still possible to save. He cannot afford to let himself be too much impressed by the real or apparent hopelessness of a situation, even if this means exposing himself to danger. Moreover, it should not be forgotten that Germany, up till the National Socialist era, was one of the most differentiated and highly civilized countries on earth, besides being, for us Swiss, a spiritual background to which we were bound by ties of blood, language, and friendship. I wanted to do everything within my feeble powers to prevent this cultural bond from being broken, for culture is our only weapon against the fearful danger of mass-mindedness.

475   If an archetype is not brought into reality consciously, there is no guarantee whatever that it will be realized in its favourable form; on the contrary, there is all the more danger of a destructive regression. It seems as if the psyche were endowed

237

with consciousness for the very purpose of preventing such destructive possibilities from happening.

476   Coming back to the question of "German psychopathy," I am as convinced as ever that National Socialism was the mass psychosis of which I have been speaking for so long. What happened in Germany can be explained, in my view, only by the existence of an abnormal state of mind. But I am open to conviction if anyone can prove to me that the phenomenology of National Socialism belongs to the normal inventory of the psyche. In Italy the mass psychosis took a somewhat milder form. Russia can plead, by way of excuse, the low level of popular education before the Revolution. But Germany was supposed to be a highly civilized country, and yet the horrors there exceeded anything the world has ever known. I therefore maintain that there are peculiar depths in the Germans which present the most violent contrast to their former high achievements. Such a condition is known in psychopathology as a dissociation, and a habitual dissociation is one of the signs of a psychopathic disposition.[17]

477   I am aware that the word "psychopathic" strikes harshly on the layman's ear, and that it conjures up all manner of horrors, such as lunatic asylums and the like. By way of explanation I should like to state that only a very small fraction of so-called psychopaths land in the asylum. The overwhelming majority of them constitute that part of the population which is alleged to be "normal." The concept of "normality" is an ideal construction. In psychology we speak of the "scope of the normal," thus implicitly admitting that the concept of normality swings between certain limits and cannot therefore be sharply defined. A rather bigger swing, and the psychic process has already entered the sphere of the abnormal. These deviations from the "norm" —and they are very common—pass unnoticed so long as they do not lead to actual signs of disease. But if definite and unmistakable symptoms occur, such as are obvious even to the layman, then the case is clearly "psychopathic" (i.e., a "suffering"— πάσχειν—of the psyche). The milder forms of psychopathy are the commonest and severe cases are rare. There are countless people who go a little bit beyond the scope of the normal, in one way

17 For the necessary qualifications of this general statement see "After the Catastrophe," pars. 423ff.

or another, either temporarily or chronically. If they get together in large numbers—which is what happens in any crowd—abnormal phenomena appear. One need only read what Le Bon[18] has to say on the "psychology of crowds" to understand what I mean: man as a particle in the mass is psychically abnormal. Ignorance of this fact is no protection against it.

478   So anyone whose ears are offended by the word "psychopathic" is at liberty to suggest a soft, soothing, comforting substitute which correctly reflects the state of mind that gave birth to National Socialism. Far from wishing to insult the German people, my object, as I have said, is to diagnose the suffering that has its roots in their psyche and is the cause of their downfall. Nothing will ever persuade me that Nazism was forced on the German people by the Freemasons, the Jews, or the wicked English—that is really too childish. I have heard that sort of thing too often in the asylum.

479   Anyone who wishes to get a vivid picture of the workings of psychopathic inferiority has only to study the way in which responsible Germans—i.e., the educated classes—react to the notorious *faits et gestes*. There is no doubt that a very large number of Germans are chiefly annoyed at having lost the war. A large proportion of them are shocked that the regime of the occupying forces is, in places, harsh, unjust, and even brutal—"after all, the war's over now." They refuse to listen to the accounts of Germany's unspeakable behaviour in Bohemia, Poland, Russia, Greece, Holland, Belgium, Norway, and France. "All kinds of regrettable things did happen, of course, but that was during the war." A slightly larger number admit the concentration camps and the "bad behaviour" in Poland and elsewhere, but in the same breath begin to enumerate the outrages committed by the English, from the Boer War on, without of course mentioning the war launched by their other psychopath, Wilhelm II. It never seems to occur to them that someone else's sin in no way excuses their own, and that their habit of accusing others merely shows up their own lack of insight.

480   Finally we come to a smaller number—the better men of the nation—who confess: *Pater, peccavi in caelum et coram te*, "we

18 *The Crowd: A Study of the Popular Mind.* Cf. also Reinwald's *Vom Geist der Massen*, which has just appeared [1946].

have our share of guilt in the desolation that has spread over the world. We know that we must bear the consequences of a war begun in a spirit of wantonness and criminality, and we would not think of trying to escape our hard fate, *not even by complaints and accusations.*" [19] Such a confession can only be answered in the words of the evangelist: "Bring forth the best robe, and put it on him; and put a ring on his hand, and shoes on his feet; and bring hither the fatted calf, and kill it; and let us eat, and be merry: For this my son was dead, and is alive again." [20] It makes us feel something of the joy that reigned in heaven over the repentant sinner, and of the discomfiture of the ninety and nine just persons.

481   Yet what meets our eye in the very next sentence? "Nevertheless, as people who have declared themselves openly and with honest conviction, as Evangelical Christians, we should and must . . . point out with due emphasis that, according to the Gospel, no one is in greater danger than he who, *secure in the consciousness of his own innocence, judges and condemns another. . . .* We cannot, indeed we should not pass over in silence the fact that foreign statesmen and their governments also played a decisive part in that first European catastrophe, through their politics both before and after 1918, *which were likewise power-politics based on injustice,* and that, consequently, they contributed their share to the inflation and the economic crisis, to the impoverishment of the German nation, *and thus prepared the ground for the dragon's teeth from which National Socialism sprang up.*"

482   In the first passage we read that no one has any intention of accusing anybody, and in the second comes the accusation. The contradiction passes unnoticed. When confession and repentance are followed by an aggressive defence, the genuineness of the repentance becomes doubtful. As it is hardly credible that the authors of this document consciously set out to sabotage the effect of their confession, we can only conclude—as is unfortunately only too true in innumerable instances where similar arguments are put forward—that there is an astounding uncon-

[19] My italics. Here I am making use of an authentic document, the authors of which I do not wish to expose by name, as they are worthy people whose shortcomings are not a personal fault but a national one.
[20] Luke 15:22f.

sciousness of the fatal impression that such an attitude is bound to create.

483 Furthermore we must ask: Has Germany openly admitted that she is conscious of her guilt, if she now "judges and condemns" others? It seems to have escaped the notice of the authors that there are plenty of people in Europe who are capable of forming their own judgment, and who are not hoodwinked by such unconscious naïvetés. Thus our document turns into a rather indiscreet monologue thoroughly in keeping with the clinical picture. Parents and teachers, judges and psychiatrists, are well acquainted with this mixture of repentance and lust for revenge, this same unconsciousness and indifference to the disastrous impression one makes, this same self-centred disregard of one's fellow men. Such an attitude defeats its object: it sets out to evoke an impression of repentance, and the next minute it defends itself by launching an attack. This manoeuvre simply makes the repentance unreal and the defence ineffectual. It is too unconscious to serve any purpose, quite unadapted and not equal to the demands of reality. There is an old saying that goes: "Sickness is diminished adaptation." The kind of adaptation here illustrated is of no value either morally or intellectually; it is inferior, and psychopathically inferior at that.

484 In saying this it is not my intention to accuse or condemn. I am obliged to mention it only because my diagnosis has been doubted.[21] A medical diagnosis is not an accusation, and an illness is not a disgrace but a misfortune. As early as 1936 I pleaded for compassion in judging the German mentality.[22] Even now I adopt the standpoint of the therapist, and therefore, in the interests of the patient, I must emphasize the necessity for complete insight without any extenuating provisos. It avails him nothing to cultivate only a half-consciousness of his condition, and to cover up his other half with illusions whose colossal dangers he has just experienced in the most terrible form. My sympathy with the lot of the Germans is great, and I am only too painfully aware that my chances of being able to help are exceedingly small. I can only hope and pray that one of the worst

---

21 Nor does my diagnosis include every individual German. I have heard statements from Germans which were spoken like a man and were not vitiated by that infantile weakness which underlies the German *Kraftmeier* style.
22 Cf. "Wotan," supra, par. 398.

dangers now threatening Germany, besides economic distress, may soon some to an end, and that is her spiritual isolation. National isolation combined with mass psychology and centralization are Germany's bane. The task she has to fulfil is not political but spiritual, and the gifts she possesses for this are practically unique. We should therefore help and support this side of her nature by all the means within our power.

*

485   I cannot bring this epilogue to a close without saying a few words about the outlook for the future. No nation has ever fallen so low as the Germans and none has ever branded itself with such a stigma, which generations will not be able to wash away. But when a pendulum swings so violently in one direction, it is capable of swinging just as far in the other—if we may apply this analogy to the psyche of a nation. I do not know whether it is justified from the ethnopsychological point of view. I only know that, in the psyche of an individual with a tendency to dissociation, there can be violent oscillations, with the result that one extreme necessarily leads to its opposite. Provided, however, that he remains in full possession of his human qualities and thus has a mean value, I am inclined to think that the minus is balanced by the plus. In other words, I believe there is a faculty for regeneration in the Germans that might be able to find the right answer to the terrific tension between the opposites which has been so evident during the past twelve years. In this endeavour Germany would not be isolated, for all the positive spiritual forces which are at work throughout the civilized world would stand by her and sustain her effort. The struggle between light and darkness has broken out everywhere. The rift runs through the whole globe, and the fire that set Germany ablaze is smouldering and glowing wherever we look. The conflagration that broke out in Germany was the outcome of psychic conditions that are universal. The real danger signal is not the fiery sign that hung over Germany, but the unleashing of atomic energy, which has given the human race the power to annihilate itself completely. The situation is about the same as if a small boy of six had been given a bag of dynamite for a birthday present. We are not one hundred per cent convinced by his assurances that no calamity will happen. Will man be able to give up toying with the idea of another war? Can we at last get

it into our heads that any government of impassioned patriots which signs the order for mobilization should immediately be executed *en bloc*?

486   How can we save the child from the dynamite which no one can take away from him? The good spirit of humanity is challenged as never before. The facts can no longer be hushed up or painted in rosy colours. Will this knowledge inspire us to a great inner transformation of mind, to a higher, maturer consciousness and sense of responsibility?

487   It is time, high time, that civilized man turned his mind to fundamental things. It is now a question of existence or non-existence, and surely this should be subjected to the most searching investigation and discussion. For the danger that threatens us now is of such dimensions as to make this last European catastrophe seem like a curtain-raiser.

IV

THE UNDISCOVERED SELF

(Present and Future)

[Written in spring 1956 and first published as *Gegenwart und Zukunft*, supplement to *Schweizer Monatshefte* (Zurich), March 1957; issued as a book (paperback) later in 1957 (Zurich). Translated from the original ms. by R. F. C. Hull. A section of the translation was published as "God, The Devil, and the Human Soul," *The Atlantic Monthly* (Boston), CC:5 (Nov., 1957; Centennial Issue); the entire translation, with revisions by the American editors, was published in book form as *The Undiscovered Self* (Boston and London, 1958), carrying the note: "This book was prompted by conversations between Dr. Jung and Dr. Carleton Smith, director of the National Arts Foundation, which brought it to the attention of the editors of the Atlantic Monthly Press," and a dedication: "To my friend Fowler McCormick." The present text is a further revision of the original translation.—EDITORS.]

1. THE PLIGHT OF THE INDIVIDUAL
IN MODERN SOCIETY

488   What will the future bring? From time immemorial this question has occupied men's minds, though not always to the same
degree. Historically, it is chiefly in times of physical, political,
economic, and spiritual distress that men's eyes turn with
anxious hope to the future, and when anticipations, utopias, and
apocalyptic visions multiply. One thinks, for instance, of the
chiliastic expectations of the Augustan age at the beginning of
the Christian era, or of the spiritual changes in the West which
accompanied the end of the first millennium. Today, as the end
of the second millennium draws near, we are again living in an
age filled with apocalyptic images of universal destruction.
What is the significance of that split, symbolized by the "Iron
Curtain," which divides humanity into two halves? What will
become of our civilization, and of man himself, if the hydrogen bombs begin to go off, or if the spiritual and moral darkness of State absolutism should spread over Europe?

489   We have no reason to take this threat lightly. Everywhere in
the West there are subversive minorities who, sheltered by our
humanitarianism and our sense of justice, hold the incendiary
torches ready, with nothing to stop the spread of their ideas except the critical reason of a single, fairly intelligent, mentally
stable stratum of the population. One should not overestimate
the thickness of this stratum. It varies from country to country
in accordance with national temperament. Also, it is regionally
dependent on public education and is subject to the influence
of acutely disturbing factors of a political and economic nature.
Taking plebiscites as a criterion, one could on an optimistic estimate put its upper limit at about forty per cent of the electorate.
A rather more pessimistic view would not be unjustified either,
since the gift of reason and critical reflection is not one of man's
outstanding peculiarities, and even where it exists it proves to

247

be wavering and inconstant, the more so, as a rule, the bigger the political groups are. The mass crushes out the insight and reflection that are still possible with the individual, and this necessarily leads to doctrinaire and authoritarian tyranny if ever the constitutional State should succumb to a fit of weakness.

490   Rational argument can be conducted with some prospect of success only so long as the emotionality of a given situation does not exceed a certain critical degree. If the affective temperature rises above this level, the possibility of reason's having any effect ceases and its place is taken by slogans and chimerical wish-fantasies. That is to say, a sort of collective possession results which rapidly develops into a psychic epidemic. Under these conditions all those elements whose existence is merely tolerated as asocial under the rule of reason come to the top. Such individuals are by no means rare curiosities to be met with only in prisons and lunatic asylums. For every manifest case of insanity there are, in my estimation, at least ten latent cases who seldom get to the point of breaking out openly but whose views and behaviour, for all their appearance of normality, are influenced unconsciously by pathological and perverse factors. There are, of course, no medical statistics on the frequency of latent psychoses—for understandable reasons. But even if their number should amount to less than ten times that of the manifest psychoses and of manifest criminality, the relatively small percentage of the population figures they represent is more than compensated for by the peculiar dangerousness of these people. Their mental state is that of a collectively excited group ruled by affective judgments and wish-fantasies. In a milieu of this kind they are the adapted ones, and consequently they feel quite at home in it. They know from their own experience the language of these conditions, and they know how to handle them. Their chimerical ideas, sustained by fanatical resentment, appeal to the collective irrationality and find fruitful soil there; they express all those motives and resentments which lurk in more normal people under the cloak of reason and insight. They are, therefore, despite their small number in comparison with the population as a whole, dangerous as sources of infection precisely because the so-called normal person possesses only a limited degree of self-knowledge.

491   Most people confuse "self-knowledge" with knowledge of their conscious ego-personalities. Anyone who has any ego-consciousness at all takes it for granted that he knows himself. But the ego knows only its own contents, not the unconscious and its contents. People measure their self-knowledge by what the average person in their social environment knows of himself, but not by the real psychic facts which are for the most part hidden from them. In this respect the psyche behaves like the body, of whose physiological and anatomical structure the average person knows very little too. Although he lives in it and with it, most of it is totally unknown to the layman, and special scientific knowledge is needed to acquaint consciousness with what is known of the body, not to speak of all that is *not* known, which also exists.

492   What is commonly called "self-knowledge" is therefore a very limited knowledge, most of it dependent on social factors, of what goes on in the human psyche. Hence one is always coming up against the prejudice that such and such a thing does not happen "with us" or "in our family" or among our friends and acquaintances. On the other hand, one meets with equally illusory assumptions about the alleged presence of qualities which merely serve to cover up the true facts of the case.

493   In this broad belt of unconsciousness, which is immune to conscious criticism and control, we stand defenceless, open to all kinds of influences and psychic infections. As with all dangers, we can guard against the risk of psychic infection only when we know what is attacking us, and how, where and when the attack will come. Since self-knowledge is a matter of getting to know the individual facts, theories are of very little help. For the more a theory lays claim to universal validity, the less capable it is of doing justice to the individual facts. Any theory based on experience is necessarily *statistical;* it formulates an *ideal average* which abolishes all exceptions at either end of the scale and replaces them by an abstract mean. This mean is quite valid, though it need not necessarily occur in reality. Despite this it figures in the theory as an unassailable fundamental fact. The exceptions at either extreme, though equally factual, do not appear in the final result at all, since they cancel each other out. If, for instance, I determine the weight of each stone in a bed of pebbles and get an average weight of five ounces, this tells

me very little about the real nature of the pebbles. Anyone who thought, on the basis of these findings, that he could pick up a pebble of five ounces at the first try would be in for a serious disappointment. Indeed, it might well happen that however long he searched he would not find a single pebble weighing exactly five ounces.

494   The statistical method shows the facts in the light of the ideal average but does not give us a picture of their empirical reality. While reflecting an indisputable aspect of reality, it can falsify the actual truth in a most misleading way. This is particularly true of theories which are based on statistics. The distinctive thing about real facts, however, is their individuality. Not to put too fine a point on it, one could say that the real picture consists of nothing but exceptions to the rule, and that, in consequence, absolute reality has predominantly the character of *irregularity*.

495   These considerations must be borne in mind whenever there is talk of a theory serving as a guide to self-knowledge. There is and can be no self-knowledge based on theoretical assumptions, for the object of this knowledge is an individual—a relative exception and an irregular phenomenon. Hence it is not the universal and the regular that characterize the individual, but rather the unique. He is not to be understood as a recurrent unit but as something unique and singular which in the last analysis can be neither known nor compared with anything else. At the same time man, as member of a species, can and must be described as a statistical unit; otherwise nothing general could be said about him. For this purpose he has to be regarded as a comparative unit. This results in a universally valid anthropology or psychology, as the case may be, with an abstract picture of man as an average unit from which all individual features have been removed. But it is precisely these features which are of paramount importance for *understanding* man. If I want to understand an individual human being, I must lay aside all scientific knowledge of the average man and discard all theories in order to adopt a completely new and unprejudiced attitude. I can only approach the task of *understanding* with a free and open mind, whereas *knowledge* of man, or insight into human character, presupposes all sorts of knowledge about mankind in general.

496   Now whether it is a question of understanding a fellow human being or of self-knowledge, I must in both cases leave all theoretical assumptions behind me. Since scientific knowledge not only enjoys universal esteem but, in the eyes of modern man, counts as the only intellectual and spiritual authority, understanding the individual obliges me to commit the *lèse majesté*, so to speak, of turning a blind eye to scientific knowledge. This is a sacrifice not lightly made, for the scientific attitude cannot rid itself so easily of its sense of responsibility. And if the psychologist happens to be a doctor who wants not only to classify his patient scientifically but also to understand him as a human being, he is threatened with a conflict of duties between the two diametrically opposed and mutually exclusive attitudes of knowledge on the one hand and understanding on the other. This conflict cannot be solved by an either/or but only by a kind of two-way thinking: doing one thing while not losing sight of the other.

497   In view of the fact that, in principle, the positive advantages of *knowledge* work specifically to the disadvantage of *understanding,* the judgment resulting therefrom is likely to be something of a paradox. Judged scientifically, the individual is nothing but a unit which repeats itself *ad infinitum* and could just as well be designated with a letter of the alphabet. For understanding, on the other hand, it is just the unique individual human being who, when stripped of all those conformities and regularities so dear to the heart of the scientist, is the supreme and only real object of investigation. The doctor, above all, should be aware of this contradiction. On the one hand, he is equipped with the statistical truths of his scientific training, and on the other, he is faced with the task of treating a sick person who, especially in the case of psychic suffering, requires *individual understanding.* The more schematic the treatment is, the more resistances it—quite rightly—calls up in the patient, and the more the cure is jeopardized. The psychotherapist sees himself compelled, willy-nilly, to regard the individuality of a patient as an essential fact in the picture and to arrange his methods of treatment accordingly. Today, over the whole field of medicine, it is recognized that the task of the doctor consists in treating the sick person, not an abstract illness.

498   This illustration from the realm of medicine is only a special

instance of the problem of education and training in general. Scientific education is based in the main on statistical truths and abstract knowledge and therefore imparts an unrealistic, rational picture of the world, in which the individual, as a merely marginal phenomenon, plays no role. The individual, however, as an irrational datum, is the true and authentic carrier of reality, the *concrete* man as opposed to the unreal ideal or "normal" man to whom the scientific statements refer. What is more, most of the natural sciences try to represent the results of their investigations as though these had come into existence without man's intervention, in such a way that the collaboration of the psyche —an indispensable factor—remains invisible. (An exception to this is modern physics, which recognizes that the observed is not independent of the observer.) So, in this respect as well, science conveys a picture of the world from which a real human psyche appears to be excluded—the very antithesis of the "humanities."

499   Under the influence of scientific assumptions, not only the psyche but the individual man and, indeed, all individual events whatsoever suffer a levelling down and a process of blurring that distorts the picture of reality into a conceptual average. We ought not to underestimate the psychological effect of the statistical world-picture: it thrusts aside the individual in favour of anonymous units that pile up into mass formations. Instead of the concrete individual, you have the names of organizations and, at the highest point, the abstract idea of the State as the principle of political reality. The moral responsibility of the individual is then inevitably replaced by the policy of the State (*raison d'état*). Instead of moral and mental differentiation of the individual, you have public welfare and the raising of the living standard. The goal and meaning of individual life (which is the only *real* life) no longer lie in individual development but in the policy of the State, which is thrust upon the individual from outside and consists in the execution of an abstract idea which ultimately tends to attract all life to itself. The individual is increasingly deprived of the moral decision as to how he should live his own life, and instead is ruled, fed, clothed, and educated as a social unit, accommodated in the appropriate housing unit, and amused in accordance with the standards that give pleasure and satisfaction to the masses. The rulers, in their turn, are just as much social units as the ruled, and are distin-

guished only by the fact that they are specialized mouthpieces of the State doctrine. They do not need to be personalities capable of judgment, but thoroughgoing specialists who are unusable outside their line of business. State policy decides what shall be taught and studied.

500 The seemingly omnipotent State doctrine is for its part manipulated in the name of State policy by those occupying the highest positions in the government, where all the power is concentrated. Whoever, by election or caprice, gets into one of these positions is subject to no higher authority; he is the State policy itself and within the limits of the situation can proceed at his own discretion. With Louis XIV he can say, "L'état c'est moi." He is thus the only individual or, at any rate, one of the few individuals who could make use of their individuality if only they knew how to differentiate themselves from the State doctrine. They are more likely, however, to be the slaves of their own fictions. Such one-sidedness is always compensated psychologically by unconscious subversive tendencies. Slavery and rebellion are inseparable correlates. Hence, rivalry for power and exaggerated distrust pervade the entire organism from top to bottom. Furthermore, in order to compensate for its chaotic formlessness, a mass always produces a "Leader," who infallibly becomes the victim of his own inflated ego-consciousness, as numerous examples in history show.

501 This development becomes logically unavoidable the moment the individual combines with the mass and thus renders himself obsolete. Apart from the agglomeration of huge masses in which the individual disappears anyway, one of the chief factors responsible for psychological mass-mindedness is scientific rationalism, which robs the individual of his foundations and his dignity. As a social unit he has lost his individuality and become a mere abstract number in the bureau of statistics. He can only play the role of an interchangeable unit of infinitesimal importance. Looked at rationally and from outside, that is exactly what he is, and from this point of view it seems positively absurd to go on talking about the value or meaning of the individual. Indeed, one can hardly imagine how one ever came to endow individual human life with so much dignity when the truth to the contrary is as plain as the palm of your hand.

502 Seen from this standpoint, the individual really is of dimin-

ishing importance and anyone who wished to dispute this would soon find himself at a loss for arguments. The fact that the individual feels himself or the members of his family or the esteemed friends in his circle to be important merely underlines the slightly comic subjectivity of his feeling. For what are the few compared with ten thousand or a hundred thousand, let alone a million? This recalls the argument of a thoughtful friend with whom I once got caught up in a huge crowd of people. Suddenly he exclaimed, "Here you have the most convincing reason for not believing in immortality: all *that lot* wants to be immortal!"

503   The bigger the crowd the more negligible the individual becomes. But if the individual, overwhelmed by the sense of his own puniness and impotence, should feel that his life has lost its meaning—which, after all, is not identical with public welfare and higher standards of living—then he is already on the road to State slavery and, without knowing or wanting it, has become its proselyte. The man who looks only outside and quails before the big battalions has nothing with which to combat the evidence of his senses and his reason. But that is just what is happening today: we are all fascinated and overawed by statistical truths and large numbers and are daily apprised of the nullity and futility of the individual personality, since it is not represented and personified by any mass organization. Conversely, those personages who strut about on the world stage and whose voices are heard far and wide seem, to the uncritical public, to be borne along on some mass movement or on the tide of public opinion and for this reason are either applauded or execrated. Since mass suggestion plays the predominant role here, it remains a moot point whether their message is their own, for which they are personally responsible, or whether they merely function as a megaphone for collective opinion.

504   Under these circumstances it is small wonder that individual judgment grows increasingly uncertain of itself and that responsibility is collectivized as much as possible, i.e., is shuffled off by the individual and delegated to a corporate body. In this way the individual becomes more and more a function of society, which in its turn usurps the function of the real life carrier, whereas, in actual fact, society is nothing more than an abstract idea like the State. Both are hypostatized, that is, have become

autonomous. The State in particular is turned into a quasi-animate personality from whom everything is expected. In reality it is only a camouflage for those individuals who know how to manipulate it. Thus the constitutional State drifts into the situation of a primitive form of society—the communism of a primitive tribe where everybody is subject to the autocratic rule of a chief or an oligarchy.

2. RELIGION AS THE COUNTERBALANCE
TO MASS-MINDEDNESS

505   In order to free the fiction of the sovereign State—in other words, the whims of the chieftains who manipulate it—from every wholesome restriction, all socio-political movements tending in this direction invariably try to cut the ground from under *religion*. For, in order to turn the individual into a function of the State, his dependence on anything else must be taken from him. Religion means dependence on and submission to the irrational facts of experience. These do not refer directly to social and physical conditions; they concern far more the individual's psychic attitude.

506   But it is possible to have an attitude to the external conditions of life only when there is a point of reference outside them. Religion gives, or claims to give, such a standpoint, thereby enabling the individual to exercise his judgment and his power of decision. It builds up a reserve, as it were, against the obvious and inevitable force of circumstances to which everyone is exposed who lives only in the outer world and has no other ground under his feet except the pavement. If statistical reality is the only one, then that is the sole authority. There is then only *one* condition, and since no contrary condition exists, judgment and decision are not only superfluous but impossible. Then the individual is bound to be a function of statistics and hence a function of the State or whatever the abstract principle of order may be called.

507   Religion, however, teaches another authority opposed to that of the "world." The doctrine of the individual's dependence on God makes just as high a claim upon him as the world does. It may even happen that the absoluteness of this claim estranges him from the world in the same way as he is estranged from himself when he succumbs to the collective mentality. He can forfeit his judgment and power of decision in the former

case (for the sake of religious doctrine) quite as much as in the latter. This is the goal which religion openly aspires to unless it compromises with the State. When it does so, I prefer to call it not "religion" but a "creed." A creed gives expression to a definite collective belief, whereas the word *religion* expresses a subjective relationship to certain metaphysical, extramundane factors. A creed is a confession of faith intended chiefly for the world at large and is thus an intramundane affair, while the meaning and purpose of religion lie in the relationship of the individual to God (Christianity, Judaism, Islam) or to the path of salvation and liberation (Buddhism). From this basic fact all ethics is derived, which without the individual's responsibility before God can be called nothing more than conventional morality.

508   Since they are compromises with mundane reality, the creeds have accordingly seen themselves obliged to undertake a progressive codification of their views, doctrines, and customs, and in so doing have externalized themselves to such an extent that the authentic religious element in them—the living relationship to and direct confrontation with their extramundane point of reference—has been thrust into the background. The denominational standpoint measures the worth and importance of the subjective religious relationship by the yardstick of traditional doctrine, and where this is not so frequent, as in Protestantism, one immediately hears talk of pietism, sectarianism, eccentricity, and so forth, as soon as anyone claims to be guided by God's will. A creed coincides with the established Church or, at any rate, forms a public institution whose members include not only true believers but vast numbers of people who can only be described as "indifferent" in matters of religion and who belong to it simply by force of habit. Here the difference between a creed and a religion becomes palpable.

509   To be the adherent of a creed, therefore, is not always a religious matter but more often a social one and, as such, it does nothing to give the individual any foundation. For this he has to depend exclusively on his relation to an authority which is not of this world. The criterion here is not lip service to a creed but the psychological fact that the life of the individual is not determined solely by the ego and its opinions or by social factors, but quite as much, if not more, by a transcendent author-

ity. It is not ethical principles, however lofty, or creeds, however orthodox, that lay the foundations for the freedom and autonomy of the individual, but simply and solely the empirical awareness, the incontrovertible experience of an intensely personal, reciprocal relationship between man and an extramundane authority which acts as a counterpoise to the "world" and its "reason."

510   This formulation will not please either the mass man or the collective believer. For the former the policy of the State is the supreme principle of thought and action. Indeed, this was the purpose for which he was enlightened, and accordingly the mass man grants the individual a right to exist only in so far as he is a function of the State. The believer, on the other hand, while admitting that the State has a moral and factual claim on him, confesses to the belief that not only man but the State that rules him is subject to the overlordship of "God," and that, in case of doubt, the supreme decision will be made by God and not by the State. Since I do not presume to any metaphysical judgments, I must leave it an open question whether the "world," i.e., the phenomenal world of man, and hence nature in general, is the "opposite" of God or not. I can only point to the fact that the psychological opposition between these two realms of experience is not only vouched for in the New Testament but is still exemplified very plainly today in the negative attitude of the dictator States to religion and of the Church to atheism and materialism.

511   Just as man, as a social being, cannot in the long run exist without a tie to the community, so the individual will never find the real justification for his existence and his own spiritual and moral autonomy anywhere except in an extramundane principle capable of relativizing the overpowering influence of external factors. The individual who is not anchored in God can offer no resistance on his own resources to the physical and moral blandishments of the world. For this he needs the evidence of inner, transcendent experience which alone can protect him from the otherwise inevitable submersion in the mass. Merely intellectual or even moral insight into the stultification and moral irresponsibility of the mass man is a negative recognition only and amounts to not much more than a wavering on the road to the atomization of the individual. It lacks the driv-

ing force of religious conviction, since it is merely rational. The dictator State has one great advantage over bourgeois reason: along with the individual it swallows up his religious forces. The State takes the place of God; that is why, seen from this angle, the socialist dictatorships are religions and State slavery is a form of worship. But the religious function cannot be dislocated and falsified in this way without giving rise to secret doubts, which are immediately repressed so as to avoid conflict with the prevailing trend towards mass-mindedness. The result, as always in such cases, is overcompensation in the form of *fanaticism,* which in its turn is used as a weapon for stamping out the least flicker of opposition. Free opinion is stifled and moral decision ruthlessly suppressed, on the plea that the end justifies the means, even the vilest. The policy of the State is exalted to a creed, the leader or party boss becomes a demigod beyond good and evil, and his votaries are honoured as heroes, martyrs, apostles, missionaries. There is only *one* truth and beside it no other. It is sacrosanct and above criticism. Anyone who thinks differently is a heretic, who, as we know from history, is threatened with all manner of unpleasant things. Only the party boss, who holds the political power in his hands, can interpret the State doctrine authentically, and he does so just as suits him.

512   When, through mass rule, the individual becomes social unit No. so-and-so and the State is elevated to the supreme principle, it is only to be expected that the religious function too will be sucked into the maelstrom. Religion, as the careful observation and taking account of certain invisible and uncontrollable factors, is an *instinctive* attitude peculiar to man, and its manifestations can be followed all through human history. Its evident purpose is to maintain the psychic balance, for the natural man has an equally natural "knowledge" of the fact that his conscious functions may at any time be thwarted by uncontrollable happenings coming from inside as well as from outside. For this reason he has always taken care that any difficult decision likely to have consequences for himself and others shall be rendered safe by suitable measures of a religious nature. Offerings are made to the invisible powers, formidable blessings are pronounced, and all kinds of solemn rites are performed. Everywhere and at all times there have been *rites d'entrée et de sortie*

whose efficacy is impugned as magic and superstition by rationalists incapable of psychological insight. But magic has above all a psychological effect whose importance should not be underestimated. The performance of a "magical" action gives the person concerned a feeling of security which is absolutely essential for carrying out a decision, because a decision is inevitably somewhat one-sided and is therefore rightly felt to be a risk. Even a dictator thinks it necessary not only to accompany his acts of State with threats but to stage them with all manner of solemnities. Brass bands, flags, banners, parades, and monster demonstrations are no different in principle from ecclesiastical processions, cannonades, and fireworks to scare off demons. Only, the suggestive parade of State power engenders a collective feeling of security which, unlike religious demonstrations, gives the individual no protection against his inner demonism. Hence he will cling all the more to the power of the State, i.e., to the mass, thus delivering himself up to it psychically as well as morally and putting the finishing touch to his social depotentiation. The State, like the Church, demands enthusiasm, self-sacrifice, and love, and if religion requires or presupposes the "fear of God," then the dictator State takes good care to provide the necessary terror.

513   When the rationalist directs the main force of his attack against the miraculous effect of the rite as asserted by tradition, he has in reality completely missed the mark. The essential point, the *psychological* effect, is overlooked, although both parties make use of it for directly opposite purposes. A similar situation prevails with regard to their respective conceptions of the goal. The goals of religion—deliverance from evil, reconciliation with God, rewards in the hereafter, and so on—turn into worldly promises about freedom from care for one's daily bread, the just distribution of material goods, universal prosperity in the future, and shorter working hours. That the fulfilment of these promises is as far off as Paradise only furnishes yet another analogy and underlines the fact that the masses have been converted from an extramundane goal to a purely worldly belief, which is extolled with exactly the same religious fervour and exclusiveness that the creeds display in the other direction.

514   In order not to repeat myself unnecessarily, I shall not enumerate all the parallels between worldly and otherworldly be-

liefs, but shall content myself with emphasizing the fact that a natural function which has existed from the beginning, like the religious function, cannot be disposed of with rationalistic and so-called enlightened criticism. You can, of course, represent the doctrinal contents of the creeds as impossible and subject them to ridicule, but such methods miss the point and do not affect the religious function which forms the basis of the creeds. Religion, in the sense of conscientious regard for the irrational factors of the psyche and individual fate, reappears—evilly distorted—in the deification of the State and the dictator: *Naturam expellas furca tamen usque recurret* (You can throw out Nature with a pitchfork, but she'll always turn up again). The leaders and dictators, having weighed up the situation correctly, are therefore doing their best to gloss over the all too obvious parallel with the deification of Caesar and to hide their real power behind the fiction of the State, though this, of course, alters nothing.[1]

515   As I have already pointed out, the dictator State, besides robbing the individual of his rights, has also cut the ground from under his feet psychically by depriving him of the metaphysical foundations of his existence. The ethical decision of the individual human being no longer counts—what alone matters is the blind movement of the masses, and the *lie* thus becomes the operative principle of political action. The State has drawn the logical conclusions from this, as the existence of many millions of State slaves completely deprived of all rights mutely testifies.

516   Both the dictator State and denominational religion lay quite particular emphasis on the idea of *community*. This is the basic ideal of "communism," and it is thrust down the throats of the people so much that it has the exact opposite of the desired effect: it inspires divisive mistrust. The Church, which is no less emphatic, appears on its side as a communal ideal, and where the Church is notoriously weak, as in Protestantism, the hope of or belief in a "communal experience" makes up for the painful lack of cohesion. As can easily be seen, "community" is an indispensable aid in the organization of masses and is therefore a two-edged weapon. Just as the addition of however many

1 Since this essay was written, in the spring of 1956, there has been a noticeable reaction in the U.S.S.R. to this objectionable state of affairs.

zeros will never make a unit, so the value of a community depends on the spiritual and moral stature of the individuals composing it. For this reason one cannot expect from the community any effect that would outweigh the suggestive influence of the environment—that is, a real and fundamental change in individuals, whether for good or for bad. Such changes can come only from the personal encounter between man and man, but not from communistic or Christian baptisms *en masse,* which do not touch the inner man. How superficial the effect of communal propaganda actually is can be seen from recent events in Eastern Europe.[2] The communal ideal reckons without its host, overlooking the individual human being, who in the end will assert his claims.

2 Added in January 1957.

3. THE POSITION OF THE WEST ON
THE QUESTION OF RELIGION

517 Confronting this development in the twentieth century of
our Christian era, the Western world stands with its heritage of
Roman law, the treasures of Judaeo-Christian ethics grounded
on metaphysics, and its ideal of the inalienable rights of man.
Anxiously it asks itself the question: How can this development
be brought to a standstill or put into reverse? It is useless to
pillory the socialist dictatorship as utopian and to condemn its
economic principles as unreasonable, because, in the first place,
the criticizing West has only itself to talk to, its arguments being heard only on this side of the Iron Curtain, and, in the second place, any economic principles you like can be put into
practice so long as you are prepared to accept the sacrifices they
entail. You can carry through any social and economic reforms
you please if, like Stalin, you let three million peasants starve to
death and have a few million unpaid labourers at your disposal.
A State of this kind has no social or economic crises to fear. So
long as its power is intact—that is to say, so long as there is a
well-disciplined and well-fed police army in the offing—it can
maintain its existence for an indefinitely long period and can
go on increasing its power to an indefinite extent. Thanks to its
excess birth-rate, it can multiply the number of its unpaid
workers almost at will in order to compete with its rivals, regardless of the world market, which is to a large measure dependent on wages. A real danger can come to it only from outside, through the threat of military attack. But this risk grows
less every year, firstly because the war potential of the dictator
States is steadily increasing, and secondly because the West cannot afford to arouse latent Russian or Chinese nationalism and
chauvinism by an attack which would have exactly the opposite
effect to the one intended.

518 So far as one can see, only one possibility remains, and that

263

is a break-down of power from within, which must, however, be left to follow its own inner development. Any support from outside at present would have little effect, in view of the existing security measures and the danger of nationalistic reactions. The absolute State has an army of fanatical missionaries to do its bidding in matters of foreign policy, and these in their turn can count on a fifth column who are guaranteed asylum under the laws and constitutions of the Western States. In addition the communes of believers, very strong in places, considerably weaken Western governments' powers of decision, whereas the West has no opportunity to exert a similar influence on the other side, though we are probably not wrong in surmising that there is a certain amount of opposition among the masses in the East. There are always upright and truth-loving people to whom lying and tyranny are hateful, but one cannot judge whether they exert any decisive influence on the masses under the police régimes.[1]

519   In view of this uncomfortable situation the question is heard again and again in the West: What can we do to counter this threat from the East? Even though the West has considerable industrial power and a sizable defence potential at its command, we cannot rest content with this, for we know that even the biggest armaments and the heaviest industry coupled with a relatively high living standard are not enough to check the psychic infection spread by religious fanaticism.

520   The West has unfortunately not yet woken up to the fact that our appeal to idealism and reason and other desirable virtues, delivered with so much enthusiasm, is mere bombination in the void. It is a puff of wind swept away in the storm of religious faith, however twisted this faith may appear to us. We are faced, not with a situation that can be overcome by rational or moral arguments, but with an unleashing of emotional forces and ideas engendered by the spirit of the times; and these, as we know from experience, are not much influenced by rational reflection and still less by moral exhortation. It has been correctly realized in many quarters that the alexipharmic, the antidote, should in this case be an equally potent faith of a different and non-materialistic kind, and that the religious attitude

1 Recent events in Poland and Hungary have shown that this opposition is more considerable than could have been foreseen.

grounded upon it would be the only effective defence against the danger of psychic infection. Unhappily, the little word "should," which never fails to appear in this connection, points to a certain weakness, if not the absence, of this desideratum. Not only does the West lack a uniform faith that could block the progress of a fanatical ideology, but, as the father of Marxist philosophy, it makes use of exactly the same intellectual assumptions, the same arguments and aims. Although the Churches in the West enjoy full freedom, they are not less full or empty than in the East. Yet they exercise no noticeable influence on the broad course of politics. The disadvantage of a creed as a public institution is that it serves two masters: on the one hand, it derives its existence from the relationship of man to God, and on the other hand, it owes a duty to the State, i.e., to the world, in which connection it can appeal to the saying "Render unto Caesar . . ." and various other admonitions in the New Testament.

521 In early times and until comparatively recently there was, therefore, talk of "powers ordained by God" (Romans 13 : 1). Today this conception is antiquated. The Churches stand for traditional and collective convictions which in the case of many of their adherents are no longer based on their own inner experience but on *unreflecting belief*, which is notoriously apt to disappear as soon as one begins thinking about it. The content of belief then comes into collision with knowledge, and it often turns out that the irrationality of the former is no match for the ratiocinations of the latter. Belief is no adequate substitute for inner experience, and where this is absent even a strong faith which came miraculously as a gift of grace may depart equally miraculously. People call faith the true religious experience, but they do not stop to consider that actually it is a secondary phenomenon arising from the fact that something happened to us in the first place which instilled πίστις into us— that is, trust and loyalty. This experience has a definite content that can be interpreted in terms of one or other of the denominational creeds. But the more this is so, the more the possibilities of these conflicts with knowledge mount up, which in themselves are quite pointless. That is to say, the standpoint of the creeds is archaic; they are full of impressive mythological symbolism which, if taken literally, comes into insufferable con-

265

flict with knowledge. But if, for instance, the statement that Christ rose from the dead is to be understood not literally but symbolically, then it is capable of various interpretations that do not conflict with knowledge and do not impair the meaning of the statement. The objection that understanding it symbolically puts an end to the Christian's hope of immortality is invalid, because long before the coming of Christianity mankind believed in a life after death and therefore had no need of the Easter event as a guarantee of immortality. The danger that a mythology understood too literally, and as taught by the Church, will suddenly be repudiated lock, stock and barrel is today greater than ever. Is it not time that the Christian mythology, instead of being wiped out, was understood symbolically for once?

522   It is still too early to say what might be the consequences of a general recognition of the fatal parallelism between the State religion of the Marxists and the State religion of the Church. The absolutist claim of a *Civitas Dei* that is represented by man bears an unfortunate resemblance to the "divinity" of the State, and the moral conclusion drawn by Ignatius Loyola from the authority of the Church ("the end sanctifies the means") anticipates the lie as a political instrument in an exceedingly dangerous way. Both demand unqualified submission to faith and thus curtail man's freedom, the one his freedom before God and the other his freedom before the State, thereby digging the grave for the individual. The fragile existence of this—so far as we know—unique carrier of life is threatened on both sides, despite their respective promises of spiritual and material idylls to come—and how many of us can in the long run fight against the proverbial wisdom of "a bird in the hand is worth two in the bush"? Besides which, the West cherishes the same "scientific" and rationalistic *Weltanschauung* with its statistical levelling-down tendency and materialistic aims as the State religion of the Eastern bloc, as I have explained above.

523   What, then, has the West, with its political and denominational schisms, to offer to modern man in his need? Nothing, unfortunately, except a variety of paths all leading to one goal which is practically indistinguishable from the Marxist ideal. It requires no special effort of understanding to see where the Communist ideology gets the certainty of its belief that time

is on its side, and that the world is ripe for conversion. The facts speak a language that is all too plain in this respect. It will not help us in the West to shut our eyes to this and not recognize our fatal vulnerability. Anyone who has once learned to submit absolutely to a collective belief and to renounce his eternal right to freedom and the equally eternal duty of individual responsibility will persist in this attitude, and will be able to march with the same credulity and the same lack of criticism in the reverse direction, if another and manifestly "better" belief is foisted upon his alleged idealism. What happened not so long ago to a civilized European nation? We accuse the Germans of having forgotten it all again already, but the truth is that we don't know for certain whether something similar might not happen elsewhere. It would not be surprising if it did and if another civilized nation succumbed to the infection of a uniform and one-sided idea. We permit ourselves the question: which countries have the biggest Communist parties? America, which—*O quae mutatio rerum!*—forms the real political backbone of Western Europe, seems to be immune because of the outspoken counterposition she has adopted, but in point of fact she is perhaps even more vulnerable than Europe, since her educational system is the most influenced by the scientific *Weltanschauung* with its statistical truths, and her mixed population finds it difficult to strike roots in a soil that is practically without history. The historical and humanistic type of education so sorely needed in such circumstances leads, on the contrary, a Cinderella existence. Though Europe possesses this latter requirement, she uses it to her own undoing in the form of nationalistic egoisms and paralysing scepticism. Common to both is the materialistic and collectivist goal, and both lack the very thing that expresses and grips the whole man, namely, an idea which puts the individual human being in the centre as the measure of all things.

524   This idea alone is enough to arouse the most violent doubts and resistances on all sides, and one could almost go so far as to assert that the valuelessness of the individual in comparison with large numbers is the one belief that meets with universal and unanimous assent. To be sure, we all say that this is the century of the common man, that he is the lord of the earth, the air, and the water, and that on his decision hangs the historical

fate of the nations. This proud picture of human grandeur is unfortunately an illusion and is counterbalanced by a reality that is very different. In this reality man is the slave and victim of the machines that have conquered space and time for him; he is intimidated and endangered by the might of the military technology which is supposed to safeguard his physical existence; his spiritual and moral freedom, though guaranteed within limits in one half of his world, is threatened with chaotic disorientation, and in the other half is abolished altogether. Finally, to add comedy to tragedy, this lord of the elements, this universal arbiter, hugs to his bosom notions which stamp his dignity as worthless and turn his autonomy into an absurdity. All his achievements and possessions do not make him bigger; on the contrary, they diminish him, as the fate of the factory-worker under the rule of a "just" distribution of goods clearly demonstrates. He pays for his share of the factory with the loss of personal property, he exchanges his freedom of movement for the doubtful pleasure of being tied to his place of employment, he forfeits all means of improving his position if he jibs against being ground down by exhausting piece-work, and if he shows any signs of intelligence, political precepts are thrust down his throat—with a bit of technical knowledge thrown in, if he is lucky. However, a roof over one's head and a daily feed for the useful animal are not to be sneezed at when the bare necessities of life may be cut off from one day to the next.

4. THE INDIVIDUAL'S UNDERSTANDING
OF HIMSELF

525   It is astounding that man, the instigator, inventor and
vehicle of all these developments, the originator of all judgments and decisions and the planner of the future, must make
himself such a *quantité négligeable*. The contradiction, the
paradoxical evaluation of humanity by man himself, is in truth
a matter for wonder, and one can only explain it as springing
from an extraordinary uncertainty of judgment—in other
words, man is an enigma to himself. This is understandable, seeing that he lacks the means of comparison necessary for self-
knowledge. He knows how to distinguish himself from the
other animals in point of anatomy and physiology, but as a conscious, reflecting being, gifted with speech, he lacks all criteria
for self-judgment. He is on this planet a unique phenomenon
which he cannot compare with anything else. The possibility
of comparison and hence of self-knowledge would arise only if
he could establish relations with quasi-human mammals in-
habiting other stars.

526   Until then man must continue to resemble a hermit who
knows that in respect of comparative anatomy he has affinities
with the anthropoids but, to judge by appearances, is extraordinarily different from his cousins in respect of his psyche. It is
just in this most important characteristic of his species that he
cannot know himself and therefore remains a mystery to himself. The differing degrees of self-knowledge within his own
species are of little significance compared with the possibilities
which would be opened out by an encounter with a creature of
similar structure but different origin. Our psyche, which is
primarily responsible for all the historical changes wrought by
the hand of man on the face of this planet, remains an insoluble puzzle and an incomprehensible wonder, an object of
abiding perplexity—a feature it shares with all Nature's secrets.

In regard to the latter we still have hope of making more discoveries and finding answers to the most difficult questions. But
in regard to the psyche and psychology there seems to be a curious hesitancy. Not only is it the youngest of the empirical sciences, but it has great difficulty in getting anywhere near its
proper object.

527   In the same way that our picture of the world had to be
freed by Copernicus from the prejudice of geocentricity, the
most strenuous efforts of a well-nigh revolutionary nature were
needed to free psychology, first from the spell of mythological
ideas, and then from the prejudice that the psyche is, on the one
hand, a mere epiphenomenon of a biochemical process in the
brain and, on the other hand, a purely personal matter. The
connection with the brain does not in itself prove that the
psyche is an epiphenomenon, a secondary function causally dependent on biochemical processes in the physical substrate.
Nevertheless, we know only too well how much the psychic
function can be disturbed by verifiable processes in the brain,
and this fact is so impressive that the subsidiary nature of the
psyche seems an almost unavoidable inference. The phenomena
of parapsychology, however, warn us to be careful, for they
point to a relativization of space and time through psychic factors which casts doubt on our naïve and overhasty explanation
in terms of psychophysical parallelism. For the sake of this explanation people deny the findings of parapsychology outright,
either for philosophical reasons or from intellectual laziness.
This can hardly be considered a scientifically responsible attitude, even though it is a popular way out of a quite extraordinary intellectual difficulty. To assess the psychic phenomenon,
we have to take account of all the other phenomena that go with
it, and accordingly we can no longer practise any psychology
that ignores the existence of the unconscious or of parapsychology.

528   The structure and physiology of the brain furnish no explanation of the psychic process. The psyche has a peculiar nature
which cannot be reduced to anything else. Like physiology, it
presents a relatively self-contained field of experience, to which
we must attribute a quite special importance because it includes
one of the two indispensable conditions for existence as such,
namely, the phenomenon of consciousness. Without conscious-

ness there would, practically speaking, be no world, for the world exists for us only in so far as it is consciously reflected by a psyche. *Consciousness is a precondition of being.* Thus the psyche is endowed with the dignity of a cosmic principle, which philosophically and in fact gives it a position co-equal with the principle of physical being. The carrier of this consciousness is the individual, who does not produce the psyche of his own volition but is, on the contrary, preformed by it and nourished by the gradual awakening of consciousness during childhood. If therefore the psyche is of overriding empirical importance, so also is the individual, who is the only immediate manifestation of the psyche.

529   This fact must be expressly emphasized for two reasons. Firstly, the individual psyche, just because of its individuality, is an exception to the statistical rule and is therefore robbed of one of its main characteristics when subjected to the levelling influence of statistical evaluation. Secondly, the Churches grant it validity only in so far as it acknowledges their dogmas—in other words, when it submits to a collective category. In both cases the will to individuality is regarded as egotistic obstinacy. Science devalues this as subjectivism, and the Churches condemn it morally as heresy and spiritual pride. As to the latter charge, it should not be forgotten that, unlike other religions, Christianity holds up before us a symbol whose content is the individual way of life of a man, the Son of Man, and that it even regards this individuation process as the incarnation and revelation of God himself. Hence the development of man into a self acquires a significance whose full implications have hardly begun to be appreciated, because too much attention to externals blocks the way to immediate inner experience. Were not the autonomy of the individual the secret longing of many people it would scarcely be able to survive the collective suppression either morally or spiritually.

530   All these obstacles make it more difficult to arrive at a correct appreciation of the human psyche, but they count for very little beside one other remarkable fact that deserves mentioning. This is the common psychiatric experience that the devaluation of the psyche and other resistances to psychological enlightenment are based in large measure on fear—on panic fear of the discoveries that might be made in the realm of the uncon-

scious. These fears are found not only among persons who are frightened by the picture Freud painted of the unconscious; they also troubled the originator of psychoanalysis himself, who confessed to me that it was necessary to make a dogma of his sexual theory because this was the sole bulwark of reason against a possible "eruption of the black flood of occultism." In these words Freud was expressing his conviction that the unconscious still harboured many things that might lend themselves to "occult" interpretation, as is in fact the case. These "archaic vestiges," or archetypal forms grounded on the instincts and giving expression to them, have a numinous quality that sometimes arouses fear. They are ineradicable, for they represent the ultimate foundations of the psyche itself. They cannot be grasped intellectually, and when one has destroyed one manifestation of them, they reappear in altered form. It is this fear of the unconscious psyche which not only impedes self-knowledge but is the gravest obstacle to a wider understanding and knowledge of psychology. Often the fear is so great that one dares not admit it even to oneself. This is a question which every religious person should consider very seriously; he might get an illuminating answer.

531   A scientifically oriented psychology is bound to proceed abstractly; that is, it removes itself just sufficiently far from its object not to lose sight of it altogether. That is why the findings of laboratory psychology are, for all practical purposes, often so remarkably unenlightening and devoid of interest. The more the individual object dominates the field of vision, the more practical, detailed, and alive will be the knowledge derived from it. This means that the objects of investigation, too, become more and more complicated and that the uncertainty of the individual factors grows in proportion to their number, thus increasing the possibility of error. Understandably enough, academic psychology is scared of this risk and prefers to avoid complex situations by asking ever simpler questions, which it can do with impunity. It has full freedom in the choice of questions it will put to Nature.

532   Medical psychology, on the other hand, is very far from being in this more or less enviable position. Here the object puts the question and not the experimenter. The analyst is confronted with facts which are not of his choosing and which he probably

never *would* choose if he were a free agent. It is the sickness or the patient himself that puts the crucial questions—in other words, Nature experiments with the doctor in expecting an answer from him. The uniqueness of the individual and of his situation stares the analyst in the face and demands an answer. His duty as a physician forces him to cope with a situation swarming with uncertainty factors. At first he will apply principles based on general experience, but he will soon realize that principles of this kind do not adequately express the facts and fail to meet the nature of the case. The deeper his understanding penetrates, the more the general principles lose their meaning. But these principles are the foundation of objective knowledge and the yardstick by which it is measured. With the growth of what both patient and doctor feel to be "understanding," the situation becomes increasingly subjectivized. What was an advantage to begin with threatens to turn into a dangerous disadvantage. Subjectivation (in technical terms, transference and countertransference) creates isolation from the environment, a social limitation which neither party wishes for but which invariably sets in when understanding predominates and is no longer balanced by knowledge. As understanding deepens, the further removed it becomes from knowledge. An ideal understanding would ultimately result in each party's unthinkingly going along with the other's experience—a state of uncritical passivity coupled with the most complete subjectivity and lack of social responsibility. Understanding carried to such lengths is in any case impossible, for it would require the virtual identification of two different individuals. Sooner or later the relationship reaches a point where one partner feels he is being forced to sacrifice his own individuality so that it may be assimilated by that of the other. This inevitable consequence breaks the understanding, for understanding also presupposes the integral preservation of the individuality of both partners. It is therefore advisable to carry understanding only to the point where the balance between understanding and knowledge is reached, for understanding at all costs is injurious to both partners.

533   This problem arises whenever complex, individual situations have to be known and understood. It is the specific task of the medical psychologist to provide just this knowledge and

273

understanding. It would also be the task of the "director of conscience" zealous in the cure of souls, were it not that his office inevitably obliges him to apply the yardstick of his denominational bias at the critical moment. As a result, the individual's right to exist as such is cut short by a collective prejudice and often curtailed in the most sensitive area. The only time this does not happen is when the dogmatic symbol, for instance the model life of Christ, is understood concretely and felt by the individual to be adequate. How far this is the case today I would prefer to leave to the judgment of others. At all events, the analyst very often has to treat patients to whom denominational limitations mean little or nothing. His profession therefore compels him to have as few preconceptions as possible. Similarly, while respecting metaphysical (i.e., non-verifiable) convictions and assertions, he will take care not to credit them with universal validity. This caution is called for because the individual traits of the patient's personality ought not to be twisted out of shape by arbitrary interventions from outside. The analyst must leave this to environmental influences, to the patient's own inner development, and—in the widest sense—to fate with its wise or unwise decrees.

534   Many people will perhaps find this heightened caution exaggerated. In view of the fact, however, that there is in any case such a multitude of reciprocal influences at work in the dialectical process between two individuals, even if it is conducted with the most tactful reserve, the responsible analyst will refrain from adding unnecessarily to the collective factors to which his patient has already succumbed. Moreover, he knows very well that the preaching of even the worthiest precepts only provokes the patient into open hostility or secret resistance and thus needlessly endangers the aim of the treatment. The psychic situation of the individual is so menaced nowadays by advertising, propaganda, and other more or less well-meant advice and suggestions that for once in his life the patient might be offered a relationship that does not repeat the nauseating "you should," "you must" and similar confessions of impotence. Against the onslaught from outside no less than against its repercussions in the psyche of the individual the analyst sees himself obliged to play the role of counsel for the defence. Fear that anarchic instincts will thereby be let loose is a possibility that

is greatly exaggerated, seeing that obvious safeguards exist within and without. Above all, there is the natural cowardice of most men to be reckoned with, not to mention morality, good taste and—last but not least—the penal code. This fear is nothing compared with the enormous effort it usually costs people to help the first stirrings of individuality into consciousness, let alone put them into effect. And where these individual impulses have broken through too boldly and unthinkingly, the analyst must protect them from the patient's own clumsy recourse to shortsightedness, ruthlessness, and cynicism.

535   As the dialectical discussion proceeds, a point is reached when an evaluation of these individual impulses becomes necessary. By that time the patient should have acquired enough certainty of judgment to enable him to act on his own insight and decision and not from the mere wish to copy convention—even if he happens to agree with collective opinion. Unless he stands firmly on his own feet, the so-called objective values profit him nothing, since they then only serve as a substitute for character and so help to suppress his individuality. Naturally, society has an indisputable right to protect itself against arrant subjectivisms, but, in so far as society is itself composed of de-individualized human beings, it is completely at the mercy of ruthless individualists. Let it band together into groups and organizations as much as it likes—it is just this banding together and the resultant extinction of the individual personality that makes it succumb so readily to a dictator. A million zeros joined together do not, unfortunately, add up to one. Ultimately everything depends on the quality of the individual, but our fatally shortsighted age thinks only in terms of large numbers and mass organizations, though one would think that the world had seen more than enough of what a well-disciplined mob can do in the hands of a single madman. Unfortunately, this realization does not seem to have penetrated very far—and our blindness is extremely dangerous. People go on blithely organizing and believing in the sovereign remedy of mass action, without the least consciousness of the fact that the most powerful organizations can be maintained only by the greatest ruthlessness of their leaders and the cheapest of slogans.

536   Curiously enough, the Churches too want to avail themselves of mass action in order to cast out the devil with Beelzebub—the

very Churches whose care is the salvation of the *individual* soul. They do not appear to have heard of the elementary axiom of mass psychology that the individual becomes morally and spiritually inferior in the mass, and for this reason they do not bother themselves overmuch with their real task of helping the individual to achieve a *metanoia,* a rebirth of the spirit—*Deo concedente.* It is, unfortunately, only too clear that if the individual is not truly regenerated in spirit, society cannot be either, for society is the sum total of individuals in need of redemption. I can therefore see it only as a delusion when the Churches try —as they apparently do—to rope the individual into some social organization and reduce him to a condition of diminished responsibility, instead of raising him out of the torpid, mindless mass and making clear to him that *he* is the one important factor and that the salvation of the world consists in the salvation of the individual soul. It is true that mass meetings parade these ideas before him and seek to impress them on his mind by dint of mass suggestion, with the melancholy result that once the intoxication has worn off the mass man promptly succumbs to another even more obvious and still louder slogan. His individual relation to God would be an effective shield against these pernicious influences. Did Christ, perchance, call his disciples to him at a mass meeting? Did the feeding of the five thousand bring him any followers who did not afterwards cry with the rest, "Crucify him!" when even the rock named Peter showed signs of wavering? And are not Jesus and Paul prototypes of those who, trusting their inner experience, have gone their individual ways in defiance of the world?

537   This argument should certainly not cause us to overlook the reality of the situation confronting the Church. When the Church tries to give shape to the amorphous mass by uniting individuals into a community of believers and to hold such an organization together with the help of suggestion, it is not only performing a great *social* service, but it also secures for the individual the inestimable boon of a meaningful form of life. These, however, are gifts which as a rule only confirm certain tendencies and do not change them. As experience unfortunately shows, the inner man remains unchanged however much community he has. His environment cannot give him as a gift something which he can win for himself only with effort and

suffering. On the contrary, a favourable environment merely strengthens the dangerous tendency to expect everything from outside—even that metamorphosis which external reality cannot provide. By this I mean a far-reaching change of the inner man, which is all the more urgent in view of the mass phenomena of today and the still greater problems of overpopulation looming in the future. It is time we asked ourselves exactly what we are lumping together in mass organizations and what constitutes the nature of the individual human being, i.e., of the real man and not the statistical man. This is hardly possible except by a new process of self-reflection.

538   All mass movements, as one might expect, slip with the greatest ease down an inclined plane made up of large numbers. Where the many are, there is security; what the many believe must of course be true; what the many want must be worth striving for, and necessary, and therefore good. In the clamour of the many resides the power to snatch wish-fulfilments by force; sweetest of all, however, is that gentle and painless slipping back into the kingdom of childhood, into the paradise of parental care, into happy-go-luckiness and irresponsibility. All the thinking and looking after are done from the top; to all questions there is an answer, and for all needs the necessary provision is made. The infantile dream-state of the mass man is so unrealistic that he never thinks to ask who is paying for this paradise. The balancing of accounts is left to a higher political or social authority, which welcomes the task, for its power is thereby increased; and the more power it has, the weaker and more helpless the individual becomes.

539   Whenever social conditions of this type develop on a large scale, the road to tyranny lies open and the freedom of the individual turns into spiritual and physical slavery. Since every tyranny is *ipso facto* immoral and ruthless, it has much more freedom in the choice of its methods than an institution which still takes account of the individual. Should such an institution come into conflict with the organized State, it is soon made aware of the very real disadvantage of its morality and therefore feels compelled to avail itself of the same methods as its opponent. In this way the evil spreads almost of necessity, even when direct infection might be avoided. The danger of infection is greater when decisive importance is attached to large numbers

and to statistical values, as is everywhere the case in our Western world. The suffocating power of the masses is paraded before our eyes in one form or another every day in the newspapers, and the insignificance of the individual is rubbed into him so thoroughly that he loses all hope of making himself heard. The outworn ideals of *liberté, égalité, fraternité* help him not at all, as he can direct this appeal only to his executioners, the spokesmen of the masses.

540 *Resistance to the organized mass can be effected only by the man who is as well organized in his individuality as the mass itself.* I fully realize that this proposition must sound well-nigh unintelligible to the man of today. The helpful medieval view that man is a microcosm, a reflection of the great cosmos in miniature, has long since dropped away from him, although the very existence of his world-embracing and world-conditioning psyche might have taught him better. Not only is the image of the macrocosm imprinted upon his psychic nature, but he also creates this image for himself on an ever-widening scale. He bears this cosmic "correspondence" within him by virtue of his reflecting consciousness on the one hand, and, on the other, thanks to the hereditary, archetypal nature of his instincts, which bind him to his environment. But his instincts not only attach him to the macrocosm, they also, in a sense, tear him apart, because his desires pull him in different directions. In this way he falls into continual conflict with himself and only very rarely succeeds in giving his life an undivided goal—for which, as a rule, he must pay very dearly by repressing other sides of his nature. One often has to ask oneself whether this kind of single-mindedness is worth forcing at all, seeing that the natural state of the human psyche consists in a jostling together of its components and in their contradictory behaviour—that is, in a certain degree of dissociation. The Buddhist name for this is attachment to the "ten thousand things." Such a condition cries out for order and synthesis.

541 Just as the chaotic movements of the crowd, all ending in mutual frustration, are impelled in a definite direction by a dictatorial will, so the individual in his dissociated state needs a directing and ordering principle. Ego-consciousness would like to let its own will play this role, but overlooks the existence of powerful unconscious factors which thwart its intentions. If it

278

wants to reach the goal of synthesis, it must first get to know the nature of these factors. It must *experience* them, or else it must possess a numinous *symbol* that expresses them and leads to their synthesis. A religious symbol that comprehended and visibly represented what is seeking expression in modern man might possibly do this; but our conception of the Christian symbol to date has certainly not been able to do so. On the contrary, that frightful world split runs right through the domains of the "Christian" white man, and our Christian outlook on life has proved powerless to prevent the recrudescence of an archaic social order like Communism.

542   This is not to say that Christianity is finished. I am, on the contrary, convinced that it is not Christianity, but our conception and interpretation of it, that has become antiquated in face of the present world situation. The Christian symbol is a living thing that carries in itself the seeds of further development. It can go on developing; it depends only on us, whether we can make up our minds to meditate again, and more thoroughly, on the Christian premises. This requires a very different attitude towards the individual, towards the microcosm of the self, from the one we have adopted hitherto. That is why nobody knows what ways of approach are open to man, what inner experiences he could still pass through and what psychic facts underlie the religious myth. Over all this hangs so universal a darkness that no one can see why he should be interested or to what end he should commit himself. Before this problem we stand helpless.

543   This is not surprising, since practically all the trump cards are in the hands of our opponents. They can appeal to the big battalions and their crushing power. Politics, science, and technology stand ranged on their side. The imposing arguments of science represent the highest degree of intellectual certainty yet achieved by the mind of man. So at least it seems to the man of today, who has received hundred-fold enlightenment concerning the backwardness and darkness of past ages and their superstitions. That his teachers have themselves gone seriously astray by making false comparisons between incommensurable factors never enters his head. All the more so as the intellectual *élite* to whom he puts his questions are almost unanimously agreed that what science regards as impossible today was impossible at all other times as well. Above all, the facts of faith, which might

give him the chance of an extramundane standpoint, are treated in the same context as the facts of science. Thus, when the individual questions the Churches and their spokesmen, to whom is entrusted the cure of souls, he is informed that to belong to a church—a decidedly worldly institution—is more or less *de rigueur;* that the facts of faith which have become questionable for him were concrete historical events; that certain ritual actions produce miraculous effects; and that the sufferings of Christ have vicariously saved him from sin and its consequences (i.e., eternal damnation). If, with the limited means at his disposal, he begins to reflect on these things, he will have to confess that he does not understand them at all and that only two possibilities remain open to him: either to believe implicitly, or to reject such statements because they are flatly incomprehensible.

544   Whereas the man of today can easily think about and understand all the "truths" dished out to him by the State, his understanding of religion is made considerably more difficult owing to the lack of explanations. ("Do you understand what you are reading?" And he said, "How can I, unless someone guides me?" Acts 8 : 30.) If, despite this, he has still not discarded all his religious convictions, this is because the religious impulse rests on an instinctive basis and is therefore a specifically human function. You can take away a man's gods, but only to give him others in return. The leaders of the mass State could not help being deified, and wherever crudities of this kind have not yet been put over by force, obsessive factors arise in their stead, charged with demonic energy—money, work, political influence, and so forth. When any natural human function gets lost, i.e., is denied conscious and intentional expression, a general disturbance results. Hence, it is quite natural that with the triumph of the Goddess of Reason a general neuroticizing of modern man should set in, a dissociation of personality analogous to the splitting of the world today by the Iron Curtain. This boundary line bristling with barbed wire runs through the psyche of modern man, no matter on which side he lives. And just as the typical neurotic is unconscious of his *shadow side,* so the normal individual, like the neurotic, sees his shadow in his neighbour or in the man beyond the great divide. It has even become a political and social duty to apostrophize the capitalism

of the one and the communism of the other as the very devil, so as to fascinate the outward eye and prevent it from looking within. But just as the neurotic, despite unconsciousness of his other side, has a dim premonition that all is not well with his psychic economy, so Western man has developed an instinctive interest in his psyche and in "psychology."

545 Thus it is that the psychiatrist is summoned willy-nilly to appear on the world stage, and questions are addressed to him which primarily concern the most intimate and hidden life of the individual, but which in the last analysis are the direct effects of the *Zeitgeist*. Because of its personal symptomatology this material is usually considered to be "neurotic"—and rightly so, since it is made up of infantile fantasies which ill accord with the contents of an adult psyche and are therefore repressed by our moral judgment, in so far as they reach consciousness at all. Most fantasies of this kind do not, in the nature of things, come to consciousness in any form, and it is very improbable, to say the least of it, that they were ever conscious and were consciously repressed. Rather, they seem to have been present from the beginning or, at any rate, to have arisen unconsciously and to have persisted in that state until the psychologist's intervention enabled them to cross the threshold of consciousness. The activation of unconscious fantasies is a process that occurs when consciousness finds itself in a situation of distress. Were that not so, the fantasies would be produced normally and would then bring no neurotic disturbances in their train. In reality, fantasies of this kind belong to the world of childhood and give rise to disturbances only when prematurely strengthened by abnormal conditions of conscious life. This is particularly likely to happen when unfavourable influences emanate from the parents, poisoning the atmosphere and producing conflicts which upset the psychic balance of the child.

546 When a neurosis breaks out in an adult, the fantasy world of childhood reappears, and one is tempted to explain the onset of the neurosis causally, as due to the presence of infantile fantasies. But that does not explain why the fantasies did not develop any pathological effects during the interim period. These effects develop only when the individual is faced with a situation which he cannot overcome by conscious means. The resultant standstill in the development of personality opens a sluice

for infantile fantasies, which, of course, are latent in everybody but do not display any activity so long as the conscious personality can continue on its way unimpeded. When the fantasies reach a certain level of intensity, they begin to break through into consciousness and create a conflict situation that becomes perceptible to the patient himself, splitting him into two personalities with different characters. The dissociation, however, had been prepared long before in the unconscious, when the energy flowing off from consciousness (because unused) reinforced the negative qualities of the unconscious and particularly the infantile traits of the personality.

547 Since the normal fantasies of a child are nothing other, at bottom, than the *imagination of the instincts,* and may thus be regarded as preliminary exercises in the use of future conscious activities, it follows that the fantasies of the neurotic, even though pathologically altered and perhaps perverted by the regression of energy, contain a core of normal instinct, the hallmark of which is adaptedness. A neurotic illness always implies an unadapted alteration and distortion of normal dynamisms and of the "imagination" proper to them. Instincts, however, are highly conservative and of extreme antiquity as regards both their dynamism and their form. Their form, when represented to the mind, appears as an *image* which expresses the nature of the instinctive impulse visually and concretely, like a picture. If we could look into the psyche of the yucca moth,[1] for instance, we would find in it a pattern of ideas, of a numinous or fascinating character, which not only compels the moth to carry out its fertilizing activity on the yucca plant but helps it to "recognize" the total situation. Instinct is anything but a blind and indefinite impulse, since it proves to be attuned and adapted to a definite external situation. This latter circumstance gives it its specific and irreducible form. Just as instinct is original and hereditary, so, too, its form is age-old, that is to say, *archetypal.* It is even older and more conservative than the body's form.

548 These biological considerations naturally apply also to *Homo sapiens,* who still remains within the framework of general biology despite the possession of consciousness, will, and

[1] This is a classic instance of the symbiosis of insect and plant. [Cf. "Instinct and the Unconscious," *The Structure and Dynamics of the Psyche,* pars. 268, 277.]

reason. The fact that our conscious activity is rooted in instinct and derives from it its dynamism as well as the basic features of its ideational forms has the same significance for human psychology as for all other members of the animal kingdom. Human knowledge consists essentially in the constant adaptation of the primordial patterns of ideas that were given us *a priori*. These need certain modifications, because, in their original form, they are suited to an archaic mode of life but not to the demands of a specifically differentiated environment. If the flow of instinctive dynamism into our life is to be maintained, as is absolutely necessary for our existence, then it is imperative that we should remould these archetypal forms into ideas which are adequate to the challenge of the present.

5. THE PHILOSOPHICAL AND THE
PSYCHOLOGICAL APPROACH TO LIFE

549   Our ideas have, however, the unfortunate but inevitable tendency to lag behind the changes in the total situation. They can hardly do otherwise, because, so long as nothing changes in the world, they remain more or less adapted and therefore function in a satisfactory way. There is then no cogent reason why they should be changed and adapted anew. Only when conditions have altered so drastically that there is an unendurable rift between the outer situation and our ideas, now become antiquated, does the general problem of our *Weltanschauung,* or philosophy of life, arise, and with it the question of how the primordial images that maintain the flow of instinctive energy are to be reoriented or readapted. They cannot simply be replaced by a new rational configuration, for this would be moulded too much by the outward situation and not enough by man's biological needs. Moreover, not only would it build no bridge to the original man, but it would block the approach to him altogether. This is in keeping with the aims of Marxist education, which seeks, like God himself, to remake man, but in the image of the State.

550   Today, our basic convictions are becoming increasingly rationalistic. Our philosophy is no longer a way of life, as it was in antiquity; it has turned into an exclusively intellectual and academic exercise. Our denominational religions with their archaic rites and conceptions—justified enough in themselves—express a view of the world which caused no great difficulties in the Middle Ages but has become strange and unintelligible to modern man. Despite this conflict with the modern scientific outlook, a deep instinct bids him hang on to ideas which, if taken literally, leave out of account all the mental developments of the last five hundred years. The obvious purpose of this is to prevent him from falling into the abyss of nihilistic despair. But

284

even when, as a rationalist, he feels impelled to criticize denominational religion as literalistic, narrow-minded, and obsolescent, he should never forget that it proclaims a doctrine whose symbols, although their interpretation may be disputed, nevertheless possess a life of their own by virtue of their archetypal character. Consequently, intellectual understanding is by no means indispensable in all cases, but is called for only when evaluation through feeling and intuition does not suffice, that is to say, in the case of people for whom the intellect carries the prime power of conviction.

551   Nothing is more characteristic and symptomatic in this respect than the gulf that has opened out between *faith* and *knowledge*. The contrast has become so enormous that one is obliged to speak of the incommensurability of these two categories and their way of looking at the world. And yet they are concerned with the same empirical world in which we live, for even the theologians tell us that faith is supported by facts that became historically perceptible in this known world of ours—namely that Christ was born as a real human being, worked many miracles and suffered his fate, died under Pontius Pilate, and rose up in the flesh after his death. Theology rejects any tendency to take the assertions of its earliest records as written myths and, accordingly, to understand them symbolically. Indeed, it is the theologians themselves who have recently made the attempt—no doubt as a concession to "knowledge"—to "demythologize" the object of their faith while drawing the line quite arbitrarily at the crucial points. But to the critical intellect it is only too obvious that myth is an integral component of all religions and therefore cannot be excluded from the assertions of faith without injuring them.

552   The rupture between faith and knowledge is a symptom of the *split consciousness* which is so characteristic of the mental disorder of our day. It is as if two different persons were making statements about the same thing, each from his own point of view, or as if one person in two different frames of mind were sketching a picture of his experience. If for "person" we substitute "modern society," it is evident that the latter is suffering from a mental dissociation, i.e., a neurotic disturbance. In view of this, it does not help matters at all if one party pulls obstinately to the right and the other to the left. This is what hap-

pens in every neurotic psyche, to its own deep distress, and it is just this distress that brings the patient to the analyst.

553 As I stated above in all brevity—while not neglecting to mention certain practical details whose omission might have perplexed the reader—the analyst has to establish a relationship with *both* halves of his patient's personality, because only from them can he put together a whole and complete man, and not merely from one half by suppression of the other half. But this suppression is just what the patient has been doing all along, for the modern *Weltanschauung* leaves him with no alternative. His individual situation is the same in principle as the collective situation. He is a social microcosm, reflecting on the smallest scale the qualities of society at large, or conversely the smallest social unit cumulatively producing the collective dissociation. The latter possibility is the more likely one, as the only direct and concrete carrier of life is the individual personality, while society and the State are conventional ideas and can claim reality only in so far as they are represented by a conglomeration of individuals.

554 Far too little attention has been paid to the fact that, for all our irreligiousness, the distinguishing mark of the Christian epoch, its highest achievement, has become the congenital vice of our age: *the supremacy of the word,* of the Logos, which stands for the central figure of our Christian faith. The word has literally become our god and so it has remained, even if we know of Christianity only from hearsay. Words like "Society" and "State" are so concretized that they are almost personified. In the opinion of the man in the street, the "State," far more than any king in history, is the inexhaustible giver of all good; the "State" is invoked, made responsible, grumbled at, and so on and so forth. Society is elevated to the rank of a supreme ethical principle; indeed, it is even credited with positively creative capacities. No one seems to notice that this worship of the word, which was necessary at a certain phase of man's mental development, has a perilous shadow side. That is to say, the moment the word, as a result of centuries of education, attains universal validity, it severs its original connection with the divine Person. There is then a personified Church, a personified State; belief in the word becomes credulity, and the word itself an infernal slogan capable of any deception. With credulity

come propaganda and advertising to dupe the citizen with political jobbery and compromises, and the lie reaches proportions never known before in the history of the world.

555   Thus the word, originally announcing the unity of all men and their union in the figure of the one great Man, has in our day become a source of suspicion and distrust of all against all. Credulity is one of our worst enemies, but that is the makeshift the neurotic always resorts to in order to quell the doubter in his own breast or to conjure him out of existence. People think you have only to "tell" a person that he "ought" to do something in order to put him on the right track. But whether he can or will do it is another matter. The psychologist has come to see that nothing is achieved by telling, persuading, admonishing, giving good advice. He must acquaint himself with all the particulars and have an authentic knowledge of the psychic inventory of his patient. He has therefore to relate to the individuality of the sufferer and feel his way into all the nooks and crannies of his mind, to a degree that far exceeds the capacity of a teacher or even of a *directeur de conscience*. His scientific objectivity, which excludes nothing, enables him to see his patient not only as a human being but also as an anthropoid, who is bound to his body like an animal. His training directs his medical interest beyond the conscious personality to the world of unconscious instinct dominated by sexuality and the power drive (or self-assertion), which correspond to the twin moral concepts of Saint Augustine: *concupiscentia* and *superbia*. The clash between these two fundamental instincts (preservation of the species and self-preservation) is the source of numerous conflicts. They are, therefore, the chief object of moral judgment, whose purpose it is to prevent instinctual collisions as far as possible.

556   As I explained earlier, instinct has two main aspects: on the one hand, that of dynamism and compulsion, and on the other, specific meaning and intention. It is highly probable that all man's psychic functions have an instinctual foundation, as is obviously the case with animals. It is easy to see that in animals instinct functions as the *spiritus rector* of all behaviour. This observation lacks certainty only when the learning capacity begins to develop, for instance in the higher apes and in man. In animals, as a result of their learning capacity, instinct under-

287

goes numerous modifications and differentiations, and in civilized man the instincts are so split up that only a few of the basic ones can be recognized with any certainty in their original form. The most important are the two fundamental instincts already mentioned and their derivatives, and these have been the exclusive concern of medical psychology so far. But in following up the ramifications of instinct investigators came upon configurations which could not with certainty be ascribed to either group. To take but one example: The discoverer of the power instinct raised the question whether an apparently indubitable expression of the sexual instinct might not be better explained as a "power arrangement," and Freud himself felt obliged to acknowledge the existence of "ego instincts" in addition to the overriding sexual instinct—a clear concession to the Adlerian standpoint. In view of this uncertainty, it is hardly surprising that in most cases neurotic symptoms can be explained, almost without contradiction, in terms of either theory. This perplexity does not mean that one or the other standpoint is erroneous or that both are. Rather, both are *relatively* valid and, unlike certain one-sided and dogmatic tendencies, admit the existence and competition of still other instincts. Although, as I have said, the question of human instinct is a far from simple matter, we shall probably not be wrong in assuming that the learning capacity, a quality almost exclusive to man, is based on the instinct for imitation found in animals. It is in the nature of this instinct to disturb other instinctive activities and eventually to modify them, as can be observed, for instance, in the songs of birds when they adopt other melodies.

557 Nothing estranges man more from the ground-plan of his instincts than his learning capacity, which turns out to be a genuine drive for progressive transformation of human modes of behaviour. It, more than anything else, is responsible for the altered conditions of his existence and the need for new adaptations which civilization brings. It is also the ultimate source of those numerous psychic disturbances and difficulties which are occasioned by man's progressive alienation from his instinctual foundation, i.e., by his uprootedness and identification with his conscious knowledge of himself, by his concern with consciousness at the expense of the unconscious. The result is that modern man knows himself only in so far as he can become con-

scious of himself—a capacity largely dependent on environmental conditions, knowledge and control of which necessitated or suggested certain modifications of his original instinctive tendencies. His consciousness therefore orients itself chiefly by observing and investigating the world around him, and it is to the latter's peculiarities that he must adapt his psychic and technical resources. This task is so exacting, and its fulfilment so profitable, that he forgets himself in the process, losing sight of his instinctual nature and putting his own conception of himself in place of his real being. In this way he slips imperceptibly into a purely conceptual world where the products of his conscious activity progressively take the place of reality.

558   Separation from his instinctual nature inevitably plunges civilized man into the conflict between conscious and unconscious, spirit and nature, knowledge and faith, a split that becomes pathological the moment his consciousness is no longer able to neglect or suppress his instinctual side. The accumulation of individuals who have got into this critical state starts off a mass movement purporting to be the champion of the suppressed. In accordance with the prevailing tendency of consciousness to seek the source of all ills in the outside world, the cry goes up for political and social changes which, it is supposed, would automatically solve the much deeper problem of split personality. Hence it is that whenever this demand is fulfilled, political and social conditions arise which bring the same ills back again in altered form. What then happens is a simple reversal: the underside comes to the top and the shadow takes the place of the light, and since the former is always anarchic and turbulent, the freedom of the "liberated" underdog must suffer Draconian curtailment. The devil is cast out with Beelzebub. All this is unavoidable, because the root of the evil is untouched and merely the counterposition has come to light.

559   The Communist revolution has debased man far lower than democratic collective psychology has done, because it robs him of his freedom not only in the social but in the moral and spiritual sphere. Aside from the political difficulties, this entailed a great psychological disadvantage for the West that had already made itself unpleasantly felt in the days of German Nazism: we can now point a finger at the shadow. He is clearly on the other side of the political frontier, while we are on the side of

good and enjoy the possession of the right ideals. Did not a well-known statesman recently confess that he had "no imagination for evil"? [1] In the name of the multitude he was expressing the fact that Western man is in danger of losing his shadow altogether, of identifying himself with his fictive personality and the world with the abstract picture painted by scientific rationalism. His spiritual and moral opponent, who is just as real as he, no longer dwells in his own breast but beyond the geographical line of division, which no longer represents an outward political barrier but splits off the conscious from the unconscious man more and more menacingly. Thinking and feeling lose their inner polarity, and where religious orientation has grown ineffective, not even a god can check the sovereign sway of unleashed psychic functions.

560　　Our rational philosophy does not bother itself with whether the other person in us, pejoratively described as the "shadow," is in sympathy with our conscious plans and intentions. Evidently it still does not know that we carry in ourselves a real shadow whose existence is grounded in our instinctual nature. No one can overlook either the dynamism or the imagery of the instincts without the gravest injury to himself. Violation or neglect of instinct has painful consequences of a physiological and psychological nature for whose treatment medical help, above all, is required.

561　　For more than fifty years we have known, or could have known, that there is an unconscious counterbalance to consciousness. Medical psychology has furnished all the necessary empirical and experimental proofs of this. There is an unconscious psychic reality which demonstrably influences consciousness and its contents. All this is known, but no practical conclusions have been drawn from this fact. We still go on thinking and acting as before, as if we were *simplex* and not *duplex*. Accordingly, we imagine ourselves to be innocuous, reasonable, and humane. We do not think of distrusting our motives or of asking ourselves how the inner man feels about the things we do in the outside world. But actually it is frivolous, superficial, and unreasonable of us, as well as psychically unhygienic, to overlook the reaction and standpoint of the unconscious. One

[1] Since these words were written, the shadow has followed up this overbright picture hotfoot with the Charge of the Light Brigade to Suez.

can regard one's stomach or heart as unimportant and worthy of contempt, but that does not prevent overeating or overexertion from having consequences that affect the whole man. Yet we think that psychic mistakes and their consequences can be got rid of with mere words, for "psychic" means less than air to most people. All the same, nobody can deny that without the psyche there would be no world at all, and still less a human world. Virtually everything depends on the human psyche and its functions. It should be worthy of all the attention we can give it, especially today, when everyone admits that the weal or woe of the future will be decided neither by the threat of wild animals, nor by natural catastrophes, nor by the danger of world-wide epidemics, but simply and solely by the psychic changes in man. It needs only an almost imperceptible disturbance of equilibrium in a few of our rulers' heads to plunge the world into blood, fire, and radioactivity. The technical means necessary for this are present on both sides. And certain conscious deliberations, uncontrolled by any inner opponent, can be put into effect all too easily, as we have seen already from the example of one "Leader." The consciousness of modern man still clings so much to external objects that he makes them exclusively responsible, as if it were on them that the decision depended. That the psychic state of certain individuals could ever emancipate itself from the behaviour of objects is something that is considered far too little, although irrationalities of this sort are observed every day and can happen to everyone.

562   The forlorn state of consciousness in our world is due primarily to loss of instinct, and the reason for this lies in the development of the human mind over the past aeon. The more power man had over nature, the more his knowledge and skill went to his head, and the deeper became his contempt for the merely natural and accidental, for all irrational data—including the objective psyche, which is everything that consciousness is not. In contrast to the subjectivism of the conscious mind the unconscious is objective, manifesting itself mainly in the form of contrary feelings, fantasies, emotions, impulses, and dreams, none of which one makes oneself but which come upon one objectively. Even today psychology is still, for the most part, the science of conscious contents, measured as far as possible by collective standards. The individual psyche has become a mere

accident, a marginal phenomenon, while the unconscious, which can manifest itself only in the real, "irrationally given" human being, has been ignored altogether. This was not the result of carelessness or of lack of knowledge, but of downright resistance to the mere possibility that there could be a second psychic authority besides the ego. It seems a positive menace to the ego that its monarchy could be doubted. The religious person, on the other hand, is accustomed to the thought of not being sole master in his own house. He believes that God, and not he himself, decides in the end. But how many of us would dare to let the will of God decide, and which of us would not feel embarrassed if he had to say how far the decision came from God himself?

The religious person, so far as one can judge, is directly influenced by the reaction of the unconscious. As a rule, he calls this the operation of *conscience*. But since the same psychic background produces reactions other than moral ones,[2] the believer is measuring his conscience by the traditional ethical standard and thus by a collective value, in which endeavour he is assiduously supported by his Church. So long as the individual can hold fast to his traditional beliefs, and the circumstances of his time do not demand stronger emphasis on individual autonomy, he can rest content with the situation. But the situation is radically altered when the worldly-minded man who is oriented to external factors and has lost his religious beliefs appears *en masse*, as is the case today. The believer is then forced onto the defensive and must catechize himself on the foundation of his beliefs. He is no longer sustained by the tremendous suggestive power of the *consensus omnium* and is keenly aware of the weakening of the Church and the precariousness of its dogmatic assumptions. To counter this, the Church recommends more faith, as if this gift of grace depended on man's good will and pleasure. The seat of faith, however, is not consciousness but spontaneous religious experience, which brings the individual's faith into immediate relation with God.

Here each of us must ask: Have I any religious experience and immediate relation to God, and hence that certainty which will keep me, as an individual, from dissolving in the crowd?

2 [Cf. infra, pars. 826ff.—EDITORS.]

6. SELF-KNOWLEDGE

565   To this question there is a positive answer only when the individual is willing to fulfil the demands of rigorous self-examination and self-knowledge. If he does this, he will not only discover some important truths about himself but will also have gained a psychological advantage: he will have succeeded in deeming himself worthy of serious attention and sympathetic interest. He will have set his hand, as it were, to a declaration of his own human dignity and taken the first step towards the foundations of his consciousness—that is, towards the unconscious, the only available source of religious experience. This is certainly not to say that what we call the unconscious is identical with God or is set up in his place. It is simply the medium from which religious experience seems to flow. As to what the further cause of such experience may be, the answer to this lies beyond the range of human knowledge. Knowledge of God is a transcendental problem.

566   The religious person enjoys a great advantage when it comes to answering the crucial question that hangs over our time like a threat: he has a clear idea of the way his subjective existence is grounded in his relation to "God." I put the word "God" in quotes in order to indicate that we are dealing with an anthropomorphic idea whose dynamism and symbolism are filtered through the medium of the unconscious psyche. Anyone who wants to can at least draw near to the source of such experiences, no matter whether he believes in God or not. Without this approach it is only in rare cases that we witness those miraculous conversions of which Paul's Damascus experience is the prototype. That religious experiences exist no longer needs proof. But it will always remain doubtful whether what metaphysics and theology call God and the gods is the real ground of these experiences. The question is idle, actually, and answers itself by reason of the subjectively overwhelming numinosity of

293

the experience. Anyone who has had it is *seized* by it and therefore not in a position to indulge in fruitless metaphysical or epistemological speculations. Absolute certainty brings its own evidence and has no need of anthropomorphic proofs.

567   In view of the general ignorance of and bias against psychology it must be accounted a misfortune that the one experience which makes sense of individual existence should seem to have its origin in a medium that is certain to catch everybody's prejudices. Once more the doubt is heard: "What good can come out of Nazareth?" The unconscious, if not regarded outright as a sort of refuse bin underneath the conscious mind, is at any rate supposed to be of "merely animal nature." In reality, however, and by definition it is of uncertain extent and constitution, so that overvaluation or undervaluation of it is pointless and can be dismissed as mere prejudice. At all events, such judgments sound very queer in the mouths of Christians, whose Lord was himself born on the straw of a stable, among the domestic animals. It would have been more to the taste of the multitude if he had got himself born in a temple. In the same way, the worldly-minded mass man looks for the numinous experience in the mass meeting, which provides an infinitely more imposing background than the individual soul. Even Church Christians share this pernicious delusion.

568   Psychology's insistence on the importance of unconscious processes for religious experience is extremely unpopular, no less with the political Right than with the Left. For the former the deciding factor is the historical revelation that came to man from outside; to the latter this is sheer nonsense, and man has no religious function at all, except belief in the party doctrine, when suddenly the most intense faith is called for. On top of this, the various creeds assert quite different things, and each of them claims to possess the absolute truth. Yet today we live in a unitary world where distances are reckoned by hours and no longer by weeks and months. Exotic races have ceased to be peepshows in ethnological museums. They have become our neighbours, and what was yesterday the private concern of the ethnologist is today a political, social, and psychological problem. Already the ideological spheres begin to touch, to interpenetrate, and the time may not be far off when the question of mutual understanding will become acute. To make oneself un-

derstood is certainly impossible without far-reaching comprehension of the other's standpoint. The insight needed for this will have repercussions on both sides. History will undoubtedly pass over those who feel it is their vocation to resist this inevitable development, however desirable and psychologically necessary it may be to cling to what is essential and good in our own tradition. Despite all the differences, the unity of mankind will assert itself irresistibly. On this card Marxist doctrine has staked its life, while the West hopes to achieve its aim with technology and economic aid. Communism has not overlooked the enormous importance of the ideological element and the universality of basic principles. The coloured races share our ideological weakness and in this respect are just as vulnerable as we are.

569   The underestimation of the psychological factor is likely to take a bitter revenge. It is therefore high time we caught up with ourselves in this matter. For the present this must remain a pious wish, because self-knowledge, as well as being highly unpopular, seems to be an unpleasantly idealistic goal, reeks of morality, and is preoccupied with the psychological shadow, which is normally denied whenever possible or at least not spoken of. The task that faces our age is indeed almost insuperably difficult. It makes the highest demands on our responsibility if we are not to be guilty of another *trahison des clercs*. It addresses itself to those leading and influential personalities who have the necessary intelligence to understand the situation our world is in. One might expect them to consult their consciences. But since it is a matter not only of intellectual understanding but of moral conclusions, there is unfortunately no cause for optimism. Nature, as we know, is not so lavish with her boons that she joins to a high intelligence the gifts of the heart also. As a rule, where one is present the other is missing, and where one capacity is present in perfection it is generally at the cost of all the others. The discrepancy between intellect and feeling, which get in each other's way at the best of times, is a particularly painful chapter in the history of the human psyche.

570   There is no sense in formulating the task that our age has forced upon us as a moral demand. We can, at best, merely make the psychological world situation so clear that it can be

seen even by the myopic, and give utterance to words and ideas which even the hard of hearing can hear. We may hope for men of understanding and men of good will, and must therefore not grow weary of reiterating those thoughts and insights which are needed. Finally, even the truth can spread and not only the popular lie.

571   With these words I should like to draw the reader's attention to the main difficulty he has to face. The horror which the dictator States have of late brought upon mankind is nothing less than the culmination of all those atrocities of which our ancestors made themselves guilty in the not so distant past. Quite apart from the barbarities and blood baths perpetrated by the Christian nations among themselves throughout European history, the European has also to answer for all the crimes he has committed against the coloured races during the process of colonization. In this respect the white man carries a very heavy burden indeed. It shows us a picture of the common human shadow that could hardly be painted in blacker colours. The evil that comes to light in man and that undoubtedly dwells within him is of gigantic proportions, so that for the Church to talk of original sin and to trace it back to Adam's relatively innocent slip-up with Eve is almost a euphemism. The case is far graver and is grossly underestimated.

572   Since it is universally believed that man *is* merely what his consciousness knows of itself, he regards himself as harmless and so adds stupidity to iniquity. He does not deny that terrible things have happened and still go on happening, but it is always "the others" who do them. And when such deeds belong to the recent or remote past, they quickly and conveniently sink into the sea of forgetfulness, and that state of chronic woolly-mindedness returns which we describe as "normality." In shocking contrast to this is the fact that nothing has finally disappeared and nothing has been made good. The evil, the guilt, the profound unease of conscience, the dark foreboding, are there before our eyes, if only we would see. Man has done these things; I am a man, who has his share of human nature; therefore I am guilty with the rest and bear unaltered and indelibly within me the capacity and the inclination to do them again at any time. Even if, juristically speaking, we were not accessories to the crime, we are always, thanks to our human nature, potential criminals. In

reality we merely lacked a suitable opportunity to be drawn into the infernal mêlée. None of us stands outside humanity's black collective shadow. Whether the crime occurred many generations back or happens today, it remains the symptom of a disposition that is always and everywhere present—and one would therefore do well to possess some "imagination for evil," for only the fool can permanently disregard the conditions of his own nature. In fact, this negligence is the best means of making him an instrument of evil. Harmlessness and naïveté are as little helpful as it would be for a cholera patient and those in his vicinity to remain unconscious of the contagiousness of the disease. On the contrary, they lead to projection of the unrecognized evil into the "other." This strengthens the opponent's position in the most effective way, because the projection carries the *fear* which we involuntarily and secretly feel for our own evil over to the other side and considerably increases the formidableness of his threat. What is even worse, our lack of insight deprives us of the *capacity to deal with evil*. Here, of course, we come up against one of the main prejudices of the Christian tradition, and one that is a great stumbling block to our policies. We should, so we are told, eschew evil and, if possible, neither touch nor mention it. For evil is also the thing of ill omen, that which is tabooed and feared. This apotropaic attitude towards evil, and the apparent circumventing of it, flatter the primitive tendency in us to shut our eyes to evil and drive it over some frontier or other, like the Old Testament scapegoat, which was supposed to carry the evil into the wilderness.

573   But if one can no longer avoid the realization that evil, without man's ever having chosen it, is lodged in human nature itself, then it bestrides the psychological stage as the equal and opposite partner of good. This realization leads straight to a psychological dualism, already unconsciously prefigured in the political world schism and in the even more unconscious dissociation in modern man himself. The dualism does not come from this realization; rather, we are in a split condition to begin with. It would be an insufferable thought that we had to take personal responsibility for so much guiltiness. We therefore prefer to localize the evil in individual criminals or groups of criminals, while washing our hands in innocence and ignoring the general proclivity to evil. This sanctimoniousness cannot be

kept up in the long run, because the evil, as experience shows, lies in man—unless, in accordance with the Christian view, one is willing to postulate a metaphysical principle of evil. The great advantage of this view is that it exonerates man's conscience of too heavy a responsibility and foists it off on the devil, in correct psychological appreciation of the fact that man is much more the victim of his psychic constitution than its inventor. Considering that the evil of our day puts everything that has ever agonized mankind in the deepest shade, one must ask oneself how it is that, for all our progress in the administration of justice, in medicine and in technology, for all our concern with life and health, monstrous engines of destruction have been invented which could easily exterminate the human race.

574   No one will maintain that the atomic physicists are a pack of criminals because it is to their efforts that we owe that peculiar flower of human ingenuity, the hydrogen bomb. The vast amount of intellectual work that went into the development of nuclear physics was put forth by men who dedicated themselves to their task with the greatest exertion and self-sacrifice, and whose moral achievement could therefore just as easily have earned them the merit of inventing something useful and beneficial to humanity. But even though the first step along the road to a momentous invention may be the outcome of a conscious decision, here, as everywhere, the spontaneous idea—the hunch or intuition—plays an important part. In other words, the unconscious collaborates too and often makes decisive contributions. So it is not the conscious effort alone that is responsible for the result; somewhere or other the unconscious, with its barely discernible goals and intentions, has its finger in the pie. If it puts a weapon in your hand, it is aiming at some kind of violence. Knowledge of the truth is the foremost goal of science, and if in pursuit of the longing for light we stumble upon an immense danger, then one has the impression more of fatality than of premeditation. It is not that present-day man is capable of greater evil than the man of antiquity or the primitive. He merely has incomparably more effective means with which to realize his propensity to evil. As his consciousness has broadened and differentiated, so his moral nature has lagged behind. That is the great problem before us today. *Reason alone no longer suffices.*

575   In theory, it lies within the power of reason to desist from experiments of such hellish scope as nuclear fission if only because of their dangerousness. But fear of the evil which one does not see in one's own bosom but always in somebody else's checks reason every time, although everyone knows that the use of this weapon means the certain end of our present human world. The fear of universal destruction may spare us the worst, yet the possibility of it will nevertheless hang over us like a dark cloud so long as no bridge is found across the world-wide psychic and political split—a bridge as certain as the existence of the hydrogen bomb. If only a world-wide consciousness could arise that all division and all fission are due to the splitting of opposites in the psyche, then we should know where to begin. But if even the smallest and most personal stirrings of the individual psyche—so insignificant in themselves—remain as unconscious and unrecognized as they have hitherto, they will go on accumulating and produce mass groupings and mass movements which cannot be subjected to reasonable control or manipulated to a good end. All direct efforts to do so are no more than shadow boxing, the most infatuated by illusion being the gladiators themselves.

576   The crux of the matter is man's own dualism, to which he knows no answer. This abyss has suddenly yawned open before him with the latest events in world history, after mankind had lived for many centuries in the comfortable belief that a unitary God had created man in his own image, as a little unity. Even today people are largely unconscious of the fact that every individual is a cell in the structure of various international organisms and is therefore causally implicated in their conflicts. He knows that as an individual being he is more or less meaningless and feels himself the victim of uncontrollable forces, but, on the other hand, he harbours within himself a dangerous shadow and adversary who is involved as an invisible helper in the dark machinations of the political monster. It is in the nature of political bodies always to see the evil in the opposite group, just as the individual has an ineradicable tendency to get rid of everything he does not know and does not want to know about himself by foisting it off on somebody else.

577   Nothing has a more divisive and alienating effect upon society than this moral complacency and lack of responsibility,

and nothing promotes understanding and *rapprochement* more than the mutual withdrawal of projections. This necessary corrective demands self-criticism, for one cannot just tell the other person to withdraw them. He does not recognize them for what they are any more than one does oneself. We can recognize our prejudices and illusions only when, from a broader psychological knowledge of ourselves and others, we are prepared to doubt the absolute rightness of our assumptions and compare them carefully and conscientiously with the objective facts. Funnily enough, "self-criticism" is an idea much in vogue in Marxist countries, but there it is subordinated to ideological considerations and must serve the State, and not truth and justice in men's dealings with one another. The mass State has no intention of promoting mutual understanding and the relationship of man to man; it strives, rather, for atomization, for the psychic isolation of the individual. The more unrelated individuals are, the more consolidated the State becomes, and vice versa.

378   There can be no doubt that in the democracies too the distance between man and man is much greater than is conducive to public welfare, let alone beneficial to our psychic needs. True, all sorts of attempts are being made to level out glaring social contrasts by appealing to people's idealism, enthusiasm, and ethical conscience; but, characteristically, one forgets to apply the necessary self-criticism, to answer the question: *Who* is making the idealistic demand? Is it, perchance, someone who jumps over his own shadow in order to hurl himself avidly on some idealistic programme that offers him a welcome alibi? How much respectability and apparent morality is there, cloaking in deceptive colours a very different inner world of darkness? One would first like to be assured that the man who talks of ideals is himself ideal, so that his words and deeds *are* more than they *seem*. To be ideal is impossible, and remains therefore an unfulfilled postulate. Since we usually have keen noses in this respect, most of the idealisms that are preached and paraded before us sound rather hollow and become acceptable only when their opposite is also openly admitted. Without this counterweight the ideal exceeds our human capacity, becomes incredible because of its humourlessness, and degenerates into bluff, albeit a well-meant one. Bluff is an illegitimate way of

overpowering and suppressing others and leads to no good.

579 Recognition of the shadow, on the other hand, leads to the modesty we need in order to acknowledge imperfection. And it is just this conscious recognition and consideration that are needed whenever a human relationship is to be established. A human relationship is not based on differentiation and perfection, for these only emphasize the differences or call forth the exact opposite; it is based, rather, on imperfection, on what is weak, helpless and in need of support—the very ground and motive for dependence. The perfect have no need of others, but weakness has, for it seeks support and does not confront its partner with anything that might force him into an inferior position and even humiliate him. This humiliation may happen only too easily when high idealism plays too prominent a role.

580 Reflections of this kind should not be taken as superfluous sentimentalities. The question of human relationship and of the inner cohesion of our society is an urgent one in view of the atomization of the pent-up mass man, whose personal relationships are undermined by general mistrust. Wherever justice is uncertain and police spying and terror are at work, human beings fall into isolation, which, of course, is the aim and purpose of the dictator State, since it is based on the greatest possible accumulation of depotentiated social units. To counter this danger, the free society needs a bond of an affective nature, a principle of a kind like *caritas*, the Christian love of your neighbour. But it is just this love for one's fellow man that suffers most of all from the lack of understanding wrought by projection. It would therefore be very much in the interest of the free society to give some thought to the question of human relationship from the psychological point of view, for in this resides its real cohesion and consequently its strength. Where love stops, power begins, and violence, and terror.

581 These reflections are not intended as an appeal to idealism, but only to promote a consciousness of the psychological situation. I do not know which is weaker: the idealism or the insight of the public. I only know that it needs time to bring about psychic changes that have any prospect of enduring. Insight that dawns slowly seems to me to have more lasting effects than a fitful idealism, which is unlikely to hold out for long.

7. THE MEANING OF SELF-KNOWLEDGE

582   What our age thinks of as the "shadow" and inferior part of
the psyche contains more than something merely negative. The
very fact that through self-knowledge, that is, by exploring our
own souls, we come upon the instincts and their world of
imagery should throw some light on the powers slumbering in
the psyche, of which we are seldom aware so long as all goes
well. They are potentialities of the greatest dynamism, and it
depends entirely on the preparedness and attitude of the conscious mind whether the irruption of these forces, and the
images and ideas associated with them, will tend towards construction or catastrophe. The psychologist seems to be the only
person who knows from experience how precarious the psychic
preparedness of modern man is, for he is the only one who sees
himself compelled to seek out in man's own nature those helpful powers and ideas which over and over have enabled him to
find the right way through darkness and danger. For this exacting work the psychologist requires all his patience; he may not
rely on any traditional oughts and musts, leaving the other person to make all the effort and contenting himself with the easy
role of adviser and admonisher. Everyone knows the futility of
preaching about things that are desirable, yet the general helplessness in this situation is so great, and the need so dire, that
one prefers to repeat the old mistake instead of racking one's
brains over a subjective problem. Besides, it is always a question
of treating one single individual only and not ten thousand,
when the trouble one takes would ostensibly have more impressive results, though one knows well enough that nothing has
happened at all unless the individual changes.

583   The effect on *all* individuals, which one would like to see
realized, may not set in for hundreds of years, for the spiritual
transformation of mankind follows the slow tread of the cen-

turies and cannot be hurried or held up by any rational process of reflection, let alone brought to fruition in one generation. What does lie within our reach, however, is the change in individuals who have, or create for themselves, an opportunity to influence others of like mind. I do not mean by persuading or preaching—I am thinking, rather, of the well-known fact that anyone who has insight into his own actions, and has thus found access to the unconscious, involuntarily exercises an influence on his environment. The deepening and broadening of his consciousness produce the kind of effect which the primitives call "mana." It is an unintentional influence on the unconscious of others, a sort of unconscious prestige, and its effect lasts only so long as it is not disturbed by conscious intention.

584   Nor is the striving for self-knowledge altogether without prospects of success, since there exists a factor which, though completely disregarded, meets our expectations halfway. This is the unconscious *Zeitgeist*. It compensates the attitude of the conscious mind and anticipates changes to come. An excellent example of this is modern art: though seeming to deal with aesthetic problems, it is really performing a work of psychological education on the public by breaking down and destroying their previous aesthetic views of what is beautiful in form and meaningful in content. The pleasingness of the artistic product is replaced by chill abstractions of the most subjective nature which brusquely slam the door on the naïve and romantic delight in the senses and on the obligatory love for the object. This tells us, in plain and universal language, that the prophetic spirit of art has turned away from the old object-relationship towards the—for the time being—dark chaos of subjectivisms. Certainly art, so far as we can judge of it, has not yet discovered in this darkness what it is that could hold all men together and give expression to their psychic wholeness. Since reflection seems to be needed for this purpose, it may be that such discoveries are reserved for other fields of endeavour.

585   Great art till now has always derived its fruitfulness from myth, from the unconscious process of symbolization which continues through the ages and, as the primordial manifestation of the human spirit, will continue to be the root of all creation in the future. The development of modern art with its seemingly nihilistic trend towards disintegration must be

understood as the symptom and symbol of a mood of universal destruction and renewal that has set its mark on our age. This mood makes itself felt everywhere, politically, socially, and philosophically. We are living in what the Greeks called the καιρός—the right moment—for a "metamorphosis of the gods," of the fundamental principles and symbols. This peculiarity of our time, which is certainly not of our conscious choosing, is the expression of the unconscious man within us who is changing. Coming generations will have to take account of this momentous transformation if humanity is not to destroy itself through the might of its own technology and science.

586   As at the beginning of the Christian era, so again today we are faced with the problem of the general moral backwardness which has failed to keep pace with our scientific, technical, and social progress. So much is at stake and so much depends on the psychological constitution of modern man. Is he capable of resisting the temptation to use his power for the purpose of staging a world conflagration? Is he conscious of the path he is treading, and what the conclusions are that must be drawn from the present world situation and his own psychic situation? Does he know that he is on the point of losing the life-preserving myth of the inner man which Christianity has treasured up for him? Does he realize what lies in store should this catastrophe ever befall him? Is he even capable of realizing that this would in fact be a catastrophe? And finally, does the individual know that *he* is the makeweight that tips the scales?

587   Happiness and contentment, equability of mind and meaningfulness of life—these can be experienced only by the individual and not by a State, which, on the one hand, is nothing but a convention agreed to by independent individuals and, on the other, continually threatens to paralyse and suppress the individual. The psychiatrist is one of those who know most about the conditions of the soul's welfare, upon which so infinitely much depends in the social sum. The social and political circumstances of the time are certainly of considerable significance, but their importance for the weal or woe of the individual has been boundlessly overestimated in so far as they are taken for the sole deciding factors. In this respect all our social goals commit the error of overlooking the psychology of the

person for whom they are intended and—very often—of promoting only his illusions.

588   I hope, therefore, that a psychiatrist, who in the course of a long life has devoted himself to the causes and consequences of psychic disorders, may be permitted to express his opinion, in all the modesty enjoined upon him as an individual, about the questions raised by the world situation today. I am neither spurred on by excessive optimism nor in love with high ideals, but am merely concerned with the fate of the individual human being—that infinitesimal unit on whom a world depends, and in whom, if we read the meaning of the Christian message aright, even God seeks his goal.

V

FLYING SAUCERS

A Modern Myth of Things Seen in the Skies

[First published as *Ein moderner Mythus: Von Dingen, die am Himmel gesehen werden* (Zurich and Stuttgart, 1958); dedicated to "Walter Niehus, the architect, with thanks for inducing me to write this little book." With the addition of the brief "supplement," this was translated by R. F. C. Hull and published under the present title (London and New York, 1959). Minor revisions have been made in the present version.—EDITORS.]

PREFACE
TO THE FIRST ENGLISH EDITION

The worldwide rumour about Flying Saucers presents a problem that challenges the psychologist for a number of reasons. The primary question—and apparently this is the most important point—is this: are they real or are they mere fantasy products? This question is by no means settled yet. If they are real, exactly what are they? If they are fantasy, why should such a rumour exist?

In this latter respect I have made an interesting and quite unexpected discovery. In 1954 I wrote an article in the Swiss weekly, *Die Weltwoche,* in which I expressed myself in a sceptical way, though I spoke with due respect of the serious opinion of a relatively large number of air specialists who believe in the reality of Ufos (unidentified flying objects). In 1958 this interview was suddenly discovered by the world press and the "news" spread like wildfire from the far West round the earth to the far East, but—alas—in distorted form. I was quoted as a saucer-believer. I issued a statement to the United Press and gave a true version of my opinion, but this time the wire went dead: nobody, so far as I know, took any notice of it, except one German newspaper.

The moral of this story is rather interesting. As the behaviour of the press is a sort of Gallup test with reference to world opinion, one must draw the conclusion that news affirming the existence of Ufos is welcome, but that scepticism seems to be undesirable. To believe that Ufos are real suits the general opinion, whereas disbelief is to be discouraged. This creates the impression that there is a tendency all over the world to believe in saucers and to want them to be real, unconsciously helped along by a press that otherwise has no sympathy with the phenomenon.

This remarkable fact in itself surely merits the psychologist's interest. Why should it be more desirable for saucers to exist than not? The following pages are an attempt to answer this question. I have relieved the text of cumbersome footnotes, except for a few which give the references for the interested reader.

C. G. JUNG

September, 1958

INTRODUCTORY

589   It is difficult to form a correct estimate of the significance of contemporary events, and the danger that our judgment will remain caught in subjectivity is great. So I am fully aware of the risk I am taking in proposing to communicate my views concerning certain contemporary events, which seem to me important, to those who are patient enough to hear me. I refer to those reports reaching us from all corners of the earth, rumours of round objects that flash through the troposphere and stratosphere and go by the name of Flying Saucers, *soucoupes,* disks, and "Ufos" (Unidentified Flying Objects). These rumours, or the possible physical existence of such objects, seem to me so significant that I feel myself compelled, as once before [1] when events of fateful consequence were brewing for Europe, to sound a note of warning. I know that, just as before, my voice is much too weak to reach the ear of the multitude. It is not presumption that drives me, but my conscience as a psychiatrist that bids me fulfil my duty and prepare those few who will hear me for coming events which are in accord with the end of an era. As we know from ancient Egyptian history, they are manifestations of psychic changes which always appear at the end of one Platonic month and at the beginning of another. Apparently they are changes in the constellation of psychic dominants, of the archetypes, or "gods" as they used to be called, which bring about, or accompany, long-lasting transformations of the collective psyche. This transformation started in the historical era and left its traces first in the passing of the aeon of Taurus into that of Aries, and then of Aries into Pisces, whose beginning coincides with the rise of Christianity. We are now nearing that great change which may be expected when the spring-point enters Aquarius.

1 "Wotan," first published in the *Neue Schweizer Rundschau,* 1936. [See supra, pars. 371ff.]

590   It would be frivolous of me to try to conceal from the reader that such reflections are not only exceedingly unpopular but even come perilously close to those turbid fantasies which becloud the minds of world-reformers and other interpreters of "signs and portents." But I must take this risk, even if it means putting my hard-won reputation for truthfulness, reliability, and capacity for scientific judgment in jeopardy. I can assure my readers that I do not do this with a light heart. I am, to be quite frank, concerned for all those who are caught unprepared by the events in question and disconcerted by their incomprehensible nature. Since, so far as I know, no one has yet felt moved to examine and set forth the possible psychic consequences of this foreseeable astrological change, I deem it my duty to do what I can in this respect. I undertake this thankless task in the expectation that my chisel will make no impression on the hard stone it encounters.

591   Some time ago I published a statement in which I considered the nature of "Flying Saucers." [2] I came to the same conclusion as Edward J. Ruppelt, one-time chief of the American Air Force's project for investigating Ufo reports.[3] The conclusion is: *something is seen, but one doesn't know what.* It is difficult, if not impossible, to form any correct idea of these objects, because they behave not like bodies but like weightless thoughts. Up till now there has been no indisputable proof of the physical existence of Ufos except for the cases picked up by radar. I have discussed the reliability of these radar observations with Professor Max Knoll, a specialist in this field. What he has to say is not encouraging. Nevertheless, there do seem to be authenticated cases where the visual observation was confirmed by a simultaneous radar echo. I would like to call the reader's attention to Keyhoe's books, which are based on official material and studiously avoid the wild speculation, naïveté, or prejudice of other publications.[4]

---

2 In an interview by Georg Gerster, *Weltwoche* (Zurich), XXII:1078 (July 9, 1954), p. 7. [See CW 18, pars. 1420ff.]

3 *The Report on Unidentified Flying Objects* (1956).

4 Major Donald E. Keyhoe, *Flying Saucers from Outer Space* (1953), and *The Flying Saucer Conspiracy* (1955). Cf. also Aimé Michel, *The Truth about Flying Saucers* (1956).

592   For a decade the physical reality of Ufos remained a very problematical matter, which was not decided one way or the other with the necessary clarity despite the mass of observational material that had accumulated in the meantime. The longer the uncertainty lasted, the greater became the probability that this obviously complicated phenomenon had an extremely important psychic component as well as a possible physical basis. This is not surprising, in that we are dealing with an ostensibly physical phenomenon distinguished on the one hand by its frequent appearances, and on the other by its strange, unknown, and indeed contradictory nature.

593   Such an object provokes, like nothing else, conscious and unconscious fantasies, the former giving rise to speculative conjectures and pure fabrications, and the latter supplying the mythological background inseparable from these provocative observations. Thus there arose a situation in which, with the best will in the world, one often did not know and could not discover whether a primary perception was followed by a phantasm or whether, conversely, a primary fantasy originating in the unconscious invaded the conscious mind with illusions and visions. The material that has become known to me during the past ten years lends support to both hypotheses. In the first case an objectively real, physical process forms the basis for an accompanying myth; in the second case an archetype creates the corresponding vision. To these two causal relationships we must add a third possibility, namely, that of a "synchronistic," i.e., acausal, meaningful coincidence—a problem that has occupied men's minds ever since the time of Geulincx, Leibniz, and Schopenhauer.[5] It is an hypothesis that has special bearing on phenomena connected with archetypal psychic processes.

594   As a psychologist, I am not qualified to contribute anything useful to the question of the physical reality of Ufos. I can concern myself only with their undoubted psychic aspect, and in what follows shall deal almost exclusively with their psychic concomitants.

[5] Cf. my paper "Synchronicity: An Acausal Connecting Principle" in *The Structure and Dynamics of the Psyche.*

1. UFOS AS RUMOURS

595   Since the things reported of Ufos not only sound incredible but seem to fly in the face of all our basic assumptions about the physical world, it is very natural that one's first reaction should be the negative one of outright rejection. Surely, we say, it's nothing but illusions, fantasies, and lies. People who report such stuff—chiefly airline pilots and ground staff—cannot be quite right in the head! What is worse, most of these stories come from America, the land of superlatives and of science fiction.

596   In order to meet this natural reaction, we shall begin by considering the Ufo reports simply as rumours, i.e., as psychic products, and shall draw from this all the conclusions that are warranted by an analytical method of procedure.

597   Regarded in this light, the Ufo reports may seem to the sceptical mind to be rather like a story that is told all over the world, but differs from an ordinary rumour in that it is expressed in the form of visions,[1] or perhaps owed its existence to them in the first place and is now kept alive by them. I would call this comparatively rare variation a *visionary rumour*. It is closely akin to the collective visions of, say, the crusaders during the siege of Jerusalem, the troops at Mons in the first World War, the faithful followers of the pope at Fatima, Portugal, etc. Apart from collective visions, there are on record cases where one or more persons see something that physically is not there. For instance, I was once at a spiritualistic séance where four of the five people present saw an object like a moon floating above the abdomen of the medium. They showed me, the fifth person present, exactly where it was, and it was absolutely incomprehensible to them that I could see nothing of the sort. I know of

1 I prefer the term "vision" to "hallucination," because the latter bears the stamp of a pathological concept, whereas a vision is a phenomenon that is by no means peculiar to pathological states.

three more cases where certain objects were seen in the clearest detail (in two of them by two persons, and in the third by one person) and could afterwards be proved to be non-existent. Two of these cases happened under my direct observation. Even people who are entirely *compos mentis* and in full possession of their senses can sometimes see things that do not exist. I do not know what the explanation is of such happenings. It is very possible that they are less rare than I am inclined to suppose. For as a rule we do not verify things we have "seen with our own eyes," and so we never get to know that actually they did not exist. I mention these somewhat remote possibilities because, in such an unusual matter as the Ufos, one has to take every aspect into account.

598   The first requisite for a visionary rumour, as distinct from an ordinary rumour, for whose dissemination nothing more is needed than popular curiosity and sensation-mongering, is always an *unusual emotion*. Its intensification into a vision and delusion of the senses, however, springs from a stronger excitation and therefore from a deeper source.

599   The signal for the Ufo stories was given by the mysterious projectiles seen over Sweden during the last two years of the war—attributed of course to the Russians—and by the reports about "Foo fighters," i.e., lights that accompanied the Allied bombers over Germany (Foo = *feu*). These were followed by the strange sightings of "Flying Saucers" in America. The impossibility of finding an earthly base for the Ufos and of explaining their physical peculiarities soon led to the conjecture of an extra-terrestrial origin. With this development the rumour got linked up with the psychology of the great panic that broke out in the United States just before the second World War, when a radio play,[2] based on a novel by H. G. Wells, about Martians invading New York, caused a regular stampede and numerous car accidents. The play evidently hit the latent emotion connected with the imminence of war.

600   The motif of an extra-terrestrial invasion was seized upon by the rumour and the Ufos were interpreted as machines controlled by intelligent beings from outer space. The apparently weightless behaviour of space-ships and their intelligent, pur-

2 [*The War of the Worlds*, radio adaptation by Orson Welles (1938).—EDITORS.]

posive movements were attributed to the superior technical knowledge and ability of the cosmic intruders. As they did no harm and refrained from all hostile acts it was assumed that their appearance over the earth was due to curiosity or to the need for aerial reconnaissance. It also seemed that airfields and atomic installations in particular held a special attraction for them, from which it was concluded that the dangerous development of atomic physics and nuclear fission had caused a certain disquiet on our neighbouring planets and necessitated a more accurate survey from the air. As a result, people felt they were being observed and spied upon from space.

601 The rumour actually gained so much official recognition that the armed forces in America set up a special bureau for collecting, analysing, and evaluating all relevant observations. This seems to have been done also in France, Italy, Sweden, the United Kingdom, and other countries. After the publication of Ruppelt's report the Saucer stories seem to have more or less vanished from the press for about a year. They were evidently no longer "news." That the interest in Ufos and, probably, the sightings of them have not ceased is shown by the recent press report that an American admiral has suggested that clubs be founded all over the country for collecting Ufo reports and investigating them in detail.

602 The rumour states that the Ufos are as a rule lens-shaped, but can also be oblong or shaped like cigars; that they shine in various colours or have a metallic glitter; [3] that from a stationary position they can reach a speed of about 10,000 miles per hour, and that at times their acceleration is such that if anything resembling a human being were steering them he would be instantly killed. In flight they turn off at angles that would be possible only to a weightless object.

603 Their flight, accordingly, resembles that of a flying insect. Like this, the Ufo can suddenly hover over an interesting object for quite a time, or circle round it inquisitively, just as suddenly to dart off again and discover new objects in its zigzag flight. Ufos are therefore not to be confused with meteorites or with reflections from so-called "temperature inversion layers." Their alleged interest in airfields and in industrial installations

3 Special emphasis should be laid on the *green* fire-balls frequently observed in the southwestern United States.

connected with nuclear fission is not always confirmed, since they are also seen in the Antarctic, in the Sahara, and in the Himalayas. For preference, however, they seem to swarm over the United States, though recent reports show that they do a good deal of flying over the Old World and in the Far East. Nobody really knows what they are looking for or want to observe. Our aeroplanes seem to arouse their curiosity, for they often fly towards them or pursue them. But they also fly away from them. Their flights do not appear to be based on any recognizable system. They behave more like groups of tourists unsystematically viewing the countryside, pausing now here for a while and now there, erratically following first one interest and then another, sometimes shooting to enormous altitudes for inexplicable reasons or performing acrobatic evolutions before the noses of exasperated pilots. Sometimes they appear to be up to five hundred yards in diameter, sometimes small as electric street-lamps. There are large mother-ships from which little Ufos slip out or in which they take shelter. They are said to be both manned and unmanned, and in the latter case are remote-controlled. According to the rumour, the occupants are about three feet high and look like human beings or, conversely, are utterly unlike us. Other reports speak of giants fifteen feet high. They are beings who are carrying out a cautious survey of the earth and considerately avoid all encounters with men or, more menacingly, are spying out landing places with a view to settling the population of a planet that has got into difficulties and colonizing the earth by force. Uncertainty in regard to the physical conditions on earth and their fear of unknown sources of infection have held them back temporarily from drastic encounters and even from attempted landings, although they possess frightful weapons which would enable them to exterminate the human race. In addition to their obviously superior technology they are credited with superior wisdom and moral goodness which would, on the other hand, enable them to save humanity. Naturally there are stories of landings, too, when the saucer-men were not only seen at close quarters but attempted to carry off a human being. Even a reliable man like Keyhoe gives us to understand that a squadron of five military aircraft plus a large seaplane were swallowed up by Ufo mother-ships in the vicinity of the Bahamas, and carried off.

604   One's hair stands on end when one reads such reports together with the documentary evidence. And when one considers
the known possibility of tracking Ufos with radar, then we have
all the essentials for an unsurpassable "science-fiction story."
Every man who prides himself on his sound common sense will
feel distinctly affronted. I shall therefore not enter here into the
various attempts at explanation to which the rumour has given
rise.

605   While I was engaged in writing this essay, it so happened
that two articles appeared more or less simultaneously in leading American newspapers, showing very clearly how the problem stands at present. The first was a report on the latest Ufo
sighting by a pilot who was flying an aircraft to Puerto Rico
with forty-four passengers. While he was over the ocean he saw
a "fiery, round object, shining with greenish white light," coming towards him at great speed. At first he thought it was a jet-
propelled aircraft, but soon saw that it was some unusual and
unknown object. In order to avoid a collision, he pulled his aircraft into such a steep climb that the passengers were shot out of
their seats and tumbled over one another. Four of them received
injuries requiring hospital attention. Seven other aircraft strung
out along the same route of about three hundred miles sighted
the same object.

606   The other article, entitled "No Flying Saucers, U.S. Expert
Says," concerns the categorical statement made by Dr. Hugh L.
Dryden, director of the National Advisory Committee for Aero-
nautics, that Ufos do not exist. One cannot but respect the unflinching scepticism of Dr. Dryden; it gives stout-hearted expression to the feeling that such preposterous rumours are an offence
to human dignity.

607   If we close our eyes a little so as to overlook certain details,
it is possible to side with the reasonable opinion of the majority
in whose name Dr. Dryden speaks, and to regard the thousands
of Ufo reports and the uproar they have created as a visionary
rumour, to be treated accordingly. They would then boil down,
objectively, to an admittedly impressive collection of mistaken
observations and conclusions into which subjective psychic
assumptions have been projected.

608   But if it is a case of psychological *projection,* there must be a

psychic cause for it. One can hardly suppose that anything of
such worldwide incidence as the Ufo legend is purely fortuitous
and of no importance whatever. The many thousands of individual testimonies must have an equally extensive causal basis.
When an assertion of this kind is corroborated practically everywhere, we are driven to assume that a corresponding motive
must be present everywhere, too. Though visionary rumours
may be caused or accompanied by all manner of outward circumstances, they are based essentially on an omnipresent emotional foundation, in this case a psychological situation common
to all mankind. The basis for this kind of rumour is an *emotional tension* having its cause in a situation of collective distress or danger, or in a vital psychic need. This condition undoubtedly exists today, in so far as the whole world is suffering
under the strain of Russian policies and their still unpredictable
consequences. In the individual, too, such phenomena as abnormal convictions, visions, illusions, etc., only occur when he is
suffering from a psychic dissociation, that is, when there is a
split between the conscious attitude and the unconscious contents opposed to it. Precisely because the conscious mind does
not know about them and is therefore confronted with a situation from which there seems to be no way out, these strange contents cannot be integrated directly but seek to express themselves indirectly, thus giving rise to unexpected and apparently
inexplicable opinions, beliefs, illusions, visions, and so forth.
Any unusual natural occurrences such as meteors, comets,
"rains of blood," a calf with two heads, and suchlike abortions
are interpreted as menacing omens, or else signs are seen in the
heavens. Things can be seen by many people independently of
one another, or even simultaneously, which are not physically
real. Also, the association-processes of many people often have a
parallelism in time and space, with the result that different people, simultaneously and independently of one another, can produce the same new ideas, as has happened numerous times in
history.

609   In addition, there are cases where the same collective cause
produces identical or similar effects, i.e., the same visionary
images and interpretations, in the very people who are least prepared for such phenomena and least inclined to believe in

them.[4] This fact gives the eyewitness accounts an air of particular credibility: it is usually emphasized that the witness is above suspicion because he was never distinguished for his lively imagination or credulousness but, on the contrary, for his cool judgment and critical reason. In just these cases the unconscious has to resort to particularly drastic measures in order to make its contents perceived. It does this most vividly by projection, by extrapolating its contents into an object, which then reflects back what had previously lain hidden in the unconscious. Projection can be observed at work everywhere, in mental illness, in ideas of persecution and hallucinations, in so-called normal people who see the mote in their brother's eye without seeing the beam in their own, and finally, in extreme form, in political propaganda.

610   Projections have what we might call different ranges, according to whether they stem from merely personal conditions or from deeper collective ones. Personal repressions and things of which we are unconscious manifest themselves in our immediate environment, in our circle of relatives and acquaintances. Collective contents, such as religious, philosophical, political and social conflicts, select projection-carriers of a corresponding kind—Freemasons, Jesuits, Jews, Capitalists, Bolsheviks, Imperialists, etc. In the threatening situation of the world today, when people are beginning to see that everything is at stake, the projection-creating fantasy soars beyond the realm of earthly organizations and powers into the heavens, into interstellar space, where the rulers of human fate, the gods, once had their abode in the planets. Our earthly world is split into two halves, and nobody knows where a helpful solution is to come from. Even people who would never have thought that a religious problem could be a serious matter that concerned them personally are beginning to ask themselves fundamental questions. Under these circumstances it would not be at all surprising if those sections of the community who ask themselves nothing were visited by "visions," by a widespread myth seriously believed in by some and rejected as absurd by others. Eye-witnesses of unimpeachable honesty announce the "signs in the heavens" which they have seen "with their own eyes," and the marvellous

4 Aimé Michel remarks that Ufos are mostly seen by people who do not believe in them or who regard the whole problem with indifference.

things they have experienced which pass human understanding.

611   All these reports have naturally resulted in a clamorous demand for explanation. Initial attempts to explain the Ufos as Russian or American inventions soon came to grief on their apparently weightless behaviour, which is unknown to earth-dwellers. Human fantasy, already toying with the idea of space-trips to the moon, therefore had no hesitation in assuming that intelligent beings of a higher order had learnt how to counteract gravitation and, by dint of using interstellar magnetic fields as sources of power, to travel through space with the speed of light. The recent atomic explosions on the earth, it was conjectured, had aroused the attention of these so very much more advanced dwellers on Mars or Venus, who were worried about possible chain-reactions and the consequent destruction of our planet. Since such a possibility would constitute a catastrophic threat to our neighbouring planets, their inhabitants felt compelled to observe how things were developing on earth, fully aware of the tremendous cataclysm our clumsy nuclear experiments might unleash. The fact that the Ufos neither land on earth nor show the least inclination to get into communication with human beings is met by the explanation that these visitors, despite their superior knowledge, are not at all certain of being well received on earth, for which reason they carefully avoid all intelligent contact with humans. But because they, as befits superior beings, conduct themselves quite inoffensively, they would do the earth no harm and are satisfied with an objective inspection of airfields and atomic installations. Just why these higher beings, who show such a burning interest in the fate of the earth, have still not found some way of communicating with us after ten years—despite their knowledge of languages—remains shrouded in darkness. Other explanations have therefore to be sought, for instance that a planet has got into difficulties, perhaps through the drying up of its water supplies, or loss of oxygen, or overpopulation, and is looking for a *pied-à-terre*. The reconnaissance patrols are going to work with the utmost care and circumspection, despite the fact that they have been giving a benefit performance in the heavens for hundreds, if not thousands, of years. Since the second World War they have appeared in masses, obviously because an imminent landing is

planned. Recently their harmlessness has been doubted. There are also stories by so-called eyewitnesses who declare they have seen Ufos landing with, of course, English-speaking occupants. These space-guests are sometimes idealized figures along the lines of technological angels who are concerned for our welfare, sometimes dwarfs with enormous heads bursting with intelligence, sometimes lemur-like creatures covered with hair and equipped with claws, or dwarfish monsters clad in armour and looking like insects.

612   There are even "eyewitnesses" like Mr. Adamski, who relates that he has flown in a Ufo and made a round trip of the moon in a few hours. He brings us the astonishing news that the side of the moon turned away from us contains atmosphere, water, forests, and settlements, without being in the least perturbed by the moon's skittishness in turning just her unhospitable side towards the earth. This physical monstrosity of a story was actually swallowed by a cultivated and well-meaning person like Edgar Sievers.[5]

613   Considering the notorious camera-mindedness of Americans, it is surprising how few "authentic" photos of Ufos seem to exist, especially as many of them are said to have been observed for several hours at relatively close quarters. I myself happen to know someone who saw a Ufo with hundreds of other people in Guatemala. He had his camera with him, but in the excitement he completely forgot to take a photo, although it was daytime and the Ufo remained visible for an hour. I have no reason to doubt the honesty of his report. He has merely strengthened my impression that Ufos are somehow not photogenic.

614   As one can see from all this, the observation and interpretation of Ufos have already led to the formation of a regular legend. Quite apart from the thousands of newspaper reports and articles there is now a whole literature on the subject, some of it humbug, some of it serious. The Ufos themselves, however, do not appear to have been impressed; as the latest observations show, they continue their way undeterred. Be that as it may, one thing is certain: they have become a *living myth*. We have here a golden opportunity of seeing how a legend is formed, and how in a difficult and dark time for humanity a miraculous tale

5 Cf. *Flying Saucers über Südafrika* (1955).

grows up of an attempted intervention by extra-terrestrial "heavenly" powers—and this at the very time when human fantasy is seriously considering the possibility of space travel and of visiting or even invading other planets. We on our side want to fly to the moon or to Mars, and on their side the inhabitants of other planets in our system, or even of the fixed stars, want to fly to us. We at least are conscious of our space-conquering aspirations, but that a corresponding extra-terrestrial tendency exists is a purely mythological conjecture, i.e., a projection.

615   Sensationalism, love of adventure, technological audacity, intellectual curiosity may appear to be sufficient motives for our futuristic fantasies, but the impulse to spin such fantasies, especially when they take such a serious form—witness the sputniks —springs from an underlying cause, namely a situation of distress and the vital need that goes with it. It could easily be conjectured that the earth is growing too small for us, that humanity would like to escape from its prison, where we are threatened not only by the hydrogen bomb but, at a still deeper level, by the prodigious increase in the population figures, which give cause for serious concern. This is a problem which people do not like to talk about, or then only with optimistic references to the incalculable possibilities of intensive food production, as if this were anything more than a postponement of the final solution. As a precautionary measure the Indian government has granted half a million pounds for birth-control propaganda, while the Russians exploit the labour-camp system as one way of skimming off the dreaded excess of births. Since the highly civilized countries of the West know how to help themselves in other ways, the immediate danger does not come from them but from the underdeveloped peoples of Asia and Africa. This is not the place to discuss the question of how far the two World Wars were an outlet for this pressing problem of keeping down the population at all costs. Nature has many ways of disposing of her surplus. Man's living space is, in fact, continually shrinking and for many races the optimum has long been exceeded. The danger of catastrophe grows in proportion as the expanding populations impinge on one another. Congestion creates fear, which looks for help from extra-terrestrial sources since it cannot be found on earth.

616   Hence there appear "signs in the heavens," superior beings

323

in the kind of space ships devised by our technological fantasy. From a fear whose cause is far from being fully understood and is therefore not conscious, there arise explanatory projections which purport to find the cause in all manner of secondary phenomena, however unsuitable. Some of these projections are so obvious that it seems almost superfluous to dig any deeper.[6] But if we want to understand a mass rumour which, it appears, is even accompanied by collective visions, we must not remain satisfied with all too rational and superficially obvious motives. The cause must strike at the roots of our existence if it is to explain such an extraordinary phenomenon as the Ufos. Although they were observed as rare curiosities in earlier centuries, they merely gave rise to the usual local rumours.

617   The universal mass rumour was reserved for our enlightened, rationalistic age. The widespread fantasy about the destruction of the world at the end of the first millennium was metaphysical in origin and needed no Ufos in order to appear rational. Heaven's intervention was quite consistent with the *Weltanschauung* of the age. But nowadays public opinion would hardly be inclined to resort to the hypothesis of a metaphysical act, otherwise innumerable parsons would already have been preaching about the warning signs in heaven. Our *Weltanschauung* does not expect anything of this sort. We would be much more inclined to think of the possibility of *psychic* disturbances and interventions, especially as our psychic equilibrium has become something of a problem since the last World War. In this respect there is increasing uncertainty. Even our historians can no longer make do with the traditional procedures in evaluating and explaining the developments that have overtaken Europe in the last few decades, but must admit that psychological and psychopathological factors are beginning to widen the horizons of historiography in an alarming way. The growing interest which the thinking public consequently evinces in psychology has already aroused the displeasure of the academies and of incompetent specialists. In spite of the palpable resistance to psychology emanating from these circles, psychologists who are conscious of their responsibilities should not be dissuaded from critically examining a mass phenomenon

6 Cf. Eugen Böhler's enlightening remarks in *Ethik und Wirtschaft* (Industrielle Organisation, Zurich, 1957).

like the Ufos, since the apparent impossibility of the Ufo reports suggests to common sense that the most likely explanation lies in a psychic disturbance.

618   We shall therefore turn our attention to the psychic aspect of the phenomenon. For this purpose we shall briefly review the central statements of the rumour. Certain objects are seen in the earth's atmosphere, both by day and by night, which are unlike any known meteorological phenomena. They are not meteors, not misidentified fixed stars, not "temperature inversions," not cloud formations, not migrating birds, not aerial balloons, not balls of fire, and certainly not the delirious products of intoxication or fever, nor the plain lies of eyewitnesses. What as a rule is seen is a body of *round* shape, disk-like or spherical, glowing or shining fierily in different colours, or, more seldom, a cigar-shaped or cylindrical figure of various sizes.[7] It is reported that occasionally they are invisible to the naked eye but leave a "blip" on the radar screen. The round bodies in particular are figures such as the unconscious produces in dreams, visions, etc. In this case they are to be regarded as *symbols* representing, in visual form, some thought that was not thought consciously, but is merely potentially present in the unconscious in invisible form and attains visibility only through the process of becoming conscious. The visible form, however, expresses the meaning of the unconscious content only approximately. In practice the meaning has to be completed by amplificatory interpretation. The unavoidable errors that result can be eliminated only through the principle of "waiting on events"; that is to say we obtain a consistent and readable text by comparing sequences of dreams dreamt by different individuals. The figures in a rumour can be subjected to the same principles of dream interpretation.

619   If we apply them to the round object—whether it be a disk or a sphere—we at once get an analogy with the symbol of totality well known to all students of depth psychology, namely the *mandala* (Sanskrit for circle). This is not by any means a new

7 The more rarely reported cigar-form may have the Zeppelin for a model. The obvious phallic comparison, i.e., a translation into sexual language, springs naturally to the lips of the people. Berliners, for instance, refer to the cigar-shaped Ufo as a "holy ghost," and the Swiss military have an even more outspoken name for observation balloons.

invention, for it can be found in all epochs and in all places, always with the same meaning, and it reappears time and again, independently of tradition, in modern individuals as the "protective" or apotropaic circle, whether in the form of the prehistoric "sun wheel," or the magic circle, or the alchemical microcosm, or a modern *symbol of order,* which organizes and embraces the psychic totality. As I have shown elsewhere,[8] in the course of the centuries the mandala has developed into a definitely psychological totality symbol, as the history of alchemy proves. I would like to show how the mandala appears in a modern person by citing the dream of a six-year-old girl. She dreamt *she stood at the entrance of a large, unknown building. There a fairy was waiting for her, who led her inside, into a long colonnade, and conducted her to a sort of central chamber, with similar colonnades converging from all sides. The fairy stepped into the centre and changed herself into a tall flame. Three snakes crawled round the fire, as if circumambulating it.*

620   Here we have a classic, archetypal childhood dream such as is not only dreamt fairly often but is sometimes drawn or painted, without any suggestion from outside, for the evident purpose of warding off disagreeable or disturbing family influences and preserving the inner balance.

621   In so far as the mandala encompasses, protects, and defends the psychic totality against outside influences and seeks to unite the inner opposites, it is at the same time a distinct *individuation symbol* and was known as such even to medieval alchemy. The soul was supposed to have the form of a sphere, on the analogy of Plato's world-soul, and we meet the same symbol in modern dreams. This symbol, by reason of its antiquity, leads us to the heavenly spheres, to Plato's "supra-celestial place" where the "Ideas" of all things are stored up. Hence there would be nothing against the naïve interpretation of Ufos as "souls." Naturally they do not represent our modern conception of the psyche, but give an involuntary archetypal or mythological picture of an unconscious content, a *rotundum,* as the alchemists called it, that expresses the totality of the individual. I have defined this spontaneous image as a symbolical representation of the *self,* by which I mean not the ego but the

[8] "Concerning Mandala Symbolism" in *The Archetypes and the Collective Unconscious.*

326

totality composed of the conscious *and* the unconscious.[9] I am not alone in this, as the Hermetic philosophy of the Middle Ages had already arrived at very similar conclusions. The archetypal character of this idea is borne out by its spontaneous recurrence in modern individuals who know nothing of any such tradition, any more than those around them. Even people who might know of it never imagine that their children could dream of anything so remote as Hermetic philosophy. In this matter the deepest and darkest ignorance prevails, which is of course the most unsuitable vehicle for a mythological tradition.

622   If the round shining objects that appear in the sky be regarded as visions, we can hardly avoid interpreting them as archetypal images. They would then be involuntary, automatic projections based on instinct, and as little as any other psychic manifestations or symptoms can they be dismissed as meaningless and merely fortuitous. Anyone with the requisite historical and psychological knowledge knows that circular symbols have played an important role in every age; in our own sphere of culture, for instance, they were not only soul symbols but "God-images." There is an old saying that "God is a circle whose centre is everywhere and the circumference nowhere." God in his omniscience, omnipotence, and omnipresence is a totality symbol *par excellence,* something round, complete, and perfect. Epiphanies of this sort are, in the tradition, often associated with fire and light. On the antique level, therefore, the Ufos could easily be conceived as "gods." They are impressive manifestations of totality whose simple, round form portrays the archetype of the self, which as we know from experience plays the chief role in uniting apparently irreconcilable opposites and is therefore best suited to compensate the split-mindedness of our age. It has a particularly important role to play among the other archetypes in that it is primarily the regulator and orderer of chaotic states, giving the personality the greatest possible unity and wholeness. It creates the image of the divine-human personality, the Primordial Man or Anthropos, a *chên-yên* (true or whole man), an Elijah who calls down fire from heaven, rises up to heaven in a fiery chariot,[10] and is a forerunner of the

9 Cf. "The Self," in *Aion.*
10 Significantly enough, Elijah also appears as an eagle, who spies out unrighteousness on earth from above.

Messiah, the dogmatized figure of Christ, as well as of Khidr, the Verdant One,[11] who is another parallel to Elijah: like him, he wanders over the earth as a human personification of Allah.

623 The present world situation is calculated as never before to arouse expectations of a redeeming, supernatural event. If these expectations have not dared to show themselves in the open, this is simply because no one is deeply rooted enough in the tradition of earlier centuries to consider an intervention from heaven as a matter of course. We have indeed strayed far from the metaphysical certainties of the Middle Ages, but not so far that our historical and psychological background is empty of all metaphysical hope.[12] Consciously, however, rationalistic enlightenment predominates, and this abhors all leanings towards the "occult." Desperate efforts are made for a "repristination" of our Christian faith, but we cannot get back to that limited world view which in former times left room for metaphysical intervention. Nor can we resuscitate a genuine Christian belief in an after-life or the equally Christian hope for an imminent end of the world that would put a definite stop to the regrettable error of Creation. Belief in this world and in the power of man has, despite assurances to the contrary, become a practical and, for the time being, irrefragable truth.

624 This attitude on the part of the overwhelming majority provides the most favourable basis for a projection, that is, for a manifestation of the unconscious background. Undeterred by rationalistic criticism, it thrusts itself to the forefront in the form of a symbolic rumour, accompanied and reinforced by the appropriate visions, and thus activates an archetype that has always expressed order, deliverance, salvation, and wholeness. It is characteristic of our time that the archetype, in contrast to its previous manifestations, should now take the form of an object, a technological construction, in order to avoid the odiousness of mythological personification. Anything that looks technological goes down without difficulty with modern man.

11 Cf. "Concerning Rebirth" in *The Archetypes and the Collective Unconscious*, pars. 240ff.

12 It is a common and totally unjustified misunderstanding on the part of scientifically trained people to say that I regard the psychic background as something "metaphysical," while on the other hand the theologians accuse me of "psychologizing" metaphysics. Both are wide of the mark: I am an empiricist, who keeps within the boundaries set for him by the theory of knowledge.

The possibility of space travel has made the unpopular idea of a metaphysical intervention much more acceptable. The apparent weightlessness of the Ufos is, of course, rather hard to digest, but then our own physicists have discovered so many things that border on the miraculous: why should not more advanced star-dwellers have discovered a way to counteract gravitation and reach the speed of light, if not more?

625   Nuclear physics has begotten in the layman's head an uncertainty of judgment that far exceeds that of the physicists and makes things appear possible which but a short while ago would have been declared nonsensical. Consequently the Ufos can easily be regarded and believed in as a physicists' miracle. I still remember, with misgivings, the time when I was convinced that something heavier than air could not fly, only to be taught a painful lesson. The apparently physical nature of the Ufos creates such insoluble puzzles for even the best brains, and on the other hand has built up such an impressive legend, that one feels tempted to take them as a ninety-nine per cent psychic product and subject them accordingly to the usual psychological interpretation. Should it be that an unknown physical phenomenon is the outward cause of the myth, this would detract nothing from the myth, for many myths have meteorological and other natural phenomena as accompanying causes which by no means explain them. A myth is essentially a product of the unconscious archetype and is therefore a symbol which requires psychological interpretation. For primitive man any object, for instance an old tin that has been thrown away, can suddenly assume the importance of a fetish. This effect is obviously not inherent in the tin, but is a psychic product.

2. UFOS IN DREAMS

626   Not only are Ufos seen, they are of course also dreamt about.
This is particularly interesting to the psychologist, because the
dreams tell us in what sense they are understood by the unconscious. In order to form anything like a complete picture of an
object reflected in the psyche, far more than an exclusively intellectual operation is required. Besides the three other functions
of feeling (valuation), sensation (reality-sense), and intuition
(perception of possibilities), we need the reaction of the unconscious, which gives a picture of the unconscious associative context. It is this total view that alone makes possible a whole
judgment on the psychic situation constellated by the object.
An exclusively intellectual approach is bound to be from fifty
to seventy-five per cent unsatisfactory.

627   By way of illustration I shall cite two dreams dreamt by an
educated lady. She had never seen a Ufo, but was interested in
the phenomenon without being able to form a definite picture of it. She did not know the Ufo literature, nor was she
acquainted with my ideas on the subject.

DREAM 1

*"I was going down the Champs Elysées in a bus, with many
other people. Suddenly the air-raid warning sounded. The bus
stopped and all the passengers jumped out, and the next moment they had disappeared into the nearest houses, banging the
doors behind them. I was the last to leave the bus. I tried to get
into a house, but all the doors with their polished brass knobs
were tightly shut, and the whole Champs Elysées was empty. I
pressed against the wall of a house and looked up at the sky: instead of the expected bombers I saw a sort of Flying Saucer, a
metallic sphere shaped like a drop. It was flying along quite*

330

*slowly from north to east, and I had the impression that I was
being observed. In the silence I heard the high heels of a woman
who was walking alone on the empty sidewalk down the Champs
Elysées. The atmosphere was most uncanny."*

DREAM 2 (ABOUT A MONTH LATER)

*"I was walking, at night, in the streets of a city. Interplane-
tary 'machines' appeared in the sky, and everyone fled. The
'machines' looked like large steel cigars. I did not flee. One of
the 'machines' spotted me and came straight towards me at an
oblique angle. I think: Professor Jung says that one should not
run away, so I stand still and look at the machine. From the
front, seen close to, it looked like a circular eye, half blue, half
white.*

*"A room in a hospital: my two chiefs come in, very worried,
and ask my sister how it was going. My sister replied that the
mere sight of the machine had burnt my whole face. Only then
did I realize that they were talking about me, and that my whole
head was bandaged, although I could not see it."*

COMMENTARY TO DREAM 1

628   The dream describes, as the exposition of the initial situation, a mass panic as at an air-raid warning. A Ufo appears, having the form of a drop. A fluid body assumes the form of a drop
when it is about to fall, from which it is clear that the Ufo is
conceived as a liquid falling from the sky, like rain. This surprising drop-form of the Ufo and the analogy with a fluid occur
in the literature.[1] Presumably it is meant to express the commonly reported changeability of the Ufo's shape. This "heavenly" fluid must be of a mysterious nature and is probably a
conception similar to that of the alchemical *aqua permanens,*
the "permanent water," which was also called "Heaven" in six-
teenth-century alchemy and stood for the *quinta essentia.* This
water is the *deus ex machina* of alchemy, the wonderful solvent,
the word *solutio* being used equally for a chemical solution and

1 A report on the case of Captain Mantell, now become a classic, speaks of the Ufo's
resemblance to a "tear drop" and says it behaved like a fluid. Cf. Wilkins, *Flying
Saucers on the Attack,* p. 90.

for the solution of a problem. Indeed, it is the great magician Mercurius himself, the dissolver and binder ("solve et coagula"), the physical and spiritual panacea, which at the same time can be something threatening and dangerous, and falls as the *aqua coelestis* from heaven.

629 Just as the alchemists speak of their "stone, which is no stone," so also of their "philosophical" water, which is no water, but quicksilver, and no ordinary Hg at that, but a "spirit" (pneuma). It represents the arcane substance, which during the alchemical operations changes from a base metal into a spiritual form, often personified as the *filius hermaphroditus, filius macrocosmi,* etc. The "water of the Philosophers" is the classic substance that transmutes the chemical elements and during their transformation is itself transformed. It is also the "redeeming spirit." These ideas began far back in the literature of antiquity, underwent further development during the Middle Ages, and even penetrated into folk-lore and fairy-tale. A very ancient text (possibly first century A.D.) says that in the stone that is found in the Nile there is a spirit. "Reach in thy hand and draw forth the spirit. That is the *exhydrargyrosis*" (the expulsion of the quicksilver). For a period of nearly seventeen hundred years we have ample testimonies to the effectiveness of this animistic archetype. Mercurius is on the one hand a metal, on the other a fluid that can easily be volatilized, i.e., changed into vapour or spirit; this was known as *spiritus Mercurii* and was regarded as a kind of panacea, saviour, and *servator mundi* (preserver of the world). Mercurius is a "bringer of healing" who "makes peace between enemies"; as the "food of immortality" he saves Creation from sickness and corruption, just as Christ saved mankind. In the language of the Church Fathers Christ is a "springing fountain," and in the same way the alchemists call Mercurius *aqua permanens, ros Gedeonis* (Gideon's dew), *vinum ardens* (fiery wine), *mare nostrum* (our sea), *sanguis* (blood), etc.

630 From many of the reports, particularly the early ones, it is evident that the Ufos can appear suddenly and vanish equally suddenly. They can be tracked by radar but remain invisible to the eye, and conversely, can be seen by the eye but not detected by radar. Ufos can make themselves invisible at will, it is said, and must obviously consist of a substance that is visible at one

moment and invisible the next. The nearest analogy to this is a volatile liquid which condenses out of an invisible state into the form of drops. In reading the old texts one can still feel the miracle of disappearance and reappearance which the alchemists beheld in the vaporization of water or quicksilver: for them it was the transformation of the "souls that had become water" (Heraclitus) into the invisible pneuma at the touch of Hermes' wand, and their descent out of the empyrean into visible form again. Zosimos of Panopolis (third century A.D.) has left us a valuable document describing this transformation, which takes place in a cooking-vessel. The fantasies born of musing over the steaming cooking-pot—one of the most ancient experiences of mankind—may also be responsible for the sudden disappearance and reappearance of the Ufo.

631   The unexpected drop-form in our dream has prompted a comparison with a central conception of alchemy, known to us not only from Europe but also from India and second century China. The extraordinariness of the Ufo is paralleled by the extraordinariness of its psychological context, which has to be adduced if we are to risk any interpretation at all. Considering the essential weirdness of the Ufo phenomenon, we cannot expect the familiar, rationalistic principles of explanation to be in any way adequate. A psychoanalytic approach to the problem could do nothing more than turn the whole idea of Ufos into a sexual fantasy, at most arriving at the conclusion that a repressed uterus was coming down from the sky. This would not fit in too badly with the old medical view of hysteria ($\H{υ}στερος$ = womb) as a "wandering of the uterus," especially in the case of a woman who had an anxiety dream. But then, what about the masculine pilots, who are the chief authors of the rumour? The language of sex is hardly more significant than any other symbolical means of expression. This type of explanation is, at bottom, just as mythological and rationalistic as the technological fables about the nature and purpose of Ufos.

632   The dreamer knew enough about psychology to realize in her second dream the necessity of not giving in to her fear and running away, as she would dearly have liked to do. But the unconscious created a situation in which this way out was barred. Consequently she had an opportunity to observe the phenomenon at close quarters. It proved to be harmless. Indeed, the

untroubled footsteps of a woman point to someone who either is not aware of it at all or is free from fear.

COMMENTARY TO DREAM 2

633   The exposition begins with the statement that it is night and dark, a time when normally everyone is asleep and dreaming. As in the previous dream, panic breaks out. A number of Ufos appear. Recalling the first commentary, we could say that the unity of the self as a supraordinate, semi-divine figure has broken up into a plurality. On a mythological level this would correspond to a plurality of gods, god-men, demons, or souls. In Hermetic philosophy the arcane substance has a "thousand names," but essentially it consists of the One and Only (i.e., God), and this principle only becomes pluralized through being split up (*multiplicatio*). The alchemists were consciously performing an *opus divinum* when they sought to free the "soul in chains," i.e., to release the demiurge distributed and imprisoned in his own creation and restore him to his original condition of unity.

634   Looked at psychologically, the plurality of the symbol of unity signifies a splitting into many independent units, into a number of "selves"; the *one* "metaphysical" principle, representing the idea of monotheism, is dissolved into a plurality of subordinate deities. From the standpoint of Christian dogma such an operation could easily be construed as archheresy, were it not that this view is contradicted by the unequivocal saying of Christ, "Ye are gods," and by the equally emphatic idea that we are all God's children, both of which presuppose man's at least potential kinship with God. From the psychological point of view the plurality of Ufos would correspond to the projection of a plurality of human individuals, the choice of symbol (spherical object) indicating that the content of the projection is not the actual people themselves, but rather their ideal psychic totality; not the empirical man as he knows himself to be from experience, but his total psyche, the conscious contents of which have still to be supplemented by the contents of the unconscious. Although we know, from our investigations, a number of things about the unconscious which give us some clue as to its nature, we are still very far from being able to sketch out

334

even a hypothetical picture that is in any way adequate. To mention only one of the greatest difficulties: there are parapsychological experiences which can no longer be denied and have to be taken into account in evaluating psychic processes. The unconscious can no longer be treated as if it were causally dependent on consciousness, since it possesses qualities which are not under conscious control. It should rather be understood as an autonomous entity acting reciprocally with consciousness.

635   The plurality of Ufos, then, is a projection of a number of psychic images of wholeness which appear in the sky because on the one hand they represent archetypes charged with energy and on the other hand are not recognized as psychic factors. The reason for this is that our present-day consciousness possesses no conceptual categories by means of which it could apprehend the nature of psychic totality. It is still in an archaic state, so to speak, where apperceptions of this kind do not occur, and accordingly the relevant contents cannot be recognized as psychic factors. Moreover, it is so trained that it must think of such images not as forms inherent in the psyche but as existing somewhere in extra-psychic, metaphysical space, or else as historical facts. When, therefore, the archetype receives from the conditions of the time and from the general psychic situation an additional charge of energy, it cannot, for the reasons I have described, be integrated directly into consciousness, but is forced to manifest itself indirectly in the form of spontaneous projections. The projected image then appears as an ostensibly physical fact independent of the individual psyche and its nature. In other words, the rounded wholeness of the mandala becomes a space ship controlled by an intelligent being. The usually lens-shaped form of the Ufos may be influenced by the fact that psychic wholeness, as the historical testimonies show, has always been characterized by certain cosmic affinities: the individual soul was thought to be of "heavenly" origin, a particle of the world soul, and hence a microcosm, a reflection of the macrocosm. Leibniz's monadology is an eloquent example of this. The macrocosm is the starry world around us, which, appearing to the naïve mind as spherical, gives the soul its traditional spherical form. Actually the astronomical heavens are filled with mainly lens-shaped agglomerations of stars, the galaxies, similar in form to that of the Ufos. This form may possibly be a con-

cession to the recent astronomical findings, for to my knowledge there are no older traditions that speak of the soul having the form of a lens. Here we may have an instance of an older tradition being modified by recent additions to knowledge, an influencing of primordial ideas by the latest acquisitions of consciousness, like the frequent substitution of automobiles and aeroplanes for animals and monsters in modern dreams.

636   It must be emphasized, however, that there is also the possibility of a natural or absolute "knowledge," when the unconscious psyche coincides with objective facts. This is a problem that has been raised by the discoveries of parapsychology. "Absolute knowledge" occurs not only in telepathy and precognition, but also in biology, for instance in the attunement of the virus of hydrophobia to the anatomy of dog and man as described by Portmann,[2] the wasp's apparent knowledge of where the motor ganglia are located in the caterpillar that is to nourish the wasp's progeny, the emission of light by certain fishes and insects with almost 100 per cent efficiency, the directional sense of carrier pigeons, the warning of earthquakes given by chickens and cats, and the amazing co-operation found in symbiotic relationships. We know, too, that the life process itself cannot be explained only by causality, but requires "intelligent" choice. The shape of the Ufos is in this sense analogous to that of the elements composing the structure of space, the galaxies, no matter how ridiculous this seems to human reason.

637   In our dream the usual lens-shaped form is replaced by the rarer cigar-form, derived apparently from the old dirigible airships. As in Dream 1 a psychoanalytic approach could resort to a female "symbol," the uterus, to explain the "drop," so here the sexual analogy of the phallic form leaps to the eye. The archaic background of the psyche has this much in common with primitive language, that they both translate unknown or incompletely understood things into instinctive and habitual forms of thought, so that Freud could, with some justification, establish that all round or hollow forms have a feminine and all oblong ones a masculine meaning, as for instance nuts and bolts, male and female pipe-joints, etc. In these cases the interest that naturally attaches to sex invites the making of such

2 "Die Bedeutung der Bilder in der lebendigen Energiewandlung."

analogies, not to speak of the amusing illustrations they provide. Still, sex is not the sole instigator of these metaphors, there is also hunger, the urge to eat and drink. In the history of religion there are not only sexual unions with the gods, they are also eaten and drunk. Even sexual attraction has become an object for these metaphors: we like a girl so much that we could "eat" her. Language is full of metaphors which express one instinct in terms of another, but we need not conclude from this that the real and essential thing is always "love" or hunger or the urge to power, etc. The main point is that every situation activates the relevant instinct, which then predominates as a vital need and decides the choice of symbol as well as its interpretation.[3]

638   Very probably there is a phallic analogy in the dream, which, in accordance with the meaning of this exceedingly archaic symbol, gives the Ufo the character of something "procreative," "fructifying," and, in the broadest sense, "penetrating." In ancient times the feeling of being "penetrated" by, or of "receiving," the god was allegorized by the sexual act.[4] But it would be a gross misunderstanding to interpret a genuine religious experience as a "repressed" sexual fantasy on account of a mere metaphor. The "penetration" can also be expressed by a sword, spear, or arrow.

639   The dreamer does not flee from the menacing aspect of the Ufo, even when she sees it coming straight at her. During this confrontation the original spherical or lens-shaped aspect reappears in the form of a circular eye. This image corresponds to the traditional eye of God, which, all-seeing, searches the hearts of men, laying bare the truth and pitilessly exposing every cranny of the soul. It is a reflection of one's insight into the total reality of one's own being.

640   The eye is half blue, half white. This corresponds to the colours of the sky, its pure blue and the whiteness of clouds that obscure its transparency. The psychic totality, the self, is a combination of opposites. Without a shadow even the self is not real. It always has two aspects, a bright and a dark, like the pre-Christian idea of God in the Old Testament, which is so much better suited to the facts of religious experience (Rev. 14:7)

---

[3] The phallus is not just a sign that indicates the penis; it is a "symbol" because it has so many other meanings.

[4] Dionysus, for instance, was invoked as *enkolpios:* 'he in the lap.'

than the Summum Bonum, based as this is on the precarious foundation of a mere syllogism (the *privatio boni*). Even the highly Christian Jacob Boehme could not escape this insight and gave eloquent expression to it in his "Forty Questions concerning the Soul."

641   The drop-shaped Ufo, suggesting a fluid substance, a sort of "water," makes way for a circular structure which not only sees, i.e., emits light (according to the old view light is equivalent to seeing), but also sends out a scorching heat. One immediately thinks of the intolerable radiance that shone from the face of Moses after he had seen God, of "Who among us shall dwell with everlasting burnings?" (Isaiah 33:14), and of the saying of Jesus: "He who is near unto me is near unto the fire."

642   Nowadays people who have an experience of this kind are more likely to go running to the doctor or psychiatrist than to the theologian. I have more than once been consulted by people who were terrified by their dreams and visions. They took them for symptoms of mental illness, possibly heralding insanity, whereas in reality they were "dreams sent by God," real and genuine religious experiences that collided with a mind unprepared, ignorant, and profoundly prejudiced. In this matter there is little choice today: anything out of the ordinary can only be pathological, for that abstraction, the "statistical average," counts as the ultimate truth, and not reality. All feeling for value is repressed in the interests of a narrow intellect and biased reason. So it is no wonder that after her Ufo experience our patient woke up in hospital with a burned face. This is only to be expected today.

643   The second dream differs from the first in that it brings out the dreamer's inner relationship to the Ufo. The Ufo has marked her out and not only turns a searching eye upon her but irradiates her with magical heat, a synonym for her own inner affectivity. Fire is the symbolical equivalent of a very strong emotion or affect, which in this case comes upon her quite unexpectedly. In spite of her justifiable fear of the Ufo she held her ground, as though it were intrinsically harmless, but is now made to realize that it is capable of sending out a deadly heat, a statement we often meet with in the Ufo literature.[5] This heat

5 Cf. Keyhoe, *The Flying Saucer Conspiracy*.

is a projection of her own unrealized emotion—of a feeling that has intensified into a physical effect but remains unrecognized. Even her facial expression was altered (burnt) by it. This recalls not only the changed face of Moses but also that of Brother Klaus after his terrifying vision of God.[6] It points to an "indelible" experience whose traces remain visible to others, because it has brought about a demonstrable change in the entire personality. Psychologically, of course, such an event betokens only a *potential* change; it has first to be integrated into consciousness. That is why Brother Klaus felt it necessary to spend long years in wearisome study and meditation until he succeeded in recognizing his terrifying vision as a vision of the Holy Trinity, in accordance with the spirit of the age. In this way he transformed the experience into an integrated conscious content that was intellectually and morally binding for him. This work has still to be done by the dreamer, and perhaps also by all those who see Ufos, dream of them, or spread rumours about them.

644 The symbols of divinity coincide with those of the self: what, on the one side, appears as a psychological experience signifying psychic wholeness, expresses on the other side the idea of God. This is not to assert a metaphysical identity of the two, but merely the empirical identity of the images representing them, which all originate in the human psyche, as our dream shows. What the metaphysical conditions are for the similarity of the images is, like everything transcendental, beyond human knowledge.

645 The motif of the isolated "God's eye," which the unconscious proffers as an interpretation of the Ufo, can be found in ancient Egyptian mythology as the "eye of Horus," who with its help healed the partial blinding of his father Osiris, caused by Set. The isolated God's eye also appears in Christian iconography.

646 In dealing with the products of the collective unconscious, all images that show an unmistakably mythological character have to be examined in their symbological context. They are the inborn language of the psyche and its structure, and, as regards their basic form, are in no sense individual acquisitions.

6 Cf. "Brother Klaus" in *Psychology and Religion, West and East.*

Despite its pre-eminent capacity for learning and for consciousness, the human psyche is a natural phenomenon like the psyche of animals, and is rooted in inborn instincts which bring their own specific forms with them and so constitute the heredity of the species. Volition, intention, and all personal differentiations are acquired late and owe their existence to a consciousness that has emancipated itself from mere instinctivity. Wherever it is a question of archetypal formations, personalistic attempts at explanation lead us astray. The method of comparative symbology, on the other hand, not only proves fruitful on scientific grounds but makes a deeper understanding possible in practice. The symbological or "amplificatory" approach produces a result that looks at first like a translation back into primitive language. And so it would be, if understanding with the help of the unconscious were a purely intellectual exercise and not one that brought our total capacities into play. In other words, besides its formal mode of manifestation the archetype possesses a numinous quality, a feeling-value that is highly effective in practice. One can be unconscious of this value, since it can be repressed artificially; but a repression has neurotic consequences, because the repressed affect still exists and simply makes an outlet for itself elsewhere, in some unsuitable place.

647   As our dream shows very clearly, the Ufo comes from the unconscious background which has always expressed itself in numinous ideas and images. It is these that give the strange phenomenon an interpretation that makes it appear in a significant light—significant not merely because they arouse dim historical memories which link up with the findings of comparative psychology, but because actual affective processes are at work.

648   Today, as never before, men pay an extraordinary amount of attention to the skies, for technological reasons. This is especially true of the airman, whose field of vision is occupied on the one hand by the complicated control apparatus before him, and on the other by the empty vastness of cosmic space. His consciousness is concentrated one-sidedly on details requiring the most careful observation, while at his back, so to speak, his unconscious strives to fill the illimitable emptiness of space. His training and his common sense both preclude him from observing all the things that might rise up from within and become visible in order to compensate for the emptiness and solitude of flight

high above the earth. Such a situation provides the ideal conditions for spontaneous psychic phenomena, as everyone knows who has lived sufficiently long in the solitude, silence, and emptiness of deserts, seas, mountains, or in primeval forests. Rationalism and boredom are essentially products of the over-indulged craving for stimulation so characteristic of urban populations. The city-dweller seeks artificial sensations to escape his boredom; the hermit does not seek them, but is plagued by them against his will.

649   We know from the life of ascetics and anchorites that, whether they would or no, and without any assistance from consciousness, spontaneous psychic phenomena rose up to compensate their biological needs: numinous fantasy images, visions and hallucinations that were evaluated either positively or negatively. Those positively evaluated derived from a sphere of the unconscious felt to be spiritual, the others obviously from the instinctual world they knew only too well, where loaded dishes and flagons and luscious meals stilled their hunger, seductive and voluptuous beings yielded themselves to their pent-up sexual desires, riches and worldly power took the place of poverty and lack of influence, and bustling crowds, noise, and music enlivened the intolerable silence and loneliness. Although it is easy to speak here of images caused by repressed wishes and to explain the projection of fantasies that way, it does not explain the visions that were evaluated positively, because these did not correspond to a repressed wish but to one that was fully conscious and therefore could not produce a projection. A psychic content can only appear as a projection when its connection with the ego personality is not recognized. For this reason the wish hypothesis must be discarded.

650   The hermits sought to attain a spiritual experience, and for this purpose they mortified the earthly man. Naturally enough the affronted world of instinct reacted with unseemly projections, but the spiritual sphere, too, responded with projections of a positive nature—most unexpectedly, to our scientific way of thinking. For the spiritual sphere had not been neglected in any way; on the contrary, it was nurtured with the greatest possible devotion by means of prayer, meditation, and other spiritual exercises. So, according to our hypothesis, it should have had no need of compensation; its one-sidedness, which insisted

on mortifying the body, was already compensated by the violent reaction on the part of the instincts. Nevertheless the spontaneous appearance of positive projections in the form of numinous images was experienced as grace and felt to be a divine revelation, and indeed they are characterized as such by the content of the visions. Psychologically speaking, these visions function in exactly the same way as the visions produced by the neglected instincts, despite the undeniable fact that the saints did everything to foster their spirituality. They did *not* mortify the spiritual man and therefore needed no compensation in this respect.

651   If, in the face of this dilemma, we cling to the proven truth of the compensation theory, we are driven to the paradoxical conclusion that, despite appearances to the contrary, the spiritual situation of the hermit was one of deficiency after all, and that it needed an appropriate compensation. Just as physical hunger is sated, at least metaphorically, by the sight of a marvellous meal, so the hunger of the soul is sated by the vision of numinous images. But it is not so easy to see why the anchorite's soul should suffer from "hunger." He stakes his whole life on earning the *panis supersubstantialis,* the "superessential bread" which alone appeases his hunger, and besides that he has the faith, doctrines, and means of grace of the Church at his disposal. Why, then, should he lack anything? All this he has, but the fact remains that he is not nourished by it and his unappeasable desire remains unfulfilled. What, obviously, he still lacks is the *actual and immediate experience of spiritual reality,* however it may turn out. Whether it presents itself to him more or less concretely or symbolically makes little difference. In any case he is not expecting the physical tangibility of any earthly thing, but rather the sublime intangibleness of a spiritual vision. This experience is, in itself, a compensation for the barrenness and emptiness of traditional forms, and accordingly he values it above all else. For in fact there appears before him, uncreated by himself, a numinous image which is just as real and "actual" (because it "acts" upon him) as the illusions spun by his neglected instincts. It is, however, as much desired by him on account of its reality and spontaneity as the illusions of his senses are undesired. So long as the numinous contents can avail themselves, in one way or another, of the traditional forms, there is no cause for disquiet. But when they betray their archa-

ism by assuming unusual and obnoxious features, the matter becomes painfully dubious. The saint then begins to doubt whether they are any less illusory than the delusions of the senses. Indeed, it may even happen that a revelation originally regarded as divine is subsequently damned as a deception of the devil. The criterion of distinction is simply and solely tradition, not reality or unreality as in the case of a real or illusory meal. The vision is a psychic phenomenon, just as are its numinous contents. Here spirit answers spirit, whereas in a fast the need for food is answered by an hallucination and not by a real meal. In the first case the bill is paid in cash, in the second case by an unbacked cheque. The one solution is satisfying, the other obviously not.

652   But in both cases the structure of the phenomenon is the same. Physical hunger needs a real meal and spiritual hunger needs a numinous content. Such contents are by nature archetypal and have always expressed themselves in the form of natural revelations, for Christian symbolism, like all other religious ideas, is based on archetypal models that go back into prehistory. The "total" character of these symbols includes every kind of human interest and instinct, thereby guaranteeing the numinosity of the archetype. That is why, in comparative religion, we so often find the religious and spiritual aspects associated with those of sexuality, hunger, aggression, power, etc. A particularly fruitful source of religious symbolism is the instinct to which most importance is attached in a given epoch or culture, or which is of most concern to the individual. There are communities in which hunger is more important than sex and vice versa. Our civilization bothers us less with food taboos than with sexual restrictions. In modern society these have come to play the role of an injured deity that is getting its own back in every sphere of human activity, including psychology, where it would reduce "spirit" to sexual repression.

653   However, a partial interpretation of the symbolism in sexual terms should be taken seriously. If man's striving for a spiritual goal is not a genuine instinct but merely the result of a particular social development, then an explanation according to sexual principles is the most appropriate and the most acceptable to reason. But even if we grant the striving for wholeness and unity the character of a genuine instinct, and base our explanation

mainly on this principle, the fact still remains that there is a close association between sexual instinct and the striving for wholeness. With the exception of religious longings, nothing challenges modern man more consciously and personally than sex. One can also say in good faith that he is possessed even more by the power instinct. This question will be decided according to temperament and one's own subjective bias. The only thing we cannot doubt is that the most important of the fundamental instincts, the religious instinct for wholeness, plays the least conspicuous part in contemporary consciousness because, as history shows, it can free itself only with the greatest effort, and with continual backslidings, from contamination with the other two instincts. These can constantly appeal to common, everyday facts known to everyone, but the instinct for wholeness requires for its evidence a more highly differentiated consciousness, thoughtfulness, reflection, responsibility, and sundry other virtues. Therefore it does not commend itself to the relatively unconscious man driven by his natural impulses, because, imprisoned in his familiar world, he clings to the commonplace, the obvious, the probable, the collectively valid, using for his motto: "Thinking is difficult, therefore let the herd pronounce judgment!" It is an enormous relief to him when something that looks complicated, unusual, puzzling and problematical can be reduced to something ordinary and banal, especially when the solution strikes him as surprisingly simple and somewhat droll. The most convenient explanations are invariably sex and the power instinct, and reduction to these two dominants gives rationalists and materialists an ill-concealed satisfaction: they have neatly disposed of an intellectually and morally uncomfortable difficulty, and on top of that can enjoy the feeling of having accomplished a useful work of enlightenment which will free the individual from unnecessary moral and social burdens. In this way they can pose as benefactors of mankind. On closer inspection, however, things look very different: the exemption of the individual from a difficult and apparently insoluble task drives sexuality into an even more pernicious repression, where it is replaced by rationalism or by soul-destroying cynicism, while the power instinct is driven towards some Socialistic ideal that has already turned half the world into the State prison of Communism. This is the exact op-

344

posite of what the striving for wholeness wants, namely, to free the individual from the compulsion of the other two instincts. The task before him comes back with all its energies unused, and reinforces, to an almost pathological degree, the very instincts that have always stood in the way of man's higher development. At all events it has a neuroticizing effect characteristic of our time and must bear most of the blame for the splitting of the individual and of the world in general. We just will not admit the shadow, and so the right hand does not know what the left is doing.

654   Correctly appraising the situation, the Catholic Church, while counting sexual sins among the "venial" ones, therefore keeps a sharp eye upon sexuality as the chief enemy in practice and ferrets it out in all corners. She thus creates an acute consciousness of sex, deleterious to weaker spirits but of advantage in promoting reflection and broadening the consciousness of the stronger. The worldly pomps of the Catholic Church for which she is reproached by the Protestants have the obvious purpose of holding the power of the spirit visibly before the natural power-instinct. This is infinitely more effective than the best logical arguments, which no one likes following. Only the tiniest fraction of the population learns anything from reflection; everything else consists in the suggestive power of ocular evidence.

655   After this digression, let us turn back to the problem of sexual interpretation. If we try to define the psychological structure of the religious experience which saves, heals, and makes whole, the simplest formula we can find would seem to be the following: *in religious experience man comes face to face with a psychically overwhelming Other*. As to the existence of this power we have only assertions to go on, but no physical or logical proofs. It comes upon man in psychic guise. We cannot explain it as exclusively spiritual, for experience would immediately compel us to retract such a judgment, since the vision, according to the psychic disposition of the individual, often assumes the form of sexuality or of some other unspiritual impulse. Only something overwhelming, no matter what form of expression it uses, can challenge the whole man and force him to react as a whole. It cannot be proved that such things happen or that they must occur, nor is there any proof that they are any-

thing more than psychic,[7] since the evidence for them rests solely on personal statements and avowals. This, in view of the crass undervaluation of the psyche in our predominantly materialistic and statistical age, sounds like a condemnation of religious experience. Consequently, the average intelligence takes refuge either in unbelief or in credulity, for to it the psyche is no more than a miserable wisp of vapour. Either there are hard-and-fast facts, or else it is nothing but illusion begotten by repressed sexuality or an over-compensated inferiority complex. As against this I have urged that the psyche be recognized as having its own peculiar reality. Despite the advances in organic chemistry, we are still very far from being able to explain consciousness as a biochemical process. On the contrary, we have to admit that chemical laws do not even explain the selective process of food assimilation, let alone the self-regulation and self-preservation of the organism. Whatever the reality of the psyche may be, it seems to coincide with the reality of life and at the same time to have a connection with the formal laws governing the inorganic world. For the psyche has yet another property which most of us would rather not admit, namely, that peculiar factor which relativizes space and time, and is now the object of intensive parapsychological research.

656   Since the discovery of the empirical unconscious the psyche and what goes on in it have become a natural fact and are no longer an arbitrary opinion, which they undoubtedly would be if they owed their existence to the caprices of a rootless consciousness. But consciousness, for all its kaleidoscopic mobility, rests as we know on the comparatively static or at least highly conservative foundation of the instincts and their specific forms, the archetypes. This world in the background[8] proves to be the opponent of consciousness, which, because of its mobility (learning capacity), is often in danger of losing its roots. That is why since earliest times men have felt compelled to perform rites for the purpose of securing the co-operation of the unconscious. In

---

[7] Neither is there any proof that they are "only" psychic!

[8] Here I must beg the reader to eschew the popular misconception that this background is "metaphysical." This view is a piece of gross carelessness of which even professional people are guilty. It is far more a question of instincts which influence not only our outward behaviour but also the psychic structure. The psyche is not an arbitrary fantasy; it is a biological fact subject to the laws of life.

a primitive world no one reckons without his host; he is constantly mindful of the gods, the spirits, of fate and the magical
qualities of time and place, rightly recognizing that man's solitary will is only a fragment of a total situation. Primitive man's
actions have a "total" character which civilized man would like
to be rid of, as though it were an unnecessary burden. Things
seem to go all right without it.

657   The great advantage of this attitude lies in the development
of a discriminating consciousness, but it has the almost equally
great disadvantage of breaking down man's original wholeness
into separate functions which conflict with one another. This
loss has made itself increasingly felt in modern times. I need
only remind you of Nietzsche's Dionysian experience of a
"breakthrough," and of that trend in German philosophy whose
most obvious symptom is the book by Ludwig Klages, *Der Geist
als Widersacher der Seele*.[9] Through this fragmentation process
one or other of the functions of consciousness becomes highly
differentiated and can then escape the control of the other functions to such an extent that it attains a kind of autonomy, constructing a world of its own into which these other functions
are admitted only so far as they can be subjugated to the dominant function. In this way consciousness loses its balance: if the
intellect predominates, then the value judgments of feeling are
weakened, and vice versa. Again, if sensation is predominant,
intuition is barred, this being the function that pays the least
attention to tangible facts; and conversely, a man with an excess
of intuition lives in a world of unproven possibilities. A useful
result of such developments is specialism, but that also promotes
a disagreeable one-sidedness.

658   It is just this capacity for one-sidedness which bids us observe things from one angle only, and if possible to reduce them
to a single principle. In psychology this attitude inevitably leads
to explanations in terms of one particular bias. For instance, in
a case of marked extraversion the whole of the psyche is traced
back to environmental influences, while in introversion it is
traced back to the hereditary psychophysical disposition and the
intellectual and emotional factors that go with it. Both explanations tend to turn the psychic apparatus into a machine. Any-

9 "The spirit as adversary of the soul."

one who tries to be equally fair to both points of view is accused of obscurantism. Yet both of them should be applied, even if a series of paradoxical statements is the result. Hence, in order to avoid multiplying the principles of explanation, one of the easily recognizable basic instincts will be preferred at the expense of the others. Nietzsche bases everything on power, Freud on pleasure and its frustration. While in Nietzsche the unconscious can be felt as a factor of some importance, and in Freud became a *sine qua non* of his theory, though without ever sloughing off the character of being something secondary and "nothing but" the result of repression, in Adler the field of vision is narrowed down to a subjective "prestige"-psychology, where the unconscious as a possibly decisive factor disappears from sight altogether. This fate has also overtaken Freud's psychoanalysis as practised by the second generation. The significant beginnings he made towards a psychology of the unconscious stopped short at a single archetype, that of the Oedipus complex, and were not developed further by the more rigorous of his pupils.

659   The evidence of the sexual instinct is, in the case of the incest complex, so patently obvious that a philosophically limited intelligence could remain satisfied with that. The same is true of Adler's subjective will to power. Both views remain caught in an instinctual premise which leaves no room for the other and so lands us in the specialist *cul de sac* of fragmentary explanation. Freud's pioneer work, on the other hand, gave access to the well-documented history of psychic phenomenology, and this allows us something like a synoptic view of the psyche. The psyche does not express itself merely in the narrow subjective sphere of the individual personality but, over and above that, in collective psychic phenomena of whose existence Freud was aware, at least in principle, as his concept of the "superego" shows. For the time being method and theory remained—and remained too long—in the hands of the psychiatrist, who of necessity is concerned only with individuals and their urgent personal problems. An investigation of fundamentals involving historical research is naturally not in his line, nor are his scientific training and his practical work of much help to him in getting at the foundations of psychological knowledge. For this reason Freud saw himself obliged to skip the—ad-

mittedly—wearisome stage of comparative psychology and press forward into the conjectural and highly uncertain prehistory of the human psyche. In so doing he lost the ground from under his feet, for he would not let himself be taught by the findings of ethnologists and historians, but transferred the insights he had gained from modern neurotics during consulting hours directly to the broad field of primitive psychology. He did not pay enough attention to the fact that under certain conditions there is a shift of emphasis and other psychic dominants come into play. The Freudian school got stuck at the Oedipus motif, i.e., the archetype of incest, and hence their views remained predominantly sexualistic. They failed to recognize that the Oedipus complex is an exclusively masculine affair, that sexuality is not the only possible dominant in the psychic process, and that incest, because it involves the religious instinct, is far more an expression of the latter than the cause of it. I will not mention my own endeavours in this field, since for most people they have remained a book with seven seals.

660   The sexual hypothesis nevertheless carries considerable power of conviction because it coincides with one of the principal instincts. The same is true of the power hypothesis, which can appeal to instincts that characterize not only the individual but also political and social movements. A *rapprochement* between the two standpoints is nowhere in sight, unless we can acknowledge the peculiar nature of the self, which embraces the individual as well as society. As experience shows, the archetypes possess the quality of "transgressivity"; they can sometimes manifest themselves in such a way that they seem to belong as much to society as to the individual; they are therefore numinous and contagious in their effects. (It is the emotional person who emotionalizes others.) In certain cases this transgressiveness also produces meaningful coincidences, i.e., acausal, synchronistic phenomena, such as the results of Rhine's ESP experiments.

661   The instincts are part of the living totality; they are articulated with and subordinate to the whole. Their release as separate entities leads to chaos and nihilism, because it breaks down the unity and totality of the individual and destroys him. It should be the task of psychotherapy, properly understood, to preserve or restore this unity. It cannot be the aim of education

349

to turn out rationalists, materialists, specialists, technicians and others of the kind who, unconscious of their origins, are precipitated abruptly into the present and contribute to the disorientation and fragmentation of society. By the same token, no psychotherapy can lead to satisfactory results if it confines itself to single aspects only. The temptation to do this is so great, and the danger of loss of instinct so threatening in the breathless tempo of modern civilization, that every expression of instinct must be watched very carefully, since it is part of the total picture and is essential for man's psychic balance.

662 For these reasons the sexual aspect of the Ufos merits our attention, as it shows that a very powerful instinct like sexuality has its share in the structure of the phenomenon. It is probably no accident that in one of the dreams we have been discussing a feminine symbol appears, and in the other a masculine, in accordance with the reports of lens-shaped and cigar-shaped Ufos, for where one appears, we may also expect its partner.

663 The vision is a symbol consisting not only of archetypal forms of thought but of instinctual elements as well, so that it can justly lay claim to be a "reality." It is not only "historical," but topical and dynamic. Hence it does not appeal only to man's conscious technological fantasies, or to his philosophical speculations, but strikes deep down into his "animal" nature. This is what we would expect a genuine symbol to do; it must affect and express the whole man. However unsatisfactory a sexual interpretation may be in this case, the contribution it makes should not be overlooked and must be given due consideration.

664 In the same way the power instinct expresses itself in both dreams; the dreamer appears in a unique situation, she is singled out, indeed "chosen" like one whose countenance is burned by the divine fire. Both interpretations, so far as they claim to be exclusive, do away with the symbolic meaning of the dreams and eliminate the individual in favour of the instinctual manifestations. The feebleness of the individual in the face of the overwhelming power of instinct is once more established. For anyone who was not yet aware of this fact, such an interpretation would of course be novel and impressive. But our dreamer does not belong to the host of ingénues, and in her case it would be pointless to reduce the dream in this way. She is, on the contrary, one of those moderns who realize what the elim-

ination of the individual means. The paralysing feeling of nothingness and lostness is compensated by the dreams: she is the only one to withstand the panic and to recognize its cause. It is at her that the unearthly thing points, and on her it leaves the visible traces of its power. She is set apart as one of the elect. Such a gesture on the part of the unconscious naturally has a useful meaning only when feelings of inferiority and the senselessness of a merely functional existence threaten to stifle the personality.

665   This case may serve as a paradigm for the widespread anxiety and insecurity of thoughtful people today, while at the same time revealing the compensating power of the unconscious.

DREAM 3

666   This dream is an excerpt from a longer dream which a 42-year-old woman patient recorded about six years ago. At the time she had heard nothing of Flying Saucers and the like. *She dreamt she was standing in a garden, when suddenly the humming of an engine became audible overhead. She sat down on the garden wall in order to see what was going on. A black metallic object appeared and circled over her: it was a huge flying spider made of metal, with great dark eyes. It was round in shape, and was a new and unique aeroplane. From the body of the spider there issued a solemn voice, loud and distinct; it uttered a prayer that was intended as an admonition and a warning to everybody, for those on earth as well as for the occupants of the spider. The gist of the prayer was: "Lead us downwards and keep us (safe) below . . . Carry us up to the height!" Adjoining the garden was a large administrative building where international decisions were being taken. Flying incredibly low, the spider passed along the windows of the building, for the obvious purpose of letting the voice influence the people inside and point out the way to peace, which was the way to the inner, secret world. They were to take reconciling decisions. There were several other spectators in the garden. She felt somewhat embarrassed because she was not fully clothed.*

COMMENTARY TO DREAM 3

667   In the preceding part of the dream the dreamer's bed had stood close to the garden wall. In her dream, therefore, she had slept under the open sky and been exposed to the free influences of Nature, which means psychologically the impersonal, collective unconscious, for this forms the counterpart to our natural environment and is always projected upon it. The wall denotes a barrier separating the immediate world of the dreamer from a more distant one (administrative building). A round metallic object appears, described as a flying spider. This description fits the Ufos. As regards the designation "spider," we are reminded of the hypothesis that Ufos are a species of insect coming from another planet and possessing a shell or carapace that shines like metal. An analogy would be the metallic-looking, chitinous covering of our beetles. Each Ufo is supposed to be a single insect, not a swarm.[10] In reading the numerous reports I must admit that I, too, was struck by the thought that the peculiar behaviour of the Ufos. was reminiscent of certain insects. To the speculative mind there is nothing inherently impossible in the idea that under other conditions Nature could express her "knowledge" in quite other ways than those mentioned earlier; for instance, instead of light-producing insects she might evolve creatures capable of "anti-gravity." In any case our technological imagination often lags a long way behind Nature's. Everything in our experience is subject to the law of gravity with one great exception: the psyche, which, as we experience it, is weightlessness itself. The psychic "object" and gravity are, to the best of our knowledge, incommensurable. They seem to be different in principle. The psyche represents the only opposite of gravity known to us. It is "anti-gravity" in the truest sense of the word. In corroboration of this we could cite the parapsychological experience of levitation and other psychic phenomena, denied only by the ignorant, which relativize time and space.

10 Sievers, *Flying Saucers über Südafrika*, p. 157, mentions Gerald Heard's hypothesis that they are a species of bees from Mars (*Is Another World Watching? The Riddle of the Flying Saucers*). Harold T. Wilkins, in *Flying Saucers on the Attack*, mentions a report of a "rain of threads," supposed to come from unknown spiders.

668   Obviously the "flying spider" is based on an unconscious fantasy of this kind. In the Ufo literature, too, reference is made to flying spiders in an attempt to explain the alleged "rain of threads" in Oloron and Gaillac.[11] Note that the dream cannot help making a concession to modern technological fantasies: it calls the spider a "new and unique aeroplane."

669   The psychic nature of the spider is shown by the fact that it contains a "voice," evidently issuing from something like a human being. This curious phenomenon reminds one of similar occurrences in insane people, who can hear voices issuing from anything or anybody. "Voices," like visions, are autonomous manifestations of the senses caused by the activity of the unconscious. "Voices from the aether" also occur in the Ufo literature.[12]

670   Emphasis is laid on the eyes, which denote seeing and the intention to see. The intention is expressed by the voice, whose message is addressed both to the earth dwellers and to the "occupants of the spider." The association with "aeroplane" here gives rise to the illogical idea of a machine that transports passengers. The passengers are evidently thought of as quasi-human, for the message is meant for them as well as for human beings. We can therefore suppose that both are simply different aspects of man, e.g., the empirical man below on earth and the spiritual man in heaven.

671   The cryptic message or "prayer" is spoken by a single voice, by a kind of prayer leader. He addresses himself to that which "leads" and "carries," and this must be the spider. We are therefore obliged to examine the symbol of the spider somewhat more closely. As we know, although this animal is quite harmless in our latitudes, it is for many people an object of horror and superstitious belief (*araignée du matin, grand chagrin; araignée du soir, grand espoir*).[13] When someone is not quite right in the head, we say in German that he "spins" and "has cobwebs in the attic." Spiders, like all animals that are not warm-blooded or have no cerebrospinal nervous system, function in dreams as symbols of a profoundly alien psychic world.

11 Aimé Michel, *The Truth about Flying Saucers.*
12 Wilkins, p. 138.
13 The horror people feel for spiders has been vividly described by Jeremias Gotthelf in his story *The Black Spider.*

So far as I can see, they express contents which, though active, are unable to reach consciousness; they have not yet entered the sphere of the cerebrospinal nervous system but are as though lodged in the deeper-lying sympathetic and parasympathetic systems. In this connection I remember the dream of a patient who had the greatest difficulty in conceiving the idea of the supraordinate totality of the psyche and felt the utmost resistance to it. He had picked up the idea from one of my books but, characteristically enough, was unable to distinguish between the ego and the self, and, because of his hereditary taint, was threatened with a pathological inflation. In this situation he dreamt that he was rummaging about in the attic of his house, looking for something. In one of the attic windows he discovered a beautiful cobweb, with a large garden-spider sitting in the centre. It was of a blue colour, and its body sparkled like a diamond.

672   The dreamer was deeply impressed by this dream, and it was, in fact, an impressive commentary on his identification with the self—all the more dangerous in view of his heredity. In such cases there is a real weakness of the ego, which cannot therefore afford any suggestion of taking second place, as that would fatally emphasize its littleness and has to be avoided at all costs. Illusions, however, are inimical to life, because they are unhealthy and sooner or later trip you up. The dream therefore attempts a kind of corrective, which, like the Delphic oracle, turns out to be ambivalent. It says in effect: "What is troubling you in the head (attic) is, though you may not know it, a rare jewel. It is like an animal that is strange to you, forming symbolically the centre of many concentric circles, reminiscent of the centre of a large or small world, like the eye of God in medieval pictures of the universe." Confronted with this, a healthy mind would fight against identification with the centre, because of the danger of paranoiac God-likeness. Anyone who gets into this spider's net is wrapped round like a cocoon and robbed of his own life. He is isolated from his fellows, so that they can no longer reach him, nor he them. He lives in the loneliness of the world creator, who is everything and has nothing outside himself. If, on top of all this, you have had an insane father, there is the danger that you will begin to "spin" your-

self, and for this reason the spider has a sinister aspect that should not be overlooked.

673   The round metallic spider of our dreamer probably has a similar meaning. It has obviously devoured a number of human beings already, or their souls, and might well be a danger to earth dwellers. That is why the prayer, which recognizes the spider as a "divine" being, requests it to lead the souls "downwards" and "keep them safe below," because they are not yet departed spirits but living earthly creatures. As such they are meant to fulfil their earthly existence with conviction and not allow themselves any spiritual inflation, otherwise they will end up in the belly of the spider. In other words, they should not set the ego in the highest place and make it the ultimate authority, but should ever be mindful of the fact that it is not sole master in its own house and is surrounded on all sides by the factor we call the unconscious. What this is in itself we do not know. We know only its paradoxical manifestations. It is our business to understand Nature, and it is no good getting impatient with her because she is so "complicated" and awkward. Not so very long ago there were medical authorities who did not "believe" in bacteria and consequently allowed twenty thousand young women to die of easily avoidable puerperal fever in Germany alone. The psychic catastrophes caused by the mental inertia of "experts" do not appear in any statistics, and from this it is concluded that they are non-existent.

674   The exhortation to remain below on earth is immediately followed by the paradoxical request: "Carry us up to the height!" One might think of the saying in *Faust:* "Then to the depths! I could as well say height: It's all the same," were it not that the dreamer has clearly separated the two processes by a hiatus. This shows that it is a sequence and not a *coincidentia oppositorum.* Evidently a moral process is envisaged, a katabasis and anabasis: the seven steps downwards and the seven steps upwards, the immersion in the *krater* followed by the ascent to the "heavenly generation" in the transformation mysteries.[14] The Mass, too, begins with the "Confiteor . . . quia peccavi nimis." Apparently one has to be "led" downwards, because it is not easy for people to descend from their heights and remain below.

14 [Cf. "Transformation Symbolism in the Mass," pars. 313, 344, 355. For *krater,* see also *Psychology and Alchemy,* par. 409, and *Alchemical Studies,* pars. 96f.— EDITORS.]

In the first place a loss of social prestige is feared, and in the second a loss of moral self-esteem when they have to admit their own darkness. Hence they avoid self-criticism to an amazing degree, preach to others, and know nothing of themselves. They are happy to possess no self-knowledge, because then nothing disturbs the rosy glow of illusions. "Below" means the bed-rock of reality, which despite all self-deceptions is there right enough. To get down to this and remain there seems to be a matter of pressing importance if it is assumed that people today are living above their proper level. An inference of such general scope is permitted by the dream, which shows the problem in terms of a human group and therefore characterizes it as a collective problem. Actually the dream has the whole of humanity in view, for the spider flies as near as possible to the windows of a building where "international decisions" are being taken. It tries to "influence" the meeting and point the way that leads to the "inner world," the way to self-knowledge. The dream expects that this will make peace possible. Accordingly the spider plays the role of a saviour who warns and brings a healing message.

675   At the end the dreamer discovers that she is insufficiently clothed. This very common dream-motif usually indicates lack of adaptation or relative unconsciousness of the situation in which one finds oneself. This reminder of one's own fallibility and negligence is particularly appropriate at a time when other people are being enlightened, for in such cases there is always a lurking danger of inflation.

676   The admonition to "remain below" has in our day given rise to theological apprehensions in various quarters. It is feared that this kind of psychology will result in a loosening of moral standards. Psychology, however, gives us a clearer knowledge not only of evil but also of good, and the danger of succumbing to the former is considerably less than when you remain unconscious of it. Nor is psychology always needed if you want to know evil. No one who goes through the world with open eyes can ignore it; moreover he is not so likely to fall into a pit as the blind man. Just as the investigation of the unconscious is suspected by theologians of Gnosticism, so an inquiry into the ethical problems it raises is accused of antinomianism and libertinism. No one in his right senses would suppose that, after a thorough confession of sin accompanied by repentance, he will

356

never sin again. It is a thousand to one that he will sin again the very next minute. Deeper psychological insight shows, in fact, that one cannot live at all without sinning "in thought, word, and deed." Only an exceedingly naïve and unconscious person could imagine that he is in a position to avoid sin. Psychology can no longer afford childish illusions of this kind; it must ensue the truth and declare that unconsciousness is not only no excuse but is actually one of the most heinous sins. Human law may exempt it from punishment, but Nature avenges herself the more mercilessly, for it is nothing to her whether a man is conscious of his sin or not. We even learn from the parable of the unjust steward that the Lord praised his servant who kept a false account because he had "done wisely," not to speak of the (expurgated) passage at Luke 6, where Christ says to the defiler of the Sabbath: "Man, if indeed thou knowest what thou doest, thou art blessed; but if thou knowest not, thou art accursed, and a transgressor of the law."

677   Increased knowledge of the unconscious brings a deeper experience of life and greater consciousness, and therefore confronts us with apparently new situations that require ethical decision. These situations have, of course, always existed, but they were not clearly grasped, either intellectually or morally, and were often left in a not unintentional half light. In this way one provides oneself with an alibi and can get out of an ethical decision. But, with deeper self-knowledge, one is often confronted with the most difficult problems of all, namely conflicts of duty, which simply cannot be decided by any moral precepts, neither those of the decalogue nor of other authorities. This is where ethical decisions really begin, for the mere observance of a codified "Thou shalt not" is not in any sense an ethical decision, but merely an act of obedience and, in certain circumstances, a convenient loophole that has nothing to do with ethics. In my long life I have never encountered a situation that made a denial of ethical principles easier for me or raised the slightest doubt in this regard; on the contrary, the ethical problem was sharpened with increasing experience and insight, and the moral responsibility became more acute. It has become clear to me that, in contrast to the general view, unconsciousness is no excuse but is far rather a transgression in the literal sense of the word. Although there are, as mentioned above, allusions to

357

this problem in the gospels, the Church has for understandable reasons not taken it up, but left the Gnostics to tackle it more seriously. As a result, Christians rely on the doctrine of the *privatio boni* and always think they know what is good and what is evil, thus substituting the moral code for the truly ethical decision, which is a *free* one. Morality consequently degenerates into legalistic behaviour, and the *felix culpa* remains stuck in the Garden of Eden. We are surprised at the decay of ethics in our century, and we contrast the standstill in this field with the progress of science and technology. But nobody is worried by the fact that a real ethos has disappeared behind a mass of moral precepts. An ethos, however, is a difficult thing that cannot be formulated and codified; it is one of those creative irrationalities upon which any true progress is based. It demands the whole man and not just a differentiated function.

678   The differentiated function undoubtedly depends on man, on his diligence, patience, perseverance, his striving for power, and his native gifts. With the aid of these things he gets on in the world and "develops." From this he has learnt that development and progress depend on man's own endeavours, his will and ability. But that is only one side of the picture. The other side shows man as he is and as he finds himself to be. Here he can alter nothing, because he is dependent on factors outside his control. Here he is not the doer, but a product that does not know how to change itself. He does not know how he came to be the unique individual he is, and he has only the scantiest knowledge of himself. Until recently he even thought that his psyche consisted of what he knew of himself and was a product of the cerebral cortex. The discovery of unconscious psychic processes more than fifty years ago is still far from being common knowledge and its implications are still not recognized. Modern man still does not realize that he is entirely dependent on the co-operation of the unconscious, which can actually cut short the very next sentence he proposes to speak. He is unaware that he is continuously sustained by something, while all the time he regards himself exclusively as the doer. He depends on and is sustained by an entity he does not know, but of which he has intimations that "occurred" to—or, as we can more fitly say, *revealed themselves* to—long-forgotten forbears in the grey

dawn of history. Whence did they come? Obviously from the unconscious processes, from that so-called unconscious which still
precedes consciousness in every new human life, as the mother
precedes the child. The unconscious depicts itself in dreams and
visions, as it always did, holding before us images which, unlike
the fragmented functions of consciousness, emphasize facts that
relate to the unknown whole man, and only apparently to the
function which interests us to the exclusion of all else. Although dreams usually speak the language of our particular
specialism—*canis panem somniat, piscator pisces*—they refer to
the whole, or at the very least to what man also is, namely the
utterly dependent creature he finds himself to be.

679   In his striving for freedom man feels an almost instinctive
aversion to this kind of knowledge, for he fears, not without
reason, its paralysing effect. He may admit that this dependence on unknown powers exists—no matter what they are called
—but he turns away from them as speedily as possible, as from
a threatening obstacle. So long as everything appears to go well,
this attitude may even be an advantage; but things do not always
turn out for the best, particularly today, when despite euphoria
and optimism we feel a tremor running through the foundations of our world. Our dreamer is certainly not the only person
to feel afraid. Accordingly the dream depicts a collective need
and utters a collective warning that we should descend to earth
and not rise up again unless the spider carries up those who
have remained below. For when functionalism dominates consciousness, it is the unconscious that contains the compensatory
symbol of wholeness. This is represented by the flying spider,
which alone is capable of carrying up the one-sidedness and fragmentariness of the conscious mind. There is no development
upwards unless it is facilitated by the unconscious. The conscious will alone cannot compel this creative act, and in order
to illustrate this the dream chooses the symbol of *prayer*. Since
according to the Pauline view we do not rightly know what we
should pray for, the prayer is no more than a "groaning in
travail" (Rom. 8 : 22) which expresses our impotence. This
enjoins on us an attitude that compensates the superstitious belief in man's will and ability. At the same time the spider image
denotes a regression of religious ideas to the theriomorphic symbol of supreme power, a reversion to the long forgotten stage

where a monkey or a hare personifies the redeemer. Today the Christian Lamb of God or the Dove of the Holy Ghost has, at most, the value of a metaphor. As against this it must be emphasized that in dream symbolism animals refer to instinctual processes which play a vital part in animal biology. It is these processes which determine and shape the life of an animal. For his everyday life man seems to need no instincts, especially when he is convinced of the sovereign power of his will. He ignores the meaning of instinct and devalues it to the point of atrophy, not seeing how much he endangers his very existence through loss of instinct. When therefore dreams emphasize instinct they are trying to fill a perilous gap in our adaptation to life.

680   Deviations from instinct show themselves in the form of affects, which in dreams are likewise expressed by animals. Hence uncontrolled affects are rightly regarded as bestial or primitive and should be avoided. But we cannot do this without repressing them, that is, without a splitting of consciousness. In reality we can never escape their power. Somewhere or other they will continue to operate even though they cannot be found in consciousness. At worst they manifest themselves in a neurosis or in an unconscious "arrangement" of inexplicable mishaps. The saint, who seems exempt from these weaknesses, pays for his immunity with suffering and abnegation of the earthly man, without which of course he would not be a saint. The lives of holy men show that the two sides cancel out. None can escape the chain of suffering that leads to sickness, old age and death. We can and should, for the sake of our humanity, "control" our affects and keep them in check, but we should know that we have to pay dearly for it. The choice of currency in which we wish to pay the tribute is—sometimes—even left to us.

681   Remaining down below and subordinating ourselves to a theriomorphic symbol, which seems very like an insult to our human dignity, means no more than that we should remain conscious of these simple truths and never forget that in point of anatomy and psychology the earthly man, for all his high flights, is first cousin to the anthropoids. Should it be granted to him, however, to develop into something higher without crippling his nature, he is reminded that this transformation is not his to command, for he is dependent on factors he cannot influence. He must content himself with a prayerful yearning and "groan-

ing," in the hope that something may carry him upward, since he is not likely to make a success of the Munchausen experiment. Through this attitude he constellates helpful and at the same time dangerous powers in the unconscious; helpful if he understands them, dangerous if he misunderstands them. Whatever names he may give to these creative powers and potentialities within him, their actuality remains unchanged. No one can stop a religious-minded person from calling them gods or daemons, or simply "God," for we know from experience that they act just like that. If certain people use the word "matter" in this connection, believing that they have said something, we must remind them that they have merely replaced an X by a Y and are no further forward than before. The only certain thing is our profound ignorance, which cannot even know whether we have come nearer to the solution of the great riddle or not. Nothing can carry us beyond an "It seems as if" except the perilous leap of faith, which we must leave to those who are gifted or graced for it. Every real or apparent step forward depends on an experience of facts, the verification of which is, as we know, one of the most difficult tasks confronting the human mind.

Dream 4

682   While I was engaged on this paper an acquaintance from abroad unexpectedly sent me a dream he had had on May 27, 1957. Our relationship was limited to one letter each every one or two years. He was an amateur astrologer and was interested in the question of synchronicity. He knew nothing of my preoccupation with Ufos, nor did he connect his dream in any way with the theme that interested me. His sudden and unusual decision to send me the dream comes, rather, into the category of meaningful coincidences, which statistical prejudice dismisses as irrelevant.

683   This is the dream: *"It was late afternoon or early evening, the sun low on the horizon. The sky was cloudy, and there was a veil of cloud over the sun which did not, however, prevent one from seeing quite clearly his disk in outline behind the cloud. Under such circumstances the sun was white. Suddenly he took on an aspect of extraordinary pallor. The whole western horizon*

became a dreadful pale white. And the pallor—pallor is the word that I want to stress—of the orb of day became a terrifying wanness. Then a second sun appeared in the west about the same distance above the horizon, only a little more to the north. But as we gazed intently at the sky—there were a great number of people spread over a wide area watching the heavens as I was —the second sun took on the distinctive form of a sphere in contrast with the sun's disk, or apparent disk. Simultaneously with the setting of the sun and the advent of night the sphere came speeding towards the earth.

"With the coming of the night, the whole potential of the dream was changed. Whereas words like pallor and wanness exactly describe the vanishing life, strength or potential of the sun, the sky now assumed an aspect of strength and majesty, which inspired not fear but awe. I could not say that I saw any stars, but the night sky was of that kind when thin wreaths of cloud allow an occasional star to be seen. The night certainly spoke of majesty, power and beauty.

"When the sphere approached the earth at high velocity, I thought at first that it was Jupiter in aberration from its proper orbit, but as the sphere came nearer, I saw that, though large, it was much too small for Jupiter.

"And it now became possible to discern the markings on its surface which were lines of longitude or like such, but were decorative and symbolic in character rather than geographical or mathematical. The beauty of the sphere, a subdued grey or opaque white, against the night sky must be emphasized. When we became aware that the sphere must certainly make a terrific impact upon the earth, we did, of course, feel fear, but it was fear in which awe was more predominant. It was a most awe-inspiring cosmic phenomenon. As we gazed, another and yet another sphere emerged from the horizon and sped towards the earth. Each sphere did in turn crash much as a bomb would crash, but at such a considerable distance that I, at least, could not make out the nature of the explosion or detonation or whatever it was. I think in one case, at least, I saw a flash. These spheres, then, were falling at intervals all around, but all of them . . . well beyond the point at which they might annihilate us. There appeared to be a danger of shrapnel. . . .

"Then I must have gone indoors, for I found myself talking

to a girl seated in a wicker chair, with an open large-paged note-book on her lap, much engrossed in her work. We were going—the rest of us—I think in a southwesterly direction, perhaps seeking safety, and I said to the girl had she not better come with us. The danger appeared to be great and we could hardly leave her alone there. She was quite definite in her reply. No, she would remain where she was and go on with her work. It was equally dangerous everywhere and one place was just as safe as another. I saw at once that she had reason and common-sense on her side.

"The dream ends by my being confronted with another girl, or, quite possibly, the same very competent and self-possessed young lady that I had left sitting in a wicker chair absorbed in her work. This time she was rather bigger and more realistic, and I could see her face, or at least that she was addressing me fairly and squarely. And she said in extraordinarily distinct tones: 'J— S—, you will live till eleven eight.' Nothing could surpass the clarity with which these eight words were articulated. Her authoritative way of enunciating them seemed to imply that I was to be censured for not supposing that I should live till eleven eight."

DREAMER'S COMMENTARY

684 This elaborate description was followed by the dreamer's comments, which can give us a number of hints as regards interpretation. As we should expect, he sees a climax in the sudden change of mood at the beginning of the dream, when the deathly, frightening pallor and wanness of the sunset changes into the sombre majesty of the night, and fear to awe. This, he said, was connected with his present preoccupation with the political future of Europe. On the basis of his astrological speculations he feared the coming of a world war in 1960–66. He had even felt impelled to write a letter to an eminent statesman expressing his fears. Afterwards he made the (not uncommon) discovery that his previously apprehensive and agitated mood suddenly changed into one of remarkable calm and even indifference, as though the whole affair no longer concerned him.

685 All the same, he could not explain to himself why the initial terror should be superseded by such a solemn and, as it were,

holy mood. He felt certain, however, that it was a collective and not a personal matter, and he asked himself: "Are we to suppose that by hanging on too earnestly to the daylight of civilization we lose all potential, and that as we advance into what looks a fearful night there is more prospect of strength?" It is not very easy to fit the qualifying epithet "majesty" into such an interpretation. He himself related it to the fact that "the things that come from outer space are utterly beyond our control." "We might put it in theistic language by saying that it is utterly impossible to know the counsels of God and that in eternity the night is as significant as the day. Therefore our only possible chance is to accept the rhythm of eternity as night and day, and so the inexorable majesty of the night would become a source of strength." Evidently the dream underlines this characteristic defeatism by the cosmic interlude of a stellar bombardment to which mankind is helplessly exposed.

686   The dream contains no trace of sexuality if, as the dreamer said, we disregard the meeting with the young lady. (As if every relationship to the opposite sex was always necessarily based on sexuality!) What disturbed him was the fact that the meeting took place at night. One can carry "sex-consciousness" too far, as this remark shows. The wicker chair is not exactly inviting in this respect, and for the dreamer himself it signified an excellent condition for concentrated mental work, as indicated also by the note-book.

687   As the dreamer was an ardent student of astrology the combination of the numbers eleven and eight set him a special problem. He thought of XI. 8 as the month and day of his decease. Being an elderly man of more than three score years and ten he was thoroughly justified in such reflections. His astrological calculations led him to relegate this fatal November to the year 1963, the middle of the conjectural World War. But he added cautiously that he was by no means sure.

688   The dream, he said, left behind a strange feeling of contentment, and of thankfulness that such an experience had been "vouchsafed" him. It was, indeed, a "big" dream, for the like of which many a man has been thankful, even if he did not understand it correctly.

COMMENTARY TO DREAM 4

689   The dream begins with a sunset, when the sun is hidden by clouds so that all one can see is a disk. This would emphasize the round form, a tendency confirmed by the appearance of a second disk, Jupiter, more round bodies in large numbers, "things from outer space." For these reasons the dream comes into the category of psychic Ufo phenomena.

690   The uncanny pallor of the sun is indicative of the fear that spreads over the daylight world in anticipation of catastrophic events to come. These events, much in contrast to his "daylight" views, are of unearthly origin: Jupiter, the father of the gods, seems to have left his orbit and is approaching the earth. We meet this motif in Schreber's *Memoirs:* the extraordinary happenings going on all round him compel God to "move nearer to the earth." The unconscious "interprets" the threat as a divine intervention, which manifests itself in the appearance of smaller replicas of the great Jupiter. The dreamer does not draw the obvious conclusion about Ufos and does not seem to have been influenced in his choice of symbols by any conscious concern with them.

691   Although to all appearances a cosmic catastrophe is about to happen, the fear changes into a positive mood of a solemn, holy, and reverent kind, as is fitting for an epiphany. For the dreamer, however, the coming of the god signalizes extreme danger: the heavenly bodies explode on the earth like huge bombs, thus bearing out his fear of a world war. Remarkably enough, they do not cause the expected earthquake, and the detonations seem to be of a strange and unusual nature. No destruction takes place in the vicinity of the dreamer; the hits are so far below the horizon that all he thinks he can see is a single flash. The collision with these planetoids is therefore infinitely less dangerous than it would be in reality. The main point here seems to be fear of the possibility of a third World War, and it is this that gives the scene its terrifying aspect. It is the dreamer's own interpretation, rather than the phenomenon itself, which causes him to be so agitated. Consequently the whole affair assumes a markedly psychological aspect.

692   This is immediately borne out by the meeting with the

young lady, who keeps her composure, imperturbably goes on with her work, and prophesies the date of his death. She does this in so solemn and impressive a manner that he even feels it necessary to emphasize the number of the words she uses, namely eight. That this number is more than mere chance is proved by the supposed date of death—the 8th of November. This double emphasis on the eight is not without significance, for eight is a double quaternity and, as an individuation symbol in mandalas, plays almost as great a role as the quaternity itself.[15] For lack of association material we shall suggest only a tentative interpretation of the number eleven with the help of the traditional symbolism. Ten is the perfect unfolding of unity, and the numbers one to ten have the significance of a completed cycle. $10 + 1 = 11$ therefore denotes the beginning of a new cycle. Since dream interpretation follows the principle *post hoc ergo propter hoc,* eleven leads to eight, the ogdoad, a totality symbol, and hence to an actualization of wholeness, as already suggested by the appearance of Ufos.

693   The young lady, who seems to be unknown to the dreamer, may be taken as a compensating anima figure. She represents a more complete aspect of the unconscious than the shadow, since she adds to the personality its feminine traits. As a rule she appears most clearly when the conscious mind is thoroughly acquainted with its shadow, and she exerts her greatest influence as a psychological factor when the feminine qualities of the personality are not yet integrated. If these opposites are not united, wholeness is not established, and the self as their symbol is still unconscious. But when the self is constellated it appears in projection, though its true nature is hidden by the anima, who at most alludes to it, as in this dream: the anima, with her calmness and certainty, counters the agitations of the dreamer's ego consciousness, and by mentioning the number eight points to the totality, the self, which is present in the Ufo projection.

694   The intuition of the enormous importance of the self as the organizer of the personality, and also the importance of the collective dominants or archetypes, which as so-called metaphysical principles determine the orientation of consciousness, is responsible for the solemn mood prevailing at the beginning of the

---

[15] Cf. the Cabiri scene in *Faust; Psychology and Alchemy*, pars. 203ff.

dream. It is a mood in keeping with the coming epiphany, though it is feared that this will unleash a world war or a cosmic catastrophe. The anima, however, seems to know better. Anyway the expected destruction remains invisible, there being no real cause for alarm in the dreamer's vicinity except his own subjective panic. The anima ignores his fear of a catastrophe and alludes instead to his own death, which we can well say is the real source of his fear.

695   Very often the nearness of death forcibly brings about a perfection that no effort of will and no good intentions could achieve. He is the great perfector, drawing his inexorable line under the balance-sheet of human life. In him alone is wholeness —one way or another—attained. Death is the end of the empirical man and the goal of the spiritual man, as the perspicacious Heraclitus says: "It is to Hades that they rage and celebrate their feasts." Everything that is not yet where it ought to be, that has not yet gone where it ought to have gone, fears the end, the final reckoning. We avoid as long as possible making ourselves conscious of those things which wholeness still lacks, thus preventing ourselves from becoming conscious of the self and preparing for death. The self then remains in projection. In our dream it appears as Jupiter, which in approaching the earth changes into a multitude of smaller heavenly bodies, into numberless "selves" or individual souls, and vanishes in the earth, i.e., is integrated with our world. This hints, mythologically, at an incarnation, but psychologically it is the manifestation of an unconscious process in the sphere of consciousness.

696   Speaking in the language of the dream, I would advise the dreamer to consider the universal fear of catastrophe in the light of his own death. In this connection it is significant that the conjectured year of his death falls in the middle of the critical period 1960–66. The end of the world would therefore be his own death and hence, primarily, a personal catastrophe and a subjective end. But as the symbolism of the dream unmistakably portrays a collective situation, I think it would be better to generalize the subjective aspect of the Ufo phenomenon and assume that a collective but unacknowledged fear of death is being projected on the Ufos. After the initial optimistic speculations about the visitors from space, people have recently begun to

367

discuss their possible dangerousness and the incalculable consequences of an invasion of the earth. Grounds for an unusually
intense fear of death are nowadays not far to seek: they are obvious enough, the more so as all life that is senselessly wasted and
misdirected means death too. This may account for the unnatural intensification of the fear of death in our time, when life
has lost its deeper meaning for so many people, forcing them to
exchange the life-preserving rhythm of the aeons for the dread
ticking of the clock. One would therefore wish many people the
compensating attitude of the anima in our dream, and would
recommend them to choose a motto like that of Hans Hopfer,
a native of Basel and pupil of Holbein: "Death is the last line of
things. I yield to none." [16]

DREAM 5

697   This dream comes from a woman with an academic education. It was dreamt several years ago without reference to Ufos:
*"Two women were standing on the edge of the world, seeking.
The older was taller but lame. The younger was shorter and had
her arm under that of the taller, as if supporting her. The older
one looked out with courage (I identified her in some way with
X), and the younger stood beside her with strength but feared to
look. Her head was bowed (I identified myself with this second
figure). Above was the crescent moon and the morning star. To
the right the rising sun. An elliptical, silvery object came flying
from the right. It was peopled around its rim with figures which
I think were men, cloaked figures all silvery white. The women
were awed and trembled in that unearthly, cosmic space, a position untenable except at the moment of vision."*

698   After this extremely impressive dream the dreamer immediately seized a paint brush in order to fix the vision, as shown in
Pl. I. The dream describes a typical Ufo phenomenon which,
like Dream 1, contains the motif of "manning," i.e., the presence of human beings. It obviously represents a borderline situation, as the expression "on the edge of the world" shows. Out
beyond is cosmic space with its planets and suns; or the beyond
may be the land of the dead or the unconscious. The first possibility suggests a space-ship, the technical achievement of more

[16] "Der Tod ist die letzt Lini der Ding. Ich weich kaim."

highly developed planetary beings; the second, angels of some kind or departed spirits, who come to earth in order to fetch a soul. This would refer to X, who was already in need of "support," as she was ill. Her health really did give grounds for anxiety, and in fact she died about two years after the dream. Accordingly the dreamer took it as a premonition. The third possibility, that the beyond is the unconscious, points to a personification of the latter, namely the animus in his characteristic plurality; the festive white robes of the crew suggest the idea of a marital union of opposites. This symbolism, as we know, also applies to death as a final realization of wholeness. The dreamer's view that the dream gave warning of the death of her friend may therefore be right.

699   The dream, then, uses the symbol of a disk-like Ufo manned by spirits, a space-ship that comes out of the beyond to the edge of our world in order to fetch the souls of the dead. It is not clear from the vision where the ship comes from, whether from the sun or moon or elsewhere. According to the myth in the *Acta Archelai,* it would be from the waxing moon, which increases in size according to the number of departed souls that are scooped up from the earth to the sun in twelve buckets, and from there are emptied into the moon in a purified state. The idea that the Ufo might be a sort of Charon is certainly one that I have not met in the literature so far. This is hardly surprising, firstly because "classical" allusions of this sort are a rarity in people with a modern education, and secondly because they might lead to very disagreeable conclusions. The apparent increase in Ufo sightings in recent years has caused disquiet in the popular mind and might easily give rise to the conclusion that, if so many space-ships appear from the beyond, a corresponding number of deaths may be expected. We know that such phenomena were interpreted like this in earlier centuries: they were portents of a "great dying," of war and pestilence, like the dark premonitions that underlie our modern fear. One ought not to assume that the great masses are so enlightened that hypotheses of this kind can no longer take root.

700   The Middle Ages, antiquity, and prehistory have not died out, as the "enlightened" suppose, but live on merrily in large sections of the population. Mythology and magic flourish as ever in our midst and are unknown only to those whose rationalistic

education has alienated them from their roots.[17] Quite apart from ecclesiastical symbolism, which embodies six thousand years of spiritual development and is constantly renewing itself, there are also its more disreputable relatives, magical ideas and practices which are still very much alive in spite of all education and enlightenment. One must have lived for many years in the Swiss countryside in order to become acquainted with this background, for it never appears on the surface. But once you have found the key, you stagger from one amazement to the next. Not only do you come across the primitive witch doctor in the guise of the so-called "Strudel" (wizard), you will also find blood pacts with the devil, pin-stickings and spells for drying up the milk of cattle, and regular hand-written books of magic. At the house of one of these rustic wizards I once discovered a book of this kind from the end of the nineteenth century, beginning with the Merseburg magic spell in modern High German and an incantation to Venus of unknown age. These wizards often have a large clientele from town and country. I myself have seen a collection of hundreds of letters of thanks which one of them received for successfully laying ghosts in houses and stables, for taking the curse off men and animals, and for curing all manner of ailments. For those of my readers who are unaware of these things and think I am exaggerating, I can point to the easily verifiable fact that the heyday of astrology was not in the benighted Middle Ages but is in the middle of the twentieth century, when even the newspapers do not hesitate to publish the week's horoscope. A thin layer of rootless rationalists read with satisfaction in an encyclopaedia that in the year 1723 Mr. So-and-so had horoscopes cast for his children, and yet do not know that nowadays the horoscope has almost attained the rank of a visiting card. Those who have even a nodding acquaintance with this background and are in any way affected by it obey the unwritten but strictly observed convention: "One does not speak of such things." They are only whispered about, no one admits them, for no one wants to be considered all that stupid. In reality, however, it is very different.

701   I mention these things that infest the roots of our society chiefly on account of the symbolism of our dreams, which

17 Cf. Aniela Jaffé's *Apparitions and Precognition*, which investigates strange occurrences among modern people for their mythological content.

sounds so incomprehensible to many people because it is based
on historical and contemporary facts that are unknown to them.
What would they say if I connected the dream of a quite simple
person with Wotan or Baldur? They would accuse me of learned
eccentricity, not knowing that in the same village there was a
"wizard" who had taken the spell off the dreamer's stable, using
for that purpose a book of magic that begins with the Merseburg incantation. Anyone who does not know that "Wotan's
host"—enlightenment or no enlightenment—still roams about
our Swiss cantons would accuse me of the greatest whimsicality
if I referred the anxiety dream of a city dweller on a lonely Alp
to the "blessed people" (the dead), when all the time he is
surrounded by mountainfolk for whom the "Doggeli" [18] and
Wotan's nightly cavalcade are a reality which they fear without
admitting it, and profess to know nothing about. It needs so
little to bridge the apparent abyss that yawns between the prehistoric world and the present. But we identify so much with
the fleeting consciousness of the present that we forget the "time-
lessness" of our psychic foundations. Everything that has lasted
longer, and will last longer, than the whirligig of modern political movements is regarded as fantastical nonsense that should
studiously be avoided. But in that way we succumb to the greatest psychic danger that now threatens us—rootless intellectualisms which one and all reckon without their host, i.e., without
the real man. Unfortunately people imagine that only the things
they are conscious of affect them, and that for everything unknown there is some specialist who has long made a science out
of it. This delusion is the more plausible in that nowadays it
really has become impossible for one individual to assimilate the
things which specialists know about and he doesn't. But since,
subjectively, the most effective experiences are the most individual and therefore the most improbable, the questioner will
often get no very satisfactory answer from the scientist. A typical
example of this is Menzel's book on Ufos.[19] The scientist's interest is too easily restricted to the common, the probable, the average, for that is after all the basis of every empirical science.
Nevertheless a basis has little meaning unless something can be

[18] Swiss-German expression for the nightmare or stable spook.
[19] D. H. Menzel, *Flying Saucers* (1953).

371

erected upon it that leaves room for the exceptional and extraordinary.

702   In a borderline situation such as our dream depicts we may expect something extraordinary, or rather, what seems extraordinary to us, though in reality it has always been inherent in such situations: The ship of death approaches with a corona of departed spirits, the deceased joins their company, and the multitudinous dead take the soul with them.

703   When archetypal ideas of this kind appear they invariably signify something unusual. It is not our interpretation that is far-fetched; it is merely that the dreamer's attention, caught by the many superficial aspects of the dream, has missed the main point, namely the nearness of death, which in a sense concerns her as much as her friend. We have met the motif of the "manning" of the space-ship in the dream of the metallic spider and shall meet it again in the next one. The instinctive resistance we feel for the deeper aspect of this motif may explain why it seems to play no role in the Ufo literature. We might exclaim with Faust: "Summon not the well-known throng!" But there is no need of this summons, because the fear that hangs over the world has already taken care of that.

DREAM 6

704   The following dream [20] comes from California, the classic Saucer country, so to speak. The dreamer is a young woman of 23. *"I was standing outside with someone (a man). It was night time and we seemed to be in a square or the centre of town—a circle. We were watching the sky. All of a sudden I saw something round and fluorescent coming towards us from way in the distance. I realized it was a Flying Saucer. I thought it was a ridiculous joke. It got larger and larger as it came towards us. It was a huge round circle of light. Finally it covered the entire sky. It was so close, I could see figures walking back and forth on the walk round the ship. There was a railing around it. I thought someone was playing a trick, then I thought it was real—I looked up behind me and saw someone with a movie projector. In back of us seemed to be a building, like a hotel. These*

20 I am indebted to Dr. H. Y. Kluger, Los Angeles, for this material.

people were up high and projecting this image into the sky. I told everyone. Then I seemed to be in a sort of studio. There were two producers, competitors—both old men. I kept going from one to the other discussing my part in their pictures. There were many girls involved. . . . One of the producers was directing this Flying Saucer thing. They were both making science-fiction films and I was going to have the lead in both pictures."

705   The dreamer, a young film actress, was undergoing psychological treatment for a marked dissociation of personality with all the accompanying symptoms. As usual, the dissociation expressed itself in her relations with the opposite sex, that is, in a conflict between two men who corresponded to the two incompatible halves of her personality.

COMMENTARY TO DREAM 6

706   As in the first two dreams, the dreamer was conscious of Ufos, and here as there the Ufo functions as a symbol carrier. Its appearance is even expected, since the dreamer had already put herself in a "central" position for this purpose—a square or centre of the city. This gives her a central position between the opposites, equidistant from right and left, and allowing her to see or feel both sides. In the light of this "attitude" the Ufo appears to be rather like an exemplification or "projection" of it. The dream insists on the projection character of the Ufo, since it proves to be a cinematographic operation conducted by two rival film producers. We can easily discern in these two figures the rival objects of her dissociated love choice, and hence the underlying conflict, which should be resolved in a reconciliation of opposites. The Ufo appears here in the mediating role we have met before, but it turns out to be an intentional cinematographic effect obviously lacking any reconciling significance. If we remember the important part a film producer plays in the life of a young actress, then the changing of the two rival lovers into producers suggests that the latter have acquired for her a more exalted rank or an increase in prestige. They have, so to speak, moved into the limelight of her own drama, whereas the Ufo is very much dimmed, if it has not lost its significance altogether as a mere trick. The accent has gone over

entirely to the producers; the apparently cosmic phenomenon is nothing more than a meaningless trick staged by them, and the dreamer's interest turns wholly to her professional ambitions. This seals the outcome of the solution offered by the dream.

707   It is not easy to see why the dream brings in the Ufo at all, only to dispose of it in this disappointing way. In view of the suggestive circumstances at the beginning of the dream—square, centre, circle—and the sensational significance of Ufos, obviously well known to the dreamer, this dénouement is rather unexpected. It is as though the dream wanted to say: "It is not like that at all—on the contrary. It is only a film trick, a bit of science fiction. Think, rather, that you have the chief role in the two pictures."

708   From this we can see what was the role intended for the Ufo and why it had to disappear from the scene. The personality of the dreamer takes up a central position on the stage, one that compensates the splitting into opposites and is therefore a means of overcoming the dissociation. For this a powerful affect is needed in order to enforce a consistent attitude. In the affect the pendulum movement of autonomous opposites ceases and a uniform state is produced. This is accomplished by the exciting appearance of the Ufo, which for a moment attracts all attention to itself.

709   It is clear that the Ufo phenomenon in this dream is unreal and only a means to an end, as though one called out to a person "Look out!" That is why it is immediately devalued: it is not a genuine phenomenon at all, but a trick, and the dream action now proceeds to the personal problem of the dreamer and her conflict between two men. If this well-known and very common situation means more and lasts longer than a passing uncertainty of choice, this is usually due to the fact that the problem is not taken seriously—like Buridan's ass, which could not decide which of two bundles of hay he wanted to eat first. It was an artificial problem: in reality he was not hungry. This seems to be the case with our dreamer: she means neither the one nor the other, but herself. What she really wants is told her by the dream, which changes the lovers into producers, represents the situation as a film project, and gives her the chief role in the pictures. That is what the dreamer really intends: in the interests of her profession she wants to play the chief role, that

of the young lover, regardless of any partner. But evidently she cannot quite bring it off in reality, because she is still tempted to regard her partners as real, when in fact they are only playing a role in her own drama. This does not speak very well for her artistic vocation, and she is right to feel some doubt as to its seriousness for her. In contradistinction to her vacillating conscious attitude, the dream points decidedly to her profession as her true love and thus gives her the solution to her conflict.

710   Any insight into the nature of the Ufo phenomenon is not to be expected from this dream. The Ufo is used only as a sort of alarm signal, thanks to the collective excitement occasioned by flying saucers. Interesting or even alarming as the phenomenon may be, youth has, or claims, the right to regard the problem of "him and her" as much more fascinating. In this case it is certainly right, for when one is still in the process of development the earth and its laws are of more significance than that message resounding from afar which the signs in heaven proclaim. Since youth lasts for a very long time and its peculiar state of mind is the highest that many human lives attain, this psychological limitation proves equally true of the grey-haired, whose birthdays are nothing more than nostalgic celebrations of their twentieth. At best the outcome is concentration on one's profession, any further development being regarded as a mere disturbance. Neither age nor position nor education is any protection against this psychological standstill. Human society is after all still very young, for what are three or five thousand years on a longer view!

711   I have introduced this dream as a paradigm of the way the unconscious can also deal with the problem that concerns us here. I wanted to show that the symbols cannot be interpreted in a uniform manner and that their meaning depends on many different factors. Life cannot go forward except from the place where one happens to be.

712   In the next chapter I shall discuss some pictures relating to Ufos. The painter of "The Fourth Dimension" (Pl. III), to whom I had written that certain details seemed to be connected with the strange apparitions in the skies, sent me the following dream, which he had on September 12, 1957:

375

DREAM 7

"I found myself, together with other people, on the top of a hill, looking out over a beautiful, broad, undulating landscape teeming with lush verdure.

"Suddenly a flying saucer floated into view, paused at eye-level before us and lay there, clear and shining, in the sunlight. It did not look like a machine but like a deep-sea fish, round and flat, but enormously big (about thirty to forty feet in diameter). It was speckled all over with blue, grey, and white spots. Its edges undulated and quivered all the time; they acted as oars and rudders.

"This creature began circling round us, then all at once, as though fired from a cannon, shot straight up into the blue sky, came rushing down again with inconceivable speed, and once more circled round our hill. It was obviously doing this for our benefit. (Once when it flew quite close, it seemed to be much smaller and looked like a hammer-head shark.)

"Now it had somehow landed in our vicinity. . . . An occupant got out and came straight towards me. (A semi-human woman?) The other people fled and waited at a respectful distance, looking back at us.

"The woman told me that they knew me well in that other world (from which she had come) and were watching how I fulfilled my task (mission?). She spoke in a stern, almost threatening tone and seemed to attach great importance to the charge laid upon me."

COMMENTARY TO DREAM 7

713   The occasion for the dream was the anticipation of a visit which the dreamer intended to pay me during the next few days. The exposition shows a positive, hopeful feeling of expectancy. The dramatic development begins with the sudden appearance of a Ufo, which has the obvious intention of showing itself as clearly as possible to the observer. On closer inspection he sees that it is not a machine but an animal of sorts, a deep-sea fish, something like a giant ray, which, as we know, sometimes makes attempts to fly. Its movements emphasize the relationship of the

376

Ufo to the observers. These overtures lead to a landing. A semi-human figure climbs out of the Ufo, thus revealing an intelligent human relationship between the Ufo and its observers. This impression is strengthened by the fact that it is a feminine figure which, because it is unknown and indefinite, belongs to the anima type. The numinosity of this archetype causes a panic reaction among the "people" present—in other words, the dreamer registers a subjective reaction of flight. The reason for this lies in the fateful significance of the anima figure: she is the Sphinx of Oedipus, a Cassandra, the messenger of the Grail, the "white lady" who gives warning of death, etc. This view is borne out by the message she conveys: she comes from another world where the dreamer is known, and where they watch attentively how he fulfils his "mission."

714   The anima personifies the collective unconscious,[21] the "realm of the Mothers," which, as experience shows, has a distinct tendency to influence the conscious conduct of life and, when this is not possible, to irrupt violently into consciousness in order to confront it with strange and seemingly incomprehensible contents. The Ufo in the dream is a content of this kind whose strangeness leaves nothing to be desired. The difficulty of integration is in this case so great that the dreamer's ordinary powers of comprehension fail him and he resorts to mythical means of explanation—star dwellers, angels, spirits, gods—even before he knows what he has seen. So great is the numinosity of these ideas that one never asks oneself whether it might not be a subjective perception of collective unconscious processes. For in the common estimation a subjective observation can only be either "true" or else, as a delusion of the senses or an hallucination, it can only be "untrue." The fact that the latter are also true phenomena with sufficient reasons of their own is apparently never taken into account, so long as no obviously pathological disturbance is present. There are, however, manifestations of the unconscious, even in normal people, which can be so "real" and impressive that the observer instinctively resists taking his perception as a delusion or hallucination. His instinct is right: one does not see only from outside

---

21 When the shadow, the inferior personality, is in large measure unconscious, the unconscious is represented by a masculine figure.

377

inwards, but from inside outwards. When an inner process cannot be integrated it is often projected outside. It is, indeed, the rule that a man's consciousness projects all perceptions coming from the feminine personification of the unconscious onto an anima figure, i.e., a real woman, to whom he is as much bound as he is in reality to the contents of the unconscious. This explains the fateful quality of the anima, which is also suggested in the dream by her question: How are you fulfilling your life's task ("mission"), your *raison d'être*, the meaning and purpose of your existence? This is the question of individuation, the most fateful of all questions, which was put to Oedipus in the form of the childish riddle of the Sphinx and was radically misunderstood by him. (Can one imagine an intelligent Athenian playgoer ever being taken in by the "terrible riddles" of the Sphinx?) Oedipus did not use his intelligence to see through the uncanny nature of this childishly simple and all too facile riddle, and therefore fell victim to his tragic fate, because he thought he had answered the question. It was the Sphinx itself that he ought to have answered and not its façade.

715   Just as Mephistopheles proves to be the "quintessence of the poodle," so the anima is the quintessence of the Ufo. But Mephistopheles is not the whole of *Faust,* and the anima too is only a part of the whole, which is obscurely alluded to in the deepsea fish, the "rotundum." Here the anima plays the role of the mediatrix between the unconscious and the conscious, a dual figure like the Sphinx, compounded of animal instinct (body) and specifically human qualities (head). In her body lie the forces that determine man's fate, in her head the power to modify them intelligently. (This basic idea is also reflected in the picture we shall reproduce later.) At this point the dream speaks a mythical language that makes use of conceptions of another world and of angelic beings who watch the doings of men. This vividly expresses the symbiosis of conscious and unconscious.

716   Such, at any rate, would seem to be the nearest we can get to a satisfactory explanation. With regard to the possible metaphysical background we must honestly confess our ignorance and the impossibility of proof. The unmistakable tendency of the dream is the attempt to create a psychologem which we meet again and again in this and many other forms, regardless of

whether the Ufos should be understood as concrete realities or as subjective phenomena. The psychologem is a reality in its own right. It is based on a real perception which has no need of the physical reality of Ufos, because it manifested itself long before Ufos were ever heard of.

717   The end of the dream lays special weight on the woman's message, emphasizing its seriousness, even its menacing quality. The collective parallel to this is the widespread fear that the Ufos may not be harmless after all, and that communication with other planets might have unpredictable consequences. This view is supported by the fact that the suppression of certain information by the American authorities [22] cannot be relegated entirely to the realm of fable.

718   The seriousness, indeed dangerousness, of the problem of individuation cannot be denied in an age in which the destructive effects of mass-mindedness are so clearly apparent, for individuation is the great alternative that faces our Western civilization. It is a fact that in a dictator State the individual is robbed of his freedom, and that we too are threatened by this political development and are not at all sure of the right means of defence. Hence the question arises in all urgency: are we going to let ourselves be robbed of our individual freedom, and what can we do to stop it?

719   Anxiously we look round for collective measures, thereby reinforcing the very mass-mindedness we want to fight against. There is only one remedy for the levelling effect of all collective measures, and that is to emphasize and increase the value of the individual. A fundamental change of attitude (*metanoia*) is required, a real recognition of the whole man. This can only be the business of the individual and it must begin with the individual in order to be real. That is the message of our dream, a message addressed to the dreamer from the collective, instinctual foundations of humanity. Large political and social organizations must not be ends in themselves, but merely temporary expedients. Just as it was felt necessary in America to break up the great Trusts, so the destruction of huge organizations will eventually prove to be a necessity because, like a cancerous growth, they eat away man's nature as soon as they become ends

[22] Cf. Keyhoe, *The Flying Saucer Conspiracy*.

in themselves and attain autonomy. From that moment they grow beyond man and escape his control. He becomes their victim and is sacrificed to the madness of an idea that knows no master. All great organizations in which the individual no longer counts are exposed to this danger. There seems to be only one way of countering this threat to our lives, and that is the "revaluation" of the individual.

720   So vitally important a measure cannot, however, be put into effect at will, that is, by planning and insight, because the individual human being is too small and weak. What is needed, rather, is an involuntary faith, a kind of metaphysical command, which no one can manufacture artificially with his own will and understanding. It can only come about spontaneously. A dominant of this kind underlies our dream. My suggestion that certain details of the picture might be connected with the Ufo problem was sufficient to constellate in the dreamer the archetype underlying this collective phenomenon and to give him a numinous insight into the metaphysical significance of the individual. The empirical man extends beyond his conscious boundaries, his life and fate have far more than a personal meaning. He attracts the interest of "another world"; achievements are expected of him which transcend the empirical realm and its narrow limits. The status of the individual is enhanced, and he acquires a cosmic importance. This numinous transformation is not the result of conscious intention or intellectual conviction, but is brought about by the impact of overwhelming archetypal impressions.

721   An experience of this kind is not without its dangers, because it often has an inflating effect on the individual. His ego fancies itself magnified and exalted, whereas in reality it is thrust into the background, so much so that the ego almost needs an inflation (the feeling of being one of the elect, for instance) in order not to lose the ground from under its feet, although it is precisely the inflation that lifts it off its foundations. It is not the ego that is exalted; rather, something greater than it makes its appearance: the self, a symbol that expresses the whole man. But the ego loves to think itself the whole man and therefore has the greatest difficulty in avoiding the danger of inflation. This is another reason why such experiences are shunned, indeed feared as pathological, and why the very idea

of the unconscious and any preoccupation with it is unwelcome. It was not so long ago that we were living in a primitive state of mind with its "perils of the soul"—loss of soul, states of possession, etc., which threatened the unity of the personality, that is, the ego. These dangers are still a long way from having been overcome in our civilized society. Though they no longer afflict the individual to the same degree, this is certainly not true of social or national groups on a large scale, as contemporary history shows only too clearly. They are psychic epidemics that destroy the individual.

722   In face of this danger the only thing that helps is for the individual to be seized by a powerful emotion which, instead of suppressing or destroying him, makes him whole. This can only happen when the unconscious man is added to the conscious one. The process of unification is only partly under the control of our will; for the rest it happens involuntarily. With the conscious mind we are able, at most, to get within reach of the unconscious process, and must then wait and see what will happen next. From the conscious standpoint the whole process looks like an adventure or a "quest," somewhat in the manner of Bunyan's *Pilgrim's Progress*. Esther Harding, in a detailed study,[23] has shown that in spite of the difference of language and outlook Bunyan was speaking of the same inward experiences which also befall people today when they choose the "strait and narrow" path. I would recommend her book to anyone who wants to know what the individuation process really is. To the constantly reiterated question "What can I do?" I know no other answer except "Become what you have always been," namely, the wholeness which we have lost in the midst of our civilized, conscious existence, a wholeness which we always were without knowing it. Esther Harding's book speaks such a simple and universal language that any man of good will, even though he lack specialized knowledge, can get an idea of what it is all about. He will also understand why, despite the fact that his question, "What on earth can I do in the present threatening world situation, with my feeble powers?" seems so important to him, it were better for him to do nothing and to leave things as they are. To worship collective ideals and work with the big

23 *Journey into Self.*

organizations is spectacularly meritorious, but they nevertheless dig the grave for the individual. A group is always of less value than the average run of its members, and when the group consists in the main of shirkers and good-for-nothings, what then? Then the ideals it preaches count for nothing too. Also, the right means in the hands of the wrong man work the wrong way, as a Chinese proverb informs us.

723 The message which the Ufo brings to the dreamer is a time problem that concerns us all. The signs appear in the heavens so that everyone shall see them. They bid each of us remember his own soul and his own wholeness, because this is the answer the West should give to the danger of mass-mindedness.

3. UFOS IN MODERN PAINTING

724   Whilst I was collecting the material for this essay, I happened to come across the work of a painter who, profoundly disturbed by the way things are going in the world today, has given expression to the fundamental fear of our age—the catastrophic outbreak of destructive forces which everyone dreads. It is, indeed, a law of painting to give visible shape to the dominant trends of the age, and for some time now painters have taken as their subject the disintegration of forms and the "breaking of tables," creating pictures which, abstractly detached from meaning and feeling alike, are distinguished by their "meaninglessness" as much as by their deliberate aloofness from the spectator. These painters have immersed themselves in the destructive element and have created a new conception of beauty, one that delights in the alienation of meaning and of feeling. Everything consists of debris, unorganized fragments, holes, distortions, overlappings, infantilisms, and crudities which outdo the clumsiest attempts of primitive art and belie the traditional idea of skill. Just as women's fashions find every innovation, however absurd and repellent, "beautiful," so too does modern art of this kind. It is the "beauty" of chaos. That is what this art heralds and eulogizes: the gorgeous rubbish heap of our civilization. It must be admitted that such an undertaking is productive of fear, especially when allied to the political possibilities of our catastrophic age. One can well imagine that in an epoch of the "great destroyers" it is a particular satisfaction to be at least the broom that sweeps the rubbish into the corner.

PLATE II: *The Fire Sower*

725   The painter in this case has summoned up the courage to admit the existence of a deep-rooted and universal fear and

383

express it in his art, just as other artists have dared—or were driven
—to choose as their motif the conscious and unconscious will for
destruction and to depict the collapse of our civilization in
chaos. They did this with a passionate superiority worthy of
Herostratus,[1] with no fear of the consequences. Fear, however,
is an admission of inferiority; it shrinks back from chaos and
longs for solid, tangible reality, for the continuity of what has
been, for meaning and purpose—in a word, for civilization. It
is conscious that all destruction is the result of inadequacy, and
that we lack something vital which could halt the onrush of
chaos. It must counter the fragmentariness of our world by a
striving to be healed and made whole. But since this apparently
cannot be found in the present, we cannot even conceive what
would make us whole. We have become sceptical, and chimerical ideas of world improvement stand low on the list. The old
panaceas have finally failed and are no longer trusted, or only
half-heartedly. The lack of any serviceable or even credible
ruling ideas has created a situation that resembles a *tabula rasa*
—almost anything might appear on it. The phenomenon of the
Ufos may well be just such an apparition.

726   More or less conscious of its analogy with a Ufo, the artist [2]
has painted a round, fiery object rotating in the heavens above
the darkening city. Following a naïve impulse to personification, he has given it the suggestion of a human face, so that it
became a head separated from the body to which it belongs.
Like the head, the body consists of flame. It is the gigantic figure
of a spectral "sower, who went forth to sow." He sows flames,
and instead of water fire falls from heaven. It seems to be an invisible fire, a "fire of the Philosophers," [3] for the city takes no
notice of it, nor does it start a conflagration. It falls unheeded,
apparently to no purpose, like seed from the hand of the sower.
Like an immaterial essence the fiery figure strides through the
houses of the city—*two worlds which interpenetrate yet do not
touch.*

1 Herostratus, in order to make his name immortal, burned down the temple of
Artemis in Ephesus, 365 B.C.
2 He was not a Saucer addict and had not read the Ufo literature.
3 In what follows there are a number of allusions to medieval symbolism, which
may perhaps be unknown to the reader. He will find the necessary documentation
in my book *Psychology and Alchemy.*

727   As the "Philosophers," that is, the old masters of alchemy, assure us, their "water" is at the same time "fire." Their Mercurius is *hermaphroditus* and *duplex,* a *complexio oppositorum,* the messenger of the gods, the One and All. He is moreover a Hermes *katachthonios* (subterranean Mercurius), a spirit emanating from the earth, shining bright and burning hot, heavier than metal and lighter than air, serpent and eagle at once, poisonous and alexipharmic. He is the panacea itself and the elixir of life, but on the other hand he is a deadly danger for the ignorant. For the educated person of those days, who studied the philosophy of alchemy as part of his general equipment—it was a real *religio medici*—this figure of the Fire Sower would have been full of allusions, and he would have had no difficulty in assimilating it to his stock of knowledge. For us, however, it is a disconcerting oddity, and we look round in vain for anything to compare it with, because what the conscious mind thinks is so utterly different from what the unconscious is aiming at. The picture illustrates the incommensurable nature of two worlds which interpenetrate but do not touch. One could compare it to a dream that is trying to tell the dreamer that consciously he lives in a dully rational world while all the time he is confronted with the nocturnal phantom of a *homo maximus.* Understood as a subjective reflex, the giant figure could be taken as a kind of psychological spectre of the Brocken. In that case one would have to posit a repressed megalomania of which the artist himself is afraid. The whole thing would then be shifted onto a pathological plane and would be nothing more than a neurotic self-confession slyly insinuated into the picture. The frightening spectacle of an apocalyptic world situation would be reduced to the personal, egocentric fear which everyone feels who nurses a secret megalomania—the fear that one's imagined grandeur will come to grief on colliding with reality. The tragedy of the world would be turned into the comedy of a little cock of the dung-hill. We know only too well that such jokes occur all too frequently.

728   So facile an argument is not sufficient to make this descent from the sublime to the ridiculous appear at all plausible. The significance of the figure lies not so much in its size and strangeness as in the numinosity of its unconscious symbolical background. If it were no more than a matter of personal vanity and

infantile self-assertion, the choice of a different symbol would have been far more appropriate—the figure of a successful and envied rival in one's own profession, for instance, suitably got up to impress, or one that increased the artist's status. But here everything points to the contrary: the figure is in every respect archetypal. It is of superhuman stature, like an archaic king or a god; it consists not of flesh and bone, but of fire; its head is round, like a luminary, or like the angel's in Revelation 10 : 1—"and a rainbow was upon his head, and his face was as it were the sun, and his feet as pillars of fire"—or like the starry heads of the planetary gods in medieval paintings. The head is separated from the body, as if to emphasize its independence, and could be compared to the arcane substance of the alchemists, the philosophical gold, the *aurum non vulgi,* the "head"-element or "omega"-element, a symbol that originated with Zosimos of Panopolis (third century A.D.). The spirit is a wanderer who roams over the earth, sowing fiery grains, like those gods and god-men who wander about and do miracles, whether of destruction or of healing. Psalm 104 : 4 likens God's "ministers" to a "flaming fire"; God himself is a "consuming fire." "Fire" signifies the intensity of affect and is the symbol of the Holy Ghost, who came down in the form of tongues of fire.

729   The characteristics of this fire-sowing figure are all steeped in tradition, some of them conscious and biblical, some of them derived from the inherited predisposition to reproduce similar but autochthonous ideas. The artist's more or less conscious allusion to the Ufo phenomenon throws light on the inner relationship between the two sets of ideas: the one interprets the other, because they both spring from the same source. Another picture by the same artist shows a motif in blue and white similar to that of Dream 2. A spring landscape, the blue sky arching above it, softened by silvery vapours. At one point the thin veil of cloud is pierced by a round opening, through which you can see the deep blue of the heavens. To either side of the opening there is a wedge of white cloud, so that the whole looks like an eye. Extremely realistic automobiles rush along on the road below. "They do not see it," the artist explained to me. In this picture the Ufo is replaced by the traditional eye of God, gazing from heaven.

730   These symbolical ideas are archetypal images that are not

derived from recent Ufo sightings but always existed. There are historical reports of the same kind from earlier decades and centuries. Thirty years ago, before Flying Saucers were heard of, I myself came across very similar dream-visions, for instance a multitude of little suns or gold coins falling from the sky, or the figure of a boy whose clothes were made of shining golden circles, or a wanderer in a field of stars, or the rising of a sun-like object which in the course of the visions developed into a mandala. I also remember a picture that was shown to me in 1919, of a town stretching along the edge of the sea, an ordinary modern port with smoking factory chimneys, fortifications, soldiers, etc. Above it there lay a thick bank of cloud, and above this there rolled a "severe image,"[4] a shining disk divided into quadrants by a cross. Here again we have two worlds separated by a bank of cloud and not touching.

731 From the very beginning the Ufo reports interested me as being, very possibly, symbolical rumours, and since 1947 I have collected all the books I could get hold of on the subject. Ufos seemed to me to have a good deal in common with mandala symbolism, about which I first wrote in 1927, in *The Secret of the Golden Flower*. Though one would like to give honest eye-witnesses and radar experts the benefit of the doubt, it must nevertheless be stressed that there is an unmistakable resemblance between the Ufo phenomena and certain psychic conditions which should not be overlooked in evaluating the observations. Besides affording a possible psychological explanation the comparison sheds light on the psychic compensation of the collective fear weighing on our hearts. The meaning of the rumour is not exhausted by its being explained as a causal symptom; rather, it has the value and significance of a living symbol, i.e., a dynamic factor which, because of the general ignorance and lack of understanding, has to confine itself to producing a visionary rumour. The fact that there is a numinous quality about all archetypal products is responsible not only for the spread of the rumour but also for its persistence. The numinosity of the complex has the further result that it stimulates deeper reflection and more careful research, until finally someone asks: What is the meaning of such a rumour at the present

4 Cf. *Psychology and Alchemy*, par. 203.

time? What future developments are being prepared in the unconscious of modern man? Long before Pallas Athene sprang, fully armed, from the head of All-Father Zeus, anticipatory and preparatory dreams had revolved round this theme and transmitted abortive sketches of it to the conscious mind. It depends on us whether we help coming events to birth by understanding them, and reinforce their healing effect, or whether we repress them with our prejudices, narrow-mindedness and ignorance, thus turning their effect into its opposite, into poison and destruction.

732   This brings me to a question I have been asked over and over again by my patients: What is the use of a compensation that, because of its symbolic form, is not understood by the conscious mind? Apart from those not so uncommon cases where only a little reflection is needed to understand the meaning of a dream, we can take it as a general rule that the compensation is not immediately obvious and is therefore easily overlooked. The language of the unconscious does not have the intentional clarity of conscious language; it is a condensation of numerous data, many of them subliminal, whose connection with conscious contents is not known. These data do not take the form of a directed judgment, but follow an instinctive, archaic "pattern" which, because of its mythological character, is not recognized by the reasoning mind. The reaction of the unconscious is a natural phenomenon that is not concerned to benefit or guide the personal human being, but is regulated exclusively by the demands of psychic equilibrium. Thus there are times when, as I have often seen, a dream that is not understood can still have a compensatory effect, even though as a rule conscious understanding is required on the alchemical principle "Quod natura relinquit imperfectum, ars perficit" (what nature leaves imperfect, the art perfects). Were this not so, human reflection and effort would be superfluous. For its part, the conscious mind often proves incapable of recognizing the full scope and significance of certain vital situations it has created for itself, and so challenges the unconscious to bring up the subliminal context, which, however, is written not in rational language but in an archaic one with two or more meanings. And since the metaphors it uses reach far back into the history of the human

mind, its interpreters will need historical knowledge in order to understand its meaning.

733   This is true also of our painting: it is a picture that reveals its meaning only with the aid of historical amplification. The fear from which it sprang is explained by the collision of the artist's conscious world with a strange apparition that came from an unknown region of his being. This world behind, below, and above us appears to us as the unconscious, which adds its subliminal contents to the images we consciously create. Thus there arises the figure of a *homo maximus*, an Anthropos and *fiilius hominis* of fiery nature, whose godlikeness or numinosity is proved by the fact that he immediately evokes similar figures in our minds, such as Enoch, Christ,[5] or Elijah, or the visions of Daniel and Ezekiel. Since Yahweh's fire chastises kills and consumes, the spectator is also at liberty to think of Jacob Boehme's "wrath-fire," which contains hell itself together with Lucifer. The scattered flames could therefore signify the "enthusiasm" of the Holy Ghost as well as the fire of evil passions—in other words, the extremes of emotion and affect which human nature is capable of, but which in ordinary life are prohibited, suppressed, hidden, or altogether unconscious. It is probably not without good reason that the name "Lucifer" applies to both Christ and the devil. The Temptation in Matthew 4 : 3ff. describes the split between them, and the fight against the devil and his angels exemplifies the mutual opposition and at the same time the inner relationship between the two sides of a moral judgment. An opposition exists only where two principles conflict with one another, but not where one is and the other not, or where there is only a one-sided dependence, such as when only good has substance but not evil.

734   The fiery figure is ambiguous and therefore unites the opposites. It is a "uniting symbol," a totality beyond human consciousness, making whole the fragmentariness of the merely conscious man. It is a bringer of salvation and disaster at once. What it will be, for good or ill, depends on the understanding and ethical decision of the individual. The picture is a kind of message to modern man, admonishing him to meditate on the signs that appear in the heavens and to interpret them aright.

5 "I am come to send fire on earth, and what will I, if it be already kindled?" Luke 12 : 49.

735   The reflection of the Ufo phenomenon in the artist's fantasy
has produced a picture whose basic features are similar to those
already discussed in the dreams. It belongs to another dimension, to a world of gods that seems to have no connection with
our reality. The picture gives one the impression of a vision,
beheld by one singled out and elect, who was permitted to see
what the gods do secretly on earth. The artist's interpretation
of the phenomenon is at an astronomical remove from the popular view that Ufos are controlled space machines.

PLATE III: *The Fourth Dimension*

736   Like the previous painting, this too is contemporary. In
order to avoid misunderstandings I must point out at once that
it is painted on canvas and that the peculiar treatment of the
background is not the result of the grain of wood showing
through. It was the artist's intention to represent something
growing or flowing. Similarly, he uses the skyline of a city to
emphasize a horizontal plane cutting through the picture.
Whereas Jakoby contrasts the low-lying city with the spacious
night sky, Birkhäuser has moved the horizontal upward, to indicate that the essence of the background also flows downward
through the depths of the earth. The colour of the city is a soft
dark red; the background is a light, watery, greenish blue
streaked with pale yellow and vermilion.

737   In this background there are fourteen more or less distinct
circles. Ten of them form the eyes of shadowy faces, half animal, half human. The other four look like knots in wood or like
dark objects floating about with haloes round them. From the
mouth of the large face at the top there issues a stream of water
that flows downward through the city. Neither touches the
other: two incommensurable events are taking place on two
totally different planes, one vertical, the other horizontal. Since,
on the horizontal plane, there is a three-dimensional city bathed
in a light that shines from the left of the picture and has nothing to do with the background, this background can only be
considered as a *fourth dimension*. The intersecting lines of the
two worlds form a cross (city and waterfall). The only discernible connection between the two is the downward glance of the
eyes in the large face above the city. The pronounced nostrils

and abnormally wide-apart eyes show that the face is only partly human. Of the four other faces, the only unmistakably human one is at the top left. The face at the bottom left can only be made out very faintly. If we regard the face in the middle, distinguished both by its size and by the fact that the water flows from its mouth, as the main face and as the source, then the ground structure of the picture is a quincunx:

738   This is a symbol of the *quinta essentia,* which is identical with the Philosophers' Stone. It is the circle divided into four with the centre, or the divinity extended in four directions, or the four functions of consciousness with their unitary substrate, the self. Here the quaternity has a 3 + 1 structure: three animal-daemonic faces and one human one. This peculiar feature of our picture recalls the quaternity discussed by Plato in the *Timaeus* and experienced still earlier by Ezekiel in his vision of the four seraphim. One of them had a human face, the other three had animal faces. The motif appears again in certain representations of the sons of Horus and in the emblems of the evangelists, as well as in the four gospels (three synoptic, one "Gnostic") and in the four Persons of Christian metaphysics: the Trinity and the devil. The 3 + 1 structure is a motif that runs all through alchemy and was attributed to Maria the Copt or Jewess. Goethe took it up again in the Cabiri scene in *Faust.* The number 4 as the natural division of the circle is a symbol of wholeness in alchemical philosophy, and it should not be forgotten that the central Christian symbol is a quaternity too, which, in the form of the long cross, even has the 3 + 1 structure.[6]

739   This painting, like the previous one, depicts the collision of two incommensurable worlds, vertical and horizontal, which meet only at one point: in the Sower's intention to scatter fire on the earth, and in the downward glance of the eyes.

[6] In H. G. Wells, the "time machine" seems to have three visible rods, but the fourth "has an odd, twinkling appearance, as if it were not real."

740   Coming now to the four circles [7] that are not eyes, we note that only one of them—on the extreme left—is completely round and solid-looking. The circle on the right of the mouth is light with a dark centre; a third circle appears to be emitting a whitish vapour; a fourth circle is half hidden by the flowing water. They form a differentiated quaternity in contrast to the undifferentiated ogdoad of eyes, which, if we disregard the main face, belong to a quaternity with a 3 + 1 structure.

741   It is difficult to say how much in the main face is animal and how much is human. But since it represents the "source of living water" (quintessence, *aurum potabile, aqua permanens, vinum ardens, elixir vitae*, etc.) and appears to have an animal component, its doubtfully human character is plain enough. One thinks of the figure "having the likeness of a human form" who appeared above the sapphire throne in Ezekiel's vision, and of Yahweh's wildness, which so often breaks through in the Old Testament. In Christian iconography the Trinity consists of three human persons (occasionally depicted as a tricephalus), while the fourth, the devil, is traditionally represented as half-animal. Our mandala seems to be complementary to the Christian totality.

742   One further fact deserves notice: the two lower faces, though inverted, are not reflections of the two upper ones, but are independent entities representing a lower as opposed to an upper world. Moreover, one of the two upper faces is light, the other considerably darker, with pointed ears. In contrast to this opposition the water flows uniformly from above downward, thus forming a potential. The source lies not only above the earthly horizontal but also above the middle line of the picture, so that the upper world is characterized as the source of life. Since the three-dimensional human body is ordinarily thought of as the seat of life and strength, this is compensated by placing the source in the fourth dimension. It flows from an ideal centre. The fourth dimension is therefore only apparently symmetrical,

[7] In this connection I would like to draw attention to van Gogh's *Starry Night* (1889). There the stars are painted as large shining disks, though the eye never sees them like that. Speaking of his picture, van Gogh used the expression "pantheistic frenzy," calling it the "remnant of an apocalyptic fantasy" and comparing the starry disks to a "group of living figures who are like one of us." The painting is supposed to be derived from a dream.

in reality it is asymmetrical—a problem that is of importance both to nuclear physics and to the psychology of the unconscious.

743   The "four-dimensional" background is a "vision," in the dual sense of seeing and of something seen. It seems to be a matter of pure chance that it has turned out so and not otherwise, when the merest accident could have given it a quite different appearance. The sight of these round blobs aimlessly scattered over a wishy-washy surface, most of them serving for eyes in indistinct animal-human faces lacking any definite expression, fails to arouse our interest. The picture discourages any attempt to find access to it, for the chance products of nature, if they lack aesthetic charm, have no effect on our sensibilities. Their chancefulness makes the slightest attempt to interpret them seem like empty speculation. It needs the interest of the psychologist, so often incomprehensible to the layman, to follow up a vague instinct for order, using for this purpose the most primitive of all devices, namely *counting*. When there are few or no characteristics that can be compared with one another, number remains as the ordering schema. Nevertheless, the little disks or holes are distinctly round and the majority of them are eyes. It is only by chance—I must repeat this—that numbers and other patterns appear whose exact repetition would be extremely improbable. In such cases we must refrain from all statistical or experimental thinking, for a probability test of this picture would involve astronomical figures. Investigations of this kind are only possible when a very simple experiment can be repeated over and over again in the shortest time, like Rhine's tests. Our picture is a unique and complex occurrence which from the statistical point of view is entirely meaningless. But from the psychological point of view such curiosities may be meaningful, because the conscious mind is involuntarily impressed by their numinosity. We must therefore take account of them, however improbable and irrational they may appear to be, just because they are important factors in a psychological process. But I must emphasize that nothing will have been proved.

744   Since psychology touches man on the practical side, it cannot be satisfied with averages, because these only give information about his general behaviour. Instead, it has to turn its

attention to the individual exceptions, which are murdered by statistics. The human psyche attains its true meaning not in the average but in the unique, and this does not count in a scientific procedure. Rhine's experiments have taught us, if practical experience has not already done so, that the improbable does occur, and that our picture of the world only tallies with reality when the improbable has a place in it. This point of view is anathema to the exclusively scientific attitude, despite the fact that without exceptions there would be no statistics at all. Moreover, in actual reality the exceptions are almost more important than the rule.

745   This picture allows some conclusions to be drawn as to the nature of the objects appearing in the sky. The "sky" is not the blue vault we see, nor is it the star-filled universe; it is a strange fourth dimension containing supernatural beings as well as dark disks or round holes. The background has a fluid, watery character in striking contrast to the exclusively fiery nature of the previous picture. Fire symbolizes dynamism, passion, and emotion, whereas water with its coolness and substantiality represents the passive object, detached contemplation, hence the thirst-quenching *aqua doctrinae* and the *refrigerium* [8] that puts out the fire, like the salamander of alchemy.

746   As the old masters say: "Our water is fire"—an identity which, as soon as we think about it, splits into opposites, as also does the unconscious God-image. This seeming mystery is characteristic of all that is: it is so and yet not so, especially the unconscious, whose reality we can experience only in parables. In the same way a fourth dimension can be regarded only as a mathematical fiction, an intellectual sophistry, or a revelation of the unconscious, for we have no direct experience of it.

747   The unconscious arrangement of the elements composing the picture suggests that the Ufos are subliminal contents that have become visible; that they are, in a word, archetypal figures.

PLATE IV: *Painting by Yves Tanguy*

748   This painting dates from the year 1927, thus anticipating by more than a decade the great bombings of cities. For this is

[8] The refreshing, cool water of life in paradise after the heat of purgatory.

what the picture brings to mind. As a contemporary painting is usually rather difficult to interpret, because its whole aim is to abolish meaning and form and to replace them by something strange and disconcerting, I have followed the method of showing it to as many different people as possible, in this way conducting a kind of Rorschach test. Most of them took the black and white background, which combines a minimum of intelligibility with a maximum of abstraction, to be a plane surface. This is supported by the fact that the light causes the five central forms to cast shadows. It can be seen that these shadows fall on a plane. The interpretation of this varies considerably: some thought it was a sea covered with drift ice in the Polar night, others a sea of fog at night time, others the bleak surface of a distant planet like Uranus or Neptune, and others a great city illuminated at night, situated along the edge of bays, like San Francisco or New York. The strange quincunx suspended over the "city" left most of them puzzled. Some interpreted it at once as falling bombs and explosions. The form in the middle was taken to be a sea-creature (sea-anemone, octopus, etc.) or a flower, or else a daemonic face with tangled hair (looking down to the left); others saw it as the swirling smoke of a great fire. The four figures surrounding it were understood as sea animals, puffs of smoke, fungi, or, because of the horns, as devils. The one at the top left, whose vivid yellowish-green contrasts with the dull, indeterminate tones of the others, was interpreted as poisonous smoke, a water-plant, flame, a house on fire, etc. I must admit that for me the comparison with a city at night by the sea, viewed from a considerable height as from an aeroplane, was the most convincing. The artist is said to have been a sailor originally, and would thus have had plenty of opportunities for such impressions.

749   The horizon is lost in cloudy forms over which hangs a faint circular luminosity; to the left of this is a dimly lit cloud bank (?), shaped like a cigar. In the centre of the brightness there is, as if by accident, a barely visible spot of the same colour as the yellowish-green "flame" (top left of the quincunx). A similar, but clearly visible, spot can be seen further down (centre right), directly above the city. A faint line connects it with another yellowish-green spot, apparently a continuation of the flame. The longish second spot points towards the centre of faintly

discernible concentric circles that suggest rotation. It is interesting to note that the first-mentioned spot at the top of the picture is also connected with concentric circles. Unfortunately they cannot be seen in the reproduction because it is too dark; they appear only as a circular luminosity surrounding the yellowish spot, but can be felt to the touch as lightly raised lines. Probably they were scratched on with a pointed instrument. There can be no doubt about their circular nature, which is clearly apparent in the lower concentric formation.

750 These details seem to be a matter of pure chance, the impression also given by the previous picture. Their fortuitous nature cannot be denied, but they assume a rather different aspect when submitted to a comparative procedure. As if by chance two luminous whirls with dark centres, and an equally fortuitous cigar form, appear in the night sky, together with a bright spot and a line connecting the second whirl with the flame. One can easily let one's imagination run and interpret the flame as belonging to a projectile shot out of the whirl, or, as we would now say, from a Ufo—for Ufos are said to have incendiary tendencies, among other things. Here it is sowing fire, as a distinct line connects it with the flame. There are, however, a number of other wavy lines crossing the picture, like highways or boundary lines. Have they anything to do with the phenomena in the sky? So much in this picture remains conjecture, for instance the indeterminable corporeal shapes, which, together with the "flame," form a quaternity with a 3 + 1 structure. The structure in the middle is equally difficult to interpret, but it is obviously of a different, more nebulous nature and is thereby distinguished from the others, though like them it throws a shadow.

751 The description of the picture would be incomplete if I omitted to mention an important factor which reveals itself on closer examination: the cylindrical, phallic cloud (?) is aimed straight at the topmost luminous whirl, and this could be interpreted sexualistically as cohabitation. Similarly, from the lower whirl a little flame leaps out, which is connected in turn with the big flame on the left. The latter, in psychological terms, is the One differentiated from the Three, the one differentiated function contrasted with the three undifferentiated functions, and hence the main function (or, alternatively, the inferior

function). The four together form an unfolded totality symbol, the self in its empirical aspect. The name of one of the Gnostic deities is Barbelo, "god is four." According to an early Christian idea the unity of the incarnate God rests on the four pillars of the gospels (representing the 3 + 1 structure), just as the Gnostic *monogenes* (*unigenitus*, Only Begotten) stands on the *tetrapeza* (four-footed table). Christ is the head of the Church. As God, he is the unity of the Trinity, and as the historical Son of Man and anthropos he is the prototype of the individual inner man and at the same time the culmination, goal and totality of the empirical man. Thus we arrive at an apparently fortuitous picture of a hierosgamos taking place in the heavens, followed by the birth of a saviour and his epiphany on earth.

752   The picture is distinguished by a strongly marked horizontal axis. The vertical axis is expressed by the quaternity, and, more dramatically, by the heavenly origin of the fire. The comparison with a bombing is not so far-fetched, since at the time the picture was painted this possibility was in the air, both as a memory of the past and as a premonition of the future. The Ufos in the sky and the remarkable happenings down below together constitute an impressive vertical, which could be interpreted as the intrusion of a different order of things. The accent lies without doubt on the quincunx, which we have dealt with above. It is a decidedly enigmatic structure, and this obviously accords with the artist's intention. He has undoubtedly succeeded in expressing the bleakness, coldness, lifelessness, the cosmic "inhumanness" and infinite desolation of the horizontal, despite the association "city." He thus confirms the tendency of this kind of modern art to make the object unrecognizable and to cut off the sympathy and understanding of the beholder, who, rebuffed and confused, feels thrown back on himself.

753   The psychological effect is very like that of the Rorschach test, where a purely fortuitous and irrational picture appeals to the irrational powers of the imagination and brings the observer's unconscious into play. When his extraverted interest is snubbed in this way it falls back on the "subjective factor" and increases the latter's energy charge, a phenomenon that was observed very clearly in the original association tests. The isolated stimulus word uttered by the experimenter bewilders and embarrasses the subject because it may have more than one

397

meaning. He does not quite know what to answer, and this accounts for the extraordinary variety of answers in these tests and—what is more important—for the large number of disturbed reactions [9] which are caused by the intrusion of unconscious contents.

754   The rebuffing of interest by unintelligibility results in its introversion and a constellation of the unconscious. Modern art has the same effect. We can therefore attribute to it a conscious or unconscious intention to turn the beholder's eyes away from the intelligible and enjoyable world of the senses and to enforce a revelation of the unconscious as a kind of substitute for the loss of human surroundings. This is also the intention of the association experiment and the Rorschach test: they are meant to supply information concerning the background of consciousness, and this they do with great success. The experimental set-up of modern art is evidently the same: it faces the observer with the question "How will you react? What do you think? What kind of fantasy will come up?" In other words, modern art is less concerned with the pictures it produces than with the observer and his involuntary reactions. He peers at the colours on the canvas, his interest is aroused, but all he can discover is a product that defies human understanding. He feels disappointed, and already he is thrown back on a subjective reaction which vents itself in all sorts of exclamations. Anyone who knows how to interpret these will learn a lot about the subjective disposition of the observer but next to nothing about the painting as such. For him it is no more than a psychological test. This may sound disparaging, but only for those who regard the subjective factor merely as a source of discomfort. But if they are interested in their own psyches, they will try to submit their constellated complexes to closer scrutiny.

755   Since even the boldest fantasy of the creative artist—however much it may exceed the bounds of intelligibility—is always bounded by the limits of the psyche itself, there may easily appear in his pictures unknown forms which indicate certain limiting and predetermined factors. These, in Tanguy's picture, are the quincunx, the quaternity with the 3 + 1 structure, and the "signs in the heavens," the circles and the cigar-form—in a

[9] Inhibitions, failures to react, slips of the tongue, subsequent forgetting of the answers, etc. All these are "complex-indicators."

word, the archetypes. In its attempt to leave the world of visible and intelligible appearances and to float in the boundlessness of chaos, modern art, to a still greater degree than the psychological tests, evokes complexes which have sloughed off their usual personal aspect and appear as what they originally were, namely primordial forms of the instincts. They are of a suprapersonal, collective-unconscious nature. Personal complexes arise wherever there are conflicts with the instinctual disposition. These are the points of faulty adaptation, and their sensitiveness releases affects which tear the mask of adaptedness off the face of civilized man. This also seems to be the goal that modern art is indirectly aiming at. For all the appearance of extreme arbitrariness and boundless chaos, the loss of beauty and meaning is compensated by a strengthening of the unconscious. And since this is not chaotic but pertains to the natural order of things, it is to be expected that forms and patterns will arise which are indicative of this order. This seems to be the case in the examples we have been discussing. As though by chance there appear in the chaos of possibilities unexpected ordering principles which have the closest affinities with the timeless psychic dominants, but at the same time have conjured up a collective fantasy typical of our technological age and painted it in the skies.

756   Pictures of this kind are rather rare, but not undiscoverable. For that matter, relatively few people have seen a Ufo, yet there can be no doubt about the existence of the rumour. It has even attracted the attention of hard-headed military authorities, despite the fact that for sheer improbability it outdoes anything I have said about the meaning of the pictures. Anyone who wants to get an independent idea of the scope of the Ufo legend should read Edgar Sievers' *Flying Saucers über Südafrika*. Though open to attack at many points, it gives one some notion of the efforts an intelligent and well-meaning person has to make in order to come to terms with the Ufos. It is undoubtedly a challenging matter that has caused the author to move heaven and hell. What he unfortunately lacks is a knowledge of the psychology of the unconscious, perhaps the most important thing here. His book sets forth all the earlier and recent attempts at explanation based on scientific and philosophical premises, but also, unfortunately, on unverifiable

theosophical assertions. Credulity and lack of discrimination, which elsewhere would be vices, here serve the useful purpose of bringing together a collection of heterogeneous speculations on the Ufo problem. Anyone who is interested in the psychology of the rumour will read this book with profit, for it offers a comprehensive survey of the psychic phenomenology of the Ufo.

4. PREVIOUS HISTORY OF
THE UFO PHENOMENON

757   Though the Ufos were first publicized only towards the end of the second World War, the phenomenon itself was known long before. It was observed in the first half of this century, and was described in earlier centuries and perhaps even in antiquity. In the Ufo literature there are collections of reports from various sources which need critical evaluation. I shall spare myself this task and give the reader only two examples.

PLATE V: *Basel Broadsheet, 1566*

758   This is from a broadsheet written by Samuel Coccius, "student of the Holy Scripture and of the free arts, at Basel, in the Fatherland," in August 1566. He reports that on August 7 of that year, at the time of the sunrise, "many large black globes were seen in the air, moving before the sun with great speed, and turning against each other as if fighting. Some of them became red and fiery and afterwards faded and went out."

759   As the illustration shows, this sighting was made in Basel. The dark colour of the Ufos may be due to their having been seen against the light of the rising sun. Some of them were bright and fiery. Their speed and irregular motion are typical Ufo features.

PLATE VI: *Nuremberg Broadsheet, 1561*

760   This broadsheet relates the story of a "very frightful spectacle" seen by "numerous men and women" at sunrise on April 14, 1561. They saw "globes" of a blood-red, bluish, or black colour, or "plates" in large numbers near the sun, "some three in a row, now and then four in a square, also some standing alone. And amongst these globes some blood-coloured crosses were seen." Moreover there were "two great tubes"—three in the picture—"in which three, four, and more globes were to be seen. They all began to fight one another." This went on for about an hour. Then "they all fell—as one sees in the picture—from the sun and sky down to the earth, as if everything were on fire, then it slowly faded away on the earth, producing a lot of steam." Underneath the globes was a long object, "shaped like a great black spear." Naturally this "spectacle" was interpreted as a divine warning.

761   This report, as the reader will have noted, contains certain details already known to us. Above all the "tubes," which are analogous to the cylindrical objects in the Ufo reports. These, in Ufo language, are the "mother-ships" which are said to carry the smaller, lens-shaped Ufos for long distances. The picture shows them in operation, releasing Ufos or taking them on board. Especially important, though lacking in the modern Ufo reports, are the indubitable quaternities, seen sometimes as simple crosses, sometimes as disks in the form of a cross, that is, as regular mandalas. There also seems to be a hint of the 3 + 1 motif in the dilemma of three and four. The militaristic interpretation is as characteristic of the sixteenth century as the technological one is of ours. The tubes are cannons and the globes cannonballs, and the shooting to and fro of the globes is an artillery engagement. The great black spearhead, as well as the spearshafts (?), seem to represent the masculine element, especially in its "penetrating" capacity. Similar things are reported in the Ufo literature.

762   The emphasis on the cross motif is striking. The Christian meaning of the cross can hardly be considered here, since we are dealing with a natural phenomenon, a swarm of round objects in violent motion, shooting in opposite directions and reminding the reporter of a battle. If the Ufos were living organisms, one would think of a swarm of insects rising with the sun, not to fight one another but to mate and celebrate the marriage flight. Here the cross signifies a union of opposites (vertical and horizontal), a "crossing"; as a plus sign, it is also a joining together, an addition. Where the globes are coupled together to form quaternities, they have given rise to the crossed marriage quaternio, which I have discussed in my "Psychology of the Transference." It forms the model for the primitive "cross

cousin marriage," but is also an individuation symbol, the union of the "four."

763   Columns of smoke rise up from the place where the cannon-balls have fallen, reminding us of Tanguy's picture. The moment of sunrise, the *Aurora consurgens* (Aquinas, Boehme), suggests the revelation of the light. Both reports have clear analogies not only with one another but also with the modern saucer stories and with the individual products of the unconscious today.

PLATE VII: *The Spiritual Pilgrim Discovering Another World*

764   This seventeenth-century woodcut, possibly representing a Rosicrucian illumination, comes from a source unknown to me.[1] On the right it shows the familiar world. The pilgrim, who is evidently on a *pélerinage de l'âme*, has broken through the star-strewn rim of his world and beholds another, supernatural universe filled with what look like layers of cloud or mountain ranges. In it appear the wheels of Ezekiel and disks or rainbowlike figures, obviously representing the "heavenly spheres." In these symbols we have a prototype of the Ufo vision, which is vouchsafed to the illuminati. They cannot be heavenly bodies belonging to our empirical world, but are projected "rotunda" from the inner, four-dimensional world. This is even more evident in the next picture.

PLATE VIII: *The Quickening of the Child in the Womb*

765   This picture comes from the Rupertsberg Codex *Scivias*, written by Hildegard of Bingen (12th cent.). It shows the quickening or "animation" of the child in the body of the mother. From a higher world an influx enters the foetus. This upper world has a remarkable quadratic form divided into three to correspond with the Trinity, but, unlike the latter, which is supposed to consist of three equal parts, the middle section is different from the other two. It contains round objects, whereas

[1] It was kindly placed at my disposal by D. van Houten, Bergen, Netherlands. [Later information suggests that it is a late 19th-cent. imitation.—EDITORS.]

the other two are characterized by the eye motif. Like the wheels of Ezekiel, the little rotunda are associated with eyes.

766 As Hildegard's text states, the radiance of the "countless eyes" (there are in reality twenty-four in each section) means "God's knowledge," that is, his seeing and knowing, with reference to the seven eyes of God that "run to and fro through the whole earth" (Zech. 4 : 10). The rotunda, on the other hand, are God's deeds, such as the sending of his son as a saviour (p. 127). Hildegard adds: "All, the bad as well as the good, appear in God's knowledge, for it is not ever clouded round by any darkness." The souls of men are "fireballs" (pp. 120, 126, 130, 133), so presumably the soul of Christ was also such a ball, for Hildegard interprets her vision not with reference to the growth of a human child only, but with particular reference to Christ and the Mother of God (p. 127). The square divided into three stands for the Holy Ghost entering into the child (p. 129). The procreative aspect of the Holy Ghost unites the Godhead with matter, as is clear from the sacred legend. The intermediate forms between spirit and matter are obviously the rotunda, early stages of animated bodies, filling the middle section of the square. There are thirty of them, and, however accidental this may be, the number 30 (days of the month) suggests the moon, ruler of the hylical world, whereas twenty-four (hours of the day) suggests the sun, the king. This indicates the motif of the *coniunctio* (☉ and ☽)—an instance of that unconscious readiness which later came to expression in Cusanus' definition of God as a *complexio oppositorum*. In the miniature the rotunda are fire-coloured, the fiery seeds from which human beings will sprout, a sort of pneumatic roe. This comparison is justified in so far as alchemy compares the rotunda to fish's eyes. The eyes of a fish are always open, like the eyes of God. They are synonymous with the *scintillae*, "soul-sparks." It is just possible that these alchemical allusions crept into Hildegard's text via the atoms of Democritus (*spiritus insertus atomis*).[2] Another such source may be responsible for the squareness of the Holy Ghost.

767 The square, being a quaternity, is a totality symbol in alchemy. Having four corners it signifies the earth, whereas a circular form is attributed to the spirit. Earth is feminine, spirit

[2] Macrobius, *In somnium Scipionis*, I, 14, 19.

A Ufo Vision
Painting by a patient

E. Jakoby: *The Fire Sower*

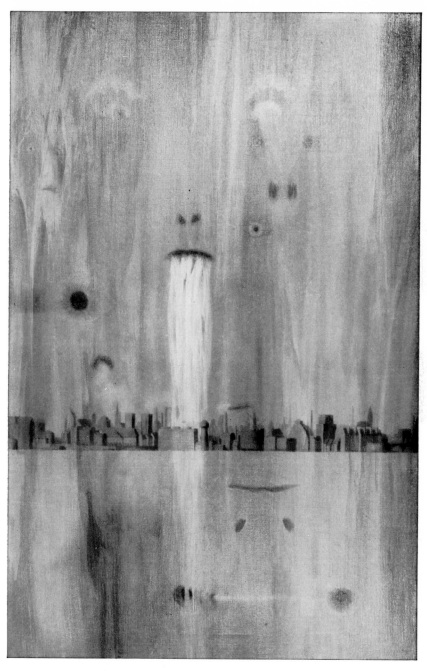

P. Birkhäuser: *The Fourth Dimension*

III

Yves Tanguy: Painting, 1927

Basel Broadsheet, 1566

Nuremberg Broadsheet, 1561

"The Spiritual Pilgrim Discovering Another World"

Woodcut, 19th (?) century

"The Quickening of the Child
in the Womb"

From the Scivias *of Hildegard von
Bingen, in a ms. of the 12th century*

VIII

masculine. The square as a symbol of the spiritual world is certainly most unusual, but becomes more intelligible when we take Hildegard's sex into account. This remarkable symbolism is reflected in the squaring of the circle—another *coniunctio oppositorum*. "Squareness" in alchemy is an important feature of the unitary substance, the *Mercurius Philosophorum sive quadratus,* and characterizes its chthonic nature, which it possesses along with spirituality (*spiritus mercurialis*). It is as much a metal as a spirit. Correspondingly, in Christian dogma, the Holy Ghost as the third Person of the Trinity does not remain a prerogative of the incarnate God, but may descend also upon sinful man. Though these ideas were not yet explicitly conscious in Hildegard's day, they were implicitly present in the collective unconscious, activated by the Christ/Mercurius analogy. This reached consciousness in the next century, but had been clearly anticipated in the writings of Zosimos of Panopolis in the third century A.D. We must emphasize, however, that there can hardly be any historical connection between the two; it is more a question of the activated archetype of the Primordial Man or Anthropos.

768 Equally characteristic of alchemy is the arithmetical structure of the Holy Ghost: he is a unity, consists of two principles (eyes and fireballs), has three parts, and is a square. This motif is known under the name of the Axiom of Maria, who lived in Alexandria in the third century and played a great role in classical alchemy.

769 The two human groups in the picture typify the fates that preside over the awakening of the soul. There are, as Hildegard says, "people who prepare good or middling or bad cheese." [3] The devil, too, has a hand in the game. The picture shows clearly, like the previous one, that the eyes and fireballs are not identical with the heavenly bodies and are differentiated

[3] "You look further and see people on the earth who carry milk in clay vessels. From this they prepare cheese. They are the people, men and women, who carry human seed in their bodies. From it arise the various generations of men. Part of the milk is fatty. It makes fatty cheese. This seed . . . produces energetic people. . . . In cleverness and discretion they master life and flourish in their works visibly before God and men. The devil does not find his place in them. Other milk is thin. This curdles into insipid cheese. This seed . . . produces weakly people. . . . A last part of the milk is mixed with corruption, and the cheese that comes from it is bitter. This seed . . . produces malformed people," etc. *Scivias*, pp. 128f.

from the stars in the background. It confirms that the fireballs are souls.

Summary

770   From the dream examples and the pictures it is evident that the unconscious, in order to portray its contents, makes use of certain fantasy elements which can be compared with the Ufo phenomenon. In dreams 1, 2, 6, and 7, and in the painting of the Fire Sower, the connection with Ufos was conscious, while in the other dreams and in two of the paintings no conscious connection could be proved. The personal relationship between the Ufo and the observing dream-subject was stressed in some of the dreams, but this is completely lacking in the paintings. In medieval paintings the personal participation in an epiphany or in suchlike visionary experiences is expressed by the visible presence of the recipient of the vision. This view does not fit at all into the programme of modern art, which is more concerned to put as great a distance as possible between the object and the spectator—like the Rorschach ink-blot, which is intentionally *tachiste* in order to avoid any suggestion of meaning and to produce a purely subjective phantasm.

771   The dreams as well as the paintings, when subjected to careful scrutiny, yield a meaningful content which could be described as an *epiphany*. In the Fire Sower this meaning can be recognized without difficulty. In the other cases an investigation in the light of comparative psychology leads to the same conclusion. For those unacquainted with the psychology of the unconscious I must emphasize that my conclusions are not the product of unbridled fantasy, as is often supposed, but are based on thorough researches into the history of symbols. It was merely in order to avoid overloading my text with annotations that I omitted practically all the references to source material. Anyone, therefore, who feels the need to test the correctness of my conclusions will have to go to the trouble of familiarizing himself with my other writings. The amplificatory method I have used for interpreting the meaning has proved fruitful when applied to historical as well as contemporary material. In the present instance it seems to me sufficiently safe to conclude that in my examples a central archetype consistently appears,

406

which I have called the archetype of the self. It takes the traditional form of an epiphany from heaven, whose nature is in several cases markedly antithetical, e.g., fire and water, corresponding to the "star of David," ✡, which consists of △ = fire and ▽ = water. The hexad is a totality symbol: 4 as the natural division of the circle, 2 as the vertical axis (zenith and nadir) —a spatial conception of totality. As a modern development of this symbol we would cite the fourth dimension in Plates II and III.

772   The *masculine-feminine antithesis* appears in the long and round objects: cigar-form and circle. These may be sexual symbols. The Chinese symbol of the *one* being, Tao, consists of *yang* (fire, hot, dry, south side of the mountain, masculine, etc.) and *yin* (dark, moist, cool, north side of the mountain, feminine). It fully corresponds, therefore, to the Jewish symbol mentioned above. The Christian equivalent can be found in the Church's doctrine of the unity of mother and son and in the androgyny of Christ, not to mention the hermaphroditic Primordial Being in many oriental and primitive religions, the "Father-Mother" of the Gnostics, and the Mercurius hermaphroditus of alchemy.

773   The third antithesis is between *Above* and *Below,* as in Plate III, where it seems to have been moved into the fourth dimension. In the other examples it constitutes the difference between what happens in the heavens and down below on earth.

774   The fourth antithesis, *unity and quaternity,* appears united in the quincunx (Pls. III, IV), the four forming, as it were, a frame for the one, accentuated as the centre. In the history of symbols, quaternity is the unfolding of unity. The one universal Being cannot be known, because it is not differentiated from anything and cannot be compared with anything. By unfolding into four it acquires distinct characteristics and can therefore be known. This is not a metaphysical argument but simply a psychological formula for describing the process by which an unconscious content becomes conscious. So long as a thing is in the unconscious it has no recognizable qualities and is consequently merged with the universal unknown, with the unconscious All and Nothing, with what the Gnostics called a "non-existent all-being." But as soon as the unconscious content enters the sphere of consciousness it has already split into the

"four," that is to say it can become an object of experience only by virtue of the four basic functions of consciousness. It is *perceived* as something that exists (sensation); it is *recognized* as this and *distinguished* from that (thinking); it is *evaluated* as pleasant or unpleasant, etc. (feeling); and finally, intuition tells us where it came from and where it is going. This cannot be perceived by the senses or thought by the intellect. Consequently the object's extension in time and what happens to it is the proper concern of intuition.

775   The splitting into four has the same significance as the division of the horizon into four quarters, or of the year into four seasons. That is, through the act of becoming conscious the four basic aspects of a whole judgment are rendered visible. This naturally does not mean that the speculative intellect could not equally well think up 360 other aspects. The four we have named are nothing more than a natural, minimal division of the circle or totality. In my work with patients the quaternity symbol crops up very frequently, the pentad very rarely, and rather less rarely the triad. Since my practice was always cosmopolitan I had plenty of occasion for comparative ethnological observations, and it struck me that the triadic mandalas invariably came from Germans. This seemed to me to have some connection with the fact that, compared with French and Anglo-Saxon literature, the typical anima figure in German novels plays a relatively insignificant role. From a totality standpoint the triadic mandala has a 4 — 1 structure as opposed to the usual 3 + 1. The fourth function is the undifferentiated or inferior function which characterizes the shadow side of the personality. When this is missing in the totality symbol there is too much emphasis on the conscious side.

776   The fifth antithesis concerns the contrast between an *enigmatic higher world and the ordinary human world.* This is the most important polarity, which is illustrated in all the examples and can therefore be taken as fundamental both to the dreams and to the pictures. The contrast seems to be intentional as well as being very striking, and, if we take this feeling into account, appears to convey something like a message. The horizontal axis of our empirical consciousness, which except for psychic contents is aware only of bodies in motion, is crossed by another order of being, a dimension of the "psychic"—for the only state-

ments we can safely make about this other order refer to the psychic, something on the one hand *mathematically abstract* and on the other hand *fabulous and mythological.* Now if we conceive numbers as having been *discovered,* and not merely *invented* as an instrument for counting, then on account of their mythological nature they belong to the realm of "godlike" human and animal figures and are just as archetypal as they. Unlike these, however, they are "real" in the sense that they are encountered in the realm of experience as *quantities* and thus form the bridge between the tangible, physical world and the imaginary. Though the latter is unreal, it is "real" in so far as it works, i.e., has an effect on us. There can be no doubt about its effectiveness, particularly at the present time. It is not the behaviour, the lack or surplus, of physical things that directly affects humanity so much as the idea we have of them, or the "imaginary" ideas by which we are obsessed.

777 The role that numbers play in mythology and in the unconscious gives food for thought. They are an aspect of the physically real as well as of the psychically imaginary. They do not only count and measure, and are not merely quantitative; they also make qualitative statements and are therefore a mysterious something midway between myth and reality, partly discovered and partly invented. Equations, for instance, that were invented as pure mathematical formulae have subsequently proved to be formulations of the quantitative behaviour of physical things. Conversely, owing to their individual qualities, numbers can be vehicles for psychic processes in the unconscious. The structure of the mandala, for instance, is intrinsically mathematical. We may exclaim with the mathematician Jacobi: "In the Olympian host Number eternally reigns."

778 These hints are merely intended to point out to the reader that the opposition between the human world and the higher world is not absolute; the two are only relatively incommensurable, for the bridge between them is not entirely lacking. Between them stands the great mediator, Number, whose reality is valid in both worlds, as an archetype in its very essence. Deviation into theosophical speculation does not help us to understand the splitting of the world picture indicated in our examples, for this is simply a matter of names and words which do not point the way to the *unus mundus* (unitary world). Number,

however, belongs to both worlds, the real and the imaginary; it is visible as well as invisible, quantitative as well as qualitative.

779   Thus it is a fact of singular importance that number also characterizes the "personal" nature of the mediating figure, that it appears as a mediator. From the psychological standpoint, and having regard to the limits set to all scientific knowledge, I have called the mediating or "uniting" symbol which necessarily proceeds from a sufficiently great tension of opposites the "self." I chose this term in order to make clear that I am concerned primarily with the formulation of empirical facts and not with dubious incursions into metaphysics. There I would trespass upon all manner of religious convictions. Living in the West, I would have to say Christ instead of "self," in the Near East it would be Khidr, in the Far East atman or Tao or the Buddha, in the Far West maybe a hare or Mondamin, and in cabalism it would be Tifereth. Our world has shrunk, and it is dawning on us that humanity is *one*, with *one* psyche. Humility is a not inconsiderable virtue which should prompt Christians, for the sake of charity—the greatest of all virtues—to set a good example and acknowledge that though there is only *one* truth it speaks in many tongues, and that if we still cannot see this it is simply due to lack of understanding. No one is so godlike that he alone knows the true word. All of us gaze into that "dark glass" in which the dark myth takes shape, adumbrating the invisible truth. In this glass the eyes of the spirit glimpse an image which we call the self, fully conscious of the fact that it is an anthropomorphic image which we have merely named but not explained. By "self" we mean psychic wholeness, but what realities underlie this concept we do not know, because psychic contents cannot be observed in their unconscious state, and moreover the psyche cannot know itself. The conscious can know the unconscious only so far as it has become conscious. We have only a very hazy idea of the changes an unconscious content undergoes in the process of becoming conscious, but no certain knowledge. The concept of psychic wholeness necessarily implies an element of transcendence on account of the existence of unconscious components. Transcendence in this sense is not equivalent to a metaphysical postulate or hypostasis; it claims to be no more than a borderline concept, to quote Kant.

780   That there is something beyond the borderline, beyond the

frontiers of knowledge, is shown by the archetypes and, most clearly of all, by numbers, which this side of the border are quantities but on the other side are autonomous psychic entities, capable of making qualitative statements which manifest themselves in *a priori* patterns of order. These patterns include not only causally explicable phenomena like dream-symbols and such, but remarkable relativizations of time and space which simply cannot be explained causally. They are the parapsychological phenomena which I have summed up under the term "synchronicity" and which have been statistically investigated by Rhine. The positive results of his experiments elevate these phenomena to the rank of undeniable facts. This brings us a little nearer to understanding the mystery of psychophysical parallelism, for we now know that a factor exists which mediates between the apparent incommensurability of body and psyche, giving matter a kind of "psychic" faculty and the psyche a kind of "materiality," by means of which the one can work on the other. That the body can work on the psyche seems to be a truism, but strictly speaking all we know is that any bodily defect or illness also expresses itself psychically. Naturally this assumption only holds good if, contrary to the popular materialistic view, the psyche is credited with an existence of its own. But materialism in its turn cannot explain how chemical changes can produce a psyche. Both views, the materialistic as well as the spiritualistic, are metaphysical prejudices. It accords better with experience to suppose that living matter has a psychic aspect, and the psyche a physical aspect. If we give due consideration to the facts of parapsychology, then the hypothesis of the psychic aspect must be extended beyond the sphere of biochemical processes to matter in general. In that case all reality would be grounded on an as yet unknown substrate possessing material and at the same time psychic qualities. In view of the trend of modern theoretical physics, this assumption should arouse fewer resistances than before. It would also do away with the awkward hypothesis of psychophysical parallelism, and afford us an opportunity to construct a new world model closer to the idea of the *unus mundus*. The "acausal" correspondences between mutually independent psychic and physical events, i.e., synchronistic phenomena, and in particular psychokinesis, would then become more understandable, for every physical event would involve a psychic one and vice versa. Such reflections are not idle speculations; they are forced on us in any serious psychological investigation of the Ufo phenomenon, as the next chapter will show.

5. UFOS CONSIDERED IN A
NON-PSYCHOLOGICAL LIGHT

781   As I said at the beginning, it was the purpose of this essay to treat the Ufos primarily as a psychological phenomenon. There were plenty of reasons for this, as is abundantly clear from the contradictory and "impossible" assertions made by the rumour. It is quite right that they should meet with criticism, scepticism, and open rejection, and if anyone should see behind them nothing more than a phantasm that deranges the minds of men and engenders rationalistic resistances, he would have nothing but our sympathy. Indeed, since conscious and unconscious fantasy, and even mendacity, obviously play an important role in building up the rumour, we could be satisfied with the psychological explanation and let it rest at that.

782   Unfortunately, however, there are good reasons why the Ufos cannot be disposed of in this simple manner. So far as I know it remains an established fact, supported by numerous observations, that Ufos have not only been seen visually but have also been picked up on the radar screen and have left traces on the photographic plate. I base myself here not only on the comprehensive reports by Ruppelt and Keyhoe, which leave no room for doubt in this regard, but also on the fact that the astrophysicist, Professor Menzel, has not succeeded, despite all his efforts, in offering a satisfying scientific explanation of even one authentic Ufo report. It boils down to nothing less than this: that either psychic projections throw back a radar echo, or else the appearance of real objects affords an opportunity for mythological projections.

783   Here I must remark that even if the Ufos are physically real, the corresponding psychic projections are not actually caused, but are only occasioned, by them. Mythical statements of this kind have always occurred, whether Ufos exist or not. These statements depend in the first place on the peculiar nature of

413

the psychic background, the collective unconscious, and for this reason have always been projected in some form. At various times all sorts of other projections have appeared in the heavens besides the saucers. This particular projection, together with its psychological context, the rumour, is specific of our age and highly characteristic of it. The dominating idea of a mediator and god who became man, after having thrust the old polytheistic beliefs into the background, is now in its turn on the point of evaporating. Untold millions of so-called Christians have lost their belief in a real and living mediator, while the believers endeavour to make their belief credible to primitive people, when it would be so much more fruitful to bestow these much needed efforts on the white man. But it is always so much easier and more affecting to talk and act *down* to people instead of *up* to them. St. Paul spoke to the populace of Athens and Rome, but what is Albert Schweitzer doing in Lambarene? People like him are needed much more urgently in Europe.

784   No Christian will contest the importance of a belief like that of the mediator, nor will he deny the consequences which the loss of it entails. So powerful an idea reflects a profound psychic need which does not simply disappear when the expression of it ceases to be valid. What happens to the energy that once kept the idea alive and dominant over the psyche? A political, social, philosophical, and religious conflict of unprecedented proportions has split the consciousness of our age. When such tremendous opposites split asunder, we may expect with certainty that the need for a saviour will make itself felt. Experience has amply confirmed that, in the psyche as in nature, a tension of opposites creates a potential which may express itself at any time in a manifestation of energy. Between above and below flows the waterfall, and between hot and cold there is a turbulent exchange of molecules. Similarly, between the psychic opposites there is generated a "uniting symbol," at first unconscious. This process is running its course in the unconscious of modern man. Between the opposites there arises spontaneously a symbol of unity and wholeness, no matter whether it reaches consciousness or not. Should something extraordinary or impressive then occur in the outside world, be it a human personality, a thing, or an idea, the unconscious content can project itself upon it, thereby investing the projection carrier with

numinous and mythical powers. Thanks to its numinosity, the projection carrier has a highly suggestive effect and grows into a saviour myth whose basic features have been repeated count-less times.

785   The impetus for the manifestation of the latent psychic con-tents was given by the Ufo. The only thing we know with tol-erable certainty about Ufos is that they possess a surface which can be seen by the eye and at the same time throws back a radar echo. Everything else is so uncertain that it must remain for the time being an unproven conjecture, or rumour, until we know more about it. We do not know, either, whether they are manned machines or a species of living creature which has appeared in our atmosphere from an unknown source. It is not likely that they are meteoric phenomena, since their behaviour does not give the impression of a process that could be inter-preted in physical terms. Their movements indicate volition and psychic relatedness, e.g., evasion and flight, perhaps even aggression and defence. Their progression in space is not in a straight line and of constant velocity like a meteor, but erratic like the flight of an insect and of varying velocity, from zero to several thousand miles per hour. The observed speeds and angles of turn are such that no earthly being could survive them any more than he could the enormous heat generated by fric-tion.

786   The simultaneous visual and radar sightings would in them-selves be a satisfactory proof of their reality. Unfortunately, well-authenticated reports show that there are also cases where the eye sees something that does not appear on the radar screen, or where an object undoubtedly picked up by radar is not seen by the eye. I will not mention other, even more remarkable reports from authoritative sources; they are so bizarre that they tax our understanding and credulity to the limit.

787   If these things are real—and by all human standards it hardly seems possible to doubt this any longer—then we are left with only two hypotheses: that of their *weightlessness* on the one hand and of their *psychic nature* on the other. This is a ques-tion I for one cannot decide. In the circumstances, however, it seemed to me advisable at least to investigate the *psychological aspect* of the phenomenon, so as to throw a little light on this complicated situation. I have limited myself to only a few

415

examples. Unfortunately, after more than ten years' study of the problem I have not managed to collect a sufficient number of observations from which more reliable conclusions could be drawn. I must therefore content myself with having sketched out a few lines for future research. Of course, next to nothing has been gained as regards a physical explanation of the phenomenon. But the psychic aspect plays so great a role that it cannot be left out of account. The discussion of it, as I have tried to show, leads to psychological problems which involve just as fantastic possibilities or impossibilities as the approach from the physical side. If military authorities have felt compelled to set up bureaus for collecting and evaluating Ufo reports, then psychology, too, has not only the right but also the duty to do what it can to shed light on this dark problem.

788   The question of anti-gravity is one which I must leave to the physicists, who alone can inform us what chances of success such an hypothesis has. The alternative hypothesis that Ufos are something psychic that is endowed with certain physical properties seems even less probable, for where should such a thing come from? If weightlessness is a hard proposition to swallow, then the notion of a materialized psychism opens a bottomless void under our feet. Parapsychology is, of course, acquainted with the fact of materialization. But this phenomenon depends on the presence of one or more mediums who exude a weighable substance, and it occurs only in their immediate vicinity. The psyche can move the body, but only inside the living organism. That something psychic, possessing material qualities and with a high charge of energy, could appear by itself high in the air at a great distance from any human mediums—this surpasses our comprehension. Here our knowledge leaves us completely in the lurch, and it is therefore pointless to speculate any further in this direction.

789   It seems to me—speaking with all due reserve—that there is a third possibility: that Ufos are real material phenomena of an unknown nature, presumably coming from outer space, which perhaps have long been visible to mankind, but otherwise have no recognizable connection with the earth or its inhabitants. In recent times, however, and just at the moment when the eyes of mankind are turned towards the heavens, partly on account of their fantasies about possible space-ships, and partly in a

figurative sense because their earthly existence is threatened, unconscious contents have projected themselves on these inexplicable heavenly phenomena and given them a significance they in no way deserve. Since they seem to have appeared more frequently after the second World War than before, it may be that they are synchronistic phenomena or "meaningful coincidences." The psychic situation of mankind and the Ufo phenomenon as a physical reality bear no recognizable causal relationship to one another, but they seem to coincide in a meaningful manner. The meaningful connection is the product on the one hand of projection and on the other of round and cylindrical forms which embody the projected meaning and have always symbolized the union of opposites.

790   Another equally "chance" coincidence is the choice of the national emblems for aircraft in the U.S.S.R. and the U.S.A.: respectively a red and white five-pointed star. For a thousand years red was regarded as the masculine and white as the feminine colour. The alchemists spoke of the *servus rubeus* (red slave) and the *femina candida* (white woman): their copulation produced the supreme union of opposites. When one speaks of Russia, one immediately thinks of "Little Father" Czar and "Little Father" Stalin. One also remembers all the talk about America being a matriarchy because the bulk of American capital is in the hands of women, not to mention Keyserling's *bon mot* about the "aunt of the nation." [1] It is clear that these parallels have nothing to do with the choice of symbols, at any rate not as a conscious causality. Comically enough—one must say—red and white are the nuptial colours. They throw an amusing light on Soviet Russia as the reluctant or unrequited lover of the *femina candida* in the White House—even if there is nothing more to it than that.

1 See infra, par. 931.

EPILOGUE

791   I had already completed my manuscript when a little book fell into my hands which I ought not to leave unmentioned: *The Secret of the Saucers*, by Orfeo M. Angelucci (1955). The author is self-taught and describes himself as a nervous individual suffering from "constitutional inadequacy." After working at various jobs he was employed as a mechanic in 1952 at the Lockheed Aircraft Corporation at Burbank, California. He seems to lack any kind of humanistic culture, but appears to have a knowledge of science that exceeds what would be expected of a person in his circumstances. He is an Americanized Italian, naïve and—if appearances do not deceive us—serious and idealistic. He makes his living now by preaching the gospel revealed to him by the Saucers. That is the reason why I mention his book.

792   His career as a prophet began with the sighting of a supposedly authentic Ufo on August 4, 1946. At the time he had no further interest in the problem. He was working in his free hours on a book entitled "The Nature of Infinite Entities," which he subsequently published at his own expense. He describes its content as "Atomic Evolution, Suspension, and Involution, Origin of the Cosmic Rays," etc. On May 23, 1952, he underwent the experience that gave him his calling. Towards 11 o'clock in the evening, he says, he felt unwell and had a "prickling" sensation in the upper half of his body, as before an electrical storm. He was working the nightshift, and as he was driving home in his car he saw a faintly red-glowing, oval-shaped object hovering over the horizon, which nobody else seemed to see. On a lonely stretch of the road, where it rose above the level of the surrounding terrain, he saw below him the glowing red disk "pulsating" near the ground only a short distance away. Suddenly it shot upwards with great speed at an angle of 30 to 40 degrees and disappeared towards the west. But

before it vanished, it released two balls of green fire from which a man's voice issued, speaking "perfect English." He could remember the words: "Don't be afraid, Orfeo, we are friends!" The voice bade him get out of the car. This he did, and, leaning against the car, he watched the two "pulsating" disks hovering a short distance in front of him. The voice explained to him that the lights were "instruments of transmission and reception" (i.e., a species of sense-organs) and that he was in direct communication with "friends from another world." It also asked him if he remembered his experience on August 4, 1946. All at once he felt very thirsty, and the voice told him: "Drink from the crystal cup you will find on the fender of your car." He drank, and it was the "most delicious beverage I had ever tasted." He felt refreshed and strengthened. The twin disks were about three feet apart. "Suddenly the area between them began to glow with a soft green light which gradually formed into a luminous three-dimensional screen." In it there appeared the heads and shoulders of two persons, a man and a woman, "being the ultimate of perfection." They had large shining eyes, and despite their supernatural perfection they seemed strangely familiar to him. They observed him and the whole scene. It seemed to him that he was in telepathic communication with them. As suddenly as it had come the vision vanished, and the fireballs reassumed their former brilliance. He heard the words, "The road will open, Orfeo," and the voice continued:

"We see the individuals of Earth as each one really is, Orfeo, and not as perceived by the limited senses of man. The people of your planet have been under observation for centuries, but have only recently been re-surveyed. Every point of progress in your society is registered with us. We know you as you do not know yourselves. Every man, woman, and child is recorded in vital statistics by means of our recording crystal disks. Each of you is infinitely more important to us than to your fellow Earthlings because you are not aware of the true mystery of your being. . . . We feel a deep sense of brotherhood toward Earth's inhabitants because of an ancient kinship of our planet with Earth. In you we can look far back in time and recreate certain aspects of our former world. With deep compassion and understanding we have watched your world going through its 'growing pains.' We ask that you look upon us simply as older brothers."

419

793   The author was also informed that the Ufos were remote-controlled by a mother-ship. The occupants of Ufos needed in reality no such vessels. As "etheric" entities they needed them only in order to manifest themselves materially to man. The Ufos could travel approximately with the speed of light. "The Speed of Light is the Speed of Truth" (i.e., quick as thought). The heavenly visitors were harmless and filled with the best intentions. "Cosmic law" forbade spectacular landings on earth. The earth was at present threatened by greater dangers than was realized.

794   After these revelations Angelucci felt exalted and strengthened. It was "as though momentarily I had transcended mortality and was somehow related to these superior beings." When the lights disappeared, it seemed to him that the everyday world had lost its reality and become an abode of shadows.

795   On July 23, 1952, he felt unwell and stayed away from work. In the evening he took a walk, and on the way back, in a lonely place, similar sensations came over him as he had felt on May 23. Combined with them was "the dulling of consciousness I had noted on that other occasion," i.e., the awareness of an *abaissement du niveau mental,* a state which is a very important precondition for the occurrence of spontaneous psychic phenomena. Suddenly he saw a luminous object on the ground before him, like an "igloo" or a "huge, misty soap bubble." This object visibly increased in solidity, and he saw something like a doorway leading into a brightly lit interior. He stepped inside, and found himself in a vaulted room, about eighteen feet in diameter. The walls were made of some "ethereal mother-of-pearl stuff."

796   Facing him was a comfortable reclining chair consisting of the same translucent, shimmering substance. Otherwise the room was empty and silent. He sat down and had the feeling that he was suspended in air. It was as if the chair moulded itself to the shape of his body of its own accord. The door shut as if there had never been a door there at all. Then he heard a kind of humming, a rhythmical sound like a vibration, which put him into a kind of semi-dream state. The room grew dark, and music came from the walls. Then it grew light again. He found on the floor a piece of metal like a coin. When he took it in his hand, it seemed to diminish in size. He had the feeling

that the Ufo was carrying him away. Suddenly something like a round window opened, about nine feet in diameter. Outside he saw a planet, the earth, from a distance of over a thousand miles, as a voice he recognized explained to him. He wept with emotion and the voice said: "Weep, Orfeo . . . we weep with you for earth and her children. For all its apparent beauty earth is a purgatorial world among the planets evolving intelligent life. Hate, selfishness, and cruelty rise from many parts of it like a dark mist." Then, he says, the craft evidently moved out into cosmic space. Through the window he saw a Ufo about one thousand feet long and ninety feet thick, consisting of a transparent crystalline substance. Music poured from it, bringing visions of harmoniously revolving planets and galaxies. The voice informed him that every being on earth was divinely created, and "upon your world the mortal shadows of those entities are working out their salvation from the plane of darkness." All these entities were either on the good side or on the bad. "We know where you stand, Orfeo." Owing to his physical weakness he had spiritual gifts, and that was why the heavenly beings could enter into communication with him. He was given to understand that the music as well as the voice emanated from this huge spaceship. It moved off slowly, and he noticed at either end of it "vortices of flame" that served as propellers, but they were also instruments for seeing and hearing, "through some method of telepathic contact."

797   On the way back they met two ordinary Ufos travelling earthwards. The voice entertained him with more explanations concerning the attitude of the higher beings to mankind: man had not kept pace morally and psychologically with his technological development, and therefore the inhabitants of other planets were trying to instil into the earth dwellers a better understanding of their present predicament and to help them particularly in the art of healing. They also wanted to put Orfeo right about Jesus Christ. Jesus, so they said, was called allegorically the son of God. In reality he was the "Lord of the Flame," "an infinite entity of the Sun" and not of earthly origin. "As the Sun spirit who sacrificed Himself for the children of woe he has become a part of the oversoul of mankind and the world spirit. In this he differs from all other cosmic teachers."

421

798 Everyone on earth has a "spiritual, unknown self which transcends the material world and consciousness and dwells eternally outside of the Time dimension in spiritual perfection within the unity of the oversoul." The sole purpose of human existence on earth is to attain reunion with the "immortal consciousness." Under the searching eye of this "great compassionate consciousness" Orfeo felt like a "crawling worm—unclean, filled with error and sin." He wept, once more to the accompaniment of appropriate music. The voice spoke and said: "Beloved friend of Earth, we baptize you now in the true light of the worlds eternal." A white flash of lightning blazed forth: his life lay clear before his eyes, and the remembrance of all his previous existences came back to him. He understood "the mystery of life." He thought he was going to die, for he knew that at this moment he was wafted into "eternity, into a timeless sea of bliss."

799 After this illuminative experience he came to himself again. Accompanied by the obligatory "etheric" music he was borne back to earth. As he left the Ufo, it suddenly vanished without trace. Afterwards, on going to bed, he noticed a burning sensation on the left side of his chest. There he found a stigma the size of a twenty-five-cent piece, an inflamed circle with a dot in the middle. He interpreted this as the "symbol of the hydrogen atom."

800 His career as an evangelist dates—true to form—from this experience. He became a witness not only of the word but of the Ufo, and was exposed to the mockery and disbelief that are the lot of the martyr. On the night of August 2 of the same year he saw, with eight other witnesses, an ordinary Ufo in the sky, which disappeared after a short time. He betook himself to the lonely spot he had previously visited, but though he didn't find the Ufo he met a figure who called out to him, "Greetings, Orfeo!" It was the same figure he had seen in the earlier vision, who wished to be called by the name of "Neptune." He was a tall handsome man with unusually large and expressive eyes. The edges of the figure rippled like water in the wind. Neptune gave him more information concerning the earth, the reasons for its lamentable conditions, and its coming redemption. Then he vanished.

801   At the beginning of September 1953 he fell into a somnambulistic state which lasted about a week. When he returned to his normal consciousness he remembered everything he had experienced during his "absence." He had been on a small "planetoid" where Neptune dwelt with his companion Lyra; or rather, he had been in heaven as Orfeo imagined it, with countless flowers, delightful odours, colours, nectar and ambrosia, noble etheric beings and, of course, almost incessant music. There he discovered that his heavenly friend was not called Neptune but Orion, and that "Neptune" had been his own name while he was still dwelling in this heavenly world. Lyra showed him particular marks of attention, to which he, the re-remembered Neptune, in accordance with his earthly nature, responded with erotic feelings, much to the horror of the celestial company. When he had dehabituated himself, with some effort, from this all-too-human reaction a *noce céleste* was celebrated, a mystic union analogous to the *coniunctio oppositorum* in alchemy.

802   With this climax I will end the account of this *pélerinage de l'âme*. Without having the faintest inkling of psychology, Angelucci has described in the greatest detail the mystic experience associated with a Ufo vision. A detailed commentary by me is hardly necessary. The story is so naïve and clear that a reader interested in psychology can see at once how far it confirms my previous conclusions. It could even be regarded as a unique document that sheds a great deal of light on the genesis and assimilation of Ufo mythology. That is why I have let Angelucci have his say.

803   The psychological experience that is associated with the Ufo consists in the vision of the *rotundum,* the symbol of wholeness and the archetype that expresses itself in mandala form. Mandalas, as we know, usually appear in situations of psychic confusion and perplexity. The archetype thereby constellated represents a pattern of order which, like a psychological "viewfinder" marked with a cross or a circle divided into four, is superimposed on the psychic chaos so that each content falls into place and the weltering confusion is held together by the protective circle. The Eastern mandalas in Mahayana Buddhism accordingly represent the cosmic, temporal, and psychological

order. At the same time they are *yantras,* instruments with whose help order is brought into being.[1]

804 As our time is characterized by fragmentation, confusion, and perplexity, this fact is also expressed in the psychology of the individual, appearing in spontaneous fantasy images, dreams, and the products of active imagination. I have observed these phenomena in my patients for forty years and have come to the conclusion that this archetype is of central importance, or rather, that it gains in importance to the degree that the importance of the ego is lost. A state of disorientation is particularly apt to depotentiate the ego.

805 Psychologically, the rotundum or mandala is a symbol of the self. The self is the archetype of order par excellence. The structure of the mandala is arithmetical, for "whole" numbers are likewise archetypes of order. This is true particularly of the number 4, the Pythagorean tetraktys. Since a state of confusion is generally the result of a psychic conflict, we find in practice that the dyad, the conjoined two, is also associated with the mandala. This appears in Angelucci's vision of the synthesis of opposites.

806 Its central position gives the symbol a high feeling-value, expressed for instance in Angelucci's stigmatization. The symbols of the self coincide with the God-images, as, for instance, the *complexio oppositorum* of Cusanus with the dyad, or the definition of God as a "circle whose centre is everywhere and the circumference nowhere" with Angelucci's sign of the hydrogen atom. He was marked not by the Christian stigmata but by the symbol of the self, of absolute wholeness or, in religious language, God. These psychological connections gave rise to the alchemical equation between Christ and the *lapis Philosophorum.*

807 The centre is frequently symbolized by an eye: the ever-open eye of the fish in alchemy, or the unsleeping "God's eye" of conscience, or the all-seeing sun. The same symbols are experienced today, not as external light-phenomena but as a psychic revelation. I would like to mention as an example the case of a woman who wrote down her experience in verse form (it had no connection with Ufos):

1 For the physiological foundations see K. W. Bash, H. Ahlenstiel, and R. Kaufmann, "Ueber Präyantraformen und ein lineares Yantra."

Vision

Light strikes the pebbled bottom
Of a deep blue pool.
Through swaying grass
A jewel flickers, gleams and turns,
Demands attention as I pass,
A staring fish-eye's glance
Attracts my mind and heart—
The fish, invisible as glass.

A shimmering silver moon,
The fish, assuming shape and form,
Evolves a whirling, swirling dance,
Intensity of light increasing,
The disk becomes a blazing golden sun,
Compelling deeper contemplation.

808   The water is the depths of the unconscious into which a ray
from the light of consciousness has penetrated. A dancing disk,
a fish's eye, swims down below in the inner darkness (instead of
flying in the heavens), and from it arises a world-illuminating
sun, an Ichthys, a *sol invictus,* an ever-open eye which reflects
the eye of the beholder and is at the same time something independent of her, a rotundum that expresses the wholeness of the
self and cannot be distinguished, except conceptually, from the
deity. "Fish" (Ichthys) and "sun" (*novus sol*) are allegories of
Christ, which like the "eye" stand for God. In the moon and
sun appear the divine mother and her son-lover, as can still be
seen today in many churches.

809   The Ufo vision follows the old rule and appears in the sky.
Orfeo's fantasies are played out in an obviously heavenly place
and his cosmic friends bear the names of stars. If they are not
antique gods and heroes they are at least angels. The author
certainly lives up to his name, for just as his wife, *née* Bor-
gianini, is in his opinion a descendant of the Borgias of unhappy memory, so he, an earthly copy of the "angels" and a
messenger bringing Eleusinian tidings of immortality, must
style himself a new Orpheus, divinely appointed to initiate us
into the mystery of the Ufo. Not even the Orphean strains are
lacking. If the name is a deliberately chosen pseudonym, we can

only say *è ben trovato*. But if it appears in his birth certificate, then the matter becomes more problematical. Today we can no longer suppose that a magical compulsion attaches to a mere name, else we should have to attribute a correspondingly sinister significance to his spouse, or the anima. Much as we would like to credit him with an intellectually rather limited, naïve good faith, it might be suspected that a "fine Italian hand" is at work. What appears impossible from the conscious standpoint can often be arranged by the unconscious with all the craftiness of nature: *Ce que diable ne peut, femme le fait.* Be that as it may, Orfeo's book is an essentially naïve production which for that very reason reveals all the more clearly the unconscious background of the Ufo phenomenon and therefore comes like a gift to the psychologist. The individuation process, the central problem of modern psychology, is plainly depicted in it in an unconscious, symbolical form which bears out our previous reflections, although the author with his somewhat primitive mentality has taken it quite literally as a concrete happening.

*

810   This epilogue was already in the press when I received word of Fred Hoyle's book, *The Black Cloud* (1957). The author is a well-known authority on astrophysics, and I was already acquainted with his two impressive volumes, *The Nature of the Universe* and *Frontiers of Astronomy.* They are brilliant expositions of the latest developments in astronomy and show their author as a bold and imaginative thinker. The fact that such an author should resort to a science-fiction story aroused my curiosity, and I read the book at once. Hoyle himself, in his preface, describes it as a "frolic," a jest, and warns against anyone identifying the views of his hero, a mathematician of genius, with his own. No intelligent reader will fall into this error, of course. Nevertheless, he will hold Professor Hoyle responsible for the authorship of his book, and he will ask what it was that induced him to tackle the Ufo problem.

811   In his "yarn" Hoyle describes how a young astronomer at the Mount Palomar observatory, while looking for supernovae to the south of Orion, discovers a dark circular patch in a dense field of stars. It is a so-called globulus, a dark cloud of gas, which, it transpires, is moving towards our solar system. At the same time, in England, considerable disturbances are detected

in the orbits of Jupiter and Saturn. The cause of this is calculated by a Cambridge mathematician, the hero of our story, to be a definite mass which, it then turns out, is located exactly at the spot where the Americans discovered the black cloud. This globulus, whose diameter is approximately equal to the distance of the sun from the earth, consists of hydrogen of fairly high density and is moving straight towards the earth at forty miles a second. It will reach the earth in about eighteen months. As the black cloud gets nearer, it causes first of all a terrible heat that kills off a large part of the life on earth. This is followed by a total extinction of light and a more than Egyptian darkness lasting for about a month—a *nigredo* like that described in the *Aurora consurgens,* a treatise ascribed to St. Thomas Aquinas: "Beholding from afar I saw a great cloud looming black over all the earth, which had absorbed the earth and covered my soul." [2]

812 When the light reappears again, there follows a period of terrible cold, which causes another appalling catastrophe. Meanwhile, the scientists in question have been shut up by the British government in their experimental location, where, thanks to the security measures they have taken, they survive the catastrophes. By observing certain remarkable ionization phenomena in the atmosphere they come to the conclusion that these are intentionally induced, and that in consequence there must be an intelligent agent in the black cloud. By means of radio they succeed in entering into communication with it, and receive answers. They learn that the cloud is five hundred million years old and is at present engaged in regenerating itself. It has taken up its position near the sun in order to recharge itself with energy. In fact, it is feeding on the sun. The scientists discover that the cloud must eliminate all radioactive substances, as these are harmful to it. This fact is also discovered by the American observers, and at their instigation the cloud is fired at with H-bombs, with the intention of "killing" it. The cloud, meanwhile, has settled in a disk round the sun, consequently threatening the earth every six months with eclipses of several weeks' duration. The English naturally have a host of questions to ask the cloud, including the "metaphysical" question concern-

2 Von Franz, ed., *Aurora Consurgens,* pp. 57 and 217ff.

ing a greater Being of still greater age, and even deeper wisdom and scientific knowledge. The cloud replies that it has already discussed the matter with other globuli but is as much in the dark about it as human beings. It is willing, however, to communicate its own greater knowledge directly to mankind. A young physicist declares himself ready to submit to the experiment. He gets into a hypnotic condition, but dies of a sort of inflammation of the brain before being able to make any communication. The Cambridge mathematician of genius now offers himself for experiment, on the condition, accepted by the cloud, that the process of communication shall take place very much more slowly. In spite of that he falls into a delirium which ends in his death. The cloud, however, has decided to quit the solar system and seek out another region of fixed stars. The sun emerges again from obscurity and everything is as before, except for the tremendous destruction of earthly life.

813   It is not difficult to see that the author has here taken up the Ufo problem so characteristic of our epoch: from outer space a round object approaches the earth and causes a world-wide catastrophe. Although the legend usually considers the catastrophic political situation, or rather nuclear fission, to be the indirect cause of the Ufo phenomenon, there are not a few people who suspect that the real danger lies in the appearance of Ufos themselves—namely an invasion of the earth by star-dwellers, which might give an unexpected and probably undesirable turn to our already questionable situation. The strange idea that the black cloud possesses a sort of nervous system, and a psyche or intelligence to match, is not an original invention of the author's, since speculative ufologists have already arrived at the hypothesis of a "sentient electrical field," and also at the idea that the Ufos are provisioning themselves with something on earth—water, oxygen, small organisms, etc., just as the cloud charged itself with solar energy.

814   The cloud causes opposite extremes of temperature and an absolute *nigredo* such as the old alchemists dreamed of. This illustrates a characteristic aspect of the psychological problem which arises when the light of day—consciousness—is directly confronted with night, the collective unconscious. Opposites of extreme intensity collide with one another, causing a disorientation and darkening of consciousness which can assume threaten-

ing proportions, as in the initial stage of a psychosis. This aspect, i.e., the analogy with a psychic catastrophe, is depicted by Hoyle as the encounter between the psychic content of the cloud and the consciousness of the two unfortunate victims. Just as earthly life is largely wiped out by the collision with the cloud, so the psyche and the life of the two scientists are destroyed by the collision with the unconscious. For although the *rotundum* is a totality symbol, it usually encounters a consciousness that is not prepared for it and does not understand it, indeed is bound to misunderstand it and therefore cannot tolerate it, because it perceives the totality only in projected form, outside itself, and cannot integrate it as a subjective phenomenon. Consciousness commits the same grave mistake as the insane person: it understands the event as a concrete external happening and not as a subjective symbolical process. The result is that the external world gets into hopeless disorder and is actually "destroyed" in so far as the patient loses his relationship to it. The author suggests the analogy with psychosis by the delirious state of the professor. It is not only the insane person who makes this fundamental mistake, but all those who take philosophical or theosophical speculations for objective realities and consider the mere fact that they believe in angels as a guarantee that such things exist in reality.

815   It is significant that it is the actual hero of the story, the mathematician of genius, who meets with disaster. No author can avoid equipping his hero with some of his own qualities and thus betraying that at least a part of himself is invested in him. What happens to the hero also happens symbolically to the author. In this case it is naturally unpleasant, for it amounts to nothing less than the fear that a collision with the unconscious would involve the destruction of the most differentiated function. It is a widespread, in fact a normal prejudice that deeper insight into unconscious motives must necessarily entail a fatal disturbance of the conscious performance. The most that can happen is an alteration of the conscious attitude. Since, in our story, everything is projected outside, mankind and all organic life on earth suffer an immense loss. The author makes no particular to-do about this; it is mentioned only as a sort of byproduct. From this we may infer a predominantly intellectual attitude of consciousness.

816 Presumably not altogether unimpressed by a hundred or more H-bombs, which might well upset its nervous system with their radioactivity, the black cloud withdraws as suddenly as it came. Nothing whatever has been learned of its contents, except that it knows as little about a metaphysical Supreme Being as we do. Nevertheless its intelligence proves unendurably high for human beings, so that it comes suspiciously near to having a divine or angel-like nature. Here the great astrophysicist joins hands with the naïve Angelucci.

817 Understood psychologically, the story is a description of fantasy-contents whose symbolical nature demonstrates their origin in the unconscious. Whenever a confrontation of this kind occurs, there is usually an attempt at integration. This is expressed in the intention of the cloud to remain for some time near the sun, in order to feed on its energy. Psychologically it would mean that the unconscious draws strength and life from its union with the sun. The sun loses no energy, but the earth and its life, signifying man, lose a great deal. Man has to pay the price for this invasion or irruption of the unconscious: his psychic life is threatened with the gravest injury.

818 What, then—psychologically speaking—is the meaning of this cosmic, or rather psychic, collision? Obviously the unconscious darkens the conscious, since no *rapprochement*, no dialectical process takes place between their contents. For the individual this means that the cloud deprives him of solar energy, in other words his consciousness is overpowered by the unconscious. This is equivalent to a general catastrophe, such as we have experienced in National Socialism and are still experiencing in the Communist inundation, where an archaic social order threatens our freedom with tyranny and slavery. Man replies to this catastrophe with his "best" weapon. Whether for this reason or from a change of mind (as seems more likely), the cloud withdraws to other regions. This means, psychologically: the unconscious, after gaining a certain amount of energy, sinks back again to its former distance. The final outcome is depressing: human consciousness and life in general suffer an incalculable loss through an incomprehensible *lusus naturae* that lacks all human meaning, a "frolic" on a cosmic scale.

819 This in turn points to something psychic that is not understood by the present. Though the nightmare is over for the sur-

vivors, from now on they live in a devastated world. Consciousness has suffered a loss of its own reality, as though the evil
dream had robbed it of something essential and made off with
it. The loss consists in missing a unique opportunity, which may
never occur again, to come to terms with the contents of the
unconscious. Although it was possible to establish an intelligent connection with the cloud, the communication of its contents proved to be unendurable and led to the death of those
who submitted to the experiment. Nothing is learnt of the contents from the other side. The encounter with the unconscious
ends bootlessly. Our knowledge is not enriched; on this point
we remain where we were before the catastrophe. The only
thing is that we are at least half a world poorer. The scientific
pioneers, the spokesmen of the *avant-garde,* prove too weak or
too immature to receive the message from the unconscious. It
remains to be seen whether this melancholy outcome is a
prophecy or a subjective confession.

820   If we compare this tale with the naïvetés of Angelucci, we
get a valuable picture of the difference between the uneducated
and the scientifically educated attitude. Both shift the problem
on to a concrete plane, the one in order to make us believe in a
saving action from heaven, the other in order to transform this
secret yet somewhat sinister expectation into an entertaining
literary joke. Both, poles apart though they are, are activated by
the same unconscious factor and make use of essentially the
same symbolism in order to express the unconscious straits we
are in.

Supplement

821   Another recent book, a novel by John Wyndham called *The
Midwich Cuckoos* (1957), attributes to a "thing," which is obviously a Ufo, a highly significant character. Of unknown but
presumably extra-terrestrial origin, this thing casts a spell on a
small, remote English village, causing man and beast to fall into
an hypnotic sleep which lasts for twenty-four hours. The zone
of sleep describes a circle round the village, and any living being that approaches instantly falls asleep when the magical line
is crossed. After twenty-four hours everybody revives, and nothing seems to have happened—on the surface.

822   Several weeks later peculiar discoveries are made: first one

and then another of the female population, and finally all its members capable of fecundation, are found to be pregnant. In due course children are born with golden eyes. When they develop, they begin to show signs of uncommon intelligence. Later it becomes known that the same miracle has befallen a village in Siberia, an Eskimo settlement, and an African village. In England, owing to the remoteness and insignificance of the locality, the village authorities succeed in hushing up a public scandal. The extraordinary intelligence of the children inevitably leads to trouble and a special school is founded for them. The amazing fact is discovered that, if one of the boys has learnt something new and hitherto unknown, all the boys know it, and the same is true of the girls, so that only one boy and one girl have to attend school. Finally the perspicacious schoolteacher can no longer doubt that the children with golden eyes represent a superior type of *Homo sapiens*. Their advanced intelligence is, moreover, coupled with a complete realization of their potential power for world domination. The question of how to deal with this menace leads to different solutions. The Africans kill the children immediately. The Eskimos expose them to the cold. The Russians, after isolating the village, destroy it by bombardment. But in England the favourite teacher introduces some boxes, apparently containing laboratory equipment but actually containing dynamite, into the schoolroom and blows himself up with all the children.

823 The peculiar parthenogenesis and the golden eyes denote kinship with the sun and characterize the children as divine progeny. Their fathers seem to have been angels of the annunciation who had come down from a "supracelestial place" to take care of the stupidity and backwardness of *Homo sapiens*. It is a divine intervention that gives evolution a definite push forward. Or, to put it in more modern terms, an advanced species of man from some other planet visits the earth in order to make biological experiments with mutation and artificial insemination. But the modern Neanderthal is in no way ready to renounce the prerogatives of the ruling race, and prefers to maintain the *status quo* by the devastating methods which have always been his final argument.

824 It is obvious that the sun children, miraculously begotten, represent an unexpected capacity for a wider and higher con-

sciousness, superseding a backward and inferior mental state. Nothing is said, however, about a higher level of feeling and morality, which would be necessary to compensate and regulate the possibilities of advanced perception and intellect. Characteristically enough, this aspect does not seem to enter the author's field of vision. It is sufficient for him that the children have a definite advantage of some kind over contemporary man. What if the children should symbolize the germ of some higher potentiality transcending the hitherto valid form of man? In that case the story looks very like a time-honoured repetition of the hero's threatened childhood and his early death through treachery. On the other hand there is something definitely suspect about these children: they are not separated individually but live in a permanent state of *participation mystique,* or unconscious identity, that precludes individual differentiation and development. Had they been spared an early extinction, they would have founded an entirely uniform society, the deadly boredom of which would have been the very ideal of a Marxist state. Thus the negative end of the story remains a matter for doubt.

VI

A PSYCHOLOGICAL VIEW
OF CONSCIENCE

———

GOOD AND EVIL IN
ANALYTICAL PSYCHOLOGY

———

INTRODUCTION TO WOLFF'S
"STUDIES IN JUNGIAN PSYCHOLOGY"

A PSYCHOLOGICAL VIEW OF CONSCIENCE [1]

825   The etymology of the word "conscience" tells us that it is a special form of "knowledge" or "consciousness." [2] The peculiarity of "conscience" is that it is a knowledge of, or certainty about, the emotional value of the ideas we have concerning the motives of our actions. According to this definition, conscience is a complex phenomenon consisting on the one hand in an elementary act of the will, or in an impulse to act for which no conscious reason can be given, and on the other hand in a judgment grounded on rational feeling. This judgment is a value judgment, and it differs from an intellectual judgment in that, besides having an objective, general, and impartial character, it reveals the subjective point of reference. A value judgment always implicates the subject, presupposing that something is good or beautiful *for me*. If, on the other hand, I say that it is good or beautiful for certain other people, this is not necessarily a value judgment but may just as well be an intellectual statement of fact. Conscience, therefore, is made up of two layers, the lower one comprising a particular psychic event, while the upper one is a kind of superstructure representing the positive or negative judgment of the subject.

826   As we might expect from the complexity of the phenomenon, its empirical phenomenology covers a very wide field. Conscience may appear as an act of conscious reflection which anticipates, accompanies, or follows certain psychic events, or as a mere emotional concomitant of them, in which case its moral character is not immediately evident. Thus, an apparently

---

1 [Originally published as "Das Gewissen in psychologischer Sicht," in *Universitas* (Stuttgart), June 1958; then in a symposium, *Das Gewissen* (Studien aus dem C. G. Jung-Institut, VII; Zurich, 1958).—EDITORS.]

2 [In the original, resp., *Gewissen, Wissen,* and *Bewusstsein.* Cf. L. *conscientia, scientia* (from *scire,* 'to know'), *conscius.*—EDITORS.]

groundless anxiety state may follow a certain action, without the subject being conscious of the least connection between them. Often the moral judgment is displaced into a dream which the subject does not understand. For example, a business man I knew was made what looked like a perfectly serious and honourable offer which, it turned out much later, would have involved him in a disastrous fraud had he accepted it. The following night after he received this offer, which as I say seemed to him quite acceptable, he dreamt that his hands and forearms were covered with black dirt. He could see no connection with the events of the previous day, because he was unable to admit to himself that the offer had touched him on the vulnerable spot: his expectation of a good business deal. I warned him about this, and he was careful enough to take certain precautions which did in fact save him from more serious harm. Had he examined the situation right at the beginning he would undoubtedly have had a bad conscience, for he would have understood that it was a "dirty business" which his morality would not have allowed him to touch. He would, as we say, have made his hands dirty. The dream represented this locution in pictorial form.

827   In this instance the classical characteristic of conscience, the *conscientia peccati* ("consciousness of sin"), is missing. Accordingly the specific feeling-tone of a bad conscience is missing too. Instead, the symbolical image of black hands appeared in a dream, calling his attention to some dirty work. In order to become conscious of his moral reaction, i.e., to feel his conscience, he had to tell the dream to me. This was an act of conscience on his part, in so far as dreams always made him feel rather uncertain. He had got this feeling of uncertainty in the course of an analysis, which showed him that dreams often contribute a great deal to self-knowledge. Without this experience he would probably have overlooked the dream.

828   From this we learn one important fact: the moral evaluation of an action, which expresses itself in the specific feeling-tone of the accompanying ideas, is not always dependent on consciousness but may function without it. Freud put forward the hypothesis that in these cases there is a repression exerted by a psychic factor, the so-called superego. But if the conscious mind is to accomplish the voluntary act of repression, we must presuppose

that there is some recognition of the moral obnoxiousness of the content to be repressed, for without this motive the corresponding impulse of the will cannot be released. But it was just this knowledge which the business man lacked, to such an extent that he not only felt no moral reaction but put only a limited trust in my warning. The reason for this was that he in no way recognized the dubious nature of the offer and therefore lacked any motive for repression. Hence the hypothesis of conscious repression cannot apply in this case.

29   What happened was in reality an unconscious act which accomplished itself as though it were conscious and intentional—as though, in other words, it were an act of conscience. It is as if the subject recognized the immorality of the offer and this recognition had released the appropriate emotional reaction. But the entire process took place subliminally, and the only trace it left behind was the dream, which, as a moral reaction, remained unconscious. "Conscience," in the sense in which we defined it above, as a "knowledge" of the ego, a *conscientia*, simply does not exist in this case. If conscience is a kind of knowledge, then it is not the empirical subject who is the knower, but rather an unconscious personality who, to all appearances, behaves like a conscious subject. It knows the dubious nature of the offer, it recognizes the acquisitive greed of the ego, which does not shrink even from illegality, and it causes the appropriate judgment to be pronounced. This means that the ego has been replaced by an unconscious personality who performs the necessary act of conscience.

30   It was these and similar experiences which led Freud to endow the superego with special significance. The Freudian superego is not, however, a natural and inherited part of the psyche's structure; it is rather the consciously acquired stock of traditional customs, the "moral code" as incorporated, for instance, in the Ten Commandments. The superego is a patriarchal legacy which, as such, is a conscious acquisition and an equally conscious possession. If it appears to be an almost unconscious factor in Freud's writings, this is due to his practical experience, which taught him that, in a surprising number of cases, the act of conscience takes place unconsciously, as in our example. Freud and his school rejected the hypothesis of inherited, instinctive modes of behaviour, termed by us arche-

439

types, as mystical and unscientific, and accordingly explained unconscious acts of conscience as repressions caused by the superego.

831   The concept of the superego contains nothing that, in itself, would not be recognized as belonging to the common stock of thought. To that extent it is identical with what we call the "moral code." The only peculiar thing about it is that one or the other aspect of the moral tradition proves unconscious in the individual case. We should also mention that Freud admitted the existence of "archaic vestiges" in the superego—of acts of conscience, therefore, which are influenced by archaic motifs. But since Freud disputed the existence of archetypes, that is, of genuine archaic modes of behaviour, we can only assume that by "archaic vestiges" he meant certain conscious traditions which may be unconscious in certain individuals. In no circumstances can it be a question of inborn types, for otherwise they would be, on his own hypothesis, inherited ideas. But that is just what he does mean, though so far as I know there are no proofs of their existence. There are, however, proofs in abundance for the hypothesis of inherited, instinctive modes of behaviour, namely the archetypes. It is therefore probable that the "archaic vestiges" in the superego are a concession to the archetypes theory and imply a fundamental doubt as to the absolute dependence of unconscious contents on consciousness. There are indeed good grounds for doubting this dependence: first, the unconscious is, ontogenetically and phylogenetically, older than consciousness, and secondly, it is a well-known fact that it can hardly be influenced, if at all, by the conscious will. It can only be repressed or suppressed, and only temporarily at that. As a rule its account has to be settled sooner or later. Were that not so, psychotherapy would be no problem. If the unconscious were dependent on consciousness, we could, by insight and application of the will, finally get the better of the unconscious, and the psyche could be completely remodelled to suit our purpose. Only unworldly idealists, rationalists, and other fanatics can indulge in such dreams. The psyche is a phenomenon not subject to our will; it is nature, and though nature can, by skill, knowledge, and patience, be modified at a few points, it cannot be changed into something artificial without profound

injury to our humanity. Man can be transformed into a sick animal but not moulded into an intellectual ideal.

832   Although people still labour under the delusion that consciousness represents the whole of the psychic man, it is nevertheless only a part, of whose relation to the whole we know very little. Since the unconscious component really is unconscious, no boundaries can be assigned to it: we cannot say where the psyche begins or ends. We know that consciousness and its contents are the modifiable part of the psyche, but the more deeply we seek to penetrate, at least indirectly, into the realm of the unconscious, the more the impression forces itself on us that we are dealing with something autonomous. We must admit that our best results, whether in education or treatment, occur when the unconscious co-operates, that is to say when the goal we are aiming at coincides with the unconscious trend of development, and that, conversely, our best methods and intentions fail when nature does not come to our aid. Without at least some degree of autonomy the common experience of the complementary or compensatory function of the unconscious would not be possible. If the unconscious were really dependent on the conscious, it could not contain more than, and other things than, consciousness contains.

833   Our dream-example and many other cases of the kind suggest that, since the subliminal moral judgment accords with the moral code, the dream has behaved in the same way as a consciousness backed by traditional moral law, and that, consequently, ordinary morality is a basic law of the unconscious or at any rate influences it. This conclusion stands in flagrant contradiction to the common experience of the autonomy of the unconscious. Although morality as such is a universal attribute of the human psyche, the same cannot be maintained of a given moral code. It cannot, therefore, be an integral part of the psyche's structure. Nevertheless, the fact remains—as our example shows—that the act of conscience operates, in principle, in exactly the same way in the unconscious as in the conscious, follows the same moral precepts, and therefore evokes the impression that the moral code also controls the unconscious process.

834   This impression is deceptive, because in practice there are just as many, and perhaps even more, examples where the

441

subliminal reaction does not conform at all to the moral code. Thus I was once consulted by a very distinguished lady—distinguished not only for her irreproachable conduct but also for her intensely "spiritual" attitude—on account of her "revolting" dreams. Her dreams did indeed deserve this epithet. She produced a whole series of extremely unsavoury dream-images all about drunken prostitutes, venereal diseases, and a lot more besides. She was horrified by these obscenities and could not understand why she, who had always striven for the highest, should be haunted by these apparitions from the abyss. She might just as well have asked why the saints are exposed to the vilest temptations. Here the moral code plays the contrary role— if it plays any role at all. Far from uttering moral exhortations, the unconscious delights in spawning every conceivable immorality, as though it had what was morally repulsive exclusively in mind. Experiences of this sort are so common and so regular that even St. Paul could confess: "For the good that I would I do not, but the evil which I would not, that I do" (Rom. 7 : 19).

835   In view of the fact that dreams lead astray as much as they exhort, it seems doubtful whether what appears to be a judgment of conscience should be evaluated as such—in other words, whether we should attribute to the unconscious a function which appears moral to us. Obviously we can understand dreams in a moral sense without at the same time assuming that the unconscious, too, connects them with any moral tendency. It seems, rather, that it pronounces moral judgments with the same objectivity with which it produces immoral fantasies. This paradox, or inner contradictoriness of conscience, has long been known to investigators of this question: besides the "right" kind of conscience there is a "wrong" one, which exaggerates, perverts, and twists evil into good and good into evil just as our own scruples do; and it does so with the same compulsiveness and with the same emotional consequences as the "right" kind of conscience. Were it not for this paradox the question of conscience would present no problem; we could then rely wholly on its decisions so far as morality is concerned. But since there is great and justified uncertainty in this regard, it needs unusual courage or—what amounts to the same thing—unshakable faith for a person simply to follow the dictates of his own conscience.

As a rule one obeys only up to a certain point, which is determined in advance by the moral code. This is where those dreaded conflicts of duty begin. Generally they are answered according to the precepts of the moral code, but only in a very few cases are they really decided by an individual act of judgment. For as soon as the moral code ceases to act as a support, conscience easily succumbs to a fit of weakness.

836   In practice it is indeed very difficult to distinguish conscience from the traditional moral precepts. For this reason it is often thought that conscience is nothing more than the suggestive effect of these precepts, and that it would not exist if no moral laws had been invented. But the phenomenon we call "conscience" is found at every level of human culture. Whether an Eskimo has a bad conscience about skinning an animal with an iron knife instead of the traditional flint one, or about leaving a friend in the lurch whom he ought to help, in both cases he feels an inner reproach, a "twinge of conscience," and in both cases the deviation from an inveterate habit or generally accepted rule produces something like a shock. For the primitive psyche anything unusual or not customary causes an emotional reaction, and the more it runs counter to the "collective representations" which almost invariably govern the prescribed mode of behaviour, the more violent the reaction will be. It is a peculiarity of the primitive mind to endow everything with mythical derivations that are meant to explain it. Thus everything that we would call pure chance is understood to be intentional and is regarded as a magical influence. Such explanations are in no sense "inventions"; they are spontaneous fantasy-products which appear without premeditation in a natural and quite involuntary way; unconscious, archetypal reactions such as are peculiar to the human psyche. Nothing could be more mistaken than to assume that a myth is something "thought up." It comes into existence of its own accord, as can be observed in all authentic products of fantasy, and particularly in dreams. It is the hybris of consciousness to pretend that everything derives from *its* primacy, despite the fact that consciousness itself demonstrably comes from an older unconscious psyche. The unity and continuity of consciousness are such late acquisitions that there is still a fear that they might get lost again.

837   So, too, our moral reactions exemplify the original behaviour

443

of the psyche, while moral laws are a late concomitant of moral behaviour, congealed into precepts. In consequence, they appear to be identical with the moral reaction, that is, with conscience. This delusion becomes obvious the moment a conflict of duty makes clear the difference between conscience and the moral code. It will then be decided which is the stronger: tradition and conventional morality, or conscience. Am I to tell the truth and thereby involve a fellow human being in catastrophe, or should I tell a lie in order to save a human life? In such dilemmas we are certainly not obeying our conscience if we stick obstinately and in all circumstances to the commandment: Thou shalt not lie. We have merely observed the moral code. But if we obey the judgment of conscience, we stand alone and have hearkened to a subjective voice, not knowing what the motives are on which it rests. No one can guarantee that he has only noble motives. We know—some of us—far too much about ourselves to pretend that we are one hundred per cent good and not egotists to the marrow. Always behind what we imagine are our best deeds stands the devil, patting us paternally on the shoulder and whispering, "Well done!"

838   Where does the true and authentic conscience, which rises above the moral code and refuses to submit to its dictates, get its justification from? What gives it the courage to assume that it is not a false conscience, a self-deception?

839   John says: "Try the spirits whether they are of God" (I John 4 : 1), an admonition we could profitably apply to ourselves. Since olden times conscience has been understood by many people less as a psychic function than as a divine intervention; indeed, its dictates were regarded as *vox Dei,* the voice of God. This view shows what value and significance were, and still are, attached to the phenomenon of conscience. The psychologist cannot disregard such an evaluation, for it too is a well-authenticated phenomenon that must be taken into account if we want to treat the idea of conscience psychologically. The question of "truth," which is usually raised here in a quite non-objective way, as to whether it has been proved that God himself speaks to us with the voice of conscience, has nothing to do with the psychological problem. The *vox Dei* is an assertion and an opinion, like the assertion that there is such a thing as conscience at all. All psychological facts which cannot be verified with the

444

help of scientific apparatus and exact methods of measurement are assertions and opinions, and, as such, are psychic realities. It is a *psychological truth* that the opinion exists that the voice of conscience is the voice of God.

840   Since, then, the phenomenon of conscience in itself does not coincide with the moral code, but is anterior to it, transcends its contents and, as already mentioned, can also be "false," the view of conscience as the voice of God becomes an extremely delicate problem. In practice it is very difficult to indicate the exact point at which the "right" conscience stops and the "false" one begins, and what the criterion is that divides one from the other. Presumably it is the moral code again, which makes it its business to know exactly what is good and what is evil. But if the voice of conscience is the voice of God, this voice must possess an incomparably higher authority than traditional morality. Anyone, therefore, who allows conscience this status should, for better or worse, put his trust in divine guidance and follow his conscience rather than give heed to conventional morality. If the believer had absolute confidence in his definition of God as the Summum Bonum, it would be easy for him to obey the inner voice, for he could be sure of never being led astray. But since, in the Lord's Prayer, we still beseech God not to lead us into temptation, this undermines the very trust the believer should have if, in the darkness of a conflict of duty, he is to obey the voice of conscience without regard to the "world" and, very possibly, act against the precepts of the moral code by "obeying God rather than men" (Acts 5 : 29).

841   Conscience—no matter on what it is based—commands the individual to obey his inner voice even at the risk of going astray. We can refuse to obey this command by an appeal to the moral code and the moral views on which it is founded, though with an uncomfortable feeling of having been disloyal. One may think what one likes about an ethos, yet an ethos is and remains an inner value, injury to which is no joke and can sometimes have very serious psychic consequences. These, admittedly, are known to relatively few people, for there are only a few who take objective account of psychic causality. The psyche is one of those things which people know least about, because no one likes to inquire into his own shadow. Even psychology is misused for the purpose of concealing the true causal

445

connections from oneself. The more "scientific" it pretends to be, the more welcome is its so-called objectivity, because this is an excellent way of getting rid of the inconvenient emotional components of conscience, notwithstanding that these are the real dynamics of the moral reaction. Without its emotional dynamism the phenomenon of conscience loses all meaning—which is, of course, the unconscious goal of the so-called "scientific" approach.

842 Conscience is, in itself, an autonomous psychic factor. All statements which do not directly deny it are agreed on this point. The clearest in this regard is the *vox Dei* concept. Here conscience is the voice of God, which often cuts sharply across our subjective intentions and may sometimes force an extremely disagreeable decision. If Freud himself attributed an almost daemonic power to the superego, although by definition it is not even a genuine conscience but merely human convention and tradition, this is in no sense an exaggeration: he was simply confirming the regular experience of the practising psychologist. Conscience is a demand that asserts itself in spite of the subject, or at any rate causes him considerable difficulties. This is not to deny that there are cases of lack of conscience. But the idea that conscience as such is only something learnt can be maintained only by those who imagine they were present on those prehistoric occasions when the first moral reactions came into existence. Conscience is far from being the only instance of an inner factor autonomously opposing the will of the subject. Every complex does that, and no one in his right senses would declare that it was "learnt" and that nobody would have a complex if it had not been hammered into him. Even domestic animals, to whom we erroneously deny a conscience, have complexes and moral reactions.

843 Primitive man regards the autonomy of the psyche as demonism and magic. This, we consider, is only what one would expect in primitive society. On closer inspection one finds, however, that the civilized man of antiquity, such as Socrates, still had his daemon and that there was a widespread and natural belief in superhuman beings who, we would suppose today, were personifications of projected unconscious contents. This belief has not, in principle, disappeared, but still persists in numerous variants. For instance, in the assumption that conscience is the

446

voice of God, or that it is a very important psychic factor (and one which manifests itself according to temperament, seeing that it usually accompanies the most differentiated function, as in the case of a "thinking" or a "feeling" morality). Again, where conscience seems to play no role, it appears indirectly in the form of compulsions or obsessions. These manifestations all go to show that the moral reaction is the outcome of an autonomous dynamism, fittingly called man's daemon, genius, guardian angel, better self, heart, inner voice, the inner and higher man, and so forth. Close beside these, beside the positive, "right" conscience, there stands the negative, "false" conscience called the devil, seducer, tempter, evil spirit, etc. Everyone who examines his conscience is confronted with this fact, and he must admit that the good exceeds the bad only by a very little, if at all. It is therefore quite in order for St. Paul to admit to having his "messenger of Satan" (II Corinthians 12 : 7). We ought to avoid sin and occasionally we can; but, as experience shows, we fall into sin again at the very next step. Only unconscious and wholly uncritical people can imagine it possible to abide in a permanent state of moral goodness. But because most people are devoid of self-criticism, permanent self-deception is the rule. A more developed consciousness brings the latent moral conflict to light, or else sharpens those opposites which are already conscious. Reason enough to eschew self-knowledge and psychology altogether and to treat the psyche with contempt!

844   There is scarcely any other psychic phenomenon that shows the polarity of the psyche in a clearer light than conscience. Its undoubted dynamism, in order to be understood at all, can only be explained in terms of energy, that is, as a potential based on opposites. Conscience brings these ever-present and necessary opposites to conscious perception. It would be a great mistake to suppose that one could ever get rid of this polarity, for it is an essential element in the psychic structure. Even if the moral reaction could be eliminated by training, the opposites would simply use a mode of expression other than the moral one. They would still continue to exist. But if the *vox Dei* conception of conscience is correct, we are faced logically with a metaphysical dilemma: either there is a dualism, and God's omnipotence is halved, or the opposites are contained in the monotheistic God-image, as for instance in the Old Testament image of

447

Yahweh, which shows us morally contradictory opposites existing side by side. This figure corresponds to a unitary image of
the psyche dynamically based on opposites, like Plato's charioteer driving the white and the black horses. Alternatively, we
must admit with Faust: "Two souls, alas, are housed within my
breast," which no human charioteer can master, as the fate of
Faust clearly indicates.

845   The psychologist can criticize metaphysics as a human assertion, but he is not in a position to make such assertions himself.
He can only establish that these assertions exist as a kind of
exclamation, well knowing that neither one nor the other
can be proved right and objectively valid, although he must
acknowledge the legitimacy of subjective assertions as such.
Assertions of this kind are manifestations of the psyche which
belong to our human nature, and there is no psychic wholeness
without them, even though one can grant them no more than
subjective validity. Thus the *vox Dei* hypothesis is another subjective exclamation, whose purpose it is to underline the numinous character of the moral reaction. Conscience is a manifestation of *mana,* of the "extraordinarily powerful," a quality which
is the especial peculiarity of archetypal ideas. For, in so far as
the moral reaction is only apparently identical with the suggestive effect of the moral code, it falls within the sphere of the
collective unconscious, exemplifying an archetypal pattern of
behaviour reaching down into the animal psyche. Experience
shows that the archetype, as a natural phenomenon, has a
morally ambivalent character, or rather, it possesses no moral
quality in itself but is amoral, like the Yahwistic God-image,
and acquires moral qualities only through the act of cognition.
Thus Yahweh is both just and unjust, kindly and cruel, truthful
and deceitful. This is eminently true of the archetype as well.
That is why the primitive form of conscience is paradoxical: to
burn a heretic is on the one hand a pious and meritorious act—
as John Hus himself ironically recognized when, bound to the
stake, he espied an old woman hobbling towards him with a
bundle of faggots, and exclaimed, "O sancta simplicitas!"—and
on the other hand a brutal manifestation of ruthless and savage
lust for revenge.

846   Both forms of conscience, the right and the false, stem from
the same source, and both therefore have approximately the

same power of conviction. This is also apparent in the symbolic designation of Christ as Lucifer ("bringer of light"), lion, raven (or *nycticorax:* night-heron), serpent, son of God, etc., all of which he shares with Satan; in the idea that the good father-god of Christianity is so vindictive that it takes the cruel sacrifice of his son to reconcile him to humanity; in the belief that the Summum Bonum has a tendency to lead such an inferior and helpless creature as man into temptation, only to consign him to eternal damnation if he is not astute enough to spot the divine trap. Faced with these insufferable paradoxes, which are an affront to our religious feelings, I would suggest reducing the notion of the *vox Dei* to the hypothesis of the archetype, for this at least is understandable and accessible to investigation. The archetype is a pattern of behaviour that has always existed, that is morally indifferent as a biological phenomenon, but possesses a powerful dynamism by means of which it can profoundly influence human behaviour.

847   The concept of the archetype has been misunderstood so often that one can hardly mention it without having to explain it anew each time. It is derived from the repeated observation that, for instance, the myths and fairytales of world literature contain definite motifs which crop up everywhere. We meet these same motifs in the fantasies, dreams, deliriums, and delusions of individuals living today. These typical images and associations are what I call archetypal ideas. The more vivid they are, the more they will be coloured by particularly strong feeling-tones. This accentuation gives them a special dynamism in our psychic life. They impress, influence, and fascinate us. They have their origin in the archetype, which in itself is an irrepresentable, unconscious, pre-existent form that seems to be part of the inherited structure of the psyche and can therefore manifest itself spontaneously anywhere, at any time. Because of its instinctual nature, the archetype underlies the feeling-toned complexes and shares their autonomy. It is also the psychic precondition of religious assertions and is responsible for the anthropomorphism of all God-images. This fact, however, affords no ground for any metaphysical judgment, whether positive or negative.

848   With this view we remain within the framework of what can be experienced and known. The *vox Dei* hypothesis is then no

more than an amplificatory tendency peculiar to the archetype—a mythological statement inseparably bound up with numinous experiences which expresses these occurrences and also seeks to explain them. By reducing them to something empirically knowable, we do not in any way prejudice their transcendence. When, for example, someone was struck by lightning, the man of antiquity believed that Zeus had hurled a thunderbolt at him. Instead of this mythical dramatization we content ourselves with the more modest explanation that a sudden discharge of electrical tension happened to take place just at the spot where this unlucky man stood under a tree. The weak point in this argument, of course, is the so-called "accident," about which several things could be said. On the primitive level there are no accidents of this sort, but only intentional designs.

849   The reduction of the act of conscience to a collision with the archetype is, by and large, a tenable explanation. On the other hand we must admit that the *psychoid* archetype, that is, its irrepresentable and unconscious essence, is not just a postulate only, but possesses qualities of a parapsychological nature which I have grouped together under the term "synchronicity." I use this term to indicate the fact that, in cases of telepathy, precognition, and similar inexplicable phenomena, one can very frequently observe an archetypal situation. This may be connected with the collective nature of the archetype, for the collective unconscious, unlike the personal unconscious, is one and the same everywhere, in all individuals, just as all biological functions and all instincts are the same in members of the same species. Apart from the more subtle *synchronicity,* we can also observe in the instincts, for instance in the migratory instinct, a distinct *synchronism.* And since the parapsychological phenomena associated with the unconscious psyche show a peculiar tendency to relativize the categories of time and space, the collective unconscious must have a spaceless and timeless quality. Consequently, there is some probability that an archetypal situation will be accompanied by synchronistic phenomena, as in the case of death, in whose vicinity such phenomena are relatively frequent.

850   As with all archetypal phenomena, the synchronicity factor must be taken into account in considering conscience. For although the voice of genuine conscience (and not just the recol-

lection of the moral code) may make itself heard in the context of an archetypal situation, it is by no means certain that the reason for this is always a subjective moral reaction. It sometimes happens that a person suffers from a decidedly bad conscience for no demonstrable reason. Naturally there are any number of cases where ignorance and self-deception offer a sufficient explanation. But this does not alter the fact that one can suddenly have a bad conscience when one is conversing with an unknown person who would have every reason to feel a bad conscience but is unconscious of it. The same is true of fear and other emotions arising from a collision with an archetype. When one is talking with somebody whose unconscious contents are "constellated," a parallel constellation arises in one's own unconscious. The same or a similar archetype is activated, and since one is less unconscious than the other person and has no reason for repression, one becomes increasingly aware of its feeling-tone in the form of a growing uneasiness of conscience. When this happens, we naturally tend to ascribe the moral reaction to ourselves, the more easily since no one, actually, has reason to enjoy a perfectly good conscience. But in the case we are discussing the self-criticism, laudable in itself, goes too far. We discover that, as soon as the conversation is ended, the bad conscience stops as suddenly as it began, and after a while it turns out that it is the other person who should take note of his bad conscience. By way of example, one thinks of cases like the one described by Heinrich Zschokke.[3] While in Brugg, he visited an inn, where he ate lunch. Opposite him sat a young man. Suddenly Zschokke saw in his mind's eye this young man standing at a desk, breaking it open, and pocketing the money he found. Zschokke even knew the exact amount and was so sure of it that he took the young man to task. The latter was so flabbergasted by Zschokke's knowledge that he made a confession on the spot.

51   This spontaneous reconstruction of an unknown fact can also be expressed in a dream, or give rise to a disagreeable feeling that cannot be put into words, or cause one to guess a situation without knowing to whom it refers. The psychoid archetype has a tendency to behave as though it were not local-

[3] *Eine Selbstschau* (1843).

ized in one person but were active in the whole environment. The fact or situation is transmitted in most cases through a subliminal perception of the affect it produces. Animals and primitives have a particularly fine nose for these things. This explanation, however, does not cover parapsychological events.

852   Experiences of this kind are the common lot of the psychotherapist, or of anybody who has frequent occasion to talk professionally, about their intimate affairs, with people with whom he has no personal relationship. One should not conclude from this that every subjective pang of conscience which seems unfounded is caused by the person one is conversing with. Such a conclusion is justified only when the ever-present guilt component in oneself proves, after mature reflection, to be an inadequate explanation of the reaction. The distinction is often a very delicate matter because, in therapy, ethical values must not be injured on either side if the treatment is to be successful. Yet what happens in the therapeutic process is only a special instance of human relationships in general. As soon as the dialogue between two people touches on something fundamental, essential, and numinous, and a certain rapport is felt, it gives rise to a phenomenon which Lévy-Bruhl fittingly called *participation mystique*. It is an unconscious identity in which two individual psychic spheres interpenetrate to such a degree that it is impossible to say what belongs to whom. If the problem is one of conscience, the guilt of the one partner is the guilt of the other, and at first there is no possibility of breaking this emotional identity. For this a special act of reflection is required. I have dwelt at some length on this problem because I wanted to show that by the concept of the archetype nothing final is meant, and that it would be wrong to suppose that the essence of conscience could be reduced to nothing but the archetype. The psychoid nature of the archetype contains very much more than can be included in a psychological explanation. It points to the sphere of the *unus mundus,* the unitary world, towards which the psychologist and the atomic physicist are converging along separate paths, producing independently of one another certain analogous auxiliary concepts. Although the first step in the cognitive process is to discriminate and divide, at the second step it will unite what has been divided, and an explanation will be satisfactory only when it achieves a synthesis.

853   For this reason I have not been able to confine myself exclusively to the psychological nature of conscience, but have had to consider its theological aspect. From this point of view it cannot be presupposed that the act of conscience is something that, of its own nature, can be treated exhaustively by means of a rational psychology. We have, rather, to give priority to the assertion which conscience itself makes—that it is a voice of God. This view is not a contrivance of the intellect, it is a primary assertion of the phenomenon itself: a numinous imperative which from ancient times has been accorded a far higher authority than the human intellect. The daemon of Socrates was not the empirical person of Socrates. Conscience as such, if regarded objectively, without rationalistic assumptions, behaves like a God so far as its demands and authority are concerned, and asserts that it is God's voice. This assertion cannot be overlooked by an objective psychology, which must also include the irrational. Nor can it be pinned down to the question of truth, for this is unanswerable anyway and for epistemological reasons has long since become obsolete. Human knowledge has to be content with constructing models which are "probable"—it would be thoughtless presumption to demand more. For just as knowledge is not faith, so faith is not knowledge. We are concerned here with things that can be disputed, that is, with knowledge, but not with indisputable faith, which precludes critical discussion at the outset. The oft-repeated paradox "knowledge through faith" seeks in vain to bridge the gulf that separates the two.

854   When, therefore, the psychologist explains genuine conscience as a collision of consciousness with a numinous archetype, he may be right. But he will have to add at once that the archetype *per se,* its psychoid essence, cannot be comprehended, that it possesses a transcendence which it shares with the unknown substance of the psyche in general. The mythical assertion of conscience that it is the voice of God is an inalienable part of its nature, the foundation of its numen. It is as much a phenomenon as conscience itself.

855   In conclusion I would like to say that conscience is a psychic reaction which one can call *moral* because it always appears when the conscious mind leaves the path of custom, of the *mores,* or suddenly recollects it. Hence in the great majority of

cases conscience signifies primarily the reaction to a real or supposed deviation from the moral code, and is for the most part identical with the primitive fear of anything unusual, not customary, and hence "immoral." As this behaviour is instinctive and, at best, only partly the result of reflection, it may be "moral" but can raise no claim to being *ethical*. It deserves this qualification only when it is reflective, when it is subjected to conscious scrutiny. And this happens only when a fundamental doubt arises as between two possible modes of moral behaviour, that is to say in a conflict of duty. A situation like this can be "solved" only by suppressing one moral reaction, upon which one has not reflected till now, in favour of another. In this case the moral code will be invoked in vain, and the judging intellect finds itself in the position of Buridan's ass between two bundles of hay. Only the creative power of the ethos that expresses the whole man can pronounce the final judgment. Like all the creative faculties in man, his ethos flows empirically from two sources: from rational consciousness and from the irrational unconscious. It is a special instance of what I have called the transcendent function, which is the discursive co-operation of conscious and unconscious factors or, in theological language, of reason and grace.

856   It is not the task of psychological understanding to broaden or to narrow the concept of conscience. "Conscience," in ordinary usage, means the consciousness of a factor which in the case of a "good conscience" affirms that a decision or an act accords with morality and, if it does not, condemns it as "immoral." This view, deriving as it does from the *mores,* from what is customary, can properly be called "moral." Distinct from this is the ethical form of conscience, which appears when two decisions or ways of acting, both affirmed to be moral and therefore regarded as "duties," collide with one another. In these cases, not foreseen by the moral code because they are mostly very individual, a judgment is required which cannot properly be called "moral" or in accord with custom. Here the decision has no custom at its disposal on which it could rely. The deciding factor appears to be something else: it proceeds not from the traditional moral code but from the unconscious foundation of the personality. The decision is drawn from dark and deep waters. It is true that these conflicts of duty are solved very

often and very conveniently by a decision in accordance with custom, that is, by suppressing one of the opposites. But this is not always so. If one is sufficiently conscientious the conflict is endured to the end, and a creative solution emerges which is produced by the constellated archetype and possesses that compelling authority not unjustly characterized as the voice of God. The nature of the solution is in accord with the deepest foundations of the personality as well as with its wholeness; it embraces conscious and unconscious and therefore transcends the ego.

857   The concept and phenomenon of conscience thus contains, when seen in a psychological light, two different factors: on the one hand a recollection of, and admonition by, the *mores;* on the other, a conflict of duty and its solution through the creation of a third standpoint. The first is the moral, and the second the ethical, aspect of conscience.

GOOD AND EVIL IN
ANALYTICAL PSYCHOLOGY [1]

858   I would like to express my warmest thanks to Professor
Seifert [2] for all he has said to us concerning the problem of the
shadow. If I comply with your wish to add a few words, it will
be about the purely empirical aspect of good and evil which the
therapist has to deal with as a concrete fact. I must confess that
I always experience difficulties when discussing the problem of
good and evil with philosophers or theologians. I have the impression that they are not talking about the thing itself, but
only about words, about the concepts which denote or refer to
it. We allow ourselves so easily to be deluded by words, we
substitute words for the whole of reality. People talk to me
about evil, or about good, and presume that I know what it is.
But I don't. When someone speaks of good or evil, it is of what
he calls good or evil, or what *he* feels as good or evil. Then he
speaks about it with great assurance, not knowing whether it
really is so or whether what he calls good or evil really corresponds to the facts. Perhaps the speaker's view of the world is
not in keeping with the real facts at all, so that an inner, subjective picture is substituted for objectivity.

859   If we wish to come to an understanding about so complex a
question as good and evil, we must start with the following
proposition: good and evil are in themselves *principles,* and we
must bear in mind that a principle exists long before us and
extends far beyond us.

1 [An extemporaneous address to the Stuttgarter Gemeinschaft "Arzt und Seelsorger," whose members travelled to Zurich to conduct the eighth annual meeting,
upon which occasion Professor Jung met the group. A transcript prepared by
Gebhard Frei was approved, with corrections, by the author and was first published in *Gut und Böse in der Psychotherapie* (ed. by Wilhelm Bitter, Stuttgart,
1959), a report of the meeting. The present translation (here revised) appeared
first in the *Journal of Analytical Psychology* (London), V (1960), 91–99.—EDITORS.]
2 [Friedrich Seifert, of Munich, a participant in the meeting.]

456

860   When we speak of good and evil we are speaking concretely of something whose deepest qualities are in reality unknown to us. Whether it is experienced as evil and sinful depends, furthermore, on our subjective judgment, as also does the extent and gravity of the sin.

861   You probably know the joke about the father confessor in Texas, to whom a young man comes with an awfully long face. "What's the matter?" he inquires. "Something terrible has happened." "But what has happened?" "I've committed murder." "How many?" This shows how differently two people can experience the same fact, the same reality. I call a certain fact bad, often without being sure that it really is so. Some things seem to me bad, though in reality they are not. For instance, after dismissing a patient I have often wanted to kick myself because I thought I had done him an injustice. Perhaps I had been too brutal or did not tell him the right thing. Next time he comes he tells me: "That was a wonderful session—just what I needed to be told." The exact opposite can also happen: I think what an excellent session it has been, what a successful dream-interpretation—and then it turns out to be all wrong.

862   Where do we get this belief, this apparent certainty, that we know what is good and what is bad? "Ye shall be as gods, knowing good and evil." Only the gods know, not us. This is profoundly true in psychology. If you take the attitude: "This thing may be very bad—but on the other hand it may not," then you have a chance of doing the right thing. But if you already know in advance you are behaving as if you were a god. We are all only limited human beings and we do not know in any fundamental sense what is good and bad in a given case. We know it only abstractly. To see through a concrete situation to the bottom is God's affair alone. We may perhaps form an opinion about it but we do not know whether it is finally valid. At most we can say cautiously: judged by such and such a standard such and such a thing is good or evil. Something that appears evil to one nation may be regarded as good by another nation. This relativity of values applies also in the realm of aesthetics: a modern work of art is for one person of supreme value, for which he is ready to lay out a large sum of money, whereas another person can make neither head nor tail of it.

863   In spite of all this we cannot simply abstain from judgment.

457

If we call good something that seems to us bad, we have in effect told a lie. If I tell someone, "What you have written is a masterpiece," thinking on the quiet that it is worth nothing, that is a lie. Maybe the lie has a positive effect on him for the moment, so that he feels flattered. But a really constructive effect is produced only when I give him the best, a positive recognition that springs from conviction, and give it moreover at the right moment. When we pass emphatic judgments we are in an emotional state of mind and are then least able to apply valid criteria.

864   My attitude to this problem is empirical, not theoretical or aprioristic. When a patient comes to the therapist he has a conflict, and the question is then how to uncover this conflict situation, which very often is unconscious, and above all to find a way out of the conflict. Probably the only thing I can do is to tell myself cautiously: we don't know exactly what's up. It seems to be such and such—but may not another interpretation be given with equal right? The situation may seem rather negative at first, but then one comes to see that this is just what the patient was fated to run into. So I say at most: I hope to God I'm doing the right thing. It may perhaps be an emotionally excessive situation, when the patient, as Albertus Magnus says, is "in an excess of affect." If we look closely we shall see that good and evil are, as I said, *principles*. The word "principle" comes from *prius*, that which is "first" or "in the beginning." The ultimate principle we can conceive of is God. Principles, when reduced to their ultimates, are simply aspects of God. Good and evil are principles of our ethical judgment, but, reduced to their ontological roots, they are "beginnings," aspects of God, names for God. Whenever, therefore, in an excess of affect, in an emotionally excessive situation, I come up against a paradoxical fact or happening, I am in the last resort encountering an aspect of God, which I cannot judge logically and cannot conquer because it is stronger than me—because, in other words, it has a numinous quality and I am face to face with what Rudolf Otto calls the *tremendum* and *fascinosum*. I cannot "conquer" a *numinosum*, I can only open myself to it, let myself be overpowered by it, trusting in its meaning. A principle is always a supraordinate thing, mightier than I am. I cannot even "conquer" the ultimate principles of physics, they simply confront

me, loom over me, as sheer facts, as laws that "prevail." Here there is something that we cannot conquer.

865   If I say in an excess of affect, "This is a rotten wine" or "This fellow is a dirty dog," I shall hardly be in a position to know whether these judgments are right. Another person might judge the same wine and the same man quite differently. We know only the surfaces of things, only how they appear to us—and so we must be very modest. How often have I wished to get rid—so it seemed to me—of some absolutely harmful tendency in a patient, and yet in a deeper sense he was perfectly right to follow it. I want, for instance, to warn somebody of the deadly danger he is running into. If I am successful I think it was a fine therapeutic achievement. Afterwards I see—if he did not take my advice—that it was just the right thing for him to run into this danger. And this raises the question: did he not *have* to be in danger of death? If he had dared nothing, if he had not risked his life, perhaps he would have been poorer by a supremely important experience. He would never have risked his life and therefore would never have gained it.

866   So in the matter of good and evil, one can, as a therapist, only hope that one is getting the facts straight, though one can never be sure. As a therapist I cannot, in any given case, deal with the problem of good and evil philosophically but can only approach it empirically. *But because I take an empirical attitude it does not mean that I relativize good and evil as such.* I see very clearly: this is evil, but the paradox is just that for this particular person in this particular situation at this particular stage of development it may be good. Contrariwise, good at the wrong moment in the wrong place may be the worst thing possible. If it were not like this everything would be so simple—too simple. If I make no *a priori* judgments and listen to the facts as they are, then I do not always know beforehand what is good for the patient and what is bad. So many factors are involved, but we cannot yet see their meaning, they appear to us veiled in the shadow, and only afterwards does light penetrate the veil. What appears "in the shadow" of the Old Testament is revealed in the New Testament in the light of truth.

867   So it is in psychology. It is presumptuous to think we can always say what is good or bad for the patient. Perhaps he knows something is really bad and does it anyway and then gets a bad

conscience. From the therapeutic, that is to say the empirical, point of view, this may be very good indeed for him. Perhaps he *has* to experience the power of evil and suffer accordingly, because only in that way can he give up his Pharisaic attitude to other people. Perhaps fate or the unconscious or God—call it what you will—had to give him a hard knock and roll him in the dirt, because only such a drastic experience could strike home, pull him out of his infantilism, and make him more mature. How can anyone find out how much he needs to be saved if he is quite sure that there is nothing he needs saving from? He sees his own shadow, his crookedness, but he turns his eyes away, does not confront himself, does not come to terms with himself, risks nothing—and then boasts before God and his fellows of his spotless white garment, which in reality he owes only to his cowardice, his regression, his super-angelic perfectionism. And instead of being ashamed, he stands in the front row of the temple and thanks God he is not as other men.

868   Such a person thinks he is justified because he knows what wrong is and avoids it. Consequently it never becomes a content of his actual life and he does not know from what he needs to be saved. Even the apocryphal saying: "Man, if thou knowest what thou dost, thou art blessed, but if thou knowest not, thou art accursed and a transgressor of the law," only gives us half a chance. A man who knows what he is doing when he commits evil may have a chance of being blessed, but in the meantime he is in hell. For the evil you do, even when you do it knowingly, is still evil and works accordingly. Yet if you had not taken this step, if you had not trodden this path, perhaps it would have been a psychic regression, a retrograde step in your inner development, a piece of infantile cowardice. Whoever thinks that by "knowing what you do" you guard against sin or save yourself from sin is wrong; on the contrary, you have steeped yourself in sin. But this saying is so paradoxical that it is terribly shocking to our ordinary feelings. The Church, however, knows of this paradox when she speaks of the *felix culpa* of our first parents (in the Liturgy for Easter Eve). If they had not sinned there would have been no *felix culpa* to bring after it the still greater miracle of the redemption. Nevertheless, evil remains evil. There is nothing for it but to accustom ourselves to thinking in paradoxes.

869   Without wishing it, we human beings are placed in situations in which the great "principles" entangle us in something,
and God leaves it to us to find a way out. Sometimes a clear
path is opened with his help, but when it really comes to the
point one has the feeling of having been abandoned by every
good spirit. In critical situations the hero always mislays his
weapon, and at such moments, as before death, we are confronted with the nakedness of this fact. And one does not know
how one got there. A thousand twists of fate all of a sudden land
you in such a situation. This is symbolically represented by
Jacob's fight with the angel at the ford. Here a man can do
nothing but stand his ground. It is a situation that challenges
him to react as a whole man. Then it may turn out that he can
no longer keep to the letter of the moral law. That is where his
most personal ethics begin: in grim confrontation with the
Absolute, in striking out on a path condemned by current
morality and the guardians of the law. And yet he may feel that
he has never been truer to his innermost nature and vocation,
and hence never nearer to the Absolute, because he alone and
the Omniscient have seen the actual situation as it were from
inside, whereas the judges and condemners see it only from
outside.

870   There is a well-known story of the young man who attained
his majority. His father said to him: "Now you are twenty. Ordinary people stick to the Bible and what the parson says. The
more intelligent mind the penal code." In other words: you are
caught between "official" religion and civic morality. When
your own conscience collides with them your most personal
ethical decisions begin, in full consciousness of your creative
freedom either to observe the moral code or not. I may, for
instance, get into a situation where, in order to keep a professional secret, I have to lie. It would be futile to shrink from
this with the excuse that I am a "moral" man. To the devil with
such self-respect!

871   I am telling you all this in order to make my attitude in
practice clear. I do not see it is my job to discuss these things
philosophically. For me they are practical matters. Of course I
am also interested in their philosophical aspect, but philosophy
butters no parsnips. The reality of good and evil consists in
things and situations that happen to you, that are too big for

461

you, where you are always as if facing death. Anything that comes upon me with this intensity I experience as numinous, no matter whether I call it divine or devilish or just "fate." Something stronger than oneself, invincible, is at work and one is up against it. The trouble is that we are so accustomed to thinking these problems out until everything is as clear as twice two makes four. But in practice it does not work like that, we do not reach a solution in principle as to how we should always act. To want one is wrong. It is the same here as with the laws of nature, which we also think of as valid everywhere. Conventional morality is exactly like classical physics: a statistical truth, a statistical wisdom. The modern physicist knows that causality is a statistical truth, but in practice he will always ask what law is valid in this particular case. So it is in the realm of morality. We should not be misled into thinking we have said something absolutely valid when we pass judgment on a particular case: this is bad, this is good. Often we have to pass judgments, we can't get out of it. Perhaps we may even say the truth, hit the mark. But to regard our judgments as absolutely valid would be nonsensical; it would mean wanting to be like God. Often even the person doing the action does not discern its inner moral quality, the sum of all the conscious and unconscious motives underlying it, and how much less those who judge the action but see it only from the outside, only its appearance, not its deepest essence. Kant rightly requires the individual and society to advance from an "ethic of action" to an "ethic of conviction." But to see into the ultimate depths of the conviction behind the action is possible only to God. Our judgment, therefore, as to what is good or evil in practice will have to be very cautious and modest, not so apodictic, as though we could see into all the darkest corners. Ideas of morality are often as widely divergent as are views on what constitutes a delicacy for the Eskimo and for ourselves.

872   My attitude, it may be objected, is empirical in the extreme, but we need such an attitude in order to find a solution. When we observe how people behave when they are faced with a situation that has to be evaluated ethically, we become aware of a strange double effect: suddenly they see both sides. They become aware not only of their moral inferiorities but also, automatically, of their good qualities. They rightly say, "I can't be as

bad as all that." To confront a person with his shadow is to show him his own light. Once one has experienced a few times what it is like to stand judgingly between the opposites, one begins to understand what is meant by the self. Anyone who perceives his shadow and his light simultaneously sees himself from two sides and thus gets in the middle.

873   That is the secret of the Eastern attitude: observing the opposites teaches the Easterner the character of Maya. It gives reality the glint of illusion. Behind the opposites and in the opposites is true reality, which sees and comprehends the whole. The Indian calls this Atman. Reflecting on ourselves we can say, "I am he who speaks good and evil," or better, "I am he through whom good and evil are spoken. The one who is in me, who voices the principles, uses me as a means of expression. He speaks through me." This corresponds to what the Indian calls Atman—that which, figuratively speaking, "breathes through" me. Not through me alone, but through all; for it is not only the individual Atman but Atman-Purusha, the universal Atman, the pneuma, who breathes through all. We use the word "self" for this, contrasting it with the little ego. From what I have said it will be clear that this self is not just a rather more conscious or intensified ego, as the words "self-conscious," "self-satisfied," etc. might lead one to suppose. What is meant by the self is not only in me but in all beings, like the Atman, like Tao. It is psychic totality.

874   It is a misunderstanding to accuse me of having made out of this an "immanent God" or a "God-substitute." I am an empiricist and as such I can demonstrate empirically the existence of a totality supraordinate to consciousness. Consciousness experiences this supraordinate totality as something numinous, as a *tremendum* or *fascinosum*. As an empiricist I am interested only in the experiential character of this totality, which in itself, ontologically considered, is indescribable. This "self" never at any time takes the place of God, though it may perhaps be a vessel for divine grace. Such misunderstandings arise from the assumption that I am an irreligious man who does not believe in God and just needs to be shown the way to belief.

875   In the history of Indian philosophy, too, there have been constant attempts not to identify the Atman with the monistically conceived Brahman (the Absolute Ground of all being),

for instance in Ramanuja as opposed to Shankara, or in Bhakti-Yoga; and Aurobindo thinks that the Indian of today has advanced so far from the level of unconsciousness to conscious realization that his Absolute can no longer have the character of a merely unconscious, impersonal cosmic force. But these are no longer questions for the pure empiricist. As an empiricist I can at least establish that the Easterner like the Westerner is lifted out of the play of Maya, or the play of the opposites, through the experience of the Atman, the "self," the higher totality. He knows that the world consists of darkness and light. I can master their polarity only by freeing myself from them by contemplating both, and so reaching a middle position. Only there am I no longer at the mercy of the opposites.

[Jung's talk appears to have ended here. Then followed an unrecorded question, evidently concerning the East.—EDITORS.]

876   We have a false picture of the East. From the East comes the humorous question: Who takes longer to be saved, the man who loves God or the man who hates him? Naturally we expect that the man who hates God takes much longer. But the Indian says: If he loves God, it takes seven years, but if he hates him only three. For the man who hates God thinks much more about him. What ruthless subtlety! But the question is absolutely right the way it is meant. It is a sort of quiz question which may be put to the educated public but not to a peasant.

877   This story reminds me of something I saw in Ceylon. Two peasants had got their carts stuck in a narrow street. One can imagine what a flood of vituperation this would have let loose here in Switzerland. But what actually happened there was this: They bowed to each other and said: "Passing disturbance, no soul." That is to say the disturbance takes place only outwardly, in the realm of Maya, and not in the realm of true reality, where it neither happened nor left a mark. One might think this almost unbelievable in such simple people. One stands amazed. But this attitude is so ingrained in them that they take it for granted. Richard Wilhelm witnessed much the same thing. Two rickshaw boys were having a fearful argument. Wilhelm thought they were going to let fly with their fists at any moment, and that blood would flow. Just then one of them rushed at the other—

but rushed past him and aimed a mighty kick at the wheel of his rickshaw, and that was the end of the argument. I myself saw two boys quarrelling and fighting with their fists, but the fists always stopped in the air, a few centimetres from the face, and no harm was done. That comes from the way these boys were brought up: it was Ceylon, where the old Buddhism still rules. It is a moral education that has become a habit, and there is nothing especially meritorious about it.

878   Now, ladies and gentlemen, have you any further questions?

[A question was asked about the devil and his special reality today, since every epoch has its own peculiar devil.]

879   The devil nowadays is something quite frightful! If you look at our situation you just cannot see where it will end. Things will go on like this as if by force. All the divine powers in creation are gradually being placed in man's hands. Through nuclear fission something tremendous has happened, tremendous power has been given to man. When Oppenheimer saw the first test of an atomic bomb the words of the Bhagavad Gita flashed into his mind: "Brighter than a thousand suns." The forces that hold the fabric of the world together have got into the hands of man, so that he even has the idea of making an artificial sun. God's powers have passed into our hands, our fallible human hands. The consequences are inconceivable. The powers themselves are not evil, but in the hands of man they are an appalling danger—in evil hands. Who says that the evil in the world we live in, that is right in front of us, is not real! Evil is terribly real, for each and every individual. If you regard the principle of evil as a reality you can just as well call it the devil. I personally find it hard to believe that the idea of the *privatio boni* still holds water.

[What should the psychotherapist do? Should he give the patient a hint of how to deal with evil, or should he urge the patient to find out for himself?]

880   You are tempting me to lay down a rule. But I would rather advise: do the one thing or do the other according to circumstances, and in your therapeutic work do not act on any *a priori,*

465

but in each case listen to what the concrete situation demands. Let that be your only *a priori*. For instance, a patient is still so unconscious that you simply *cannot* take up an attitude towards his problems. He identifies himself, like a psychotic, with his unconscious and would rather regard the analyst as crazy than understand his own inner situation. Try telling a completely unconscious mother, a sort of Kali Durga, who considers herself the best mother in the world, that she is to blame for the neurosis of her elder daughter and the unhappy marriage of her younger daughter—then you will hear something! And above all: the patient is not helped. Something must grow from inside *her*. Another patient has reached a certain level of consciousness and expects orientation from you. It would then be a great mistake not to make your attitude clear. The right thing must be said at the right time in the right place.

881   A patient should not be regarded as an inferior being whom one lays on a couch while one sits behind him like a god, letting a word drop now and then. Everything suggestive of illness should be avoided. The patient is tending in this direction anyway and would like nothing better than to take refuge in illness: ". . . now I can give up, now I must just lie there, now I am good and sick." Illness too is a solution of sorts, a way of disposing of life's problems: "I am ill, now the doctor must help!" As a therapist I mustn't be naïve. Unless the patient should really be in bed he should be treated like a normal person, indeed like a partner. That provides a sound basis for the treatment. People often come to me expecting me to let loose some medical magic. Then they are disappointed when I treat them as normal people and myself act like a normal man. One patient had experienced only the strong silent god sitting behind the couch. As soon as I began to talk to her she said astonished, almost horrified: "But you're expressing your affects, you're even telling me what you think!" Naturally I have affects and show them. Nothing is more important than this: every human being should be taken as a real human being and treated according to his peculiarities.

882   Therefore I say to the young psychotherapist: Learn the best, know the best—and then forget everything when you face the patient. No one has yet become a good surgeon by learning the text-books off by heart. Yet the danger that faces us today is

that the whole of reality will be replaced by words. This accounts for that terrible lack of instinct in modern man, particularly the city-dweller. He lacks all contact with the life and breath of nature. He knows a rabbit or a cow only from the illustrated paper, the dictionary, or the movies, and thinks he knows what it is really like—and is then amazed that cowsheds "smell," because the dictionary didn't say so. It is the same with the danger of making a diagnosis. One knows that this disease is treated by So-and-so in chapter seventeen, and one thinks that this is the important thing. But the poor patient goes on suffering.

883   People speak sometimes of "overcoming" evil. But have we the power to overcome it? It should be remembered, first, that "good" and "evil" are only our judgment in a given situation, or, to put it differently, that certain "principles" have taken possession of our judgment. Secondly, it is often impossible to speak of overcoming evil, because at such times we are in a "closed" situation, in an aporia, where whatever we choose is not good. The important thing is to be aware that we are then in a numinous situation, surrounded on all sides by God, who can bring about either the one or the other and often does. There are plenty of examples of this in the Old Testament. Or think of Teresa of Avila when she had a mishap on a journey: the coach broke down while crossing a small river and she fell into the icy water. "Lord, how can you permit such things?" "Well, that's how I treat my friends." "Aha, that's why you have so few!" Teresa had got into a situation where evil—in this case physical evil—was done to her; she did not know how to integrate it, but nevertheless felt God's immediate presence. That is how the "principles," the "primordial powers," approach a person—they put him in a numinous situation where there is no rational solution, where he does not feel himself the maker and master of the situation, but rather that it is God. No one can then foresee what will happen. Often we cannot say in such situations how the problem of good and evil will work out. We have to put our trust in the higher powers.

884   If I am faced with this problem in analysis I may say: "Well, let's wait and see what the dreams turn up, or whether higher powers will intervene, perhaps through illness or death. In any case don't decide. You and I are not God."

885   In making the shadow conscious we must be very careful that the unconscious does not play yet another trick and prevent a real confrontation with the shadow. A patient may see the darkness in himself for a moment, but the next moment he tells himself that it is not so bad after all, a mere bagatelle. Or else he exaggerates his remorse, because it is so nice to have such a wonderful remorseful feeling, to enjoy it like a warm eiderdown on a cold winter's morning when one should be getting up. This dishonesty, this refusal to see, ensures that there will be no confrontation with the shadow. Yet if there were a confrontation, then with increasing consciousness the good and the positive features would come to light too. We must therefore beware of the danger of wallowing in affects—remorse, melancholy, etc.—because they are seductive. It is easy enough to pride oneself on being able to feel such beautiful regrets. That is why people love plays, films, or preachers that move them to tears, because they can then enjoy their own emotions.

886   In the course of our discussion we heard the word "esoteric." [3] It is said, for instance, that the psychology of the unconscious leads to an esoteric form of ethics. But we have to be careful in using such a word. Esotericism means mystification. Yet we never know the real secrets, even the so-called esotericists do not know them. Esotericists—at least earlier—were supposed not to reveal their secrets. But the real secrets cannot be revealed. Nor is it possible to make an "esoteric" science out of them, for the simple reason that they are not known. What are called esoteric secrets are mostly artificial secrets, not real ones. Man needs to have secrets, and since he has no notion of the real ones he fakes them. But the real ones come to him out of the depths of the unconscious, and then he may reveal things which he ought really to have kept secret. Here again we see the numinous character of the reality in the background. It is not we who have secrets, it is the real secrets that have us.

[3] [Presumably in one of the other talks in this symposium.—Editors.]

INTRODUCTION TO TONI WOLFF'S
"STUDIES IN JUNGIAN PSYCHOLOGY"[1]

887   In writing this introduction I am discharging a debt of
thanks: the author of the essays printed in this volume was my
friend and collaborator for more than forty years, until her untimely death in 1953, at the age of sixty-five. She took an active
part in all phases of the development of analytical psychology,
and to her we owe the expression "complex psychology" as a
designation for this field of research. Her collaboration was not
confined to working out practical methods of analysis and to the
task of theoretical formulation, both of which have found visible expression in the published material. She also helped me
to carry out, over a period of forty years, a "silent experiment"
in group psychology, an experiment which constitutes the life
of the Psychological Club in Zurich.

888   This small group of thirty to seventy members was founded
in 1916, and it owes its existence to the realization that analytical treatment (including the "psychoanalytic" method) is a
dialectical process between two individuals, and therefore gives
results which are necessarily onesided from the collective and
social point of view. The individual personality of the analyst
represents only one of the infinite possibilities of adaptation
which life offers as well as demands. This should not be taken
to mean that analysis is a discussion between two individuals
who are, at bottom, hopelessly incommensurable, or is nothing
more than an approximation between them. Human personality is certainly not individual only, it is also collective, and to
such a degree that the individual is rather like an underprivi-
leged minority. Every so-called normal person represents the
species *Homo sapiens* and can therefore be regarded as the measure of things human, or as a general example of human

1 [Translated from the Vorrede to Toni Wolff, *Studien zu C. G. Jungs Psychologie*
(Zurich, 1959), pp. 7–14.—EDITORS.]

behaviour. For this reason, a large part of the analytical work takes place on levels which are common to all, or at any rate most, individuals, and which do not require the discussion of individual differences. The longer the discussion is intentionally restricted to what is common, collective, and average—that is, to theoretical suppositions—the closer it comes to the danger-point where the specifically individual features of the patient are suppressed.

889   Thanks to her high natural intelligence and quite exceptional psychological insight, the author was one of the first to recognize the extraordinary importance of this psychotherapeutic problem, and devoted herself to it with particular zeal. For many years she was president of the Club and so had a unique opportunity to collect observations on group psychology. For in a group we see operating all those psychic events which are never constellated by an individual, or may even be unintentionally suppressed. A male analyst, for example, can never constellate the reactions which a woman would release if she were in his place. These modes of behaviour therefore remain latent; or if they appear at all, there is no critical eye to separate the wheat from the chaff. At best they remain hanging in mid-air as theoretical speculations; they are not experienced as realities and so cannot be recognized for what they are. Only what the analyst has become conscious of through his own experience can become an object for psychological discussion. Other objects, which may be put up for discussion by the patient should they reach his consciousness, come to grief on the unconsciousness of the analyst at this particular point. If he can divest himself of his authority, he may be able to compensate for his own defective experience by the experience of another. But there is always a danger that he will counter the psychological reality by some schematic theorem, because his fear of feeling inferior prevents him from admitting his defect. This danger is particularly great for the analyst, who is always expected to show authority. As a result, it happens all too easily that the balance between theoretical prejudice and uncritical acceptance can no longer be preserved, so that the analyst is unable to distinguish between justified and unjustified resistances on the part of his patient.

890   This problem, a very important one in practice, led the

author to pay particular attention to the typical modes of behaviour, especially of women. As every intelligent person knows, a typology of this sort does not aim in the least at a statistical classification; its purpose is to afford insight into the structure of normal modes of behaviour. These are typical forms of reaction whose existence is quite justified, and which should not be regarded as pathological merely because the analyst belongs to a different type. A typology is therefore designed, first and foremost, as an aid to a psychological critique of knowledge. Empirical psychology is so rich that one can set up hundreds of typological criteria without necessarily endowing any one of them with special significance, unless it happened to be a particularly common and instructive criterion. The valuable thing here is the critical attempt to prevent oneself from taking one's own prejudices as the criterion of normality. Unfortunately, this happens only too easily; for instance, extraversion is "normal," but introversion is pathological auto-eroticism.

891 Her study of the difficulties that arise in a group provided the author with a mass of empirical material of which she made valuable use. Like the individual, a group is influenced by numerous typical factors, such as the family milieu, society, politics, outlook on life, religion. The bigger the group, the more the individuals composing it function as a collective entity, which is so powerful that it can reduce individual consciousness to the point of extinction, and it does this the more easily if the individual lacks spiritual possessions of his own with an individual stamp. The group and what belongs to it cover up the lack of genuine individuality, just as parents act as substitutes for everything lacking in their children. In this respect the group exerts a seductive influence, for nothing is easier than a perseveration of infantile ways or a return to them. Only the man who knows how to acquire spiritual possessions of his own is proof against this danger.

892 Group observations have confirmed over and over again that the group subtly entices its members into mutual imitation and dependence, thereby holding out the promise of sparing them a painful confrontation with themselves. People still do not realize that fate will reach them all the same, if not directly then indirectly. A State that protects us from everything also takes away from us everything that makes life worth living. We need

not stress the social advantages of living in a group, let alone the necessary and vital protection afforded by society. They are known to everyone. On the other hand, nobody likes or dares to mention in so many words the negative effects of group-existence, because this might bring up the frightening problem of self-knowledge and individuation. In any analytical treatment that seeks to be a psychological process of dialectic between two individuals the odious question is bound to arise: What is mine and what is thine?

893   The answer to this question necessitates a thorough examination of psychic contents, of meanings and values, on a plane beyond the collective "should" and "must." A much needed consideration of what is essential to the individual proves to be the first task, for no one can get anywhere near independence unless he is conscious of his own singularity. Belief in general rules and precepts will never make a man anything more than a collective being, whereas in reality he is an individual different from others and should therefore be in possession of his own individual consciousness. Without the physical and spiritual possessions that go with this he is in danger of being submerged in the collective. As this runs counter to the specific, biological urge of man to develop an individually differentiated consciousness, a great variety of injurious effects may be produced.

894   The more "scientific" our education attempts to be, the more it orients itself by general precepts and thus suppresses the individual development of the child. One of these general precepts states: "The individuality of the child should be taken into account and protected."

895   This principle, praiseworthy in itself, is reduced to absurdity in practice if the numerous peculiarities of the child are not adjusted to the values of the collectivity. One is then protecting and developing merely the peculiarities, without considering whether they will be useful or harmful to the child later on in social life. He is being robbed of the important experience that peculiarities are not admissible just because he has them. Their differentiation and evaluation demand so much tact, experience, and sense of values on the part of the educator that the above precept cannot be realized without danger to the pupil. It is very likely that too general an application of the principle will produce unadapted individualists rather than individuals

capable of adaptation. The former are ruled by a ruthless ego, but the latter recognize the existence of factors which are equal if not superior to their own will.

896   The possession of individual peculiarities is neither a merit nor, in itself, a valuable gift of nature. It is "just one of those things," and it becomes significant only to the degree that consciousness reflects upon it, evaluates it, and subjects it to ethical decision. The authority needed for this is represented by the educator. It has to be supposed that he himself really *is* such an authority. But he can become so only when he has accomplished the act of self-knowledge on himself. Otherwise children are the first to find out that he merely *talks,* but *is* not. He has a right to peculiarities only if he has earned them, and only by earning them does he possess authority, in other words, self-reliance and individuality. These can never be obtained by mollycoddling one's own desires.

897   These educational commonplaces seem to have been generally forgotten today. Ignorance of them is one of the chief causes of the terrifying increase in juvenile delinquency. Since nobody is educated by general precepts and by giving peculiarities free rein, the young person loses all sense for authority and thus falls a victim to his inner chaos of undifferentiated values. The development of his personality comes to a standstill, he feels himself to be suppressed, robbed of his individual nature. That is why, paradoxically, the juvenile delinquent struggles to regain his birthright, and even goes to the length of committing a crime in order to take by force something that shall be irrevocably "his." It is a collective protest against the levelling platitudes of the so-called scientific view of the world, and against the destruction of the instinctual and emotional forces which results from it.

898   The spiritual and moral value of a group is measured by the average value of its individual members. If they are without value, then no group ideal can help. Group experiences therefore always lead back to the question of the value of the individual and his development.

899   The author of these essays accordingly turned her attention to the psychic contents of the individuals composing a group, and to the discussion of them for the purpose of intensifying

473

consciousness. The peculiar nature of discussions of this kind, which the layman often finds very puzzling, is due to the fact that they are not philosophical in the conventional sense, but are psychological. That is to say, they are concerned with the affects, emotions, and values of individuals, and their subject-matter is taken not from the abstract world of concepts but from everyday life, from the experiences, dreams, and fantasies of individual human beings. The discussion tries to bring order into this chaos of disconnected and uncomprehended details by examining their unknown connections with the human mind in general in the light of consciousness, so far as this is possible with the help of understanding and of our present means of communication. This therapeutic activity is naturally not philosophy in the current sense of the word, even though those who are not familiar with the psychological material always make the mistake of confusing purely empirical and pragmatic terms with philosophical concepts, or of taking them as metaphysical assertions.

900   For anyone who knows the material these essays are uncommonly instructive and stimulating. They will tell the educated layman many things about which the learned specialists have little to say. They are answers to questions which affect the psyche of our contemporaries far more closely than those given by the academic specialist. Though the latter would certainly do well, in the interests of scientific objectivity, to exclude from his work all feeling-values, and, in particular, all subjective reactions and excursions into neighbouring territories in which he himself is a layman, the psychologist is ill-advised to disregard the emotional connections and analogies which are the essence of psychic life. In order to sketch an adequate picture of psychic events, and of the manifold connections between them, he must stress just those aspects which the specialist anxiously excludes from his field of study. An empirical psychology of complex phenomena therefore occupies a difficult position in the world of specialism. Whereas the specialist, guided by general principles, pushes forward to an ever more exact understanding of the smallest details, the empirical psychologist has to start from a very limited field in which he himself is the only expert—an expert, that is to say, in his personal knowledge of himself. But

474

even here he will find it exceedingly difficult to rid himself of the prejudice that what he is practising is some kind of "objective psychology." If he really has any talent in this respect, he will soon discover that he is surrounded by a number of similar experts who all have assumptions of their own and, like him, are inclined to regard their personal prejudices as generally valid psychological knowledge. Empirical knowledge, however, is composed of numerous individual observations by numerous individual observers, who have previously assured themselves of the identity of their methods of observation as well as of the objects observed. Because complex psychic phenomena are amenable to experimental methods only in minimal degree, we have to depend on descriptions of them, and can attempt to interpret them only by means of amplification and comparison. This procedure is the exact opposite of what the specialist is at pains to achieve. He wants to know the object in its truest essence and in all its peculiarity; whereas the comparative psychologist, in order to understand its irrational and apparently accidental details, must not fight shy even of the most obvious and superficial analogies, however fortuitous they may seem, because they serve as bridges for psychic associations. Just as he horrifies the philosopher who has no interest in psychology by what must seem to him a special brand of inferior philosophy, so he annoys the scientific specialist unacquainted with psychotherapeutic problems by the inexactitude and superficiality of his "fantastic" analogies. What then must he expect of the theologian, whose propositions he blasphemously regards as "statements" of the psyche, i.e., as psychic products, reducing them to the same level as the statements of other religions, which are one and all erroneous?

901 Psychological treatment, taken in its widest sense, seeks the values that satisfy the psychic needs of contemporary man, so that he shall not fall victim to the destructive influence of mass psychology. Words like "should" and "must" are useless remedies that have long since lost their efficacy. In order to find a proper remedy we need a knowledge of the real and whole man, and this is not possible without taking account of all those spheres of knowledge which immediately affect him and his conduct of life.

902   Several of the essays in this volume bear witness to the efforts
which the author has made in this regard. They are visible
examples of the endeavour of complex psychology to fill the
gap which the invasion of the natural sciences has created in
the higher education of man.

VII

REVIEWS AND SHORT ARTICLES

THE SWISS LINE IN THE
EUROPEAN SPECTRUM [1]

903   Count Keyserling is a phenomenon that needs to be judged
with extreme caution. On no account should one think the
judgment final; the phenomenon is far too complex. There is
no merit in stressing its darker aspects, for they fairly leap to
the eye. Moreover, so much light emanates from Keyserling that
one wonders whether these shadows are not an integral part of
him—not just a physical concomitant, so to speak, but the necessary condition for his peculiar intuitive capacity. Light presupposes darkness. Darkness fosters vision, obscurity demands clarifi-
cation, diversity calls for unity and discord for harmony.

904   It is easy to poke fun at Keyserling as an aristocrat who peers
at the world through a monocle. Keyserling is not to be taken
as a joke, though he himself suffers from the delusion that his
book was written with a sense of humour. I do not find his book
humorous; his style is mordant, and often one hears the crack
of a whip. Instead of evoking hearty laughter it makes one think.
What Keyserling calls humour is a light, jesting, sometimes brilliant manner, but cold to the touch and lacking in geniality, a
cavalier wit—in short, a mock-humour. His humour is put on; it
is one of the many ways of lending wings to his intuition and
keeping it soaring high above the weltering darkness; a pardon-
able attempt to lighten what is, at bottom, an extremely difficult task. The thoughtful reader will not misunderstand this
alleged joker, for he will guess that the book is Keyserling himself, in the act of approaching the earth from afar, and Europe
in particular.

1 [First published as "Die Bedeutung der schweizerischen Linie im Spektrum
Europas," *Neue Schweizer Rundschau* (Zurich), XXIV (21st year), (1928), 6, 1–11,
469–79. The article is in effect a review of Count Hermann Keyserling's *Das Spektrum Europas* [The Spectrum of Europe] (Heidelberg, 1928), trans. by Maurice
Samuel as *Europe* (New York and London, 1928). The quotations in the present
version are trans. from the original.—EDITORS.]

905   What! Take Keyserling seriously? Regardless of his own different personal opinion, I think we should be well advised not
to treat him with levity and shrug off his book as a "humorous
one." His attempt to get a bird's-eye view of Europe is no mean
achievement. The chief value and meaning of the book, as I
see it, is that it gives clear expression to the need for the intellectual today to wean himself from the purely rational point of
view. It bears witness to a psychological reality which has vanished from sight ever since the days of a common Latin language,
the one universal Christian Church, and a universal Gothic
style, so completely that one never even thinks of it. Keyserling
advocates a return to a psychological view of the world, where
nations are seen as functions, as the various activities and expressions of the one, great, indivisible man. This view is tre-
mendously idealistic, not to say "metaphysical," and is indisputable proof of Keyserling's remoteness from the earth. The
stand he has taken has the undeniable character of spirituality,
with all the advantages and disadvantages this entails.

906   In order to proclaim these welcome tidings, Keyserling needs
his world-scorning, aristocratic stance, as it gives him the necessary elevation, distance, and solitude. If he should need a monocle as well, I would not hold it against him, for I know what
ulterior purpose it serves. Even the "megalomania" of which
he has so often been accused (though in this book of Keyserling's it expresses itself in much milder form than in his other
writings) is an excusable adjunct, being nothing other than a
somewhat too convulsive effort to hold his own against the
whole world. It is a declaration flung in the face of nothingness,
incomprehensible only to those who have never lost their foot-
hold on the earth. Megalomania simply keeps one's courage up;
otherwise it signifies nothing.

907   Keyserling hails from the far-away regions of the spirit, hence
he has trouble in understanding what he sees on earth. He talks
such a lot about "meaning" only because he is looking for it.
And one certainly has to look for it, for at first one sees only nonsense, especially in our present-day world. It is, indeed, extremely difficult to glimpse a meaning anywhere. And the search
for it is hopelessly complicated by the fact that there are far too
many "meanings" already—millions of short-lived, short-sighted,
short-winded *ad hoc* meanings which seem uncommonly sensible

to all who are struck with them, the more so the more senseless they are. This dreary spectacle becomes quite dismaying when we turn our gaze from the limited and less lugubrious sphere of the individual and see it parading as the alleged "soul of the nation." Keyserling is condemned to begin at the most senseless and hopeless end—with an attempt to understand the national psyche. Every harsh word, every crack of the whip, every distortion of judgment becomes fully understandable as an involuntary expression of his irritation and impatience with this thankless, tightly knotted, refractory material. Keyserling *has* to boast of being a Russian, a German, a Frenchman as well as a Balt; he has to name himself in one breath with Napoleon, Socrates, and Genghis Khan in order to escape the thousand tentacles of the national psyche and be able to think and judge. He cannot allow himself to belong to any nation, not even to the human race. He is neither "human" nor "inhuman," he is a unique phenomenon. Unfortunately, psychology has no acceptable name for this quality, but at any rate it is one which enables Keyserling to see humanity from the outside.

908   This cosmic view of humanity—to use a term that suits his comet-like psychology—comprehensive though it is, is limited by the earth's visibility. It is confined to daylight, and takes no account of things that are under the earth. Whatever may be perceived on the broad surface, Keyserling sees brilliantly. The chapters on Italy and Holland are superb. With regard to France, he has hit the nail on its head (which is Paris), but the Frenchman buried in the countryside remains invisible, essential though he is to the picture. In Spain Keyserling saw, no doubt correctly, the still surviving Gothic man, without naming him as such. That part of the Englishman which is hidden in the earth and sea has received the name of the "beast-man"— not very complimentary, but objectively correct. Somehow I am not satisfied with his Germany, but I know of no one who could have made a better job of it. Austria has planted her cosy culture very evidently in Vienna; as an Alpine country she is stuck in the earth and for Keyserling invisible. Russia, Rumania, Hungary, Greece, and Turkey I know nothing of from personal experience.

909   And now for Switzerland, which concerns us so closely and so painfully! Undeniably, Switzerland comes off worst. Keyser-

ling has named me, together with Herr Badrutt of St. Moritz, the model Swiss, which must have astonished and delighted Herr Badrutt even more than it did me. However, I deserve this elevation in status probably less than he does, seeing that I have been Swiss for some five hundred years only on my mother's side, but on my father's side only for one hundred and six years (as C. A. Bernoulli pointed out in the *Basler Nachrichten* when my family-tree was questioned). I must therefore beg the reader to see my "relatively Swiss" attitude as the result of my little more than hundred-year-old Swiss nationality.

910   I admit unblushingly that Keyserling's criticism of the visible Swiss character, however harsh and fault-finding, is absolutely true. The fewer illusions we have in this respect the better for us. We ought to know how we look from the outside, and we should be grateful that he has been so unsparing. It is unfortunately impossible to deny that to every unpleasant sentence he has written about us, we could add at least half a dozen highly illustrative examples from our daily experience.[2] It is indeed an unedifying picture which he has painted of our Switzerland. The good things he mentions pale into insignificance beside the bad. I must own that I felt insulted and irritated by some of them. This is because willy-nilly we identify ourselves with the nation, chalking up its supposed good qualities to our own account, and attributing our own bad qualities to others. This unconscious symbiosis is practically unavoidable, but it has the disadvantage that the more we hide behind the nation the less conscious we are of ourselves. As soon, therefore, as I became aware of my ruffled national pride, I read the chapter on Switzerland as though Keyserling had been writing about me personally, and behold! my irritation vanished.

911   It became clear to me that when I took his criticism personally, I found I was being judged only from the outside. We have to put up with such criticism, of course; but the essential thing is that we should be able to stand up to our judgment of ourselves. From outside this attitude looks like self-righteousness, but it is so only if we are incapable of criticizing ourselves. If

2 At a family gathering someone noticed that a certain relative was cut by everyone. Wondering what the reason might be for this behaviour, he asked the lady of the house. "He does terrible things, he's a dreadful person."—Well, what's he done?—"He's living on his capital!"

we can exercise self-criticism, criticism from outside will affect us only on the outside and not pierce to the heart, for we feel that we have a sterner critic within us than any who could judge us from without. And anyway, there are as many opinions as there are heads to think them. We come to realize that our own judgment has as much value as the judgment of others. One cannot please everybody, therefore it is better to be at peace with oneself. "One claps his eyes on it, another a price on it, a third man despises it—what does it matter?" [3] Keyserling pitches on this genuine piece of Swiss wisdom and exclaims indignantly: "For any cultured person or someone in a higher social position this way of thinking, inimical to all values, is merely irresponsible and unprincipled."

912   Herein lies the most glaring difference between the man of the Keyserling breed and the Swiss. The judgment of others is not in itself a standard of value, it may be no more than a useful piece of information. The individual has a right, indeed it is his duty, to set up and apply his own standard of value. In the last resort ethics are the concern of the individual, as Albert Schweitzer has pointed out so forcefully. And for that matter, what is the attitude of the aristocrat? Does he bother about the judgment of others? Sitting on his peak he can look down superciliously on the multitude, unmoved by the hubbub of opinion. ("The dogs bark, but the caravan passes on.") Why shouldn't the least aristocratic of nations do the same? Or is it a case of "quod licet Jovi, non licet bovi"? But this would be to forget that the word "subject" (*Untertan*) has not existed in Switzerland for a very long time and that, historically, the psychological attitude of the Swiss, including the one-time "subject lands," was moulded not by the latter but by the thirteen members of the old Confederation. The fact remains that the typical Swiss attitude of not bothering about the opinions of others bears a curious resemblance to the attitude of the aristocrat. I admire that blunt Swiss who sits in his modest house and lets the world know that he has his own sense of values and can let the opinions of others roll off him. He is an "aristocrat" in his way, not "audessus de la mêlée," like the feudal lord of the manor, but—captious as this sounds—"au-dessous de la mêlée." I am not just

3 "Der eine betracht's, der andere acht's, der dritte veracht's, was machts!"

playing with words: the tumult and the shouting are always found where the opposites clash, and that is always midway between above and below. Above is aristocratic, below unaristocratic. The aristocrat, so long as he remains above, is outside the mêlée; the non-aristocrat, so long as he remains below, equally so. Above and below have always been brothers, as we learn from the wise saying in the *Tabula smaragdina*: "Heaven above, heaven below."

913   "Aristocratic" and "unaristocratic" are value-judgments, subjective and arbitrary, and are therefore best left out of the discussion. The very word "aristocrat" is a value-judgment. Let us speak rather of the "man of the spirit" and the "man of earth." The spirit, as we know, is always above, a shining, fiery, aerial being, a mighty rushing wind, while the earth lies below, solid and dark and cold. This perennial image is expressed in the *yang* and *yin* of classical Chinese philosophy. The "man of the spirit" represents the *yang* principle; his chief characteristic is an attitude conditioned by ideas, often called "idealistic" or "spiritual." The "man of earth" represents *yin,* and he is characterized by an earth-bound attitude. *Yang* and *yin* are deadly enemies who need one another. The man whose attitude is permeated by the earth under his feet is the exponent of a principle that leaves nothing to be desired in the way of aristocratic panache, for it is the eternal adversary and partner of the spirit. Keyserling's man is the aristocrat of *yang,* the Swiss the aristocrat of *yin.* So at least does Keyserling conceive him, when he calls him the non-aristocrat *par excellence.* I fully agree, but with the proviso that this judgment includes all those nations and parts of nations upon whom nature has set her mighty seal.

914   Our loveliest mountain, which dominates Switzerland far and wide, is called the Jungfrau—the "Virgin." The Virgin Mary is the female patron saint of the Swiss. Of her Tertullian says: ". . . that virgin earth, not yet watered by the rains," and Augustine: "Truth has arisen from the earth, because Christ is born of a virgin." These are living reminders that the virgin mother is the earth. From olden times the astrological sign for Switzerland was either Virgo or Taurus; both are earth-signs, a sure indication that the earthy character of the Swiss had not escaped the old astrologers. From the earth-boundness of the Swiss come all their bad as well as their good qualities: their

down-to-earthness, their limited outlook, their non-spirituality, their parsimony, stolidity, stubbornness, dislike of foreigners, mistrustfulness, as well as that awful *Schwizerdütsch* and their refusal to be bothered, or to put it in political terms, their neutrality. Switzerland consists of numerous valleys, depressions in the earth's crust, in which the settlements of man are embedded. Nowhere are there measureless plains, where it is a matter of indifference where a man lives; nowhere is there a coast against which the ocean beats with its lore of distant lands. Buried deep in the backbone of the continent, sunk in the earth, the Alpine dweller lives like a troglodyte, surrounded by more powerful nations that are linked with the wide world, that expand into colonies or can grow rich on the treasures of their soil. The Swiss cling to what they have, for the others, the more powerful ones, have grabbed everything else. Under no circumstances will the Swiss be robbed of their own. Their country is small, their possessions limited. If they lose what they have, what is going to replace it?

915   From this comes their national resentment, which, as Keyserling rightly remarks, is not unlike that of the Jews. This is understandable enough, since the Jews as a people are in the same precarious situation and are forced to develop the same defence-mechanisms. Resentment is a defence reaction against the threat of interference.

916   There are two kinds of interference which cause the hackles of the Swiss to rise: political and spiritual. Everyone can understand why they should defend themselves to the utmost against political interference, and this utmost is the art of neutrality born of necessity. But why they should defend themselves against spiritual interference is rather more mysterious. It is, however, a fact, as I can confirm from my own experience. English, American, and German patients are far more open to new ideas than the Swiss. A new idea for the Swiss is always something of a risk; it is like an unknown, dangerous animal, which must if possible be circumvented or else approached with extreme caution. (This, I may add, accounts for the remarkably poor intuitive capacity of the Swiss.)

917   Thus far, I find everything quite as it should be. I believe that the spirit is a dangerous thing and I do not believe in its paramountcy. I believe only in the Word become flesh, in the

spirit-filled body, where *yang* and *yin* are wedded into a living form.

918   The danger inherent in the spirit is that it will uproot man, bear him away from the earth and inspire him to Icarian flights, only to let him plunge into the bottomless sea. The chthonic man is rightly afraid of this and instinctively defends himself against it, but in the most unpleasant way—by his "resentment." Conversely, the man of the spirit fears and loathes the prison of the earth. It is, at bottom, the same kind of prejudice which the intuitive type has in regard to the sensation type: he confuses the latter with his own inferior sensation function. Naturally the sensation type has the same prejudice against the intuitive. When the two clash, both are aggrieved, because they feel that their most essential values have been misunderstood. The "other" in us always seems alien and unacceptable; but if we let ourselves be aggrieved the feeling sinks in, and we are the richer for this little bit of self-knowledge.

919   The unpleasant reaction Keyserling has evoked in Switzerland is not a sign of repudiation—it merely proves that the cap fits. Everybody reads him, and his book is discussed at every social gathering. An influence like this is usually not unilateral. Something emanating from Switzerland has had its effect on Keyserling, as every attentive reader will have observed; and this something is indigenous to Switzerland.

920   If it be true that we are the most backward, conservative, stiff-necked, self-righteous, smug, and churlish of all European nations, this would mean that in Switzerland the European is truly at home in his geographical and psychological centre. There he is attached to the earth, unconcerned, self-reliant, conservative, and backward—in other words, still intimately connected with the past, occupying a neutral position between the fluctuating and contradictory aspirations and opinions of the other nations or functions. That wouldn't be a bad role for the Swiss: to act as Europe's centre of gravity.

921   I do not wish to evoke the impression that I am trying to turn our national vices into a virtue. I do not deny the ugly side of the earthbound character, but I take it as a given fact and am merely trying to discover what its meaning might be for Europe. We need not be ashamed of ourselves as a nation, nor can we alter its character. Only the individual can alter or improve him-

self, provided he can outgrow his national prejudices in the course of his psychic development. The national character is imprinted on a man as a fate he has not chosen—like a beautiful or an ugly body. It is not the will of individuals that moulds the destinies of nations, but suprapersonal factors, the spirit and the earth, which work in mysterious ways and in unfathomable darkness. It is useless to attack or to praise nations since no one can alter them. Moreover the "nation" (like the "state") is a personified concept that corresponds in reality only to a specific nuance of the individual psyche. The nation has no life of its own apart from the individual, and is therefore not an end in itself. It is nothing but an inborn character, and this may be a handicap or an advantage, and is at best only a means to an end. Thus in many ways it is an advantage to have been imprinted with the English national character in one's cradle. You can then travel in the most god-forsaken countries and when anybody asks, "Are you a foreigner?" you can answer, "No, I am English" (as Schmitz tells in his autobiography).[4] This blissful self-assurance is enviable, but not in itself a merit.

922   By logically transforming nations into functions, Keyserling destroys their fictitious substance, though Europe would still continue to exist as a substantial unity. With the help of this conception he breaks through our nationalistic limitations: responsibility to the nation is legitimate only in so far as it answers to the needs of Europe as a whole. A nation can no longer be its own fulfilment; it can fulfil itself only as one function within a functional system. Does neutral Switzerland, with its backward, earthy nature, fulfil any meaningful function in the European system? I think we must answer this question affirmatively. The answer to political or cultural questions need not be only: Progress and Change, but also: Stand still! Hold fast! These days one can doubt in good faith whether the condition of Europe shows any change for the better since the war. Opinions, as we know, are very divided, and we have just heard Spengler's lamentations on the decline of the West. Progress can occasionally go down-hill, and in the face of a dangerously rapid tempo standing still can be a life-saver. Nations, too, get tired and long for political and social stabilization. The Pax Romana meant a good deal to the Roman Empire.

4 [See bibliography.]

923   All life is individual life, in which alone the ultimate meaning is to be found. Here I would like to quote the deepest thought in Keyserling's book: "If we now lift ourselves to the highest point of view attainable by earthbound man, we must say: The ultimate goal does not lie in the fulfilment of nations as such; how could it ever have been thought otherwise? Their life is only a means to a higher end; were it not so, no pessimism would be black enough." From this point of view, of course, the nation as an outward characteristic of a human society is a negligible factor. What would it then matter to the individual whether his "nation" lay peacefully ruminating in a lush meadow or not? But wasn't it the highest ambition of some of the wisest rulers to achieve precisely this? Is it so certain, then, that this state of stagnation is absolutely worthless? One of the most fundamental characteristics of every civilization is the quality of permanence, something created by man and wrested from the meaningless flux of nature. Every house, every bridge, every street, is a witness to the value of duration in the midst of change.

924   The neutral stability of Switzerland, despite all the disadvantages of our national character, seems to me to mean more for the European psyche than Keyserling is willing to admit. From his lofty point of view Switzerland must appear just as he describes it. And so indeed it is, seen from the outside. It is the diametrical opposite of Keyserling's nature, its earthiness contradicts his intuitive temperament, for which mere existence is an abomination. That is why he waxes so indignant about people who have money and do not spend it. Why should they spend it, if saving it gives them more pleasure? For other people, spending is a pleasure. But saving is the standstill that Keyserling dreads, and spending the liberating movement for which every intuitive longs. What Keyserling holds against Switzerland is, in the last analysis, its whole *raison d'être*. The Swiss national character that has been built up over the centuries was not formed by chance; it is a meaningful response to the dangerously undermining influence of the environment. We Swiss should certainly understand why a mind like Keyserling's judges us so harshly, but he should also understand that the very things he taxes us with belong to our most necessary possessions.

THE RISE OF A NEW WORLD [1]

925   "The Rise of a New World" is the subtitle of the German
edition of Keyserling's *America Set Free,* and is in every respect
the most succinct résumé of the theme of the book. For this book
is not purely and simply about America, any more than *The
Spectrum of Europe* was purely and simply about Europe. It
presents an extremely variegated picture that glitters in all the
colours of the rainbow, sombre and gay, pessimistic and optimistic—a veritable spectrum, which is often more like a spectre,
of America. The immediate cause of its birth is the abrasive
surface of the transatlantic continent, across which Keyserling's
aerial and procreative spirit flew, crackling and striking sparks
as it went. The book is like an independent organism that ex-
hibits as many characteristic features of its mother as of its
father. This is particularly evident in the fact that America has
become for the author a symbol of the rise of a new world. At
first it looks as if this "new world" was America, but at the end
of the book it becomes clear that the new world includes old
Europe—that is, ourselves. "The Rise of a New World" is as
much concerned with Europe as with America, for the book is
the product of the mutual impact of Keyserling and the United
States. (Another book of his will deal with South America.[2]) One
must bear this fact in mind, because it provides a clue to a correct understanding of the book's subjectivity. It is not unintentionally subjective, as if by regrettable accident, but is meant
to be so. To this it owes its dual aspect: America seen through

1 [First published as "Der Aufgang einer neuen Welt," *Neue Zürcher Zeitung*
(Zurich), no. 2378, iv (Dec. 7, 1930): a review of Count Hermann Keyserling's
Amerika; Der Aufgang einer Neuen Welt (Stuttgart, 1930), trans. anon. as *America
Set Free* (New York and London, 1930). This translation of Jung's article is new, but
the Keyserling quotations are from the English edition.—EDITORS.]
2 [*South-American Meditations* (1932).]

European eyes. Unavoidably, European psychology is translated into American terms that sound foreign to our ears, and this gives rise to a disconcerting and fascinating play of light and shadow, through which two fundamentally incommensurable worlds are alternately compared and contrasted.

926   Never before have I realized more clearly how difficult, if not impossible, it is fully to understand anything foreign, and to give an exhaustive account of it. A purely objective comparison would remain stuck in superficialities. Hence anyone who undertakes a comparison must call upon all his subjectivity for assistance if he is to produce a picture that will really tell us something about the foreigner. One should never read Keyserling in the belief that what he says about something is really so—or even that he thinks it is. Temperamental and downright as his utterances are, they are never hypostatizations. He simply expresses his opinion, and for this we can only be grateful. This book contains a wealth of the most deliberate, serious, and trenchant opinions, and there is every advantage to be gained from reflecting on them, even if one does not agree with them at first, if at all. Judging by my own experience of life in America, I have no fundamental objection to make against Keyserling's views. I begin to have misgivings only when he sets foot on that most hazardous territory of all, namely that of prognosis. But apart from that, his picture of America is splendidly compendious. The most striking thing is the fact that—very much in contrast with his standpoint in *The Spectrum of Europe*—he lets the American *earth* have its say. The immensity and massiveness of the continent must have done something to him. He feels its primeval, not yet "humanized" character. He misses the "psychic atmosphere" in the North American landscape. "No gods have yet sprung from its union with man," America has "no soul yet," because the conquerors of a foreign land "may take their bodies with them, but not their souls."

927   This categorical judgment certainly sounds rather bleak, but Keyserling has said something very true which offers a key to the locked recesses of American psychology. His analysis does not, to be sure, penetrate to these depths, but it does move within the wide field of American phenomenology, which, from the psychological point of view, offers material that is well-nigh inexhaustible. The vastness of the continental land-mass, the pre-

ponderance of immense open spaces, produce, so the author thinks, an atmosphere which resembles that of Russia and Central Asia. This bold comparison is a leitmotif of the book, and it comes up again and again in his discussion of the contrasting parallel between American private enterprise and Russian Bolshevism. "[America's] very spirit is one of width and vastness. This spirit of width and vastness is similar to that of Russia and Central Asia, and entirely different from that of Europe" (p. 70). That is why America might be compared, not with Europe, but with China (p. 73). For this reason America should not be ashamed of her Babbitts. "Babbitt . . . is today the soundest and most reliable representative of the entire continent" (p. 75), precisely because he is the type who is closest to the earth. This type will survive and, in time, will cause all European, and particularly all Anglo-Saxon, influences to disappear.

928   Keyserling regards the philosophers Emerson and William James as "contrasting ideologists" (p. 100). Dewey, on the other hand, he regards as the "most representative American" (p. 112), and the reasons he gives for this are not bad. He has an equally convincing view of the founder of Behaviourism, John B. Watson, as *the* American psychologist, and adds that his "psychology" means as little to the European as does Dewey's "philosophy." To make up for this, Dewey means all the more to the Asiatic (i.e., Russia and China), because his philosophy is really "psychology bent on education" (p. 113). The fact that Dewey's importance extends even to Asia (an example being the educational reforms in China) proves the curious similarity of their respective psychic situations despite all the differences. Here again Keyserling, it seems to me, hits the mark, for in Asia as well as in the chaotic mixture of races and cultures in America there is a social and educational problem of first rank to be faced. The European emigrant is rejuvenated on American soil; in that primitive atmosphere he can revert to the psychological patterns of his youth—hence his adolescent psychology with all the educational problems this entails. As a matter of fact, the moral condition of post-war youth in America presents the country with an immense educational task, compared with which other cultural tasks that seem of more importance to the European must inevitably take second place.

929   Keyserling considers that the ideal of a high living standard
is the mainspring of American morality. It expresses itself in
the idea of "social service," and also in the idea of social welfare. Keyserling calls this the "animal ideal" (p. 158). "What
animal, if it could think, would not enlist under the banner of
the highest possible standard of living?" exclaims Keyserling
(p. 164). And it is this ideal that constitutes the essential core
of the typically American outlook on life: behaviourism. Watson
is therefore "one of the foremost representatives of what the
United States stood for in the twentieth century" (p. 167). At
the same time, behaviourism provides the intellectual link with
Bolshevist psychology. For this reason the American, for all his
hustling, is mentally the most passive of men (p. 271), and
"American civilization is the most uniform that has ever
existed." "The ideal of health, then, contributes in its turn to
the animalization of the American. But the same is true of education as it is generally understood. It is becoming more and
more a form of training such as animals can be submitted to."

930   This mental condition goes hand in hand with the lack of
authority in the States. "The State and the Government are not
considered as institutions ranging above the private individual.
On the contrary, they are supposed to be mere executives of his
will" (p. 235). "Every American citizen rejoices in [American
political institutions] and will do his utmost to uphold their
prestige in foreign countries. But as regards his own person he
views them in a totally different light. At home he is, first and
last, a private entrepreneur" (p. 236). "The United States are
one gigantic Canton Appenzell—the most provincial province
in Switzerland" (pp. 237–38).

931   There is no lack of *bons mots* in this book, for instance the
club-woman as the "aunt of the nation," who does her best to
deprive her naughty little nephew of alcohol, on the ground that
it is injurious to health. There is also the crack about the "kindergarten" (p. 271) psychology of adult Americans, and many
other entertainingly apt drolleries.

932   The chapter on "The Overrated Child" seems to me the best
in the book. "America," we are told, "is fundamentally the land
of the overrated child" (p. 267)—an expression of the nation's
youthfulness and at the same time an attempt to perpetuate it.
What Keyserling has to say about the relation of the sexes and

of members of the family to one another, and about parents, husbands and wives, marriage, the upbringing of children, the demasculinization of men and the masculinization of women is very well worth reading, not merely because it concerns America but because we Europeans can learn something from it of value to ourselves. Anyone who still does not know how much the American way of life is infecting Europe's upper classes, just as Asiatic Bolshevism is seeping into European Communism, should take this opportunity to find out. Europe is dangerously close to becoming a mere hyphen between America and Asia. It cannot yet be said that the European has "only the fearful choice" between Americanization and Bolshevism. Europe, thank God, still exists in her own right. But we should realize all the more clearly how far the Americanization of the social upper crust has advanced. That is why I wish Keyserling as devoted a public in Europe as in America. Above all, one should not let oneself be irritated, even when it sometimes looks as if a nasty-tempered dog were mercilessly shaking its victim, or as if a universal schoolmaster were giving the boys good advice for their journey through life. One should never get annoyed with Keyserling, for at bottom he means it well. And how often he hits the mark! Everything he says about America from the European point of view may be arbitrary, cock-eyed, or just plain wrong, and yet the thoughtful European can derive plenty of stimulation from this book, not only for himself as a European, collective being, but for himself as an individual. After all, the American is a human being like ourselves, and his ideals and moral motives belong to the same Christian era as ours. Hence any criticism of him affects us as well. The reader will be particularly impressed by this in the final chapter, on "Spirituality." Here Keyserling seems to be talking about America, but in reality he is making a profession of faith, and expressing a hope for the future, which apply to Europe in a higher sense than to America, although they are also of profound significance for any American living in a Christian era.

933   It had never struck me so clearly before how much Keyserling is the mouthpiece of the collective spirit, until I read this chapter. One might easily expect from Keyserling, the "intellectual aristocrat," lofty pronouncements borne along on the rarefied breezes that blow from the differentiated academic

mind. But nothing of the sort happens here. On the contrary, he speaks of things that are not only remote from the academic mind, but are unknown to it and are even regarded with contempt. They are things which really do concern the psyche of modern man, which do not appear on the surface, but which become visible to anyone who is interested in the background and who has occasion to speak with people who usually do not talk very loudly. But the "silent ones in the land" are greater in number than the makers of noise. In this chapter, Keyserling speaks from the background, and to those who dwell in the background. Here he is no longer the *enfant terrible,* no longer the brilliant talker; here he grips you. We hear a Keyserling who commands attention, one who speaks with the voice of many, and so gives expression to a great time of change. The man of this age undoubtedly speaks through him when he rates understanding above faith and experience above a credo. The individual, "master of himself and freed from the shackles of tradition, is beginning to understand the old truths, in so far as they are truths which in earlier times were simply accepted on authority, in a new and personal way. At the very time when the old forms are disintegrating, advanced minorities are beginning to experience their essential meaning, their living and immortal substance, more profoundly than at any time since the golden age of Christianity, when Greek thinkers were giving shape to the Christian view of the world. This means nothing less than that the age of the Holy Ghost is now at hand" (p. 464).

934   Who would have thought that? Or rather, who actually thinks like that? Who are these "advanced minorities"? Where are they? I will tell you: your next-door neighbours, the Meiers and the Müllers, of whom you would never have expected it, think like that. Sometimes they know it and sometimes they don't. If they do, they conceal this knowledge more carefully than the worst scandal. Nowadays it is no longer the old-fashioned objects of modesty that are guarded by a feeling of shame, but a secret spirituality. There are millions of people today who make "spiritual" experiments on themselves, and who are so shamefully conscious of their incompetent and illegimate behaviour that more often than not they close their eyes to what they are doing. Their numbers justify Keyserling in speaking out so confidently, in saying something so unprece-

dented and so unbelievable that he should know that all
Churches, all academies, all governments, and all joint-stock
companies will shake their wise and venerable heads at it. How
many of these "silent ones in the land" would dare to shake the
good Count democratically by the hand on the strength of this
confession?

LA RÉVOLUTION MONDIALE [1]

935   It is perhaps a sign of the times that in his new book, *La Révolution mondiale et la responsabilité de l'Esprit,* Keyserling addresses his public in French. One feels oneself transported back to the eighteenth century in Germany, when not only statesmen but philosophers and scholars preferred a more refined, cultured, and elegant language like French to their complicated and clumsy German, politely dressing up their subject in a courtly Sunday suit. *La Révolution mondiale* is certainly not a subject that calls for any such old-fashioned allurements, so it must be quite other reasons that impelled the author to write in French. I wish the book had been written in German, for, in my unqualified opinion, its spirit is as un-French as it could possibly be. Even the words "la responsabilité de l'esprit" expresses a kind of "spirit" (*Geist*) that can hardly be imputed to the French "esprit." Keyserling looks foreign and odd in French dress. German or perhaps Russian expresses the peculiar nature of his spirituality much better. If his public had been Chinese, or people who could read Chinese, both they and he would have benefited had he written in Chinese characters.

936   Every Chinese character is a complicated structure of meaning, in which sometimes whole families of ideas are gathered under one roof. Characters such as these are admirably suited to reproduce the infinite, protean diversity of Keyserling's ideas, and at the same time vague enough to convey to the reader all those flashes of intuition that are so typical of Keyserling's mind. They would also give the reader the great satisfaction of thinking that he had perceived all this for himself. But in French it sounds as if Keyserling alone had perceived everything.

[1] [First published as "Ein neues Buch von Keyserling," *Basler Nachrichten,* Sonntagsblatt [Sunday Supplement], XXVIII:19 (May 13, 1934), 78–79. The article is a review of Keyserling's *La Révolution mondiale et la responsabilité de l'Esprit* (Paris, 1934), quotations of which have been translated from the French.—EDITORS.]

937   The book shows Keyserling's reaction to what is going on in the world today, just as his earlier book, *South-American Meditations*, describes the impact which South America, a continent that is not controllable by the spirit, made upon him. It is no doubt from this book that the "telluric powers" are derived, whose revolt the author feels to be the cause and content of the present European crisis. They seem to him—no doubt again in recollection of the South American *gana*-world—to be essentially passive, not only in need of direction by the spirit, but capable of being so directed. The spiritual and the telluric are the contrapuntal poles of this book and also of the world crisis. Nietzsche's "slave-insurrection in morals" changes here into a mass-insurrection against the spirit. Keyserling is clear-sighted enough to see that this revolt is not just a negative phenomenon but that it also has its positive side; it turns out that the revolt of the "telluric" man brings with it an efflorescence of "faith and courage." "The primordial expressions of the spirit are courage and faith, and its eternal prototype is the religious spirit." A certain amount of barbarization is inevitable, but "the rebirth of blind faith . . . is simply a sign of the renewal of youth, and thus of increased vitality."

938   In order to find the criterion for contemporary events, Keyserling harks back to the rise of Islam and, even more, to that of Christianity. For him we are in the midst of a "world change," and it is no longer a question of social or political happenings, of "repentance," and certainly not of leadership, planned economy, and the like. He has set his picture of our contemporary world in the widest possible framework, filling it with a multitude of aspects and cross-relationships which are all, at bottom, products of his own congenitally mixed nature. His heritage, stemming from a diversity of widely separated races and peoples as well as from all sorts of different cultural levels, produces in Keyserling an enormous range of reactions and points of view which give this book, like all his others, its glitter and variety. He is no doubt speaking from his own most personal experience when he says: "Consequently, there is only one attitude which is appropriate: to take human nature as it is, in all the diversity of its strata and all its queer disequilibrium."

939   This sentence holds good for the author but not for the masses, for in the latter case we should have no substitute

497

"uniformity" for "diversity" and "hopeless balance" for "disequilibrium." The masses as we know follow the law of their own inertia and seek, if disturbed, to restore the state of balance as speedily as possible, no matter how uncomfortable it may be. In this respect the masses are uncommonly "telluric." No wonder these "telluric powers" seem to Keyserling the most unspiritual thing imaginable. For him the "spirit" is its polar opposite. This is a genuinely Western point of view, and in this matter, therefore, Keyserling feels himself at odds with classical philosophy, which, he says, makes this Western antithesis unreal. One can only ask oneself whether such an opposition between heaven and earth has always existed, and whether the *I Ching* may not be right after all, when it says that heaven and earth only occasionally draw apart and come into conflict with one another. Chinese wisdom regards this state merely as a passing one that contradicts the ordinances of heaven. Heaven and earth belong together, *yang* and *yin* give birth to one another and devour one another in a way that accords with the heavenly order of things. Europeans take it for granted that crocodiles are wicked, man-eating monsters, but the primitive takes just the opposite view, for to his way of thinking crocodiles eat people only in exceptional circumstances, and then only when they have been put up to it by a hostile medicine-man. If one is the crocodile's brother, then there is no danger at all. So, too, we in the West have perpetuated the purely exceptional opposition between heaven and earth, and, as a result, find ourselves in a perpetual state of ethical conflict. The Chinese believe in what Nietzsche called the "spirit of gravity," and the dragon, which we like to think lives in gloomy caverns, sparkles for them in the heavens as a merry firework, and drives away the magic wrought by evil spirits. For the Chinese, "spirit" does not signify order, meaning, and everything that is good; on the contrary, it is a fiery and sometimes dangerous power.

940   It might therefore be objected that the "telluric powers" are not at all unspiritual, but are, on the contrary, endowed with a dangerous spirit, a spirit so powerful that the spirit of the West must indeed reflect with all its might on its "responsibility," compiling, as in Keyserling's book, a list of "should"s and "must"s, though "with how little success," as the author resignedly remarks.

941   I fear Keyserling makes rather too much use of a spirit which in the past found itself in hopeless opposition to the earth. "Accepting human nature as it is" means nothing less than swallowing the "telluric essence"—which constitutes "eighty per cent of man's nature"—as a bitter medicine, however unspiritual it may be. It almost seems as if this time earth might have something to say to heaven, and that, consequently, the aerial spirit had better pay attention. When Keyserling hopes to save the "spirit" by appealing to "creative understanding," he seems to me to be entrapped in the idea—so typical of the age of enlightenment and progress—that in the end everything can be understood. But the earth will show us clearly enough that there are some things man will never understand, that there are times when the spirit is completely darkened because it needs to be reborn. We should not try to escape this night by "understanding," nor shall we ever succeed in soaring above the chaos by adopting a positive attitude to everything. ("What is needed today is an *absolutely* positive attitude towards everything that, on the empirical level, is different from oneself.") The "telluric powers" will do their utmost to convince us that we are neither reasonable, nor spiritual, nor capable of understanding, nor positive, nor God knows what, for the essence of the old spirit consisted precisely in the conceit that we were all these things. Keyserling brands American pragmatism as "profoundly unspiritual" (I hope, by the way, he doesn't mean William James!), but by his "positive attitude" he runs the risk of succumbing to Schiller's brand of pragmatism—anything rather than capitulate.

942   How can that religious renewal, predicted by Keyserling as necessary and imminent, come about at all unless our much-vaunted spirit—which wants to understand everything and take a positive attitude to everything, and, above all, feels responsible for our ethical behaviour—can gracefully die? It has indeed become a human spirit, fallible and limited; it "needs a death" in order to be renewed, and it cannot do this by itself. What does the supremacy of the "telluric powers" mean, except that the "spirit" has once again grown weak with age, because it has been too much humanized?

943   Keyserling takes up Nietzsche's idea of a "cultural monastery," stimulated thereto by the "Entretiens sur l'avenir de l'esprit européen" organized by the French under the presidency

of Paul Valéry, which took place in Paris in October 1933,[2] and was the immediate occasion of *La Révolution mondiale*. He says: "In short, the solution we advocate has a good deal in common with that offered by the monasteries at the beginning of the Middle Ages." What moving spirits will belong to the New Order?

Of what kind would the men be who were capable of giving direction to the masses who now determine the course of history? Surely the very men we have been describing: absolutely free, haughtily independent, concerned with quality alone, conscious of their uniqueness, determined to acknowledge no authority outside themselves, proud to be a tiny minority, as active mentally as the mob is passive. Men whose consciousness is naturally centred on a plane superior to earthly happenings, to country, to race, to social or political necessities; men who in their deepest aspirations are completely free of all external considerations, of glory, influence, status; ascetics, in short, of a single pattern, forming a nobility of a kind hitherto unknown.

944   The heaping together of paintings by Old Masters in museums is a catastrophe; likewise, a collection of a hundred Great Brains makes one big fathead. An "Order" is constituted, firstly, by the grace of God, and secondly, by a majority of highly insignificant people. Those noble souls who float before the eyes of the author will constitute an order, or will be fit to be received into such, when (in keeping with the author's list of qualities) they (1) are conscious of their lack of freedom, (2) humbly recognize their dependence, (3) have forgotten their so-called uniqueness, (4) can adapt to the eternal powers outside themselves, (5) can endure being a small minority, (6) have their natural centre of consciousness in their earth, in their race, and in social and political necessities, and (lastly) when, through the presence of God, which curiously enough always coincides with a time of great distress, there has grown up in them a need for true human fellowship from a profound experience of the nullity of human existence.

945   If our esteemed author, Count Keyserling, were to become

2 [The third in a series of "Conversations," actually organized by the Permanent Committee of Arts and Letters of the League of Nations and conducted by the International Institute of Intellectual Co-operation in various cities from 1932 to 1938. Keyserling represented Germany at the meeting in question. Cf. Valéry, *History and Politics*, pp. 531ff. and 541ff.—EDITORS.]

a lay brother charged with working in the kitchens of the cultural monastery, then I would believe in the feasibility of this idea, but not before. I even believe that the reader would be doing the book an injustice if he took such ideas quite literally. Ideas are images for something, and not its essence; they are symbols, and even symptoms. By taking them literally we block the approach to Keyserling's world of ideas. He is, in the truest sense, the mouthpiece of the *Zeitgeist,* or, to be more accurate, the *Zeitgeist* of the spiritual man. When one takes him like this, even his cultural monastery presents no difficulty: it is symptomatic of that chiliastic mood which no conscious person nowadays should dismiss as worthless. The time is as great as one thinks it, and man grows to the stature of the time. Keyserling's mediumistic gifts have gathered together the loose, fluttering, fragmentary thoughts of a whole epoch. Like Ortega y Gasset, he condenses the symptomatic utterances of the collective spirit, speaking through a thousand tongues, into a single discourse addressed to his contemporaries. That is why everyone will hear his own voice in this discourse. And because it is extremely useful and desirable to know what one is thinking (which is not always the case, by any means), one should read this book assiduously. There is probably no other work which describes the spiritual imponderabilia of our age more lucidly than *La Révolution mondiale.*

THE COMPLICATIONS OF
AMERICAN PSYCHOLOGY [1]

946   It would never occur to the naïve European to regard the psychology of the average American as particularly complicated or even sophisticated. On the contrary he is rather impressed by the simplicity and straightforwardness of American thought and manners. He likes to think of Americans as being a very active, business-like, and astonishingly efficient people, concentrated upon a single goal (viz., the yellow god), and a bit handicapped by what certain English magazines call "Americana"—something on the border-line of mild insanity, "colonials are liable to be a bit odd, don't you know, like our South African cousins."

947   Thus, when I have to say something serious about Americans and their peculiar psychology, my European audience is not shocked exactly, but at all events somewhat puzzled and inclined to disapprove. What the Americans will feel about my ideas, remains to be seen.

948   In 1909 I paid my first short visit to the United States. This was my first impression of the American people as a whole; before that I had known individuals only. I remember, when walking through the streets of Buffalo, I came across hundreds of workmen leaving a factory. The naïve European traveller I was then could not help remarking to his American companion: "I really had no idea there was such an amazing amount of Indian blood in your people." "What," said he, "Indian blood? I bet there is not one drop of it in this whole crowd." I replied: "But don't you see their faces? They are more Indian than European." Whereupon I was informed that probably most of these workmen were of Irish, Scottish, and German extraction without a trace of Indian blood in their veins. I was puzzled and half in-

1 [Written in English and first published as "Your Negroid and Indian Behavior," *Forum* (New York), LXXXIII (1930):4, 193–99. Slightly revised stylistically for publication here.—EDITORS.]

credulous. Subsequently I learned to see how ridiculous my hypothesis had been. Nevertheless, the impression of facial similarity remained and later years only enhanced it. As Professor Boas maintains, there are even measurable anatomical changes in many American immigrants, changes which are already noticeable in the second generation. His findings, however, have not been accepted by other authorities.

949 I remember a New York family of German immigrants of which three of the children were born in Germany and four in America. The latter were unmistakably Americans, the first three were clearly Germans. To a keen European eye there is an indefinable yet undeniable something in the whole makeup of the born American that distinguishes him from the born European. It is not so much in the anatomical features as in the general behaviour, physical and mental. One finds it in the language, the gestures, the mentality, in the movements of the body, and in certain things even more subtle than that.

950 When I returned from America, I was left with the peculiarly dissatisfied feeling of one who has somehow missed the point. I had to confess that I was unable "to size them up." I only knew that a subtle difference existed between the American and the European, just as it does between the Australian and the South African. You can say many witty or clever things about that difference, and yet you miss the point somehow. But another impression also stuck in my mind. I had not noticed it at first, but it kept on coming back like all those things that have a certain importance and yet have not been understood. I was once the guest of a pretty stiff and solemn New England family of a rather terrifying respectability. It felt almost like home. (There are very conservative and highly respectable folk in Switzerland, too. We might even better the American record in this respect.) There were Negro servants waiting at table. I felt at first as if I were eating lunch in a circus and I found myself diffidently scrutinizing the dishes, looking for the imprint of those black fingers. A solemnity brooded over the meal for which I could see no reason, but I supposed it was the solemnity or serenity of great virtue or something like that which vibrated through the room. At all events nobody laughed. Everyone was just too nice and too polite. Eventually I could stand it no longer, and I began to crack jokes for better or worse. These

were greeted with condescending smiles. But I could not arouse that hearty and generous American laugh which I love and admire. "Well," I thought, "Indian blood, wooden faces, camouflaged Mongols, why not try some Chinese on them?" So I came to my last story, really a good one—and no sooner had I finished than right behind my chair an enormous avalanche of laughter broke loose. It was the Negro servant, and it was the real American laughter, that grand, unrestrained, unsophisticated laughter revealing rows of teeth, tongue, palate, everything, just a trifle exaggerated perhaps and certainly less than sixteen years old. How I loved that African brother.

951   I admit it is a rather foolish story, all the more so as I could not then see the reason why the incident should stick in my mind. Only much later did I discover the underlying significance of this and of that other impression I had received at Buffalo.

952   Our convictions often have a humble origin. I do not hesitate, therefore, to tell my reader exactly how my ideas about American psychology started. Those two little impressions really hold in a nutshell everything I subsequently learned in the course of twenty-five years' work with American patients.

953   The American laugh is most impressive. Laughing is a very important emotional expression and one learns a lot about character from a careful observation of the way people laugh. There are people who suffer from a crippled laughter. It's just painful to see them laugh and the sound of that shrill, evil, compressed rattle almost makes you sick. America as a nation can laugh, and that means a lot. There is still a childlikeness, a soundness of emotion, an immediate rapport with your fellow being.

954   This laughter goes hand in hand with a remarkable vivacity and a great ease of expression. Americans are great talkers. Gossip and chattering spill over into monstrously big newspapers. The talking goes on even when you are reading. The style of "good" American writing is a talking style. When it is not too flat, it is just as refreshing and exhilarating for us Europeans as your laughter. But often, alas, it is just chattering, the vibrating noise of a big ant-heap.

955   One of the greatest advantages of the American language is its slang. I am far from sniffing at American slang, on the contrary I like it profoundly. Slang means a language in the making,

a thing fully alive. Its images are not worn-out and worm-eaten metaphors, pale reflections hallowed by immemorial age, smooth, correct, and concise conventions, but figures full of life, carrying all the stamina of their earthly origin, and the incomparable flavour of local conditions peculiar to the strange and unprejudiced soil of a new country. One feels a new current of strange life in the flow of the old English language, and one wonders where it comes from. Is it the new country only? I doubt it.

956   The way the American moves shows a strong tendency to nonchalance. When we analyse the way he walks, how he wears his hat, how he holds his cigar, how he speaks, we discover a marked nonchalance. One hears an unusual amount of unrestrained voices in the talk going on around one. There is a lack of restraint in the way people sit, sometimes at the expense of your furniture, or on Sundays you see streets punctuated with feet showing over the window-sills. There is a tendency to move with loose joints, with a minimum of innervation. In speech one notices this nonchalance in an insufficient innervation of the soft palate, which causes the nasal intonation that is so common with Americans. The swaying hip which you can observe in primitive, particularly Negro women is frequently seen in American women, and the swinging gait of the man is fairly usual.

957   The most amazing feature of American life is its boundless publicity. Everybody has to meet everybody, and they even seem to enjoy this enormity. To a central European such as I am, this American publicity of life, the lack of distance between people, the absence of hedges or fences round the gardens, the belief in popularity, the gossip columns of the newspapers, the open doors in the houses (one can look from the street right through the sitting-room and the adjoining bedroom into the backyard and beyond), the defencelessness of the individual against the onslaught of the press, all this is more than disgusting, it is positively terrifying. You are immediately swallowed by a hot and all-engulfing wave of desirousness and emotional incontinence. You are simply reduced to a particle in the mass, with no other hope or expectation than the illusory goals of an eager and excited collectivity. You just swim for life, that's all. You feel free—that's the queerest thing—yet the collective movement grips you faster than any old gnarled roots in European soil

would have done. Even your head gets immersed. There is a peculiar lack of restraint about the emotions of an American collectivity. You see it in the eagerness and in the hustle of everyday life, in all sorts of enthusiasms, in orgiastic sectarian outbursts, in the violence of public admiration and opprobrium. The overwhelming influence of collective emotions spreads into everything. If it were possible, everything would be done collectively, because there seems to be an astonishingly feeble resistance to collective influences. It is true that collective action is always less laborious than an individual attempt. The momentum of collective action carries much further than even concentrated individual effort, since it makes people unaware of themselves and heedless of risks. On the other hand, it easily goes too far and leads people into situations which individual deliberation would hardly ever have chosen. It has a decidedly flattening influence on people's psychology.

958   You see this particularly in the American sex problem as it had developed since the war. There is a marked tendency to promiscuity, which shows not only in the frequency of divorces but quite particularly in the peculiar liberation from sex prejudices in the younger generation. As an inevitable consequence the individual rapport between the sexes will suffer. An easy access never calls forth and therefore never develops the values of character, and at the same time it is a most serious obstacle to any deeper mutual understanding. Such an understanding, without which no real love can exist, is reached only by overcoming all the difficulties due to the psychological difference between the sexes. Promiscuity paralyses all these efforts by offering easy opportunities of escape. Individual rapport becomes quite superfluous. But the more a so-called unprejudiced freedom and easy promiscuity prevail, the more love becomes flat and degenerates into transitory sex interludes. The most recent developments in the field of sexual morality tend toward sexual primitivity, analogous to the instability of the moral habits of primitive peoples, where under the influence of collective emotion all sex taboos instantly disappear.

959   All American life seems to be the life of the big settlement—real town-life. Even the smallest settlement denies itself the character of a village and tends to become a city. The town rules the whole style of living, even in the country. It seems as though

everything were collective and standardized. Once on a visit to a so-called camp with so-called country life, a European friend who was travelling with me whispered to me in a quiet moment: "I bet they even have a text-book on how to camp," and—there it was, evilly glistening in red and gold upon the shelf!

960   The country is wonderful, nay, just divine, still with the faint perfume of unhistorical eternity in the air, and those lovely crickets not yet shy of man. They don't know yet that they are living in America, like some Navahos. And the bullfrog talks in the night with his prehistoric booming voice. Beautiful immense nights, and days blessed with sunshine. There is real country and nobody seems to be up to it, certainly not that hustling, noisily chattering, motoring townfolk. They are not even down to it, as the Red Indians are, with whom one feels peculiarly at ease because they are obviously under the spell of their country and not on top of it. So there at last is the peace of God.

961   I know the mother-nations of North America pretty well, but I would be completely at a loss to explain, if I relied solely on the theory of heredity, how the Americans descended from them acquired their striking peculiarities. One might suppose that some of them were the product of the old pioneer and colonist attitude. But I fail to see how the particular qualities I have mentioned have anything to do with the character of the early farmer colonist. There is a much better hypothesis to explain the peculiarities of the American temperament. It is the fact that the States are pervaded by the Negro, that most striking and suggestive figure. Some States are particularly black, a fact that may astonish the naïve European, who thinks of America as a white nation. It is not wholly white, if you please, but piebald. It cannot be helped, it just is so.

962   What is more contagious than to live side by side with a rather primitive people? Go to Africa and see what happens. When it is so obvious that you stumble over it, you call it "going black." But if it is not so obvious it is explained as "the sun." In India it is always the sun. In reality it is a mitigated going black, counterbalanced by a particularly stiffnecked conventionality (with its subdivisions of righteousness and conspicuous respectability). Under the pressure of all this conventionality people simply dry up, though they make the sun responsible. It is much easier for us Europeans to be a trifle

immoral, or at least a bit lax, because we do not have to maintain the moral standard against the heavy downward pull of primitive life. The inferior man has a tremendous pull because he fascinates the inferior layers of our psyche, which has lived through untold ages of similar conditions—"on revient toujours à ses premiers amours." He reminds us—or not so much our conscious as our unconscious mind—not only of childhood but of our prehistory, which would take us back not more than about twelve hundred years so far as the Germanic races are concerned. The barbarian in us is still wonderfully strong and he yields easily to the lure of his youthful memories. Therefore he needs very definite defences. The Latin peoples being older don't need to be so much on their guard, hence their approach to the coloured man is different.

963   But the defences of the Germanic man reach only as far as consciousness reaches. Below the threshold of consciousness the contagion meets with little resistance. Just as the coloured man lives in your cities and even within your houses, so also he lives under your skin, subconsciously. Naturally it works both ways. Just as every Jew has a Christ complex, so every Negro has a white complex and every American a Negro complex. As a rule the coloured man would give anything to change his skin, and the white man hates to admit that he has been touched by the black.

964   Now for the facts. What about that American laughter? What about the boundless noisy sociality? The pleasure in movement and in stunts of all sorts? The loose-jointed walk, the Negroid dancing and music? The rhythm of jazz is the same as the *n'goma,* the African dance. You can dance the Central African *n'goma* with all its jumping and rocking, its swinging shoulders and hips, to American jazz. American music is most obviously pervaded by the African rhythm and the African melody.

965   It would be difficult not to see that the coloured man, with his primitive motility, his expressive emotionality, his childlike directness, his sense of music and rhythm, his funny and picturesque language, has infected the American "behaviour." As any psychologist and any doctor knows, nothing is more contagious than tics, stammering, choreic movements, signs of emotion, above all laughter and peculiarities of speech. Even if your

mind and heart are elsewhere, even if you don't understand a joke in a foreign language, you can't help smiling when everybody else smiles. Stammering can have a most infectious quality, so that you hardly can refrain from imitating it involuntarily. Melody and rhythm are most insidious, they can obsess you for days, and as to language it is most disturbing how its metaphors and different ways of pronunciation affect you, beginning with some apologetic quotation, and then because you just can't help it.

966   The white man is a most terrific problem to the Negro, and whenever you affect somebody so profoundly, then, in a mysterious way, something comes back from him to yourself. The Negro by his mere presence is a source of temperamental and mimetic infection, which the European can't help noticing just as much as he sees the hopeless gap between the American and the African Negro. Racial infection is a most serious mental and moral problem where the primitive outnumbers the white man. America has this problem only in a relative degree, because the whites far outnumber the coloured. Apparently he can assimilate the primitive influence with little risk to himself. What would happen if there were a considerable increase in the coloured population is another matter.

967   I am quite convinced that some American peculiarities can be traced back directly to the coloured man, while others result from a compensatory defence against his laxity. But they remain externals leaving the inner quick of the American character untouched, which is not the case where "going black" is concerned. Since I am not a behaviourist, I take leave to suppose that you are still very far from the real man when you observe only his behaviour. I regard behaviour as a mere husk that conceals the living substance within. Thus I can discern the white man clearly enough through his slightly Negroid mannerisms, and my question is: Is this American white man nothing but a simple white man, or is he in some way different from the European representative of the species? I believe there is a marked difference between them within as well as without. European magazines have recently published pictures of well-known Americans in Indian headdress, and some Red Indians in European costume in the opposite column, with the question: Who are the Indians?

968   This is not just a joke. There is something in it that can hardly be denied. It may seem mysterious and unbelievable, yet it is a fact that can be observed in other countries just as well. Man can be assimilated by a country. There is an x and a y in the air and in the soil of a country, which slowly permeate and assimilate him to the type of the aboriginal inhabitant, even to the point of slightly remodelling his physical features. The verification of such facts in terms of exact measurement, overwhelmingly obvious though they sometimes are, is—I admit—exceedingly difficult. But there are many such things that elude all our means of exact scientific verification despite their obvious and indubitable character. Think of all the subtleties of expression in the eyes, gestures, and intonation. In practice everybody goes by them and no idiot could misunderstand them, yet one is faced with a most ticklish task when it comes to giving an absolutely scientific description of them. I know a man who could tell from a series of photographs of Jews of different countries with almost infallible certainty: This is a Polish, that a Cossack, and that a German Jew, and so on.

969   Undoubtedly there are these subtle indications in man: sometimes they lurk in the lines of his face, sometimes in his gestures, his facial expression, the look in his eyes, and sometimes in his psyche, that shines forth through the transparent veil of his body. At all events it is often possible to tell in what country he was born. I know quite a number of cases where children of purely European parents were born in Eastern countries and exhibited the marks of their respective birthplaces either in the imponderabilia of their appearance or in their mental make-up or in both, and to such a degree that not only I myself but other people who were entirely ignorant of the circumstances could make the diagnosis. The foreign country somehow gets under the skin of those born in it. Certain very primitive tribes are convinced that it is not possible to usurp foreign territory, because the children born there would inherit the wrong ancestor-spirits who dwell in the trees, the rocks, and the water of that country. There seems to be some subtle truth in this primitive intuition.

970   That would mean that the spirit of the Indian gets at the American from within and without. Indeed, there is often an astonishing likeness in the cast of the American face to that of

the Red Indian, more I think in the men's faces than in the women's. But women are always the more conservative element in spite of their conspicuous affectation of modernity. It is a paradox certainly, yet such is human nature.

971   The external assimilation to the peculiarities of a country is a thing one could almost expect. There is nothing astonishing in it. But the external similarity is feeble in comparison with the less visible but all the more intense influence on the mind. It is just as though the mind were an infinitely more sensitive and suggestible medium than the body. It is probable that long before the body reacts the mind has already undergone considerable changes, changes that are not obvious to the individual himself or to his immediate circle, but only to an outsider. Thus I would not expect the average American, who has not lived for some years in Europe, to realize how different his mental attitude is from the European's, just as I would not expect the average European to be able to discern his difference from the American. That is the reason why so many things that are really characteristic of a country seem to be merely odd or ridiculous: the conditions from which they arise are either not known or not understood. They wouldn't be odd or ridiculous if one could feel the local atmosphere to which they belong and which makes them perfectly comprehensible and logical.

972   Almost every great country has its collective attitude, which one might call its genius or *spiritus loci*. Sometimes you can catch it in a formula, sometimes it is more elusive, yet nonetheless it is indescribably present as a sort of atmosphere that permeates everything, the look of the people, their speech, behaviour, clothing, smell, their interests, ideals, politics, philosophy, art, and even their religion. In a well-defined civilization with a solid historical background, such as for instance the French, you can easily discover the keynote of the French *esprit:* it is "la gloire," a most marked prestige psychology in its noblest as well as its most ridiculous forms. You find it in their speech, gestures, beliefs, in the style of everything, in politics and even in science.

973   In Germany it is the "Idea" that is impersonated by everybody. There are no ordinary human beings, you are "Herr Professor" or "Herr Geheimrat," "Herr Oberrechnungsrat," and even longer things than that. Sometimes the German idea is

right and sometimes it is wrong, but it never ceases to be an idea whether it belongs to the highest philosophy or is merely a foolish bias. Even when you die in Germany, you don't die in mere human misery, you die in the ideal form of "Hausbesitzersgattin" or something of the sort.

974   England's innermost truth and at the same time her most valuable contribution to the assets of the human family is the "gentleman," rescued from the dusty chivalry of the early Middle Ages and now penetrating into the remotest corner of modern English life. It is an ultimate principle that never fails to carry conviction, the shining armour of the perfect knight in soul and body, and the miserable coffin of poor natural feelings.

975   But could one "size up" other countries like Italy, Austria, Spain, Netherlands, Switzerland, just as easily? They are all very characteristic countries, yet their spirit is more difficult to catch. It would need not one word but at least a couple of sentences. America is also one of those countries that are not settled by one shot. European prejudice would say: Money. But only people who have no idea of what money means to Americans can think like that. Yes, if they themselves are Americans, it would be money. But America is not as simple as that. Of course there is any amount of ordinary materialism in America as everywhere else, but also a most admirable idealism which hardly finds its equal anywhere else. Money with us has still something of the magic of the old taboo, dating from the times when any money business like banking, or usury, was considered dishonest. It is still something of a forbidden pleasure in the old countries. That is why it is good form with us to hush up money matters. The American, unhampered by the burden of historical conditions, can make and spend money for what it is worth. America is peculiarly free from the spell of money, yet she makes a lot of it. How can the European understand this puzzle?

976   America has a principle or idea or attitude, but it is surely not money. Often, when I was searching through the conscious and the unconscious mind of my American patients and pupils, I found something which I can only describe as a sort of Heroic Ideal. Your most idealistic effort is concerned with bringing out the best in every man, and when you find a good man you naturally support him and push him on, until at last he is liable to collapse from sheer exertion, success, and triumph. It is done

in every family, where ambitious mothers egg their boys on with the idea that they must be heroes of some sort, or you find it in the factory, where the whole system anxiously tries to get the best man into the best place. Or again in the schools where every child is trained to be brave, courageous, efficient, and a "good sport," a hero in short. There is no record which people will not kill themselves to break, even if it is the most appalling nonsense. The moving pictures abound with heroes of every description. American applause holds the world's record. The "great" and "famous" man gets mobbed by enthusiastic crowds, whatever he may be "great" in; even Valentino got his full share. In Germany you are great if your titles are two yards long, in England if you are a gentleman as well, in France if you coincide with the prestige of the country. In small countries there is, as a rule, no greatness when you are alive, because things need to be small, therefore it is usually posthumous. America is perhaps the only country where "greatness" is unrestricted, because it expresses the most fundamental hopes, desires, ambitions, and convictions of the nation.

977   I admit that to an American these things seem to be fairly natural, but not to a European. There are many Europeans who are infected by feelings of inferiority when they contact America and meet her heroic ideal. As a rule they don't admit it, and so they boast of Europe all the louder or begin to ridicule the many things in America which are open to criticism, such as roughness, brutality and primitivity. Often they get their first and decisive shock in the custom-house, so that their appetite is ruined for the rest of the States. It is inevitable that the heroic attitude should be coupled with a sort of primitivity, because it has always been the ideal of a somewhat sporty, primitive society. And this is where the real historical spirit of the Red Man enters the game. Look at your sports! They are the toughest, the most reckless, and the most efficient in the world. The idea of mere play has almost entirely disappeared, while in other parts of the world the idea of play still prevails rather than that of professional sport. Your sport demands a training that is almost cruel and an application that is almost inhuman. Your sportsmen are gladiators, every inch of them, and the excitement of the spectators derives from ancient instincts that are akin to bloodlust. Your students go through initiations and form secret

societies like the best among barbarous tribes. Secret societies of every description abound all over the country from the Ku Klux Klan to the Knights of Columbus, and their rites are analogous to any primitive mystery religion. America has resuscitated the ghosts of Spiritualism, of which she is the original home, and cures diseases by Christian Science, which has more to do with the shaman's mental healing than with any recognizable kind of science. Moreover it is proving to be pretty effective, just as were the cures of the shaman.

978   The old European inheritance looks rather pale beside these vigorous primitive influences. Have you ever compared the skyline of New York or any great American city with that of a pueblo like Taos? And did you see how the houses pile up to towers towards the centre? Without conscious imitation the American unconsciously fills out the spectral outline of the Red Man's mind and temperament.

979   There is nothing miraculous about this. It always has been so: the conqueror overcomes the old inhabitant in the body but succumbs to his spirit. Rome at the zenith of her power contained within her walls all the mystery cults of the East; yet the spirit of the humblest among them, a Jewish mystery society, transformed the greatest of all cities from top to bottom. The conqueror gets the wrong ancestor-spirits, the primitives would say: I like this picturesque way of putting it. It is pithy and expresses every conceivable implication.

980   People rarely want to know what a thing is in itself, they want to know whether it is favourable or unfavourable, advisable or evil, as if there were indubitably good or bad things. Things are as we take them. Moreover, anything that moves is a risk. Thus a nation in the making is naturally a big risk, to itself as well as others. It is certainly not my task to play the role of a prophet or of a ridiculous adviser of nations, and moreover there is nothing to give advice about. Facts are neither favourable nor unfavourable; they are merely interesting. And the most interesting of all is that this childlike, impetuous, "naïve" America has probably the most complicated psychology of all nations.

THE DREAMLIKE WORLD OF INDIA[1]

981   A first impression of a country is very often like meeting a person for the first time: your impression may be quite inaccurate, even definitely wrong in many respects, yet you are likely to perceive certain qualities or certain shadows which would very probably be blurred by the more accurate impressions of a second or third visit. My reader would make a great mistake if he were to take any statements I make about India for gospel truth. Think of a man coming to Europe for the first time in his life; he spends some six to seven weeks travelling from Lisbon to Moscow and from Norway to Sicily, he does not understand a single European language except English and he has a most superficial knowledge of the peoples, their history, and their actual life. Would he be likely to produce anything more than a mildly delirious phantasmagoria of hasty impressions, snapshot sentiments, and impatient opinions? I am afraid he would have little chance of escaping the charge of utter incompetence and inadequacy. I am very much in the same position in daring to say anything about India. I am told that I have the excuse of being a psychologist, and therefore am supposed to see more, or at least something peculiar which other fellows might be expected to overlook. I do not know. I must leave the final verdict to my reader.

982   The flat expanse of Bombay and its low dark green hills, rising almost suddenly above the horizon, give you the feeling of the vastness of a continent behind. This impression explains my first reaction directly I disembarked: I took a car and went out of town, away into the country. That felt a great deal better— yellow grass, dusty fields, native huts, great, dark-green, weird banyan trees, sickly palmyra palms sucked dry of their life-juice

1 [Written in English and first published in *Asia* (New York), XXXIX (1939):1, 5–8. —EDITORS.]

515

(it is run into bottles near the top to make palm-wine, which I never tasted), emaciated cattle, thin-legged men, the colourful saris of women, all in leisurely haste or in hasty leisure, with no need of being explained or of explaining themselves, because obviously they are what they are. They were unconcerned and unimpressed; I was the only one who did not belong to India. We drove through a strip of jungle near a blue lake. We pulled up suddenly, but instead of having run over a lurking tiger we found ourselves in the midst of a native movie-scene: something presumably was going to happen to a white girl, dressed up as a *dompteuse* escaped from a circus. Cameras, megaphone, and excited shirt-sleeves were in full action—the shock was so great that we instinctively stepped on the gas. After this I felt that I could go back to the city, which I had not yet really seen.

983 The Anglo-Indian style of architecture of the past fifty years is not interesting, but it gives a peculiar character to Bombay, as if one had already seen it somewhere else. It has more to do with the "English character" than with India. I make an exception of the "Gateway of India," that huge portal at the head of the royal road to Delhi. In a way it repeats the splendid ambition to be found in the "Gate of Victory," built by Akbar the Great in Fatehpur-Sikri, that soon-deserted town lying in ruins— red sandstone glowing in the Indian sun for long centuries, past and to come—a wave that crashed on the shore of time and left a strip of foam.

984 That is India, as I saw her: certain things last forever— yellow plains, green spirit-trees, dark-brown boulders of gigantic size, emerald-green watered fields, crowned by that metaphysical fringe of ice and rock away up north, that inexorable barrier beyond human conception. The other things unroll like a film, unimaginably rich in colour and shape, ever-changing, lasting a few days or a few centuries, but essentially transitory, dreamlike, a multi-coloured veil of *maya*. Today it is the still youthful British Empire that is going to leave a mark on India, like the empire of the Moguls, like Alexander the Great, like number-less dynasties of native kings, like the Aryan invaders—yet India somehow never changes her majestic face. Human life appears to be curiously flimsy in every respect. The native town of Bombay seems to be a jumble of incidentally piled-up human habitations. The people carry on an apparently meaningless life,

eagerly, busily, noisily. They die and are born in ceaseless waves, always much the same, a gigantic monotony of endlessly repeated life.

985 In all that flimsiness and vain tumult, one is conscious of immeasurable age with no history. After all why should there be recorded history? In a country like India one does not really miss it. All her native greatness is in any case anonymous and impersonal, like the greatness of Babylon and Egypt. History makes sense in European countries, where, in a relatively recent, barbarous, and unhistorical past, things began to take shape. Castles, temples, and cities were built, roads and bridges were made, and the peoples discovered that they had names, that they lived somewhere, that their cities multiplied and that their world grew bigger every century. When they saw that things developed, they naturally became interested in the changes of things, and it seemed worth while to record beginnings and later developments—for everything was going somewhere, and everybody hoped for unheard-of possibilities and improvements in the future, spiritual as well as secular.

986 But in India there seems to be nothing that has not lived a hundred thousand times before. Even the unique individual of today has already lived innumerable times in past ages. The world itself is nothing but a renewal of world existence, which has happened many times before. Even India's greatest individual, the unique Gautama Buddha, was preceded by more than a score of other Buddhas and is still not the last. No wonder, then, that the gods too have their numerous avatars. *Plus ça change, plus c'est la même chose*—why any history under such circumstances? Moreover, time is relative: the yogi sees the past as well as the future. If you walk the "noble eightfold path," you will remember what you were ten thousand lives ago. Space is relative: the yogi walks in his spirit-body with the speed of thought over lands, seas, and heavens. What you call real—all the good and ill of human life—is illusion. What you call unreal—sentimental, grotesque, obscene, monstrous, blood-curdling gods—unexpectedly becomes self-evident reality when you listen for half a hot night to an incessant, clever drumming that shakes up the dormant solar plexus of the European. He is used to regarding his head as the only instrument for grasping the world, and the *kathakali,* as he follows it with his eyes, would remain

517

a grotesque dance were it not for the drumming that creates a
new reality rising from the bowels.

987   A walk through the bustle of Bombay's bazaars set me thinking. I had felt the impact of the dreamlike world of India. I am
convinced that the average Hindu does not feel his world as
dreamlike: on the contrary, his every reaction shows how much
he is impressed and gripped by its realities. If he were not en-
thralled by his world, he would not need his religious and philo-
sophic teaching about the Great Illusion, any more than we
ourselves would need the Christian message of love if we were
other than we are. (The essence of teaching is to convey knowledge of things about which we know too little!) Perhaps I myself had been thrown into a dreamlike state by moving among
fairytale figures of the Thousand and One Nights. My own
world of European consciousness had become peculiarly thin,
like a network of telegraph wires high above the ground, stretching in straight lines all over the surface of an earth looking
treacherously like a geographic globe.

988   It is quite possible that India is the real world, and that the
white man lives in a madhouse of abstractions. To be born, to
die, to be sick, greedy, dirty, childish, ridiculously vain, miserable, hungry, vicious; to be manifestly stuck in illiterate unconsciousness, to be suspended in a narrow universe of good and
evil gods and to be protected by charms and helpful *mantras,*
that is perhaps the real life, life as it was meant to be, the life of
the earth. Life in India has not yet withdrawn into the capsule
of the head. It is still the whole body that lives. No wonder the
European feels dreamlike: the complete life of India is something of which he merely dreams. When you walk with naked
feet, how can you ever forget the earth? It needs all the acro-
batics of the higher yoga to make you unconscious of the earth.
One would need some sort of yoga if one tried seriously to live
in India. But I did not see one European in India who really
lived there. They were all living in Europe, that is, in a sort of
bottle filled with European air. One would surely go under
without the insulating glass wall; one would be drowned in all
the things which we Europeans have conquered in our imagination. In India they become formidable realities directly you
step beyond the glass wall.

*

989   Northern India is characterized by the fact that it is part of the immense Asiatic continent. I noticed a frequent note of harshness in the way the people talked to each other, recalling harassed camel-drivers or irritable horse-dealers. The variety of Asiatic costumes here supersedes the immaculate whiteness of the mild plant-eaters. Women's dresses are gay and provocative. The many Pathans, proud, unconcerned, and ruthless, and the bearded Sikhs, with their contradictory character—over-masculine brutality combined with melting sentimentality—give a strong Asiatic tinge to the appearance of the masses. The architecture shows clearly how much the Hindu element has succumbed to the predominating Asiatic influence. Even the temples of Benares are small and not very impressive, if it were not for their noisiness and dirt. Shiva, the destroyer, and the bloodthirsty and blood-curdling Kali seem to be in the foreground. The fat, elephant-headed Ganesha is also much in demand to bring good luck.

990   In comparison, Islam seems to be a superior, more spiritual, and more advanced religion. Its mosques are pure and beautiful, and of course wholly Asiatic. There is not much mind about it, but a great deal of feeling. The cult is one wailing outcry for the All-Merciful. It is a desire, an ardent longing and even greed for God; I would not call it love. But there is love, the most poetic, most exquisite love of beauty in these old Moguls. In a world of tyranny and cruelty, a heavenly dream crystallized in stone: the Taj Mahal. I cannot conceal my unmitigated admiration for this supreme flower, for this jewel beyond price, and I marvel at that love which discovered the genius of Shah Jehan and used it as an instrument of self-realization. This is the one place in the world where the—alas—all too invisible and all too jealously guarded beauty of the Islamic Eros has been revealed by a well-nigh divine miracle. It is the delicate secret of the rose gardens of Shiraz and of the silent patios of Arabian palaces, torn out of the heart of a great lover by a cruel and incurable loss. The mosques of the Moguls and their tombs may be pure and austere, their *divans*, or audience halls, may be of impeccable beauty, but the Taj Mahal is a revelation. It is thoroughly un-Indian. It is more like a plant that could thrive and flower in the rich Indian earth as it could nowhere else. It is Eros in its purest form; there is nothing mysterious, nothing symbolic

about it. It is the sublime expression of human love for a human being.

991   On the same plains of Northern India, almost two thousand years before the time of the Moguls, the spirit of India had borne its ripest fruit, the very essence of its life, the perfect Lord Buddha. Not very far from Agra and Delhi is the hill of Sanchi with its famous stupa. We were there on a brisk morning. The intense light and the extraordinary clarity of the air brought out every detail. There on the top of a rocky hill, with a distant view over the plains of India, you behold a huge globe of masonry, half-buried in the earth. According to the *Maha-Parinibbana-Sutta,* Buddha himself indicated the way in which his remains were to be buried. He took two rice bowls and covered the one with the other. The visible stupa is just the bowl on top. One has to imagine the lower one, buried in the earth. The roundness, a symbol of perfection since olden days, seems a suitable as well as an expressive monument for a Tathagata. It is of immense simplicity, austerity, and lucidity, perfectly in keeping with the simplicity, austerity, and lucidity of Buddha's teaching.

992   There is something unspeakably solemn about this place in its exalted loneliness, as if it were still witnessing the moment in the history of India when the greatest genius of her race formulated her supreme truth. This place, together with its architecture, its silence, and its peace beyond all turmoils of the heart, its very forgetfulness of human emotions, is truly and essentially Indian; it is as much the "secret" of India as the Taj Mahal is the secret of Islam. And just as the perfume of Islamic culture still lingers in the air, so Buddha, though forgotten on the surface, is still the secret breath of life in modern Hinduism. He is suffered at least to be an avatar of Vishnu.

*

993   Travelling with the British delegates to the Indian Science Congress in Calcutta, I was hustled through a good many dinners and receptions. I had a chance at these to talk to educated Indian women. This was a novelty. Their costume stamps them as women. It is the most becoming, the most stylish and, at the same time, the most meaningful dress ever devised by women. I hope fervently that the sexual disease of the West, which tries to transform woman into a sort of awkward boy, will not creep into

India in the wake of that fad "scientific education." It would be a loss to the whole world if the Indian woman should cease to wear her native costume. India (and perhaps China, which I do not know) is practically the only civilized country where one can see on living models how women can and should dress.

994   The costume of the Indian woman conveys far more than the meaningless half-nakedness of the Western woman's evening dress. There is something left which can be unveiled or revealed, and, on the other hand, one's taste is not offended by the sight of aesthetic flaws. The European evening dress is one of the most obvious symptoms of our sexual morbidity: it is compounded of shamelessness, exhibitionism, impotent provocation, and a ridiculous attempt to make the relation between the sexes cheap and easy. Yet everybody is, or ought to be, profoundly aware of the fact that the secret of sexual attraction is neither cheap nor easy, but is one of the demons which no "scientific education" has yet mastered. Women's fashions with us are mostly invented by men: you can guess the result. After having exhausted all the means of producing the semblance of a fertile brood-mare with corsets and bustles, they are now trying to create the adolescent hermaphrodite, an athletic, semimasculine body, despite the fact that the body of the Northern woman already has a painful tendency toward bony coarseness. They try coeducation in order to make the sexes equal to each other, instead of stressing the difference. But the worst sight—oh—is the women in trousers parading the decks! I often wondered if they knew how mercilessly ugly they looked. Usually they were very decent middle-class types and were not smart at all, but only touched by the current rage for hermaphroditosis. It is a sad truth, but the European woman, and particularly her hopelessly wrong dress, put up no show at all when compared with the dignity and elegance of the Indian woman and her costume. Even fat women have a chance in India; with us they can only starve themselves to death.

995   Talking of costumes, I must say that the Hindu man is too fond of ease and coolness. He wears a long piece of cotton cloth wound round and between his legs. The front of the legs is well covered, but the back is ridiculously bare. There is something effeminate and babyish about it. You simply cannot imagine a soldier with such garlands of cloth between his legs. Many wear

a shirt over this or a European jacket. It is quaint, but not very masculine. The northern type of costume is Persian and looks fine and manly. The garland type is chiefly southern, perhaps because of the matriarchal trend which prevails in the south. The "garland" looks like a sort of overgrown diaper. It is an essentially unwarlike dress and suits the pacifist mentality of the Hindu perfectly.

996   A real fight, in such a contrivance, is well-nigh impossible. The combatants would be trapped in no time by the many circumvolutions of their ridiculous sheets. Yet they are free with words and gestures, but, when you are expecting the worst, they confine themselves to attacking the other's shirt and diaper. I once watched two boys of about eight or nine having a heated quarrel over a game. They came to blows. We can all remember pretty well what a fight between boys at that age means. But the performance of the Hindu boys was really worth seeing: they struck out violently, but the dangerous-looking fists remained miraculously arrested about an inch from the enemy's face—and afterwards it was exactly as if they had had a really good fight! They are profoundly civilized. This was in the south; the Mohammedan element in the north is probably much nearer the real stuff when it comes to a fight.

*

997   The impression of softness that the Hindu conveys points to a predominance of the feminine element in the family, presumably of the *mother*. It seems to be a style which is dependent on old matriarchal traditions. The educated Hindu has very much the character of the "family boy," of the "good" son, who knows that he has to deal with a mother and, moreover, knows how to do it. But one gets much the same impression from the women. They show a studied and stylish kind of modesty and inconspicuousness, which immediately gives you the feeling of dealing with an extremely domesticated and socialized person. There is no harshness or arrogance, no mannishness or stridency in their voice. This is a most agreeable contrast to certain European women I have known, whose strained, overloud, and spastic voices betray a peculiarly forced and unnatural attitude.

998   I had many opportunities to study the English voice in India. Voices are treacherous; they reveal far too much. You marvel at the fantastic efforts people make to sound gay, fresh,

welcoming, enterprising, jolly, benevolent, full of good comrade-
ship, and so on. And you know it is merely an attempt to cover
up the real truth, which is very much the reverse. It makes you
tired listening to those unnatural sounds, and you long for somebody to say something unkind or brutally offensive. You cannot
help noticing how a great number of perfectly nice and decent
Englishmen elaborately imitate a he-man voice, God knows why.
It sounds as if they were trying to impress the world with their
throaty rumbling tones, or as if they were addressing a political
meeting, which has to be convinced of the profound honesty
and sincerity of the speaker. The usual brand is the bass voice,
of the colonel for instance, or the master of a household of
numerous children and servants who must be duly impressed.
The Father Christmas voice is a special variety, usually affected
by academically trained specimens. I discovered that particularly
terrific boomers were quite modest and decent chaps, with a
noticeable feeling of inferiority. What a superhuman burden it
is to be the overlords of a continent like India!

999   The Indians speak without affectation. They represent nothing. They belong to the three hundred and sixty million people
of India. The women represent less than nothing. They belong
to large families incidentally and geographically living in a
country called India. And you have to adapt yourself to the
family and know how to talk and how to behave, when twenty-
five to thirty members of a family are crowded together in a
small house, with a grandmother on top. That teaches you to
speak modestly, carefully, politely. It explains that small twitter-
ing voice and that flowerlike behaviour. The crowding together
in families has the contrary effect with us. It makes people
nervous, irritable, rough, and even violent. But India takes the
family seriously. There is no amateurishness or sentimentality
about it. It is understood to be the indispensable form of life,
inescapable, necessary, and self-evident. It needs a religion to
break this law and to make "homelessness" the first step to saintliness. It certainly seems as if Indians would be unusually pleasant and easy to live with, particularly the women; and, if the
style were the whole man, Indian life would be almost ideal.
But softness of manners and sweetness of voice are also a part of
secrecy and diplomacy. I guess Indians are just human, and so
no generalization is quite true.

1000   As a matter of fact, you stub your toes time and again against a peculiar obliqueness when you ask for definite information. You often find then that people are less concerned with your question than with deliberations about your possible motives or about how it would be possible to wriggle out of a tight corner without getting hurt. Overcrowding has surely much to do with this widespread and very characteristic defect in the Indian character, for only the art of deception can preserve the privacy of the individual in a crowd. The woman's whole manner is directed towards the mother as well as the man. To the former she is a daughter, to the latter the woman whose skilful behaviour gives him a reasonable chance to feel like a man. At least I did not meet a single "battleship," so typical of the Western drawing-room, the sight of which makes a man feel about as comfortable as a mouse drowning before breakfast in cold water.

1001   The Indians mean and are meant to live in India. Therefore they have settled down to a degree of domestication which we cannot attain, even with the aid of ideals and frantic moral efforts. Our migrations have not yet come to an end. It was only a short while ago that the Anglo-Saxons immigrated from northern Germany to their new homeland. The Normans arrived there from Scandinavia, via northern France, quite a while later, and it is much the same with practically every nation in Europe. Our motto is still: *ubi bene, ibi patria.* Because of this truth we are all fervent patriots. Because we still can and will wander, we imagine that we can live more or less anywhere. Not yet convinced that we ought to be able to get along with one another in closely packed families, we feel that we can afford to quarrel, for there is still good open country "out West" if things come to the worst. At least it seems so. But it is no longer quite true. Even the Englishman is not settled in India; he is really condemned to serve his term there and to make the best of it. Hence all those hopeful, jolly, eager, energetic, powerful voices issue from people who are thinking and dreaming of spring in Sussex.

WHAT INDIA CAN TEACH US [1]

1002   India lies between the Asiatic north and the Pacific south, between Tibet and Ceylon. India ends abruptly at the foothills of the Himalaya, and at Adam's Bridge. At one end, a Mongolian world begins, at the other, the "paradise" of a South Sea island. Ceylon is as strangely different from India as is Tibet. Curiously enough, at either end one finds the "spoor of the elephant," as the Pali Canon [2] calls the teaching of the Lord Buddha.

1003   Why has India lost her greatest light, Buddha's path of redemption, that glorious synthesis of philosophy and *opus divinum*? It is common knowledge that mankind can never remain on an apex of illumination and spiritual endeavour. Buddha was an untimely intruder, upsetting the historical process, which afterwards got the better of him. Indian religion is like a *vimana*, or pagoda. The gods climb over one another like ants, from the elephants carved on the base to the abstract lotus which crowns the top of the building. In the long run, the gods become philosophical concepts. Buddha, a spiritual pioneer for the whole world, said, and tried to make it true, that the enlightened man is even the teacher and redeemer of his gods (not their stupid denier, as Western "enlightenment" will have it). This was obviously too much, because the Indian mind was not at all ready to integrate the gods to such an extent as to make them psychologically dependent upon man's mental condition. How Buddha himself could obtain such insight without losing himself in a complete mental inflation borders on a miracle. (But any genius is a miracle.)

1004   Buddha disturbed the historical process by interfering with

1 [Written in English and first published in *Asia* (New York), XXXIX (1939):2, 97–98.—EDITORS.]

2 [The body of Southern Buddhist Sacred Writings.—EDITORS.]

the slow transformation of the gods into ideas. The true genius nearly always intrudes and disturbs. He speaks to a temporal world out of a world eternal. Thus he says the wrong things at the right time. Eternal truths are never true at any given moment in history. The process of transformation has to make a halt in order to digest and assimilate the utterly impractical things that the genius has produced from the storehouse of eternity. Yet the genius is the healer of his time, because anything he reveals of eternal truth is healing.

1005   The remote goal of the transformation process, however, is very much what Buddha intended. But to get there is possible neither in one generation nor in ten. It obviously takes much longer, thousands of years at all events, since the intended transformation cannot be realized without an enormous development of human consciousness. It can only be "believed," which is what Buddha's, as well as Christ's, followers obviously did, assuming—as "believers" always do—that belief is the whole thing. Belief is a great thing, to be sure, but it is a substitute for a conscious reality which the Christians wisely relegate to a life in the hereafter. This "hereafter" is really the intended future of mankind, anticipated by religious intuition.

1006   Buddha has disappeared from Indian life and religion more than we could ever imagine Christ disappearing in the aftermath of some future catastrophe to Christianity, more even than the Greco-Roman religions have disappeared from present-day Christianity. India is not ungrateful to her master minds. There is a considerable revival of interest in classical philosophy. Universities like Calcutta and Benares have important philosophy departments. Yet the main emphasis is laid on classical Hindu philosophy and its vast Sanskrit literature. The Pali Canon is not precisely within their scope. Buddha does not represent a proper philosophy. He challenges man! This is not exactly what philosophy wants. It, like any other science, needs a good deal of intellectual free play, undisturbed by moral and human entanglements. But also, small and fragmentary people must be able to "do something about it" without getting fatally involved in big issues far beyond their powers of endurance and accomplishment. This is on the right road after all, though it is indeed a *longissima via*. The divine impatience of a genius may disturb or even upset the small man. But after a few generations he will reassert himself by sheer force of numbers, and this too seems to be right.

1007   I am now going to say something which may offend my Indian friends, but actually no offence is intended. I have, so it seems to me, observed the peculiar fact that an Indian, inasmuch as he is really Indian, does not think, at least not what we call "think." *He rather perceives the thought.* He resembles the primitive in this respect. I do not say that he *is* primitive, but that the process of his thinking reminds me of the primitive way of thought-production. The primitive's reasoning is mainly an unconscious function, and he perceives its results. We should expect such a peculiarity in any civilization which has enjoyed an almost unbroken continuity from primitive times.

1008   Our western evolution from a primitive level was suddenly interrupted by the invasion of a psychology and spirituality belonging to a much higher level of civilization. Our case was not so bad as that of the Negroes or the Polynesians, who found themselves suddenly confronted with the infinitely higher civilization of the white man, but in essence it was the same. We were stopped in the midst of a still barbarous polytheism, which was eradicated or suppressed in the course of centuries and not so very long ago. I suppose that this fact has given a peculiar twist to the Western mind. Our mental existence was transformed into something which it had not yet reached and which it could not yet truly be. And this could only be brought about by a dissociation between the conscious part of the mind and the unconscious. It was a liberation of consciousness from the burden of irrationality and instinctive impulsiveness at the expense of the totality of the individual. Man became split into a conscious and an unconscious personality. The conscious personality could be domesticated, because it was separated from the natural and primitive man. Thus we became highly disciplined, organized, and rational on one side, but the other side remained a suppressed primitive, cut off from education and civilization.

1009   This explains our many relapses into the most appalling barbarity, and it also explains the really terrible fact that, the higher we climb the mountain of scientific and technical achievement, the more dangerous and diabolical becomes the misuse of our inventions. Think of the great triumph of the human mind, the power to fly: we have accomplished the age-old dream of humanity! And think of the bombing raids of modern warfare! Is this what civilization means? Is it not rather a convincing demonstration of the fact that, when our mind went up to conquer the skies, our other man, that suppressed barbarous individual, went down to hell? Certainly our civilization can be proud of its achievements, yet we have to be ashamed of ourselves.

1010   This surely is not the only way in which man can become civilized, at all events it is not an ideal way. One could think of another more satisfactory possibility. Instead of differentiating only one side of man, one could differentiate the whole man. By burdening the conscious man with the earthbound weight of his primitive side one could avoid that fatal dissociation between an upper and a lower half. Of course it would be no mean *tour de force* to experiment with the white man of today along these lines. It would obviously lead to devilishly intricate moral and intellectual problems. But, if the white man does not succeed in destroying his own race with his brilliant inventions, he will eventually have to settle down to a desperately serious course of self-education.

1011   Whatever the ultimate fate of the white man may be, we can at least behold one example of a civilization which has brought every essential trace of primitivity with it, embracing the whole man from top to bottom. India's civilization and psychology resemble her temples, which represent the universe in their sculptures, including man and all his aspects and activities, whether as saint or brute. That is presumably the reason why India seems so dreamlike: one gets pushed back into the unconscious, into that unredeemed, uncivilized, aboriginal world, of which we only dream, since our consciousness denies it. India represents the other way of civilizing man, the way without suppression, without violence, without rationalism. You see them there side by side, in the same town, in the same street, in the same temple, within the same square mile: the most highly cultivated mind and the primitive. In the mental make-up of the most spiritual you discern the traits of the living primitive, and in the melancholy eyes of the illiterate half-naked villager you divine an unconscious knowledge of mysterious truths.

1012   I say all this in order to explain what I mean by not-thinking. I could just as well say: Thank heaven there is a man left who has not learned to think, but is still able to perceive his thoughts, as if they were visions or living things; a man who has transformed, or is still going to transform, his gods into visible thoughts based upon the reality of the instincts. He has rescued his gods, and they live with him. It is true that it is an irrational life, full of crudeness, gruesomeness, misery, disease, and death, yet somehow complete, satisfactory and of an unfathomable emotional beauty. It is true that the logical processes of India are funny, and it is bewildering to see how fragments of Western science live peacefully side by side with what we, shortsightedly, would call superstitions. Indians do not mind seemingly intolerable contradictions. If they exist, they are the peculiarity of such thinking, and man is not responsible for them. He does not make them, since thoughts appear by themselves. The Indian does not fish out infinitesimal details from the universe. His ambition is to have a vision of the whole. He does not yet know that you can screw the living world up tightly between two concepts. Did you ever stop to think how much of the conqueror (not to say thief or robber) lies in that very term "concept"? It comes from the Latin *concipere*, 'to take something by grasping it thoroughly.' That is how we get at the world. But Indian "thinking" is an increase of vision and not a predatory raid into the yet unconquered realms of nature.

1013   If you want to learn the greatest lesson India can teach you, wrap yourself in the cloak of your moral superiority, go to the Black Pagoda of Konarak, sit down in the shadow of the mighty ruin that is still covered with the most amazing collection of obscenities, read Murray's cunning old *Handbook for India,* which tells you how to be properly shocked by this lamentable state of affairs, and how you should go into the temples in the evening, because in the lamplight they look if possible "more [and how beautifully!] wicked"; and then analyse carefully and with the utmost honesty all your reactions, feelings, and thoughts. It will take you quite a while, but in the end, if you have done good work, you will have learned something about yourself, and about the white man in general, which you have probably never heard from any one else. I think, if you can afford it, a trip to India is on the whole most edifying and, from a psychological point of view, most advisable, although it may give you considerable headaches.

APPENDIX

EDITORIAL (1933) [1]

1014   Owing to the resignation of Professor Kretschmer, the president of the General Medical Society for Psychotherapy,[2] the presidency and with it the administration of the *Zentralblatt für Psychotherapie* have fallen to me. This change coincided with the great political upheaval in Germany. Although as a science psychotherapy has nothing to do with politics, fate has willed it that I should take over the editorship of the *Zentralblatt* at a moment when the state of affairs in psychotherapy is marked by a confusion of doctrines and views not unlike the previous state of affairs in politics. One-sided and mutually exclusive methods of observation have exerted too far-reaching an influence not only on specialized medical opinion but also on the psychological views of many educated laymen. The resulting contradictions have only been sharpened by the spread of my own—very different—ideas, so that we can well speak of confusion being worse confounded. It will therefore be the primary task of the *Zentralblatt* to give impartial appreciation to all objective contributions, and to promote an over-all view which will do greater justice to the basic facts of the human psyche than has been the case up till now. The differences which actually do exist between Germanic and Jewish psychology and which have long been known to every intelligent person are no longer to be glossed over, and this can only be beneficial to science. In psychology more than in any other science there is a "personal equation," disregard of which falsifies the practical and theoretical findings.

1 [Published in the *Zentralblatt für Psychotherapie und ihre Grenzgebiete* (Leipzig), VI:3 (Dec., 1933), 139–40.—EDITORS.]
2 [Allgemeine Ärztliche Gesellschaft für Psychotherapie. Founded 1928, with Dr. Robert Sommer as first president. In 1930, Professor Ernst Kretschmer became president and Jung vice-president.]

At the same time I should like to state expressly that this implies no depreciation of Semitic psychology,[3] any more than it is a depreciation of the Chinese to speak of the peculiar psychology of the Oriental.

1015   Psychotherapy has long ceased to be an exclusive province for specialists. The interest of the whole world is directed upon the psychological discoveries of medical men. Psychotherapy will therefore be obliged to take the whole of the psyche into account when constructing its theories, and to extend its vision beyond the merely pathological and personal. The efforts of the *Zentral-blatt* will be directed to this end.

C. G. JUNG

[3] [Jung implemented this principle in the International Society. Cf. infra, Circular Letter, pars. 1035ff., and also par. 1060.—EDITORS.]

A REJOINDER TO DR. BALLY[1]

I

1016   I wish to discuss no surmises with Dr. Bally, but prefer to report the facts which led me to take over the editorship of the *Zentralblatt für Psychotherapie.* About three years ago I was elected honorary [vice-] president of the General Medical Society for Psychotherapy. When, owing to the political upheaval, Professor Kretschmer resigned from the presidency, and the Society like so many other scientific organizations in Germany received a profound shock, some leading members pressed me—I may say, fervently—to take the chair. This, I would expressly emphasize, was the presidency not of the *German* but of the *International* Society, as is stated in the issue from which Dr. Bally quotes.[2] Thus a moral conflict arose for me as it would for any decent man in this situation. Should I, as a prudent neutral, withdraw into security this side of the frontier and wash

---

[1] [Published under "Zeitgenössisches" in the *Neue Zürcher Zeitung,* CLV (1934), no. 437, p. 1, and no. 443, p. 1 (March 13 and 14). The article by the Swiss psychiatrist. Dr. G. Bally was published under the title "Deutschstämmige Psychotherapie?" in the same periodical, no. 343 (Feb. 27). Cf. infra, par. 1034, n. 5.—EDITORS.]

[2] [*Zentralblatt für Psychotherapie,* VI:3 (Dec., 1933), 142ff. The confusion no doubt arose because the General Medical Society for Psychotherapy was dominated by the Germans, who held the main executive positions. Its membership was, however, international, and the congresses were international in character. Upon Kretschmer's resignation (Apr. 6, 1933), Jung was probably for a short time acting president, by virtue of his position as vice-president. Almost at once, however, with the agreement of his colleagues, he reorganized the society so as to make it formally international. Jung was then elected president of this International General Medical Society for Psychotherapy. The statutes were ratified at a congress at Bad Nauheim, May 10–13, 1934: cf. the *Zentralblatt,* VII:3 (1934, month not indicated). The society's headquarters were located in Switzerland. A separate German society, under the presidency of Prof. M. H. Göring, was founded in Berlin on Sept. 15, 1933, as the German section of the International Society (VI:3, pp. 140ff.). —EDITORS.]

535

my hands in innocence, or should I—as I was well aware—risk my skin and expose myself to the inevitable misunderstandings which no one escapes who, from higher necessity, has to make a pact with the existing political powers in Germany? Should I sacrifice the interests of science, loyalty to colleagues, the friendship which attaches me to some German physicians, and the living link with the humanities afforded by a common language—sacrifice all this to egotistic comfort and my different political sentiments? I have seen too much of the distress of the German middle class, learned too much about the boundless misery that often marks the life of a German doctor today, know too much about the general spiritual wretchedness to be able to evade my plain human duty under the shabby cloak of political subterfuge. Consequently no other course remained for me but to answer for my friends with the weight of my name and independent position.

1017 As conditions then were, a single stroke of the pen in high places would have sufficed to sweep all psychotherapy [3] under the table. That had to be prevented at all costs for the sake of suffering humanity, doctors, and—last but not least—science and civilization.

1018 Anybody who has the least notion about present-day Germany knows that no newspaper, no society, nothing, absolutely nothing can exist unless it has been *gleichgeschaltet* (conformed) by the government. Consequently the organization of a journal or a society is an affair that has two sides. I can wish, but whether things will turn out as I wish is another question, the decision for which rests neither with me nor with my colleagues. Anyone who has to deal with Germany today knows how rapidly things can alter, how one unforeseen decree follows another, and how the political scene changes like lightning. It is quite impossible to keep abreast of events from abroad, when even inside Germany people are unable, with the best will in the world, to get the political authorities to adopt a clear and binding attitude.

1019 Since the German section of the International Society *has* to be *gleichgeschaltet,* and since, moreover, the *Zentralblatt* is published in Germany, there naturally arose so many difficulties that more than once we doubted the possibility of a reorganization. One of these concerned the oath of allegiance and the

3 [In Germany.—EDITORS.]

"purity of political sentiment" required of the German Society. We in Switzerland can hardly understand such a thing, but we are immediately in the picture if we transport ourselves back three or four centuries to a time when the Church had totalitarian presumptions. Barbed wire had not been invented then, so there were probably no concentration camps; instead, the Church used large quantities of faggots. The "modernist" oath of today is a pale and feeble offshoot of an earlier, much more robust and palpable *Gleichschaltung*. As the authority of the Church fades, the State becomes the Church, since the totalitarian claim is bound to come out somewhere. First it was Socialism that entered into the Catholic heritage and again is experimenting with the crassest kind of *Gleichschaltung*—not, indeed, with a view to buttressing up the kingdom of heaven but to producing an equally millenarian state of bliss (or its substitute) on earth. Russian Communism has therefore, quite logically, become the totalitarian Church, where even the poorest mouse emits the Bolshevist squeak. No wonder National Socialism makes the same claims! It is only consistent with the logic of history that after an age of clerical *Gleichschaltung* the turn should come for one practised by the secular State.

1020   But even in such an age the spirit is at work in science, in art, philosophy, and religious experience, heedless of whether the contemporary situation be favourable or unfavourable, for there is something in man that is of divine nature and is not condemned to its own treadmill and imprisoned in its own structure. This spirit wants to live—which is why old Galileo, when they had done torturing him, recanted, and afterwards, so the story goes, said "But it does move"—only very softly, I'll wager. Martyrdom is a singular calling for which one must have a special gift. Therefore it seems to me at least as intelligent not to worry the high inquisition for a while with the exciting news that one has discovered the moons of Jupiter without the authorization of Aristotle. Galileo had the childlike eyes of the great discoverer and was not at all wise to his *gleichgeschaltet* age. Were he alive today he could sun himself on the beach at Los Angeles in company with Einstein and would be a made man, since a liberal age worships God in the form of science. But the "metamorphosis of the gods" rolls rumbling on and the State becomes lord of this world: more than half Europe is al-

537

ready swallowed up. Science and every healing art get seven fat years, then come the seven lean. They must learn to adapt themselves. To protest is ridiculous—how protest against an avalanche? It is better to look out. Science has no interest in calling down avalanches; it must preserve its intellectual heritage even under the changed conditions.

1021   That is how things stand today. Neither I nor my German colleagues are responsible for them. If the German section of the Society wants to exist at all the oath of allegiance is inescapable, as any reasonable person will understand. It was therefore planned that the managing editor of the *Zentralblatt*, Dr. Cimbal of Hamburg, would bring out a special issue with statements by leading German psychotherapists, together with a signed introductory statement by the president of the German Society, Professor Göring of Elberfeld, for exclusive circulation in Germany. Such, too, were the instructions which I gave to the managing editor. To my great surprise and disappointment Professor Göring's political manifesto was suddenly printed in the current issue of the *Zentralblatt* [VI:3]. I do not doubt that there were inside political reasons for this, but it was one of those lamentable tactical gaffes which were the bane of German foreign policy even in the Wilhelm era. In this way my name unexpectedly appeared over a National Socialist manifesto, which to me personally was anything but agreeable. And yet after all— what is help or friendship that costs nothing? The incident is naturally so incriminating as to put my editorship seriously in question.

1022   In Germany everything *must* be "German" at present if it is to survive. Even the healing art must be "German," and this for political reasons. From the standpoint of medicine itself, it is unimportant whether it is called "German" or "French," but it is extremely important that it should live, even if under undeniably difficult conditions, as I know only too well. It is a cheap jibe to ridicule "Germanic psychotherapy," but a very different thing to have to rescue medicine for humanity's sake from the seething chaos of revolution. It is easy to stand by and be funny when the main point is to get a young and insecure science into a place of safety during an earthquake, and that was my aim in helping to reorganize the psychotherapeutic movement in Germany. Medicine has nothing to do with politics—

I only wish it had!—and therefore it can and should be practised for the good of suffering humanity under all governments. If the doctors of Petersburg [*sic*] or Moscow had sought my help I would have acceded without hesitation, because I am concerned with human beings and not with Bolsheviks—and if I was then inevitably branded a Bolshevik it would have bothered me just as little. Man after all still has a soul and is not just an ox fatted for political slaughter. If I am called into the arena for the sake of the soul I shall follow the call wherever it may be. This naïve belief of mine in the human soul may, from the Olympian standpoint of a hypertrophied intellect or of partisan blindness, appear laughable, suspect, unpatriotic, and God knows what. I do not pride myself on being a good Christian, but I do believe in the saying, "Render unto Caesar the things that are Caesar's, and unto God the things that are God's." The doctor who, in wartime, gives his help to the wounded of the other side will surely not be held a traitor to his country.

II

1023   There is no sense in us doctors facing the National Socialist regime as if we were a party. As doctors we are first and foremost men who serve our fellows, if necessary under all the aggravations of a given political situation. We are neither obliged nor called upon to make protests from a sudden access of untimely political zeal and thus gravely to endanger our medical activity. My support of the German doctors has nothing to do with any political attitude. If it is interpreted politically—which has doubtless happened already or soon will—the interpretations are a reflection on those who make them. I have never been in a position to stop the formation of myths.

1024   Admittedly I was incautious, so incautious as to do the very thing most open to misunderstanding at the present moment: I have tabled the Jewish question. This I did deliberately. My esteemed critic appears to have forgotten that the first rule of psychotherapy is to talk in the greatest detail about all the things that are the most ticklish and dangerous, and the most misunderstood. The Jewish problem is a regular complex, a festering wound, and no responsible doctor could bring himself to apply methods of medical hush-hush in this matter.

1025   As to the difference between Jewish and "Aryan-Germanic-Christian-European" psychology, it can of course hardly be seen in the individual products of science as a whole. But we are not so much concerned with these as with the fundamental fact that in psychology the object of knowledge is at the same time the organ of knowledge, which is true of no other science. It has therefore been doubted in all sincerity whether psychology is possible as a science at all. In keeping with this doubt I suggested years ago that every psychological theory should be criticized in the first instance as a subjective confession. For, if the organ of knowledge is its own object, we have every reason to examine the nature of that organ very closely indeed, since the subjective premise is at once the object of knowledge which is therefore limited from the start. This subjective premise is identical with our psychic idiosyncrasy. The idiosyncrasy is conditioned (1) by the individual, (2) by the family, (3) by the nation, race, climate, locality, and history.

1026   I have in my time been accused of "Swiss wooden-headedness." Not that I have anything against possessing the national vices of the Swiss; I am also quite ready to suppose that I am a bigoted Swiss in every respect. I am perfectly content to let my psychological confession, my so-called "theories," be criticized as a product of Swiss wooden-headedness or queer-headedness, as betraying the sinister influence of my theological and medical forbears, and, in general, of our Christian and German heritage, as exemplified for instance by Schiller and Meister Eckhart. I am not affronted when people call me "Teutonically confused," "mystical," "moralistic," etc. I am proud of my subjective premises, I love the Swiss earth in them, I am grateful to my theological forbears for having passed on to me the Christian premise, and I also admit my so-called "father complex": I do not want to knuckle under to any "fathers" and never shall (see "queer-headedness").

1027   May it not therefore be said that there is a Jewish psychology too, which admits the prejudice of its blood and its history? And may it not be asked wherein lie the peculiar differences between an essentially Jewish and an essentially Christian outlook? Can it really be maintained that I alone among psychologists have a special organ of knowledge with a subjective bias, whereas the Jew is apparently insulted to the core if one assumes him to be a Jew? Presumably he would not have one assume that his insights are the products of a mere cipher, or that his brain emerged only today from the featureless ocean of non-history. I must confess my total inability to understand why it should be a crime to speak of "Jewish" psychology.

1028   If I were in the position—as Dr. Bally supposes me to be—of not being able to point to a single difference between the two psychologies, it would amount to exactly the same thing as not being able to make plausible the difference between the peculiarities of the English and the Americans, or the French and the Germans. I have not invented these differences; you can read about them in innumerable books and newspapers; as jokes they are on everybody's tongue, and anyone who fails to see that there are one or two psychological differences between Frenchmen and Germans must have come from the back of beyond and know nothing about our European madhouse. Are we really to believe that a tribe which has wandered through history for several thousand years as "God's chosen people" was not put up to such an idea by some quite special psychological peculiarity? If no differences exist, how do we recognize Jews at all?

1029   Psychological differences obtain between all nations and races, and even between the inhabitants of Zurich, Basel, and Bern. (Where else would all the good jokes come from?) There are in fact differences between families and between individuals. That is why I attack every levelling psychology when it raises a claim to universal validity, as for instance the Freudian and the Adlerian. All levelling produces hatred and venom in the suppressed and misjudged; it prevents any broad human understanding. All branches of mankind unite in one stem—yes, but what is a stem without separate branches? Why this ridiculous touchiness when anybody dares to say anything about the psychological difference between Jews and Christians? Every child knows that differences exist.

1030   It seems to be generally assumed that in tabling the discussion of ethnological differences my sole purpose was to blurt out my "notorious" anti-Semitism. Apparently no one believes that I—and others—might also have something good and appreciative to say. Whatever it be, and however critical it be, I would never have the audacity to maintain that "ten tribes are accursed and two alone holy." That saying comes from no Christian. My criticism and appreciation will always keep well outside this glaring contrast, and will contain nothing that cannot be discussed civilly.

1031   I express no value-judgments, nor do I intend any veiled ones. I have been engaged for many years on the problem of imponderable differences which everybody knows and nobody can really define. They are among the most difficult problems of psychology and probably for that reason are a taboo area which none may enter on pain of death. To many people it is an insult if one credits them with a special psychological idiosyncrasy, and in dealing with parties and nations one must be even more careful. That is why any investigation of these imponderables is so extraordinarily difficult, because, as well as doing his work, the investigator has to perform a grotesque egg-balancing dance around highly charged sensibilities. It is high time the practising psychologist understood more about these psychic imponderabilia, because from them arise a good half of the things that go wrong in the world. Anyone who could define the nature of these imponderable differences would truly have gazed deep into the mystery of the human soul. For my part, I do not belong to those savants who concern themselves exclusively with what is known already—an extremely useful activity, no doubt—but prefer to sniff around territories where nothing is yet known.

1032   Consequently I am amused to find myself cast in the role of the nitwit who is unable to spot a single difference between Jews and Christians. It is, in spite of Bally, an undoubted fact that the difference exists, just as water existed before the chemist discovered H_2O; but it cannot be grasped as yet, because all the views that have been put forward so far are unsatisfactory. These purely cognitive difficulties have, however, nothing to do with the question of whether the imponderables exist. I intend shortly to publish a few no doubt very inadequate and arguable *aperçus* on this subject. I am as little capable as anybody else of putting forward anything final, but I shall be content if I succeed in provoking discussion. I would like to bring the parties together round a conference-table, so that they could at last get to know and acknowledge their differences. Very often this sort of knowledge is the way to understanding. I wish I could do the same for the brothers in enmity on the left and right of the Rhine. Naturally nothing like this can be attempted without inviting the kicks of both sides.

1033 Would the cure be successful? The possibility of defeat in a good cause has never alarmed me.

1034 But, my public will object, why raise the Jewish problem today of all days and in Germany of all places? Pardon me, I raised it long ago, as anybody knows who is acquainted with the literature. I did not speak about it only since the revolution; I have been officially campaigning for criticism of subjective psychological premises as a necessary reform in psychology ever since 1913.[4] This has nothing to do with the form of the German state. If I am to be exploited for political ends, there's nothing I can do to stop it. Or can anyone stop anything he pleases in Germany? It is rather late in the day for my critical attitude to attract attention only now, and it is, alas, characteristic that it should be construed in such a way as to suggest that Nazism alone has lent wings to my criticism. It is, I frankly admit, a highly unfortunate and disconcerting coincidence that my scientific programme should, without any assistance of mine and against my express wish, have been lined up with a political manifesto. But an event of this kind, although regrettable in itself, often has the consequence of ventilating problems which would otherwise be sedulously avoided.[5]

[4] [Actually, a short while before, when Jung stipulated that the analyst must be analysed. The first reference to this occurs in "The Theory of Psychoanalysis" (1913), in *Freud and Psychoanalysis*, pars. 447–50 (cf. "Some Crucial Points in Psychoanalysis," ibid., pp. 252f.). Cf also "A Contribution to the Study of Psychological Types" (1913), in *Psychological Types*, pars. 88off.; "On Psychological Understanding" (1914), in *The Psychogenesis of Mental Disease*, pars. 419f.; *Psychological Types* (orig. 1921), pars. 88ff., 601; "A Psychological Theory of Types" (1927), ibid., pars. 919f.; "Freud and Jung: Contrasts" (1929), in *Freud and Psychoanalysis*; "Introduction to Kranefeldt's 'Secret Ways of the Mind'" (1939), ibid., pars. 747, 757f.—EDITORS.]

[5] [When the foregoing "Rejoinder to Dr. Bally" was published in the *Neue Zürcher Zeitung*, a prefatory note by the Editor stated: "Dr. Bally, in his article 'Deutschstämmige Psychotherapie?', was in our view entitled to take up Dr. Jung's programme as outlined in the *Zentralblatt für Psychotherapie* [VI:3] and to express his astonishment that though Dr. Jung started from the teachings of Freud and quite legitimately departed from them, he did not in his scientific writings support his opposition with the differences between Christian-Germanic and Semitic psychology, but only at this present juncture acknowledges the 'super-

psychology of the racial psychologists.' " In the issue of March 15, 1934 (CLV, 457), Jung replied as follows:

["In the Editor's prefatory note to my article, it is stated that I started from the teachings of Freud. I did not start from Freud, but from Eugen Bleuler and Pierre Janet, who were my immediate teachers. When I took up the cudgels for Freud in public, I already had a scientific position that was widely known on account of my association experiments, conducted independently of Freud, and the theory of complexes based upon them. My collaboration was qualified by an objection in principle to the sexual theory, and it lasted up to the time when Freud identified in principle his sexual theory with his method.

["The assertion that I acknowledge racial psychology only at this present juncture is incorrect. In 1927 I wrote: 'Thus it is a quite unpardonable mistake to accept the conclusions of a Jewish psychology as generally valid. Nobody would dream of taking Chinese or Indian psychology as binding upon ourselves. The cheap accusation of anti-Semitism that has been levelled at me on the ground of this criticism is about as intelligent as accusing me of an anti-Chinese prejudice.' ["The Relations between the Ego and the Unconscious" (Coll. Works, Vol. 7), par. 240, n. 8.] And in June 1918 I wrote: 'In my opinion this problem does not exist for the Jews. The Jew already had the culture of the ancient world and on top of that has taken over the culture of the nations amongst whom he dwells. He has two cultures, paradoxical as that may sound. He is domesticated to a higher degree than we are, but he is badly at a loss for that quality in man which roots him to the earth and draws new strength from below. This chthonic quality is found in dangerous concentration in the Germanic peoples. Naturally the Aryan European has not noticed any signs of this for a very long time, but perhaps he is beginning to notice it in the present war; and again, perhaps not. The Jew has too little of this quality—where has he his own earth underfoot? The mystery of the earth is no joke and no paradox.' " (Supra, par. 18.)—EDITORS.]

CIRCULAR LETTER (1934) [1]

Esteemed colleagues:

1035   At the last Congress [2] of the International General Medical Society for Psychotherapy, it was decided to constitute the Society in the form of national groups.[3] Therefore, national groups have now been formed or are being formed in the various countries that were represented at the Congress (Denmark, Germany, Netherlands, Sweden, and Switzerland). The conditions of membership in these national groups vary according to the local by-laws. Because of the political circumstances and because national groups do not yet exist in all countries, so that individuals as such cannot join their respective groups, it has been decided that association with a national group is on a purely voluntary basis; in other words, individual membership is possible within the framework of the International General Medical Society for Psychotherapy.[4]

1 [Inserted as a separate sheet in the *Zentralblatt*, VII:6 (Dec., 1934). The stipulations are based on the statutes of the Society, printed ibid., VII:3.—EDITORS.]

2 [At this, the 7th Congress for Psychotherapy, May, 1934, at Bad Nauheim, the statutes of the International General Medical Society for Psychotherapy were ratified. Jung's presidential address to the Congress may have been extempore; a ms. cannot be traced, but there is a summary of it in the *Zentralblatt*, VII:3. It seems to have been much the same in substance as the "Contribution to a Discussion on Psychotherapy" (infra, pars. 1060ff.).

[At the same Congress, Jung delivered a lecture, "Über Komplextheorie," previously delivered on May 5 at the Federal Polytechnic Institute, Zurich, and published the same year as "Allgemeines zur Komplextheorie." Cf. "A Review of the Complex Theory," *Coll. Works*, Vol. 8, pars. 194ff.

[For Jung's presidential address to the 8th Congress, held in March 1935, also at Bad Nauheim, see pars. 1055ff.]

3 [In order to prevent any national group dominating the Society, it was stipulated in the statutes that no national group could muster more than 40 per cent voting strength.]

4 [By this means, German Jews could remain members of the International Society though ejected from the German national group (cf. infra, par. 1060).]

1036   The International Society is neutral as to politics and creed. Persons wishing to become members of it are invited to communicate with the general secretariat of the International Society, represented by Dr. W. Cimbal, Altona, or with the president's general secretary, Dr. C. A. Meier, Burghölzli, Zurich.

1037   The organ of the Society is the *Zentralblatt für Psychotherapie*, Verlag S. Hirzel, Leipzig; subscription to members, 15 Reichsmarks per year, post-paid.

1038   We therefore respectfully invite you to join the International General Medical Society for Psychotherapy.

Dr. C. G. Jung

Zurich-Küsnacht
December 1, 1934

EDITORIAL (1935) [1]

1039   Although severely shaken by contemporary events, the International General Medical Society for Psychotherapy and its organ the *Zentralblatt* have consolidated their position during the past year, which began with the Congress at Bad Nauheim.[2]

1040   Psychotherapy, after outgrowing the initial chaos of unsystematized tricks and techniques used by all branches of medicine that came into contact with the neuroses, gradually developed into a discipline whose scope and content entitled it to be called "medical psychology," and to be accounted a specialized subject on its own. At one time its arsenal of knowledge consisted merely of a few tags of popular wisdom, a dose of "sound common sense," and a tip or two from suggestion therapy; but today it has become an extensive field of science with continually widening problems. These undoubtedly raise, and have already raised, philosophical issues. The proper subject of medical psychology—the sick psyche—cannot be artificially separated from its wider background, the human psyche in general, though in practice this separation is effected by the illness itself. And although it is necessary to trace the deviations of pathological psychic development in all its details, in evaluating its findings medical research must in the end take its stand on normal observations and average values. As a result, any psychopathology that claims to be practical is inevitably led beyond itself into the sphere of normal psychology, and thus into the domain of philosophy. This is one of the many overlappings so characteristic of modern medicine: one has only to think of physiological chemistry and microbiology. Thus what began as psychotherapy has become an independent branch of science which has already swallowed up all that was formerly meant by psychopathology.

1 [Published in the *Zentralblatt*, VIII:1 (1935, month not indicated), 1–5.—EDITORS.]
2 [The 7th Congress for Psychotherapy. See supra, pars. 1016, n. 2, and 1035, n. 2.]

Today no psychopathology is conceivable that could get along without the insights and discoveries of the psychotherapists.

1041 For a long time past, practical psychological treatment has driven the specialist to elaborate his views in the form of theories, because these are indispensable for an orderly presentation of the empirical facts. Science cannot exist without hypotheses. But if hypotheses are made, intellectual integrity inevitably demands, in my view, a criticism of the premises. An hypothesis does not rest only on the apparent testimony of experience, it rests also on the judgment of the observer. If criticism of the premises underlying a judgment is needed anywhere, it is needed in psychology. (This is not the place for lengthy philosophical discussions, therefore a hint must suffice.)

1042 The accusation has been made in certain quarters that the newer psychotherapy is concerned too much with philosophical problems and not enough with the minutiae of case-histories. This accusation must be emphatically rebutted, because philosophical problems belong in the highest degree to any empirical study of the psyche, as fit subjects both for research and for philosophical criticism. The empirical intellect, occupying itself with the minutiae of case-histories, involuntarily imports its own philosophical premises not only into the arrangement but also into the judgment of the material, and even into the apparently objective presentation of the data. If psychotherapists today are beginning to talk about a *Weltanschauung,* a philosophy of life, this merely proves that they have discovered the existence of certain broad assumptions which were formerly overlooked in the most ingenuous manner. What is the use of even the most accurate and punctilious work if it is prejudiced by an unavowed assumption? Any science worthy of the name must criticize its own assumptions. Freud himself did not shrink from the major philosophical task of debunking religious assumptions "once and for all." His intellectual development shows very clearly how the problems of medical psychology logically culminate in criticism, or at any rate polemical discussion, of its own premises. A departure of this kind is not an aberration; it is the positive duty of any growing science, and moreover it brings about a broadening, deepening, and enriching of its discoveries.

1043   Since psychotherapy purports to be a method of healing, it must include among its aims the need to change a less adapted attitude, such as we see in every morbid state, into a normally adapted attitude. The adaptedness of a psychic system, however, is always related to the situation of the moment, and is therefore not fixed in an unchanging pattern. Adaptedness is not a permanént and permanently valid state which, once reached, can be maintained for ever; it is a continually advancing process which has as its indispensable premise the constant observation of changes occurring both within and without. A system of healing that fails to take account of the epoch-making *représentations collectives* of a political, economic, philosophical, or religious nature, or assiduously refuses to recognize them as actual forces, hardly deserves the name of therapy. It is more a deviation into a pathologically exaggerated attitude of protest which is the very reverse of adapted. Adaptedness as a criterion of cure is absolutely necessary, though of course it is not the only one.

1044   Discussion of general assumptions and leading ideas is a most important item in the present phase of psychotherapy, because it brings into the limelight assumptions that tacitly exist and are all the more dangerous for that reason. In no circumstances can psychotherapy be a single method or a single system. Individuals and their temperaments vary so fundamentally that all forms of schematism and dogmatism cannot be got rid of quickly enough if psychotherapy is not to come to a dead end.

1045   The peculiar nature of psychogenic insecurity and disease, as well as their enormous incidence, make the extension of psychotherapy to wider fields an urgent necessity, more particularly because paedogogics, by definition, does not bother about the education of adults, and the churches have nothing to say to vast numbers of people. The churches, it is true, have only themselves to blame if people confuse religion with a creed and, seeing no need to believe in anything, promptly take that as a proof that religion is superfluous. Experience shows that religion is, at the very least, a psychic fact that has existed from time immemorial and expresses itself in a thousand different forms. Protestant theology, strangely deluded, calls this view "psychologism" and in so doing robs itself of the most effective means of combatting man's insecurity—the confessional, which the Catholic Church has wisely appropriated for the benefit of mankind. Modern psychotherapy has no such aspirations, but often it is virtually compelled to assume spiritual guidance in a realm that properly and originally belonged to the pastoral cure of souls, and is thus faced with an educative task which makes the most exacting demands on the knowledge and competence of the therapist. Though he may decline to cope with them on the plea of professional incompetence, they are really quite manageable if only he will fulfil the necessary conditions. At this point practical treatment impinges directly upon such questions as a philosophy of life, and there is no sense whatever in brushing them aside as irrelevant, thus cutting the patient off from that much needed relationship and adaptation to the great problems of the age and condemning him to a neurotic hole-and-corner existence. That would be the very thing that psychotherapy does *not* envisage.

1046   The human psyche, even when in a pathological condition, is a complex whole actuated not only by instinctual processes and personal relationships but by the spiritual needs and suprapersonal currents of the time. And just as the general practitioner is rightly expected to know the *normal* anatomy and physiology of the body he has to treat, so the psychotherapist will sooner or later feel constrained to know everything that is of vital importance to the life of the psyche. He will, in short, have to approach psychology as one of the humane sciences. That this may prove inconvenient to a doctor trained mainly in the natural sciences is altogether understandable; but the growth of medicine has demonstrated again and again that its disciples, after a little hesitation, were ready to learn more. Psychotherapy is an intermediate field of research which requires the collaboration of many different branches of learning. It will be the task of the future to decide very carefully wherein the competence of each branch lies.

1047   In accordance with the line of development suggested here, the next Congresses will be concerned on the one hand with the specifically medical relations between psychology and endocrinology, and on the other hand with its relation, as a humane science, to oriental symbolism.

1048   During the past year the organization of the International Society has made, in some part, satisfactory progress. The German group was, at the time of the last Congress, already firmly organized under the direction of Professor Göring. Since then there have been added a Dutch group, the "Netherlands Society for Psychotherapy," with thirty-two members under the presidency of Dr. van der Hoop in Amsterdam, and a Danish group with ten members under the presidency of Dr. O. Brüel in Copenhagen. Finally, a Swiss group with fourteen members under the presidency of the undersigned was recently founded in Zurich, bearing the name of the "Swiss Society for Practical Psychology."

1049 The difficulties of establishing relations with neurological and psychiatric societies, not unknown elsewhere, have placed considerable obstacles in the way of founding a Swedish group by Dr. Poul Bjerre in Stockholm, so that no agreement has been reached up to the present.

1050 The work of the groups outside Germany is organized in different ways. Copenhagen has two or three meetings a year, with lectures on specialized subjects. Amsterdam has four meetings a year. Zurich has a meeting every month, with a common programme of work in which, at present, the psychology of dreams is being worked out systematically.

1051 The fragmentation of psychology into various schools and into even more numerous separate theories makes it desirable that discussion in the spirit of collaboration among colleagues should be fostered more than ever in the future. In this way certain misunderstandings would be removed and many questions clarified which at present remain unsolved for want of co-operation.

C. G. JUNG

EDITORIAL NOTE (1935) [1]

1052   Earlier, a Scandinavian and a Dutch issue were published by the *Zentralblatt*, and a Swiss issue is now being presented this year. As Switzerland is a trilingual country, we have not hesitated to include a contribution in French (by Professor Baudouin, Geneva). There are also two contributions in English by two writers who have spent several years studying in Zurich. They are H. G. Baynes, London, who was my assistant for several years, and Esther Harding, New York, author of the deservedly well-known works *The Way of All Women* and *Woman's Mysteries*. Although English is not one of the three official languages of Switzerland, unofficially it is the fourth, as is shown among other things by the fact that for years I have been invited to give English lectures in Zurich.

1053   The greatest danger that threatens psychology is one-sidedness and insistence on a single standpoint. In order to do justice to the phenomena of the psyche, a variety of viewpoints is needed. Just as there are points of view based on race psychology, so also there are national ones, and we may welcome it as an enrichment of our experience that we have succeeded in including in our issues contributions from the Romance and the Anglo-Saxon mind.

1054   The problems of psychiatry are not simplified by concentrating on one single aspect to the exclusion of all the others, for each individual psychic fact is decisively influenced by its relation to the whole; indeed, its real significance can be discovered only when its position in the whole has been ascertained. It would therefore seem more valuable at present to map out the scope of the whole than to investigate individual psychic processes in detail, on a general assumption that is as uncon-

1 [Published in the *Zentralblatt*, VIII:2 (1935, month not indicated), 65.—EDITORS.]

scious as it is incorrect. To this end we need the *consensus gentium,* which is in any case the foundation stone of an international Society and its organ. To promote international collaboration is one of the cultural characteristics of Switzerland, and this should also give the Swiss issue its own peculiar stamp.

C. G. JUNG

PRESIDENTIAL ADDRESS TO THE
8TH GENERAL MEDICAL CONGRESS FOR
PSYCHOTHERAPY, BAD NAUHEIM, 1935 [1]

1055 It is now a year since the International Medical Society for Psychotherapy was founded. During that year the German group has been organized under the successful leadership of Dr. Göring. Then the Netherlands Society for Psychotherapy joined the International Society under the leadership of Dr. van der Hoop. In Copenhagen, a Danish group was organized by Dr. Brüel. A Swiss group has recently been founded in Zurich under my presidency. Dr. Bjerre writes to me from Stockholm that, owing to external difficulties, it has so far not been possible for him to organize a Swedish group. Let us hope that the second year in the life of our Society will find him more successful. A little while ago Professor Stransky, of Vienna, got in touch with me about the founding of an Austrian group, so there appears to be a good chance that the Society will also include Austria.

1056 It seems, however, that it is not particularly easy to bring all those doctors and psychologists who are concerned with psychotherapy or applied psychology into a neutral organization. The reasons for this—apart from the fact that some of them may have become understandably tired of societies—fall into two groups. The first comprises all those difficulties which a young science always has to contend with. Psychotherapy is still a child that is not very sure of itself. Moreover, it has two elder sisters who watch over its growth with somewhat mixed feelings and often dispute its right to independence. These sisters are psychiatry and neurology. Although there are praiseworthy exceptions among the practitioners of these sciences, psychotherapy, being pre-eminently psychological in its outlook and its methods, has as a rule eked out an exceedingly scanty existence under their

1 [March 27–30, 1935. Previously unpublished. Cf. supra, par. 1039.—EDITORS.]

auspices. I do not want to reproach them for this, for both psychiatry and neurology have a perfect right to their own special problems, which have little enough in common with those of psychotherapy. On the other hand, it is not permissible for them to claim a right to take psychotherapy under their wing merely because the one is concerned with mental diseases and the other with nervous diseases. The functional psychological disturbances, or psychoneuroses, are by nature a special field impinging neither on the psychiatric clinic nor on the domain of neurology. Modern psychotherapy has developed beyond that early stage of its career when it was nothing more than fatherly advice or suggestion with or without hypnosis, and has become a proper method of psychological treatment for the use of specialists. This fact is overlooked not only by the public but, all too often, by doctors as well.

1057 The other reasons why the organization of our professional colleagues meets with difficulties have to do with psychological cross-currents within the profession itself. Objective discussion among professionals is not yet possible to the degree that a strictly scientific approach would require. There are certain groups of doctors who put forward theories with totalitarian pretensions and barricade themselves against criticism to such an extent that their scientific convictions are more like a confession of faith. This kind of attitude is a substitute for religion, though no objection could be made to this if only it were admitted. On the contrary, we could understand very well that it is the psychotherapists who feel most acutely the need for religious convictions, since the religions are in fact the oldest systems for healing the sufferings of the soul. But unlike religious ideas, these psychological theories are notably intellectualistic as well as anti-religious. Thus, we are confronted with the uncomfortable fact that in psychotherapy there are not only different theories—which in itself would be a matter for congratulation—but different convictions which are apparently indisputable—a phenomenon that is otherwise found only in the realm of political or religious controversy.

1058 In the face of all these difficulties, the International Society maintains, first of all, that psychotherapy is an independent branch of medicine and, secondly, that scientific truths cannot be substantiated by uncritical and one-sided convictions. Accordingly, it welcomes adherents of all schools so far as they are willing to adopt an objective standpoint.

1059   I therefore earnestly hope that in the course of time all those of our colleagues who wish to see psychotherapy developing along broader lines will associate themselves with us.

CONTRIBUTION TO A DISCUSSION ON PSYCHOTHERAPY [1]

1060   I can only agree with the general statements and intentions of the report we have just heard.[2] The same difficulties that exist in Switzerland for psychotherapy also exist abroad. As a member of the board of the International Society I have sought for years to bring about understanding between the different schools of psychotherapy. No less than three works have been written by members of my school (W. M. Kranefeldt, G. R. Heyer, Gerhard Adler), which all endeavour to give a fair survey of the different scientific standpoints. I had been honorary president of the Society for several years when the revolution in Germany broke out. The then president resigned, and a group of leading German psychotherapists came to me with the request that I take over the presidency, firstly in order to support a beleaguered psychotherapy in its struggle for existence, and secondly in order to preserve its international contacts. Out of regard for the position of psychotherapy in Europe I felt I had no right to withdraw from this difficult and painful task, and therefore decided to accept the presidency of the International Society. In doing so, I was not for one moment unaware that in these days it is a matter of the greatest difficulty to establish an international association without excluding Germany, although it is a *medical* society far removed from any political activity. The *Gleich-*

---

1 [In May 1935, Dr. W. Morgenthaler, an official of the Swiss section of the International General Medical Society for Psychotherapy, organized a symposium on "Psychotherapy in Switzerland." Jung delivered a lecture entitled "What Is Psychotherapy?" (*Coll. Works*, Vol. 16, pars. 28ff.). A discussion followed, and Jung contributed the present remarks (styled "Votum C. G. Jung"), which were published in the *Schweizerische Ärztezeitung für Standesfragen* (Bern), XVI (1935): 26, 345f., together with his lecture (pp. 335ff.).—EDITORS.]

2 [By Dr. Morgenthaler.—EDITORS.]

557

schaltung [3] of the German group was inevitable. Protest would simply have put an end to psychotherapy in Germany. In these circumstances one had to be content with saving what was possible. Jewish doctors are excluded from the German group by the Aryan regulations, but I have succeeded in getting the draft of the international statutes amended so that German Jewish doctors can individually become members of the Society as a whole.[4] National groups now exist in the Netherlands, Denmark, and Switzerland. The Freudian spirit of sectarianism put the greatest obstacles in the way of an Austrian group, and a political campaign was started in the press by the corresponding elements in Switzerland. These regrettable attempts to render objective discussion impossible from the start by sowing political suspicion on the one hand and sectarian discord on the other should not prevent fair-minded doctors who have the scientific development of their work at heart from doing their utmost to reach agreement. I have therefore gladly accepted the invitation to take part in the programme of work proposed by the planning committee.

1061　For a variety of reasons it is probably better if psychotherapists, with a view to safeguarding their scientific and professional interests, do not constitute a group within a psychiatric society. The divergence of interests is too great for direct collaboration to be profitable. In Germany too the separation of psychotherapy from psychiatry has proved to be a compelling necessity. But if psychotherapy is to achieve its independence, its representatives must for better or worse gather round the conference table and lay aside the autistic fads and fancies which have been so very rightly stressed by Dr. Morgenthaler.

1062　It is, in my humble opinion, high time for psychotherapists to become conscious of their social responsibilities. The concept of psychotherapy has reached the wider public; there are large numbers of psychotherapists—so many that one can without exaggeration speak of them as a "profession"; a copious literature exists and has an eager following; and finally psychotherapy, originally the concern of medical men, has come to extend so far beyond its original boundaries that its oldest initia-

3 [See supra, par. 1018.]
4 [See supra, pars. 1035ff.]

tor, Freud himself, today thinks very differently about lay therapy from what he did before. The psychotherapist is now firmly entrenched with the public, so his social responsibility has already begun. But it becomes an urgent problem in view of the incontrovertible fact that the practice of psychotherapy today is largely in the hands of "medical laymen." To anticipate at once, I am not speaking of those incompetent and irresponsible quacks whom the law is quite capable of catching, but of altogether serious teachers and psychologists whose previous training enables them to exert an educative influence. Since applied psychotherapy is largely educative in essence, it can hardly refrain from collaborating with the educator without impoverishing itself. Just as the medical practitioner makes plentiful use of lay assistants, and is even dependent on them in large measure, so the psychotherapist has need of auxiliary methods which he is bound to leave to helpers who are not medically trained. I need only mention physiotherapy and its various uses, special educative techniques, and so on. In my opinion it would be quite wrong for medical psychotherapists to shun these natural fellow-workers and brand them all quacks. On the other hand, the doctor has every interest in not allowing the pretentious aspirations that are fostered in numerous pedagogic institutes and in certain philosophy departments to run riot; instead, he will gradually confine the various fields of activity within their proper limits by wise collaboration. But if he shuts his eyes to the very existence of legitimate psychological workers, he not only fails to eliminate those tendencies by this ostrich policy, but denies himself the much-needed insight into the manifold branches of educational therapy today, and, furthermore, deprives them of the one essential: eventual medical surveillance and control. The International Medical Society for Psychotherapy is concerning itself in a positive way with the problem of practising psychologists and technical assistants when it clearly recognizes the dangers of a wildly proliferating and medically uncontrollable psychological lay movement.

1063   Recently, as so often in the course of the last twenty years, it has been asserted that lay interest in psychological questions is on the decrease and that, because neuroses are either endocrine disturbances or mild forms of psychosis, all psychotherapy is superfluous. I would like to utter an urgent warning against such errors. Various psychological trends may fall out of fashion, but psychological problems in general are far more deeply rooted in the public than is realized outside the psychotherapeutic profession. In this respect the psychotherapist is faced with social responsibilities which sooner or later will make closer association with his fellow-workers an absolute necessity, quite apart from the economic considerations to which Dr. Morgenthaler has drawn attention.

PRESIDENTIAL ADDRESS TO THE
9TH INTERNATIONAL MEDICAL CONGRESS FOR
PSYCHOTHERAPY, COPENHAGEN, 1937 [1]

1064   For the first time our Society is convening here in Copenhagen, at the friendly invitation of the Scandinavian national
groups. Our decision to hold the Congress outside its previous
confines demonstrates its international nature. The Society has
long felt the need not only to overcome the geographical and
linguistic barriers but, even more important, to extend the frontiers of medical psychotherapy as a science. However much the
psychotherapist in his practical work must concentrate on the
individual patient and on the most minute details, as a scientist
he needs a viewpoint that widens his horizon, not just for his
own sake, but for that of his patients, whose almost limitless
differences demand of him a correspondingly broad understanding. Any narrow adherence to artificial limits would be a catastrophe for our science, whether these limits be national, political,
linguistic, religious, or philosophical. Although every investigator is limited as an individual, and must work within his
individual limits, his self-limitation loses all meaning if there
is no living contact with the diversity of other points of view. So
if in the course of the last few years we have succeeded, despite
considerable external difficulties, not only in preserving our
original Society but in establishing its internationality on a
series of national groups—German, Dutch, Danish, Swedish,
Austrian, and Swiss—we have at least laid the foundations of its
further development. It is our liveliest wish to welcome our
French and English colleagues also as future members of our
Society. At a time like this, when historical necessity lays so
much stress on the development of national individuality, the
problem of international relationships becomes equally urgent
by way of compensation. The nations of Europe form a Euro-

1 [October 2–4, 1937. Previously unpublished.]

pean family, which like every family has its own special spirit. However far apart the political goals may lie, they rest ultimately on the common European psyche, with whose aspects the practising psychologist should be familiar.

1065   You will I am sure agree with me that the conditions for an international organization are extremely precarious today. But this should not deter us from doing everything in our power, however limited it may be in these unfavourable times, to preserve the human and psychic ties of the European family and also to practise in the international sphere what we daily seek to inculcate in our patients. By this I mean the avoidance of that basic evil, *projections upon our neighbour*. For everything that exists there are, as we know only too well, sufficient reasons, and only a bad psychologist will fail to appreciate their full significance. It is the task of our science to understand and classify all varieties of human behaviour. Faced with such a bewildering diversity of aspects and viewpoints, psychology can continue to function only if it abandons all hasty commitment to dogmas and doctrinaire convictions and allows every view to express itself freely so far as there are sufficient reasons to support it. In science there is no spirit of sectarianism which decides the truth. Being the science of the psyche, psychology is the sum total of what the psyche says about itself. Hence everything is psychologically true that psychologically exists. But the things that psychologically exist are innumerable. I can therefore wish nothing better for our Society, and in particular for this Congress, than that every opinion should be expressed and listened to, and that as many nations as possible should make their own particular contribution to the total picture of the European psyche.

1066   I still have the painful duty of recalling a loss that our Society has suffered during the past year. Robert Sommer, the co-founder and for many years the first president of the General Medical Society for Psychotherapy, died on February 3rd. Thanks to his wide knowledge of philosophy and psychology, and especially of familial research, he was drawn to our special field and its working hypotheses. His decision to throw in his lot with us and his readiness to collaborate with our endeavours deserve not only our heartfelt thanks but also the highest praise, as this happened at a time when the psychological point of view in medicine was still open to public attack. In these circumstances it was an act of courage that made psychotherapy possible in Germany and to a large extent kept it alive. Sommer's support for psychotherapy was, together with Eugen Bleuler's, of decisive importance for the further development of the new ideas.

1067   I would like to ask you to rise from your seats in memory of our loyal friend and supporter.

1068   Ladies and Gentlemen, the 9th Congress of the International General Medical Society for Psychotherapy is opened. To the organizing committee, and to Dr. Brüel and Dr. Bjerre in particular, I express the Society's thanks for the invitation as well as for the work of preparing the Congress. I now leave the floor to Dr. Brüel.

PRESIDENTIAL ADDRESS TO THE
10TH INTERNATIONAL MEDICAL CONGRESS FOR PSYCHOTHERAPY, OXFORD, 1938 [1]

1069   When we met at Copenhagen last year, it was the first time that our Congress had been held outside Germany. And soon afterwards our British colleagues suggested arranging a meeting in England. It has always been my desire to establish a line of communication between continental psychological medicine and England, where, within the last ten years, so much has been done for the cause of psychotherapy and where there are already so many physicians interested either in the treatment of neuroses or in the psychological aspect of illness in general. I am sure that I speak in the name of all my continental colleagues when I express my profound gratitude to this good town of Oxford, of ancient fame, to our English friends, and to all those whose benevolence and friendly support has made the organization of the Congress possible. We are deeply indebted to the organizing committee, in particular to Dr. Baynes, Dr. Strauss, and Dr. Squires, for their generous advice and help.

1070   Before we begin the actual work I should like, if you will permit me, to make some remarks about the way in which the general intentions of our Congress should be understood. One of the most serious obstacles to collaboration in the field of psychotherapy is the peculiar fact of there being different schools of thought which are apparently incompatible with each other. Not that such a fact would be any novelty in the history of medicine, but it is an annoying encumbrance which has delayed the union and collaboration of the numerous workers in the field of psychotherapy. Medical psychology is still a delicate plant which needs careful nursing if it is to lead a reasonably independent existence in the near future. But how can anyone take care of its development when not even its own representatives are at one among themselves as to what the thing is? It has recently

1 [July 29 – August 2, 1938. Delivered in English; previously unpublished.]

become a serious question, in more countries than one, whether psychotherapy could or should be taught at the universities. Many physicians have realized that quite ordinary diseases are accompanied by psychological disturbances which are causally related to the organic ailment. Psychiatrists have become aware that even psychoses often have a remarkably psychological aspect, and psychotherapists have found that borderline cases, ominously labelled as schizophrenia, are not inaccessible to psychological treatment. In education, considerable use has already been made of the psychological points of view elaborated by medical psychologists. And even the clergy, Catholic as well as Protestant, are beginning to be interested in our work, because they are human beings like ourselves who are burdened and even harassed at times by the intricate moral problems of the people who consult them. We can safely speak of an enormous increase of public interest in our work within the last ten years. Interest in psychology is serious in our day and is no longer a ridiculous fad as it was twenty years ago. Today we ought to think hard and make a serious effort to bring together all men of good will in our profession, in order to meet the needs and demands of the time. In Switzerland we had a committee for psychotherapy elected by the Swiss Society of Psychiatry many years ago. And, as one might expect, for as many years nothing happened. Recently, however, we made a move, but one of our faculties of medicine said: "What are you going to teach? You do not even agree with each other about your own theories."

1071   This remark hits the nail on the head. Yet the nail of psychotherapy has several heads and only one of these is struck by this criticism. Those who are not professionally acquainted with psychology do not realize that it includes a very large and equally important practical part which has little or nothing to do with a particular theory. But it is the latter which is loudly proclaimed before the public, and thus the prejudice is aroused that psychotherapy amounts to nothing but the preaching of a particular theory. This is a gross mistake. As a matter of fact each psychotherapist in his practical work follows a line that is more or less common to all his colleagues (provided they do not use hypnotism). And each of them, no matter to what school he belongs, follows his own line because he knows from experience that good work demands the whole man and is never achieved by mere routine or by a theoretical creed. The very nature of the cases we are treating forces us occasionally to change our method or our theoretical explanation. We know that a neurosis is not a typical infection by a specific microbe, but the morbid development of the whole of a personality. We also know that the originators of psychological theories are human beings with an individual psychic predisposition, the one more prone to a certain kind of opinion or interpretation than the other. On the one hand we have to deal with very individual patients and on the other hand we make use of opinions which are only very relatively valid. These truths are incontestable. They should warn us against any fixed standpoint and they should turn our minds to what we actually do with our patients, rather than to a meaningless dispute about opinions.

1072   The Swiss Committee of Psychotherapy has made the attempt to formulate those points about which all psychotherapists, working along the lines of psychological analysis, could agree. The democratic spirit of Switzerland has helped us to avoid all absolutism and we succeeded in producing Fourteen Points of mutual agreement.[2] President Wilson's noble attempt seems to have stood godfather to our little enterprise. There are people who doubt whether the League of Nations really works. But our enterprise in Switzerland has already worked. We are ready now to start an Institute of Psychotherapy.

1073   Our fourteen points, which I am presently going to discuss, have been ridiculed as a lukewarm compromise that skates over the most tremendous differences of opinion. That is exactly what we intended to do. If you want to quarrel about opinions, you can spend the rest of your life doing so. But we wanted to get something done, and you cannot do that by endless philosophical discussions about the ultimate meaning of the psyche. Each school had to sacrifice some of its hobby-horses and to abandon stiff-necked resistance to other points of view. Something little short of a miracle happened: our admittedly lukewarm and

2 ["The fourteen points dealt with medical procedure, psychogenesis, diagnosis, exploration, material (including all possible forms of human expression, behaviour, controlled language, the language of free association, of fantasy, of dreams, of symptoms and symptomatic actions), aetiology, the unconscious, fixation, conscious realization, analysis and interpretation, transference, ontogenic reduction, phylogenic reduction, and therapy."—*Zentralblatt*, XI (1939):1–2, p. 2.—EDITORS.]

superficial formulations brought about a cordial collaboration between people who formerly thought they were miles apart from each other. If my colleagues understand that psychotherapy is our common cause, then there is a hope it will find a well-merited place among the other branches of medical science.

BIBLIOGRAPHY

BIBLIOGRAPHY

Acta Archelai. See HEGEMONIUS.

ANGELUCCI, ORFEO M. *The Secret of the Saucers.* Amherst (Wis.), 1955.

Annalen der Naturphilosophie. Edited by Wilhelm Ostwald. Leipzig, 1902– .

ANQUETIL DU PERRON, ABRAHAM HYACINTHE. *Oupnek'hat (id est, Secretum tegendum) . . . in Latinum conversum . . . studio et opere Anquetil du Perron.* Strasbourg, 1801–2. 2 vols.

Anthropophyteia. Jahrbücher für folkloristische Erhebungen und Forschungen zur Entwicklungsgeschichte der geschlechtlichen Moral. Edited by Friedrich H. Krauss. Leipzig, 1904–13. 10 vols.

AUGUSTINE, SAINT. *Sermo 189.* See MIGNE, *P.L.,* vol. 38, cols. 1005–7.

Aurora Consurgens. See FRANZ, MARIE-LOUISE VON.

BALLY, G. "Deutschstämmige Psychotherapie?" *Neue Zürcher Zeitung,* CLV: 343 (Feb. 27, 1934).

BASH, K. W., AHLENSTIEL, H., and KAUFMANN, R. "Ueber Präyantraformen und ein lineares Yantra." In: *Studien zur analytischen Psychologie C. G. Jungs.* Zurich, 1955. (I, 205–228.)

BELLOWS, HENRY ADAMS (ed. and trans.). *The Poetic Edda.* (Scandinavian Classics, 21, 22.) New York, 1923. 2 vols. in one. ("Voluspo," I, 1–27.)

BENOÎT, PIERRE. *Atlantida.* Translated by Mary C. Tongue and Mary Ross. New York, 1920. (Original: *L'Atlantide.* Paris, 1920.)

BÖHLER, EUGEN. *Ethik und Wirtschaft.* Zurich (Industrielle Organization), 1957.

[ECKHART, MEISTER.] *Meister Eckhart.* [Works.] Translated by C. de B. Evans. London, 1924–52. 2 vols.

Entretiens: L'Avenir de l'esprit européen. (League of Nations: International Institute of Intellectual Co-operation.) Paris, 1934.

FOERSTER-NIETZSCHE, ELIZABETH (ed.). *Der werdende Nietzsche*. Munich, 1924.

FOREL, AUGUSTE. *The Sexual Question*. Adapted from the 2nd German edition by C. F. Marshall. Revised edn., New York, 1925. (Original: *Die sexuelle Frage*. Munich, 1905.)

FRANZ, MARIE-LOUISE VON (ed.). *Aurora Consurgens: A Document Attributed to Thomas Aquinas on the Problem of Opposites in Alchemy*. Translated by R.F.C. Hull and A.S.B. Glover. New York (Bollingen Series LXXVII) and London. 1966.

FREUD, SIGMUND. *The Future of an Illusion*. Translated by W. D. Robson-Scott. In: Standard Edn.,* 21. 1961.

———. *The Interpretation of Dreams*. Translated by James Strachey. In: Standard Edn.,* 4 and 5. 1953.

———. *The Psychopathology of Everyday Life*. Translated by Alan Tyson. In: Standard Edn.,* 6. 1961 (dated 1960).

———. *Totem and Taboo*. Translated by James Strachey. In: Standard Edn.,* 13. 1955.

FÜRST, EMMA. "Statistical Investigations on Word-Associations and on Familial Agreement in Reaction Type among Uneducated Persons." In: *Studies in Word-Association,* under the direction of C. G. Jung. Translated by M. D. Eder. London, 1918; New York, 1919. (Pp. 407–445.)

GEORGE, STEFAN. *Werke*. Gesamt-Ausgabe. Endgültige Fassung. Berlin, 1927–34. 18 vols.

GOETHE, JOHANN WOLFGANG VON. *Faust, Parts One and Two*. Translated by Philip Wayne. (Penguin Classics.) Harmondsworth and Baltimore, 1949, 1959.

———. *Werke*. Edited by Ernst Beutler. (Gedenkausgabe.) Zurich, 1948–54. 24 vols. (Vols. I–II: Sämtliche Gedichte.)

GOETZ, BRUNO. *Deutsche Dichtung*. Lucerne, 1935.

* The Standard Edition of the Complete Psychological Works of Sigmund Freud, translated from the German under the general editorship of James Strachey, in collaboration with Anna Freud, assisted by Alix Strachey and Alan Tyson. London.

——. *Das Reich ohne Raum*. Potsdam, 1919; 2nd enl. edn., Constance, 1925.

GOTTHELF, JEREMIAS (pseudonym of Albert Bitzius). *The Black Spider*. Translated by H. M. Waidson. London, 1958. (Original: *Die schwarze Spinne*.)

HAGGARD, H. RIDER. *Ayesha: the Return of She*. London, 1905.

——. *She*. London, 1887.

——. *Wisdom's Daughter*. London, [1923].

HARDING, M. ESTHER. *Journey into Self*. New York, 1956.

——. *The Way of All Women*. London and New York, 1933.

——. *Women's Mysteries, Ancient and Modern*. London and New York, 1935.

HASTINGS, JAMES (ed.). *Encyclopaedia of Religion and Ethics*. Edinburgh and New York, 1908–27. 13 vols.

HAUER, (JACOB) WILHELM. *Deutsche Gottschau: Grundzüge eines deutschen Glaubens*. Stuttgart, 1935.

HAY, AGNES BLANCHE MARIE. *The Evil Vineyard*. London and New York, 1923.

HEARD, [HENRY FITZ]GERALD. *Is Another World Watching? The Riddle of the Flying Saucers*. London, 1950; New York, 1951.

HEGEMONIUS. *Acta Archelai*. Edited by Charles Henry Beeson. (Griechische christliche Schriftsteller.) Leipzig, 1906.

HERMES TRISMEGISTUS. *The Emerald Table (Tabula Smaragdina)*. In: *The Lives of the Alchymistical Philosophers*. London, 1815; repr. 1955. (Pp. 383–84.)

HILDEGARD OF BINGEN, SAINT. *Wisse die Wege; Scivias*. Translated (into German) and edited by Maria Böckeler. Salzburg, 1955.

HÖLDERLIN, JOHANN CHRISTIAN FRIEDRICH. *Gedichte*. Edited by Franz Zinkermagel. Leipzig, 1922.

HOYLE, FRED. *The Black Cloud*. London, 1957.

——. *Frontiers of Astronomy*. London, 1955.

——. *The Nature of the Universe*. London, 1950.

IRENAEUS. *Adversus* [or *Contra*] *haereses libri quinque.* In: *The Writings of Irenaeus.* Translated by Alexander Roberts and W. H. Rambaut. (Ante-Nicene Christian Library, 5, 9.) Edinburgh, 1868–9. 2 vols.

JAFFÉ, ANIELA. *Apparitions and Precognition. A Study from the Point of View of C. G. Jung's Analytical Psychology.* Translated by Vera Klein Williams and Mary Elliot. New Hyde Park (N.Y.) and London, 1963.

JONES, ERNEST. *Sigmund Freud: Life and Work.* London, 1953–57. 3 vols. (New York edn. differently paged.)

JOYCE, JAMES. *Ulysses.* Paris, 1922.

JUNG, CARL GUSTAV. *Aion.* (Collected Works, 9, ii.*) 1959; 2nd edn., 1968.

————. *Alchemical Studies.* (Collected Works, 13.) 1968.

————. *The Archetypes and the Collective Unconscious.* (Collected Works, 9, i.) 1959; 2nd edn., 1968.

————. "Brother Klaus." In: *Psychology and Religion: West and East,* q.v.

————. *Collected Papers on Analytical Psychology.* Edited by Constance E. Long; translated by various persons. London and New York, 1916; 2nd edn., 1917.

————. "Concerning Mandala Symbolism." In: *The Archetypes and the Collective Unconscious,* q.v.

————. "Concerning Rebirth." In: *The Archetypes and the Collective Unconscious,* q.v.

————. "A Contribution to the Study of Psychological Types." In: *Psychological Types.* (Collected Works, 6.*) (Alternative source: *Collected Papers on Analytical Psychology,* q.v.)

————. *Contributions to Analytical Psychology.* Translated by C. F. and H. G. Baynes. London and New York, 1928.

————. *The Development of Personality.* (Collected Works, 17.) 1954.

————. *Essays on Contemporary Events.* Translated by Elizabeth Welsh, Barbara Hannah, and Mary Briner. London, 1947.

* For details of the Collected Works, see the list at the end of this volume.

——. "Freud and Jung: Contrasts." In: *Freud and Psychoanalysis,* q.v.

——. *Freud and Psychoanalysis.* (Collected Works, 4.) 1961.

——. "General Aspects of Dream Psychology." In: *The Structure and Dynamics of the Psyche,* q.v.

——. "Instinct and the Unconscious." In: *The Structure and Dynamics of the Psyche,* q.v.

——. "Introduction to Kranefeldt's *Secret Ways of the Mind.*" In: *Freud and Psychoanalysis,* q.v.

——. "Marriage as a Psychological Relationship." In: *The Development of Personality,* q.v.

——. *Modern Man in Search of a Soul.* Translated by W. S. Dell and Cary F. Baynes. London and New York, 1933.

——. "On Psychological Understanding." In: *The Psychogenesis of Mental Disease,* q.v.

——. *The Practice of Psychotherapy.* (Collected Works, 16.) 1954; 2nd edn., 1966.

——. *Psychiatric Studies.* (Collected Works, 1.) 1957; 2nd edn., 1970.

——. *The Psychogenesis of Mental Disease.* (Collected Works, 3.) 1960.

——. "The Psychological Foundations of Belief in Spirits." In: *The Structure and Dynamics of the Psyche,* q.v.

——. "A Psychological Theory of Types." In: *Psychological Types,* q.v. (Alternative source: *Modern Man in Search of a Soul,* q.v.)

——. *Psychological Types.* (Collected Works, 6.*) (Alternative source: Translation by H. G. Baynes. London and New York, 1923.)

——. *Psychology and Alchemy.* (Collected Works, 12.) 1953; 2nd edn., 1968.

——. "Psychology and Religion." In: *Psychology and Religion: West and East,* q.v.

——. *Psychology and Religion: West and East.* (Collected Works, 11.) 1958; 2nd edn., 1969.

——. "The Psychology of the Transference." In: *The Practice of Psychotherapy,* q.v.

575

——. "Psychotherapy and a Philosophy of Life." In: *The Practice of Psychotherapy*, q.v.

——. "A Review of the Complex Theory." In: *The Structure and Dynamics of the Psyche*, q.v.

——. "The Relations between the Ego and the Unconscious." In: *Two Essays on Analytical Psychology*, q.v.

——. *The Structure and Dynamics of the Psyche*. (Collected Works, 8.) 1960; 2nd edn., 1969.

——. "The Structure of the Psyche." In: *The Structure and Dynamics of the Psyche*, q.v.

——. "The Structure of the Unconscious." In: *Two Essays on Analytical Psychology*, q.v.

——. *Symbols of Transformation*. (Collected Works, 5.) 1956.

——. "Synchronicity: an Acausal Connecting Principle." In: *The Structure and Dynamics of the Psyche*, q.v.

——. "The Theory of Psychoanalysis." In: *Freud and Psychoanalysis,* q.v.

——. "Transformation Symbolism in the Mass." In: *Psychology and Religion: West and East,* q.v.

——. *Two Essays on Analytical Psychology*. (Collected Works, 7.) 1953; 2nd edn., 1966.

——. "What Is Psychotherapy?" In: *The Practice of Psychotherapy*.

——. See also WILHELM, RICHARD.

JUNGER, ERNST. *On the Marble Cliffs*. Translated by Stuart Hood. London, 1947. (Original: *Auf den Marmorklippen*.)

KERNER, JUSTINUS. *The Seeress of Prevorst*. Translated by Mrs. [Catherine] Crowe. New York, 1859. (Original: *Die Seherin von Prevorst*. Stuttgart and Tübingen, 1829. 2 vols.)

KEYHOE, DONALD EDWARD. *The Flying Saucer Conspiracy*. London, 1957.

——. *Flying Saucers from Outer Space*. New York, 1953; London, 1954.

KEYSERLING, COUNT HERMANN. *America Set Free*. New York and London, 1929. (Original: *Amerika. Der Aufgang einer neuen Welt*. Stuttgart and Berlin, 1930.)

――. *The Book of Marriage.* Translated by W. H. Hilton-Brown and others. New York, [1926]. (Original: *Das Ehe-Buch.* Celle, 1925.)

――. *Europe.* Translated by Maurice Samuel. New York and London, 1928. (Original: *Das Spektrum Europas.* Heidelberg, 1928.)

――. *Mensch und Erde.* (Der Leuchter, 8.) Darmstadt, 1927.

――. *La Révolution mondiale et la responsabilité de l'Esprit.* Paris, 1934.

――. *South-American Meditations.* Translated by Therese Duerr. New York and London, 1932. (Original: *Südamerikanische Meditationen.* Stuttgart, 1932.)

KLAGES, LUDWIG. *Der Geist als Widersacher der Seele.* 2nd edn., Leipzig, 1937.

――. *Vom cosmogonischen Eros.* Jena, 1922.

KRAFFT-EBING, RICHARD VON. *Psychopathia Sexualis.* Adapted from the 12th German edition by F. J. Rebman. New York, 1925. (Original: Stuttgart, 1886.)

LE BON, GUSTAVE. *The Crowd, a Study of the Popular Mind.* London, 1896.

MACROBIUS, AMBROSIUS THEODOSIUS. *Commentarium in Somnium Scipionis.* In: *Opera.* Edited by F. Eyssenhardt. Leipzig, 1893. For translation, see: *Commentary on the Dream of Scipio.* Translated by William Harris Stahl. (Records of Civilization, Sources and Studies, 48.) New York, 1952.

MENZEL, DONALD HOWARD. *Flying Saucers.* Cambridge (Mass.) and London, 1953.

MICHEL, AIMÉ. *The Truth about Flying Saucers.* London, 1957. (Original: *Lueurs sur les soucoupes volantes.* Paris, 1954.)

MIGNE, JACQUES PAUL (ed.). *Patrologiae cursus completus.* Latin series. Paris, 1844–64. 221 vols. (This work is referred to as "Migne, *P.L.*")

[MURRAY, JOHN.] *Murray's Handbook for Travellers in India, Burma, and Ceylon.* London, 1891; 17th edn., 1955.

NIETZSCHE, FRIEDRICH WILHELM. *Beyond Good and Evil.* Translated by Helen Zimmern. Edinburgh and London, 1907.

———. *The Birth of Tragedy.* Translated by William A. Haussmann. London, 1909.

———. *Thus Spoke Zarathustra.* See: *The Portable Nietzsche.* Selected and translated by Walter Kaufmann. New York, 1954.

———. *Werke.* Leipzig, [1930–32]. 8 vols. ("An den Mistral," V, 495; "To the Unknown God," V, 457–58.)

NINCK, MARTIN. *Wotan und germanische Schicksalsglaube.* Jena, 1935.

NOSTRADAMUS, MICHEL (Nostredame). *The Complete Prophecies of Nostradamus.* Translated and edited by Henry C. Roberts. New York, 1949. (Original: *Vrayes Centuries et prophéties de Maistre Michel Nostredame.* Amsterdam, 1667.)

OSTWALD. See: *Annalen der Naturphilosophie.*

PORTMANN, ADOLF. "Die Bedeutung der Bilder in der lebendigen Energiewandlung." In: *Eranos-Jahrbuch 1952* (XXI). Zurich, 1953.

REINWALD, PAUL. *Vom Geist der Massen.* Zurich, 1946.

ROUSSEAU, JEAN-JACQUES. *The Confessions.* The anonymous translation into English of 1783 and 1790 revised and completed by A. S. B. Glover. New York, 1955.

RUPPELT, EDWARD J. *Report on Unidentified Flying Objects.* London and New York, 1956.

SCHMITZ, OSCAR A. H. [Autobiography, I:] *Die Geister des Hauses; Jugenderinnerungen.* [II:] *Dämon Welt; Jahre der Entwicklung.* [III:] *Ergo Sum; Jahre des Reifens.* Munich, 1925–27. 3 vols.

———. *Psychoanalyse und Yoga.* Darmstadt, 1923.

SCHREBER, DANIEL PAUL. *Memoirs of My Nervous Illness.* Translated by Ida Macalpine and Richard A. Hunter. London, 1955. (Original: *Denkwürdigkeiten eines Nervenkranken.* Leipzig, 1903.)

SIEVERS, EDGAR. *Flying Saucers über Südafrika.* Pretoria, 1955.

Tabula smaragdina. See HERMES.

TERTULLIAN. *Adversus Judaeos.* See Migne, *P.L.,* vol. 2, cols. 595–642.

VALÉRY, PAUL. *History and Politics.* Translated by Denise Folliot and Jackson Mathews. (Collected Works, edited by Jackson Mathews, 10.) New York (Bollingen Series XLV) and London, 1962.

VIRGIL. [*Eclogues.*] *The Pastoral Poems.* The text of the Eclogues, with a translation by E. V. Rieu. (Penguin Classics.) Harmondsworth and Baltimore, 1954.

WELLS, HERBERT GEORGE. *The Time Machine.* London, 1895.

——. *The War of the Worlds.* London, 1898.

WILHELM, RICHARD (trans.). *The Secret of the Golden Flower.* With a foreword and commentary by C. G. Jung. Translated from the German by Cary F. Baynes. New edn., London and New York, 1962.

WILKINS, HAROLD TOM. *Flying Saucers on the Attack.* London, n.d. [1954.]

WOLFF, TONI. *Studien zu C. G. Jungs Psychologie.* Zurich, 1959.

WYNDHAM, JOHN. *The Midwich Cuckoos.* London and New York, 1957.

ZSCHOKKE, JOHANN HEINRICH DANIEL. *Eine Selbstschau.* 3rd edn., Aarau, 1843.

INDEX

INDEX

A

abaissement du niveau mental, 420
abstinence, sexual, 109
Abyssinia, 179
acausal phenomena, *see* synchronicity
acceleration, of Ufos, 316
accidents, 450; as omens, 61
Acta Archelai, 369
Acts of the Apostles, 40, 280, 445
Adam, 296
Adam's Bridge, 525
Adamski, George, 322
adaptation: diminished, 241; neurosis and, 162; psychological, and projection, 25; psychotherapy and, 549; will to, 161, 169
adaptedness, 282
Adler, Alfred, 14, 160, 161, 164*f*, 288, 348, 541
Adler, Gerhard, 557
adultery, 120, 123, 129
aeroplanes, 317
aesthetics, values in, 457
affect(s): control of, 360; excess of, 458, 459; deviations from instinct as, 360; uncontrolled, 360; wallowing in, 468
Africa, 66, 136, 152; and Christianity, 89; hysteria in, 19; white and black in, 47
afterlife, belief in, 328
aggression, and religion, 343
Ahasuerus, 181
Ahlenstiel, H., 424*n*
airman, as observer, 340
Akbar the Great, 516
Alberich, 186
Albertus Magnus, 458

alchemy, 331*f*, 334, 385*f*, 394, 404*f*; colours in, 417; Hildegard and, 404; Holy Ghost in, 405; mandala in, 326; three plus one motif in, 39; water in, 332, 333
Alexander the Great, 516
Allah, 192, 328
all-being, non-existent, 407
Allgemeine Ärztliche Gesellschaft für Psychotherapie, 533, 535, 537, 538
Alps, 115
America, 94, 379, 417, 489*ff*; communism and, 267; conscious and unconscious in, 49; divorce in, 120; Ufos in, 315*ff*; Indianization in, 13, 45*f*, 502, 510*f*; lack of soul in, 490; national spirit of, 512; Negroes in, 46*f*, 508*f*; North, Germanic colonization of, 45; South, 497; *see also* psychology
American(s): and Europeans, differences, 503, 509; Negro complex of, 508
American Indians, 507
Americanization, 91, 493
Amorites, 192
amplification, 325, 340, 389, 406
Amsterdam, 551
anabasis, 355
analysis: a dialectical process, 469; training, 159, 163; *see also* psychoanalysis
analyst, sex of, and patient's reactions, 470
ancestor-spirits, 510
anchorites, 341
angel(s), 369; guardian, 447; of Rev. 10 : 1, 386
Angelucci, Orfeo M., 418*ff*, 430, 431

Anglo-Saxons, 524
anima, 366*f*, 376, 426; as archetype, 38*ff*; and collective unconscious, 377*f*; fateful quality of, 378; feminine character, 118; figure, projection on to, 378; in German literature, 408; as mediatrix, 378; and Ufo, 378
animal magnetism, 15
animals: Christianity and, 22; domestic, complexes in, 446; as dream symbols, 360; instinct in, 287
animism, primitive, 211
animosity, 40
animus, 119, 369; as archetype, 38, 41*ff*
Anquetil du Perron, A. H., 85, 86
Antarctic, 317
anteaters, 57
Anthropophyteia, 87
Anthropos, 327, 389, 405; Christ as, 397; *see also* man, primordial
anthroposophy, 16, 83, 84, 87
anti-gravity, 352, 416; *see also* weightlessness
antinomianism, 356
anti-Semitism, 166, 181, 213, 541, 544*n*
antithesis(-es), *see* opposites
anxiety, seat of, 170; anxiety states, 143, 146
apes, 287
Appenzell, 492
apperceptions, 9
aqua caelestis, see *aqua permanens*
aqua doctrinae, 394
aqua permanens, 331, 332, 392
Aquarius, 311
Aquinas, *see* Thomas Aquinas
arcane substance, 334, 386
archetype(s), 313, 327*f*, 335, 366, 411; ambivalence of, 237; amorality of, 448; analogy with watercourse, 189; autonomy of, 449; bipolar, 229; change in constellation of, 311; foundation of consciousness, 346; Freud and, 439*f*; manifestation in child, 32*f*; and myth, 329;

nature of, 31, 219, 449; numinosity of, 272, 340, 343; of order, 328; psychoid nature of, 450, 451, 452, 453; recognition of, 32*ff*; of self, 407; in Tanguy picture, 398*f*; transgressiveness of, 349; Wotan as, 187
architecture, Indian, 516, 519
Aries, 311
arrangement, 360
arrow, 337
art; expressionist, 83; modern, 140, 210, 303, 383; ——, psychology of, 146; ——, and unconscious, 398; "symbol" of, 19
Aryan, *see* Germanic
ascetics, 341
Asia, Central, 491
ass, 66
assimilation, of man to country, 510*f*
association: experiments, 544*n*; processes, parallel, 319; tests, 30, 397*f*
astrologer, 361, 364
astrology, 59, 83, 84, 87, 90, 312, 364, 484; current, 370; *see also* horoscopes
asymmetry, of fourth dimension, 392*f*
atheism, 258
atman, 35, 410, 463, 464; -Purusha, 463
atomic energy, 242, 321
atomic physics, *see* physics
atoms, of Democritus, 404
attic, 354
attitude(s): collective national, 511; earth-bound, and spiritual, 484; positive, Keyserling and, 498*f*
Augustine, St., 287, 484
Augustus, era of, 141, 247
Aurobindo, Shri, 464
aurora borealis, 186
Aurora consurgens, 403, 427
aurum non vulgi, 386
aurum potabile, 392
Auschwitz, 196
Australian primitives, 49

Austria, 481, 512, 554, 558
authoritarian principle, 153
average, statistical, 328, 393*f*
Axiom of Maria, *see* Maria

B

Babbitt, 491
Bach, Johann Sebastian, 79
Bad Nauheim: 7th Congress, 535*n*,
   545*n*, 547; 8th Congress, 554
Badrutt, Hans, 482
Bahamas, 317
Baldur, 190*n*, 371
Bally, G., 535*ff*
baptism, 67; *en masse*, 262
barbarians, and Germanic mental-
   ity, 14
Barbelo, 397
Basel, 401
Bash, K. W., 424*n*
ba-soul, 42
Baudouin, C., 552
Baynes, H. Godwin, 552, 564
bear, 65
"beast, blond," 13, 212, 219, 227
Beauchamp, Christine L., 125
beauty, 67, 69; modern art and, 383
Beelzebub, 275
beetles, 352
behaviour: American, 508; and real
   man, 509; typology of, 471
behaviourism, 491, 492
behaviourists, 70
belief: and reality, 526; unreflect-
   ing, 265
Benares, 519, 526
Benoît, Pierre, 39*f*, 43, 44
Bergson, Henri, 147
Berlin, 236
Bernheim, H., 172
Bernoulli, C. A., 482
berserker, 185, 186, 213, 214
Besant, Annie, 44, 86
Bhagavad Gita, 465
Bhakti-Yoga, 464
Binet, Alfred, 4

biology: knowledge and, 336; and
   man, 282*f*; and the psyche, 7, 17
birds, song of, 288
Birkhäuser, P., 390, Pl. III
birth control, *see* contraception
birthplace, indications of, in children, 510
Bismarck, Otto Eduard Leopold
   von, 208
Bjerre, Poul, 551, 554, 563
"black, going," 121, 507, 509
Blavatsky, Mme. Helena, 86
Bleuler, Eugen, 544*n*, 563
blood: Mercurius as, 332; rains of,
   319
Boas, Franz, 45, 503
body: rediscovery of, 93*f*; and
   psyche/spirit, relation, 94, 411
Boehme, Jacob, 338, 389, 403
Boer War, 239
Böhler, Eugen, 324*n*
Bolsheviks/Bolshevism, 87, 88, 320,
   491, 493; and behaviourism, 492;
   and totalitarianism, 537
Bombay, 515*ff*
bombings, of cities, 394
borderline cases, 565
boredom, 341
Borgias, the, 425
boy, in golden clothes, 387
Brahman, 463
brain: and fantasies, 10; and psyche,
   270
bread, superessential, 342
"breakthrough," 347
breath, as spirit, 72
British Empire, 516
broadsheets, illustrating Ufos, 401*f*,
   Pls. V, VI
Brocken, spectre of, 385
Buchenwald, 196
Brüel, O., 551, 554, 563
Buddha, 92, 410, 517, 520, 525*f*
Buddhism, 153, 257, 278, 525*f*; and
   animals, 22; and compassion, 98;
   in Europe, 16; mandalas in, 423;
   monasticism and, 40
Buffalo (New York), 46*n*, 502

bull: dream-symbol, 20f; sacrifice of, 21
Bunyan, John, 381
Burckhardt, Johann Jakob, 213
bureau, Ufo recording, 316
Buridan's ass, 374, 454
bush-soul, 65f

C

cabalism, 410
Cabiri, see *Faust*
Calcutta, 520, 526
California, 372
calves, two-headed, 319
cannons, 402
capital, living on one's, 482n
Capitalists, 320
Carpocrates, 131
case-histories, 548
Cassandra, 377
catastrophe(s): cosmic, 367; psychic, 355
categories, Kantian, 10
caterpillar, 336
Catholic Church: and confession, 549; and Fascism, 190; and sexuality, 345
cats, and earthquakes, 336
causality, 54ff; life-process and, 336; psychic, 445
censorship, 209
cerebrospinal nervous system, 353f
Ceylon, 464f, 525
chain-reactions, atomic, 321
Chamberlain, Houston Stewart, 186
Chamberlain, Neville, 205, 206
Champs Élysées, 330f
chance, 55f, 66ff; grouping of chance occurrences, 60; primitives and, 443
chaos, 384
character: changes of, 139; national, 486f
Charcot, J. M., 172
chariot, fiery, 327
Charon, 369

chauffeur, as culture-hero, 93
cheese, Hildegard on, 405
chemistry, physiological, 547
chên-yên, 327
chickens, and earthquakes, 336
child: overrated, 492; in womb, quickening of, 403ff, Pl. 8
children: indication of birthplace in, 510; and student marriages, 103f
China/Chinese, 89, 521; alchemy in, 333; and America, 491; characters, 496; philosophy, 142; psychological consciousness in, 165; science in, 90; and spirit, 498
choking, 5
Christ, 328, 334, 389, 410; androgyny of, 407; fish as symbol of, 141, 425; as "fountain," 332; head of Church, 397; historicity of, 285; and *lapis*, 424; Nietzschean travesty of, 213; and Mercurius, 405; and Sabbath-breaker, 357; soul of, as ball, 404; as sun, 425; symbols of, 449; temptation of, 389; and Wotan, 180; *see also* Anthropos; Jesus
Christianity, 89, 92, 115, 187, 257, 279, 526; in Africa, 89; Asiatic origin of, 91; barbarian element in, 14; and bull sacrifice, 21; and Christian Science, 48; French Revolution and, 16; and Germanic peoples, 12f, 190n; and individuation process, 271; repristinization of, 328; rise of, 311, 497; in Roman Empire, 92; and slavery, 121
Christian Science, 16, 48, 84, 514
chthonic: portion of psyche, 31; quality, in man, 13
Church(es), 549; Christian, 77, 153, 480; ——, and guilt, 196; as communal ideal, 261; and mass action, 275f; and politics, 265; and the psyche, 271; totalitarianism in, 537; *see also* Catholic Church
cigar-form, 407; in Tanguy painting, 396; of Ufos, 325, 336

Cilicia, 91
Cimbal, W., 538, 546
cinema, 93
circle: antithesis to cigar-form, 407; apotropaic/magic, 326; God as, 327, 424; quadripartite, 391; squaring of, 405; *see also* mandala
cities, and culture, 115, 341
city, symbol in picture, 395, 397
civilization(s): American, uniformity of, 492; collapse of, 142; regeneration of, 143
clergy, and psychotherapy, 565
cloud, black, 426*ff*
Coccius, Samuel, 401
coeducation, 521
coffin, symbol in Nietzsche, 182
cohabitation, 396
coincidence, meaningful, *see* synchronicity
coincidentia oppositorum, 355; *see also* opposites; *complexio; coniunctio*
coins; falling from sky, 387; symbols on, 47
Coleridge, Samuel Taylor, 158
collective man, *see* man, collective
collectiveness, American, 506
colours: masculine/feminine, 417; red/white, 417
coloured races, 295, 296; and American man, 508; reactions to, 508; *see also* Negro
comets, 319
communism, 289, 537; archaic social order, 279, 430; Bolshevism and, 493; ideal of, 261; ideology of, 266*f*, 295; primitive, 255; State prison of, 344; Communist revolution, 289
community, idea of, 261
compassion, 98
compensation: psychic / psychological, 141, 219, 220, 342; ——, in history, 121, 142; purpose of unconscious, 388; *see also* compensatory function
compensatory function, of uncon-

scious, 18*ff*, 23, 43, 86, 118, 152, 219
complexes: awareness of, 225; Jewish, 539; modern art and, 399; theory of, 544*n*
complex-indicators, 398*n*
complexio oppositorum: God as, 404, 424; Mercurius as, 385; see also *coincidentia oppositorum;* opposites; *coniunctio*
complex-proneness, 34
compulsions, conscience and, 447
concentration, among primitives, 54
concentration camps, 196, 239
concept, implications of term, 529
conception and fantasy, relation, 313
concupiscence/*concupiscentia,* 160*f*, 287
Condillac, Étienne de, 173
confessional, 549
Confiteor, 355
Confucianism, 153
coniunctio, 404; *oppositorum,* 405, 423; see also *coincidentia; complexio*
conscience, 292, 424; moral and ethical, 454*f*; morality of 453*f*; nature of, 437*f*; paradox of, 442; relation to moral precepts, 443; "right" and "false," 445; and synchronicity, 450*f*; see also *vox Dei*
conscientia peccati, 438
consciousness/conscious mind: adaptive function of, 11; axis of, 408; not biochemically explicable, 346; cosmic, 136*f*; dawn of, 139; differentiation of, 136; discriminating, 347; disintegration of, 139; ego-, 136, 137, 145, 149, 249; founded on archetypes, 346; group-, 136; higher, 433; onesidedness of, 15; precondition of being, 271; present-day, 75; relation to whole man, 441; split, 285, 360; and unconscious, dissociation, 527; ——, relation, 334; *see also* unconscious
consensus omnium, 292

"container," 122, 123
contraception, 101, 122, 323
contrasexuality, 118f
conventionality, 507
conversion, 293
Copenhagen, 551, 554, 561
Copernicus, 270
Corinthians (II), 447
costume, see dress
Couéism, 157
countertransference, 273
counting, 393, 409
courtesan, 39
creation, error of, 328
credulity, 286f
creed: ambivalence of, 265; religion and, difference, 257
crime, collective, 200
criminal: pale, 202, 215; statistical, 199
crisis, 140
crocodile(s), 51f, 56, 64, 498
cross, 391, 402
crowds, psychology of, see psychology, mass
cruelty, in dream symbols, 219, 220
Crusaders, 314
culture: creation of, 132; development of, 12
cure of souls, 550
Cusanus, Nicolaus, 404, 424
cynicism, 344

D

Dadaism, 27
daemon, 447; Socrates', 446, 453
dancing, in America, and African, 508
danger, collective, 319
Daniel, 389
David, star of, see star
death: fear of, 368; irrationalism and, 181n; as perfector, 367; primitives and, 51, 72; ship of, 372; synchronistic phenomena and, 450; and Ufos, 369

defence: aggressive, German, 240; resentment as, 485
Delhi, 516
delinquency, juvenile, 473
deliverance, archetype of, 328
delusion, 377; see also hallucination
demiurge, 334
democracy, 154, 224f
Democritus, 404
demons: fear of, 19; psychic forces as, 211
Denmark, 545, 551, 554
destroyers, great, epoch of, 383
destruction of world, see millennium
detective story, 93
Deussen, Paul, 91
development, man's, 358
devil(s), 69, 298; and conscience, 447; contemporary, 465; delusions of, 343; as half animal, 392; as Lucifer, 389; as a neurosis, 155; pacts with, 370; and pathological states, 146f; Trinity and, 391, 392; Wotan and, 181
dew, of Gideon, 332
Dewey, John, 491
dictators: deification of, 261; and external solemnities, 260
differentiation: of whole man, 528; see also functions
dimension, fourth, 390, 392ff, 407
Dionysus: and Apollo, 181n, 187; enkolpios, 337n; Wotan and, 180, 181, 185, 188, 189; -Zagreus, 213, 214
direction, sense of, in primitives, 53
director of conscience, 274, 287
discovery, age of, 84
disintegration, in painting, 383
disks, starry, 392n
disparagement, euphemistic, 171
Disraeli, Benjamin, 141
dissociation, 278, 282, 373; of conscious and unconscious, 527; hysteria and, 203, 207; in modern society, 285; phenomena of, 139; psychic, 64, 319; psychopathic, 238; in Roman world, 140

distress, situation of, 323
divans, 519
divination, 59
divinity, symbols of, 339
divorce, 120, 506
doctor: analysis of, 159; approach to individual, 273, 466f; personality of, and therapy, 159f
Doggeli, 371n
Don Juan, 120
dogma, and truth, 158
Dornach, 87
Dove, of Holy Ghost, 360
dragon, 498
dreams, 11f, 33, 144ff; always of oneself, 151f; of Americans, Indian/Negro symbols in, 47; "big," 152; with collective meaning, 152; as compensatory, 20, 388; distortion of, 151; among Elgonyi, 63; interpretation of, 150ff; modern symbols in, 336; moral judgments and, 438, 442; and psychoanalysis, 164; sent by God, 338; soul symbol in, 326; specialism of, 359; symptoms of unconscious, 151; Ufos in, 330ff, 406; and unconscious psychic activity, 218; IN-STANCES OF DREAMS (in order of occurrence in text): woman singing hymns, and bull in agony, 20; being attacked by mamba, 62; drunken tramp in ditch, 151; drunken prostitute in gutter, 151; fairy changing into flame, 326; flying saucer over Champs Elysées, 330f; burnt face as result of seeing interplanetary machine, 331, 334f; flying spider over international gathering, 351ff; cobweb in attic, 354; pallid sun and sphere, 361ff; two women on edge of world, 368ff; flying saucers in California, 372f; flying saucer resembling fish, 376ff; arms covered with dirt, 438
dress: European, 521; Indian, 520ff
drop, Ufo as, 331, 333, 336

Dryden, Hugh L., 318
dualism: psychological, 297, 299; and *vox Dei* conception, 447
duplication of cases, law of, 59
durée créatrice, 147
duty, conflicts of, 357, 444, 445, 454f
dyad, 424
"dying, great," 369

E

eagle, 327n
earth: and heaven, interrelation, 498; low opinion of, entertained by Ufo occupants, 421; man of, 484; square as symbol of, 404
earthquakes, animal warnings of, 336
East, significance of, 114
Eckhart, Meister, 190, 191, 216, 540
ecstasy, 181n, 213
Edda, 191ff
Eddy, Mary Baker, 84
Eden, Garden of, 358
Edomites, 192
education: of adults, 549; American, 267, 491, 492; German, 222; and individuality, 473; Marxist, 284; medical psychology and, 565; one-sidedness of modern, 153; scientific, and the individual, 252
effeminacy, 41, 107
eggs, Easter, 72
Église gnostique de la France, 83
ego: depotentiation of, 424; inflation of, 211, 253, 356, 380; instincts, 288; as seat of anxiety, 170; and self, 149, 463
ego-consciousness, *see* consciousness
egoism, primitive, 137
Egypt: concept of soul in, 42; Mithraism and, 91; mythology, 339; psyche in, 78
eight, the number, 366
Einherjer, 188
Einstein, Albert, 89, 537
Eisleben, 184
élan vital, 147

electricity, 8
elements, transformation/transmutation of, 332
eleven, the number, 366
Elgon, Mount, 57, 61
Elgonyi, 64, 71
Elijah, 327f, 389
elixir of life/*elixir vitae*, 385, 392
Ellis, H. Havelock, 87
emblems, national aircraft, 417
Emerson, Ralph Waldo, 491
emotion: signs of, infective, 508; unusual, 315; *see also* affects
enantiodromia, 82
end of the world, 328, 367
endocrinology, 550
energy, 7f; of archetypes, 335; conservation of, 86; mana and, 69; need of goal for, 122
English: German attitude to, 239; national character of, 487; national idea, 512
Englishman, as "beast-man," 481
Enlightenment, Age of the, 16, 235
Enoch, 389
enthusiasm, 389
environment, and extraversion, 347
epidemics, psychic, 235, 248, 249, 264f, 381
epiphany, 406f
equality, 154; psychic, 137
equations, 409
Ergreifer/Ergriffener/Ergriffenheit, 184f, 189, 191
Eros, 7, 123, 124, 125, 133; cosmogonic, 181; Islamic, 519
esotericism, 468
ESP (extra-sensory perception), 349
esprit and spirit, 496
ethics, 257, 357f; of action and conviction, 462; and individual, 483; Judaeo-Christian, 263; primitive and civilized, 53
Eulenspiegel, Till, 143
Europe: collective guilt of, 196ff; non-European view of, 211; relation of Switzerland to, 486; relation to East and West, 114

Eurydice, 213
evangelists, emblems of, 391
evil, 356; by contagion, 199; imagination in, 290, 297; knowledge of, 457ff; need to realize, 297; "overcoming," 467; reality of, 465; and unconsciousness, 82; *see also* good; *privatio boni*
exceptions, and probability, 394
exclusiveness, in marriage relation, 123
exhydrargyrosis, 332
expectations, of supernatural events, 328
experience: communal, 261; religious, 293, 345f
expiation, 200
explosions, atomic, 321
expressionism, 83
extra-sensory perception, *see* ESP
extraversion, 142, 347, 471
eye(s), 353, 424f; blue/white, in dream, 331, 337; evil, 211; fishes', 404, 424, 425; of God, 339, 386, 424; ——, seven, 404; golden, 432; in Hildegard's vision, 404f; of Horus, 339; as symbol, 337, 392f, 403ff
Ezekiel, 389, 391, 392, 403, 404

F

face, burned, 331, 338f, 350
fairy, 326
fairytales, 26, 33, 219, 332, 449
faith, 84, 265, 292, 362; demythologization of, 285; and knowledge, 285, 453
faithfulness, in marriage, 131
family, Indian, 522, 523
family romance, 164
fanaticism, 259
fantasies: of ascetics, 341; and problem of perception, 313; infantile, 281f; infantile-perverse, 162, 167; mythological, 9f; perverse, 80; sexual, 105f; unconscious, activation of, 281

Faria, 172
fascinosum, 458, 463
Fascism, 190
Fatehpur-Sikri, 516
father, archetype of, 35*f*, 190; complex, 540
Fatima, 314
Faust, see Goethe
fear(s): children's, 33; collective, compensation of, 387; devaluation of psyche and, 271; expression in art, 383; and inferiority, 384; nocturnal, 33; projection and, 297, 324
feeling: as feminine virtue, 41; function of, 330, 347, 408, *see also* functions, four; *see also* intellect
felix culpa, 358, 460
femina candida, 417
fetishes, 15, 329
fifth column, 264
fights, Indian, 522
filius hermaphroditus / macrocosmi, 332
filius hominis, 389
film producers, 372*f*
fire: divine epiphany and, 327; God as, 386; of the Philosophers, 384*f*; in star of David, 407; as symbol, 384, 389; —— of emotion, 338, 394; tongues of, 386; *see also* water
fireballs, 404*ff*; green, 316*n*, 419
Fire Sower, 383*ff*, 406, Pl. 2
fish: Christ as, 141; deep-sea, 376; dream of Ufo resembling, 376*f*
fission, nuclear, 299, 316, 428, 465
flagstaff, missionary's, 58
flight of Ufos, nature of, 316*f*, 415
flirting, 110
fluid, Ufo as, 331
flying saucers, *see* Ufos
Foerster-Nietzsche, Elizabeth, 183
foetus, 403
folklore, 332
"Foo fighters," 315
food of immortality, 332
food production, 323
forces, psychic, 185

foreigners, 81
Forel, August, 103, 172
forms: disintegration of, 383; sexual significance of, 336
fountain, Christ as, 332
four, the number, 391, 408; archetype of order, 424; as division of circle, 407; union of the, 403; *see also* quaternity
fourteen points, of psychotherapeutic agreement, 566
Fourth Dimension, 375*f*, 390*ff*, Pl. III
France, 316; Keyserling and, 481; national keynote, 511; psychology in, 4
Franz, Marie-Louise von, 427*n*
freedom: in East and West, 114; and morality, 229; striving for, 359; threat to individual, 379
free love, 111
Freemasons, 239, 320
French Revolution, 15, 16, 85
frenzy, pantheistic, 392
Freud, Sigmund, 90, 124, 160, 161, 162, 169*ff*, 541, 558; and analysis of therapist, 159; attitude of, 164*f*; and "archaic vestiges," 440; and dream interpretation, 150; on ego and anxiety, 170; and ego instincts, 288; and evil nature of psyche, 85, 87; *Future of an Illusion, The,* 172; and incest prohibition, 33; *Interpretation of Dreams, The,* 88, 163; and lay therapy, 559; materialistic bias of, 164; and meaning of forms, 336; and occultism, 272; and perverse fantasies, 80; and prehistory of psyche, 349; *Psychopathology of Everyday Life, The,* 30; reductive attitude, 14; relation to Jung, 544*n*; and religion, 548; on sublimation, 171; and superego, 348, 438*ff*, 446
Freidenkaiser, 222
friendship, homosexual, 107
frigidity: animus and, 119; sexual, 106

Fulfilment, Great, 207
function(s): autonomy of, 347; compensatory, *see* compensatory function; conflicting, 347; four, 330, 391, 408; ——, differentiation of, 347, 358, 396; transcendent, 454; *see also* feeling; intellect; intuition; sensation; thinking
furor teutonicus, 185
Fürst, Emma, 37*n*
Futurism, 27
Fylgja, 188

G

Gaillac, 353
gait, of Americans, 505
galaxies, 335, 336
Galileo, 537
gana-world, South American, 497
Ganesha, 519
Gate of Victory, 516
Gateway of India, 516
genealogies, feminine passion for, 43
General Medical Society for Psychotherapy, *see* Allgemeine Ärtzliche Gesellschaft für Psychotherapie
Genesis, Book of, 139*f*
Genghis Khan, 481
genius, 447, 525*f*
gentleman, the, 512
George, Stefan, 181 & *n*
German Faith movement, 190*f*
Germanic peoples/Germans: collective hysteria of, 204; collective unconscious in, 219; and coloured man, 508; hysteria in, 207*ff*; psychology of, 13, 165*f*, 210; and triadic mandalas, 408; as victims, 192; Wotan and the, 186
Germany, 186*ff*, 222*ff*; inferiority feelings in, 203; Gnosticism in, 83; and mass psychology, 222; mass psychosis of, 233, 235; Keyserling and, 481; national keynote, 511*f*; psychological problem of, 227*ff*; psychopathology in, 4; *see also*

Gleichschaltung; National Socialism
Gerster, Georg, 312
Gestapo, 232
Geulincx, Arnold, 313
ghosts, 69
giants, 317
Gideon, *see* dew
glass, broken, 60
Gleichschaltung, in Germany, 535*ff*, 558
globes, black, 401
globulus, 426
gloire, la, 510
Gnosticism/Gnostics, 356; and evil, 358; "Father-Mother" in, 407; four in, 397; modern, 83
God/gods: Buddhist view, 525; childish view of, 185; claims on individual, 256*f*; Greek, 189; inner, 155; loving *v.* hating, 464; man's kinship with, 334; Old Testament idea of, 337; personifications of psychic forces, 185, 211; principles and, 458; relation to, 293; and religious experiences, 293; and the State, 258; symbols of, and self, 339; totality symbol, 327; Ufos as, 327; unconscious powers as, 361; voice of, see *vox Dei; see also* circle; God-image
"God-Almightiness," 215
God-image(s), 327*f*; anthropomorphism of, 449; father as, 36; opposites in, 394; return of, 214; symbols of self and, 424; Yahwistic, morality of, 448
Godless, movement of, 180
God-substitute, 463
Goebbels, Josef, 204*f*, 236
Goethe, J. W. von, 16, 40, 43, 75*n*, 98, 135, 144, 146, 172, 190*n*, 203, 207, 213, 355, 366*n*, 391, 448
Goetz, Bruno, 184, 187*n*
gold, philosophical, 386; see also *aurum*
good: and evil, relativity of, 459; knowledge of, 456*ff*

Göring, Hermann, 204f
Göring, M. H., 538, 551, 554
Gospel(s), 142; four, 391, 397
Gothic: man, 481; style, 480
Gottesminne, 98
Gotthelf, Jeremias, 353n
grace, 342
Grail, messenger of, 377
gravitation, 321, 329, 352; see also weightlessness
gravity, spirit of, 498
greatness, national conceptions of, 513
Greco-Roman religions, and Christianity, 526
Greece, 481
Greek temperament, and Germanic, 189
grex segregatus, 184
group: effects on members, 471f; factors influencing, 471; inferiority to individuals, 382
group-consciousness, see consciousness
group psychology, 470
Guatemala, 322
guilt: collective, 195ff, 210, 217; consciousness of, 215f; Germany and, 340f; legal and psychic, 195
Gustloff, Sigmund, 190n

H

Haggard, H. Rider, 39, 40, 43, 44
hallucination(s), 314n, 320, 377
Hänsel and Gretel, 33
Harding, M. Esther, 381, 552
hare, 360, 410
Hartmann, Eduard von, 3
Hauer, Wilhelm, 190f
Hauffe, Frau, 125
Hay, Marie, 44
Heard, Gerald, 352n
heart, 447
heat: emitted by Ufos, 338; magical, 338
heaven: and earth, interrelation, 498; intervention from, 328; water as, 331
Heine, Heinrich, 203
Helen: of Troy, 40, 213; companion of Simon Magus, 40
Heraclitus, 82, 333, 367
Herbart, Johann Friedrich, 173
herd instinct, 219
hereafter, the, 526
heredity, 340, 507; and introversion, 347
heresy, 271
hermaphrodite, 407; see also filius hermaphroditus; Mercurius
hermaphroditosis, 521
Hermes, 188; katachthonios, 385; see also Mercurius
Hermetic philosophy, 327, 334
hermits, 341
Hero of Alexandria, 79
hero-archetype/motif, 44, 47f
Herostratus, 80, 384
Herrenvolk, 210
hexad, 407
Heyer, G. R., 552
hierosgamos, 397
Hildegard of Bingen, 403ff, Pl. VIII
Himalayas, 91, 317
historians, 324
history: conflict with, 130; contemporary, therapist and, 177; Indian attitude to, 517; psychological factors and, 324; subjective in, 148f
Hitler, Adolf, 185, 186, 203ff, 222f, 236; movement, and Wotan, 180; see also National Socialism
Holbein, Hans, 81
Hölderlin, Friedrich, 16, 94
Holland, see Netherlands
Holy Ghost, 386, 404, 405; age of, 494; in alchemy, 405; arithmetical structure of, 405; descent on man, 405; Dove of, 360; enthusiasm of, 389; as nickname for Ufo, 325n
homelessness, 523
homo maximus, 86, 385, 389
Homo sapiens, 282, 432, 469

homosexuality: female, 99, 108, 119; among students, 99*f*, 105, 107*f*
Hopfer, Hans, 368
horoscopes, 85, 317
horse, white, and Wotan, 180
Horus: eye of, 339; sons of, 391
Hoyle, Fred, 426*ff*
humanitarianism, 81
humanity: cosmic view of, 481; as ideal, 154; oneness of, 410
humour, Keyserling's, 479*f*, 492
Hungary, 264*n*, 481
hunger, 337; and religion, 343; spiritual, 343
huntsman, wild, 181; in Nietzsche, 183
Hus, John, 448
hydrogen atom, 422, 424
hydrogen bomb, 298*f*
hydrophobia, 336
hyenas, 61
Hyperboreans, 84
hypnosis, 555
hypnotism, 16, 157
hypotheses, necessity of, 548
hysteria, 6, 173, 202*ff*, 206*f*; national, 210; Ufos and, 333

I

I Ching, 498
Ichthys, 425
idea(s): adaptation of primordial, 283; German, 511*f*; inherited, 10, 440; lag in, 284; lucky, 145; new, 230; ——, Swiss and, 485; Platonic, 326; power of, over psyche, 24
ideal, heroic, 512*f*
idealism(s), 300; in America, 512
identification: of child with parents, 37; with nation, 482
identity, unconscious, 37; see also *participation mystique*
illness, as defence, 466
illusion(s), 319, 354; in adolescents, 105; of anchorites, 342; reality as, 517

image(s): "austere," 387; mythological, 339
imago, parental, 36*ff*
imitation, instinct for, 288
immortality, 44, 70*f*, 79, 266
Imperialists, 320
improbable, occurrence of the, 394
incest: archetype of, 349; complex, 348; and religious instinct, 349; tendency, 33*f*
independence, social, women and, 117
indeterminacy, 90
India, 507, 515*ff*, 525*ff*; and alchemy, 333; and birth control, 323; civilization and primitivity in, 528; as part of Asia, 519; and Western culture, 196; wholeness of life in, 518
Indian Science Congress, 520
Indians, American, *see* America
individual: diminishing importance of, 253*f*; need of individual consciousness, 472; as resultant, 70; revaluation of, 380; salvation of, 276; understanding the, 251
individuation, 378, 379, 381, 426; Christianity and, 271; seriousness of problem, 379; symbol of, 326, 403
industrialization, 222
inertia, psychic, 139
infantilism, 460; and neurosis, 161*f*
infection: psychic, *see* epidemic, psychic; racial, 509
inferiority(-ies), psychopathic, 204, 207, 233, 239
inferiority complex, 346
inferiority feelings, 202*f*, 513, 523
infinite, hungering for, 207
inflation, 354, 356, 381, 525; of ego, *see* ego; spiritual, 355
inhibitions, 398*f*
initiation: in modern America, 514; rites of, 38; and sportsmen's training, 48
insane: unconscious in the, 4; "voices" and, 68

insanity, 338; epidemic, 212, 248; latent, 248; moral, 161
insects, 352
instinct(s): in animals, 287; archetypal, 282; atrophy of, in civilized man, 19; basis of consciousness, 346; and choice of symbols, 337, 343; deviations from, 360; dream emphasis on, 360; imagination of, 282, 290; lack of contact with, 467; loss of, 291; and love, 98; migratory, 450; modern art and, 399; in primitive, 32; and psyche, 7f, 340; religious, 344, 349; two aspects, 287; and unconscious, 18; and wholeness, 345, 349f
integration, of unconscious contents, 221, 236
intellect: and feeling, discrepancy 295; function of, 347f, 408
intellectualisms, 371
intention, 340
International General Medical Society for Psychotherapy, 536, 545, 547, 550f, 554, 555, 557, 559, 561f
International Institute of Intellectual Co-operation, 499n
internationalism, 93
interpretation, "low-down," 167f
inter-planetary travel, 323
intonation, American, 505
introversion, 347, 398, 471
intuition: function of, 330, 408; lack of, in Swiss, 485; and sensation, 486; and unconscious, 18, 298
invasion, extra-terrestrial, 315f
inventions, misuse of, 528
Irenaeus, 40n
Irma (Freudian patient), 163
Iron Curtain, 247, 263, 280
irrationalism/irrationality, 181; collective, 248
irregularity, and absolute reality, 250
Isaiah, 338
Islam, 257; in India, 519; rise of, 497
isms, 49, 234

isolation: individual, State and, 300f; national, Germany's, 242
Italy, 190, 205, 238, 316, 481, 512; ancient, slavery in, 121

J

Jacob, 461
Jacobi, Karl G. J., 409
Jaffé, Aniela, 370n
Jakoby, E., 390, Pl. II
James, William, 491, 499
Janet, Pierre, 4, 5, 172, 544n
jazz, 508
Jerusalem, 201; Siege of, 314
Jesuits, 320
Jesus, 76, 276, 338; German view, 186; Ufo pilots' view of, 421; see also Christ
Jews: Christ-complex of, 508; and Christians, difference, 542; differences among, 45; and membership of International Society for Psychotherapy, 545n, 558; and Nazism, 239; projection on, 181, 320; psychological consciousness of, 165f; and race theories, 202; two cultures of, 13f, 544n; resentment in, 485; see also psychology, Jewish
Jew, Wandering, 181
John, First Epistle of, 444
jokes, 541
Josephus, 201
Joyce, James, 210
Judaism, 257
Jung, Carl Gustav: Keyserling and, 482; and Nazis, 232

WORKS: *Aion*, 41n, 141n, 327n; *Alchemical Studies*, 235n, 355n; "Brother Klaus," 339n; *Collected Papers on Analytical Psychology*, 233n, 234n, 543n; "Concerning Mandala Symbolism," 326n; "Concerning Rebirth," 328n; *Contributions to Analytical Psychology*, 29n, 97n, 113n, 234n;

Jung *(cont.)*
Development of Personality, 122*n*, 236*n*; *Essays on Contemporary Events*, 177*n*, 179*n*, 194*n*, 218*n*, 227*n*; "Freud and Jung: Contrasts," 543*n*; "General Aspects of Dream Psychology," 235*n*; "Instinct and the Unconscious," 32*n*, 282*n*; "Marriage as a Psychological Relationship," 122; *Psychiatric Studies*, 125*n*; *Psychological Types*, 543*n*; *Psychology and Alchemy*, 355*n*, 366*n*, 384*n*, 387*n*; "Psychology and Religion," 231*n*, 232*n*; "Psychology of the Transference, The," 402; "Psychotherapy Today," 177*n*; "Relations Between the Ego and the Unconscious, The," 228*n*, 544*n*; "Review of the Complex Theory, A," 545*n*; *Structure and Dynamics of the Psyche, The*, 29*n*, 32*n*, 234*n*, 235*n*, 282*n*, 313*n*; "Structure of the Unconscious, The," 228*n*; *Symbols of Transformation*, 47; "Synchronicity: An Acausal Connecting Principle," 313*n*; "Theory of Psychoanalysis, The," 543*n*; "Transformation Symbolism in the Mass," 355*n*; *Two Essays on Analytical Psychology*, 38*n*, 41*n*, 228*n*, 229*n*, 234*n*; "What Is Psychotherapy?", 557*n*; with Wilhelm: *The Secret of the Golden Flower*, 235, 387

Jünger, Ernst, 214
Jungfrau, 484
Jupiter, 362, 365, 367

K

Kabras forest, 61
kairos/καιρός, 191, 304
Kali, 519; —— Durga, 466
Kant, Immanuel, 410, 462
karma, 88
ka-soul, 42

katabasis, 355
Kathakali, 517
Kaufmann, R., 424*n*
Keyhoe, Donald E., 312, 317, 338*n*, 379*n*, 413
Keyserling, Count Hermann, 93, 417, 479*ff*, 489*ff*, 496*ff*
Khidr, 328, 410
Kitoshi, 61
Klages, Ludwig, 181, 347
Klaus, Brother, 339
Kluger, H. Y., 372
Knights of Columbus, 514
Knoll, Max, 312
knowledge: absolute, 336; and belief, 265; and faith, 285, 453; organ and object of, 540; tree of, 140; and understanding, of man, 250, 273
Konarak: Black Pagoda, 529
Krafft-Ebing, Richard von, 103
Kranefeldt, W. M., 557
krater, 355
Kretschmer, Ernst, 533, 535
Kreuger, Ivar, 142
Krishnamurti, 86
Kronos, 188, 189
Ku Klux Klan, 514
Kundalini yoga, 84
kwei-soul, 29
Kyffhäuser, 186

L

labour camps, 323
lady, white, 377
Lamb of God, 360
Lambarene, 414
landings, from Ufos, 317, 322
Langmann, Dr. (clergyman), 190*n*
language, affective results of, 509
lapis philosophorum, see stone, philosophers'
Latin, 480
Latins, and coloured men, 508
laughter, American, 46, 504, 508
law, Roman, 263
laymen, as therapists, 554

leader(s), 154, 230, 253; of mob, 220; *see also* mass(es)
League of Nations, 189, 499*n*
learning capacity, 287, 288
Le Bon, Gustave, 239
legends, 219; formation of, 322*f*
Leibniz, G. W., 313, 335
lens-shape, of Ufos, 335*f*
leopard-woman, 64, 66
levitation, 352
Lévy-Bruhl, Lucien, 37, 51, 52, 64, 65, 452
liaisons, sexual, among students, 106*f*
liar, pathological, see *pseudologia phantastica*
libertinism, 356
libido, 8
lie, and political action, 261, 266
Liébeault, A.-A., 326
life, negation of, 181*n*
life-instinct, 147
light: divine epiphany and, 327; emission by fish and insects, 336
lion, symbol of Christ and Satan, 449
living standard, 492
Lockheed Aircraft Corporation, 418
Logos: as male principle, 123, 124; supremacy of, 286
Los Angeles, 537
Louis XIV, 253
love, 97*f*; conjugal, 98; development of ideal, 110; and faith, 112; and hygiene, 102; kinds of, 97*f*; and marriage, 123; of neighbour, 301; and sexuality, 6*f*, 98*ff*, 112; for things, 118
love choice, and parents, 38*f*
Loyola, Ignatius, 266
Lucifer, 389, 449
Luke, Gospel of, 240, 357, 389*n*

M

machine, man and the, 268
Macrobius, 404*n*
macrocosm and microcosm, 335

maenads, 185
magic: books, 371; primitives and, 51, 446; psychological effect of, 260; science of the jungle, 63; in Switzerland, 371
magnetic fields, interstellar, 321
Maha-Parinibbana Sutta, 520
Mahatmas, 91
Mahayana, *see* Buddhism
Maidenek, 196
Main, river, 181
majesty, 364
mamba, 61
man: Christ as prototype and goal of, 397; collective/mass, 229*f*, 258; ——, atomization of, 301; demasculinization of, 493; inner/higher, 447; Primordial, 327, 405, *see also* Anthropos
mana, 63, 68, 69, 72, 303, 448; *see also* personality
mandala(s), 221, 366; cross-shaped, 402; mathematical structure of, 409, 424; as space ship, 335; as totality symbol, 326; triadic, and Germans, 408; and Ufos, 387, 423*f*
"manning," 368, 372
Mantell, Capt., 331*n*
mare nostrum, 332
Maria the Copt/Jewess, 391; Axiom of, 405
marriage: cross-cousin, 402*f*; medieval, 125*f*; and mother archetype, 35; "perfect," 120, 126; problems, 128; quaternio, 402; and the student, 100*f*, 103*ff*; trial, 111*f*; women and, 120*ff*
Mars, 321, 323
Martians, 315
Mary, Virgin, as patron of Swiss, 484
masculine-feminine antithesis, 407
Marxism, 265, 295
Mass, the, 355
mass(es), 275*ff*; anonymity of, 154, 230; Churches and, 275*f*; industrialized, 200; leaders and, 154, 230, 253, 275; and manifestation of archetypes, 229; resistance to,

mass (es) *(cont.)*
278; "telluric," 498; *see also* man, collective/mass; psychology, mass
mass meeting, and numinous experience, 294
mass-mindedness, 379, 382
masturbation, 104; effects of, 109*f*; mutual, 107
materialism/materialists, 70, 223, 258, 344, 411, 512; and psyche, 411
materialization, 416
matriarchy, in America, 417
matter, 361; physicist and, 147; and psyche, 411
Matthew, Gospel of, 389
Max Müller, Frederick, 91
Maya, 463, 464, 516
Mayer, Robert, 15
meaning, search for, 480
mediator: loss of belief in, 414; number as, 410
medicine, and politics, 538*f*
medicine-man, 59, 66, 68, 498
mediums, spiritualistic, 416
megalomania, 89, 385; Keyserling's, 480
Meier, C. A., 546
melody, infectiveness of, 509
Menzel, D. H., 371, 413
Mephistopheles, 144, 172, 207, 215, 378
Mercurius, 332; *duplex/hermaphroditus,* 385, 407; metal, and spirit, 332; Philosophorum, 405; quadratus, 405; subterranean, 385; *see also* Hermes; spiritus
Mercury, 188
Merseburg spell, 371, 372
Mesmer, Friedrich Anton, 15, 172
Messiah, 44, 328
metamorphosis of the gods, 304
metanoia, 276, 379
metaphors, 337
metaphysics, 215, 448; Christian, 391; fear of, 185; Jung and, 328; psychologizing, 328*n*
meteors/meteorites, 316, 319
M'ganga, 59

Michel, Aimé, 312, 320*n*, 353*n*
microbiology, 547
microcosm: alchemical, 326; man as, 278, 286; soul as, 335
Middle Ages, 326, 369; adultery in, 120; and anima, 41; world-view of, 81, 328
Midwich Cuckoos, The, 431*ff*
migrations, European, 524
milk, drying up, 370
millennium, 80; first, end of, 247, 324
Mimir, 192, 194
mind: causal concept of, 29; conscious, *see* consciousness; influence of country on, 511; meaning of, 30; *see also* psyche
Minne, 188 & *n*
missionaries, Christian, 89
Mithraism, 21, 91
mob, 275; formation of, 220; *see also* mass(es)
modern man: and power instinct, 344; and unconscious, 358
Moguls/Mogul Empire, 516, 519
monadology, 335
monastery, cultural, 499*ff*
monasticism, ideals of, 40
Mondamin, 410
money, American attitude to, 512
monogenes, 397
monotheism, 334
Mons, battle of, 314
month, Platonic, 311
mood(s): changes of, 139; in woman, 119
moon, 321, 323, 404; further side of, 322; as symbol of divine mother, 425; visionary, 314; waxing, and departed souls, 369
moral code, 440*ff*; and religion, 461
morality: alteration of, 116; primitives and, 53; and the unconscious, 441
Morgenthaler, W., 557*n*, 558, 560
mortification, 342
Moses, 338, 339
mosque, 180

mother: archetype of, 34f, 36; in India, 522; and son, unity of, 407
Mothers, realm of, 377
mother-ships, 402, 420
Mountain Lake, 68
movement, in Americans, 505
multiplicatio, 334
mungu, 72
Murray, John: Handbook for India, 529
museums, 500
music: American, 508; atonal, 210; "etheric," 420ff
Mussolini, Arnaldo, 205
Mussolini, Benito, 205
mysteries: ancient, 10; Gnostic, 16
mystery religions, 16, 92
mystical instruction, 118
mystics, and love, 98
myth(s), 9, 26, 449; age of, and Wotan, 187; art and, 303; autogenesis of, 443; and dreams, 219; integral to religion, 285; living, Ufos as, 322; natural bases of, 329
mythology: Christian, symbolical understanding of, 266; Egyptian, 339; modern, 369

N

nadir, 407
names: and magical compulsion, 426; of tribes, 136
Napoleon, 481
narcissism, 99, 160
nation(s): "aunt of," 492; as functions of mankind, 480, 487; identification with, 482; and individual, relation, 27, 488; personified, 487
nationalism, fear of, 263
National Socialism, 166, 237ff, 289, 430, 537ff, 543; Wotan and, 184, 192
nature: man and, 66; and unconscious, 23
Navahos, 507
Negro: American, 46f, 507; —— and African, gap between, 509; European assimilation to, 121; white complex of, 508, 509
Neptune (Ufo pilot), 423
Netherlands, 481, 512, 553; Society for Psychotherapy, 551, 554
neurology, and psychotherapy, 554f
neurosis, 39, 120, 138, 159, 219; and adaptation, 162; affects whole personality, 566; alternative explanations, 160; cardiac, 159; child's, and parents' psychology, 34; concupiscence and, 160; hysterical, 203, see also hysteria; infantile fantasies and, 281; learning to bear, 169; loss of, 167; as new name for devil, 146f, 155; positive aspects, 167, 169; and psychotherapy, 559; reason for, in the present, 171; symptoms of, and instincts, 288; uncontrolled affects and, 360
neutrality, Swiss, 485
New Testament, 258
n'goma, 508
Nicholas of Cusa, see Cusanus
Nietzsche, F. W., 14, 86, 98, 113, 121, 131, 181, 182f, 202, 203, 212, 214f, 347, 348, 497, 498; feminine side in, 213
nightmare(s), 34; Nietzsche's, 183
nigredo, 427, 428
Nile, 332
Ninck, Martin, 188f
normality, concept of, 238, 296
Normans, 524
Nostradamus (Michel Nostredame), 179
"nothing but," 8, 23, 144, 162, 168, 170, 171, 348
Notre Dame (Paris), 85, 86
novels, and sex, 102f
number(s): archetypal aspect, 409ff, 424; as mediator, 410; see also dyad; hexad; ogdoad; pentad; quaternity; quincunx; tetraktys; three plus one motif; triad; two; four; eight; ten; twenty-four: thirty

numinosum/numinosity/numinous, 340, 342*f*, 377, 380, 385, 387, 393, 415, 458
Nuremberg, 401
nutrition, function of, 6
nycticorax, 449

O

Oannes, 141
oath, modernist, 537
obliqueness, Indian, 524
observer, in physics, 252
obsessions/obsessional ideas, 143, 146; conscience and, 447
occultism, 3, 272, 328
occupants, of Ufos, 317
occurrences, unusual, as omens, 319
octopus, 395
Odin, 187*n*; *see also* Wotan
Oedipus, 378; complex/motif, 348, 349
ogdoad, 366, 392
Oldenberg, Hermann, 91
Old Masters, 500
Old Testament, 190*n*, 392, 447, 467
Oloron, 353
omens, 58*ff*, 319
One, the, 334
one-sidedness, 93, 130, 253, 347, 552; of conscious mind, 15; Freud's, 160; of modern education, 153
opinion: psychotherapy and, 158; in women, 119
opium trade, 89
Oppenheimer, Robert J., 465
opposites: above/below, 407, 484; aristocratic/unaristocratic, 484; collision of, 428*f*; fire/water, 407; higher world/human world, 408*f*; masculine/feminine, 407; psychic, and conscience, 447; reconciliation of, 373; self as combination of, 337; tension of, 410, 414; union of, 327, 369, 402, 417; unity /quaternity, 407*f*; *see also* antitheses; *coincidentia oppositorum; complexio oppositorum*

opus divinum, 334
organizations, large, 379*f*
Origen, 98
Orpheus, 425
Ortega y Gasset, José, 501
Orthodox Church, Eastern, 180
Osiris, 339
Ostwald, Wilhelm, 103
"other" in us, 152, 169*f*, 486
Otto, Rudolf, 458
Oupnek'hat, 85
overcrowding, in India, 524
overpopulation, 277, 323
Oxford, 564

P

paedagogics, 549
painting: medieval, 406; modern, pathological element in, 210; ——, and Ufos, 383*ff*
Pali Canon, 525, 526
Pallas Athene, 388
panacea, 332, 383, 385
Papuans, 64
Paracelsus, 211
Paradise, 139
parallelism, psychophysical, 270, 411
parapsychology / parapsychological phenomena, 83, 84, 335, 411; and absolute knowledge, 336; and materialization, 416; and relativization of space/time, 270, 450
parents: as archetypes, 34*ff*; influences from, and conflicts, 281
Paris, 481
Parsifal, 214
parthenogenesis, 432
participation mystique, 37*f*, 64, 65, 67, 75, 195, 433, 452
Pathans, 519
Paul, St., 129, 276, 293, 414, 442, 447; Greek mother of, 186
passivity, woman's, 117
pax Romana, 487
peculiarities, individual, 472*f*
pélerinage de l'âme, 403, 423
penetration, 337, 402

pentad, 408
Pentecost, 189
perception(s): of conscious and unconscious, 18; subliminal, 9
perils of the soul, 139, 172, 186, 381
permanence, civilization and, 487
persecution, ideas of, 320
persona, 127
personality: dissociation of, 203, 373, *see also* dissociation; mana, 69, 70; of portions of psyche, 67; splitting of, 207, 282, 289
persuasion, 157
perversions, sexual, 99*f*
Pforta, 183
phallus, 337
Philemon and Baucis, 207, 213
Philistines, 182
philosophy: in India, 526; and modern age, 180; psychopathology and, 547
photographing Ufos, 322
phrases, familiar, and disruption of consciousness, 138
phylogeny, 32, 33
physics, 89, 462; atomic/nuclear, 298, 316, 329, 393, 452; and observer, 252; theoretical, 411
physiotherapy, 559
pictures, "meaningless," 383
pietism, 257
pigeons, carrier, 336
Pilgrim, Spiritual, 403, Pl. VII
pin-sticking, 370
Pisces, 141, 311
"plan, great," 205*f*
planets: and atomic explosions, 321; reconnaissance from, 321
Plato, 98, 198, 326, 391, 448
platonic relationships, 109*f*, 123
play, and sport, 513
pleasure principle, 160; Freud and, 348
plurality, of "selves," 334
Pluto, 188
pneuma, 35, 72, 189, 332, 463
Poimandres, 189
Poland, 239, 264*n*

polis, 99
politics: individual's part in, 299; relation to therapy, 178, 538*ff*
population, increasing, 323
polygamy, 89
Polynesia/Polynesians, 89, 527
Portmann, Adolf, 336
possession, 139, 146, 211, 214, 381; collective, 248; see also *Ergreifer*
power, drive/principle/will to, 27, 135, 147, 155, 287, 349; Adler and, 161, 165, 348; Catholic Church and, 345; instinct, 344; in mob leader, 220
powers: arbitrary, 66, 69; telluric, 497*f*
"power-word," 48
pragmatism, 499
prayer, 351, 353, 359
precognition, 336, 450
"prelogical" mind, 51*ff*
present: consciousness of, 75*ff*; meaning of, 115
prestige psychology, 348
presuppositions, of primitive, 54
"Prevorst, Seeress of," 124
priest, Catholic, 118
primitives: and ancestral inheritance, 510; and autonomous psyche, 446; and causality, 56; concentration among, 54; and death, 51; and dreams, 150; and fetish, 329; and morals, 53; and mystical instruction, 118; neurotics among, 19; projection among, 26, 65; and psyche, 11*f*; psychology of, 136; senses of, 53; and sex, 103; thought-production among, 527; "totality" in, 347; unpsychological, 63; and the unusual, 137
primitivity: in dream symbols, 219, 220; elements of, in India, 528*f*; sexual, 506
Primordial Being, 407
principles, 458, 467
privatio boni, 338, 358, 465
problem(s): personal, attitude to, 78;

problem(s) (*cont.*)
sexual, discussion of, 123; woman's, 114
proficiency, 76
projection(s): 25*f*, 65, 69, 318, 320, 562; on to anima figure, 378; appearance as physical facts, 335; ascetics and, 341; basis of, 328; carriers of, 320; explanatory, 324; instinctual and spiritual, 341; mandala as, 327; among primitives, 64, 68; and radar, 413; return of, to origin, 214; Ufos and, 318*ff*, 323, 373, 417; of unrecognized evil, 297; withdrawal of, 300; *see also* fear
promiscuity, sexual, 506
propaganda, political, 320
propitiation, rites of, 19
prostitution: and love, 100; and marriage, 40, 120; tolerated, 120; in Uganda, 89
Protestantism, 257, 261; in Germany, 190; theology of, 549
Psalms, 386
pseudologia phantastica, 203, 205
pseudo-moderns, 76*f*
psychasthenia, 6
psyche: analogy with building, 31; building up of, 70; cannot know itself, 410; child's, and parents, 34; collective, 80, 86, 137; complexity of, 7, 550; current undervaluation of, 346; differences in, 137*f*; not an epiphenomenon, 270; European, 562; fascination of, 90, 92, 93; German, 186; importance of, 291; individual differences, 135; inside and outside, 78; materialized, 416; and matter, relation of, 411; national, 481; a natural phenomenon, 340; not subject to will, 440; objective, 147; peculiar nature of, 270*f*; polarity of, 447; prehistory of, Freud and, 349; reality of, 346; two-sided, 141; unity of, 146; weightless, 352
psychiatrist, 348

psychiatry, and psychotherapy, 554*f*
psychism, materialized, Ufo as, 416
psychoanalysis: and attitude to sex, 102; beginning of, 4; Freudian, 83, 85, 163, 348; as technique, 163*f*; and Ufos, 333; and yoga, 90; *see also* analysis; Freud
psychogenic disturbances, 5*f*
psychokinesis, 411
psychologem, 378*f*
Psychological Club of Zurich, 469
psychologism, 144, 549
psychology: abstract approach of, 272; academic, 272; American, 490*ff*, 502*ff*; analytical, sources of, 16; Chinese, 90; comparative, 340; complex, 469; and complexes, 225; criminal, 233; current interest in, 83, 324; "dirty-joke," 168; "discovery" of, 79; and evil, 356; Freudian, 90, *see also* psychoanalysis; Jewish and Germanic, 533, 540*ff*; layman's attitude to, 134*ff*; mass, 222, 225, 228*f*, 239, 276; ——, German proneness to, 219, 222; medical, psychotherapy as, 547; national, 233; practice and theory in, 565; of primitives, 136; recent origin of, 137; as a science, 540; and therapy, 157*f*; Western man's interest in, 281; woman's, 116, 123*f*
psychoneuroses, 555
psychopathology, 124; and experimental psychology, 4; French, 16; and psychotherapy, 547*f*
psychopathy, 238; German, 232, 238; national, 233
psychotherapy: confusion in, 533; Germanic, 538; as medical psychology, 547; need for wider field, 549; as profession, 558; and psychiatry, separation of, 558; as relationship, 164; schools of, 158, 564; scope of, 17; task of, 349; as a technique, 157*ff*, 168; and universities, 565; *see also* neurology; psychiatry; therapy

puberty; and metabolism, 105; psychological, 104, 106
publicity, American, 505*f*
Pueblo Indians, 61, 65, 89, 211
puer aeternus, 181
puerperal fever, 355
Puerto Rico, 318
puff-adder, 61
Punch, 186
Pyramids, 79

Q

quaternio, marriage, 402
quaternity, 366, 391*f*, 396, 398, 402, 404; square as, 404; and unity, 407
quicksilver, 332, 333; *see also* Mercurius
quietism, Eastern, 91
quincunx, 391, 395, 397, 398, 407
quintessence/*quinta essentia,* 331, 391, 392

R

rabbi, 20
radar, 312, 318, 325, 332, 413, 415
Ramanuja, 464
rationalism: and city dwelling, 341; scientific, 253; and sexuality, 344
rationalists, 344; and neurosis, 167
raven, 449
ray (fish), 376
reality: lack of, 208; spiritual, lack of experience of, 342
Reason, Goddess of, 85, 280
reconnaissance, aerial, 316
red, masculine colour, 417
redeemer, personified as animal, 360
rééducation de la volonté, 157
Reformation, 153, 213
refrigerium, 394
regression, 160, 237
Reich, German: founding of, 212; "thousand-year," 190, 215
Reichstag fire, 199
reincarnation, 88; and anima, 43
Reinwald, 239

relationship: doctor-patient, 164, 274; human, and imperfection, 301
relativization, of space and time, 270, 346, 450
relativism, 90
relativity, 89
religion(s): decline of, and psyche, 79, 83; difficulty of understanding, 280; Elgonyi and, 71*f;* goals of, 260; and hero-motif, 48; instinctive nature of, 259; inter-War development, 180; and massmindedness, 256*ff;* modern contempt for, 93; "night," 33; a psychic fact, 549; as psychotherapeutic, 172; and psychotherapy, 555; State, 266; and unconscious, 19
religious activity, 155
religious experience, psychological structure of, 345
representations, collective, 51*f,* 60, 71, 443, 549
repression(s), 5*f,* 160, 320; neurotic consequences of, 340; sexual, and "spirit," 343; of sexuality, 345; superego and, 438*f*
resentment(s): of chthonic man, 486; early, 164; Swiss, 485
resistance(s), 162, 470
respectability, 129
restraint, lack of, American, 506
restrictions, sexual, 343
resurrection, Christ's, symbolism of, 266
Revelation, Book of, 337, 386
revelations, divine, visions as, 342
revolution: Communist, *see* Communism; French, *see* French Revolution
Rhine, J. B., 349, 393, 394, 411
Rhineland, 181
rhythm, infectiveness of, 509
Ribot, Théodore, 4
rickshaw boys, 465
riddle, of Sphinx, 378
rites: effects of, 260; and unconscious, 346

rites d'entrée et de sortie, 200, 259
romance, and marriage, 102
Roman empire, 487
Romans, Epistle to the, 265, 359, 442
Rome: absence of technical progress, 79; Asianization of, 91; germ of regeneration in, 143; malaise in post-classical, 140; and mystery cults, 514; imported religions, 16; slavery in, 121
restlessness, 49
Rorschach test, 395, 397, 398, 406
ros Gedeonis, 332
Rosicrucians, 403
rotundum(-a), 326, 378, 404, 423*f*, 425, 429
Rousseau, Jean-Jacques, 108
Rumania, 481
rumour(s): mass, 324; requisites for, 315; symbolic, 328; Ufo as symbolical, 387; visionary, 314, 318*f*
Rupertsberg codex, 403
Ruppelt, Edward J., 312, 316, 413
Russia, 114*n*, 196, 261*n*, 481; and America, 491; education in pre-revolutionary, 238; labour camps, 323; policy of, 319; red as colour of, 417; religion in, 180, 190; Tsarist, 115

S

Sabbath, defiler of, 357
Sahara, 317
saints, 360; and dreams, 146
salamander, 394
Salpêtrière, 4
salvation, archetype of, 328
Sanchi, 520
sanctions, Christianity and, 215
sanguis, 332
Saqqara, 79
Satan, symbols of, 449
saving and spending, 488
saviour, 356; birth and epiphany of, 397
scapegoat, 297

Schiller, Friedrich, 18, 499, 540
schizoid states, 139
schizophrenia, 565
Schmitz, Oscar, 90, 487
Schopenhauer, Arthur, 16, 86, 147, 313
Schreber, Daniel Paul, 365
Schuler, Alfred, 181 & *n*
Schwabing, 206
Schweitzer, Albert, 414, 483
science, 81, 82, 279; Chinese, 90; and the exceptional, 371*f*; *v.* faith, 84; and the individual, 252
scintillae, 404
"sea, our," 332
sea-anemone, 395
séance, 314
secrets, 468
sectarianism, 257
security, 91*f*; magic and, 260; material, 81
Seifert, Friedrich, 456 & *n*
self: appearance of, 380; archetype of, 406*f*; ——, Ufo as, 327; archetype of order, 424; better, 447; breaking up of unity of, 334; as combination of opposites, 337; and ego, 149, 463; as mediating symbol, 410; organizer of personality, 366; as psychic wholeness, 410; symbols of, 326, 424*ff*; *see also* ego
self-assertion, 160; *see also* power drive
self-control, 41
self-criticism, 300, 356, 447, 482*f*
self-knowledge, 151*f*, 248*ff*, 269, 293*ff*, 356; in therapist, 163
self-preservation, 200*f*, 287
"selves," multiplication of, 334
sensation, function of: 330, 347, 408; and frigidity, 106; and intuition, 486; *see also* functions, four
seraphim, four, 391
serpent: in Paradise, 140; symbol of Christ and Satan, 449
servator mundi, 332
servus rubeus, 417

Set, 339
sex(uality), 287; aggressive, in women, 119; in America, 492, 506; Catholic Church and, 345; and forms, 336*ff;* Freudian view, 7, 348*f;* and love, *see* love; in men and women, 104; and metaphor, 337; primitives and, 103; and psyche, 135, 147; and religion, 343, 345; repressed, 155, 344, 346; study of, 90; and symbolism, 343*f;* Ufos and, 333; and unconscious, 6*f*, 23; in women, and marriage, 123*f*
shadow, 215, 345, 366, 377*n;* collective, of humanity, 296*f;* confrontation with, 463, 468; discovery of, 216; Hitler as representing, 223; ignorance of, in hysterics, 207; inescapable, 170; man's, and woman, 113, 127; necessary to self, 337; projection of, 203; recognition of, 300*f;* unconsciousness of, 280*f;* Western man and, 290
Shah Jehan, 519
Shakespeare, 156
shaman/shamanism, 15, 16, 48, 514
Shankara, 464
shape(s): sexual significance of, 336; of Ufos, 317, 325, 335*f*
shark, 376
sheep sacrifices, 181
shen-soul, 29
Shiraz, 519
Shiva, 519
shofar, 20
Siegfried, 190*n*
Sievers, Edgar, 322, 352*n*, 399
"signs in the heavens," 320, 323, 398
Sikhs, 519
Simon Magus, 40
sin, 356*f;* original, 296
size, of Ufos, 317
skyscrapers, 514
slang, American, 504*f*
slaves, 121
Sleipnir, 184
slips of the tongue, 398*n*
slogans, 248, 276

smiling, infective, 509
Smith, Hélène, 125
snakes, dream-symbol, 19; *see also* serpent
social democracy, 77
social service, 492
socialism, 537
societies, secret, American, 514
Society for Psychical Research, British, 234
society, abstract nature of, 254*f*
Socrates, 76, 446, 453, 481
solar plexus, 517
sol invictus, 425
solstice, 181
solution/solvent, 331*f*
Sommer, Robert, 533*n*, 562
Son of God, Christ and Satan as, 449
Son of Man, 271, 397
soul(s): concept of, 42*f;* ——, Chinese, 29; "in chains," 334; individual, and world soul, 335; loss of, 139, 381; "nations of the," 86; of the nation, 481; perils of, *see* perils; as sphere, 326, 335; Ufos as, 326; universality of, 67; wandering, 64; *see also* world-soul
soul-force, 15
soul-sparks, 404
space-ships/travel, 315*f*, 321, 323, 324, 329, 369, 421; *see also* Ufos
Spain, 115, 481, 512; Civil War in, 190
spear(s), 337, 402
specialization, growth of, 79
speech: English, 522*f;* Indian, 522, 523; peculiarities of, 508
speed, of Ufos, 316
spells, 371
Spengler, Oswald, 487
sphere: dream figure, 362; soul as, 326
Sphinx, 377; riddle of, 378
spider, flying, 351*ff*, 359
Spinoza, Benedict/Baruch, 20, 98
spirit(s): alchemical water as, 332; ancestral, 69; and body, relation of, 94; breath as, 72; collective,

spirit(s) (cont.)
501; danger of, 486; evil, 447, see also demon, devil; man of the, 484; Mercurius as, 332, see also Mercurius; primitive man and, 11, 52; symbolized by circle, 404; and telluric powers, 498f
spiritualism, 15, 48, 67f, 83, 84, 87, 514
spirituality, secret, 494
spiritus loci, 511
spiritus Mercurii/mercurialis, 332, 405
spittle, 72
split, psychic, 139; split-mindedness, 327; see also consciousness; dissociation; personality
spring-point, 311
sport, 93; in America, 48, 513
sputniks, 323
square, 404f
Squires, H. C., 564
"stab in the back," 208
Stalin, J. V., 263
stammering, 508f
star of David, 407
star, as aircraft emblem, 417
State: American view of, 492; deification of, 261; dependence on, 201, 221; goals of, 260; and individual, 225f, 252ff, 256, 258; as personality, 255, 286; and religion, 259f; Welfare, 201
statistical method / statistics, 249f, 394
Steiner, Rudolf, 84
stepmother, 37
steward, unjust, 357
stigmatization, 422, 424
Stockholm, 551, 554
stone: found in Nile, 332; Philosophers', 391, 424; see also lapis
storm-god, 184
Stransky, Erwin, 554
stratosphere, 311
Strauss, Dr., 564
Strudel, 370
stupa, 520

subjective factor, energy charge of, 397
subject status, Swiss and, 483
sublimation, 8, 160, 171
substitute formation, 161
Suez, 290
suffering, chain of, 360
suggestion(s), 70, 157; mass, 234, 254, 276; therapy, 547
suicide, 41
Summum Bonum, 445, 449
sun, 424; allegory of Christ, 425; dream-figure, 361f; Elgonyi and, 72; falling from sky, 387; Pueblo view of, 68
sun children, 432f
sun wheel, 326
superbia, 287
superego, 348, 438, 439f, 446; archaic vestiges in, 440
Superman, 203, 208, 212, 213, 214
Sweden, 315, 316
Swedenborg, Emanuel, 86
Swiss, character of, 484ff
Swiss Committee of Psychotherapy, 566
Swiss Society for Practical Psychology, 551
Swiss Society of Psychiatry, 565
Switzerland, 103, 186, 200, 224, 512; as Europe's centre of gravity, 486; function in Europe, 487; and German guilt, 196; Keyserling and, 481ff; magic in, 370, 371
sword, 337
symbiosis, 336; of conscious and unconscious, 378
symbol(s), 11, 279; circular, 327; collective, in dreams, 152; creation of, 18; individuation, 326; religious, archetypal character of, 285; of self and of divinity, 339; theriomorphic, 360; Ufos as, 325, 387; union of rational and irrational in, 18; uniting, 389, 407, 414; see also totality
symbol-creating function, 18, 19, 23
symbolism: Christian, archetypal

nature, 343; ecclesiastical, 370; neurotic, ambiguity of, 169; oriental, psychology and, 548; sexual interpretation, 343
symbology, comparative, 340
synchronicity, 313, 349, 361, 411, 417, 450
synchronism, 450

T

table, four-footed, 397
table-turning, 15
Tabula smaragdina, 484
Taj Mahal, 519, 520
talking, Americans and, 504
Tanguy, Yves, 394*ff*, 403, Pl. IV
Tao, 407, 410, 463
Taos, 514
Taurus, 311, 484
tear-drop, Ufo as, 331*n*
technique, psychotherapy and, 157*ff*
technology, 328
telepathy, 336, 450
telluric man/masses, 497*f*
temperature inversion layers, 316, 325
temptation of Jesus, 389
ten, the number, 366
Ten Commandments, 439
tension, emotional, 319
Teresa of Avila, 467
tetraktys, 424
tetrapeza, 397
Teutschenthal, 184
theocracy, 231
theories, statistical, 249
Theosophy, 16, 83, 84, 87, 88, 90, 91
therapist, *see* doctor
thinking: *see* functions, four; intellect
thirty, the number, 404
Thomas Aquinas, 403, 427
thought: Indians and, 527, 529; primitives and, 12
threads, rain of, 352*n*, 353
three plus one motif, 391, 392, 397, 402, 408

thriller, vogue for, 199
thunderbolt, 450
Tibet, 91, 525
tics, 508
Tifereth, 410
time machine, 391*n*
totalitarianism, 221, 536*f*
totality: Christian, 392; consciousness and, 335; God as symbol of, 327; symbols of, 404, 407; *see also* mandala; wholeness
town, in America, 506*f*
tradition, as criterion, 343
transference, 160, 273
transformation: Buddhism and, 526; of souls into water, 333
trauma, infantile sexual, 171
tremendum, 458, 463
triad, 408
tricephalus, 392
Trinity, Holy, 391, 403; Christ and, 397; and the devil, 392; iconography of, 392; vision of, 339
troposphere, 311
trusts, 379
tubes, seen in sky, 402
Turkey, 481
twenty-four, the number, 404
twilight state, hysterical, 208
two, as vertical axis, 407
tyranny, 277

U

Ufos, 311*ff*, 415; appearance and disappearance, 332*f*; as archetypal images, 327; in dreams, 330*ff*; in history, 401*ff*; materiality of, 416*f*; not photogenic, 322; occupants of, 317, 321*f*; plurality of, 334*f*; as portents of death, 369; psychic nature of, 415; and radar, 332, 415; sexual aspects, 333, 350*f*; shapes, 325, 336; *see also* acceleration; drop; flight; size; speed
Uganda, 89
"ugliest Man," 131

uncleanness, magical, 197
unconscious, 147, 290, 334*f*; autonomy of, 335, 441; collective/suprapersonal, 10*ff*, 138, 219, 377; ——, unity of, 450; compensation, theory of, 15, 17, 23, 219, 388; contents of, 8*f*, 18; denial of, 3; dependence on consciousness, doubts regarding, 440; discovery of, 211*f*, 358; dreams as symptoms of, 151, 218; early use of term, 3; fear of, 119; Freudian concept, 5, 30; Germanic, tensions in, 166, 219; guiding function, 23; language of, 17; nature of, 30; objectivity of, 291; personal, 9; projection of, 25; psychic forces and, 185; psychoanalysis and, 4; and religious experience, 293; in religious persons, 292; uniting symbol in, 414; *see also* consciousness; dissociation; compensatory
unconsciousness: Jewish, and Aryan, 165; of mass man, 75; as sin, 357; woman's, 117, 119
understanding, 499; *see also* knowledge
unemployed, in Germany, 180, 205
unigenitus, 397
United Kingdom, 316
United States, *see* America
unity: focus of, 143; of individual, 349; of mankind, 295; and quaternity, 407; symbol of, 414; *see also* totality; wholeness
universities, 565
unus mundus, 409, 411, 452
Upanishads, 85, 191
U.S.S.R., *see* Russia
uterus, 333, 336

V

Valentino, Rudolph, 513
Valéry, Paul, 499*n*, 500
Valhalla, 190*n*
Valkyries, 186, 188

van Gogh, Vincent, 392*n*
van der Hoop, Dr., 551, 554
van Houten, D., 403*n*
venereal diseases, 89, 102
Venus, 321; incantation to, 371
Verdant One, 328
Vienna, 235, 481, 554
vimana, 525
vinum ardens, 332, 392
violence, in dream-symbols, 219, 220
Virgil, 121
Virgo, 484
Vishnu, 520
vision, and hallucination, 314*n*
visions: collective, 314, 319, 320, 324; of Saints, 342; as symbol, 350
voice(s): 353; English, 522*f*; inner, 447
volatilization, 332
volition, 340
Voluspo, 192*f*, 194
vox Dei, 444*f*, 446*ff*, 453

W

Wagalaweia songs, 186
Wagner, Richard, 184, 186*n*, 212, 214
war: outlawing, 77; preparation for, 82; *see also* World War I
Warens, Madame de, 108
wasp, 336
water: permanent/of the Philosophers/philosophical, 331*f*, 385; in star of David, 407; source of living, 392; symbol of passivity, 394; that is fire, 385, 394; as unconscious, 425; see also *aqua permanens*
Watson, John B., 491, 492
weightlessness, 315, 316, 321, 329, 352, 415
Weimar Republic, 180
Weizsäcker, Viktor von, 166*n*
welfare, social, 154, 492
Welfare State, 201
Welles, Orson, 315*n*

Wells, H. G., 315, 391n

Weltanschauung, of psychotherapy, 548

West and East, differences, 114

wheels, in Ezekiel's vision, 403

white, feminine colour, 417

white man, Pueblo view of, 89, 211

White House, 417

wholeness, 339; archetype of, 328, 335; death and, 367; four as symbol of, 391; instinct for, 344f; psychic, cosmic affinities, 335; ——, images of, 335; and sexuality, 344; symbol of, 339, 414; and transcendence, 410; *see also* individuation; totality; unity

Wilhelm II, 239

Wilhelm, Richard, 90, 91, 235, 464

Wilkins, Harold T., 331n, 352n, 353n

will to power, *see* power

wind: god of, 187f; Hermes and, 188f; symbol in Nietzsche, 182

wine, fiery, 332

wish-fantasies, 164f, 169, 248

wish-fulfilment, 160, 162, 277

wishes, repressed/suppressed, 5, 341

witchcraft, 11, 52, 69; dreams and, 150

witch-doctor, 370

witch-motif, 33

wizards, 371, 372

Wolff, Toni, 469–70

woman (women): conservatism of, 511; Dionysus and, 185; dress, 520f; Indian, 520f, 522· male attachment to older, 108; man's image of, 39; mental masculinization of, 119; and psychology, 125; relation to man's world, 116; and social independence, 117; unmarried, surplus of, 120; *see also* anima

"wooden-headedness," Swiss, 540

word(s): magical, 147; personification of, 286f; *see also* Logos

world: end of, 328, 367; higher and human, 408f; lower and upper,

392; vertical and horizontal, 391f

world-soul, 326; and individual souls, 335

World War I, 77, 80, 130, 179, 208, 220, 221, 233, 314; woman and, 116

World War II, 222

World War III, 364f

Wotan, 194, 214, 371; archetype of, 187f, 189; cavalcade of, 371; as *Ergreifer,* 185; oak(s) of, 85, 184; resurrection of, 180

wrath-fire, 389

writing, American, 504

Wunsch, 188 & n

Wyndham, John, 431ff

Y

Yahweh, 192, 448; fire of, 389; wildness of, 392

yang, see *yin*

yantras, 424

yin and *yang,* 35, 142, 407, 484, 486, 498

yoga, 518; and psychoanalysis, 90; *see also* Bhakti-Yoga; Kundalini yoga

yogi, 517

youth, 375

Youth Movement, German, 180

yucca moth, 282

Z

Zagreus, *see* Dionysus

Zarathustra, *see* Nietzsche

Zechariah, Book of, 404

Zeitgeist, 281, 303, 501

zenith, 407

zeppelin, 325n

Zeus, 189, 388, 450

Zosimos, 333, 386, 405

Zschokke, Heinrich, 451

Zurich, 551, 554

THE COLLECTED WORKS OF

C. G. JUNG

T HE PUBLICATION of the first complete edition, in English, of the works of C. G. Jung was undertaken by Routledge and Kegan Paul, Ltd., in England and by Bollingen Foundation in the United States. The American edition is number XX in Bollingen Series, which since 1967 has been published by Princeton University Press. The edition contains revised versions of works previously published, such as *Psychology of the Unconscious*, which is now entitled *Symbols of Transformation*; works originally written in English, such as *Psychology and Religion*; works not previously translated, such as *Aion*; and, in general, new translations of virtually all of Professor Jung's writings. Prior to his death, in 1961, the author supervised the textual revision, which in some cases is extensive. Sir Herbert Read (d. 1968), Dr. Michael Fordham, and Dr. Gerhard Adler compose the Editorial Committee; the translator is R. F. C. Hull (except for Volume 2) and William McGuire is executive editor.

The price of the volumes varies according to size; they are sold separately, and may also be obtained on standing order. Several of the volumes are extensively illustrated. Each volume contains an index and in most a bibliography; the final volumes will contain a complete bibliography of Professor Jung's writings and a general index to the entire edition.

In the following list, dates of original publication are given in parentheses (of original composition, in brackets). Multiple dates indicate revisions.

*1. PSYCHIATRIC STUDIES

On the Psychology and Pathology of So-Called Occult Phenomena
(1902)
On Hysterical Misreading (1904)
Cryptomnesia (1905)
On Manic Mood Disorder (1903)
A Case of Hysterical Stupor in a Prisoner in Detention (1902)
On Simulated Insanity (1903)
A Medical Opinion on a Case of Simulated Insanity (1904)
A Third and Final Opinion on Two Contradictory Psychiatric Diag-
noses (1906)
On the Psychological Diagnosis of Facts (1905)

†2. EXPERIMENTAL RESEARCHES

Translated by Leopold Stein in collaboration with Diana Riviere

STUDIES IN WORD ASSOCIATION (1904–7, 1910)
The Associations of Normal Subjects (by Jung and F. Riklin)
An Analysis of the Associations of an Epileptic
The Reaction-Time Ratio in the Association Experiment
Experimental Observations on the Faculty of Memory
Psychoanalysis and Association Experiments
The Psychological Diagnosis of Evidence
Association, Dream, and Hysterical Symptom
The Psychopathological Significance of the Association Experiment
Disturbances in Reproduction in the Association Experiment
The Association Method
The Family Constellation
PSYCHOPHYSICAL RESEARCHES (1907–8)
On the Psychophysical Relations of the Association Experiment
Psychophysical Investigations with the Galvanometer and Pneumo-
graph in Normal and Insane Individuals (by F. Peterson and
Jung)
Further Investigations on the Galvanic Phenomenon and Respiration
in Normal and Insane Individuals (by C. Ricksher and Jung)
Appendix: Statistical Details of Enlistment (1906); New Aspects of
Criminal Psychology (1908); The Psychological Methods of
Investigation Used in the Psychiatric Clinic of the University of
Zurich (1910); On the Doctrine of Complexes ([1911] 1913); On
the Psychological Diagnosis of Evidence (1937)

* Published 1957; 2nd edn., 1970.   † Published 1973.

*3. THE PSYCHOGENESIS OF MENTAL DISEASE
   The Psychology of Dementia Praecox (1907)
   The Content of the Psychoses (1908/1914)
   On Psychological Understanding (1914)
   A Criticism of Bleuler's Theory of Schizophrenic Negativism (1911)
   On the Importance of the Unconscious in Psychopathology (1914)
   On the Problem of Psychogenesis in Mental Disease (1919)
   Mental Disease and the Psyche (1928)
   On the Psychogenesis of Schizophrenia (1939)
   Recent Thoughts on Schizophrenia (1957)
   Schizophrenia (1958)

†4. FREUD AND PSYCHOANALYSIS
   Freud's Theory of Hysteria: A Reply to Aschaffenburg (1906)
   The Freudian Theory of Hysteria (1908)
   The Analysis of Dreams (1909)
   A Contribution to the Psychology of Rumour (1910–11)
   On the Significance of Number Dreams (1910–11)
   Morton Prince, "The Mechanism and Interpretation of Dreams": A
       Critical Review (1911)
   On the Criticism of Psychoanalysis (1910)
   Concerning Psychoanalysis (1912)
   The Theory of Psychoanalysis (1913)
   General Aspects of Psychoanalysis (1913)
   Psychoanalysis and Neurosis (1916)
   Some Crucial Points in Psychoanalysis: A Correspondence between
       Dr. Jung and Dr. Loÿ (1914)
   Prefaces to "Collected Papers on Analytical Psychology" (1916, 1917)
   The Significance of the Father in the Destiny of the Individual
       (1909/1949)
   Introduction to Kranefeldt's "Secret Ways of the Mind" (1930)
   Freud and Jung: Contrasts (1929)

‡5. SYMBOLS OF TRANSFORMATION (1911–12/1952)
   PART I
   Introduction
   Two Kinds of Thinking
   The Miller Fantasies: Anamnesis
   The Hymn of Creation
   The Song of the Moth   (continued)

* Published 1960.   † Published 1961.
‡ Published 1956; 2nd edn., 1967. (65 plates, 43 text figures.)

5. (*continued*)

PART II
Introduction
The Concept of Libido
The Transformation of Libido
The Origin of the Hero
Symbols of the Mother and of Rebirth
The Battle for Deliverance from the Mother
The Dual Mother
The Sacrifice
Epilogue
Appendix: The Miller Fantasies

*6. PSYCHOLOGICAL TYPES (1921)
Introduction
The Problem of Types in the History of Classical and Medieval
   Thought
Schiller's Ideas on the Type Problem
The Apollinian and the Dionysian
The Type Problem in Human Character
The Type Problem in Poetry
The Type Problem in Psychopathology
The Type Problem in Aesthetics
The Type Problem in Modern Philosophy
The Type Problem in Biography
General Description of the Types
Definitions
Epilogue
Four Papers on Psychological Typology (1913, 1925, 1931, 1936)

†7. TWO ESSAYS ON ANALYTICAL PSYCHOLOGY
On the Psychology of the Unconscious (1917/1926/1943)
The Relations between the Ego and the Unconscious (1928)
Appendix: New Paths in Psychology (1912); The Structure of the
   Unconscious (1916) (new versions, with variants, 1966)

‡8. THE STRUCTURE AND DYNAMICS OF THE PSYCHE
On Psychic Energy (1928)
The Transcendent Function ([1916]/1957)
A Review of the Complex Theory (1934)
The Significance of Constitution and Heredity in Psychology (1929)

* Published 1971.   † Published 1953; 2nd edn., 1966.
‡ Published 1960; 2nd edn., 1969.

Psychological Factors Determining Human Behavior (1937)
Instinct and the Unconscious (1919)
The Structure of the Psyche (1927/1931)
On the Nature of the Psyche (1947/1954)
General Aspects of Dream Psychology (1916/1948)
On the Nature of Dreams (1945/1948)
The Psychological Foundations of Belief in Spirits (1920/1948)
Spirit and Life (1926)
Basic Postulates of Analytical Psychology (1931)
Analytical Psychology and *Weltanschauung* (1928/1931)
The Real and the Surreal (1933)
The Stages of Life (1930–1931)
The Soul and Death (1934)
Synchronicity: An Acausal Connecting Principle (1952)
Appendix: On Synchronicity (1951)

*9. PART I. THE ARCHETYPES AND THE
COLLECTIVE UNCONSCIOUS
Archetypes of the Collective Unconscious (1934/1954)
The Concept of the Collective Unconscious (1936)
Concerning the Archetypes, with Special Reference to the Anima
   Concept (1936/1954)
Psychological Aspects of the Mother Archetype (1938/1954)
Concerning Rebirth (1940/1950)
The Psychology of the Child Archetype (1940)
The Psychological Aspects of the Kore (1941)
The Phenomenology of the Spirit in Fairytales (1945/1948)
On the Psychology of the Trickster-Figure (1954)
Conscious, Unconscious, and Individuation (1939)
A Study in the Process of Individuation (1934/1950)
Concerning Mandala Symbolism (1950)
Appendix: Mandalas (1955)

*9. PART II. AION (1951)
   RESEARCHES INTO THE PHENOMENOLOGY OF THE SELF
The Ego
The Shadow
The Syzygy: Anima and Animus
The Self
Christ, a Symbol of the Self
The Sign of the Fishes   (*continued*)

* Published 1959; 2nd edn., 1968. (Part I: 79 plates, with 29 in colour.)

9. (*continued*)
The Prophecies of Nostradamus
The Historical Significance of the Fish
The Ambivalence of the Fish Symbol
The Fish in Alchemy
The Alchemical Interpretation of the Fish
Background to the Psychology of Christian Alchemical Symbolism
Gnostic Symbols of the Self
The Structure and Dynamics of the Self
Conclusion

*10. CIVILIZATION IN TRANSITION
The Role of the Unconscious (1918)
Mind and Earth (1927/1931)
Archaic Man (1931)
The Spiritual Problem of Modern Man (1928/1931)
The Love Problem of a Student (1928)
Woman in Europe (1927)
The Meaning of Psychology for Modern Man (1933/1934)
The State of Psychotherapy Today (1934)
Preface and Epilogue to "Essays on Contemporary Events" (1946)
Wotan (1936)
After the Catastrophe (1945)
The Fight with the Shadow (1946)
The Undiscovered Self (Present and Future) (1957)
Flying Saucers: A Modern Myth (1958)
A Psychological View of Conscience (1958)
Good and Evil in Analytical Psychology (1959)
Introduction to Wolff's "Studies in Jungian Psychology" (1959)
The Swiss Line in the European Spectrum (1928)
Reviews of Keyserling's "America Set Free" (1930) and "La Révolution Mondiale" (1934)
The Complications of American Psychology (1930)
The Dreamlike World of India (1939)
What India Can Teach Us (1939)
Appendix: Documents (1933–1938)

†11. PSYCHOLOGY AND RELIGION: WEST AND EAST
WESTERN RELIGION
Psychology and Religion (The Terry Lectures) (1938/1940)

* Published 1964; 2nd edn., 1970. (8 plates.)
† Published 1958; 2nd edn., 1969.

A Psychological Approach to the Dogma of the Trinity (1942/1948)
Transformation Symbolism in the Mass (1942/1954)
Forewords to White's "God and the Unconscious" and Werblowsky's
    "Lucifer and Prometheus" (1952)
Brother Klaus (1933)
Psychotherapists or the Clergy (1932)
Psychoanalysis and the Cure of Souls (1928)
Answer to Job (1952)

    EASTERN RELIGION

Psychological Commentaries on "The Tibetan Book of the Great
    Liberation" (1939/1954) and "The Tibetan Book of the Dead"
    (1935/1953)
Yoga and the West (1936)
Foreword to Suzuki's "Introduction to Zen Buddhism" (1939)
The Psychology of Eastern Meditation (1943)
The Holy Men of India: Introduction to Zimmer's "Der Weg zum
    Selbst" (1944)
Foreword to the "I Ching" (1950)

*12. PSYCHOLOGY AND ALCHEMY (1944)
Prefatory note to the English Edition ([1951?] added 1967)
Introduction to the Religious and Psychological Problems of Alchemy
Individual Dream Symbolism in Relation to Alchemy (1936)
Religious Ideas in Alchemy (1937)
Epilogue

†13. ALCHEMICAL STUDIES
Commentary on "The Secret of the Golden Flower" (1929)
The Visions of Zosimos (1938/1954)
Paracelsus as a Spiritual Phenomenon (1942)
The Spirit Mercurius (1943/1948)
The Philosophical Tree (1945/1954)

‡14. MYSTERIUM CONIUNCTIONIS (1955-56)
    AN INQUIRY INTO THE SEPARATION AND
    SYNTHESIS OF PSYCHIC OPPOSITES IN ALCHEMY
The Components of the Coniunctio
The Paradoxa
The Personification of the Opposites
Rex and Regina   (continued)

* Published 1953; 2nd edn., completely revised, 1968. (270 illustrations.)
† Published 1968. (50 plates, 4 text figures.)
‡ Published 1963; 2nd edn., 1970. (10 plates.)

14. (*continued*)
Adam and Eve
The Conjunction

*15. THE SPIRIT IN MAN, ART, AND LITERATURE
Paracelsus (1929)
Paracelsus the Physician (1941)
Sigmund Freud in His Historical Setting (1932)
In Memory of Sigmund Freud (1939)
Richard Wilhelm: In Memoriam (1930)
On the Relation of Analytical Psychology to Poetry (1922)
Psychology and Literature (1930/1950)
"Ulysses": A Monologue (1932)
Picasso (1932)

†16. THE PRACTICE OF PSYCHOTHERAPY
GENERAL PROBLEMS OF PSYCHOTHERAPY
Principles of Practical Psychotherapy (1935)
What Is Psychotherapy? (1935)
Some Aspects of Modern Psychotherapy (1930)
The Aims of Psychotherapy (1931)
Problems of Modern Psychotherapy (1929)
Psychotherapy and a Philosophy of Life (1943)
Medicine and Psychotherapy (1945)
Psychotherapy Today (1945)
Fundamental Questions of Psychotherapy (1951)
SPECIFIC PROBLEMS OF PSYCHOTHERAPY
The Therapeutic Value of Abreaction (1921/1928)
The Practical Use of Dream-Analysis (1934)
The Psychology of the Transference (1946)
Appendix: The Realities of Practical Psychotherapy ([1937] added, 1966)

‡17. THE DEVELOPMENT OF PERSONALITY
Psychic Conflicts in a Child (1910/1946)
Introduction to Wickes's "Analyses der Kinderseele" (1927/1931)
Child Development and Education (1928)
Analytical Psychology and Education: Three Lectures (1926/1946)
The Gifted Child (1943)
The Significance of the Unconscious in Individual Education (1928)

* Published 1966.
† Published 1954; 2nd edn., revised and augmented, 1966. (13 illustrations.)
‡ Published 1954.

The Development of Personality (1934)
Marriage as a Psychological Relationship (1925)

18. THE SYMBOLIC LIFE
Miscellaneous Writings

19. BIBLIOGRAPHY OF C. G. JUNG'S WRITINGS

20. GENERAL INDEX TO THE COLLECTED WORKS

See also:

C. G. JUNG: LETTERS

Selected and edited by Gerhard Adler, in collaboration with Aniela Jaffé.
Translations from the German by R.F.C. Hull.
VOL. 1: 1906–1950
VOL. 2: 1951–1961

THE FREUD/JUNG LETTERS
Edited by William McGuire, translated by
Ralph Manheim and R.F.C. Hull